Rethinking The Good

OXFORD ETHICS SERIES
Series Editor: Derek Parfit, All Souls College, Oxford University

THE LIMITS OF MORALITY
Shelly Kagan

PERFECTIONISM
Thomas Hurka

INEQUALITY
Larry S. Temkin

MORALITY, MORTALITY, Volume I
Death and Whom to Save from It
F. M. Kamm

MORALITY, MORTALITY, Volume II
Rights, Duties, and Status
F. M. Kamm

SUFFERING AND MORAL RESPONSIBILITY
Jamie Mayerfeld

MORAL DEMANDS IN NONIDEAL THEORY
Liam B. Murphy

THE ETHICS OF KILLING
Problems at the Margins of Life
Jeff McMahan

INTRICATE ETHICS
Rights, Responsibilities, and Permissible Harm
F. M. Kamm

RETHINKING THE GOOD
Moral Ideals and the Nature of Practical Reasoning
Larry S. Temkin

Rethinking The Good

MORAL IDEALS AND THE NATURE OF
PRACTICAL REASONING

Larry S. Temkin

OXFORD
UNIVERSITY PRESS

OXFORD
UNIVERSITY PRESS

Oxford University Press, Inc., publishes works that further
Oxford University's objective of excellence
in research, scholarship, and education.

Oxford   New York
Auckland   Cape Town   Dar es Salaam   Hong Kong   Karachi
Kuala Lumpur   Madrid   Melbourne   Mexico City   Nairobi
New Delhi   Shanghai   Taipei   Toronto

With offices in
Argentina   Austria   Brazil   Chile   Czech Republic   France   Greece
Guatemala   Hungary   Italy   Japan   Poland   Portugal   Singapore
South Korea   Switzerland   Thailand   Turkey   Ukraine   Vietnam

Copyright © 2012 Oxford University Press

Published by Oxford University Press, Inc.
198 Madison Avenue, New York, New York 10016

www.oup.com

Oxford is a registered trademark of Oxford University Press

All rights reserved. No part of this publication may be reproduced,
stored in a retrieval system, or transmitted, in any form or by any means,
electronic, mechanical, photocopying, recording, or otherwise,
without the prior permission of Oxford University Press.

Library of Congress Cataloging-in-Publication Data
Temkin, Larry S.
Rethinking the good : moral ideals and the nature of practical reasoning / Larry S. Temkin.
   p. cm.—(Oxford ethics series)
Includes bibliographical references (p.   ) and index.
ISBN 978-0-19-975944-6 (alk. paper)
1. Ethics.   2. Good and evil.   3. Practical reason.   I. Title.
BJ1031.T395 2011
170—dc22   2011004595

1 3 5 7 9 8 6 4 2

Printed in the United States of America
on acid-free paper

To
Derek and Shelly
Bud and Lee
Daniel, Andrea, and Rebecca
And, especially, Meg

PREFACE

The initial idea that eventually gave rise to this book occurred to me many years ago, when I was still a graduate student at Princeton University. It was 1977, and I was sitting in on a seminar by a visiting professor who I had been *told* was one of the great living philosophers; but I confess that up until that point I had never heard of him. The professor was presenting an early version of a typescript that he would eventually publish some seven years later. The professor, the typescript, and the seminar were quite literally awe inspiring, and they profoundly changed the direction of my philosophical thinking, and indeed my life.

The typescript—of *Reasons and Persons*[1]—was *filled* with fascinating arguments and claims, but one problem that particularly gripped me was the earliest version of Derek Parfit's the *Mere Addition Paradox*. As the Paradox goes, there are three alternatives, A, B, and A+, and it *appears* that, all things considered, A is better than B, and B is better than A+, but that, all things considered, A is *not* better than A+.[2] Noting that "all-things-considered better than" is a transitive relation, Parfit claimed that the three judgments were *inconsistent* and that one of them had to go. The paradox lay in the fact that each of the three inconsistent judgments seemed *extremely* plausible, so that even though it was clear that at least one of them had to be rejected, it was hard to see how any of them could actually be given up.

I was utterly taken with the Mere Addition Paradox. I went round and round in my head considering which of Parfit's three judgments to reject and kept coming up with the thought that it might be a mistake to give *any* of them up. This led me to entertain a rather radical thought. Perhaps it *would* be a mistake to reject any of the three judgments. Perhaps each of the three judgments is, in fact, *true*. *Perhaps* the lesson to be learned from the Mere Addition Paradox is that "all-things-considered better than" is *not* a transitive relation.

As I thought about the Mere Addition Paradox more and more, I warmed up to this conjecture, and I managed to convince myself that it was an idea worth pursuing. At that point, I made an appointment to meet with a teacher of mine, Tom Nagel, in order to run my idea by him. I remember sitting in Nagel's office and explaining that I had been thinking about Parfit's Mere Addition Paradox a lot, and I thought that *perhaps* the lesson to be learned from Parfit's

---

[1] Oxford: Oxford University Press, 1984.
[2] On the Mere Addition Paradox, see chapter 19 of *Reasons and Persons*.

paradox was that "all-things-considered better than" was *not* a transitive relation. Nagel scrunched up his face in what looked to me to be a combination of pity, bewilderment, and scorn and then said, in words I shall never forget, "Larry, I wouldn't understand what someone *meant* who claimed that *all things considered, A* is better than *B*, and *all things considered, B* is better than *C*, but *all things considered, A* is *not* better than *C*." That was pretty much the end of our conversation; for Nagel, it was part of the meanings of the words "all-things-considered better than" that "all-things-considered better than" was a transitive relation. Needless to say, I left Nagel's office feeling utterly deflated about the prospect that my radical conjecture might be true.

Deflated, but not completely defeated, I decided to run my idea past another professor of mine, Tim Scanlon. Once again, I made an appointment, and sitting in Scanlon's office I raised the possibility that perhaps the lesson to be learned from Parfit's Mere Addition Paradox was that "all-things-considered better than" was not a transitive relation. My conversation with Scanlon lasted a bit longer than my conversation with Nagel, but basically he echoed the view that Nagel had expressed. Scanlon, too, suggested that it was an *analytic* truth that "all-things-considered better than" was a transitive relation.

I tried one last time. I ran my idea by Parfit himself, since it was *his* paradox! I thought that if anyone might be open to my idea it would be Derek. After all, Derek would understand better than anyone else the full force of the considerations leading to my conjecture; moreover, if I was right, it would make the Mere Addition Paradox even more revolutionary and significant than anyone had previously imagined. Derek was extremely kind and patient with me, but at the end of the day he sided with Nagel and Scanlon. My conjecture *couldn't* be true, given the meanings of the words "all-things-considered better than."

Stubborn, but not *completely* crazy, at that point I abandoned my thought. Nagel, Scanlon, and Parfit were three of the greatest living moral philosophers; I was a punk graduate student. I turned my attention to other issues and soon began working on a topic that would engage me for many years to come, the topic of equality.

Six years later, in the fall of 1983, I taught an undergraduate class on the typescript of *Reasons and Persons*. I was at Rice University at the time, and two of my students, Richard Dees and Martin Halbert, were as taken with the Mere Addition Paradox as I had been originally. Each week, for the entire semester, each of them came to my office, separately, to argue that the Mere Addition Paradox failed. Each week, I explained to them why their latest objection to the Paradox missed the mark. Their passion for the Paradox reignited my own, and by the end of the semester I was convinced that the Mere Addition Paradox *did* fail, although not for any of the reasons that Dees or Halbert had suggested. Rather, it failed for reasons that supported my original conjecture about the Paradox. Specifically, I became convinced that in presenting his arguments in support of the Mere Addition Paradox, Parfit implicitly relied on a set of claims that, if correct, vindicated each of the particular judgments that gave rise to the Paradox, but also entailed that "all-things-considered better than" was not a transitive relation.

The following year, I wrote up a 125-page draft of my first article on this book's topic, "Intransitivity and the Mere Addition Paradox,"[3] and sent it off to Parfit. A year passed before I heard anything from Derek about my paper. Then, during a visit to Rice, Derek relayed the following story. My paper had arrived just as *Reasons and Persons* was heading off to press, and having worked for many months, without interruption, to get to that stage, he was thoroughly exhausted, and didn't have the heart or energy to read what I'd sent. But he took my work with him on a later trip to India, carried it partway up a mountain, and then, with one of the world's tallest peaks looming in the distance, he sat down, cross-legged, and finally read my draft. Derek told me that he couldn't remember ever having read a more impressive paper. He then added that he thought that my paper had destroyed the greatest flower of ten years of his life, but that he didn't mind!

This story is, of course, much more of a testimony to Derek's character and generosity (not to mention the poorness of his memory!) than it is to the quality of the draft I had sent him. But you can imagine the impact that his over-the-top remarks had on a young assistant professor. They convinced me that it was worth pursuing the line that I had first come up with in graduate school, and I have been doing so, off and on, ever since. The path has been a long one, and it has taken many unexpected twists and turns. As is common in philosophy, one argument and topic led to another, and I found myself addressing many issues that never occurred to me when I first began thinking about the Mere Addition Paradox. The result is the book that is now in your hands.

East Brunswick, New Jersey
June 2011

Postscript. Tim Scanlon has since abandoned his view that it is analytically true that "all-things-considered better than" is a transitive relation. Further, he now grants that there may be an important "all-thing-considered better than" relation that is not transitive. Derek Parfit continues to believe that "all-things-considered better than" can be used with a meaning that must refer to a transitive relation, but he grants that my arguments show that there is another "all-things-considered better than" relation that is fundamental for practical reasoning that is not transitive. I don't know Tom Nagel's current view of the matter. Alas, ever since that initial day in his office I've been afraid to ask him! L.T.

---

[3] *Philosophy and Public Affairs* 16 (1987): 138–87.

ACKNOWLEDGMENTS

In finishing a book that one has spent much of one's life on, there is an acute awareness of the inadequacy of any set of acknowledgments. So many people have given me feedback and support over the years that it would be impossible to adequately thank them all. So let me begin with a general acknowledgment and apology. I am truly grateful to everyone who has had a hand in shaping this book. I am also deeply sorry to anyone I have inadvertently omitted, and to the many people listed here who have not been given their full due.

First, many thanks to Mike Atkins for convincing me, in the spring of 2009, to bring this book to fruition and to leave further work for another occasion; also, more important, for his lifelong friendship.

Second, I'd like to thank the copyeditor and production assistants at Oxford University Press for their careful and judicious contributions to this book. Among those deserving special mention are Hari Kumar, Natalie Johnson, and Lucy Randall. I am also grateful to Peter Momtchiloff for his support of this project from its earliest stages and, especially, to Peter Ohlin for his encouragement, enthusiasm, and patience throughout the many years I have been working on this book.

Chapter 3 draws on "A 'New' Principle of Aggregation," *Philosophical Issues* 15 (2005): 218–34; chapter 4 draws on "Aggregation within Lives," in *Utilitarianism: The Aggregation Question*, ed. Ellen F. Paul, Fred D. Miller, and Jeffrey Paul (Cambridge: Cambridge University Press, 2009), 1–29; chapter 5 draws on "A Continuum Argument for Intransitivity," *Philosophy and Public Affairs* 25 (1996): 175–210; chapters 11 and 12 draw on "Intransitivity and the Mere Addition Paradox," *Philosophy and Public Affairs* 16 (1987): 138–87, and on "Rethinking the Good, Moral Ideals and the Nature of Practical Reasoning," in *Reading Parfit*, ed. Jonathan Dancy (Oxford: Basil Blackwell, 1997), 290–344; chapter 8 draws on "Worries about Continuity, Transitivity, Expected Utility Theory, and Practical Reasoning," in *Exploring Practical Philosophy*, ed. Dan Egonsson, Jonas Josefsson, Björn Petersson, and Toni Rønnow-Rasmussen (Burlington: Ashgate, 2001), 95–108; and appendix E draws on "Intransitivity and the Person-Affecting Principle: A Response," *Philosophy and Phenomenological Research* 59 (1999): 777–84. I am grateful to the editors of *Philosophical Issues, Philosophy and Public Affairs*, Basil Blackwell, Oxford University Press, Ashgate Publishing Limited, and *Philosophy and Phenomenological Research* for their permission to include material from those articles.

Much of this book was written during research leaves. For some of the most productive years of my life, I am indebted to fellowships from the National Humanities Center (1984–85), Harvard's Program in Ethics and the Professions (1994–95, since renamed the Edmond J. Safra Center for Ethics), All Souls College (1999–2000), the National Institutes of Health, Department of Clinical Bioethics (2005–6), and the Australian National University (January–June 2008). Helping to make those years interesting and enjoyable were my hosts, staffs, and colleagues. Although I can't name them all, I would be remiss if I didn't mention Kent Mullikin, Leon Kass, Jeff Hunter, and Tom Regan (NHC); Dennis Thompson, Jean McVeigh, Helen Hawkins, Ted Aaberg, and Dan Wikler (HPEP); Warden John Davies, Julie Edwards, Derek Parfit, and Jerry Cohen (ASC); Zeke Emanuel, Becky Chen, David Wendler, Marion Danis, Christine Grady, and Frank Miller (NIH); and Robert Goodin, Di Crosse, David Chalmers, Alan Hájek, Thomas Pogge, and Christian Barry (ANU).

In the spring of 2010, I taught an eight-day seminar on my book at the University of Oslo. To my hosts, Carsten Hansen and Eyjólfur Emilsson, as well as the students, many thanks for your warm hospitality and feedback.

For the past ten years, I have received great support from my department chairs: Robert Matthews, Peter Klein, Brian McLaughlin, and Barry Loewer; and also from many administrators at Rutgers, the State University of New Jersey, especially, Barry Qualls. Also, I am enormously grateful to Dick Foley, Peter Klein, and, especially, Ruth Chang, for their roles in bringing me to Rutgers.

My current and former students and colleagues, both at Rutgers and at Rice University, have been a great source of pleasure, learning, and inspiration. And thanks to the wonderful staff at both Rutgers and Rice: Pauline Mitchell, Mercedes Diaz, Ann Lipovsky, Stacey Messing, Matt Wosniak, Carole Dachowicz, Susan Viola, Miranda Robinson, and Sue Brod.

I'd like to thank my teachers at Wisconsin: Michael Byrd, Fred Dretske, Robert Hambourger, Zane Parks, Marcus Singer, and, especially, Dennis Stampe; and also at Princeton: Paul Benacerraf, Michael Frede, Gil Harman, David Lewis, Tom Nagel, Tim Scanlon, and Margaret Wilson. And for their ongoing friendship and support, I'd also like to thank Dan Brock, Alan Code, Jerry Cohen, Keith DeRose, Frankie Egan, Zeke Emanuel, James Fishkin, Alvin Goldman, Peter Kivy, Doug Husak, Mark Kulstad, Bob Matthews, Tim Maudlin, Vishnya Maudlin, Howard McGary, Don Morrison, Ingmar Persson, Barry Qualls, Joseph Raz, Tim Scanlon, Gordon Schochet, Amartya Sen, Peter Singer, Holly Smith, Ernie Sosa, Dennis Thompson, and Dan Wikler.

To all those who have given me comments on this book's topics, many thanks. These people include Miguel Alzola, Marcello Antosh, Gustaf Arrhenius, Nick Beckstead, Jonathan Bennett, Ken Binmore, David Bourget, Baruch Brody, Joshua Burton, Tim Campbell, Alan Carter, Alan Code, Jerry Cohen, Tyler Cowen, Jonathan Dancy, Marion Danis, Keith DeRose, Kai Draper, Nir

Eyal, Waqas Farid, Christoph Fehige, Fred Feldman, Geoffrey Ferrari, Charles Fried, Alex Friedman, David Gauthier, Richard Grandy, Preston Green, Jim Griffin, Alan Hájek, Carsten Hansen, Gil Harman, Liz Harman, Carl Hoefer, Heine Holman, Susan Hurley, Cornelius Jakhelln, Michael Johnson, Olin Joynton, Evelyn Keyes, Chris Knapp, Keith Krebs, Stuart Kurtz, Michael Licciardi, Jerry Massey, Tim Maudlin, Dan McCormack, Liam Murphy, Tom Nagel, Jan Narveson, Alastair Norcross, Nikolaj Nottelmann, Toby Ord, Ingmar Persson, Wlodek Rabinowicz, Peter Railton, Melinda Roberts, John Roemer, Tim Scanlon, Peter Schweinsberg, Stefan Sciaraffa, Amartya Sen, Michael Sherry, Ernie Sosa, Jason Stanley, Gregory Trianosky, Peter Unger, Carlos Valdivia, Peter Vallentyne, J. David Velleman, Gerardo Vildostegui, Alex Voorhoeve, Robert Wachbroit, David Wasserman, Ryan Wasserman, Michael Weber, Andrew White, Jennifer Whiting, Dan Wikler, and Evan Williams.

Yitzhak Benbaji, Oscar Horta, and Gerard Vong deserve special mention for their very helpful comments on large portions of the book.

Ruth Chang, Shelly Kagan, Frances Kamm, and Jeff McMahan have given me enormously beneficial comments on several chapters. I am deeply indebted to them for their unstinting criticisms, and for the spirit of collegiality with which they have given them! My life has been greatly enriched, philosophically and otherwise, by our regular meetings.

I shall always be indebted to Richard Dees and Martin Halbert, already mentioned in my preface. But for their relentless worrying about Parfit's Mere Addition Paradox, I might never have returned to the issue that so vexed me in graduate school and that is so central to this book.

I owe thanks to Jake Nebel, for his help with the copyedited pages, the page proofs, and the final index. I also owe a tremendous debt of gratitude to Nick Beckstead and Tim Campbell, who not only gave me very helpful feedback on the book, but also were invaluable in the book's preparation. In addition to helping with the copyedited pages and the page proofs, they tirelessly and cheerfully proofed earlier drafts of the typescript and created the book's index, the bibliography, the lists of diagrams and examples, the abstracts, and so much more.

Mikhail Valdman and Jake Ross never fail to give me prompt, and enormously helpful, responses when I seek their advice. Mikhail commented on the entire draft, and I have revised the book at many points thanks to him. Jake commented on substantial portions of the book, and his insightful criticisms forced me to significantly revise my presentation of several of the book's key chapters.

Five others deserve separate mention.

Stuart Rachels was one of the first philosophers to respond to my article "Intransitivity and the Mere Addition Paradox,"[1] and to challenge the transi-

---

[1] *Philosophy and Public Affairs* 16 (1987): 138–87.

tivity of the "all-things-considered better than" relation. He gave me extensive feedback on my early articles, and his own work on the topic was pathbreaking. Rachels's spectrum argument from torture to headaches[2] inspired a great deal of my own work on the topic, including chapter 5 of this book.[3] For many, Rachels's example, and its variants, is the most compelling challenge to the transitivity of the "all-things-considered better than" relation.

John Broome has been giving me useful feedback regarding this book's topics since before we knew each other! Derek Parfit sent him an early draft of my "Intransitivity and the Mere Addition Paradox" back in 1985—without my name on it—and John responded with an extremely perceptive set of comments addressed to "anon." Derek forwarded John's comments to me, and we have been in contact about these issues ever since. I regard John as my harshest critic—and a good friend. I have learned much from his work,[4] and from our many discussions.

I have profited from many useful discussions with Roger Crisp over the years, and his many judicious comments on the entire book improved it greatly. Beyond that, Roger has been a trusted friend, valuable critic, and source of encouragement for more than fifteen years. I greatly appreciate everything that he has done for me.

Shelly Kagan is, along with Derek Parfit, the best philosophical critic I know; and he gave me 117 pages of incredibly insightful single-spaced comments. I spent four full months responding to Shelly's comments, and there are few pages that have not been revised in light of his acute suggestions. I know that I have not adequately dealt with all of Shelly's worries. But thanks to his efforts, this book is vastly better than it otherwise would have been. I can't thank him enough.

Derek Parfit is the editor of this series. He is also my teacher and mentor. My philosophical debt to Derek will be apparent throughout this book. Time and again, my arguments were inspired by his *Reasons and Persons*.[5] However, my debt to Derek extends far beyond his written work. We have had many hundreds of hours of conversations, and each time I have learned from his deep insights, penetrating criticisms, and unrivaled originality. Beyond that, Derek has been an unwavering source of support and motivation. For much of my career, I have written with an audience of one in mind—Derek. It has always been my hope that one day I would produce a work worthy of all the

---

[2] Originally presented in his unpublished Philosophy, Politics and Economics thesis, "A Theory of Beneficence" (Oxford University, 1993).

[3] It also served as the basis of my article "A Continuum Argument for Intransitivity," *Philosophy and Public Affairs* 25 (1996): 175–210.

[4] Especially from his two great books, *Weighing Goods* (Oxford: Basil Blackwell, 1991) and *Weighing Lives* (Oxford: Oxford University Press, 2004).

[5] Oxford: Oxford University Press, 1984.

time and encouragement that he has generously given me. Like the God that Nietzsche claims we invented, I know that my debt to Derek exceeds my ability to repay it. But perhaps this book, inspired by Derek, is a fitting tribute to his impact on me and my regard for him.

Next, a few personal acknowledgments to my wonderfully loving, and close-knit, family. I shan't name all of my aunts, uncles, cousins, nieces, nephews, in-laws and brothers- and sisters-in-law—but they have all played an important part in my life.

My grandparents, Louis and Lee Temkin and Abraham and Faye Sigman, are long gone. But they were very dear to me, and they helped shape me, and my life prospects, in countless ways that made my life as a philosopher possible.

My parents, Bud and Lee Temkin, are the foundation on which my life has been built. There are few really important lessons that I have learned in my life that I didn't learn from them. My parents taught me what it is to support and love someone wholeheartedly and unconditionally, but not blindly. Those aspects of my character that I take the most pride in, I owe to them.

My sister and brothers, Terrie, Mark, and Ron, have all played a major role in my life. Besides the great affection we have for each other, I appreciate all they have done on behalf of our family—much more than their fair share, I'm afraid.

My children, Daniel, Andrea, and Rebecca, are an unending source of joy and pride. They have also been great eye-openers for me. They have taught me that there is so much more to life than philosophy—for example, volleyball! When I was a teen, my grandmother once told me that when my father was born, she loved him so much that she thought it was unholy. At the time, I utterly failed to comprehend her meaning; I dismissed her comment as just so much neo-Victorian hyperbole. Stripped of its religious connotations, I understand it now.

Finally, I want to thank Meg, for sharing my life with me since we were sixteen. All that I owe to everyone else named in these acknowledgments, overwhelming as it is, is a pittance in comparison with what I owe to Meg. She is my rock, the one who provides stability and direction to me and my children. She is also my enabler, the one who has made a wonderful home for us wherever we have moved so that I could pursue my philosophy. Without Meg, I couldn't have focused on my work the way that I have during my life. Without her, this book would never have been written.

CONTENTS

1. **Introduction** 3
   1.1. Overview of the Book 4
   1.2. A Guide to the Material 5
   1.3. Intuitions 6
   1.4. Impossibility Arguments and Juggling 9
   1.5. Some Terminology 10
   1.6. Hammers and Nails 18
   1.7. Final Remarks 19

2. **Aggregation and Problems about Trade-offs: Many-Person Spectrum Arguments** 23
   2.1. Aggregation: A General Schema 24
   2.2. Some Standard Views Regarding Trade-offs between Quality and Number 26
   2.3. The Problem of Additive Aggregation 34
   2.4. Jake Ross's Principle 39
   2.5. A Worry about Consistency 45
   2.6. Some Initial Worries and Preliminary Responses 52
   2.7. Extending the Results to Various Ideals 60
   2.8. Concluding Remarks 65

3. **A "New" Principle of Aggregation** 67
   3.1. The Disperse Additional Burdens View 67
   3.2. The Disperse Additional Burdens View and the Levelling Down Objection 75
   3.3. Worries about Iteration 79
   3.4. The Bad Old Days and Harmless Torturers 80
   3.5. Anti-Additive-Aggregationist Principles, Prisoner's Dilemmas, and Each-We Dilemmas 85

4. **On the Separateness of Individuals, Compensation, and Aggregation within Lives** 96
   4.1. On the Separateness of Individuals: Sidgwick, Rawls, and Nozick 96
   4.2. Compensation versus Moral Balancing 101
   4.3. Compensation, Prudential Balancing, and Additivity 108

5. Aggregation and Problems about Trade-offs within Lives: Single-Person Spectrum Arguments 129
5.1. The Third Standard View 129
5.2. Another Worry about Consistency 132
5.3. A Powerful Example: From Torture to Mosquito Bites 134
5.4. Refining Views One through Four and Clarifying the Example 139
5.5. An Objection to View Three: Invoking Principles of Decomposition and Recombination 145
5.6. A Proportionality Argument against View Three 152
5.7. Trusting Our Intuitions Regarding Inordinate Lengths of Time 154

6. Exploring Transitivity: Part I 162
6.1. Transitive and Nontransitive Relations 163
6.2. Incommensurability/Incomparability and Conditions Where Transitivity Either Fails to Apply or Fails 171
6.3. Rough Comparability 176
6.4. Rational Decision Making and the Nontransitivity of Not Worse Than 183
6.5. Rational Preferences and the Money Pump 185
6.6. The Importance of Global and Strategic Reasoning 188

7. Exploring Transitivity: Part II 194
7.1. The Nontransitivity of Permissibility 195
7.2. The Nontransitivity of Moral Obligatoriness 197
7.3. The Obligatoriness Relation and Another Possible Money Pump 201
7.4. From Obligatoriness to Better Than: On the Right and the Good, and the Inheritability of Nontransitivity 203
7.5. Defending the Transitivity of the Obligatoriness Relation: A Fine-Grained Solution 214
7.6. "All-Things-Considered Better Than": The Underlying Conditions That Might Make It a Transitive or Nontransitive Relation 217
7.7. Introducing the Internal Aspects and Essentially Comparative Views 228

8. Expected Utility Theory/Expected Value Theory 232
8.1. Clarifying My Target 232
8.2. A Brief Characterization of Expected Utility Theory and Expected Value Theory 233
8.3. On the Relation between Rough Comparability and Expected Value Theory 237

8.4. The Principle of Continuity   245
    8.4.1. Examining Continuity: "Easy" Cases versus "Extreme" Cases   246
    8.4.2. From Safe Bets to High-Stakes Bets: The Challenge   249
    8.4.3. Objections and Responses   253
    8.4.4. J. Ross's Principle Revisited   261
8.5. Concluding Remarks   262

9. Spectrum Arguments: Objections and Replies   265
9.1. Different Kinds, Different Criteria   265
9.2. Sorites Paradoxes   277
    9.2.1. The Purported Analogy   277
    9.2.2. Disanalogies   278
    9.2.3. Nonnormative Spectrum Arguments   284
9.3. Heuristics and Similarity-Based Arguments   296

10. On the Value of Utility and Two Models for Combining Ideals   313
10.1. Preliminary Remarks   313
10.2. A Standard Model for Utility and a Standard Model for Combining Ideals   315
10.3. Is *All* Utility Noninstrumentally or Intrinsically Valuable?   317
10.4. Total versus Average Utility   319
10.5. Revisiting the Repugnant Conclusion   324
10.6. The Capped Model for Ideals   328
10.7. Upper and Lower Limits for Different Kinds of Utility   335
10.8. Complications to Consider for a Capped Model of Utility   338
10.9. Contrasting the Capped Model with the Standard Model for Utility   343
10.10. Shared Formal or Structural Features of Ideals   351
10.11. Concluding Remark   360

11. On the Nature of Moral Ideals: Part I   363
11.1. The Mere Addition Paradox   364
11.2. Illuminating the Mere Addition Paradox: Parfit's Implicit Appeal to an Essentially Comparative View of Moral Ideals   366
11.3. The Internal Aspects View of Moral Ideals   383
11.4. An Independence of Irrelevant Alternatives Principle   387
11.5. On the Relevance of Mere Addition   390
11.6. Reconsidering the Mere Addition Paradox on the Internal Aspects View   394
11.7. Is the Mere Addition Paradox Genuinely Paradoxical?   388

12. On the Nature of Moral Ideals: Part II 401
- 12.1. Reconsidering the Essentially Comparative View 402
- 12.2. Narrow Person-Affecting Views 416
- 12.3. The Narrow Person-Affecting View: Objections and Responses 422
- 12.4. Impersonal Views versus Person-Affecting Views: More Examples Illuminating the Powerful Appeal of Narrow Person-Affecting Considerations 434
- 12.5. Restricting the Scope of Essentially Comparative Ideals 445
- 12.6. Another Reason to Accept Essentially Comparative Views: Revisiting "How More Than France Exists" 448
- 12.7. Two Further Reasons to Accept an Essentially Comparative View 452

13. Juggling to Preserve Transitivity 457
- 13.1. Fine-Grained Solutions 457
- 13.2. The Time Trade-off Method 465
- 13.3. A Sports Analogy 468
- 13.4. Reflective Equilibrium 471
- 13.5. Another Impossibility Result 475

14. Conclusion 477
- 14.1. Topics Canvassed 477
- 14.2. Lessons Learned 479
- 14.3. Work Remaining 488
- 14.4. On the (Ir)Relevance of Meaning or Logic to Whether "All-Things-Considered Better Than" Is a Transitive Relation 494
- 14.5. Some Responses to My Views 497
- 14.6. On the Appropriateness of (Sometimes) Embracing Incredible or Inconsistent Views 499
- 14.7. Moral and Practical Dilemmas 508
- 14.8. Skepticism 514
- 14.9. Final Remarks 520

Appendices 522
- A Worries about Duration and Number 522
- B On the Relations between Quantity, Quality, Duration, and Number 526
- C A New Version of the Paradox of the Heap 531
- D Three Further Objections to Spectrum Arguments 534
  - D.1. Vagueness and Indeterminacy 534

        D.2. Zeno's Paradox   538
        D.3. Finding a Uniquely Best Alternative along a
            Spectrum   540
   E Norcross's Argument for Restricting the Scope of the Narrow
      Person-Affecting View   545
   F Lexical Priority in Defense of the Axiom of Transitivity   554
   G Book Summary   558
        G.1. Chapter 1   558
        G.2. Chapter 2   559
        G.3. Chapter 3   560
        G.4. Chapter 4   561
        G.5. Chapter 5   561
        G.6. Chapter 6   563
        G.7. Chapter 7   564
        G.8. Chapter 8   566
        G.9. Chapter 9   566
        G.10. Chapter 10   567
        G.11. Chapter 11   568
        G.12. Chapter 12   569
        G.13. Chapter 13   570
        G.14. Chapter 14   571
        G.16. Appendices   572

Bibliography   575
Index   583
List of Diagrams   605
List of Cases and Examples   607
List of Principles and Views   611

Rethinking The Good

1

Introduction

John Rawls once wrote, "All ethical doctrines worth our attention take consequences into account in judging rightness. One which did not would simply be irrational, crazy."[1] Surely, Rawls is right. As important as nonconsequential concerns are, in many cases consequences matter. Often, we either need or want to determine the best outcome "all things considered." Moreover, this is so not only in the "ethical" domain, but also in the practical domain more generally. Many times, we are interested in determining the best outcomes for ourselves, our families, our groups, or our societies. Thus, echoing Rawls, all plausible theories of practical reasoning must give an adequate account of the assessment and ranking of outcomes. Unfortunately, an adequate account has not yet been given; nor is one on the horizon.

Many years ago, when I began this book, I hoped to provide such an account—or at least an outline of what such an account would look like or how it might be developed. My aims are different now. Largely, they are to illuminate some of the key assumptions to which many are firmly committed regarding the nature of the good, moral ideals, and practical reasoning. These assumptions have a central role to play in the development of an adequate account for ranking outcomes. But, unfortunately, as we will see, deep tensions between some of the assumptions raise fundamental, and perhaps insuperable, difficulties. Accordingly, the prospects now seem dim for developing an account for ranking outcomes that accommodates all of the key assumptions.

Many of this book's results are negative. Indeed, some believe that if this book's arguments were sound, they would constitute a serious case for skepticism about practical reasoning.[2] Accordingly, those who are not skeptics may

---

[1] *A Theory of Justice* (Cambridge, MA: Harvard University Press, 1971), 30.
[2] Derek Parfit has expressed such a view to me in discussion; see section 14.8.

be convinced that this book's arguments must not be sound, even if it isn't apparent where, exactly, they go wrong. In my conclusion, I discuss the nature of the skepticism my arguments may seem to support, and how such skepticism differs from other forms of skepticism that have been offered. But I might note that I, myself, am not a skeptic. Accordingly, I retain the hope that even if this book's arguments are sound, we will be able to avoid the morass of practical skepticism, even if it is not yet clear how best to do that.

Ultimately, this book forces us to reexamine and revise some of our deepest beliefs about the nature of the good, moral ideals, and practical reasoning. But it doesn't dictate which of those beliefs should be revised or how they should be revised. Still, for reasons that will become clear later, I believe that whatever revisions we ultimately make will have far-reaching practical and theoretical implications.

1.1 Overview of the Book

This book addresses many topics. A central one is the topic of aggregation. I consider a number of widely held views about how we should aggregate benefits and burdens both between and within lives, to generate all-things-considered rankings of different alternatives. In chapters 2 through 5, I will characterize and address two approaches to aggregating benefits and burdens: an *additive-aggregationist* approach and an *anti-additive-aggregationist* approach. I will consider implications, problems, and objections confronting each approach, as well as responses that these might prompt. Ultimately, I will contend that an *additive-aggregationist* approach is deeply plausible and relevant for comparing *some* alternatives, while an *anti-additive-aggregationist* approach is deeply plausible and relevant for comparing *other* alternatives.

A second central topic that will also be addressed in chapters 2 through 5, as well as in chapters 8 and 9, is the nature and significance of various *Spectrum Arguments*. These are, in essence, impossibility arguments, and they demonstrate a surprising inconsistency between several views to which most people are deeply wedded. The key views are the relevance and significance of the additive-aggregationist approach for comparing some, nearby, alternatives along certain spectrums, the relevance and significance of the anti-additive-aggregationist approach for comparing some, far apart, alternatives along those spectrums, and the *Axiom of Transitivity*, which holds that "all-things-considered better than" is a transitive relation. I will closely explore various Spectrum Arguments, including numerous objections and responses to which they give rise. In doing this, I will contend that giving up any of the Spectrum Arguments' inconsistent views will have practical and theoretical implications that will be extremely difficult for most people to accept.

As indicated, one of the key views underlying my Spectrum Arguments is the Axiom of Transitivity. A third central topic that will be explored throughout this work, but especially in chapters 6, 7, and 13, is the status of the Axiom of Transitivity, and various related Axioms of Transitivity, such as the views that "equally as good as" and "at least as good as" are transitive relations. I will explore the nature of transitivity and the general conditions which account for whether a relation is, or is not, transitive. I will show that a number of important normative relations are *nontransitive* (a notion defined later, in section 1.5), including the "not worse than" relation (understood as expressing the relation of *rough comparability*, as defined in chapter 6), the "permissibility" relation (permissible to do rather than), and the "obligatoriness" relation (ought to do rather than). I will then consider whether the nontransitivity of these other normative relations provides reason to believe that the "all-things-considered better than" relation may also be nontransitive. Ultimately, I will argue that whether or not the various Axioms of Transitivity hold depends on the nature of ideals.

Accordingly, a fourth central topic of this book will be to explore the nature of ideals and, in particular, to examine two rival conceptions of ideals, which I call the *Internal Aspects View* and the *Essentially Comparative View*. After having been implicitly in play in earlier chapters, these views will be explicitly introduced in chapter 7 and then be the main focus of chapters 11 and 12. I will argue that each of these views has great plausibility, and that to give either of them up would have radical implications.

In exploring these topics, numerous important issues will arise, two of which will receive special treatment in chapters devoted to them. In particular, chapter 8 will address concerns about the foundations of *Expected Utility Theory*, and its analogue *Expected Value Theory*; chapter 10 will present and consider two models for combining moral ideals in arriving at all-things-considered judgments, a *Standard* (uncapped) model and a *Capped* model.

Throughout this work, I will show that many of the beliefs to which people are most committed are inconsistent, or have surprising and often deeply implausible implications. I also hope to show that, for most people, coming to terms with the results of this book will require a major shift in their understanding of the good, moral ideals, and practical reasoning.

1.2 A Guide to the Material

Every author wants his or her book read in its entirety. But this is a long book. Accordingly, while there is reason to read this book in the order it is written, let me provide some information that might help those interested in reading a coherent subset of the book.

First, let me note that certain chapters naturally go together. This is so of chapters 2 and 3, 4 and 5, 6 and 7, and 11 and 12. While many chapters could be read independently of the others, in general, one would be better served reading the first of a paired set of chapters before the second.

Chapters 1 through 7 and 10 through 12 are the most central, so one might read those chapters most carefully, and in that order. But let me emphasize that chapters 10 through 12, especially 11 and 12, are of fundamental importance to understanding this book. So, even if one decides to skip or skim some earlier chapters, those chapters should be read.

Notwithstanding the foregoing, I note that chapters 1 through 5 are likely to be more accessible to undergraduates than some of the other chapters and might be usefully taught independently of the other chapters.

Chapters 9 and 13 deal with important objections that have been raised to my arguments. These chapters might be skipped or skimmed if one doesn't share any of the objections or worries addressed in those chapters. Similarly, if one has some of the concerns addressed in those chapters, but not others, one might simply read those sections relevant to addressing one's particular concerns.

Chapter 8 concerns the foundations of Expected Utility Theory, and its analogue Expected Value Theory. I think this chapter is important and should be of interest to most of this book's readers, but it is likely to be of most relevance to followers of Expected Utility Theory and those subjects that partly depend on it, such as game theory, decision theory, and economics.

Chapter 14 concludes the book with a straightforward recapitulation of the topics canvassed, lessons learned, and work remaining, as well as some reflections on the book's implications. Some readers may want to skip or skim different sections of the conclusion, depending on their interests in the topics canvassed.

Most readers will safely ignore appendices A through F, though I expect that different readers will find one or another of those appendices of value depending on their interests.

Finally, for those who won't be reading the book in its entirety, a summary of each chapter's main claims is given—without arguments, of course—in appendix G.

1.3 Intuitions

Let me say a few words about the role that intuitions play in my arguments. We have intuitive judgments about particular cases, actual or hypothetical, as well as about general principles. In addition, we have both initial, pretheoretical, intuitive judgments, and firm, considered, ones. According to Henry Sidgwick, and many others, such intuitive judgments provide the starting point for moral theory.[3] For Sidgwick, the task of moral philosophy is largely one of seeking a coherent, systematic, and non–ad hoc way of accommodating and explaining many of our pretheoretical intuitive judgments as well as most of our firm, considered, ones. Moreover, ideally, the method sought should offer a plausible and principled way of assessing, and where appropriate revising, people's intuitive judgments about both particular cases and general principles. John Rawls's view about the desirability of seeking a state of *reflective equilibrium* with respect to one's pre- and posttheoretical intuitions and judgments expresses a position that is similar to Sidgwick's in its essential methodological tenets, even if it differs in its details.[4]

There are serious questions about Sidgwick's methodological approach. One of the most important concerns the normative status of its results. Why should we believe that any results yielded by such a methodological approach correspond with the *truth* about morality, if there is such a thing, rather than merely *cohere* with most of our initial beliefs? Presumably, if there is an answer to this question it lies with a position that might be called *rational intuitionism*. *Roughly*, on such a view, there are moral facts; these moral facts provide reasons to believe certain things; a fully rational person is, in the right circumstances, responsive to all the reasons that there are; a fortiori, a fully rational person will, in the right circumstances, form appropriate beliefs in response to the reasons provided by the moral facts; and, finally, these appropriately formed beliefs either constitute or generate at least some of our moral intuitions and judgments.

I confess that I am tempted to some version of rational intuitionism, so construed. But I will not try to defend such a view, as doing so would require another book, and there is nothing in this book that commits me to such a position. The key point is that an appeal to intuitions is appropriate and defensible on a wide range of normative theories and meta-ethical views, including both realist and nonrealist conceptions. For example, on the views that ethics is invented or constructed, or that it reflects our sentiments or attitudes, we may still appropriately look to our intuitions to help illuminate what ethical standards we might choose to adopt, or which ethical principles would accurately reflect our sentiments and attitudes.

A second important question about Sidgwick's approach concerns whether the task he has in mind is achievable. It seems reasonable to *seek* a coherent, systematic, and non–ad hoc method of accommodating and explaining many of our pretheoretical intuitive judgments and most of our firm considered ones; but this doesn't mean that there is good reason to expect that we will actually *arrive* at such a method. Indeed, Sidgwick him-

---

[3] See Sidgwick's *The Methods of Ethics*, 7th ed. (London: Macmillan, 1907).
[4] See Rawls's *A Theory of Justice*, 20–22, 48–51, 120, 432, 434, and 579.

self was acutely aware that his approach failed to reconcile some of our deepest beliefs about the nature of rationality and morality.[5] So, it is an important and open question how to respond to our moral intuitions, if we are unable to arrive at a method for dealing with them of the sort that Sidgwick seeks.

I agree, then, that serious questions can be raised about Sidgwick's methodological approach. But I share his conviction that our moral intuitions about both particular cases and general principles are the *starting point* for moral theory. Our moral intuitions provide the data, as it were, with which moral theory must concern itself. Accordingly, in this book there is a lot of attention paid to identifying our moral intuitions about a host of actual and hypothetical cases, as well as our intuitions about a host of general moral or practical principles and ideals.

Some people may hope to "do away" with the role of intuitions in normative theory. But I believe that this is a fool's quest. In my judgment, appeal to intuitions is an indispensable staple of normative theory. Thus, it is no accident that such appeals clearly appear in the most important writings of many of the best contemporary moral and political theorists.[6] Of course, we must be prepared to subject our intuitions to critical scrutiny, and to revise or reject them in the light of such scrutiny. But, ultimately, I believe that all plausible normative theories are grounded on intuitions.

In sum, I take our intuitive judgments seriously, as features of our response to the world that need to be understood, explained, and, where possible, accommodated. Getting clear on our intuitions is not the last step in moral theorizing, but it is a crucially important step, and one that must come very near or at the beginning of such theorizing.

---

[5] Derek Parfit writes that "when asked about his book [*The Methods of Ethics*], Sidgwick said that its first word was *Ethics*, and its last *failure*" (in his *Reasons and Persons* [Oxford: Oxford University Press, 1984], 443). Sidgwick's response reflected his belief that moral theory had to provide an answer to Glaucon's challenge, "Why should I be moral?" (from Plato's *The Republic*, trans. Allan Bloom [New York: Basic Books, 1968]), and that to do this successfully moral theory had to establish that either prudence and morality never conflicted, or that if they did, one ought to act morally insofar as one was rational. However, Sidgwick believed that his masterpiece couldn't answer this fundamental problem for moral theory because it couldn't reconcile his beliefs about the nature of individual rationality—including his belief that it was always rational (even if not uniquely so) to act in one's own best interest—with his beliefs about what morality demanded of us—including his belief that morality sometimes required us to act contrary to our best interests.

[6] This point will be obvious to anyone with even a passing acquaintance with the literature of the last forty years. See, for example, the writings of G. A. Cohen, Philippa Foot, Thomas Hurka, Shelly Kagan, Frances Kamm, Jeff McMahan, Thomas Nagel, Robert Nozick, Derek Parfit, John Rawls, Joseph Raz, Thomas Scanlon, Amartya Sen, Judith Thomson, and Bernard Williams. (I trust those whom I have not named here will forgive me, as I couldn't possibly list *all* of the excellent philosophers who make significant appeal to intuitions in their work.)

1.4 Impossibility Arguments and Juggling

Most people accept the transitivity of the "better than" relation, where a relation, R, is transitive, if and only if for all a, b, and c, if aRb and bRc, then aRc. Applied to the assessment of outcomes, the transitivity of "better than" entails that if, all things considered, A is a better outcome than B, and B is a better outcome than C, then, all things considered, A is a better outcome than C.

In earlier writings, I claimed to have arguments for the conclusion that "all-things-considered better than" is not a transitive relation.[7] This was misleading, at best. My considered view of the matter is different. I believe that over the years I have developed some arguments showing that a number of views that many people find deeply compelling are incompatible. If I were an economist, I might call these arguments *impossibility* arguments. Since I am not an economist, I generally don't. Nor do I formalize my arguments symbolically. Still, in essence, I think a significant part of what is going on in this work is the development of a number of impossibility arguments. Some of these are fairly straightforward, involving just a few positions that are presented over the course of a few pages. Others are much more complicated, involving many different complexly related positions that are developed over the course of many chapters.

Impossibility arguments reveal that one cannot *consistently* maintain each of several positions. Of course, so understood, every deductively sound argument constitutes an impossibility argument. What makes an impossibility argument interesting and significant depends on the nature of its inconsistent positions; more particularly, on how deeply we are wedded to them, and how significant the implications would be of giving any of them up. Suffice it to say, I believe that many of us are deeply wedded to each of the inconsistent positions I identify, and that to give up any of them would have far-reaching and deeply implausible implications. A large part of this book's aim is to consider various arguments that can be given for and against the different conflicting positions, to explore what positions stand or fall together, and to illuminate some of the implications of accepting or rejecting the different positions.

One of the views that is at stake in my arguments is the view that all plausible or important "all-things-considered better than" relations are transitive. But I want to emphasize, here, that in this book I am *not* arguing that we should reject this view. Like many, I see the power and appeal of the view that all plausible or important "all-things-considered better than" relations are transitive. Like many, I see the tremendous upheaval that would result in our practical and theoretical reasoning if we gave such a view up. So, like many, I am loath

---

[7] See, especially, "A Continuum Argument for Intransitivity," *Philosophy and Public Affairs* 25 (1996): 175–210.

to deny the view in question. The problem is that I am *also* loath to give up any of the other views that my arguments reveal to be inconsistent with it.

So, my current state is akin to that of a juggler who finds himself juggling too many balls, each of which is precious and important. He knows that he can't keep juggling all of the balls indefinitely, but he can't seriously imagine letting any of them drop. As ball one heads to the ground he has to decide whether to let it fall, or whether to catch it and let some other ball fall instead. Perhaps he initially decides to catch ball one, and then, as ball two heads to the ground, to catch that as well in his other hand. But as he watches ball three head toward the ground he realizes that he just can't let that fall. So he quickly throws ball one in the air, and catches ball three. But at this point ball four may be headed to the ground, so he may quickly throw ball two in the air and catch ball four before it hits the ground. But at this point ball one is on its way down, and he will once again have to decide between ball one and one of the other balls in his hand. And so it will continue, as long as he is able to successfully juggle all the balls. Eventually, it seems he will have to let several of them drop, but he is desperate to avoid that. So he keeps juggling—hoping, perhaps, that he will discover some solution to his predicament, though at present he has no reason to believe that this is possible.

1.5 Some Terminology

In this book, I shall often consider judgments of the form "other things equal, it would be better if *A* rather than *B*" or "all things considered, *A* is better than *B*," where *A* and *B* are alternative outcomes or possible states of affairs. Such claims are to be understood as claims about the relative merits of the outcomes from an *impartial* perspective. On some accounts, the impartial perspective corresponds to the perspective of an "ideal observer" or a "rational impartial spectator" who does not himself have any deontological or agent-relative reasons to favor one outcome over another.[8] Such a claim expresses an evaluative judgment about what we think there is most reason to want, or what would be most *desirable*, from an impartial perspective, rather than a narrowly moral judgment about what we *ought to do*.

---

[8] So understood, the impartial perspective is still capable of giving due weight to partial or agent-relative considerations insofar as they have a moral value that is relevant to the goodness of outcomes. If, for example, it is morally important that parents provide especially for their own children, the impartial perspective can value an outcome in which parents fulfill their parental duties over an alternative in which parents abandon their children, even if the alternatives are equal in all other respects. However, while *Tom* has reason to favor an alternative in which his children fare well and his neighbor's children do not over an alternative in which his neighbor's children fare well and his children do not, other things equal, there is no reason to regard one of those alternatives as *better* than the other from the *impartial* perspective.

This last point is worth emphasizing. The claim that, other things equal, A is better than B, reflects the judgment that from an impartial perspective there would be most reason to prefer the former outcome to obtain rather than the latter and, analogously, greater reason, from that perspective, to regret an outcome where B obtained rather than A, other things equal. But, importantly, such a claim is not about what we *ought to do*, all things considered; nor does it entail that it is always obligatory, or even always permissible, to produce outcome A rather than outcome B. Such implications would follow on certain consequentialist moral theories, but I am not taking a stand on the truth of such theories in this book.

As indicated in my preface, many people have believed that it is an *analytic* truth that "all-things-considered better than" is a transitive relation. Others have believed that it is a *logical* truth that "all-things-considered better than" is a transitive relation. Thus, some have suggested that while my arguments may be interesting and significant, and while they may force us to recognize that there is a normatively significant relation that is intransitive, the relation in question *can't* be an "all-things-considered better than" relation.[9] Accordingly, one might think that I should recast my arguments, showing that there is a conflict between several of our deepest beliefs and the transitivity of a significant normative relation that might be called the *choiceworthiness* relation, or the *preferability* relation, where, roughly, we might say that one outcome is more choiceworthy or preferable than another if, faced with the two outcomes, there would be most reason to hope that the one was realized from an impartial perspective.[10] One advantage of recasting my arguments this way is that I might prevent some potential readers—including, perhaps, virtually all economists—from dismissing my arguments out of hand for even raising the nonsensical possibility of challenging an analytical or logical truth.

I see the attractions of this position, and so for many years I did, indeed, couch my arguments in terms of the notion of "preferability" instead of the notion of "all-things-considered better than." The thought, of course, was that preferability, as I introduced it, could be seen to have a significant role in normative reasoning, but that even if it *seemed* as if the "preferability" relation *better* be transitive, there would be no antecedent insistence that such a relation *must* be transitive, for analytical or logical reasons.

However, as I circulated drafts of this book and gave many lectures based on it, it became increasingly clear that introducing the notion of "preferability" was unnecessarily distracting and confusing. Most readers and audiences

---

[9] For example, this view has been expressed by John Broome (in *Weighing Lives* [Oxford: Oxford University Press, 2004], 62) and was previously held by Derek Parfit (in discussion). Parfit no longer holds this view, though Broome still does.

[10] Derek Parfit once suggested this position to me, offering it as a friendly amendment to my approach.

inferred that the notion of "preferability" just *was* a notion of "all-things-considered better than," and they urged that I simply put the relevant arguments in terms of a conflict between certain of our deep beliefs and the view that any plausible candidate for an "all-things-considered better than" relation must be transitive. Moreover, and more important, in countless discussions over the years, it became clear that some people were led by my arguments to conclude that there is at least one important "all-things-considered better than" relation that is not transitive, that many others were at least *tempted* by that position, and that most people were at least *open* to that possibility. By contrast, I am pretty sure that no one would have been open to the possibility of rejecting a genuinely analytic truth, like "all bachelors are unmarried males," or a genuinely logical truth, like "all As are A" or "if $A \to B$, and A, then B."

Wittgenstein's famous claim that "meaning is use"[11] is controversial and notoriously difficult to unpack. But based on the reactions I have received to my work, it is pretty clear to me that as many people actually *use* the notion of "all-things-considered better than," the claim that every plausible or important "all-things-considered better than" relation must be transitive is neither analytically nor logically true. Accordingly, in this book, I have decided to cast my arguments in terms of the notion of "all-things-considered better than," rather than in terms of my previously introduced notion of "preferability."

Let me say a bit more about this. I don't deny that there may be *a* use of the notion of "all-things-considered better than" where it is either a conceptual or logical truth that the relation of "all-things-considered better than" is transitive. Indeed, as we will see in later chapters, if we take "better than" to be the comparative of "goodness," and "goodness" to be an internal feature of outcomes, then it *will* be a logical truth that "all-things-considered better than" is transitive. Something like this is how John Broome uses the notion of "better than,"[12] and I readily grant that this usage is hardly idiosyncratic. Accordingly, I agree that *if* one uses the notion of "better than" to express Broome's conception, then the "all-things-considered better than" relation *couldn't* be intransitive.

However, in that case, a different question arises, concerning the scope of the notion in question. We may have assumed that the notion of "better than" that is analytically or logically transitive covers a large part of the normative realm, applying to and enabling us to compare all or most alternatives. But we may *learn*, as a result of this book's considerations, that the scope and significance of that particular conception of "better than" is

---

[11] See Wittgenstein's *Philosophical Investigations*, where this claim is repeated and discussed throughout the text. A classic translation is G. E. M. Anscombe's (2nd ed., Oxford: Blackwell, 1958).

[12] See *Weighing Lives*, sections 2.1 and 4.1.

severely limited. That is, we may learn that often the comparisons we are most interested in for normative purposes are not comparisons in terms of the "all-things-considered better than" relation *as Broome and others understand it*, and that their notion does not play the central role in practical reasoning that it has been thought to.

On the other hand, I believe that there is *another* use of the notion of "all-things-considered better than" that is wider and less restricted than the one that guarantees the transitivity of "better than" as a matter of logic or the meanings of words. This use is connected with what might be called a *reason-implying* sense of "better than." Roughly, on this use, outcome A is better than outcome B, all things considered, if one would have more reason to prefer A to be realized than B, from an impartial perspective. Moreover, importantly, on the reason-implying sense of "better than" that I have in mind here, and with which I will be principally concerned throughout this book, it is an open question—determined neither by the meanings of the words nor by logic alone—whether "all-things-considered better than" is a transitive relation. The answer to that question will turn on the nature of ideals. As we will see, if the view of ideals that I call the *Internal Aspects View* turns out to be correct, then "all-things-considered better than" in my reasoning-implying sense *will* be a transitive relation. If, however, the view of ideals that I call the *Essentially Comparative View* turns out to be correct, then "all-things-considered better than" in my reason-implying sense need *not* be a transitive relation. But the key point to note is that my reason-implying sense of "better than" doesn't dictate which view of ideals is correct, which is why it is an open question, on my reason-implying sense of "better than," whether or not "all-things-considered better than" is a transitive relation.

This issue is very important and is worth further clarification and emphasis. Many people may have implicitly assumed that there is only a single use of the notion of "all-things-considered better than." But just as there may be many senses of "ought"—for example, "ought" morally, "ought" prudentially, "ought" rationally, "ought" epistemologically (to believe), "ought" subjectively (given what one desires or believes), "ought" objectively (given what is most desirable or true)—so there may be many senses of "all-things-considered better than." I am granting that on *some* senses of "all-things-considered better than," "all-things-considered better than" is a transitive relation by definition or as a matter of logic. But I am suggesting that on at least *one* important sense of "all-things-considered better than"—a reason-implying sense that is central to practical reasoning—"all-things-considered better than" is not transitive as a matter of definition or logic. Rather, on the reason-implying sense of the notion of "all-things-considered better than" with which I am mainly concerned in this book, it is an open question whether the "all-things-considered better than" relation is transitive, a question that turns on the correct view about the nature of ideals.

Note, there may be more than one reason-implying sense of "all-things-considered better than." Consider, for example, three possible people, John, Jack, and Jane. John, a committed utilitarian, claims that "all things considered" *A* is better than *B* and *B* is better than *C*. In claiming this, John may be invoking a reason-implying sense of "all-things-considered better than." Believing that utility is the *only* factor that is relevant and significant for assessing the goodness of outcomes, John believes that from the impartial perspective there is most reason to prefer *A* to *B* and *B* to *C*. Jack, a committed egalitarian, may contend that "all things considered" *B* is better than *A* and *C* is better than *B*. In claiming this, Jack, too, may be invoking a reason-implying sense of "all-things-considered better than." Believing that equality is the *only* factor that is relevant and significant for assessing the goodness of outcomes, Jack believes that from the impartial perspective there is most reason to prefer *B* to *A* and *C* to *B*. Jane, the most reasonable of the three, believes that "all things considered" *A* is better than *B* and *C* is better than *B*. In claiming this, Jane may also be invoking a reason-implying sense of "all-things-considered better than." Believing that many different factors are relevant and significant for comparing outcomes, including utility and equality, but others factors as well, Jane believes that from the impartial perspective there is most reason to prefer *A* to *B* and *C* to *B*.

As presented so far, John, Jack, and Jane may all be invoking the *same* reason-implying sense of "all-things-considered better than": *my* reason-implying sense according to which for any two outcomes *X* and *Y*, *X* is better than *Y* *all things considered* if and only if there is most reason to prefer *X* to *Y* from an impartial perspective after accurately taking into account *all* of the factors that are relevant and significant for comparing such outcomes from that perspective. That is, it may be that the differences in judgments between John, Jack, and Jane simply reflect the differences in their views about what factors *are* relevant and significant for assessing the goodness of outcomes from the impartial perspective. Suppose, however, that after much dispute, it became apparent that when John claimed that *A* is better than *B* all things considered, he was using the notion of "all-things-considered better than" in a *utilitarian* reason-implying sense, meaning that what he intended by his claim was simply that *insofar* as one focused on utility, there would be most reason to prefer *A* to *B* from an impartial perspective. In that case, there need be no reason for Jack or Jane to dispute John's claim that *A* is better than *B* all things considered. Although they *might* want to claim that John's sense of "all-things-considered better than" is somewhat misleading or infelicitous, they might do better to simply grant that *A is* better than *B*, in the *utilitarian* reason-implying sense of "all-things-considered better than," but to argue that *that* sense of "all-things-considered better than" is not the most central or important one for the purposes of practical reasoning.

I have gone on regarding this at some length, because I believe that some people use the notion of "all-things-considered better than" in different senses than I am using it in this work. In claiming that X is better than Y all things considered, some may be using it in a non-reason-implying sense, and others may be using it in a reason-implying sense that *restricts* the factors that one can consider in assessing and comparing outcomes to the *intrinsic* value of such outcomes or, as I shall put it in this work, to factors that are wholly *internal* to those outcomes. As indicated, I don't want to deny that one *can* use the notion of "all-things-considered better than" in such senses—that, for example, there is a plausible and coherent sense of "all-things-considered better than" that we might call the *internal aspects reason-implying* sense of "all-things-considered better than." However, I want to emphasize that in this work I will usually be employing a wider, less restricted, notion of "all-things-considered better than." Thus, as noted previously, on *my* reason-implying sense of "all-things-considered better than," to say that X is better than Y *all things considered* is simply to contend that there is most reason to prefer X to Y from an impartial perspective after accurately taking into account *all* of the factors that are relevant and significant for comparing such outcomes from that perspective, where this doesn't set, in advance, any restrictions or preconditions on what factors might actually *be* relevant or significant for such comparisons or on what the nature of those factors must be like. As the book unfolds, I hope it will become clear that the wide, less restricted, reason-implying sense of "all-things-considered better than" that I employ in this work is a central and important one—indeed it may be *the* most central and important one—for practical reasoning.

Accordingly, when, in this work, I am discussing the notions of "better than" and "all-things-considered better than," and the related notions of "worse than," "equally as good as," "at least as good as," and so on, I am employing my wide, less restricted, reason-implying sense of those notions. So understood, my arguments cannot be dismissed out of hand as unintelligible or contrary to logic merely because they raise the *possibility* that "all-things-considered better than" might not be a transitive relation. Also, importantly, when I write, as I do throughout this book, about *the* "better than" relation, or *the* "all-things-considered better than" relation, this should *not* be construed as my believing or implying that there can only be *one* "better than" relation or *one* "all-things-considered better than" relation. Rather, I am simply saving words in my presentation of the issues. Unless context makes plain that I am using such expressions otherwise, all such expressions simply refer to *my* wide, less restricted, reason-implying sense of such notions. Having labored this point as much as I have, here at the beginning, I hope and trust that the reader will remember this point throughout the book, and that I will not have to remind the reader on each occasion of the sense in which I am using the notion of "all-things-considered better than" and its cognates.[13]

Having said all that, here, as elsewhere, I don't really care much about merely terminological matters. People can use terms more or less as they see fit, and if some readers want to *insist* that, given how *they* understand the notion of "all-things-considered better than," it *must* be a transitive relation, analytically or logically, so that any purported notion of "all-things-considered better than" that does not entail that the relation is transitive is necessarily unintelligible or self-contradictory, then I'll invite such readers to think about my arguments in different terms. However, that won't change the fact that this book raises a host of deep and substantive issues for our understanding of practical reasoning,[14] or the fact that substantive issues can never be settled by terminological fiat.

Next, let me introduce some terminology. I shall say that a relation R is *intransitive*, if there are any three outcomes, a, b, and c, such that aRb, and bRc, but it might not be the case that aRc. Note, on my terminology, to say of a relation that it is intransitive is equivalent to saying that it is *not* a transitive relation, nothing more. It does not commit one to the strong view that for all a, b, and c, if aRb, and bRc, then cRa; nor does it even commit one to the weaker view that there has to be at least one set of outcomes, a, b, and c, where aRb, bRc, and cRa. Of course, if a relation R has such implications then it *will* be intransitive, but the point is that there are various ways in which it might be true that it is not the case that aRc, without its being true that cRa. So, for example, if R is the "better than" relation, in addition to c's being better than a, other ways in which it would not be the case that a is better than c would be if a and c were equal, or only roughly comparable (see chapter 6).

---

[13] I am grateful to Derek Parfit whose pressing led me to emphasize the preceding remarks as much as I did. Parfit was concerned that some people who used the notion of "all-things-considered better than" in a sense other than the one I am principally concerned with would fail to take the results of this book as seriously as they should, and would be puzzled or object to my later discussions of "the" "all-things-considered better than" relation which did not involve their own favored sense of that notion. In fact, Parfit urged that to avoid confusion I rewrite *each* subsequent reference to the "all-things-considered better than" relation, to spell out that I am referring to *my* wide, less restricted, reason-implying sense of that notion, and he is unlikely to be satisfied with the prophylactic remarks that I have provided here, as lengthy as they are. However, since this particular concern of Parfit's didn't come to my attention until *after* my typescript had already been submitted to the copyeditor, and since to fully accommodate them would have required rewriting literally thousands of sentences, affecting nearly every page of the typescript, I have decided to address them once, carefully, here in my introductory chapter. I hope and trust that what I have provided here will be sufficient to prevent the confusions or objections that Parfit thought might otherwise needlessly arise in the minds of some readers.

[14] As, for example, both Broome and Parfit recognize, despite differing from me in their understanding of the notion of "all-things-considered better than." See, for example, section 4.1 of Broome's *Weighing Lives*, especially page 62. Parfit has conveyed this sentiment to me in conversation on many occasions.

Now, let me introduce a bit of nonstandard terminology. In some cases it *appears* that a certain relation, R, both applies to some alternatives and is intransitive. But, as we will see later, in some of those cases we may decide not that the relation R is actually intransitive, but that the relation R doesn't actually apply, simpliciter, to the cases in question. Hence, as we might put it, it isn't really that the notion of transitivity *fails*, but that it *fails to apply*, because there is no single relation, R, that actually applies to the different alternatives, such that for some outcomes a, b, and c, aRb, and bRc, but it is not the case that aRc. Moreover, in some cases there may be disagreement as to whether we should say that transitivity actually fails for a given set of rankings, or whether, appearances to the contrary, it fails to apply to the set of rankings in question. Accordingly, for expository purposes, I shall use the terminology of *nontransitivity* to be neutral between these two positions. In particular, there will be some cases where a given relation, R, seemingly applies to a set of alternatives where I shall say that relation R is nontransitive, leaving it open whether R actually applies to the set of alternatives and generates an intransitive ranking of those alternatives, or whether R fails to generate a transitive ranking across those alternatives because R doesn't actually apply across the different alternatives, and hence doesn't generate a set of rankings that either meet or fail to meet the criterion for transitivity.

Clearly, my notion of nontransitivity is broader than my notion of intransitivity, as all intransitive relations will be nontransitive, but not vice versa. As we will see, the "permissible to do rather than" relation is nontransitive in my sense. As we will also see, the "all-things-considered better than" relation may also be nontransitive. If so, this may be deeply problematic for practical reasoning, whatever the underlying source of its being nontransitive.

Finally, let me note the following. Some people believe that many of the worries raised in this book are best understood not as worries about the transitivity of the "all-things-considered better than" relation, per se, but as worries about the notion of *comparability* and, more particularly, as worries about the ultimate intelligibility of making all-things-considered comparisons between different outcomes with respect to their goodness.[15] I shall return to this kind of position in my concluding chapter. But, for now, let me acknowledge that I have no strong objections if someone wants to think about my arguments along the lines suggested. Although my impossibility arguments typically have, as one of their premises, the claim that "all-things-considered better than" is a transitive relation, and so can be seen to raise worries about the transitivity of the "all-things-considered better than" relation, I think it is compatible with the spirit of my arguments to focus on the worries that they raise about comparing outcomes in terms of goodness, all things considered, rather than to get bogged down on the

---

[15] I have heard this suggestion from a number of people over the years in various audiences I have addressed, including, most recently, from an audience member at the University of Oslo.

narrower question of whether they could or couldn't show that "all-things-considered better than" in my wide reason-implying sense isn't a transitive relation.

1.6 Hammers and Nails

There is an old adage that to a person with a hammer everything looks like a nail. This adage guards against taking a single approach to every problem we confront. There is a strong temptation to take a tool that we have mastered and that we find particularly effective for solving one task, and to try to apply it to solve other tasks for which it is ill-suited. The result of doing this is often to arrive at forced, or bludgeoned, solutions that don't do justice to the subtlety and complexity of the problems we actually face. This is particularly a danger in the normative realm, where it is sometimes less clear than it is in other realms that one has arrived at an unacceptable or failed solution. (Carpenters who use a hammer, rather than a sander, to make a chair leg fit may produce a cracked chair that collapses under the weight of an occupant.)

Total utilitarians have a simple, powerful, elegant theory that generates a straightforward answer to most normative questions. But most people agree that the theory gets things terribly wrong in certain cases, and that such a theory is simply too crude, on its own, to capture the full complexity of moral thinking. But many people, including many philosophers, economists, game theorists, and decision theorists, are attracted to modern-day descendants of total utilitarianism, such as cost-benefit analysis, and Expected Utility Theory for dealing with uncertainty. Such theories are also simple, powerful, and elegant, and like total utilitarianism they, too, generate straightforward answers to many practical questions. But, as plausible and useful as these theories are, for certain purposes, they, too, get things terribly wrong in certain cases and are too crude, on their own, to capture the full complexity of practical reasoning. Or so I believe, anyway.

Thomas Nagel expresses a similar view, warning us of the dangers of cooking "up a unified but artificial system like cost-benefit analysis, which will grind out decisions on any problem presented to it."[16] Nagel parenthetically grants that "such systems may be useful if their claims and scope of operation are less ambitious" but contends, "What is needed instead is a mixed strategy, combining systematic results where these are applicable with less systematic judgments to fill in the gaps."[17]

---

[16] "The Fragmentation of Value," in *Mortal Questions* (Cambridge: Cambridge University Press, 1979), 131. Nagel appended a footnote to the word "analysis" that reads: "See Lawrence Tribe, 'Policy Science: Analysis or Ideology?' *Philosophy and Public Affairs* 11 (Fall 1972): 66–110."

[17] "The Fragmentation of Value," 139.

More generally, Nagel conveys some of his "philosophical sympathies and antipathies" as follows:

> I believe one should trust problems over solutions, intuition over arguments, and pluralistic discord over systematic harmony. Simplicity and elegance are never reasons to think that a philosophical theory is true: on the contrary, they are usually grounds for thinking it is false.... If arguments or systematic theoretical considerations lead to results that seem intuitively not to make sense, or if a neat solution to a problem does not remove the conviction that the problem is still there... then something is wrong with the argument and more work needs to be done.... Superficiality is as hard to avoid in philosophy as it is anywhere else. It is too easy to reach solutions that fail to do justice to the difficulty of the problems. All one can do is try to maintain a desire for answers, a tolerance for long periods without any, an unwillingness to brush aside unexplained intuitions, and an adherence to reasonable standards of clear expression and cogent argument.[18]

I share Nagel's sentiments. Indeed, the spirit of his perspective infuses my thinking throughout this book.

1.7 Final Remarks

Many of this book's claims are put in terms of moral ideals, moral judgments, moral reasoning, and so on. Some people restrict the use of the word "moral" so that it only applies to the narrow category of duties or "what we owe to each other."[19] I use the word "moral" more broadly. For me, questions about right and wrong, virtue and vice, and good and bad all lie within the purview of moral theory. So, for example, I think all of the following are fundamentally moral questions: whether it is obligatory, permissible, or prohibited to perform a certain action; whether it is (morally) desirable to develop a certain character or set of character traits so as to be a certain kind of person or so as to lead a certain kind of life; and whether one life, set of principles or institutions, or outcome is better or worse than another.

Much of this book is put in terms of moral questions, broadly construed, but there is also discussion of prudential questions, such as what makes one

---

[18] *Mortal Questions*, x–xii.
[19] I take this phrase from Thomas Scanlon's excellent book *What We Owe to Each Other* (Cambridge, MA: Harvard University Press, 1998). Scanlon is one of many philosophers who favor a narrow construal of the notion of "moral."

life a better life than another in self-interested, as opposed to moral, terms. Moreover, although much of my discussion concerns morality, many of my arguments and claims straightforwardly apply to practical reasoning more generally. So, for example, while I directly discuss two different models for moral ideals, the considerations I present apply, mutatis mutandis, to two different models for practical ideals generally, including prudential ideals. Often my discussion of the notion of "all-things-considered better than" focuses on moral cases; but the considerations I present in support of those cases will generally apply to the notion of "all-things-considered better than" simpliciter, when both moral and nonmoral factors would have to be considered and each given their due weight.

Some people claim not to be able to make *sense* of such claims as "one outcome is better than another all things considered." This is especially so when such comparisons would require aggregating across different people in order to arrive at such judgments. Some economists are attracted to such a view because of metaphysical and/or epistemological worries about the problem of interpersonal comparisons. Specifically, some may doubt that there even *could* be a fact of the matter about whether one person is worse off than another in the way that there would need to be for interpersonal comparisons and aggregations across persons to be meaningful. Alternatively, they may simply doubt that we could ever *know* what we would need to know for such comparisons and aggregations to be meaningful.

Additionally, some philosophers worry that ranking outcomes involves a kind of conceptual confusion. On one such view, only sentient beings can be well off or poorly off, so only sentient beings can be better or worse off than other sentient beings. Since outcomes are not *themselves* sentient—even if some of their *members* are—it makes no sense to attribute states of well-being to outcomes, or to rank some outcomes as better or worse off than others. Robert Nozick may hold such a view. He writes:

> Why not...hold that some persons have to bear some costs that benefit other people more, for the sake of the overall social good? But there is no *social entity* with a good that undergoes some sacrifice for its own good. There are only individual people, with their own individual lives. Using one of these people for the benefit of others, uses him and benefits the others. Nothing more. What happens is that something is done to him for the sake of others. Talk of an overall social good covers this up.[20]

It is hardly self-evident what to make of this intriguing passage, but clearly Nozick doesn't think societies or outcomes are the *kinds* of entities to have a

---

[20] *Anarchy, State, and Utopia* (New York: Basic Books, 1974), 33.

good. This *suggests* that, for Nozick, only sentient beings have goods; so that while we might talk of improving the overall good of an individual, it is deeply wrongheaded to talk of improving the overall social good. In claiming that *nothing more* occurs when one uses one person to benefit another other than that the one person is used and the other benefited, Nozick seems to be implying that it would be illegitimate to claim that such an event might make the *outcome* better. Thus, for Nozick, in comparing two outcomes it makes sense to say that one outcome might be better for some individuals, while the other outcome might be better for other individuals, but we must resist the temptation to aggregate across the different individuals in the outcomes so as to arrive at a judgment as to which of the two *outcomes* was better overall.[21]

I don't want to minimize the economists' worries about interpersonal utility comparisons, nor make light of the worries raised by people like Nozick, but here I want to echo my opening quotation from Rawls. Any ethical theory that doesn't take consequences into account, and isn't prepared to rank some outcomes as better or worse than others, "would simply be irrational, crazy." Or, to put the point more gently, such a theory would be committed to deep skepticism about a large part of the moral domain. We may find ourselves *forced* to such deep skepticism at the end of the day. But it is a view to be avoided if at all possible.

To modify a famous example of Hume's, suppose there were two possible alternatives. In *A*, millions of people flourish in all the ways that matter most, but one person, John, suffers a scratched finger. In *B*, John avoids having his finger scratched and is just as well off in all other respects as he would be in *A*, but everyone *else* suffers excruciatingly and then dies. On the view under consideration, we can rightfully claim that *A* would be *vastly* better than *B* for millions of people, while *B* would only be incrementally better than *A* for *one* person, John. But the truth of such claims does *not* license our claiming that *A* would be a better outcome than *B*. Indeed, on the view in question, we couldn't even claim that an outcome, *C*, where there were billions of good people in Heaven, would be better than an outcome, *D*, where there were billions of different good people in Hell. All we could say is that *C* would be extraordinarily good for the particular billions of people in Heaven, while *D* would be extraordinarily bad for the particular billions of people in Hell.

Suffice it to say, I reject this view of the matter. I think it makes perfect sense to claim that *A* and *C* would be vastly better outcomes than *B* and *D*, respectively. Moreover, I think that the truth of that claim has moral significance. Among other things, the fact that *A* and *C* would be vastly better out-

---

[21] Another philosopher who has deep worries about the intelligibility of saying that one outcome is better than another all things considered is Philippa Foot. See "Utilitarianism and the Virtues," in *Moral Dilemmas: And Other Topics in Moral Philosophy* (Oxford: Clarendon Press, 2002), 59–77. (I am grateful to Matthew Hanser for providing me with this cite.)

comes than *B* and *D* means that there is powerful reason to both prefer and promote *A* and *C* over *B* and *D* if faced with those alternatives. Of course, in saying this I am not denying that other factors might *also* be relevant to our decision were we ever to face a choice between such alternatives.

Having stated my position about this matter, I shall not try to defend it, as doing so would take me far afield from this book's main focus. Instead, let me just freely grant that one of this book's underlying assumptions is that some outcomes can be better or worse than others. Though not completely uncontroversial, I believe that most people will (rightly!) grant me that assumption. In any event, even among those who worry about whether *outcomes* are the kinds of entities that could be good or bad, or better or worse than other outcomes, most agree that a sentient *individual's* life could be good or bad, or made better or worse by different events. And many of the worries I raise about comparisons between different outcomes are also raised about comparisons between different ways that an individual life might go. More generally, much of this book raises questions about the nature of the good, moral ideals, and practical reasoning that should be of interest even to those who doubt whether one outcome can be better than another.

Let me end this introduction by commenting on another passage of Nagel's. At the end of his introduction to *The View from Nowhere* Nagel writes:

> I do not feel equal to the problems treated in this book. They seem to me to require an order of intelligence wholly different from mine. Others who have tried to address the central questions of philosophy will recognize the feeling.[22]

Here, as earlier, I share Nagel's sentiments. As indicated at the beginning of this introduction, I once hoped to solve the problems introduced in this book. I no longer feel up to that task. But I hold out the hope that this book will move others to take up my challenges. Perhaps, as a result of our combined efforts, we will one day have a much better idea not only of what we do believe, but of what we should believe, regarding the nature of the good, moral ideals, and practical reasoning.

---

[22] *The View from Nowhere* (New York: Oxford University Press, 1986), 12.

2

Aggregation and Problems about Trade-offs
MANY-PERSON SPECTRUM ARGUMENTS

Practical decisions often involve issues of trade-offs. Sometimes trade-offs involve different kinds of benefits, burdens, or competing ideals. Thus, we must often decide how much increases or improvement in certain benefits, burdens, or ideals would offset decreases or worsening in other benefits, burdens, or ideals. Sometimes trade-offs concern quality versus number, or duration versus number. Thus, we might have to decide whether a fewer number of benefits of higher quality or longer duration offset a larger number of benefits of lesser quality or shorter duration. Moreover, questions about trade-offs can arise for single individuals, within lives, or for groups of individuals, between lives. Often, our most perplexing practical decisions revolve around the difficulties we face in resolving trade-off issues.

I shall not directly enter the familiar debates concerning trade-offs between different kinds of benefits, burdens, or ideals. So, for example, I shall not consider to what extent one should be willing to trade off between happiness, virtue, equality, utility, freedom, security, justice, or perfection. These are important questions, but they have long been staples of moral theory, and of social and political philosophy. Instead, I shall focus on other questions about trade-offs.

In this chapter, I begin by presenting a general schema of aggregation. I then present several Standard Views about trade-offs between quality and number, focusing on cases where the trade-offs involve different individuals. My aim, here, is neither to attack nor to defend these views. Instead, I want to articulate them and then raise questions about their consistency and implications. In appendix A, I note that similar views and questions may hold regarding trade-offs between duration and number. As we will see, the views and questions I discuss raise deep issues for both theory and practice. These issues will occupy us for much of the book.

Usually, people speak of trade-offs between quality and *quantity*, rather than quality and number. But as I discuss in appendix B, this may be misleading. Though it may sound a bit odd, in some normative contexts quantity includes quality as one of its components. Thus, it is more perspicuous to frame my discussion in terms of trade-offs between quality and number, rather than quality and quantity.

Although this is mainly a book of moral and practical theory, it will help to put my claims in concrete terms. Correspondingly, I shall focus my discussion of aggregation and trade-offs in terms of health care, together with a few non-health-related examples. However, I trust it will be evident that the issues I am raising are both general and deep, and extend well beyond the realm of health care and my other limited examples.

2.1 Aggregation: A General Schema

Aggregation is the process or method of combining different parts into a whole. In ethics, there are principles of aggregation for assessing individual lives. Basically, these tell us how the different elements or components of individual lives combine to affect the goodness, comparative quality, or desirability of those lives. Likewise, there are principles of aggregation for assessing outcomes. Basically, these tell us how the different elements or components of outcomes combine to affect the goodness, comparative quality, or desirability of those outcomes.

It is often *assumed* that the relevant components to be combined in assessing the goodness or desirability of outcomes are the individual lives of sentient beings, or perhaps the goodness or desirability of the individual sentient lives within those outcomes. But more inclusive conceptions of relevant components are possible. For example, some people might believe that the continued existence of certain nations, groups, customs, or cultures contributes to the goodness of the outcomes of which they are a part, over and above the impact which their continued existence has on the individual sentient lives in those outcomes. Similarly, some people believe that the existence of natural wonders, like the Grand Canyon, Mount Everest, or Victoria Falls, or of unspoiled wildernesses or jungles, or of different species of flora and fauna, contributes to the value of the earth over and above the impact which their existence has on the lives of sentient beings. Likewise, some perfectionists believe that there is value in the existence of great works of art, music, poetry, or architecture, beyond the extent to which such works affect the lives of sentient individuals. For now, I take no stand on what kinds of factors might be relevant to the goodness of outcomes, or how they might contribute to such goodness. But a principle of aggregation for assessing outcomes must give *due* weight to *each* of the factors that the full theory of the good deems relevant to the goodness of outcomes; combining them in *whatever* way is ultimately dictated by the full theory of the good.

In philosophy, aggregation is often associated with simple summing. This is partly the legacy of classical utilitarianism, which is often associated with an aggregative approach to ethics for assessing both individual lives and outcomes. As classical utilitarianism is frequently interpreted, the goodness or desirability of a person's life is just the sum total—that is, a simple additive function—of the positive and negative experiences, or utility, contained within that life. Likewise, the goodness or desirability of an outcome is just the sum total—again, a simple additive function—of the positive and negative experiences, or utility, contained in each sentient life within that outcome.

Although aggregation is often associated with simple summing, *additive* aggregation is but one of many ways of combining the different elements relevant to the goodness of lives or outcomes, to generate an assessment of the comparative desirability of those lives or outcomes. Indeed, as I shall use the notion, a principle of aggregation will be *any* function from the relevant elements—whatever those turn out to be—to the assessment of the goodness or comparative desirability of the item being assessed, say, lives or outcomes. So, for example, one might have principles of aggregation that focused on averages, like average utilitarianism, or on weighted totals, like prioritarianism,[1] or on the highest or best achievements, like some forms of perfectionism, or on the well-being of those who are worst off, like maximin. Thus, as I use the notion, a principle of aggregation may accommodate distributive considerations in assessing individual lives or outcomes. How *much* good obtains in lives or outcomes may or may not matter as much as *how* that good is *distributed* within lives or outcomes.

---

[1] *Prioritarianism* is the term I now use to describe the position Parfit has called the *Priority View*, and that I previously called *extended humanitarianism*. Roughly, on this view one wants everyone to fare as well as possible, but the worse off someone is in absolute terms the greater weight is attached to improving their situation. Parfit discussed the Priority View in his famous article "Equality or Priority?" The Lindley Lecture, University of Kansas, 1991; reprinted in *The Ideal of Equality*, ed. Matthew Clayton and Andrew Williams (London: Macmillan; New York: St. Martin's Press, 2000), 81–125. I introduced the term *prioritarianism* in my "Equality, Priority, and the Levelling Down Objection," in *The Ideal of Equality*, 126–61, and have discussed it in many other places as well, including chapter 9 of *Inequality* (New York: Oxford University Press, 1993); "Egalitarianism Defended," *Ethics* 113 (2003): 764–82; "Equality, Priority, or What?" *Economics and Philosophy* 19 (2003): 61–88; and "Harmful Goods, Harmless Bads," in *Value, Welfare and Morality*, ed. R. G. Frey and Christopher Morris (Cambridge: Cambridge University Press, 1993), 290–324. My first discussion of this topic appeared in early drafts of my 1983 Princeton PhD dissertation, "Inequality." This discussion helped define and motivate prioritarianism—which I then called *extended humanitarianism*—as an alternative to *genuine egalitarianism*—which I now call noninstrumental egalitarianism. I noted that prioritarianism was often conflated with egalitarianism, could avoid the *Levelling Down Objection* (see chapter 3), and might appear to many as the most plausible alternative to egalitarianism.

2.2 Some Standard Views Regarding Trade-offs between Quality and Number

Most believe:

> (*N*) Other things equal, numbers matter, at least for many values and many contexts.

Examples of *N*: other things equal, it would be better if there were 5,000 cases of AIDS rather than 10,000; 1 million cases of dehydration rather than 10 million; 90 broken arms rather than 100; 80,000 cases of measles rather than 100,000; and 15 cases of acne rather than 25. As I said I would, here and later I employ health-related examples to illustrate the view under discussion, and I have varied both the numbers and the severity of the illnesses to illustrate *N*'s robustness. The view that other things equal numbers matter applies across the *full range* of medical conditions, and across most alternatives more generally.

The "other things equal" clause is important. Twenty-five cases of *mild* acne, or 10 million cases of *slight* dehydration might, of course, be better than 10 cases of *severe* acne, or 1 million cases of *severe* dehydration, respectively. Likewise, *perhaps* 10,000 cases of AIDS in an elderly group that would soon die anyway would be better than 5,000 cases of AIDS in a group of young mothers with dependent small children. Similarly, context matters. So, 80,000 cases of childhood measles might ravage a poor rural society whose total childhood population is 100,000, whereas 100,000 cases of childhood measles might have little impact on a wealthy developed society whose childhood population was 100 million. But, assuming other things *are* equal, the preceding examples seem right, illustrating *N*'s plausibility.

As emphasized in chapter 1, in this work the claim that "other things equal, it would be better if there were 5,000 AIDS cases rather than 10,000" is to be understood as a claim about the relative merits of the two outcomes from an impartial perspective. Such a claim expresses an evaluative judgment about what there would be most reason to prefer, or what would be most *desirable*, from an impartial perspective. It is not a claim about what we *ought to do*, all things considered; nor does it entail that it is always obligatory, or even always permissible, to produce an outcome involving 5,000 AIDS cases, rather than one involving 10,000 AIDS cases.

There may be some values or contexts for which numbers don't matter.[2] Clearly, there is nothing normatively significant about the *mere fact* that there are *more* atoms than planets in the universe. Likewise, there is no reason to believe that an outcome that had *more* electrons would be better than one that

---

[2] I am grateful to Jim Griffin for pressing me to clarify this point. My argument does not depend on the claim that numbers matter for *all* values and contexts. It is sufficient for my purposes if numbers matter in the way I suggest they do for the kinds of cases I consider in my arguments.

had *fewer*, simply in virtue of the fact that it had a *greater number* of electrons. In addition, there may be *some* values for which numbers are irrelevant. Perhaps on some versions of perfectionism two instances of "perfection" or "near perfection" are no better than one. So, for example, a world in which a second artist independently created a painting indistinguishable from Da Vinci's *Mona Lisa* might be no better regarding perfection than the actual world in which only one such painting was independently created. And perhaps, though I don't find this view plausible myself, on some views of perfection a world including *many distinct* works of great art would be no better regarding perfection than a world including just *one* work of great art, as long as the one work of great art would be as great as any of the many possible distinct works.[3] Still, in many contexts and for many values, numbers matter. Other things equal, if freedom or justice or utility is genuinely valuable, it is better if more rather than fewer people are free or get what they deserve or have high levels of utility.

Not everyone believes that numbers matter in the moral realm.[4] Indeed, the philosophical literature is replete with bold claims, ingenious examples, and clever arguments purporting to show that numbers don't matter. However, I find the relevant examples and arguments woefully inadequate to undermine the overwhelming plausibility of *N*, the view that numbers matter. And I am hardly alone. As controversial as the topic of trade-offs is, I venture that *no* administrator in a major national or international health organization denies

---

[3] Some extreme perfectionists might grant *tie-breaking* weight to numbers, and admit that a world with many equally good works would be better than a world with fewer equally good works, but would still deny that numbers have *much* significance, contending that a *single* great work of art would be better than *any* number of works of art that weren't quite as good.

[4] For example, John Taurek explicitly denies that numbers should count in his rich and widely discussed article "Should the Numbers Count?" *Philosophy and Public Affairs* 6 (1977): 293–316. In an important respect, Taurek can be seen as following Kant, insofar as Kant argues that *persons* have infinite worth, and as such that they are not replaceable and one cannot "trade off" between one person and another for moral purposes. In particular, Kant famously believed that you can't treat people merely as a means to the ends of others and thought that this implied that you can't sacrifice one person for the greater good of others (see Kant's *Grounding for the Metaphysics of Morals*, trans. James W. Ellington [Indianapolis: Hackett, 1981], especially the second section). Other authors who follow Kant in raising serious questions about whether numbers count in all cases include Bernard Williams and Elizabeth Anscombe. See the concluding comments of "2. The structure of consequentialism," in Williams's "A Critique of Utilitarianism," in *Utilitarianism: For and Against*, with J. J. C. Smart (Cambridge: Cambridge University Press, 1973), and also Anscombe's "Modern Moral Philosophy," *Philosophy* 33 (1958): 1–19. Also, as indicated in chapter 1, some authors like Nozick, Foot, and Thomson have doubts as to the intelligibility of assessing the goodness of outcomes; a fortiori, these authors will have doubts about numbers counting in the moral realm for purposes of ranking the goodness of outcomes.

Shelly Kagan challenges a number of widely held assumptions about additivity in his fascinating article "The Additive Fallacy," *Ethics* 99 (1988): 5–31. Moreover, while I think that numbers surely count in the moral realm, in a large range of cases, much of this book takes up the claim that numbers do not always count, and that even when they do count they may not count in the simple additive way that many people implicitly assume. On the latter point, see chapter 10.

N. More generally, most reject the view that numbers don't matter, and they are surely right (so I assert without argument) to do so.[5]

The "other things equal" clause renders N exceedingly weak. Stronger positions can be reached by relaxing the clause. Thus, one might hold that if other things are *virtually* equal, or *nearly* equal, or *fairly* equal, or even *sufficiently* equal, numbers matter (here, and in what follows, I omit the qualifier "for many values and in many contexts"). So, for example, in the medical context, one might hold that as long as the difference in severity of two illnesses is not *too* great, it would be better if a smaller number of people suffered from the severer illness, than if a *sufficiently* larger number of people suffered from the less severe illness.

Many regard qualifiers like "too" and "sufficiently" as "weasel" words. Correspondingly, they regard their presence in the preceding formulation with suspicion, rendering the content of the claim vague or indeterminate. But this is a case where the qualifiers simply render the claim as modest as one likes—and hence more defensible.[6] So, while there may be disputes as to whether the preceding formulation actually applies in any particular case, we don't have to settle those disputes to recognize the overwhelming plausibility of the view it expresses. Indeed, I believe that in principle virtually everyone would accept, at least initially, the foregoing view.

Consider, for example, the following possibilities. It might be widely agreed that for certain types of cases, pancreatic cancer is worse than AIDS, psychosis worse than manic depression, stroke worse than heart attack, broken arm worse than broken leg, mumps worse than measles, and warts worse than acne. Even so, it might be acknowledged that for each pair of alternatives the difference in severity of the illnesses is sufficiently small that it would be better (in my wide reason-implying sense) if a smaller number of people had the severer illness, than if a sufficiently larger number of people had the less severe illness. Thus, it might be claimed that, other things equal, it would be better for there to be 1,000 cases of pancreatic cancer, than 5,000 AIDS cases, 10 cases of psychosis rather than 30 cases of manic depression, 25,000 strokes rather than 50,000 heart attacks, 60 broken arms rather than 100 broken legs, 100,000 cases of mumps rather than 500,000 cases of measles, and 7,000 cases of warts rather than 20,000 cases of acne.

Of course, the actual illnesses and numbers I've used here are merely for illustrative purposes. People will make different judgments regarding the

---

[5] For a compelling response to the view that numbers don't count, see Derek Parfit's "Innumerate Ethics," *Philosophy and Public Affairs* 78 (1978): 285–301.

[6] When I was in graduate school, Tim Scanlon used to advise us to make our claims "weaker and therefore stronger." What he meant was that it was better to make a modest claim that was defensible than a bolder claim that was not. Often I'll follow Tim's usage and talk about "weak" and "strong" claims, where a "weak" claim is just a modest claim that is generally uncontroversial or easily defended, and a "strong" claim is one that is often controversial or relatively hard to defend.

relative severity of each illness, and, correspondingly, people will make different judgments about how many of the lesser illnesses would have to obtain before that would be worse than a given number of instances of the greater illness. Nevertheless, I submit that there would be widespread agreement regarding the general view. Where differences in severity of illnesses are not *too* great, numbers matter, and once again this view applies across the *full range* of medical conditions.

There are various equivalent ways of characterizing the position I have been describing.[7] One natural way would be in terms of trade-offs between different harms and the number of people experiencing those harms. Another would be in terms of trade-offs between different benefits and the number of people experiencing those benefits. And yet another would be in terms of trade-offs between both harms and benefits and the number of people experiencing those harms and benefits. Let me briefly illustrate this. Suppose that John is facing a given harm A, and Mary a different harm B, and that if x happened John's harm would be prevented but not Mary's, while if y happened Mary's harm would be prevented but not John's. Someone who judged that it would be better if x happened rather than y might justify their claim in any of three ways. First, they might defend the view that A is a worse harm than B. Second, they might defend the view that x provides greater benefits than y, as John benefits more from not suffering A than Mary would benefit from not suffering B. Third, they might appeal to both benefits and harms, and point out that together the benefit to John and harm to Mary from x obtaining are better than the benefit to Mary and harm to John from y obtaining. There are, I think, both a technical philosophical usage of the terms "benefits" and "harms" and a well-understood ordinary use of those terms for many contexts where each of the three claims in question would be equivalent in the sense of having the same truth conditions.[8] That is, understood in the way I have in mind, any one of the preceding claims will be true or defensible if and only if the other two are also true or defensible.

So, in presenting the views about trade-offs discussed in this book we have a choice between equivalent ways of doing so. Depending on the context, sometimes I may put my point in terms of harms, sometimes in terms of

---

[7] I am grateful to Shelly Kagan for suggesting that I clarify the point made in this paragraph and the following one, to avoid unnecessary confusion in the minds of some readers when I move from examples involving "harms" to general principles about "benefits."

[8] This is not to deny that there are also contexts in which ordinary usage assiduously distinguishes between benefits and harms. For example, in ordinary usage I do not *harm* my neighbor when I decide not to *benefit* him by giving him my life's savings. These issues are connected with assumptions about baselines and counterfactuals that I shall not pursue here. Still, there is a common usage according to which, if my neighbor is not yet sick but currently faces the prospect of misery or death from an approaching illness or catastrophe, then I *benefit* my neighbor if I prevent the harms in question from befalling him. This is the sense I am appealing to throughout this book, unless I indicate otherwise.

benefits, and sometimes in terms of both benefits and harms. But my canonical formulation of the views I discuss will typically be put in terms of benefits.

Accordingly, let me name and state the general view about trade-offs that I was describing earlier as follows:

> *The First Standard View (FSV)—Trade-offs between Quality and Number Are Sometimes Desirable*: In general, an outcome where a larger number of people have a lower quality benefit is better than an outcome where a smaller number of people have a higher quality benefit, *if* the number receiving the lower quality benefit is "sufficiently" greater than the number receiving the higher quality benefit, and *if* the differences in the initial situations of the people benefited and the degrees to which they are benefited are not "too" great.

In *FSV*, and in what follows, the assumptions that "differences in the initial situations...are not 'too' great," or that people are "similarly situated," serve as "everything *else* is *roughly* equal" clauses. Thus, we don't assume that some people are saints, and others sinners, or that if some people were benefited they would significantly improve society, while if others were benefited they would have no effect, or an adverse effect, on society, or that some are much better off than the others in other respects than the benefits or illnesses we are considering. So, for our purposes, the only salient differences to consider are the number of people affected and the varying degrees to which they would be affected by benefits or illnesses. So understood, few reject the First Standard View. Still, it will be useful to name and state the opposing view. I do so as follows:

> *The No Trade-offs View (NTOV)—No Trade-offs between Quality and Number Are Desirable*: An outcome where a larger number of people have a lower quality benefit is not better than an outcome where a smaller number of similarly situated people have a higher quality benefit, *even if* the number of people receiving benefits in the former outcome is "much" greater than the number of people receiving benefits in the latter outcome, and *even if* the differences in the degrees to which the similarly situated people in the different outcomes are benefited are "very" small.

The No Trade-offs View may have philosophical supporters attracted to it on some pure theoretical grounds. But if it does, it doesn't have many. It is an extreme view that should be rejected.

Some advocates of Rawls's *maximin principle* may initially dispute my claim regarding the implausibility of the No Trade-offs View—where the maximin principle assesses the justice of a society's principles and institutions in terms of the extent to which those principles and institutions maximize the long-term expectations of society's least fortunate group.[9] This view gives *lexical priority* to society's worst-off group, in that it will rank one set of principles and institutions as more just than another if the long-term expectations of society's worst-off group are higher under the one set of principles and institutions than the other, *regardless* of how society's other groups fare under the different principles and institutions. Since those who believe in giving lexical priority to the worst-off are committed to giving even very small benefits to the worst-off group rather than very large benefits to a better-off group, it seems they might also be committed to aiding even a few members of the worst-off group rather than any number of members of a better-off group. Hence, as suggested, such people may want to accept the No Trade-offs View.

Two points might be made about this. First, Rawls has given us a principle of social *justice*, and we may think that this is more conclusive for the question of what a society can legitimately or rightly *do*, than it is for the question of what makes one outcome *better* than another. As central as the notion of social justice is to political theory, it is only *one* component relevant to the assessment of an outcome's *goodness*. Thus, the First Standard View may be plausible regarding the overall ranking of the *goodness* of outcomes, *even if* Rawlsian considerations of social justice would often dictate that a society ought not to *act* so as to produce the better outcome.

Second, and more important, Rawls's maximin principle is weakest *precisely* in its insistence on giving *lexical* priority to the worst-off *even in cases where the differences between the worst-off and others better off are small*. But these are *exactly* the kinds of cases where the First Standard View applies. Other things equal, it is extremely hard to believe that it would be *better*—and not merely socially more *just* (though, frankly, it is *also* very hard to believe that it would actually be more just!)—to benefit a *few* people who are badly off by just a *little*, rather than a *lot* of people who are *almost* as badly off by a *lot*.[10]

In those cases where the differences in people's initial situations are small, it seems that the plausibility of giving lexical priority to the members of the worst-off group can only be maintained by insisting that either *all* of the people

---

[9] See *A Theory of Justice* (Cambridge, MA: Harvard University Press, 1971), section 26.

[10] Strictly speaking, for Rawls the members of society's worst-off group need not actually be badly off in *absolute* terms; it is sufficient that they are badly off *relative to the other members of their society*. For what it is worth, I think whatever intuitive plausibility there is to the view that one should give *lexical* priority to the members of society's worst-off group in those cases where the people in question are *actually* badly off, in absolute terms—and, as indicated in the text, I don't think there is much intuitive plausibility to even this position where people who are *almost* as badly off as the members of the worst-off group are concerned—almost completely disappears in those cases where the members of the worst-off group aren't actually *badly off*, in absolute terms, but only relatively so. I also think that my view about this is supported by the *reasoning* Rawls presents in justifying the conditions under which it is appropriate to accept a maximin principle of justice, but shall not pursue that here. For the reasoning in question, see section 26 of *A Theory of Justice*.

concerned are members of the worst-off group, or *none* of them are. And, of course, on either move there would be no reason for proponents of maximin to oppose the First Standard View.[11] Thus, I continue to hold—though I haven't actually *argued* for it—that the No Trade-offs View is an extreme view that should be rejected, and that principles like maximin are not, ultimately, to be followed in those cases where they conflict with the First Standard View.[12]

In addition to the view that Trade-offs between Quality and Number are Sometimes Desirable, most people accept the following:

> *The Second Standard View (SSV)—Trade-offs between Quality and Number Are Sometimes Undesirable Even When Vast Numbers Are at Stake*: If the quality of one kind of benefit is "sufficiently" low, and the quality of another kind of benefit is "sufficiently" high, then an outcome in which a relatively small number of people received the higher quality benefit would be better than one in which virtually any number of (otherwise) similarly situated people received the lower quality benefit.

SSV could be fleshed out more. As stated, it leaves open whether the "sufficiently" small/large benefit has to be *actually* small/large measured in some *absolute* way, or only small/large *relative* to the overall condition of the person, or to the larger/smaller benefit. Similarly, as stated, *SSV* leaves open whether the difference between the smaller and larger benefit has to be large, and if so, whether it has to be actually large, measured in some absolute terms, or only relatively large, measured as a function of the conditions of the people or the benefits themselves.[13]

Eventually, it would be useful and interesting to work out all the details determining when *SSV* holds. But I shall not do that here. For now, it is sufficient to see that there *are* cases where *SSV* seems deeply plausible, as this is all I need

---

[11] Actually, as Shelly Kagan has pointed out to me, this argument is slightly oversimplified. On a *lexical* version of the maximin principle, one seeks first to maximize the expectations of the worst-off group, and having done that to then maximize the expectations of the next worst-off group, and so on. So, if all of the people in question are deemed to be members of the worst-off group, that will be the end of the story, but not otherwise, as the same issue can arise again later on the lexical version of maximin. Given this, the argument of the text would have to be iterated for each successive group to which the advocate of maximin might turn.

[12] This does not entail that we have to *reject* principles like maximin if they conflict with the First Standard View. Perhaps we should continue to give them weight. But I am suggesting that so far there is good reason to think that our final all-things-considered judgments should track the First Standard View rather than principles like maximin in those cases where they conflict. (I say "so far," because in the face of the whole of this book's considerations, some people may ultimately decide that the First Standard View has to be rejected, notwithstanding its great plausibility.)

[13] The reader will note that similar questions might arise regarding the First Standard View. But they might seem more pressing for the Second Standard View than the First, which is why I mention them here.

for my current argument. And, indeed, examples where such a principle seems plausible abound. Thus, virtually all agree that, other things equal, it would be worse if fifty people suffered from AIDS, quadriplegia, severe psychosis, or being deaf, dumb, and blind, than if virtually *any* number of people suffered from a minor nosebleed, a slight cold, a sprained finger, or a short mild headache.

It isn't that nosebleeds, colds, sprains, and headaches don't matter. They do. They are conditions of ill health, albeit mild ones, and other things equal they make a claim on our sympathy and resources, although not a particularly strong one. But we *don't* think that the claims of those suffering from such minor afflictions *add up* in the way they would need to to outweigh the overwhelmingly powerful claims of those suffering from AIDS, paraplegia, dementia, or being deaf, dumb, and blind.

As before, though most people accept the Second Standard View, it will be useful to name and state the opposing view.

The Unlimited Trade-offs View (UTOV)—Trade-offs of Number for Quality Are Always, in Principle, Desirable: No matter *how* low the quality of one kind benefit (as long as it is positive), and no matter *how* high the quality of another kind of benefit (as long as it is finite), an outcome with a "sufficiently" large number of people receiving the low-quality benefits will be better than an outcome with a smaller number of (otherwise) similarly situated people receiving the high-quality benefits.[14]

---

[14] The astute reader—which naturally includes *all* readers of this book, and especially *you*—will note that strictly speaking the Unlimited Trade-offs View is not *necessarily* opposed to the Second Standard View. The Unlimited Trade-offs View may be compatible with the Second Standard View due to the qualifier "virtually" that appears in the Second Standard View. Nevertheless, as I intend them to be interpreted, the spirit of the Unlimited Trade-offs View *is* opposed to the spirit of the Second Standard View. One could convey the opposition more rigorously by further qualifying the different positions. For example, one could note that advocates of the Second Standard View will maintain the view in question unless, perhaps, the number of people receiving the smaller benefits is *astronomically* large (and perhaps even then), and then spell out just how large "astronomically" large would have to be before they might doubt the claim in question. Then, one might further explicate the Unlimited Trade-offs View by noting that the number of people necessary to qualify as "sufficiently" large needn't be "astronomically" large. I have chosen not to characterize the Unlimited Trade-offs View and the Second Standard View in such terms, because doing so properly would be both complex and cumbersome. But I trust it is now evident that the Unlimited Trade-offs View and the Second Standard View could be spelled out so that they genuinely oppose each other, and that I intend them to be interpreted accordingly. Similar remarks apply to the purported opposition between some of the positions I describe later.

Note, it is arguable that anyone willing to accept a position like the Second Standard View for any cases where the number of people receiving the smaller benefits is not "astronomically" large should be willing to accept it even in cases where the number of people receiving the smaller benefits *are* astronomically large, and hence I should simply drop the qualifier "virtually" from my characterization of the Second Standard View. And once the qualifier "virtually" is dropped, then the Second Standard View *is* straightforwardly opposed by the Unlimited Trade-offs View. I am sympathetic to this position, but I know of people who would readily accept the qualified version of the Second Standard View, but

Unlike the No Trade-offs View, it would be misleading to call the Unlimited Trade-offs View "extreme." Indeed, it would be accepted by most of those enamored by Expected Utility Theory, including total utilitarians, and most game theorists, decision theorists, and economists. Nevertheless, I think most people accept the Second Standard View and reject the Unlimited Trade-offs View. Moreover, there are powerful reasons to do so. Let us briefly consider some of those reasons.

2.3 The Problem of Additive Aggregation

The Second Standard View—that Trade-offs between Quality and Number Are Sometimes Undesirable Even When Vast Numbers Are at Stake—reflects a powerful anti-additive-aggregationist position that philosophers have widely discussed as an objection to total utilitarianism. It can be referred to as *the problem of additive aggregation*. (It might be more perspicuous to call the position in question the problem of *simple* additive aggregation, but for simplicity(!) here, and in what follows, I usually omit the "simple.")

Let me note two examples opposing additive aggregation.

The first is Derek Parfit's *Repugnant Conclusion*: "For any possible population of at least ten billion people, all with a very high quality of life, there must be some much larger imaginable population whose existence, if other things are equal, would be better, even though its members have lives that are barely worth living."[15]

The second is what I call the *Lollipops for Life* case. Suppose there were two alternative universes. In one, countless people would each receive many licks of different lollipops over the course of their lives. Unfortunately, there would also be one innocent person who suffered unbearable agony for fifty years before eventually dying a slow, lonely, torturous death. In the second universe, each of the countless people would receive *one* less lick of a lollipop over the course of their lives, but the innocent person would be spared the agony and instead live a full, rich life. Which universe would be better?

---

who claim to have no views whatsoever, or at least no confidence in their views, about any cases where astronomically large numbers are involved. Correspondingly, I cautiously include the qualifier "virtually" so that my arguments will have force for as many people as possible. That is, I am slightly limiting the scope of the Second Standard View so as to expand the reach of my overall argument.

[15] *Reasons and Persons* (Oxford: Oxford University Press, 1984), 388. Parfit's arguments concerning the Repugnant Conclusion are fascinating and, as indicated in my preface, together with the related considerations he presents—especially the Mere Addition Paradox—they first sparked my interest in intransitivity. See part 4 of *Reasons and Persons*, and my "Intransitivity and the Mere Addition Paradox," *Philosophy and Public Affairs* 16 (1987): 138–87. Parfit's seminal publication on this topic was "Future Generations: Further Problems," *Philosophy and Public Affairs* 11 (1982): 113–72.

Most people firmly believe that the Repugnant Conclusion is, indeed, repugnant. They believe that an outcome, *A*, of at least 10 billion people, all with a very high quality of life, would be better than an outcome, *Z*, with a large population all of whom have lives that are barely worth living, no matter *how many* people live in *Z*. Similarly, most firmly believe that no matter *how many* people would get the *one* extra lollipop lick, the universe without the extra licks would be better than the universe with it, if the latter, but not the former, involved an innocent person suffering fifty years of unbearable agony followed by a slow, lonely, torturous death.

Notoriously, total utilitarians reject these claims. However counterintuitive it may seem, they are committed to the simple additive-aggregationist view that if only there are *enough* people in *Z*, *Z* would be better than *A*, and if only *enough* people get an extra lick, the universe with the extra lollipop licks would be better than the one without them.

Should we regard such examples as serious objections to total utilitarianism? Total utilitarians, of course, think not. They deny that the so-called problem of additive aggregation is in fact a problem. Insisting that more of the good is better than less of the good, they offer a number of sophisticated explanations for why we have the intuitions we do about such cases, arguing, in essence, that our intuitions were not developed to adequately respond to such wild science-fiction-type cases involving unimaginably large numbers of relatively small amounts. Correspondingly, they contend that we don't intuitively grasp how *much* total good is dispersed among *Z*'s innumerable masses, or how *much* total pleasure would be enjoyed by countless people each getting one extra lick of a lollipop.

For the total utilitarian, then, no matter *how* small the amount of good may be in a life that is barely worth living, or *how* small the amount of pleasure may be from one lick of a lollipop, if only there are *enough* such lives, or licks, *eventually* the total amount of good or pleasure will outweigh, and then be better than, *any* finite amount of good or pain that might be balanced off against it. Here, our understanding supposedly leads us to recognize truths that our imagination fails to appreciate; both the Repugnant Conclusion and the Lollipops for Life example can be rejected as objections to utilitarianism.

The utilitarian's position is coherent and admirably consistent. But despite the powerful appeal of coherence and consistency, few people are willing to bite the bullet and accept the total utilitarian's response to the Repugnant Conclusion and the Lollipops for Life example. I believe they are right not to do so.

Before going on, it is worth noting that views similar to the anti-additive-aggregationist position are, albeit for different reasons, endorsed by philosophers representing a wide range of philosophical positions.

For example, Jim Griffin, a sophisticated pluralist, claims that there are incommensurabilities of the form: enough of *A* outranks any amount of *B*. According to Griffin, such incommensurabilities reflect discontinuity between values, which involves "the suspension of addition;...we have a positive value that, no matter how often a certain amount is added to itself, cannot become greater than another positive value, and cannot, not because with piling up we get diminishing value or even disvalue...but because they are the sort of value that, even remaining constant, cannot add up to some other value."[16]

To exemplify his view, Griffin imagines a spectrum of art ranging from the very best of Rembrandt, Vermeer, and de Hooch all the way (down!) to contemporary kitsch. Griffin suggests that though the "kicks" of kitsch are real, they are different from the genuine appreciation of beauty—so much so that, other things equal, it would be rationally defensible to prefer fifty years appreciating the beauty of Rembrandt, Vermeer, and de Hooch to any number of years of enjoying the kicks of kitsch.[17]

Likewise, Frances Kamm, a distinguished deontologist, challenges the additive-aggregationist view. So, for example, she writes, "There are no number of headaches such that we should prevent them rather than certainly save a few lives."[18]

Similarly, Thomas Scanlon, a prominent contractualist, argues at length against the aggregationist model. In support of his contention, he offers the following example:

> Suppose that Jones has suffered an accident in the transmitter room of a television station. Electrical equipment has fallen on his arm, and we cannot rescue him without turning off the transmitter for fifteen minutes. A World Cup match is in progress, watched by many people, and it will not be over for an hour. Jones's injury will not get any worse if we wait, but his hand has been mashed and he is receiving extremely painful electrical shocks. Should we rescue him now or wait until the

---

[16] *Well-Being: Its Meaning, Measurement, and Moral Importance* (Oxford: Clarendon Press, 1986), 85.

[17] *Well-Being*, 86.

[18] This quotation is taken from page 3 of a typescript that Kamm originally wrote for the World Health Organization, entitled "Health and Equity." She echoes this point in a later article when she writes, in criticism of Peter Singer, that "as a strict aggregationist, if he [Singer] had a choice between saving a few thousand people dying of starvation or else curing the headaches of each of an enormous number of people, he should do the latter" ("Aggregation, Allocating Scarce Resources, and the Disabled," *Social Philosophy and Policy* 26 [2009]: 155). Kamm has also argued against additive aggregation in support of a view of hers which she calls the *Principle of Irrelevant Utilities* (see note 27). For example, in the published version of her "Health and Equity" she writes that if two people, C and D, are facing losses, then "so long as what is at stake for C and D is large, *no number of...small losses occurring in each of many people should be aggregated on D's side* so as to outweigh giving C an equal chance of avoiding the large loss" (in *Summary Measures of Population Health*, ed. C. J. L. Murray et al. [Geneva: World Health Organization, 2002], 690). Kamm has argued extensively against additive-aggregation in many of her works, including *Morality, Mortality, Vol. I: Death and Whom to Save from It* (New York: Oxford University Press, 1993) and *Intricate Ethics: Rights, Responsibilities, and Permissible Harm* (New York: Oxford University Press, 2007).

match is over? Does the right thing to do depend on how many people are watching—whether it is one million or five million or a hundred million? It seems to me that we should not wait, no matter how many viewers there are.[19]

Now, strictly speaking, Griffin, Kamm, and Scanlon are not addressing the question of goodness or desirability of different outcomes with which I have been concerned.[20] Nevertheless, while they hold three very distinct moral views, each can be counted as allies in the anti-additive-aggregationist camp. Each offers considerations that fit well with the Second Standard View, that Trade-offs between Quality and Number Are Sometimes Undesirable Even When Vast Numbers Are at Stake.

Suffice it to say, I think Griffin, Kamm, and Scanlon are right, insofar as they implicitly challenge the additive aggregationist's position. Likewise, I find it compellingly plausible that we should *not* trade off lollipop licks for lives, and should agree, with Parfit, that the Repugnant Conclusion *is* genuinely repugnant. I conclude that there are, indeed, powerful reasons to reject the Unlimited Trade-offs View, and to accept the Second Standard View.

Let me say a bit more about the additive aggregationist's position which I will call, for simplicity, the *Additive-Aggregationist Position*. The position I have in mind may incorporate a number of elements, including each of the following: first, benefits and burdens, or well-being, or what has traditionally been called *utility* is morally significant and relevant for comparing outcomes; second, in comparing outcomes, *more* utility is *better* than *less* utility; third, how *much* utility an outcome contains, as a whole, is a simple *additive* function of the utilities of *each* sentient individual in that outcome; fourth, the total utility of each sentient being is determined by a simple *additive* function of the "local" utilities possessed by that individual over the course of her life, day by day, or perhaps moment by moment; fifth, the relation between how good an outcome is regarding utility and how good it is regarding other ideals is thought to be such that as long as one outcome is better than another regarding utility by *enough*, then the one outcome will also be better all things considered (in my wide reason-implying sense); and, perhaps, sixth, which would account for the fifth element, how good an outcome is, all things considered, is an additive function of how good it is with respect to each individual ideal that is relevant to assessing the goodness of outcomes.

Thus, the Additive-Aggregationist Position is in fact a complex position involving a number of elements, and one might vary these elements in different ways to generate different versions of an Additive-Aggregationist

---

[19] *What We Owe to Each Other* (Cambridge, MA: Harvard University Press, 1998), 235.
[20] Griffin talks about what would be "rationally defensible to prefer," Kamm about what we "should" or "shouldn't" do, and Scanlon about what it would be "right" to do.

Position.[21] Hence, what I am calling "the" Additive-Aggregationist Position is actually a family of views. Perhaps the most familiar and popular member of the family is the view discussed previously, *total utilitarianism*, which combines the first four elements of the Additive-Aggregationist Position with the view that utility is the *only* ideal that is relevant for assessing outcomes, thereby making the fifth and sixth elements trivially true, and implying that one outcome is better than another all things considered if it has more total utility.

Given the stature of utilitarianism as one of the most important and influential moral theories, much of my discussion of the Additive-Aggregationist Position, and its opposing view, which I'll simply call the *Anti-Additive-Aggregationist Position*, will implicitly have total utilitarianism in mind as the exemplar of the Additive-Aggregationist Position. But I hope it will be apparent how my claims and arguments could be modified to address other members of the additive-aggregationist family. Furthermore, in chapter 10, I'll explore in more detail a general version of the Additive-Aggregationist Position that regards utility as but one important moral ideal, among others, when I discuss what is perhaps the most natural and standard way of thinking about the value of utility and its relation to other moral ideals.

Given the complex nature of the Additive-Aggregationist Position, those who reject it in those cases where it entails the Unlimited Trade-offs View in favor of the Second Standard View may do so for very different reasons. Some may do so because they balk at the additive-aggregationist reasoning involved in its third, fourth, or sixth elements. But some may actually accept the elements of the view that are straightforwardly additive, but reject the view because of its other elements, and what those elements commit one to, *given* the additive-aggregationist reasoning underlying the third, fourth, and sixth elements. As important, many may *accept* additive-aggregationist reasoning in *some* contexts and domains, and yet reject such reasoning in *other* contexts and domains.[22] This accords with a natural and plausible description of why many people accept *both* the First and Second Standard Views. For a large class of cases, to which the First Standard View applies, additive-aggregationist reasoning seems plausible; but for another large class of cases, to which the Second Standard View applies, anti-additive-aggregationist reasoning seems plausible. The importance of this observation, and its defense, will be addressed throughout much of this book.

---

[21] I am grateful to Shelly Kagan for calling to my attention the importance of emphasizing this point.

[22] This idea accords with Joseph Raz's view that there can be *conditional ideals*, in the sense of ideals that have value in some circumstances but not others (see, e.g., *The Morality of Freedom* [Oxford: Oxford University Press, 1986]). Similar claims are made by Frances Kamm, when she defends her *Principle of Contextual Interaction* in *Morality, Mortality, Vol. I*, and by Shelly Kagan in his article "The Additive Fallacy."

2.4 Jake Ross's Principle

I have presented considerations supporting the view that in certain contexts anti-additive-aggregationist reasoning is more plausible than additive-aggregationist reasoning. I would next like to present a view of Jake Ross's,[23] supporting the claim that in certain contexts it would be most rational to *follow* the dictates of the Anti-Additive-Aggregationist Position *even if* one had most reason to *believe* that the Additive-Aggregationist Position was correct. As we will see, Ross's view has a bearing at many points throughout this book.

To illuminate Ross's view, it will help to consider two variations of an example he gives.

> *Gnats versus Cannibals, Case I*: One is about to be cast on an island occupied by pockets of either annoying gnats or hungry cannibals. One can take either of two maps to follow. Gnat Map will tell you where all the gnats are if, in fact, it is Gnat Island; Cannibal Map will tell you where all the cannibals are if, in fact, it is Cannibal Island. Correspondingly, Gnat Map will enable one to effectively avoid any gnats, but will be useless if the island is populated by cannibals. Similarly, Cannibal Map will enable one to effectively avoid any cannibals, but will be useless if the island is infested with gnats. Unfortunately, you don't know, for sure, whether you are landing on Gnat or Cannibal Island.

> *Gnats versus Cannibals, Case II*: With one notable exception, everything is the same as in case I. The exception is this. In case II, Cannibal Island is densely populated. Accordingly, Cannibal Map reveals that there is no way of avoiding the cannibals if one is being cast upon Cannibal Island. Whatever path one takes, if one is on Cannibal Island one will be promptly captured and eaten.

Which map should you take to guide you on the island in the two cases? Ross argues, convincingly, that in case *I*, it would generally be *most* rational to take Cannibal Map with you, even if one had good reason to *believe* that in all probability you were landing on Gnat Island. For example, even if one knew that there was a 95 percent chance you would be landing on Gnat Island, and only a 5 percent chance you would be landing on Cannibal Island, it would *still* make sense to follow Cannibal Map—that is, to act *as if* the island were populated with cannibals rather than gnats—in navigating the island. The reason for this is roughly that what you stand to *gain* by following the map that you have most reason to believe is the *correct* one is basically *insignificant* in comparison with what you stand to *lose* by following that map if, in fact, what

---

[23] Presented in his pathbreaking article "Rejecting Ethical Deflationism," *Ethics* 116 (2006): 742–68.

you have most reason to believe is false. Likewise, what you stand to gain by following the map that you have most reason to believe is the *incorrect* one is vastly more important than what you stand to lose by following that map, if your belief about that map turns out to be false.

Ross also argues, convincingly, that in case *II*, it would be most rational to take Gnat Map with you, and this is so even if one thought that there was only a slim chance that you would be landing on Gnat Island rather than Cannibal Island. So, for example, even if one had good reason to believe that there was a 95 percent chance one was landing on Cannibal Island, and only a 5 percent chance one was landing on Gnat Island, one should still proceed *as if* Gnat Map is the correct map. After all, if Cannibal Map *is* the correct map, it won't matter *at all* what one does when one lands on the island, as all paths and options will be equally bad. A fortiori, in the likely event that that you are being cast on Cannibal Island, it won't matter *which* map you are following. On the other hand, in the unlikely event that you are being cast on Gnat Island, Cannibal Map will be useless, while Gnat Map will enable you to effectively avoid annoying gnat bites. Accordingly, in case *II*, you have everything to gain and nothing to lose by taking and following Gnat Map.[24]

Reflecting and expanding upon such considerations, Ross arrives at several important conclusions regarding the circumstances in which it is rational to *follow* certain theories for the purposes of practical reasoning; acting *as if* they were true, even if one has most reason to *believe* that another theory is, in fact, more likely to *be* true. Oversimplifying, let me sum up and combine some of Ross's key results as follows.

> *J. Ross's Principle*: Clause 1: Given any two theories, T_1 and T_2, it is rational to *follow* T_2 in one's practical deliberations, even if one believes that T_1 is more likely to be true than T_2, as long as one gives *some* credence to the possibility of T_2's being true, and T_1 evaluates all of one's options as equally desirable. So, given options $O_1, O_2, O_3, \ldots, O_n$, if T_1 judges all the options as equivalent, while T_2 judges one of the options, say O_p, as superior to the others, as long as one has some credence in T_2 it is *rational* to *follow* T_2 and choose O_p, *even if* one has most reason to *believe* that T_1 is the correct theory. In such a case, one has everything to gain and nothing to lose by acting *as if* T_2 were the correct theory and following its dictates. Clause 2: similarly, if T_1 judges that there is little to choose between one's options, while T_2 judges that it makes a great difference which of one's options one chooses, then as long as one believes there is a "decent" chance that T_2

---

[24] Some readers will recognize the reasoning underlying Ross's judgment about case *II* as the reasoning that is embodied by the *Sure-Thing Principle*. I will briefly discuss the Sure-Thing Principle in chapter 8.

might be true, it will often be rational to follow the dictates of T_2, even if in fact one has more credence in T_1 than in T_2.

Now, in fact, Ross gives a carefully worked out formula for determining exactly when we should follow T_2, rather than T_1, in the case where T_2 judges that there is a great difference between one's options, and T_1 judges that there is only a small difference between one's options. Though interesting and important, the precise details of Ross's account need not detain us here. For my purposes, it is sufficient to recognize the basic truth expressed by J. Ross's Principle. For practical purposes, it can often be *rational* to act *as if* a given theory is true, even if, in fact, one has greater credence in rival theories. This will be so if the theory that one has less credence in favors one option, while rival theories regard all the options as equivalent (clause *1*); or, often, if the theory that one has less credence in judges that there is a great difference between one's options, while rival theories judge that there is little difference between one's options (clause *2*).

Let us now apply J. Ross's Principle to some of the cases we have been considering. Consider a variation of Parfit's Repugnant Conclusion. Suppose that *A* and *Z* were related in such a way that multiplying the value of each *A* life times the number of people in *A*, and multiplying the value of each *Z* life times the number of people in *Z*, *A* and *Z* would be equally good on the Additive-Aggregationist Position. We know that on the Anti-Additive-Aggregationist Position, *A* would be judged as much better than *Z*. Now, as we have seen, many people find the view that *Z* might be as good as *A* repugnant. So, many people will in fact attach much *more* credence to the Anti-Additive-Aggregationist Position than to the Additive-Aggregationist Position for comparing such alternatives. But suppose, for a moment, that one was inclined to attach *more* credence to the Additive-Aggregationist Position than to the Anti-Additive-Aggregationist Position. Even so, as long as one attached *some* credence to the Anti-Additive-Aggregationist Position, it is clear that if one was given a choice between two alternatives like *A* and *Z*, which were related in the manner described, it would be rational to choose *A*, in accordance with clause *1* of J. Ross's Principle. After all, if the Additive-Aggregationist Position *is* the correct principle for choosing between such outcomes, one won't go *wrong* by choosing *A*, while if the Anti-Additive-Aggregationist Position is the correct principle for choosing between such outcomes, one will go terribly wrong by choosing *Z*. So, in the case described, one has lots to gain and nothing to lose by acting *as if* the Anti-Additive-Aggregationist Position is correct, even if one *believes* otherwise. Accordingly, if one ever actually faced such a choice, it would be *practically* rational to choose *A*, and *practically* irrational to choose *Z*.[25]

---

[25] Readers familiar with the shortcomings of Pascal's Wager will recognize that this argument depends on the assumption that there isn't another theory for assessing outcomes in which we have comparable credence that balances out the Anti-Additive-Aggregationist Position, by judging that *Z* is

Some people will have doubts as to whether *A* could ever be *exactly* as good as *Z* on any of our views about how to assess outcomes. But we can relax this assumption. Consider all those cases where, according to the Additive-Aggregationist Position, *Z* would actually be *better* than *A*, but not by a lot. Unless we are convinced that there is very little or no chance that the Anti-Additive-Aggregationist Position could be correct for comparing such alternatives, it could still be practically rational to choose *Z* rather than *A*, if faced with such alternatives. After all, given that the difference between choosing *A* and *Z* would be fairly small if the Additive-Aggregationist Position is correct, while the difference between choosing *A* and *Z* would be huge if the Anti-Additive-Aggregationist Position is correct, in accordance with the clause 2 of J. Ross's Principle it will often be *practically* rational to choose as if the Anti-Additive-Aggregationist Position is correct, even if one attaches greater credence to the Additive-Aggregationist Position.

Similar considerations apply to my Lollipops for Life case, and to any other case where there is a conflict between the Additive-Aggregationist Position and the Anti-Additive-Aggregationist Position. *As long as* there would be little or no difference between the alternatives if the Additive-Aggregationist Position were correct, while there would be a major difference between the alternatives if the Anti-Additive-Aggregationist Position were correct, then as long as we have some credence in both views, it will generally be rational to follow the dictates of the Anti-Additive-Aggregationist Position in our practical deliberations even if, in fact, we attach greater credence to the Additive-Aggregationist Position.[26]

Although I have been discussing cases where J. Ross's Principle would tell us to follow the Anti-Additive-Aggregationist Position rather than the Additive-Aggregationist Position, even if we had greater credence in the latter, it is important to recognize that J. Ross's Principle is neutral between those positions; indeed, it is neutral between all positions, principles, or

---

in fact much better than *A*, and to the same extent to which *A* is supposed to be better than *Z* on the Anti-Additive-Aggregationist Position. But there is, in fact, no such additional theory. This is why the considerations I offer here succeed, where Pascal's analogous argument in support of the view that we all have reason to believe in the Christian God fails. (Pascal's argument also involves problems of infinity; whereas my argument does not.)

[26] The first qualification here is crucial. There might be a version of the Repugnant Conclusion such that the number of people in *Z* was *so* vast, that *Z* was judged as much better than *A* according to the Additive-Aggregationist Position. In that case, J. Ross's Principle would not apply, and it would *not* be practically rational to choose *A* rather than *Z* if one had greater credence in the Additive-Aggregationist Position than the Anti-Additive-Aggregationist Position. J. Ross's Principle only comes into play in helping to choose between which theories or principles to follow, each of which we have some credence in, in those cases where there is little or no difference between the alternatives according to all but one of the theories or principles, but a great difference between the alternatives according to the other theory or principle. (Again, my remarks here are oversimplified for ease of presentation, but I trust the point is clear enough.)

theories in which we might have credence. So, there will be cases where J. Ross's Principle would tell us to follow the Additive-Aggregationist Position rather than the Anti-Additive-Aggregationist Position, even if we had more credence in the latter. To illustrate this, let us consider one of the spectrums discussed earlier, and the kind of Anti-Additive-Aggregationist Position which only assessed outcomes by focusing on the different levels people were at in those outcomes, and not on the number of people at each level. On the Anti-Additive-Aggregationist Position, an outcome in which n people suffered from a given illness would be worse than an outcome in which two or three times as many people suffered from an illness that was almost, but not quite, as bad, since, in assessing those outcomes, it would only pay attention to the quality of the lives of the people affected. Still, since, by hypothesis, the quality of lives in the second outcome would only be *slightly* better than the quality of lives in the first outcome, the difference between choosing the first or second outcomes would be quite small on the Anti-Additive-Aggregationist Position currently under discussion. On the other hand, the difference between the two outcomes would be very large on the Additive-Aggregationist Position, which pays attention not only to the *quality* of lives but to the *number* of people affected by each illness. It follows from clause 2 of J. Ross's Principle, that it would probably be rational to choose between the outcomes in question *as if* the Additive-Aggregationist Position were correct, even if, in fact, one attached greater credence to the Anti-Additive-Aggregationist Position. After all, for *such* comparisons, what one gains if one follows the Anti-Additive-Aggregationist Position, and that position is, in fact, correct, is basically insignificant in comparison with what loses if one follows that position and it is, in fact, incorrect.

In the preceding sections, I claimed that most people believe that additive-aggregationist reasoning is relevant for comparing alternatives that are near each other on the spectrums I considered, while anti-additive-aggregationist reasoning is relevant for comparing alternatives that are at the opposite ends of the spectrums I considered. Although my discussion was couched in terms of people's judgments about the goodness of outcomes, I might have added the further claim that given a choice between two alternatives that were near each other on my spectrums, most people would almost certainly choose in accordance with additive-aggregationist reasoning, while given a choice between two alternatives that were far apart on my spectrums, most people would almost certainly choose in accordance with anti-additive-aggregationist reasoning. Indeed, at the risk of sounding overly rhetorical, I think many people would regard it as *crazy* to choose between such outcomes in any other ways than the ones I have suggested, if they were actually *confronted* with such choices for people about whom they cared. This section's considerations support the *practical rationality* of such choices, even if people's *beliefs* are not as I have claimed them to be.

As long as people have credence in both positions, and as long as there are no other rival positions that would have a significant bearing on their choices, it will be practically rational to choose as if additive-aggregationist reasoning is correct for alternatives that are near each other on my spectrums, even if one has greater credence in the Anti-Additive-Aggregationist Position; but, by the same token, it will often be practically rational to choose as if anti-additive-aggregationist reasoning is correct for alternatives that are far apart on my spectrums, even if one has greater credence in the Additive-Aggregationist Position. This is one of the important lessons to be drawn from J. Ross's Principle.[27]

---

[27] Frances Kamm worries about J. Ross's Principle, because she thinks it is incompatible with her *Principle of Irrelevant Utilities*. It is instructive to consider Kamm's worry. (Kamm raised this worry in discussion; on her Principle of Irrelevant Utilities, see *Morality, Mortality, Vol. I*, 144–64.)

Kamm has argued that if we had to choose which of two strangers to save, Bill or Kathy, our deontological obligation to treat them impartially would require that we give them an equal chance of being saved, say, by flipping a fair coin to decide whom to save. Kamm explicitly rejects the consequentialist view that if, by hypothesis, saving Bill or Kathy would be equally good, then if, by saving Bill, we would *also* save a flower, then we should save Bill and the flower rather than only save Kathy. Kamm does not deny that, by hypothesis, the *outcome* where we save Bill and the flower would be a slightly better *outcome* than the outcome where we save Kathy alone (the example assumes that saving each of the people would have equally good effects and that, in addition, some people would receive a small amount of pleasure from the flower); but she contends that in matters of life or death, we cannot let our *choice* of who lives or dies be determined by such a trivial matter as whether the outcome would be slightly better if we saved one person rather than another. On Kamm's view, the extra pleasure people might derive from the saved flower is an *irrelevant utility*, in the sense that we must regard such a minor utility as irrelevant in making such a momentous *decision* as who lives and who dies. Thus, for Kamm, if the choice is between saving Bill and a flower, or Kathy alone, we must *still* flip a coin, or find another equivalent way of ensuring that we are treating them impartially by giving them each an equal chance at being saved.

Kamm worries that if we accept J. Ross's Principle, her arguments in favor of the Principle of Irrelevant Utilities are all for naught. She believes that if Ross is right we should choose between Bill and Kathy *as if* utilitarianism is the right view, *even if* we give greater credence to Kamm's own view of the matter. This is because Kamm grants that the outcome in which we save Bill and the flower would be no worse than the outcome in which we save Kathy alone, while the utilitarian thinks the former would be *better* than the latter. So, it would seem, on Ross's reasoning, we have everything to gain and nothing to lose by saving Bill and the flower.

Not everyone is persuaded about Kamm's Principle of Irrelevant Utilities. And no doubt some will argue against it by appeal to Rossian or Sure-Thing-type reasoning. But Kamm's worry about J. Ross's Principle is based on a misunderstanding of his view. J. Ross's Principle applies to principles or theories; it tells us which principle or theory it is practically rational to *follow* in certain circumstances. It does not apply to *outcomes* except, indirectly, insofar as competing theories themselves apply to outcomes.

As indicated, Kamm grants that the *outcome* in which Bill and the flower are saved would be at least as good as (and in fact better than) the *outcome* in which Kathy alone is saved; but she explicitly *denies* that our decision about who should live should be guided solely by considerations of how the outcomes compare. To the contrary, she has mustered powerful examples purporting to show that the deontological requirement of treating people impartially *precludes* our allowing such a decision to be influenced by an irrelevant utility like the extra pleasure people would receive from a saved flower. Given this, far from being incompatible with Kamm's view, if anything, J. Ross's Principle provides practical support for the very conclusion Kamm advocates! (cont.)

2.5 A Worry about Consistency

I have presented various views that people hold, and suggested that there are powerful reasons to hold them. Let me next suggest that, together, these views raise deep worries about consistency.

In chapter 1, I noted that most people accept the transitivity of the "better than" relation; that is, they accept that if *A* is better than *B*, and *B* better than *C*, then *A* is better than *C*. However, the Standard Views discussed in section 2.2 are inconsistent with the transitivity of "better than." At least, this is so given one further very plausible assumption that I shall soon make explicit. As the book unfolds, we will see that the inconsistency in question raises major questions about our understanding of practical reasoning and the nature of the good.

First, the plausible assumption that underlies the purported inconsistency. The assumption is just that there is, or at least could be, a spectrum of benefits, ranging from the very great to the very minor, such that one could make a series of pairwise comparisons of benefits across the spectrum, where the First Standard View would apply to all pairwise comparisons involving benefits that were "near" each other on the spectrum, while the Second Standard View would apply to all pairwise comparisons of benefits at opposite ends of the spectrum. Applied to the medical context, the assumption holds that there is, or at least *could be*, a spectrum of illnesses ranging from the very serious to the very mild, such that one could make a series of pairwise comparisons of illnesses across the spectrum, where the *FSV* would apply to all pairwise comparisons involving illnesses that were "near" each other on the spectrum, while the *SSV* would apply to all pairwise comparisons of illnesses at opposite ends of the spectrum.

In a moment, I'll give some reasonably concrete examples illustrating how the inconsistency I have in mind might actually arise in the real world. But, first, let me give a simple abstract schema making plain the problem I have in mind.

Suppose we attach credence to two theories, a consequentialist theory like utilitarianism, and a nonconsequentialist theory like Kamm's. And suppose we must decide whether to save Bill and a flower, or Kathy alone. The consequentialist view will favor saving Bill and the flower, and letting the extra utility gained from the flower be the deciding factor in the decision. But since the extra utility from the flower is, by hypothesis, quite minimal, there won't be a *significant* moral difference between the two alternatives on the consequentialist theory. On Kamm's theory, on the other hand, there will be a *big* moral difference between choosing between Bill and Kathy on the basis of a coin flip, and choosing between them on the basis of the "irrelevant" utility of an extra flower. The latter would be *deeply* wrong, and would be *strongly* prohibited. A fortiori, in the case Kamm has described, there is, morally, a lot to gain and little to lose by following Kamm's Theory, while there is, morally, a lot to lose and little to gain by following the consequentialist theory. Thus, in accordance with the second clause of J. Ross's Principle, if we are aiming at doing the best we can morally, it may be *practically* rational to *follow* Kamm's theory and act *as if* it is the true theory, *even if* we give greater credence to consequentialism. Naturally, the practical rationality of following Kamm's theory if we want to do the best we can morally will be even stronger, on Ross's view, if, in fact, we are persuaded by Kamm's arguments and give her theory more credence than consequentialism.

Suppose, for simplicity, that we divide the spectrum of negative well-being into ten basic levels, with level 10 involving the worst negative elements people endure, and level 1 involving the mildest negative elements people endure. Suppose, further, that we think that where there is a difference of only one between people's levels, the First Standard View applies, but that where there is a difference of nine between people's levels, the Second Standard View applies. Intuitively, this just means that we think that differences in well-being between people who are in adjacent levels of the well-being spectrum are sufficiently small that it would be better if a smaller number of people had to endure being at level 10, 9, 8, 7, 6, 5, 4, 3, or 2, than if a "sufficiently" larger number of people had to endure being at level 9, 8, 7, 6, 5, 4, 3, 2, or 1, respectively; but that we think the differences in well-being between people who are at the opposite ends of the negative well-being spectrum are so large that it would be better if virtually any number of people had to endure being at level 1 than if some number of people had to endure being at level 10. This means that there will be some numbers of people, $k, l, m, n, o, p, q, r, s$, and t, where $t > s > r > q > p > o > n > m > l > k$, such that, in accordance with the First Standard View, we think it would be better if k people were at level 10 than if l people were at level 9; better if l people were at level 9 than if m people were at level 8; better if m people were at level 8 than if n people were at level 7; and so on. But also, in accordance with the Second Standard View, we think it would be better if t people were at level 1 than if k people were at level 10.[28]

Here, as elsewhere, the particular scale for negative well-being that I've chosen is arbitrary and merely for illustrative purposes. But it suffices to show the inconsistency between the Standard Views I've discussed about the desirability of different trade-offs between quality and number and the transitivity of "better than." Let $A, B, C, D, E, F, G, H, I$, and J be outcomes where there are k people at level 10, l people at level 9, m people at level 8, n people at level 7, o people at level 6, p people at level 5, q people at level 4, r people at level 3, s people at level 2, and t people at level 1, respectively. Then, as we have just seen, on the First Standard View, A would be better than B, B better than C, C better than D, D better than E, E better than F, F better than G, G better than H, H better than I, and I better than J. If "better than" is a transitive relation, this entails that A, an outcome where k people were at level 10, experiencing the worst negative elements that humans endure, would be better than J, an

---

[28] Many people who believe the qualified claim in the text will also believe the stronger claim that it would be better to prevent or cure even *one* person from suffering the severely negative effects of being at level 10 than *any* number of people from suffering mild negative effects of being at level 1. I incline toward this view myself. However, the weaker claim is all I need for my arguments to succeed, and since some people may accept the weaker claim who worry about the stronger claim, and anyone who accepts the stronger claim will also accept the weaker claim, it is the weaker claim I employ in my argument. See note 6.

outcome where *t* people were at level 1, experiencing the mildest negative elements that humans endure. But, as we have seen, on the Second Standard View *A* is *not* better than *J*. Thus, it appears that one *must* reject the First Standard View, the Second Standard View, or the transitivity of "better than." Alternatively, one must contend that there *couldn't be* a spectrum of negative well-being whose members stand together in the relations that 1 through 10 are purported to, such that the First Standard View would apply to the pairwise comparisons between outcomes whose members were in adjacent levels along that spectrum, but the Second Standard View would apply to the pairwise comparisons between outcomes whose members were in levels at the opposite ends of the well-being spectrum. Here we have an outright inconsistency, from which it seems to follow that *something has to go!*[29] But what? I believe that the claim that there *couldn't* be a spectrum of negative well-being of the sort the argument depends on will be extremely difficult to defend, but that *giving up any of the other three views will require major revision in our practical and theoretical thinking*.

This discussion has been abstract. Let us consider some simple examples. Consider first a spectrum of depression from which one might periodically suffer for the duration of one's life. Suppose that the spectrum is divided into eight levels, with level 1 being the mildest and level 8 being the most serious, where the different levels are depicted as follows:

8, being very seriously depressed (on average) 6 days a week
7, being quite seriously depressed 5 days a week
6, being seriously depressed 4 days a week
5, being fairly seriously depressed 3 days a week
4, being pretty depressed 2 days a week
3, being depressed 1 day a week
2, being awfully down in the dumps once every two weeks
1, being pretty down once a month

These descriptions are admittedly simplified, but they describe a spectrum of depressions such that many would agree about the desirability of trade-offs between quality and number for cases "near" each other on the spectrum, but reject such trade-offs for cases at the opposite ends of the spectrum.

For example, I believe the following might be true. It might be better if outcome *A* occurred, in which 10 people suffered from level 8 depression,

---

[29] Virtually every clear-thinking philosopher or logician worth her salt will regard the "seems to follow" as deeply misleading and wholly unnecessary. Where an outright inconsistency obtains something *has* to go, there is no "seems to follow" about it! This is almost certainly right. However, in my concluding chapter I raise some worries about the absolute certainty of even this most fundamental of logical positions. Of course, the ultimate strength of those worries will be for the reader to decide.

than if outcome *B* occurred, in which 50 people suffered from level 7 depression. Although there would be general agreement that it was worse to be very seriously depressed 6 days a week for the duration of one's life, than to be quite seriously depressed 5 days a week for the duration of one's life, from an impartial perspective there would be most reason to prefer the outcome in which "only" 10 people suffered the former illness to the outcome in which 50 people suffered the latter illness—an illness which though less bad than the former illness, was certainly of a similar order of magnitude in terms of the suffering and negative impact that it would have on its victims. Similarly, it might be better if outcome *B* occurred, in which 50 people suffered from level 7 depression, than if *C* occurred, in which 200 suffered from level 6 depression; if *C* occurred than if *D* occurred, in which 800 suffered from level 5 depression; if *D* occurred than if *E* occurred, in which 2,000 suffered from level 4 depression; if *E* occurred, than if *F* occurred, in which 6,000 suffered from level 3 depression; if *F* occurred, than if *G* occurred, in which 20,000 suffered from level 2 depression; and if *G* occurred, than if *H* occurred, in which 100,000 suffered from level 1 depression. In each of the pairwise comparisons, the second illness is less severe than the first, but they are "close enough" in severity that the much greater number of affected people seemingly licenses the trade-off in question. That is, these are the *kinds* of cases where trade-offs between quality and number seem desirable, in accordance with the First Standard View.[30]

If "better than" is transitive, the preceding entails that outcome *A* might be better than outcome *H*; that is, that it might be better if 10 people suffered from level 8 depression, than if 100,000 people suffered from level 1 depression. But this is a position many would reject. The gap in severity between level 8 depression and level 1 depression is *so* large that the Second Standard View seemingly applies. Correspondingly, most would think it better if 100,000 people were "pretty down" once a month for the duration of their lives, than if 10 people were seriously depressed six days a week for the duration of their lives. Indeed, many people would think it better if 1 million or even 10 million people were "pretty down" once a month for the duration of their lives, than if 10 people were seriously depressed six days a week for the duration of their lives.

---

[30] For those people who are looking for systematic regularity in the progression of my example's numbers, you won't find any! But it isn't needed, either. I have chosen an example which involves nice round numbers, and for which the judgments generated by the First Standard View would be plausible, but where the progression doesn't explode out of our intuitively graspable range. That is all I need for my purposes, and I think I have succeeded. But as I note later, here as elsewhere, there is nothing special about the particular levels of depression and numbers I have chosen. All I need for my argument to succeed is that there could be even *one* spectrum of outcomes of the sort I have suggested where our judgments about how the different outcomes compared would track the judgments given here. I believe my example is enough to suggest that this could, indeed, be the case, even if the reader would favor a spectrum of cases which differed in its precise details from the one I have given here.

Not everyone will agree with this last judgment, of course. But serious, lifelong, clinical depression is among the cruelest fates that can befall a human. Arguably, it is as bad as, or worse than, being a quadriplegic, severely mentally retarded, or deaf, dumb, and blind.[31] Indeed, I suspect that most people who have had to spend three or four years in refugee, prisoner of war, or even concentration camps, and have had to suffer the pain, indignity, and humiliation of rape, torture, and starvation in such camps, have probably, nonetheless, had lives that were, *on the whole*, less crushing than the lives of most people who have had to suffer from serious, lifelong, clinical depression. Bearing this in mind, if one could push a button that would spare even ten people from such a horrible cruel fate, or a different button what would spare hundreds of thousands or even millions of people from being "pretty down" once a month, I think many people, and perhaps most, would, in fact, push the first button. Moreover, in doing this they would believe, in accordance with the Second Standard View, that they were producing the better outcome.

Notice, one might balk at my vague descriptions of the different levels of depression, and hence be uncertain as to whether one should agree about the desirability of the different trade-offs given the particular numbers I've chosen. But I don't think this substantially affects my point. Suppose, for example, one thinks that the gap between being very seriously depressed 6 days a week and being quite seriously depressed 5 days a week is larger than I realize, so that in fact it would be better if even *50* people suffered the latter than if 10 people suffered the former. So make it *100* people, or *200* people! Is it really plausible to think that it wouldn't be better if only 10 people suffered the severer depression than if 100 or 200 suffered the lesser, but still quite serious, depression? I think not. Alternatively, one could always insert an intermediate illness between the two described and then rerun the argument with an extra step. In either case the total numbers of people involved in the various trade-offs would become larger, but this wouldn't change most people's convictions about the relevance of the First Standard View for comparing "near" alternatives on the spectrum, and the relevance of the Second Standard View for comparing

---

[31] For an account of just how crushing serious depression really is, see Peter Kramer's *Against Depression* (New York: Viking, 2005). Indeed, Kramer would argue that I have understated just how bad depression is. For example, in his book he writes, "Because public health dollars are scarce, statisticians have worked to quantify the harm diseases cause. Their findings have surprised even the researchers who devised the major studies: Depression is the most devastating disease known to mankind" (150). He also notes, "Among the chronic diseases of midlife, depression was (by 1990) already the most burdensome, and not by a small margin. Major depression accounted for almost 20 percent of all disability-adjusted life years lost for women in developed countries—more than three times the burden imposed by the next most impairing illness. The story was similar in developing regions: depression was still the fourth most burdensome disease (after conditions that affect the very young) and the most disabling disease for both men and women age fifteen to forty-four. In the 2020 projections, depression becomes the single most disabling disease in developing regions" (152).

alternatives at the opposite ends of the spectrum. The fundamental tension remains between the First Standard View, the Second Standard View, and the transitivity of "better than."

Before going on, let me add the following. Some people distinguish between the *direct* impact an illness has on one's life and its *indirect* impact. So, for example, it might be argued that what makes constant serious depression so bad is not merely the direct impact it has on one's physical and psychological well-being (lost weight, listlessness, feelings of hopelessness, and so on), but the indirect impact (making it difficult to keep a job, engage in enjoyable activities, or maintain significant personal relationships). In my examples, I am assuming that both the direct and the indirect impact *on the affected individuals* are relevant to our assessment of the outcomes. So, in essence, my claim is that there is, or could be, a spectrum of illnesses such that when one took account of *both* the direct and the indirect impact of each illness *on its victim*, the First Standard View seems plausible for comparing outcomes involving illnesses that are "near" each other on the spectrum, and the Second Standard View seems plausible for comparing outcomes involving illnesses that are at opposite ends of the spectrum. Importantly, however, my "other things equal clause" is intended to rule out any direct or indirect effects that an individual's benefits or burdens have on *third* parties. So, for example, I don't deny that there may be real-world statistical truths of the following sort: in an outcome where 100,000 people were down in the dumps once a month, over time, there might be more car accidents than otherwise, leading to the ruin of 20 lives. Given such a truth, one might be tempted to judge that an outcome where 10 people suffered constant severe depression would be better than one where 100,000 were down in the dumps occasionally, because what one would *really* be judging, implicitly, is that an outcome where 10 people suffered constant severe depression would be better than one where 100,000 were down in the dumps occasionally *and* 20 people had ruined lives! I would accept *that* judgment, but I am interested in a different comparison. I am exploring counterfactual comparisons of the following sort: taking account of both the direct and indirect ways in which each person *herself* would be affected by her illness, how would an outcome where 10 people suffered constant severe depression compare with one where 100,000 people were down in the dumps occasionally, and there *were* no other relevant differences between the outcomes? It is such "pure" cases that my "other things equal" clause is partly intended to pick out, and it is crucial to bear this in mind, if my examples are to serve their purpose.

Let me next briefly present a second, analogous, example. Consider the following alternatives:

A, 10 people go through life without two arms and a leg
B, 50 people go through life without one arm, a leg, and a hand

C, 200 people go through life without an arm and a leg
D, 800 people go through life without an arm and a foot
E, 2,000 people go through life without an arm
F, 6,000 people go through life without a hand
G, 20,000 people go through life without three fingers
H, 100,000 people go through life without a finger
I, 400,000 people go through life without the top third of one finger

As described, I think most would agree that for "near" members of the preceding handicap spectrum (*A* and *B*, *B* and *C*, *C* and *D*, etc.), the First Standard View would apply, so that trade-offs between quality and number would be appropriate. So, while there might be some disagreements about the exact numbers that would be necessary to license any particular trade-offs, in principle, one might agree that *A* is better than *B*, *B* is better than *C*, *C* is better than *D*, and so on.[32] If "better than" is transitive, this entails that *A* is better than *I*. But most would, I think, reject this. Appealing to the Second Standard View, many would claim that the difference in severity between *A*'s and *I*'s handicaps is *so* great, that for such outcomes trade-offs between quality and number are undesirable. They would contend that it would be worse if 10 people went through life without two arms and a leg, than if 400,000—or, for that matter, 4 million or 40 million—people went through life without the top third of one finger. (Note, here, as throughout, there is an implicit "all things considered" clause; so, for example, we are not to assume that with so many missing thirds of people's fingers there would be more accidents, and hence more ruined lives for that reason.) As before, there is an inconsistency between the First Standard View, the Second Standard View, and the transitivity of "better than."

---

[32] There is, of course, a vast psychological literature attesting to the phenomenon of *adaptive preference formation*, whereby humans have a great capacity to adapt to, identify with, and endorse the circumstances in which they find themselves. So, just as some members of the deaf community do not think of themselves as "disadvantaged" or "handicapped" relative to members of the hearing community, no doubt some people who had to go through life without two arms and a leg might not think of themselves as disadvantaged or handicapped relative to people who had to go through life without one arm, a leg, and a hand. I do not wish to minimize the importance of the value people put on their own lives "from the inside," nor to be making any controversial claims about the relative value of lives with different physical and psychological capacities; still, I hope there can be agreement that from an impartial ex ante perspective *some* spectrum of alternatives analogous to the one I gave might be ordered in the way suggested. We might agree that a "handicapped" person's life was just as *valuable*, morally, as a "normal" person's life, but still think that in most contexts there is good reason to try to prevent people from being "handicapped" if we can. Similarly, we might think that an outcome in which someone "only" had to overcome or adapt to the loss of one arm, a leg, and a hand would, generally, be better than an outcome in which someone had to overcome or adapt to the loss of both arms and a leg; but, in accordance with the text, we may agree that the outcome in which "only" ten people had to overcome or adapt to the latter condition would generally be better than one in which *fifty* people had to overcome or adapt to the former condition. I am grateful to Roger Crisp for reminding me (in correspondence) that some people may worry about my example here because of people's adaptability to "handicaps."

To focus our thinking, the preceding examples have involved trade-offs between similar kinds of illnesses or disabilities: depression in the one case and physical handicaps in the other. But I hope it is clear that the same problem will arise when confronting trade-offs between different kinds of illnesses or disabilities. The point is that illnesses can range in severity from the very bad to the relatively mild. *Any* illness might be put on a spectrum of the sort I've been discussing, and we will have to choose which of the many illnesses to address with our limited resources. Sometimes our choices might be determined by deontological or agent-relative considerations. But often, especially at government or international levels, we will want our choices to be at least partially guided by considerations of which outcome would be best. We will feel the pull of the impartial perspective and seek to promote the best outcome—the one there is most reason to prefer from the impartial perspective. But in such cases, how are we to choose, when it seems quality and number are *both* relevant for certain comparisons, *only* quality is relevant for others, and the transitivity of "better than" seemingly breaks down given these apparent facts?

2.6 Some Initial Worries and Preliminary Responses

There are many worries one might have regarding the argument to this point. Most of these will be considered in more detail in later chapters, but let me introduce a few of them here, and offer some preliminary responses.

Consider again Jim Griffin's position, noted earlier. But for the sake of our discussion, let us reformulate his claims in a way he may not approve of: that is, in terms of "better than," rather than in terms of what it may be rationally defensible to *prefer*. So, the reformulated position might be put as follows. There are incommensurabilities of the form: enough of A outranks any amount of B, so that an outcome involving "enough" of A will be better than an outcome involving any amount of B. Such incommensurabilities reflect *discontinuity* between values, and this involves "the suspension of addition; . . . we have a positive value that, no matter how often a certain amount is added to itself, cannot become greater than another positive value, and cannot, not because with piling up we get diminishing value or even disvalue . . . but because they are the sort of value that, even remaining constant, cannot add up to some other value."[33] So, for example, there might be a spectrum of artworks ranging from Rembrandt, Vermeer, and the like, at one end of the spectrum, to contemporary kitsch, at the other end, such that, though the "kicks" of kitsch are real, they are vastly different from the appreciation of beauty, and this is so in such a way that, other things equal, an outcome involving fifty years of appreciating

---

[33] *Well-Being*, 85.

the beauty of Rembrandts, Vermeers, and the like would be better than an outcome involving *any* number of years of enjoying the kicks of kitsch.[34]

First, it might be claimed that if A and B really are *incommensurable*, then it makes no *sense* to claim that "enough" of A might *outweigh* any amount of B. This claim raises a multitude of issues, but at bottom, it conflates the category of the *incommensurable* with the category of the *incomparable*. The claim about incommensurability is a claim that there is no common scale on which As and Bs can both be put, such that Bs can be seen as proportionate in value to As. But one can have comparability without proportionality. So, for example, suppose that all human lives were, necessarily, of finite value, and all angel lives were, necessarily, of infinite value. Then, one might plausibly claim that human and angel lives were incommensurable, meaning that there was no common scale on which both kinds of lives could be put, such that one could say of any human life that it was proportionate, to a certain fixed degree, to an angel life, and meaning that no number of human lives would be more valuable than an angel life. But this wouldn't mean that one couldn't *compare* the two lives. One *can* compare them: a single angel life outweighs, in value, any amount of human lives. Correspondingly, other things equal, an outcome containing an angel life will be better than an outcome containing no angels (or other similar beings) and any number of human lives.

Second, it might be claimed that if there is a genuine discontinuity between the value of appreciating a Rembrandt and the value of enjoying kitsch, then they can't be put on a common scale. So, in essence, Rembrandts are one kind of art (say, "high" art), kitsch is another kind of art (say, "low" art), and while there may be a spectrum of high art, each of whose members could be compared on an appropriate scale of value, and a spectrum of low art, each of whose members could be compared on an appropriate scale of value, there won't be a *single* spectrum of art that includes both high art and low art. Alternatively, it might be claimed that even if we grant that there is a single spectrum of art including both high art and low art, there *must* be a break along that spectrum such that on one side of the break there is high art, and on the other side there is not. This is where discontinuity of value will arise, as the art

---

[34] *Well-Being*, 86. Here is a different example. For purposes of adding color accents to a room, it might be that the colors red and blue are *incommensurable, in the sense* that there is no common scale on which red and blue can both be put, such that we can meaningfully say that a given shade, or amount, of blue is worth, or proportionate to, a given shade or amount of red. In particular, it would be silly to claim that if it were true that adding blue accents had a positive impact on the aesthetics of the room, then as long as one added *enough* of them this would have to improve the room more than adding some number of red accents. This might clearly be false. But this doesn't mean that the red and blue accents are not comparable. To the contrary, it may well be the case that for a given room red accents (of any shade or amount) would be better than blue ones (of any shade or amount). To be sure, the color analogy is strained in certain respects. Still, I think it helps illuminate the important distinction between *incommensurability* and *incomparability*.

on one side of the break will be valued in accordance with a scale appropriate for evaluating high art, and the art on the other side will be valued in accordance with a scale appropriate for evaluating non–high art. But, importantly, one won't be able to compare the artworks on opposite sides of the break by any of the scales appropriate to comparing artworks on the same side of the break; such artworks will simply be incommensurable, and so the First Standard View won't even *apply* to that pair. Hence, we can't generate the series of pairwise comparisons across the full spectrum of cases, which is necessary for there to be a violation of transitivity.

Similar remarks might be made regarding discontinuities in the domains of benefits, burdens, and illnesses. These might be thought to challenge either my argument's so-called empirical premise or the First Standard View's general applicability. I shall discuss some of these worries in more detail later, but for now let me note the following.

Even if one grants that Rembrandts are one "kind" of art ("high" art) and kitsch another("low" art), they are still both kinds of *art*. Correspondingly, it seems that both kinds of art *could* be placed on a *single* spectrum, that would range from "high" art at one end of the spectrum to "low" art at the other, and that, in principle, there could be artworks of varying degrees of quality spread throughout the rest of the spectrum. This thought is buttressed by the fact that tiny differences of degree, if there are *enough* of them, can amount to a difference in kind. Given this, there is, indeed, every reason to believe that one could have a single spectrum of artworks, each of which differed in quality by only a tiny degree from its nearby neighbors, that ranged from high art (Rembrandts) at one end to low art (kitsch) at the other. Similar claims hold for benefits, burdens, and illnesses. Correspondingly, my argument's empirical premise retains its plausibility even if one thinks that there may be discontinuities of value in the domains in question.

As for the view that discontinuity commits us to believing that we must employ one scale for comparing works of high art and another scale for comparing works of low art, this is terribly important, but both mistaken and misleading. Here is what may be true. It may be that in comparing works of high art *with each other*, and works of low art *with each other*, we appeal to the very *same* set of criteria, which in essence involves comparing them in terms of a particular scale of value. More generally, it may be that whenever we compare artworks of sufficiently *similar* quality, we compare them in terms of the very same set of criteria, which is to say that we appeal to a scale of value that we deem appropriate for *such* comparisons. But that is compatible with thinking that if we compare artworks of sufficiently *different* quality, say "high" art with "low" art, then we must appeal to a *different* set of criteria, which is to say that we deem a different scale of value appropriate for making *such* comparisons. Similar remarks would also apply to benefits, burdens, and illnesses. On such a conception, there could be discontinuities in value of the sort Griffin discusses—where for certain As and Bs "enough" of A might outweigh any amount of B, according to the criteria, and hence scale, appropriate for comparing As with Bs. But this would be consistent with the possibility that A and B could be placed on opposite ends of a *single* spectrum, and that the First Standard View would express the relevant criteria, and hence imply the appropriate scale, *not* for comparing As with Bs, but for comparing those alternatives that were *near* each other on the spectrum.

Thus, even if one granted that there *must* be a sharp break on the art spectrum, such that on one side of the break there is high art and on the other side there is not high art, it would *not* follow that there would be a discontinuity in value of the sort Griffin recognizes between artworks immediately adjacent to each other on each side of *that* break. This is because the art spectrum might be divided into a multitude of categories, ranging, let us suppose, from high art, to very good art, to good art, to fine art, to decent art, to fair art, to okay art, to low art. Griffin's view need not commit him to think that at *each* point where there is a "break" in the spectrum from one category to the next there is discontinuity, and hence incommensurability. So, in particular, Griffin can readily grant that there is no discontinuity between the worst example of high art and the best example of non–high art, which in this case would be the best example of very good art. His view is simply that there is discontinuity between *high* art and *low* art. A fortiori, Griffin could accept that a principle like the First Standard View *would* be appropriate for comparing certain outcomes involving high art with certain outcomes involving very good art, even if it would not be appropriate for comparing high art with low art. Similar remarks would apply to my spectra involving benefits, burdens, and illnesses.

The view I have sketched raises huge issues, and it will be developed further, and explored at length, in later chapters. My point here is just to introduce one way of thinking about the claim that there may be discontinuities in value of the sort Griffin discusses that does not automatically entail the rejection of either my argument's empirical premise or the First Standard View.

Some people will object to Griffin's claim that we could have "a positive value that, no matter how often a certain amount is added to itself, cannot become greater than another positive value, and cannot, not because with piling up we get diminishing value or even disvalue... but because they are the sort of value that, even remaining constant, cannot add up to some other value."[35] Such a claim may sound incoherent. After all, if, as many believe, positive values can be accurately represented by positive real numbers, then no matter how small the real number representing one positive value may be, if that number is "added to itself" often enough, the resulting sum *will* exceed the

---

[35] *Well-Being*, 85.

positive real number accurately representing another positive value, no matter how valuable the other positive value may be (and, hence, no matter how large the real number accurately representing that value).

Griffin, of course, wouldn't deny the mathematical truth expressed in the preceding sentence. But he would insist that it misrepresents his view, a view that recognizes the possibility of incommensurable values, and that insists on the "suspension of addition" when comparing alternatives involving such values. Consider the following simple analogy. A student's overall grade might be based on her performance on three papers, or on her performance on those papers, together with any extra papers the teacher allows her to submit in order to try to improve her grade. Among the options for determining final grades, a teacher might average all the student's grades, or just use the top three grades. On either of those options, a student who submits three A papers will receive a higher grade than a student who hands in all C papers, no matter *how* many papers she submits. Suppose that we say a 4 represents the positive value of an A paper, and a 2 the positive value of a C paper. I think this is the kind of case Griffin has in mind, in suggesting that we can have "a positive value that, no matter how often a certain amount is added to itself, cannot become greater than another positive value, and cannot, not because with piling up we get diminishing value or even disvalue...but because they are the sort of value that, even remaining constant, cannot add up to some other value."[36]

Of course Griffin recognizes that if you *added* the values of each of three C papers, they would total 6, and that would be greater than the positive value of a single A paper, 4. But one needn't believe that the overall value of three C papers exceeds the value of an A paper because one can plausibly deny that one should employ a simple additive function in determining the overall value of a series of papers. Note, as Griffin rightly observes, it isn't that one believes that the value of a second C paper is *diminished* relative to the value of a first C second paper, or that it actually has *disvalue*, as if, for example, the value of a second C paper should be represented by a 1 or −1. To the contrary, one can rightly believe that the value of each C paper remains constant, 2; with each being *just as* valuable, as a paper, as its predecessor. Even so, no matter *how many* C papers "pile up," they will never surpass the value of three A papers. This is the view many of us have about the value of papers, the view Griffin has about low art versus high art, and the view that I have suggested many hold regarding "minor" benefits, burdens, or illnesses versus "major" benefits, burdens, or illnesses.

As stated, Griffin's view may be liable to misunderstanding, but it is not incoherent. It may well be that there are sorts of value, such as the value of a C paper, "that, even remaining constant, cannot add up to some other value," such

---

[36] *Well-Being*, 85.

as the value of an *A* paper. Having said that, there is a different charge that may be laid at the feet of someone like me, who accepts a position like Griffin's. It might be claimed that although, considered by *itself*, such a view is not *incoherent*, such a view *is inconsistent* with certain of our other deep beliefs. But, of course, I accept that charge. Indeed I insist on it! The gist of this chapter is to argue for precisely that position, and the task of much of this book is to explore the foundations and ramifications of that fact.

Return to the question of whether there might be discontinuities in various spectra such that the First Standard View might be implausible even for comparing alternatives that were "near" each other on the spectra. It might be argued that benefits and burdens can be placed on a single large spectrum, with very great benefits at one end, and very great burdens at the other, and that somewhere along the spectrum one would pass through three alternatives that were very near each other, one of which was a very slight benefit, one of which was a very slight burden, and another, between them, which was neutral in terms of benefits and burdens, or perhaps *indeterminate*, in the sense of being neither a benefit nor a burden without exactly being "neutral." It might then be argued that there would be sharp discontinuities between the slight benefit and the slight burden, or even between the neutral or indeterminate condition and the slight benefit or slight burden. Given this, it might be further claimed that the First Standard View fails for comparing outcomes involving such alternatives, even though they are "near" each other on the spectrum in question. Similarly, some might argue that among severe burdens, there might be a threshold such that a tiny increase in a really severe burden might transform a life from one that is barely worth living into one that is no longer worth living, and that though these burdens would lie "near" each other on the spectrum, the First Standard View would be implausible for comparing outcomes involving such alternatives.

But why should we accept this? Consider the following example. Imagine that a human life free of burdens has a level of 100, which is very much worth living. Imagine also that a human life filled with 99 burdens has a level of 1, which is barely worth living. Finally, imagine that a human life filled with 101 burdens has a level of −1, which is barely worth not living. Now suppose that there were 500 people at level 100, 10 people at level −1, and 20, 30, or 50 people at level 1. If we could remove the burdens of one of the two groups of people, I think it is clear that it would be *better* if we removed the burdens of the larger group of people at level 1, than of the smaller group of people at level −1.

It is true that the people at level 1 have lives worth living while those at level −1 do not, and other things equal that should make us want to benefit the people at −1 more than the people at 1. But even so, the differences between the two groups are very small. Both sets of lives are burdened *almost* as much as each other. Indeed, the lives of those at level 1 are *so* burdened that if they were only slightly more burdened their lives would no longer be worth living and they would be no better off than those at level −1. Given this, it seems perfectly appropriate to follow the First Standard View when it comes to making trade-offs between the two groups.

But, for now, let me not insist on this point. The First Standard View was worded the way it was to acknowledge that there may be *some* discontinuities of the sort imagined here. Perhaps the First Standard View isn't plausible when comparing lives involving slight benefits with lives involving slight burdens, or with lives involving neutral or indeterminate conditions; or when comparing lives that are so burdened as to be barely worth living, with slightly more burdened lives that are not worth living. Still, *all* I need for my argument to succeed is that there is even *one* range of cases on a spectrum such that the First Standard View would be plausible for comparing the cases that were *near* each other *within that range*, and the Second Standard View would be plausible for comparing the cases that were at the opposite ends of that range.

It is no accident that many of my examples take place on one side of the neutral point between benefits and burdens. So, I often focus on trade-offs between high-quality benefits and low-quality benefits, or between large burdens and small burdens (measured in terms of the negative impact that they have on the quality of a life). Likewise, most of my examples could easily be constructed so as not to cross the threshold between a life worth living and a life not worth living. For example, one needn't believe that the life of a quadriplegic, or someone deaf, dumb, and blind, can't be worth living, in order to believe that it would be worse if fifty people suffered from quadriplegia, or being deaf, dumb and blind, than if virtually *any* number of people suffered from a minor nosebleed, a slight cold, a sprained finger, or a short, mild headache.

Importantly, then, I am open to the claim that there may be *some* thresholds, or discontinuities, along some spectra such that the First Standard View would be implausible for comparing outcomes involving certain alternatives that were "near" each other along one of the relevant spectra. But all this shows is that the First Standard View has some limits in its scope, not that it is false. The fact is that the First Standard View is a deeply plausible view that seemingly applies to a wide range of cases. Moreover, importantly, many of the cases to which it *does* seemingly apply involve a spectrum of alternatives for which the Second Standard View *also* seemingly applies for the alternatives at the opposite ends of the spectrum, where the judgments yielded by the two views are inconsistent with the transitivity of "better than." This is the crucially important fact that this chapter is intended to illuminate, and which serves as the starting point for much of this book's work.

Finally, it may be argued that, despite appearances to the contrary, there *isn't* any *inconsistency* between the First Standard View, the Second Standard View, and the transitivity of "better than." Let me explain.

In essence, the First Standard View applies the criteria of *quality times number* to a certain set of cases. The Second Standard View, on the other hand, basically only employs the criterion of *quality*, when comparing certain cases. Clearly, then, since the First and Second Standard Views are employing *different* criteria for assessing outcomes, the notion of transitivity doesn't *apply* to the sets of judgments yielded by the different criteria. "Better than" is a transitive relation *only* when comparing outcomes in terms of the *very same* criteria. If *A* is better than *B*, in terms of the criteria relevant to judging good tennis players, and *B* is better than *C*, in terms of the criteria relevant to judging good husbands, *nothing* follows about whether *A* is better than *C*, whether as a tennis player, a good husband, or anything else. So, it isn't ever "better than" *simpliciter* that is transitive, it is always "better than with respect to some *x*," that is transitive, such as "being a better tennis player than," or "being a better father than."

When, for a given spectrum, the First Standard View tells us that *A* is better than *B*, *B* better than *C*,..., and *Y* better than *Z*, it is telling us that *A* is better than *B with respect to quality and number*, *B* is better than *C with respect to quality and number*, and so on. In this context, the claim that "better than" is a transitive relation entails that *A* is better than *Z with respect to quality and number*. But this is true. *A is* better than *Z* with respect to *quality and number*. Likewise, when the Second Standard View tells us that *Z* is better than *A*, it is telling us that *Z* is better than *A with respect to quality alone*. And, indeed, *Z is* better than *A* with respect to quality alone. But there is no conflict with transitivity here either, since *with respect to quality alone, Z* is better than *Y, Y* better than *X*,..., and *B* better than *A*, which, by transitivity, entails the appropriate result that *Z* is better than *A with respect to quality alone*. So, on this line of reasoning, there is no conflict between the First Standard View, the Second Standard View, and the transitivity of "better than."

The First Standard View reflects the fact that the members of the spectrum stand to each other in one relation. The Second Standard View reflects the fact that the members of the spectrum *also* stand to each other in a *different* relation. Both views are true, and each of the relations in question *is* transitive. Since transitivity simply holds that for any *given* relation, *R*, if *aRb*, and *bRc*, then *aRc*, there is no *failure* of transitivity if *aRb*, and *bRc*, but aR_1c; where *R* and R_1 are *distinct* relations. Thus, one might conclude that in examples of the sort I have been considering, there *is* no failure of transitivity, and no inconsistency of the sort I have claimed. Insofar as one focuses on a single relation— whether it be the "better than with respect to quality and number" relation or the "better than with respect to quality alone" relation—transitivity applies *and* holds, but insofar as one makes comparisons involving two relations, which, in essence, all my examples do, transitivity doesn't *fail*, it simply *fails to apply*.

I believe that the preceding analysis gets to the very heart of what is going on in *all* of the cases discussed in this work where it may appear that there is a failure of transitivity. But notice, the essence of this move *is* to deny the First Standard View and/or the Second Standard View. Advocates of the First Standard View don't simply hold that *A* is better than *B with respect to quality and number*; they hold that *A* is better than *B all things considered*, *because* it is better with respect to quality and number. That is, they can admit that if outcomes were ranked in virtue of *quality alone*, then *B* would be better than *A*; but they believe that *in comparisons like those involving A and B*, how two outcomes compare *all things considered* is *not* determined by how they compare with respect to quality alone, but that quality *and* number are relevant for making *such* comparisons. Likewise, advocates of the Second Standard View don't simply hold that *Z* is better than *A with respect to quality alone*; they hold that *Z* is better than *A all things considered*, *because* it is better with respect to quality alone. That is, they can admit that if outcomes were ranked in virtue of a multiplicative function of quality *and* number, then *A* would be better than *Z*; but they believe that *in comparisons like those involving A and Z*, how two outcomes compare *all things considered* is *not* determined by how they compare with respect to quality *and* number, but that quality *alone* is relevant for making *such* comparisons. That is, intuitively, both the First and Second Standard Views reflect judgments about when one outcome is better than another *all things considered*. Given this, they *are* inconsistent with "*all-things-considered better than*" being a transitive relation. Thus, we still face a quandary. We must reject the notion that "all-things-considered better than" (in my wide reason-implying sense) is a transitive relation, or we must reject the notion that the First and Second Standard Views each reflects all things considered judgments (in my wide reason-implying sense). *One* of them might reflect an all things considered judgment, but not *both*.

I shall explore this line of thinking more deeply as the book progresses. But for now, let me simply add the following. In thinking about my cases, we *may* come to decide that there is a *failure* of transitivity, in particular, that "all-things-considered better than" (in my wide reason-implying sense) is not a transitive relation. Alternatively, we may conclude that when we are considering the notion of "all-things-considered better than" in my wide reason-implying sense—which, I have claimed, may be the most important sense of "all-things-considered better than" for practical reasoning—there is never a *failure* of transitivity, but simply a range of cases where insofar as transitivity applies it holds, and insofar at it *appears* not to hold, it simply *fails to apply*. The claim that there may be a range of cases where transitivity fails to apply may not seem to be particularly surprising or worrying. However, as we will see, a full understanding of this issue may have significant implications for our understanding of the good, moral ideals, and the nature of practical reasoning.

2.7 Extending the Results to Various Ideals

The First and Second Standard Views reflect many people's attitudes to trade-offs between quality and number, but they have been framed in terms of benefits, and all of my examples involve trade-offs with respect to utility (or welfare or well-being). Understandably, then, many people will regard the First and Second Standard Views as relevant to the ideal of utility. Since most people accept that utility is at least one ideal, among others, that is relevant to assessing the goodness of outcomes, and since most people accept both the First and Second Standard Views as I have formulated them, in this book I shall usually focus on examples involving utility to make my points. However, it is worth noting, and bearing in mind throughout our ensuing discussion, that similar problems and issues that arise for utility may also arise for certain other ideals.

Consider, for example, the ideal of freedom. I believe that most people who care about freedom would accept analogues of the First and Second Standard Views with respect to freedom. That is, I believe that most people who care about freedom would accept each of the following positions:

The First Standard View for Freedom (FSVF)—Trade-offs between Individual Freedom and Numbers Are Sometimes Desirable: In general, an outcome where a number of people have their freedoms infringed to a certain extent will be better, regarding freedom, than an outcome where a larger number of people have their freedoms infringed to a lesser extent, *if* the difference in the extent to which the people's freedoms are infringed in the two outcomes is not "too" great, and *if* the number of people whose freedoms would be infringed to the lesser extent is "sufficiently" larger than the number of people whose freedoms would be infringed to the (slightly) larger extent.

The Second Standard View for Freedom (SSVF)—Trade-offs between Individual Freedom and Numbers Are Sometimes Undesirable Even When Vast Numbers Are at Stake: If the infringements of freedom in one outcome would be extremely severe, and the infringements of freedom in another outcome would be basically inconsequential, then an outcome in which a relatively large group of people suffered the severe infringements of freedom would be worse, regarding freedom, than an outcome in which virtually any number of people suffered the basically inconsequential infringements of freedom.

Like the First Standard View, the First Standard View for Freedom reflects an additive-aggregationist approach for comparing certain outcomes with respect to freedom. Like the Second Standard View, the Second Standard View for Freedom reflects an anti-additive-aggregationist approach for comparing certain outcomes with respect to freedom. As with the First and Second Standard Views as originally formulated, I believe that both views are extremely plausible and would be difficult to reject. But, as should be apparent, together, *FSVF* and *SSVF* are incompatible with the transitivity of the "all-things-considered better than" relation, given a plausible assumption. The assumption is just that there is, or could be, a spectrum of alternatives, ranging from a large group of people suffering the most egregious form of slavery at one end, to a vastly larger group of people suffering a basically inconsequential infringement of their freedom on the other end (perhaps, for example, they have to display a passport to the authorities whenever they enter or exit their country!), such that the First Standard View for Freedom would be relevant for comparing all "nearby" alternatives of the spectrum, and the Second Standard View for Freedom would be relevant for comparing the alternatives at the opposite ends of the spectrum.

In that case, the First Standard View for Freedom would imply that, regarding freedom, the spectrum's first alternative was better than the second, the spectrum's second alternative was better than the third, the third alternative was better than the fourth, and so on. So, if "all-things-considered better than" is a transitive relation, the additive-aggregationist reasoning of the First Standard View for Freedom would imply that, regarding freedom, the spectrum's first alternative is better than the last. But, by hypothesis, the spectrum's first alternative may involve a million people suffering the most egregious form of slavery, while the spectrum's last alternative may involve a vast population that is perfectly free, except that they have to display their passports whenever they enter or exit their country. In accordance with the anti-additive-aggregationist reasoning of the Second Standard View for Freedom, I believe that most advocates of freedom would reject the conclusion that the spectrum's first alternative was better than the last regarding freedom.

Hence, familiarly, one must reject the First Standard View for Freedom, the Second Standard View for Freedom, the plausible assumption that there could be a spectrum of alternatives whose members were related in the manner described, or the view that "all-things-considered better than" is a transitive relation. Here, as before, something has to go, but for most advocates of freedom, giving up any of these views will not be easy.

Let us consider one other example, the ideal of equality. I believe that most people who care about equality would accept analogues of the First and Second Standard Views with respect to inequality. That is, I believe that most people who care about equality would accept each of the following positions:

The First Standard View for Equality (FSVE)—Trade-offs between Inequality Gaps and Numbers Are Sometimes Desirable: In general, an outcome with a larger gap between the better- and worse-off will be better, regarding inequality, than an outcome with a smaller gap between the better- and worse-off, *if* the difference in the size of the gaps in the two outcomes is "sufficiently" small, and *if* the number of people who are worse off, and hence who have individual complaints with respect to inequality, is "sufficiently larger" in the outcome where the gap between the better- and worse-off is (slightly) smaller.

The Second Standard View for Equality (SSVE)—Trade-offs between Inequality Gaps and Numbers Are Sometimes Undesirable Even When Vast Numbers Are at Stake: If the size of the gap between the better- and worse-off in one outcome is extremely large, and the size of the gap between the better- and worse-off in a second outcome is extremely small, then as long as there is a large number of people in the first outcome's worse-off group, the first outcome will be worse, regarding inequality, than the second, no matter how many people there are in the second outcome's (slightly) worse-off group.

Again, like the First Standard View, the First Standard View for Equality reflects an additive-aggregationist approach for comparing certain outcomes with respect to inequality.[37] In addition, like the Second Standard View, the Second Standard View for Equality reflects an anti-additive-aggregationist approach for comparing certain outcomes with respect to inequality. As with the First and Second Standard Views as originally formulated, I believe that both views are extremely plausible and would be difficult to reject. But, as should be apparent, together, *FSVE* and *SSVE* are incompatible with the transitivity of the "all-things-considered better than" relation, given a plausible assumption. The assumption is just that there is, or could be, a spectrum of alternatives, ranging from one in which a large group of people are *enormously* worse off than all the other members of their alternative (so that the gaps between the better- and worse-off are *huge*), to one in which a vastly larger group of people are *barely* worse off than the other members of their outcome (so that the gaps between the better- and worse-off are *tiny*), such that the First Standard View for Equality would be relevant for comparing all "nearby" alternatives of the spectrum, and the Second Standard View for Equality would be relevant for comparing the alternatives at the opposite ends of the spectrum. I might add that the spectrum might also involve the further features that: all better-off members are equally, and extremely, well off regardless of which alternative they are in; the worse-off members of the spectrum's first alternative are horribly badly off; the worse-off members of each "later" alternative of the spectrum are just *slightly* better off than the worse-off members of the immediately preceding alternative of the spectrum; and, finally, that the worse-off members of the last alternative, being *barely* worse off than

---

[37] In my book *Inequality*, I argued that the notion of equality is enormously complex. In particular, I argued that a number of plausible aspects underlie the notion of equality and showed that many of these involve combining different ways of measuring an individual's complaint regarding inequality with different ways of combining individual complaints to arrive at an all-things-considered judgment of how bad an outcome is regarding inequality. Six of these different aspects involve either an *Additive Principle of Equality* or a *Weighted Additive Principle of Equality*. Each of these reflects an additive-aggregationist approach for measuring inequality which would entail the First Standard View for Equality. See chapters 2 and 7 of *Inequality*.

their alternative's better-off members, are themselves extremely well off (though not *quite* as extremely well off as their barely better-off compatriots).

Given such a spectrum, the First Standard View for Equality would imply that, regarding inequality, the spectrum's first alternative was better than the second, the spectrum's second alternative was better than the third, the third was better than the fourth, and so on. So, if "all-things-considered better than" is a transitive relation, the additive-aggregationist reasoning of the First Standard View for Equality would imply that, regarding inequality, the spectrum's first alternative is better than the last. However, the spectrum's first alternative may involve millions of people being *enormously* worse off than all of the other members of their outcome, while the spectrum's last alternative may involve a vast population all of whose members are *almost* equally well off, and as well or almost as well off as the very best-off members of the spectrum's first alternative. In accordance with the anti-additive-aggregationist reasoning of the Second Standard View for Equality, I believe that most advocates of equality would reject the conclusion that the spectrum's first alternative was better than the last regarding inequality.[38]

Hence, unsurprisingly, one must reject the First Standard View for Equality, the Second Standard View for Equality, the plausible assumption that there could be a spectrum of alternatives whose members were related in the manner described, or the view that "all-things-considered better than" is a transitive relation. Here, as before, something has to go, but, for most advocates of equality, giving up any of these views will not be easy.

Having shown how positions like the First and Second Standard Views could be extended to other ideals like freedom and equality, I shall, as indicated earlier, mostly focus on cases and arguments involving benefits or burdens in terms of utility (welfare or well-being). In many ways, these are the simplest and least controversial cases to consider, and they are sufficient for

---

[38] The view that the spectrum's first alternative would be better than the last regarding inequality is a version of a position that I called the *Repellant Conclusion* in *Inequality* (see chapter 7, especially sections 7.7–7.9). The Repellant Conclusion is an implication for egalitarians analogous to Derek Parfit's Repugnant Conclusion (see chapter 17 of *Reasons and Persons*). Here, I make plain, in a way that I did not in *Inequality*, how additive-aggregationist reasoning of the sort that underlies the First Standard View for Equality entails the Repellant Conclusion, and how anti-additive-aggregationist reasoning of the sort that underlies the Second Standard View for Equality explains our resistance to the Repellant Conclusion. In sections 7.8 and 7.9 of *Inequality*, I discuss various ways one might try to resist the Repellant Conclusion. These ways are taken up in chapter 10, in the context of my discussing how one might respond to Parfit's Repugnant Conclusion.

I am indebted to Oscar Horta for seeing the connection between my discussion of the Repellant Conclusion in *Inequality* and this book's discussion of the conflict between different approaches to additive-aggregation, and for urging that I include a discussion of this connection in this book. Indeed, it is due to Horta's prodding, for which I am grateful, that I have included this section, extending my discussion of the First and Second Standard Views beyond the realm of utility (welfare or well-being) to the ideals of freedom and equality.

establishing this book's central claims. However, as noted earlier, it is worth bearing in mind, throughout this book, that the considerations I am discussing about additive-aggregationist and anti-additive-aggregationist reasoning will apply to various ideals within the normative realm, and hence have broad implications across that realm.

2.8 Concluding Remarks

In this chapter we have seen that the First and Second Standard Views are seemingly inconsistent with the transitivity of "better than." At least, this is so given the plausible assumption that there is, or at least could be, a spectrum of benefits, ranging from very high quality benefits to very low quality benefits, such that the First Standard View would be relevant for comparing outcomes involving benefits that were "near" each other on the spectrum, and the Second Standard View would be relevant for comparing outcomes involving benefits that were "far apart" on the spectrum. Thus, we are faced with a dilemma. We must either show that there *couldn't be* a spectrum of benefits that stand together in the relation suggested, or we must give up the First Standard View, the Second Standard View, or the transitivity of "better than."

I find it extremely hard to believe that there *couldn't* be the kind of spectrum described, and in fact this chapter presents several spectrums that appear to fit the model in question. But, for many, it will be extremely difficult to reject either the First Standard View or the Second Standard View. This suggests that we should be prepared to reject the transitivity of "better than." I *am* prepared, at least in principle, to reject the transitivity of "better than." But I also believe that doing so has grave implications. Just how grave these implications are will become evident as the book unfolds, but I think that they are sufficiently grave that they will force many to reexamine their commitments to the First and Second Standard Views. In the end, I am not sure which of the three inconsistent views should be given up, but I'm pretty sure that for most people giving up any of them will require major revisions in their thinking about the nature of moral ideals and practical reasoning. The full extent to which this is so will become more apparent later.

Next, let me say a bit more about the status of, and relation between, the First and Second Standard Views. The First Standard View recognizes that there is a large class of cases where it seems the relative merits of two outcomes is a function of the *quantity* of benefits in those outcomes; where, in this context, concern for quantity is understood as a concern that takes account of an outcome's quality, duration, and number of benefits (see appendix B). And, indeed, often it seems that the better of two outcomes—the one there is most reason to prefer from an impartial perspective—just *is* the one with the greatest *quantity* of benefits so understood. On the other hand, the Second Standard

View recognizes that there is another class of cases where it seems the relative merits of two outcomes is *not* simply a function of the *quantity* of benefits and burdens in those outcomes, even when quantity *includes* quality as one of its components. On the Second Standard View, what matters is how the quantity of benefits and burdens is *distributed* within or between lives. Accordingly, advocates of the Second Standard View needn't deny that the *quantity* of benefits may be *greater* in an outcome where many people have been spared a minor head cold, than in an outcome where only ten people have been spared severe dementia, but they deny that the outcome with the greater *quantity* of benefits—so measured—is *better*, all things considered, than the outcome with fewer total benefits. On their view, the *distribution* of benefits in the outcomes is such that there is most reason to prefer the outcome with the fewer benefits from an impartial perspective.

The First Standard View embodies an additive-aggregationist approach for assessing a *certain* class of cases. The Second Standard View rejects the additive-aggregationist approach for a *different* class of cases. As suggested earlier, this holds the clue as to why we might ultimately come to accept either that "all-things-considered better than" is not a transitive relation, or that the notion of "all-things-considered better than"—which is a transitive relation—fails to *apply* to the cases I have considered. We shall explore this point further in later chapters.

Naturally, purists might insist that either the additive-aggregationist approach should be accepted *everywhere* or it should be accepted *nowhere*. But here, as elsewhere, the middle ground seems, at least initially, most plausible. An additive-aggregationist approach seems plausible in some cases, but not in others.

This chapter has introduced a certain kind of argument, one I call a *Spectrum Argument*, which illuminates an apparent inconsistency between some deeply held beliefs. I shall present other examples of such arguments in later chapters. But first, I want to discuss a "new" principle of aggregation, suggested by the Second Standard View, that seems relevant to the assessment of outcomes. Let us turn to that next.

3

A "New" Principle of Aggregation

This chapter further explores problems about trade-offs. It does this by examining a "new" principle of aggregation: the *Disperse Additional Burdens View*—short for the more cumbersome *Disperse Additional Burdens So as to Prevent Any Individual from Having to Bear a Substantial Additional Burden*.[1] I call this a "new" principle of aggregation because it is not typically distinguished, or discussed, as a distinct principle in the philosophical literature. Nevertheless, this principle reflects familiar modes of reasoning. In fact, I believe that it can be seen as a natural extension of chapter 2's Second Standard View. Unsurprisingly, then, I believe this principle is plausible, and one that plays an important role in the assessment of outcomes. However, worries arise when one considers iterated applications of the principle. This chapter aims to illuminate this principle and the worries it generates. As we will see, we may have to either reject this principle or refuse to allow ourselves to be repeatedly guided by it.

Some principles of aggregation are *complete*. For any two alternatives, they generate a comparative ranking of those alternatives. But a principle of aggregation may also be *incomplete*. It may rank some, but not all, alternatives in comparison with each other. The principle of aggregation this chapter explores is incomplete.

3.1 The Disperse Additional Burdens View

I believe most people accept the following:

The Disperse Additional Burdens View: In general, if additional burdens are dispersed among different people, it is better for a given total

---

[1] My terminology here is slightly different from what I used in previous work to refer to the position in question. Specifically, the Disperse Additional Burdens View corresponds to what I previously called the *Minimize Great Additional Burdens View* in "A 'New' Principle of Aggregation," *Philosophical Issues* 15 (2005): 218–34. I am grateful to Mikhail Valdman for suggesting the simpler name.

burden to be dispersed among a vastly larger number of people, so that the additional burden any single person has to bear within her life is "relatively small," than for a smaller total burden to fall on just a few, such that their additional burden is substantial.

The Disperse Additional Burdens View reflects the anti-additive-aggregationist position of chapter 2's Second Standard View, but it differs from that view in two ways. First, the Disperse Additional Burdens View is couched in terms of burdens rather than benefits. Second, the Disperse Additional Burdens View drops the "similarly situated" clause that was included in the Second Standard View. Let me comment on each of these differences.

The first difference is not substantive. This is because, as suggested in chapter 2, one can always regard questions about the distribution of burdens as questions about the distribution of benefits (the benefits of not bearing burdens!) and vice versa. Accordingly, I might have presented the view in question in terms of benefits. Had I done so, I would have characterized it as follows.

> *The Consolidate Additional Benefits View*: In general, if additional benefits are dispersed among different people, it is better for a given total benefit to be consolidated among a few people, such that each person's additional benefit is substantial, than for a larger total benefit to be dispersed among a vastly larger number of people, so that the additional benefit any single person receives within her life is "relatively small."

So this raises the question as to why, in this chapter, I have decided to put the view I have in mind in terms of burdens rather than benefits. I confess that I do so for rhetorical, rather than philosophical, reasons. Over the years, I have found that most people find either formulation plausible and important, but that some people who are strongly attracted to the view when it is couched in terms of burdens have some doubts about the view when it is couched in terms of benefits. This is somewhat odd, given their equivalence, but seems to reflect the familiar phenomenon of *framing effects*, according to which people's intuitions about equivalent cases may differ considerably depending on how the cases are framed.[2] Rather than get bogged down in a series of speculative and unnecessary arguments for why some people's intuitions are sometimes misled when the view is cast in terms of benefits rather than burdens, I have, unsur-

---

[2] The psychology literature on framing effects is vast. A classic paper on the topic is Daniel Kahneman and Amos Tversky's "The Framing of Decisions and the Psychology of Choice," *Science* 211 (1981): 453–58. See also *Judgment under Uncertainty: Heuristics and Biases*, ed. Daniel Kahneman, Paul Slovic, and Amos Tversky (Cambridge: Cambridge University Press, 1982).

prisingly, decided to present my official formulation in terms of the frame that best suits my purposes![3] Since I believe the view in question *is* plausible and important, and since most people see that when it is put in terms of burdens, I think it is appropriate to do this. But, to be fair, I will also put a few examples in terms of benefits, and trust that most readers will continue to see the force of the view I'm describing.[4]

The second difference is significant. By dropping the "similarly situated" clause of chapter 2's Second Standard View, the Disperse Additional Burdens View doesn't merely maintain that among people equally well off, it is better if many people receive minor burdens than if a few people receive great burdens. It holds that it is better if many people receive minor burdens than if a few people receive great burdens, even among people that aren't equally well off, and in particular, *even if those who would receive the minor burdens were initially much worse off than those who would receive the great burdens*, and even if those who would receive the minor burdens would remain as badly off, or even worse off, than those who would receive the great burdens. This feature of the Disperse Additional Burdens View makes it more controversial than chapter 2's Second Standard View, and, as we will see, it has worrisome implications. Nevertheless, on reflection, I believe that many find the Disperse Additional Burdens View compelling, at least for those cases where if many people have their burdens increased a "little" this would have relatively little overall

---

[3] But I'll speculate this much: I suspect that some people's intuitions about these cases are being (mis)guided by deontological considerations, which distinguish between harming someone and merely failing to benefit someone, where the former is generally regarded as wrong, while the latter is generally regarded as permissible. Distinctions of that kind are familiar, controversial, and much discussed in the literature. But even if one grants importance to such distinctions for deontological purposes, I think they are irrelevant to the question I am concerned with here, since my question is about the goodness of alternative outcomes, rather than about whether it is permissible, required, or prohibited to bring about one outcome rather than another. If one focuses on the question about goodness, the claim I have made here and in chapter 2 about the relationship between benefits and burdens should, I hope, be defensible.

[4] In earlier drafts of this book I dealt with this issue differently. I conveyed my sense that the Disperse Additional Burdens View and the Consolidate Additional Benefits View are actually equivalent, but nevertheless treated them as separate views. This enabled me to avoid "privileging" one characterization over the other. More important, it enabled me to finesse the fact that some people who accept the Disperse Additional Burdens View nevertheless have worries about the Consolidate Additional Benefits View. By treating the views as distinct, I was, in essence, making room for some readers to accept both views, and for others to only accept one. Since it is enough, for my purposes, that most people would accept the Disperse Additional Burdens View, I thought it unnecessary to insist or show that readers who accepted that view but had doubts about the Consolidate Additional Benefits View were making a mistake. However, Shelly Kagan found it misleading and confusing that I should treat the Disperse Additional Burdens and Consolidate Additional Benefits Views as separate, even for the sake of accommodating as many readers as possible. Given my view of the relation between benefits and burdens, he urged that I treat them as equivalent characterizations of a single view. Though there are some advantages to my previous approach, I think Kagan is right about this and have altered my presentation accordingly.

impact on their lives, whereas if a few people have their burdens increased "substantially" this would have a substantial impact on their lives. Importantly, the Disperse Additional Burdens View is not necessarily plausible as an *all-things-considered* judgment, but I think it represents an important principle that underlies and influences many people's judgments about the desirability of alternative outcomes.

Let us further explore the nature and appeal of the Disperse Additional Burdens View. One question that arises is whether the Disperse Additional Burdens View is only plausible when one assumes that the additional burdens shared by the many are "trivial." For example, one might readily admit that no number of pin pricks spread out among innumerable masses would outweigh a substantial burden felt by a few, but wonder if a similar judgment ever holds when the many's burdens are nontrivial. So consider the following case.

Suppose we have to choose between 100,000 people each suffering great pain for a *week*, or 10 people suffering great pain for fifty *years*. And suppose that we were only judging the outcomes in terms of the suffering in those outcomes of those experiencing the pains. In addition, suppose that, by hypothesis, each week of pain is just as bad as any other in terms of the suffering of its subject; so, in particular, the impact of a week's pain in terms of suffering is neither increasing nor decreasing with each passing week. Surely, suffering great pain for a week is not a trivial matter. Still, I think many would judge that, other things equal, the former situation would be better than the latter, and this is so even though in the former case there would be a greater *total* amount of suffering—100,000 weeks, rather than 26,000 weeks. This judgment accords with the Disperse Additional Burdens View, if we assume that as bad as a week of great pain is, it would only increase the burden in a person's life a "little," in the sense that it would have relatively little overall impact on a person's life, whereas fifty *years* of pain would have a *substantial* impact on a person's life. Of course, if we imagined that the week of pain had a substantial and lasting impact on each person's life, the Disperse Additional Burdens View would no longer apply, and we might well make a different judgment about which of the two outcomes was better. Still, it seems that the Disperse Additional Burdens View can be plausibly applied in at least some cases where the many's additional burdens would be nontrivial, yet still have relatively little overall impact on their lives.

As is well known, the simple additive-aggregationist model of total utilitarianism is opposed by the well-known anti-additive-aggregationist principles of equality and maximin. Whereas the former view assesses the goodness of outcomes solely in terms of how *much* utility or well-being obtains in the outcomes, the latter views assess the goodness of outcomes in terms of how the utility or well-being in the outcomes is *distributed* among its members, with equality favoring outcomes in which well-being is distributed so that differences in well-being between the better- and worse-off are as small as possible, and maximin favoring outcomes in which well-being is distributed so that the members of the worst-off group are as well off as possible. Given this, some might wonder whether our anti-additive-aggregationist views are best captured by the ideals of equality and maximin, and whether the appeal of the Disperse Additional Burdens View ultimately rests on the plausibility of those other views. More particularly, one might question whether the Disperse Additional Burdens View is really a "new" view after all, or just a repackaged variation of the older, more familiar, ideals of equality or maximin.[5]

On reflection, I believe that the Disperse Additional Burdens View is a plausible principle in its own right, and is distinct from both equality and maximin. To see this, let us consider a variation of Tim Scanlon's example against additive aggregation, presented in chapter 2.

Recall that in Scanlon's imagined case, Jones is experiencing extremely painful electrical shocks, and that we cannot rescue him for an hour unless we interrupt television transmission of a World Cup match. Scanlon claims that we should rescue Jones immediately, no matter how many viewers there are. Now suppose we add some details to Scanlon's example. Suppose that Jones has led a remarkably pain-free life, and in fact would still be among society's best-off members even if he were to suffer an hour of extremely painful shocks. Suppose further that among those who are enjoying watching the match are some of society's worst-off members.

In such a case, both equality and maximin would line up *with* utility to *oppose* helping Jones immediately. And certainly the reasons for helping Jones are less strong than they would be if Jones were among the worst-off and the viewers among the best-off. Nevertheless, I think Scanlon would contend that we should still help Jones immediately,[6] and important elements of our thinking support such a view. One such element, I believe, is the Disperse Additional Burdens View.

Unfortunately, the preceding example is not pure. Partly, our judgment may turn on strong intuitions about the urgency or primacy of relieving extreme pain, which we may think always trumps the "trivial" pleasure of watching a sporting event. So let us alter Scanlon's example. First, imagine that the match will continue for three hours, so that Jones will suffer three hours of extremely painful shocks unless we turn off the transmitter. Next, imagine that

---

[5] The considerations presented next would also apply, mutatis mutandis, to the more recently discussed and now widely accepted distributive principle prioritarianism. Prioritarianism can be interpreted as a generalized, and less extreme, version of maximin, which gives extra weight to the importance of helping someone the worse off they are in absolute terms, but which does not give lexical priority to helping the very worst off. On prioritarianism, see Derek Parfit's "Equality or Priority?" and my "Equality, Priority, and the Levelling Down Objection," in *The Ideal of Equality*, ed. Matthew Clayton and Andrew Williams (London: Macmillan; New York: St. Martin's Press, 2000), 81–125 and 126–61.

[6] My view here is based on conversations I have had with Scanlon about this issue.

among the worst-off people watching the game are 100 who have a chronic illness that produces pain of the same intensity as Jones is suffering while being shocked. In particular, imagine that each minute of pain that Jones will endure will produce the same degree of suffering in him, and that that is the same as the degree of suffering felt by those with the chronic illness during each minute that they are in pain. Imagine further that the 100 with the chronic illness are such rabid fans that watching the game distracts them from their pain, effectively serving as a psychological anesthetic. Finally, imagine that one only needs to turn the transmitter off for two minutes to rescue Jones.

If one rescues Jones, 100 people who are among the worst-off will each suffer *two* additional minutes of intense pain, for a total of 200 (extra) minutes of intense pain. In addition, many millions of others will suffer aggravation from having the match interrupted. On the other hand, if one waits till the match is over, one "merely" allows one of society's best-off members—Jones—to suffer excruciating shocks for three hours.

Here, considerations of the urgency and primacy of intense pain apply to *both* choices, with the total *amount* of intense pain being greater if one rescues Jones, 200 minutes versus 180 minutes. As earlier, considerations of equality, maximin, and total utility all support waiting until the match concludes before helping Jones. Moreover, we may assume that perfectionist ideals are neutral between these alternatives, as neither alternative better affects beauty, truth, the advancement of society, and so on. (Crudely, *perfectionism* is an ideal which values that which is "best" or "highest" in human or global achievements. On different versions of perfectionism, the best outcome might be the one with the "greatest" achievements in social, political, moral, cultural, intellectual, or individual development.) Even so, it seems that there is strong reason to help Jones immediately, at least some of which is provided by the Disperse Additional Burdens View. In one respect, at least, it seems better for millions to suffer aggravation from having a match interrupted and 100 people to suffer intensely for two extra *minutes*, than for one person to have to suffer intensely for three consecutive *hours*.[7]

Let me be clear. There are many factors that might support the intuition that we ought to help Jones that do not appeal to the Disperse Additional Burdens View, and have nothing to do with the relative desirability of the different outcomes. For example, assuming that Jones is "right there, in front of us" with a pressing need, many may feel that there are special deontological, agent-relative, or contractualist reasons why what we ought to *do* is to help Jones. And, indeed, Scanlon's discussion of his example focuses on his understanding

---

[7] Mikhail Valdman notes, in correspondence, that it is important in this example that Jones's pain be for three straight hours. If Jones suffered a total of three hours of pain, but in ten-second increments spread out over a long life, we'd feel very differently about the trade-off in question. I agree. I discuss issues of aggregation within a life in the next two chapters.

of "what we owe to each other," and doesn't appeal to the relative desirability of the different outcomes. Even so, I believe that in an important respect the outcome in which Jones is spared the burden of great pain for three hours is *better* than the outcome in which 100 worse-off people are spared (an additional) two minutes of comparable pain, and millions of others are spared the aggravation of having a World Cup broadcast interrupted. Specifically, I believe that the shorter instances of pain and frustration spread out over many people don't "add up" in the way they would need to in order to outweigh the significance of the pain Jones would suffer if we don't help him. Underlying this view, I suggest, is the Disperse Additional Burdens View.[8]

Note, the claim that in an important respect the outcome where Jones doesn't suffer will be better than the one where he does is ambiguous. On one reading it is trivially true. On the other it is significant. Unsurprisingly, I intend the significant reading! Let me explain.

It is trivially true that the outcome where Jones doesn't suffer is better in *one* respect than the outcome in which he does, insofar at it is better *for Jones*. The *significant* claim is that in one respect the *overall* total and distribution of pain is better in the outcome where Jones doesn't suffer. This is the claim I am making earlier, and it relies on a principle of aggregation like the Disperse Additional Burdens View. This substantive principle tells us that, for the purposes of evaluating the goodness of outcomes, burdens do not aggregate in a certain way, so that lots of "minor" burdens spread across many may not outweigh "major" burdens shouldered by a few, even if, in some sense, the *total* amount of burden is greater in the former case than in the latter.

The difference between the trivial and the significant reading is easily illustrated by considering a different case. Suppose that in one outcome Jones would suffer mild pain for one minute, but nobody else would suffer at all; while in a second outcome Jones wouldn't suffer at all, but hundreds of others would suffer greatly. On the trivial reading, there would still be *one* respect in which the second outcome was better than the first. After all, the second

---

[8] Shelly Kagan recognizes that we need more than equality and maximin to account for our intuitions in this case; but he wonders whether we need to appeal to the Disperse Additional Burdens View rather than simply the Second Standard View of chapter 2. But, as presented, the Second Standard View had a "similarly situated" clause which the Disperse Additional Burdens View lacks. The point of this example is to illustrate that we do, indeed, find the kind of anti-additive-aggregationist position expressed by the Second Standard View plausible even in cases where the person who would be spared the much greater burden is initially much better off than those who would be spared the lesser burden. That is, as chapter 2 shows, most people find the Second Standard View plausible, but as this example shows, they also find the bolder Disperse Additional Burdens View plausible.

Importantly, unless we consider examples like the revised case of Jones, we won't have a true test for whether or not our judgments are actually turning on egalitarian or maximin considerations. After all, if people start off "similarly situated," then failing to spare someone the much greater burden will produce an outcome which is much worse in terms of equality or maximin than will failing to spare lots more people a much smaller burden.

outcome *would* be better *for Jones*, and this would give us *some* reason, though not much, to prefer the second outcome to the first. Still, in this case the Disperse Additional Burdens View does not apply, and it is clear that *overall* the amount and distribution of burdens in the second outcome is much worse than that in the first. This doesn't yet mean that the first outcome is better than the second *all things considered*, since we don't know how the two outcomes compare with respect to other ideals, like justice, freedom, equality, or perfection. Still, it seems clear that the burdens of the many aggregate in such a way that, overall, the first outcome is better than the second in an important respect.[9] Thus, throughout this work, when I claim that there is an important respect in which one outcome is better than another, I am making the substantive, overall claim, not the trivial one that focuses on the plight of a particular individual.

Though suggestive, the preceding example is open to two criticisms. First, since even extreme pain may not seem "substantial" if it lasts "only" three hours (at least if it belongs to someone else(!)—think back to the last time you were in genuinely extreme pain for even five minutes, say from a bee sting, or an exposed nerve in your tooth, or a virulent bout of food poisoning), it may be doubted whether the Disperse Additional Burdens View really applies to my version of Scanlon's example. Second, as implied earlier, it may be doubted whether one can safely generalize from examples involving "trivial" costs, like two *minutes* of pain or aggravation. Correspondingly, it will be helpful to consider another example.

Earlier, I claimed that 100,000 people each suffering great pain for a week would be, in at least one important respect, better than 10 people suffering great pain for fifty years, and that this is so even though suffering great pain for a week is clearly nontrivial. Let me next urge that this is an extremely robust intuition that survives in the face of conflicting intuitions generated by equality, maximin, and utility.

Suppose that each of 100,000 people currently faces the prospect of suffering great pain for fifty years, while ten people currently have pain-free prospects. In outcome *A*, the 10 people will *also* face the prospect of fifty *years* of great pain. In outcome *B*, the 10 people continue to have pain-free prospects, but each of the 100,000 will face the prospect of an additional *week* of pain. *A* would be better than *B* regarding equality, maximin, and utility. But I think many would agree that *B* seems better in an important respect, and *perhaps* even all things considered. This judgment is supported by the Disperse Addi-

---

[9] As I acknowledge in chapter 1, not everyone believes this, as some people, like Robert Nozick, Philippa Foot, and Judith Thomson, have doubts about the meaningfulness of any claim that one outcome is better than another. Still, as I note in chapter 1, I find such a position utterly incredible, and I believe that most others will as well, though I recognize that some people believe the arguments of this book buttress the position in question.

tional Burdens View, at least on the assumption that to those already facing the prospect of suffering for fifty *years*, one additional *week* will have relatively little impact on the overall quality of their lives, while to those originally facing pain-free prospects, suffering for fifty *years* will have a substantial impact on the overall quality of their lives.

I conclude, then, that the Disperse Additional Burdens View is plausible even in cases where the many's burdens are clearly nontrivial, and that its force is distinct from that of other anti-additive-aggregationist principles like equality and maximin.

Finally, as suggested previously, I note that all of these claims might have been put in terms of benefits rather than burdens. If one imagines that action *x* would produce an outcome where a few people would benefit *substantially* by many additional years of food, medicine, or shelter, while action *y* would produce an outcome where many people would benefit a small amount by just a few additional hours, or days, of food, medicine, or shelter, I believe that most people would agree that in *one* important respect *x* would produce a better outcome than *y*, in accordance with the anti-additive-aggregationist reasoning of the Disperse Additional Burdens View (or its equivalent, the Consolidate Additional Benefits View). That is, I think most people would agree that there is an important respect in which *x*'s outcome would be *better* than *y*'s, *even if x*'s outcome wouldn't be better than *y*'s in terms of other familiar ideals such as maximin, equality, utility, or perfection.

3.2 The Disperse Additional Burdens View and the Levelling Down Objection

One of the most prevalent and influential objections to egalitarianism is the *Levelling Down Objection*. An example of the Levelling Down Objection may be made with the aid of diagram 3.2.A, where the column heights represent how well off people are, and the widths represent the number of people in each group.

Imagine that *II* is a world where half are blind, and *I* is a world where all are. One *could* always transform *II* into *I* by putting out the eyes of the sighted. But surely it would be abominable to do this. Hence, many have thought, inequality doesn't matter, or at least it doesn't matter very much.

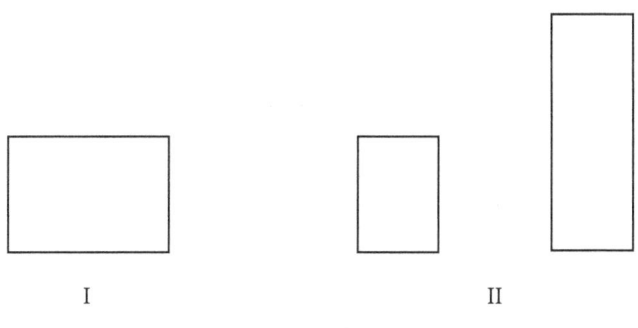

DIAGRAM 3.2.A

Elsewhere, I have argued that the Levelling Down Objection does *not* succeed in establishing that inequality doesn't matter, or even that it doesn't matter very much.[10] All it establishes is that inequality is not *all* that matters, and that in certain cases, at least, inequality doesn't matter more than every other ideal *combined*. These, of course, are points that egalitarians have long recognized and accepted. I shall not repeat my arguments for those conclusions here. Instead, I'd like to suggest that the spirit of the Disperse Additional Burdens View may partly underlie our firm conviction that *I* is much worse than *II*, in diagram 3.2.A.

Strictly speaking, the Disperse Additional Burdens View doesn't apply to the comparison between *I* and *II*. But, as I say, I think its spirit does. After all, if one believes, in accordance with the Disperse Additional Burdens View, that it is better if a small additional burden is added to the lives of many, than if a great additional burden is added to the lives of a few, then surely one will also believe that it is better if *no* additional burden is borne by many, than if some people's burdens are increased substantially. We might call this a *limiting case* of the Disperse Additional Burdens View. Applied to *I* and *II*, this view regards *II* as clearly better than *I*, since it spares half the population the substantial burden of being blind, with *no* additional burden to the many who would be blind in either outcome.

Because *II* is so much better than *I* in other respects, it is easy to overlook the extent to which our judgment about *I* and *II* might derive force from the spirit of the Disperse Additional Burdens View. After all, *II* is better than *I* regarding utility, perfectionism (we may presume), and maximin (at least if we accept a lexical version of the maximin principle, that would have us first maximize the expectations of the worst-off group and then minimize the size of that group). Indeed, I, myself, discussed the Levelling Down Objection for many years without noting any connection with the spirit of the Disperse Additional Burdens View. Still, I believe that most people who would oppose levelling down the sighted to the level of the blind would *also* oppose levelling down some of the sighted to the level of the nearly blind, even if this slightly improved the situation of countless people who were blind. Moreover, I don't think this is merely a judgment about what we ought or ought not to *do*. Rather, I think many believe that a situation in which some people have normal eyesight would be better than one in which they suffer near blindness, even if in the latter situation the lives of many blind people were *slightly* improved so that they were now "only" almost completely blind rather than completely blind. More generally, in accordance with the Disperse Additional Burdens View, I think many believe that an outcome where some are spared a significant

---

[10] See, for example, chapter 9 of *Inequality* (New York: Oxford University Press, 1993); "Equality, Priority, and the Levelling Down Objection," in *The Ideal of Equality*, ed. Matthew Clayton and Andrew Williams (London: Macmillan; New York: St. Martin's Press, 2000), 126–61; "Personal versus Impersonal Principles: Reconsidering the Slogan," *Theoria* 69 (2003): 20–30; "Egalitarianism Defended," *Ethics* 113 (2003): 764–82; and "Equality, Priority, or What?" *Economics and Philosophy* 19 (2003): 61–88.

burden would be better than one where they must bear such a burden, but many others would be spared a minor burden.

Consider diagram 3.2.B.

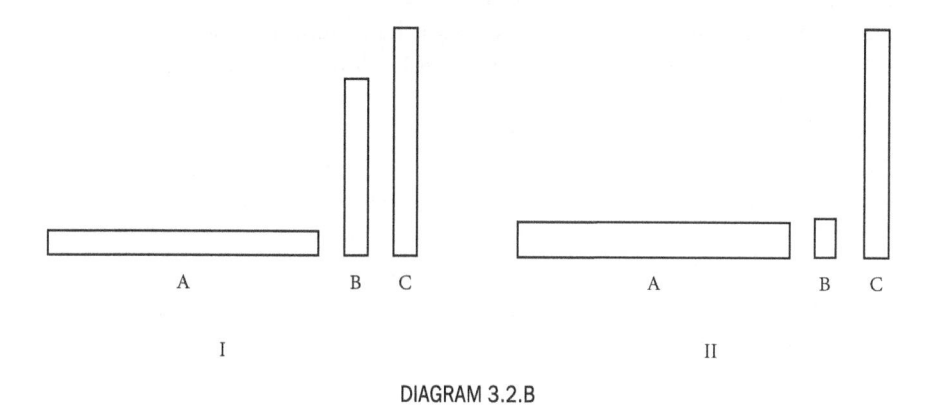

DIAGRAM 3.2.B

In case *I*, let *A* represent a group who are not well off, *B* a much smaller group who are very well off, and *C* the people who are best off, and whose lives determine the extent to which case *I* achieves the goals of perfectionism. Most agree that it would be *clearly* undesirable if case *I*'s *B* group was levelled down to the level of the *A* group. Would the many who are *so* confident about this judgment completely change their minds if they were told that in fact the situation would be like that depicted in case *II* of diagram 3.2.B? In case *II*, let us suppose, the *C* group is unaffected, so the level of perfection is unchanged, the *B* group is lowered almost to the level of the case *I*'s *A* group, and this has a substantial negative impact on their lives, and the *A* group benefits slightly, and nontrivially, though not enough to have a significant impact on the overall quality of their lives. I suspect most staunch opponents of "mere" levelling down in cases like diagram 3.2.A would not suddenly become strong proponents of "redistributive" levelling down in cases like diagram 3.2.B. But in diagram 3.2.B, not only is the "levelled-down" situation better regarding equality, which was also the case in diagram 3.2.A, but, we may suppose, unlike in diagram 3.2.A, the "levelled-down" situation is better regarding utility and maximin, and no worse regarding perfection. Here, it seems, any temptation to hang on to the view that "redistributive" levelling down should still be opposed is best attributed to a position like the Disperse Additional Burdens View.

Considering diagram 3.2.B, I suspect that many will believe that the increases in utility, maximin, and equality accompanying the levelling down of the *B* group in case *II* will be outweighed by the substantial extra burden placed on the *B* group in order to achieve those increases.[11] However, my aim here is

---

[11] See chapter 10 for a discussion of what I call the Capped Model for Ideals which would explain, and perhaps vindicate, such a judgment.

not to insist that case *I* is better than case *II all things considered*. Perhaps it isn't. Still, I believe that most will agree that there is *one* important respect in which the overall distribution in case *I* is better than that in case *II*. This is, I think, attributable to the power and influence of a position like the Disperse Additional Burdens View. And, of course, if I am right that such a view provides strong intuitive support for opposing levelling down in diagram 3.2.B, there is good reason to suppose that the spirit of that view also provides strong intuitive support for opposing levelling down in cases like diagram 3.2.A. Unfortunately, however, as implied earlier, it was easy to overlook the role that the spirit of the Disperse Additional Burdens View might have been playing in our judgments about such cases, since in those cases other more familiar ideals, like utility, perfectionism, and maximin, as well as welfarist and person-affecting intuitions, also oppose levelling down.[12]

The Disperse Additional Burdens View partly underlies and supports some common attitudes about charitable contributions. Most people deny that they have a moral obligation to do everything they possibly can to help the world's needy. Typically, they believe in deontological, or agent-relative, duties or permissions, that license them to devote most of their time, effort, and resources to their own projects and commitments, or to providing for their loved ones. Still, many would admit that from an impartial perspective, aiding the needy would improve the situation, even if it involved substantial additional burden in their lives, as long as it significantly enhanced the life prospects of enough of the needy to outweigh the attendant losses to themselves and their loved ones. On the other hand, many find it hard to believe that heavily burdening themselves to aid the needy would improve the situation, if doing so would merely improve the lives of *lots* of needy by just a *little*. They

---

[12] Mikhail Valdman pointed out, in correspondence, that an unreflective bias in favor of the status quo may also influence our intuitions about some of the cases I have been discussing. For example, regarding diagram 3.2.B, if one assumes case *I* as the starting point, a status quo bias might make many loath to change it into case *II* by lowering the *B* group significantly, even if the *A* group benefited slightly from our doing so. But by the same token, if one assumes case *II* as the starting point, a status quo bias might make many of those same people loath to change it into a situation like case *I*, via a "tax" on the *A* group that benefited the *B* group. And similarly, Valdman wrote, in the classic levelling-down case, "it seems much easier to convince someone that there would be nothing good about making the sighted blind than it would be to convince someone that, starting from a position of equality in which everyone is blind, that nothing of value would be lost by performing a sight-restoring operation on just half the people," and this might be partially explained by a status quo bias that many unreflectively have. Of course, as Valdman recognizes, even if there is a status quo bias that influences our judgments about such cases, those judgments may also be influenced by other factors, including the Disperse Additional Burdens View. Furthermore, we may think that our judgments about such cases are indefensible insofar as they rest on a status quo bias, or that if the status quo bias is relevant at all, it is only relevant to the deontological question of what we might be permitted, required, or impermissible to do. My question concerns the comparative goodness of the different outcomes, and if we make judgments of the sort I have suggested regarding that question, I think many will think such judgments are at least partially defensible insofar as they rest on the Disperse Additional Burdens View.

see the point, from an impartial perspective, of making substantial sacrifices for the sake of substantial gains to others, but they don't see the point of making substantial sacrifices if such sacrifices fail to have a significant impact on the lives of others. This view is supported by the Disperse Additional Burdens View, and it helps explain the well-known phenomenon of certain charities identifying particular individuals who will be the recipient of one's contributions, and who will be significantly benefited by one's donation.

3.3 Worries about Iteration

Let me next turn to a worry concerning the Disperse Additional Burdens View. Suppose, in accordance with the Disperse Additional Burdens View, one agrees that it would be better to spare one person from suffering fifty years than each of 10,000 people from suffering one week, and that this is true in most cases independently of how well off the 10,000 people are both in absolute terms and relative to the one person. This immediately raises a problem of iteration.

Imagine facing a similar choice many times. Specifically, imagine that in each of many cases one can prevent a different person from suffering fifty years alone, or the *same* 10,000 people from suffering for one (extra) week. The first time we face such a choice we think it better to spare the single person, leaving each of the 10,000 to suffer a week. The second time, we again think it better to spare the different single person, leaving each of the 10,000 to suffer but one additional week. And so on. Given what we said earlier, we might make the same decision *each* time. Thus, even when the 10,000 people will already have suffered for 100, 1,000, or even 2,000 weeks, we might think it better for each to suffer just 1 more *week*, than for some other person to have to suffer *fifty years*. But the result of making such decisions, one at a time, is that after making 2,600 decisions, *10,000* people will each suffer for fifty years, rather than 2,600! And if anything is clear, in this murky and treacherous area, it is that it is better for 2,600 people to suffer fifty years each, than for 10,000 people to do so. Thus, a sequence of choices, *each* of which apparently produces the best outcome given the alternatives, produces a final outcome that is *clearly* worse than the one that would have been produced had different—seemingly inferior—choices been made.

Here is a variation. Suppose that if an international agency like the World Health Organization (WHO) invests its resources in curing one illness, it will effectively prolong 1,000 people's lives by *fifty years*. Alternatively, if WHO invests its resources in attacking another illness that affects 2 million people, it will prolong their lives by *one month*. Although in the first case, WHO would be keeping people alive a total of 600,000 extra months, and in the second case it would be keeping people alive a total of 2 million extra months, in accordance with the Disperse Additional Burdens View, I think many would agree that the first outcome would be better than the second. Yet, were WHO to face and make the same choice with a different group of 1,000, but the same group of 2 million involved each time, after 600 such choices WHO would have prolonged the lives of 600,000 people for fifty years rather than 2 million people for fifty years!

Finally, similar considerations apply to hunger relief. Given the choice between relieving hunger for 1,000 people for fifty *years*, or 4 million people for a *week*, many would agree that the former would be better. And this is so, even though the former "only" eliminates 2.6 million weeks of hunger rather than 4 million weeks of hunger. In accordance with the Disperse Additional Burdens View, many believe it is better to consolidate the benefits of one's resources so as to make a significant impact for some, rather than disperse them so as to make a relatively small difference for many. Yet here, as before, iterations of this policy could lead to terrible results. As a result of a sequence of 2,600 choices one might make—each of which seemingly brought about the better result among the available alternatives—one would only have fed 2.6 million people for fifty years, rather than 4 million.

The preceding suggests the following practical result. National and international organizations are often in a position to trade off between helping or burdening a few people a lot, or many people a little. When this occurs, such organizations must pay close attention to the nature and possibility of iterations. If an organization can help a few people a lot, or many people a little, it makes a great difference whether they will face similar choices many times, and also whether it will be the same or different people who are affected each time. If the choice-situation is rare, it may be morally imperative to help the few a lot. Similarly, if the choice-situation is frequent, but different people will be involved each time, it may again be morally imperative to choose, on each occasion, so as to help the few a lot, rather than the many a little. But if the choice-situation is frequent enough, and the opportunity obtains to help the *same* large group on each occasion, then it may be imperative to help the large group repeatedly, even if one is only helping the members of that group a little each time. In such a case, one must look at the *combined* effects of one's actions taken as a *complete set*, as in fact, one would then be helping a large group of people a *lot*, over time. Here, as elsewhere in practical reasoning, it would be disastrous to consider each action separately from the larger context of which it is a part.

3.4 The Bad Old Days and Harmless Torturers

My discussion, both in this chapter and in chapter 2, was sparked by two examples of Derek Parfit's. Let me next present his two examples, and then sketch how they influenced my thinking.

> *The Bad Old Days.* A thousand torturers have a thousand victims. At the start of each day, each of the victims is already feeling mild pain.

Each of the torturers turns a switch a thousand times on some instrument. Each turning of a switch affects some victim's pain in a way that is imperceptible. But, after each torturer has turned his switch a thousand times, he has inflicted severe pain on his victim.

The Harmless Torturers. In the Bad Old Days, each torturer inflicted severe pain on one victim. Things have now changed. Each of the thousand torturers presses a button, thereby turning the switch once on each of the thousand instruments. The victims suffer the same severe pain. But none of the torturers makes any victim's pain perceptibly worse.[13]

Parfit used these examples to illuminate a host of intriguing topics, including whether there can be imperceptible harms and benefits, whether someone's pain can become less painful, or less bad, by an amount too small to be noticed, and whether an act can be wrong, because of its effects on other people, even if none of the people could ever notice any difference. Among his conclusions, Parfit showed that it can be a great mistake to overlook, or ignore, imperceptible or trivial harms or benefits. Parfit is surely right about this, but as I thought about his examples, and numerous variations of them, I came to the view that such examples had fascinating implications regarding aggregation, and that these implications extended well beyond cases involving imperceptible or trivial harms or benefits.

I began by simplifying Parfit's alternatives. Suppose that I faced a single choice. I could push a red button or a blue button. If I pushed the red button, a single individual would receive 1,000 jolts of electricity, such that each individual jolt, by itself, would be imperceptible or trivial, but together they would cause the individual to suffer excruciating pain. If I pushed the blue button, each of 1,000 individuals would receive a single jolt of electricity, whose effect on him would be imperceptible or trivial. Faced with such a choice, it seemed clear that I *should* push the blue button, and that this *wasn't* merely for deontological or agent-relative reasons. Rather, it seemed clear that the outcome in which one person suffered excruciating pain would be *worse* than the outcome in which 1,000 people were made imperceptibly or trivially worse off. Next, I noticed that this intuition was both powerful and robust. For many cases, at least, I felt the same way whether the one individual was initially well off or poorly off, and whether the 1,000 individuals were initially well off or poorly off. The clearest case, of course, was where I imagined the one person

---

[13] *Reasons and Persons* (Oxford: Oxford University Press, 1984), pt. 1, chap. 1, sec. 29, p. 80. In note 44 for part 1 (511) Parfit suggests that his presentation and discussion of the Harmless Torturers "derives entirely from the stimulus of...[a] brilliant example" of Jonathan Glover's which can be found on pages 174–75 of Glover's "It Makes No Difference Whether or Not I Do It," *Proceedings of the Aristotelian Society*, supplemental volume 49 (1975): 171–90.

was initially poorly off and the 1,000 people were initially well off, but even when I assumed the one person was initially much better off than the 1,000, it seemed clear that there was an important respect in which it would be better to make the 1,000 imperceptibly or trivially even worse off, than to make the one person suffer excruciating pain he would otherwise avoid.

I next considered cases where there were more than 1,000 people connected to the blue button, each of whom would receive a single jolt of electricity. My firm conviction that the outcome would be better if I pushed the blue button than if I pushed the red button didn't waver if I imagined 1,010 people would be connected to the blue button, each of whom would receive one jolt of electricity. Was my conviction about such cases just a "mistake of moral mathematics"?[14] On reflection, I thought not. This wasn't an instance of the common tendency to overlook or ignore imperceptible or trivial harms or benefits; rather, I *fully attended* to the effects on the many, but came to the considered judgment that the trivial or imperceptible pains of the many *just didn't add up* in the way they would need to, to outweigh the significant pain of the one.

Yet another variation of the example confirmed my thinking about such cases. In this variation, if I pushed the red button, one person would suffer intense pain for 1,000 straight days. If I pushed the blue button, 1,010 people would suffer intense pain for one day each. Here there is no illusion that suffering intense pain for a day would be "imperceptible" or "trivial," no tendency to mistakenly overlook or ignore the effects on the many that pushing the blue button would have. I am acutely aware that the effects of my pushing the blue button would be bad for each of the 1,010 people who experienced them, and I would think it quite bad for so *many* people to have to suffer as a result of my choice. Indeed, in this case, unlike those involving imperceptible or trivial burdens, it is clear that there are morally compelling reasons to go to great lengths, if necessary, to avoid pushing the blue button. Still, faced with such a choice, in most cases I think I should push the blue button rather than the red button, and as earlier, I think this not merely for deontological or agent-relative reasons. Though neither imperceptible nor trivial, typically, one day of intense pain will have a relatively small impact on someone's life, while 1,000 straight days of intense pain will have a significant impact on someone's life. In such cases, at least, it seems that many instances of the former spread across different lives would be better than one instance of the latter.

Consideration of such examples led me to distinguish and to recognize the force of chapter 2's First and Second Standard Views, as well as this chapter's Disperse Additional Burdens View. But, of course, just as Parfit pointed

---

[14] In chapter 3 of *Reasons and Persons*, "Five Mistakes in Moral Mathematics," Parfit identifies the tendency to overlook or ignore imperceptible or trivial harms or benefits as one of the "mistakes of moral mathematics" to which we are prone.

out that *from the standpoint of the victims* the *outcome* produced by the Harmless Torturers was *just as bad* as that produced by the Bad Old Days, it was apparent that the non-additive-aggregationist views I favored faced the problems of iteration noted in section 3.3. Thus, faced with the choice of pushing the red button once or the blue button once, I would think it better to push the blue button. Faced with the choice of pushing the red button a second time, this time connected to a new individual, or the blue button a second time, connected to the same 1,010 individuals, I would again think it better to push the blue button. And so on. Even if I'd already pushed the blue button 999 times, I think it might be better for each of the 1,010 people to suffer *one* additional day of intense pain, than for a new individual to have to suffer *1,000* straight days of intense pain. At least, there is an important respect in which an outcome where 1,010 people suffer 1,000 straight days of intense pain and a separate individual is spared 1,000 straight days of intense pain seems better than one where the 1,010 people will suffer 999 straight days of intense pain (anyway!) and in addition a separate individual will suffer 1,000 straight days of intense pain. But, of course, if I face such choices repeatedly, and push the blue button each time in accordance with my anti-additive-aggregative reasoning, after 1,000 such choices I will have produced an outcome that is *clearly* inferior to the one I would have produced had I pushed the red button each time. In the former case, 1,010 people suffer intensely for 1,000 straight days; in the latter "only" 1,000 do so.

Let us explore this issue further. When I consider each red or blue button choice *separately*, it seems there is an anti-additive-aggregationist reason to push the blue button, in accordance with the Disperse Additional Burdens View. However, when I consider 1,000 such decisions *collectively*, it is clear that I would produce a better outcome if I pushed the red rather than the blue button on each occasion. Why? The reason is simple. The collective result of 1,000 red-button pushes is that 1,000 people suffer greatly for 1,000 days. The collective result of 1,000 blue-button pushes is that 1,010 people suffer greatly for 1,000 days. Between *these* alternatives there is no issue of trading off between small additional burdens for many and large additional burdens for a few. There are just large burdens for many, or the *same* large burdens for more. Hence, for these alternatives the Disperse Additional Burdens View—which *licenses* my pushing of the blue button when each choice is considered *separately*—is silent. It simply doesn't *apply* to the alternatives that consist in the *collective* consequences of my actions. Thus, the collective result of pushing the red button each time is clearly better than the collective result of pushing the blue button each time, in accordance with chapter 2's principle *N*, that other things equal, numbers matter.

Given the foregoing, it may seem that for any fixed set of alternatives, it will be a simple matter to determine whether we should adopt a red-button or blue-button strategy. If we will face the choice once, or but a few times, we should be blue-button pushers. If we face such a choice "many" times—such that the outcomes produced by our actions *considered collectively* are such that the Disperse Additional Burdens View no longer applies to them—we should be red-button pushers. Unfortunately, however, this simple approach for cases where we face such a choice many times is theoretically unstable for familiar reasons.[15] After all, as rational agents, we needn't restrict ourselves to a simple all-red or all-blue strategy. Rather, we can adopt mixed strategies so as to produce the best outcome. That is, we can "defect" from the all-red choice just once, or twice, or a "small" number of times. But once one considers such mixed strategies, and allows *any* "defections," it is difficult to justify any particular "stopping point" between the all-red strategy and the clearly inferior all-blue strategy.

Let me spell out the difficulty here. Suppose I know, in advance, that I shall face the red-button or blue-button choice 1,000 times. This can be seen as involving 1,001 distinct alternatives. On the first alternative, I push the red button each time, and the blue button not at all. On the second alternative, I push the red button 999 times, and the blue button once. On the third alternative, I push the red button 998 times, and the blue button twice. And so on. On the 1,001st alternative, I push the red button 0 times, and the blue button 1,000 times. I start with the clear conviction that the first alternative is better than the last: better that 1,000 people suffer intensely for 1,000 days, while 1,010 other people don't, than that 1,010 people suffer intensely for 1,000 days, while 1,000 other people don't. But I then think that the second alternative may be better than the first: better that 999 people suffer intensely for 1,000 days, 1 person doesn't suffer, and 1,010 others each suffer for *one* day, than that 1,000 people suffer intensely for 1,000 day while 1,010 others don't suffer. I may think this in accordance with the Disperse Additional Burdens View, which applies to these alternatives and licenses the trade-off between the substantial burden for one person and the relatively small burden for many others. Next, I consider the second and third alternatives. Again, I may think the third alternative is better than the second: better that 998 people suffer intensely for 1,000 days, 2 people don't suffer, and 1,010 others each suffer for 2 days, than

---

[15] There has been a great deal of discussion of these kinds of issues in the literature. On the problem of instability, and what we might do in response to it, see Jon Elster's *Ulysses and the Sirens: Studies in Rationality and Irrationality* (Cambridge: Cambridge University Press, 1984), Ned McClennen's *Rationality and Dynamic Choice: Foundational Explorations* (New York: Cambridge University Press, 1990), and David Gauthier's *Morals by Agreement* (Oxford: Oxford University Press, 1986). Roughly, the notions of precommitment (Elster), bounded rationality (McLennen), and constrained maximizing (Gauthier) are developed and defended as rational strategies for imposing a kind of consistency on ourselves or the world, so as to prevent ourselves from following what we would most want to do or what the best theory of rationality would prescribe that we do at some points in the future, in the face of predictable changes in circumstances or desires, in order to give us the best chance, over time, of actually living the life that we (now) most value or that would be best according to that very theory of rationality. See, also, part 1 of Parfit's *Reasons and Persons*, and Tom Nagel's *The Possibility of Altruism* (Oxford: Oxford University Press, 1970).

that 999 people suffer intensely for 1,000 days, 1 person doesn't suffer, and 1,010 others each suffer for 1 day. Again, my judgment might be guided by the Disperse Additional Burdens View, which applies to these alternatives. Likewise, I might think that the fourth alternative is better than the third, the fifth better than the fourth, and so on. For *each* pair of "adjacent" alternatives from the 1st through the 1,001st, I might think that the "later" alternative is better than the "earlier" one in accordance with the Disperse Additional Burdens View. But then this might lead me to think it would be better to "defect" from the all-red strategy once rather than not at all, twice rather than once, three times rather than twice, and so on. Here, the problem of iteration combines with the issue of transitivity discussed in chapter 2 to generate a theoretical dilemma. For any alternative short of the all-blue strategy, there is another available alternative that seems better. But, of course, reasoning in such a manner would seemingly lead one, via iteration and transitivity, to adopt the all-blue alternative, which we *know* is inferior to the all-red one.

One can see, then, how reflection on variations of Parfit's examples might lead one to recognize both the power of anti-additive-aggregationist principles, and the problems of iteration and the intransitivity of the "better than" relation to which they lead. They also give rise to insights about *Prisoner's Dilemmas* and *Each-We Dilemmas*, to which I turn next.

3.5 Anti-Additive-Aggregationist Principles, Prisoner's Dilemmas, and Each-We Dilemmas

Prisoner's Dilemmas have been widely discussed.[16] Classic Prisoner's Dilemmas involved conflicts between two self-interested individuals. But I shall use the term *Prisoner's Dilemmas* to include the cases involving more than two people that raise similar problems. Parfit calls such cases *Many Person Prisoner's*

---

[16] My presentation of Prisoner's Dilemmas is heavily influenced by part 1 of *Reasons and Persons*. But a small sample of the literature on the topic includes Robert Axelrod's "The Emergence of Cooperation among Egoists,"*American Political Science Review* 75 (1981): 306–18, and *The Evolution of Cooperation* (New York: Basic Books, 1984); Jonathan Bendor's "In Good Times and Bad: Reciprocity in an Uncertain World," *American Journal of Political Science* 31 (1987): 531–58; Kenneth Binmore's *Playing Fair: Game Theory and the Social Contract* 1 (Cambridge, MA: MIT Press, 1994); David Gauthier's *Morals by Agreement*; Garret Hardin's "The Tragedy of the Commons," *Science* 162 (1968):1243–48; Nigel Howard's *Paradoxes of Rationality* (Cambridge, MA: MIT Press, 1971); J. V. Howard's "Cooperation in the Prisoner's Dilemma," *Theory and Decision* 24 (1988): 203–13; Susan Hurley's "Newcomb's Problem, Prisoners' Dilemma, and Collective Action," *Synthese* 86 (1991): 173–96; Gregory Kavka's *Hobbesian Moral and Political Theory* (Princeton, NJ: Princeton University Press), 1986; David Lewis's "Prisoner's Dilemma Is a Newcomb Problem," *Philosophy and Public Affairs* 8 (1979): 235–40; Thomas Schelling's *The Strategy of Conflict* (Cambridge, MA: Harvard University Press, 1960); Brian Skyrms's *The Dynamics of Rational Deliberation* (Cambridge, MA: Harvard University Press, 1990); and Robert Trivers's "The Evolution of Reciprocal Altruism," *Quarterly Review of Biology* 46 (1971): 35–57.

Dilemmas, but for our purposes it is unnecessarily cumbersome to distinguish between two-person and many-person cases.[17]

In a Prisoner's Dilemma, each of a group of individuals could benefit herself to a certain extent, or other group members, collectively, even more. If each person had to act separately, there was no way to "bind" the acts together such that whatever one person chose the others would also have to choose, no one person's act would significantly affect the actions that would be chosen by many others, there wasn't a possibility of "retaliation" by the other group members, and one wouldn't be facing similar choices in the future, then each person would be best off, in self-interested terms, if she chose to benefit herself. After all, if I am facing a genuine Prisoner's Dilemma, then I *know* the following will be true. If others benefit me, and I benefit myself, I'm better off in purely self-interested terms than if they benefit me and I benefit *them*; and likewise, if they benefit themselves, and I benefit me, I'm better off in self-interested terms than if they benefit themselves and I benefit them. Hence, in such situations, *whatever anyone else chooses*, I'm best off in self-interested terms if I act so as to benefit myself. But, that is true of *each* person facing a Prisoner's Dilemma. Hence, each member of the group has self-interested reasons to benefit herself. But, in a Prisoner's Dilemma, if *each* person acts in her own best interest, they, *together*, are worse off. Indeed, together, they may be *much* worse off than they would have been, if each had acted on behalf of the others, rather than on behalf of herself.

Here is an exaggerated example. Eleven people face a one-time-only choice of giving themselves 10 units of happiness, or each of the other ten people 100 units of happiness. There is no possibility of communication, binding the choices together, retaliation, or redistribution after the fact. In such a case, each person is better off in purely self-interested terms if she gives herself the 10 units of happiness. This *ensures* that she will end up with 10 more units of happiness than she would otherwise have, *whatever everyone else decides*. But, of course, if each person acts in this way, each person will only end up with 10 units of happiness—the 10 she gives herself; while if each person acted on behalf of others, *together* they would produce 1,000 units of happiness for each group member. That is, each person would benefit 100 units from the choices of each of the other ten people, and clearly they would all be *much* better off than they would be if each person acted self-interestedly.

In Prisoner's Dilemmas, people would fare better if they were all motivated to act on behalf of others, or guided by the Kantian question "What if everybody did what I will choose to do?" rather than if they were all motivated

---

[17] This section has been greatly revised in light of some acute worries that Shelly Kagan raised to an earlier draft. Whether or not my revisions are sufficient to meet all of Shelly's worries, I am grateful to him for forcing me to refine my claims and arguments.

to act self-interestedly. Correspondingly, some have seen Prisoner's Dilemmas as vindicating, at least for a certain class of cases, the importance of being moral rather than merely self-interested. Interestingly, however, Derek Parfit has suggested that not all moral theories avoid Prisoner's Dilemmas, and that in fact Common-Sense Morality faces moral analogues of the standard Prisoner's Dilemmas.

Parfit reasons as follows. On Common-Sense Morality, people have special duties or obligations toward those with whom they have special relationships. For instance, doctors, lawyers, priests, and teachers have, respectively, *special* obligations to their *own* patients, clients, parishioners, and students. Likewise, each of us has special obligations to our family and friends. So, for example, Parfit suggests that given the choice between saving her *own* child or saving two children who are strangers, Common-Sense Morality requires that a parent save her own child. But, then, suppose that two parents face the following situation. Each parent has three children facing death. Each can save one of her own children, or two children of the other parent. Moreover, suppose that each parent knows that unless she saves her own child, that child will die for sure, as the other parent will only be in a position to save her other two children. If we assume that the case involves the standard features of the classic Prisoner's Dilemma—namely, that each parent has to act separately, that there is no way for the parents to "bind" their acts together such that whatever one parent chooses the other would also have to choose, that there isn't a possibility of "retaliation" by the other parent after the fact, and that the parents wouldn't face similar choices in the future—then it appears that according to Common-Sense Morality each parent ought to save her *own* child. After all, each parent knows *for sure* that the fate of one of her children lies wholly in her hands, and that she can ensure that child's survival simply by giving it the priority over two strangers that Common-Sense Morality dictates that she should. Moreover, each parent knows that *whatever* decision the other parent makes, she will inevitably do what is best for *her* children by saving her own child, as doing this will save one more of her children than would otherwise be saved. Specifically, by saving her own child, each parent ensures that either one of her children is saved, rather than none, or that all three of her children are saved rather than two, depending on what the other parent chooses. In such a case, then, it seems that Common-Sense Morality will say that each parent *ought* to save her own child. But, of course, if each does this, *together* they will only save two of their children—one apiece—rather than the four they would have saved if each had saved two of the other parent's children.

In cases like the foregoing, Common-Sense Morality seemingly directs us to do what is best for our children; but if *each* of us does what is best for our children, then we, *together*, produce an outcome that is *worse* for our children. Reflecting on such cases, Parfit suggests that for each classic Prisoner's Dilemma involving self-interest, there may be an analogous Prisoner's

Dilemma involving Common-Sense Morality that rides "piggyback," as it were, on the original dilemma. Thus, just as it may be in *my* interest to pollute, have more children, grow more crops, or drive my car rather than take public transportation—even if this imposes a greater *total* burden on others than the burden I would bear if I refrained from such activities—so it may be in the interests of my children, or family, for me to pollute, have more children, grow more crops, or drive my car rather than take public transportation—even if this imposes a greater *total* burden on the children or families of others than the burden that my children or families would have to bear if I refrained from such activities. Assuming that the actions in question are not violating anyone else's rights, Common-Sense Morality may direct me, and others, to do the actions in question *for the sake of* those to whom we have the *special obligation* of providing for their well-being. But, of course, if *each* of many people acts in such a way, they, *together*, will be much worse-off, as the collective burden imposed on the community will exceed the individual benefits derived from such choices.

Parfit analyzes Prisoner's Dilemmas as examples of what he calls *Each-We Dilemmas*. He suggests that Each-We Dilemmas only arise for so-called *agent-relative* theories, theories that prescribe distinct aims (or reasons for acting) to different agents. Thus, the Self-Interest Theory of rationality gives to each agent the distinct aim of providing for his *own* well-being, and these aims conflict in the standard Prisoner's Dilemmas. Likewise, Common-Sense Morality gives to each agent the distinct aim of providing for the well-being of her *own* family, and these aims conflict in the analogues of the Prisoner's Dilemmas Parfit discusses. By contrast, Parfit contends, "Consequentialist theories cannot produce such [Each-We] Dilemmas.... this is because these theories are *agent-neutral*, giving to all agents common aims."[18] It is, Parfit thinks, a significant advantage of agent-neutral over agent-relative moral theories that, because they give to all agents common aims, they are able to avoid moral analogues of the standard Prisoner's Dilemmas.

Consider a consequentialist theory that gives to each agent the common aim of promoting the best outcome, and which treats each agent's interests equally for the purposes of evaluating outcomes. Such a theory would tell each agent to give 100 units of happiness to each of ten others, rather than 10 units of happiness to himself, and hence would avoid the unpalatable consequences that the Self-Interest Theory faces in the first kind of Prisoner's Dilemma discussed earlier. Likewise, such a theory would tell each agent to save two children of another parent rather than only one of his own children, and hence would avoid the unpalatable consequences that Common-Sense Morality purportedly faces in the second kind of Prisoner's Dilemma discussed earlier.

---

[18] Parfit, *Reasons and Persons*, 91.

Parfit's analysis of Prisoner's Dilemmas in terms of Each-We Dilemmas is illuminating, but this chapter's considerations suggest that he is mistaken in thinking that consequentialist theories avoid moral analogues of Prisoner's Dilemmas altogether. As seen, consequentialist moralities *will* be able to avoid *some* of the moral analogues of Prisoner's Dilemmas facing Common-Sense Morality, namely, those that arise in certain contexts because Common-Sense Morality gives different people distinct, and conflicting, agent-relative aims. But moral analogues of the Prisoner's Dilemmas can arise even for consequentialist theories that give everyone common, agent-neutral, aims. Specifically, this can happen for any consequentialist theory that rejects the simple additive-aggregationist approach for comparing all outcomes, in favor of an additive-aggregationist approach for comparing some outcomes, but a non-additive-aggregationist approach for comparing others.

Consider, again, the Disperse Additional Burdens View. I believe there is nothing about consequentialist, or agent-neutral, theories *as such* that requires them to *rule out* the Disperse Additional Burdens View as incoherent, unintelligible, or indefensible. Thus, just as consequentialists might value equality or justice, so they might believe that the outcome in which a given total burden was dispersed among a vastly larger number of people, so that the additional burden any single person had to bear within her life was "relatively small," would be better than the outcome in which a smaller total burden fell on just a few, such that their additional burden was substantial. Correspondingly, a consequentialist theory might well give everyone the common, agent-neutral aim of acting in accordance with the Disperse Additional Burdens View, so as to bring about the best outcome.

Suppose, then, consequentialists find themselves facing the red-button/blue-button scenario of section 3.3. If each consequentialist has to act separately, there is no way for them to "bind" their acts together, there isn't an issue of "retaliation" or redistribution after the fact, and they wouldn't be facing similar choices in the future, then wouldn't each consequentialist rightly choose to push the blue button, in accordance with his common agent-neutral aim of promoting the best available outcome? That is, each consequentialist would recognize that *whatever choices his fellow consequentialists make*, his choice is between an outcome where n people suffer intensely for 1,000 days, and 1,010 people suffer for x days, and one where $n - 1$ people suffer intensely for 1,000 days, and 1,010 people suffer for $x + 1$ days. Correspondingly, in accordance with the Disperse Additional Burdens View, he knows that *whatever* everyone else does, he *will* produce the best available outcome by pushing the blue button. But, of course, this is true for *each* consequentialist, and we know that if *each* consequentialist produces the best available outcome, *together* they will produce a worse outcome, one where 1,010 people suffer for 1,000 days, rather than one where 1,000 people suffer for 1,000 days. Here, I submit, we have a moral analogue of the Prisoner's Dilemma for consequentialists.

I suggest, then, that Parfit was mistaken in thinking that only agent-relative theories face analogues of the Prisoner's Dilemmas. Agent-neutral theories can as well—at least, agent-neutral theories that endorse non-additive-aggregationist principles for certain kinds of comparisons.

Parfit's mistake was in thinking that Each-We Dilemmas *only* arise when a theory gives individuals distinct *aims* whose pursuit would conflict with the aims the theory would prescribe for the collectivity. As we have just seen, Each-We Dilemmas can *also* arise from the fact that the factors that are relevant and significant for comparing a particular outcome of type A with a particular outcome of type B can be different from the factors that are relevant and significant for comparing a particular outcome A^* with a particular outcome B^*, where, A^* and B^* are the outcomes that obtain, respectively, after a large number of particular outcomes of types A and B have been instantiated.

Even if I am a consequentialist, I cannot always control the options I face. As a consequentialist, I have to choose the *best* of whatever options are available *to me at the time of acting*. I can, of course, and must, pay attention to the impact that my choices will have on others, as well as the impact that other people's choices will have on the effects of my choices. But if, taking full account of such information, I would produce the best outcome by producing an outcome of type A rather than an outcome of type B, then that is what I ought to do according to consequentialism. So, even if I recognize that, *together*, I and others will collectively face a *series* of choices which could result in outcomes A^* or B^*, it doesn't follow that I, or others, ever face a choice between A^* or B^*. It follows that even if *each* of us *successfully* acts in accordance with the aim of producing the best available outcome *from the options available to each of us*, we, *together*, may nonetheless produce a *worse* outcome than we would have produced had we each acted wrongly in consequentialist terms given the alternatives that we faced. In particular, it may be that A-type outcomes are better than B-type outcomes, given the factors that are relevant and significant for making *those* comparisons, while an A^* outcome is worse than a B^* outcome, given the factors that are relevant and significant for making *those* comparisons. This is why even consequentialists can face moral analogues of the Prisoner's Dilemmas. Contrary to Parfit's suggestion, even consequentialists can face Each-We Dilemmas.

Although I believe Parfit was mistaken in suggesting that only agent-relative theories could face Each-We Dilemmas, we might still believe that he has highlighted an important difference between agent-relative and agent-neutral theories. To see this, let us distinguish between the kind of Each-We Dilemma that Parfit identified and the kind that I have identified, as follows. Let us call the kind of dilemma that can arise if individuals have distinct aims a *Distinct Aims Each-We Dilemma*, and the kind of dilemma that can arise if individuals recognize the relevance and significance of different factors for making different comparisons—and in particular the relevance and significance of additive-aggregationist principles for some comparisons and the relevance and significance of anti-additive aggregationist principles for other comparisons—a *Distinct Factors Each-We Dilemma*. Then it is important to see, as Parfit has shown us, that *only* agent-relative theories face *Distinct Aims Each-We Dilemmas*; so, insofar as one regards the latter as problematic, that may seem to count in favor of agent-neutral theories. But *both* agent-relative and agent-neutral theories can face Distinct Factors Each-We Dilemmas; so, however problematic the latter may seem, it provides no reason to favor an agent-relative approach over an agent-neutral approach, or vice versa.

There is a related point to be emphasized here. The reasoning that *underlies* the Distinct Factors Each-We Dilemmas—namely, that anti-additive-aggregationist reasoning is relevant and significant for some comparisons, but not others—is *independent* of the reasonings that underlie the agent-relative and agent-neutral perspectives. Thus, in particular, if one is attracted to the former reasoning, one can combine it with either of the latter two perspectives; similarly, if one is attracted to either of the latter two perspectives, one *can* combine it with the former reasoning if one finds such reasoning intuitively compelling, but one doesn't *have* to if one finds such reasoning objectionable. The situation is otherwise regarding the reasoning that underlies the Distinct Aims Each-We Dilemmas. As Parfit has shown, such reasoning is intimately connected with, or perhaps is equivalent to, the reasoning that underlies the agent-relative perspective, and is incompatible with the reasoning that underlies the agent-neutral perspective. Thus, any significant concerns one might have about Distinct Aims Each-We Dilemmas *must* count as significant concerns about the agent-relative perspective, and hence as reason to favor an agent-neutral perspective over an agent-relative one.

Thus, even if Parfit is mistaken in claiming that agent-neutral theories can't face Each-We Dilemmas, there is something to his view that there may be *special* reason to be worried about agent-relative theories, insofar as such theories, unlike agent-relative ones, give rise to Distinct Aims Each-We Dilemmas. But, having said that, let me add two qualifying remarks. First, even if one grants that there is *one* important respect in which agent-neutral theories are more plausible than agent-relative theories, it remains an open question not even addressed, let alone settled, by anything said here, whether agent-neutral theories are more plausible than agent-relative theories *all things considered*. Second, *if* one finds the reasoning underlying Distinct Factors Each-We Dilemmas compelling, as many do, this may lessen the sting of Parfit's objection that agent-relative theories face Distinct Aims Each-We Dilemmas. That is, we may decide that we have to accept *some* Each-We Dilemmas in any event, because we are convinced that additive-aggregationist reasoning is relevant for some comparisons, while anti-additive-aggregationist reasoning is relevant for other comparisons. But having decided this, on independent grounds, it may not seem too objectionable to accept some *other* Each-We Dilemmas, as well, if doing so enables us to capture certain fundamental views that can only be captured by an agent-relative theory.

So, while we might have thought that, all things considered, the combination of an agent-relative theory with its various advantages and disadvantages, including the fact that it gives rise to Each-We Dilemmas, is less plausible than an agent-neutral theory that doesn't give rise to Each-We Dilemmas, we might ultimately decide that, all things considered, the combination of an agent-relative theory with its various advantages and disadvantages, including the fact that it gives rise to *both* Distinct Aims and Distinct Factors Each-We Dilemmas, is more plausible than an agent-neutral theory with its various advantages and disadvantages, including the fact that it gives rise to Distinct Factors Each-We Dilemmas. I haven't argued that this is so, of course. But recognizing that both agent-relative theories and agent-neutral theories can face certain kinds of Each-We Dilemmas changes the dynamic of Parfit's argument. Consequently, we may want to reconsider how much of an objection, if any, it really is to agent-relative theories that they face Distinct Aims Each-We Dilemmas *in addition* to the Distinct Factors Each-We Dilemmas that agent-neutral theories *also* face.[19]

---

[19] Derek Parfit balks at my discussion here. He grants that I may be making an important point about the nature and implications of agent-neutral theories, but he insists that as he has defined Each-We Dilemmas, agent-neutral theories can't face them. I have two responses to this, one charitable and one less charitable. Let me begin with the charitable response.

As noted in chapter 1, people can define terms in any way they see fit. If Parfit has defined the term Each-We Dilemmas in such a way as to preclude the possibility of agent-neutral theories giving rise to Each-We Dilemmas so be it; it is certainly his prerogative to do so. But we may gently ask whether or not this is the most useful definition for those words, or whether there is another notion in the same ballpark that it would be more useful to refer to via the words "Each-We Dilemmas." More particularly, I might claim that I have offered an alternative definition of "Each-We Dilemmas" that I commend to the reader. That is, I suggest that my definition slightly improves on the one Parfit gives, and that the notion I discuss offers an even more useful and illuminating way of thinking about different theories than the one Parfit discusses.

If Parfit prefers that I not use his words, for which he has already given a precise definition, I invite anyone who is interested in the exercise to come up with another name for the position I have described. Alternatively, I might distinguish my position from Parfit's by simply adding an "*" to the name of my position. So, my claim would be that there are two different kinds of Each-We Dilemmas*, Distinct Aims Each-We Dilemmas*—which are equivalent to what Parfit calls Each-We Dilemmas—and Distinct Factors Each-We Dilemmas*. The whole rest of my discussion would proceed exactly as it did in the text, but with the added "*" at every point where I currently use the words "Each-We Dilemmas." As should be plain, and as Parfit readily accepts, the slight change in terminology would not affect the substance of my remarks at all.

The less generous response to Parfit's claim, which I don't want to labor given the availability of the ready-to-hand generous response, is simply that as I read and reread the relevant sections of *Reasons and Persons* (sections 21 and 32), I don't see that Parfit actually has given us a definition of "Each-We Dilemmas" which precludes the possibility that agent-neutral theories could give rise to them. It is plain that Parfit thinks he has given such a definition, but frankly, I can't find it.

Parfit tells us that a theory faces Each-We Dilemmas if "there might be cases where, if each does better in this theory's terms, we do worse, and vice versa" (*Reasons and Persons*, 91). He then adds that

Distinct Aims Each-We Dilemmas are important, and have received the most attention. But, ultimately, I believe that Distinct Factors Each-We Dilemmas are more disturbing. Let me explain why.

Given the possibility of finding oneself facing a Distinct Aims Each-We Dilemma, it is clear what option I should seek if it were solely up to me. For example, in accordance with the Self-Interest Theory, I should seek the option where everyone else acts on my behalf, and I also act on my behalf; and in accordance with Common-Sense Morality, I should seek the option where everyone else acts on behalf of those to whom I have special obligations, and I also act on

---

"Consequentialist theories cannot produce such Dilemmas. As we saw in section 21, this is because these theories are agent-neutral, giving to all common aims" (91). But when one looks at section 21, there is no discussion of Each-We Dilemmas, but rather a discussion of when a theory is directly collectively self-defeating. And what Parfit presents is the definition that a theory T is directly collectively self-defeating when

(1) it is certain that, if we all successfully follow T, we will thereby cause our T-given aims to be worse achieved than they would have been if none of us had successfully followed T, or

(2) our acts will cause our T-given aims to be best achieved only if we do not successfully follow T. (*Reasons and Persons*, 54)

together with a series of claims purporting to show that no agent-neutral theory can be directly collectively self-defeating. It appears, then, that Parfit is committed to the view that a theory faces Each-We Dilemmas if and only if it cannot be directly collectively self-defeating.

But I think my arguments presented in this section and in section 3.4 establish that, contra Parfit, agent-neutral theories can be directly collectively self-defeating. (Note, Parfit's definition is intended to establish that a theory is directly collectively self-defeating as long as there are some cases where clauses 1 or 2 applies. He is certainly not making the stronger, indefensible claim that in order to be directly collectively self-defeating clauses 1 or 2 must apply for all cases. If that were his claim, then even his paradigmatic examples of theories that are directly collectively self-defeating, the Self-Interest Theory and Common-Sense Morality, would not be so.)

I don't want to simply repeat the many long arguments of sections 3.4 and 3.5. However, as Parfit rightly notes, "We successfully follow C when each does the act which, of the acts that are possible for him, makes the outcome best" (*Reasons and Persons*, 54, emphases added). It follows that when each of us is facing the red-button/blue-button choice of section 3.4, we will be successfully following C when each of us pushes the blue button. This is because, for each person it is true that whatever anyone else does, one brings about the best available outcome by pushing the blue button. As noted in this section, each person's choice is not between bringing about an outcome in which everyone pushes the red button or everyone pushes the blue button; rather, each person faces the much more limited choice of whether or not he should push the red or blue button. Given that choice, each person acts rightly according to C if and only if she pushes the blue button. And this is so, even though if she were given the choice between an outcome in which everyone pushes the red button and one in which everyone pushes the blue button, C would clearly direct her to choose the former.

So, by the lights of C, we have successfully followed C when each of us has pushed the blue button. But in this kind of case both clauses of Parfit's definition of when a theory is directly collectively self-defeating are met. In accordance with clause 1, it is certain that, having all successfully followed C, we thereby caused our C-given aims to be worse achieved than they would have been if none of us had successfully followed C, since the outcome in which everyone pushes the blue button is undeniably worse according to C than the outcome in which everyone pushes the blue button. Likewise, in accordance with clause 2, our acts will cause our C-given aims to be best achieved only if we do not successfully follow C, since only if we each act wrongly by C's lights, and push the red button, will we promote the best outcome by C's lights. (cont.)

behalf of those to whom I have special obligations. In addition, recognizing that others would have the same reasons to seek the options that would be best for themselves or those to whom they have special obligations, and recognizing that this would have disastrous consequences, I and others would have compelling reasons to open up lines of communication between us, if that were possible, and to arrive at a set of enforceable agreements whereby we would each have sufficient incentive to follow a compromise path that would not involve our acting as the Self-Interest Theory or Common-Sense Morality would otherwise tell us to act. As importantly, were we able to do this, I believe that it would be apparent what the enforceable agreements would require of us.

For example, if each of us could benefit ourselves by 10, or ten other individuals by 10, it is *clear* that if we were able to do so, the Self-Interest Theory would countenance our arriving at an enforceable agreement whereby each of us benefited others by 10 (thereby guaranteeing, this example assumes, that each of us would in fact end up much better off than we would if we didn't arrive at such an agreement). Likewise, if each of us could benefit those to whom we had special obligations by 10, or those to whom other people had special obligations by 20, it is *clear* that if we were able to do so, Common-Sense Morality would countenance our arriving at an enforceable agreement whereby each of us benefited the people that others had special obligations toward by 20 (again, thereby guaranteeing, this example assumes, that each of those to whom we had special obligations would in fact end up much better off than they would if we didn't arrive at such an agreement).

Therefore, as troubling as Distinct Aims Each-We Dilemmas are, it is clear what we should aim for if we could dictate what is to happen, and also clear how we should compromise to bring about the best outcome if we are able to do so. However, Distinct Factors Each-We Dilemmas are another matter. The problem with such dilemmas is that it isn't even clear what we should aim for if we could dictate what is to happen, nor is it clear what we, collectively, should compromise on, if we were able to reach any compromise of our choosing. This is because in a Distinct Factors Each-We Dilemma it isn't clear what the best

---

As indicated, then, I think the examples I discuss in this section and the previous one meet Parfit's definition for when a theory can be directly collectively self-defeating, and in so doing establish, as I claimed, that agent-neutral theories can face Each-We Dilemmas even as Parfit has defined and characterized that notion. But as I indicated earlier, though I believe this is true, there is no reason for me to insist on this position, given the availability of the uncontroversial response noted previously. There is a perfectly plausible, straightforward, and important sense in which agent-neutral theories can face Each-We Dilemmas, or at least Each-We Dilemmas*, and it behooves us to recognize and come to terms with that fact. (Note, this whole discussion assumes that agent-neutral theories might accept anti-additive-aggregationist positions like the Disperse Additional Burdens View for comparing some outcomes but not others. As I have shown, it is that assumption that makes it possible for agent-neutral theories to face Each-We Dilemmas. Accordingly, if one could successfully argue that no agent-neutral theories can accept the kind of view in question, that would be a substantive argument in support of the claim that Parfit was making on terminological grounds.)

outcome is, or even that there *is* such an outcome. Worse yet, it seems that for any outcome that we might choose, individually *or* collectively, there is another available outcome that we might have chosen instead, which would have been even better.

For example, in our red-button/blue-button case, we know that the all-blue-button outcome, where 1,010 people suffer intensely for 1,000 days, is clearly inferior to the all-red-button outcome, where only 1,000 people suffer intensely for 1,000 days, but that only tells us how we should choose between *those two particular outcomes*. In accordance with the Disperse Additional Burdens View, it appears that rather than have everyone push the red button we should coordinate our selections so that 999 people push the red button and 1 person pushes the blue button, since that would produce an outcome better than the one in which everyone pushes the red button. But then, as we have seen, it also appears we should coordinate our selections so that 998 people push the red button and 2 people push the blue button, since that would produce an outcome even better than the one in which 999 people push the red button and 1 person pushes the blue button. And so on. Here, we have the problem of iteration discussed in the previous section, and there seems to be no stable, non–ad hoc stopping point before the clearly unpalatable solution of each person pushing the blue button.

I think, then, that as important as Distinct Aims Each-We Dilemmas are, Distinct Factors Each-We Dilemmas are even more disturbing. It is difficult to know how to respond to them even if we allow communication and enforceable agreements. Of course, one "solution" to such dilemmas is to simply abandon the anti-additive-aggregationist approach reflected in such positions as the Disperse Additional Burdens View. But for the reasons discussed in this chapter and chapter 2, this solution is difficult to accept. Whether other solutions might be better will be considered in subsequent chapters.

*****

In this chapter, I presented a "new" principle of aggregation, the Disperse Additional Burdens View. A natural extension of chapter 2's Second Standard View, the view is an anti-additive-aggregationist principle that governs the permissibility of trade-offs involving large benefits or burdens for some, versus small benefits or burdens for many. In assessing the Disperse Additional Burdens View, I expanded on and reinforced many of the worries raised in chapter 2. We saw that there are many cases where the Disperse Additional Burdens View seems compelling. But we also saw that the principle is incomplete, applying to some alternatives but not others in such a way as to raise problems of iteration, resist a stable solution to those problems, and pose a threat to the transitivity of the "better than" relation. As we will see in the following chapters, similar problems arise in a multitude of areas.

4

On the Separateness of Individuals, Compensation, and Aggregation within Lives

Chapters 2 and 3 dealt with aggregation and problems about trade-offs between lives. In this chapter, and the next, I will argue that similar issues arise regarding aggregation and trade-offs within lives. Intrapersonal problems about aggregation have been less widely recognized than their interpersonal counterparts, and they are perhaps of less practical significance. However, they raise similar theoretical questions that are deeply problematic.

In this chapter, I begin by commenting on two related factors that have obscured the fact that there are problems about aggregation within lives: the separateness of individuals, and the possibility of compensation within a life, but not between lives. I then consider various reasons to reject a simple additive-aggregationist approach for measuring the goodness of an individual life. The considerations presented here will help illuminate chapter 5, where problems about trade-offs within lives are discussed.

4.1 On the Separateness of Individuals: Sidgwick, Rawls, and Nozick

In Book *III* of *The Methods of Ethics*,[1] Henry Sidgwick provides the basis of an ingenious argument for utilitarianism. Sidgwick begins with a "rational intuition" about Prudence, or Rational Self-Love, which he describes as an "equal and impartial concern for all parts of our conscious life."[2] Of this intuition he writes:

> We might express it concisely by saying "that Hereafter *as such* is to be regarded neither less nor more than Now." ... All the

---

[1] 7th ed., London: Macmillan, 1907.
[2] *The Methods of Ethics*, 124 n. 1.

principle affirms is that the mere difference of priority and posteriority in time is not a reasonable ground for having more regard to the consciousness of one moment than to that of another. The form in which it practically presents itself to most men is "that a smaller present good is not to be preferred to a greater future good" (allowing for differences of certainty).... the principle... is equally applicable to any... interpretation of "one's own good," in which good is conceived as a mathematical whole, of which the integrant parts are realized in different parts or moments of a lifetime.[3]

Sidgwick next adds a "rational intuition" about "Universal Good." He claims:

We have formed the notion of Universal Good by comparison and integration of the goods of all individual human—or sentient—existences. And here again, just as in the former case, by considering the relation of the integrant parts to the whole and to each other, I obtain the self-evident principle that the good of any one individual is of no more importance from the point of view... of the Universe, than the good of any other.... And it is evident to me that as a rational being I am bound to aim at good generally... not merely at a particular part of it.[4]

Sidgwick concludes:

From these two rational intuitions we may deduce...the maxim of Benevolence in an abstract form: viz. that each one is morally bound to regard the good of any other individual as much as his own, except in so far as he judges it to be less, when impartially viewed, or less certainly knowable or attainable by him.[5]

This argument provides the basis for classical utilitarianism only given certain assumptions. One assumption is that when Rational Self-Love, or as most people would now call it, *rational self-interest*, conceives "one's own good" as a "mathematical whole, of which the integrant parts are realized in different parts or moments of a lifetime," it is conceiving an individual's good as composed of the amounts of good contained in the different moments of the individual's life *added* together. Moreover, the view "that a smaller present good is not to be preferred to a greater future good" has to be interpreted as a special instance of the general claim that rational self-interest is concerned with the individual's life going as well as possible, and that this involves the life having as *much* good as possible. That is, rational self-interest must be understood as

---

[3] *The Methods of Ethics*, 381.
[4] *The Methods of Ethics*, 382.
[5] *The Methods of Ethics*, 382.

an *optimizing* view that involves *additive maximization*, according to which rationality aims at the *best* achievable life, where this is the one with the greatest *sum total* of good contained within the different moments of that life. Similarly, then, Sidgwick believes that the Universal Good is composed of the good of each sentient individual, added together, where the best outcome will be the one with the greatest sum total of individual goods. Correspondingly, since Sidgwick believes that rational beings are "bound to aim at good generally, [and]...not merely at a particular part of it," rational beings must be utilitarians, and act so as to maximize the good.

Now, strictly speaking, most of the logical work of the argument is done by the second premise. But the first premise "softens up" the reader so as to make the second premise seem more plausible. Intuitively, Sidgwick is reasoning as follows. Rationality requires that I be impartial between the different moments of my life. So, I should be willing to accept less in one moment, so as to receive even more in another, as that will make my life go better, overall. Likewise, in accordance with "the self-evident principle that the good of any one individual is of no more importance...than the good of any other," rationality requires that I be impartial between lives. Correspondingly, Sidgwick suggests, I should be willing to promote less good in one life, so as to promote even more good in another, as that will make the outcome, or "Universal Good," go better, overall.

Rawls recognizes this basis for classical utilitarianism. He suggests that on utilitarianism "the principle of choice for an association of men is interpreted as an extension of the principle of choice for one man."[6] He then observes that "the striking feature of the utilitarian view of justice is that it does not matter, except indirectly, how [the] sum of satisfactions is distributed among individuals, any more than it matters, except indirectly, how one man distributes his satisfactions over time. The correct distribution in either case is that which yields the maximum fulfillment."[7] Rawls's response to utilitarianism, and the Sidgwickian line underlying it, is both famous and, to most nonutilitarians, crushing: "Utilitarianism does not take seriously the distinction between individuals."[8]

Interestingly, Rawls does not challenge Sidgwick's characterization of the demands of rational self-interest. He allows that perhaps it is rational in my own case to pursue trade-offs between the different *moments of my life* so as to maximize the total amount of good that *I* experience over the course of my life. But he denies that in pursuing the good of society—Sidgwick's Universal Good—we should similarly permit or require trade-offs between different *people* so as to maximize the total amount of good in *society*. Rawls recognizes the striking difference between someone choosing for *herself*, to have less at

---

[6] *A Theory of Justice* (Cambridge, MA: Harvard University Press, 1971), 24.
[7] *A Theory of Justice*, 26.
[8] *A Theory of Justice*, 27.

one moment, so that she might have even more at other moments over the course of her life, and someone imposing a loss on someone *else*, so that *other* persons might have more, collectively. Setting aside important questions about autonomy and rights that arise in comparing these cases, it appears that in the former case the one who loses is *also* the gainer, she is the *beneficiary* of the loss. Thus, in the former case there isn't *really* a loser, just a winner. In the latter case, the one who loses really *is* a loser. Her situation has helped promote the greater good, but *all* the benefits of *her* loss accrue to *others*. In essence, her welfare has been *sacrificed* for the greater good.

Robert Nozick echoes these themes. He writes:

> Individually, we each sometimes choose to undergo some pain or sacrifice for a greater benefit or to avoid a greater harm: we go to the dentist to avoid worse suffering later; we do some unpleasant work for its results.... In each case, some cost is borne for the sake of the greater overall good. Why not, *similarly*, hold that some persons have to bear some costs that benefit other persons more, for the sake of the overall social good? But there is no *social entity* with a good that undergoes some sacrifice for its own good. There are only ... different individual people, with their own individual lives. Using one of these people for the benefit of others, uses him and benefits the others. Nothing more. What happens is that something is done to him for the sake of others.... To use a person in this way does not sufficiently respect and take account of the fact that he is a separate person,[9] that his is the only life he has. *He* does not get some overbalancing good from his sacrifice.[10]

Nozick employs such claims in defense of his notion of moral side constraints, and in particular his view that there is "a libertarian side constraint that prohibits aggression against another."[11] Moreover, as indicated in chapter 1, I believe that such considerations underlie the serious skepticism that some feel about assessing the goodness or badness of outcomes per se. But even among those who reject Nozick's libertarian side constraints, who believe that some outcomes are better or worse than others, and who accept that *some* trade-offs between people are desirable, most find the Rawls-Nozick line about the separateness of individuals compelling against the simple additive-aggregationist approach of classical utilitarianism.

---

[9] At this point Nozick has a note, 5, citing Rawls on the separateness of individuals; specifically, citing sections 5, 6, and 30 of *A Theory of Justice*. See *Anarchy, State, and Utopia* (New York: Basic Books, 1974), 32–33.
[10] *Anarchy, State, and Utopia*, 32–33.
[11] *Anarchy, State, and Utopia*, 33.

Rawls, of course, was developing a theory of social justice; his goal was to determine the correct principles and institutions of a just society. Nozick was likewise concerned with the principles that would govern a just society, though his views about moral side constraints also have direct implications about the moral obligations of individuals. Neither Rawls nor Nozick was principally concerned with developing theories of the goodness of outcomes. Still, I believe that most people who find Rawls's and Nozick's claims about the separateness of individuals compelling also believe that this is relevant to the assessment of outcomes. In particular, once doubts about additive aggregation across lives have been raised, there is ample room for considerations of distribution to enter into the assessment of outcomes, so that what matters is not merely how *much* good obtains, but how that good is *distributed*. In this context, the appeal of chapter 2's Second Standard View and chapter 3's Disperse Additional Burdens View may be unsurprising. *Given the separateness of individuals*, it is natural to suppose that *of course* one should prefer tiny burdens for many rather than huge burdens for one, or a huge benefit for one rather than tiny benefits for many, because the tiny burdens or benefits of the many don't *add up across lives* in the way they would need to to outweigh the significant impact on the single individual life that the huge benefit or burden would have. Thus, the anti-additive-aggregationist principles discussed so far may seem like natural extensions of the now familiar and widely accepted point about the separateness of individuals.

For many, Rawls's and Nozick's points about the separateness of individuals—which have obvious Kantian roots[12]—have crystallized the importance of anti-additive-aggregationist principles in assessing the goodness of outcomes. Unfortunately, however, I believe that their focus on the separateness of individuals, together with the fact that they left the Sidgwickian conception of rational self-interest largely unchallenged, helped obscure both the basis and the scope of anti-additive-aggregationist principles. In fact, I believe that the Second Standard View and the Disperse Additional Burdens View are *not* simply extensions of the familiar point about the separateness of individuals, and do *not* rely on that point for their plausibility. Specifically, I believe that analogues of such views are also relevant for assessing the goodness of individual lives, so that they apply *within*, as well as between, lives. If this is right, then we should reject Sidgwick's conception of rational self-interest that many, including both Rawls and Nozick, seem willing to grant.[13] The view here

---

[12] See Kant's *Groundwork for the Metaphysics of Morals*, trans. James W. Ellington (Indianapolis: Hackett, 1981), especially the second section. Both Rawls, in *A Theory of Justice*, and Nozick in *Anarchy, State, and Utopia*, acknowledge their debt to Kant on this point.

[13] It is possible that Rawls and Nozick merely grant Sidgwick his conception of rational self-interest "for the sake of argument." Still, I think it is fair to claim that Sidgwick was expressing the conception of individual self-interest that has dominated Western thought since Plato. A notable recent challenge to this conception is presented by Derek Parfit in part 2 of his *Reasons and Persons* (Oxford: Oxford University Press, 1984).

needn't involve rejecting the optimizing element of Sidgwick's conception, according to which one aims at the *best* achievable human life (though one might want to reject such a view on independent grounds);[14] rather, it involves rejecting the simple additive-aggregationist assumption according to which the *best* life is the one with the greatest *sum total* of goods spread throughout the life. In section 4.3, I shall offer various examples and considerations in support of this position. But first, it will be useful to distinguish the issue of compensation from the issue of moral balancing.

4.2 Compensation versus Moral Balancing

In part 3 of *Reasons and Persons*, Derek Parfit claims that advocates of the point about the separateness of individuals often conflate the issue of compensation with the issue of moral balancing.[15] I think he is right. When Nozick points out that when someone is used for the benefit of others "*He* does not get some over-balancing good from his sacrifice,"[16] this is undeniable as a point about *compensation*. The one who is burdened is *not* compensated by the fact that others may benefit even more than he has been burdened by his "sacrifice." But, as Parfit rightly notes, despite the rhetorical tone of Nozick's remarks, this fact about compensation doesn't *settle* the question of whether the moral balance of benefits versus burdens is sufficient to make the outcome better, or possibly even to warrant "sacrificing" the one for the others. Consider diagram 4.2.A.

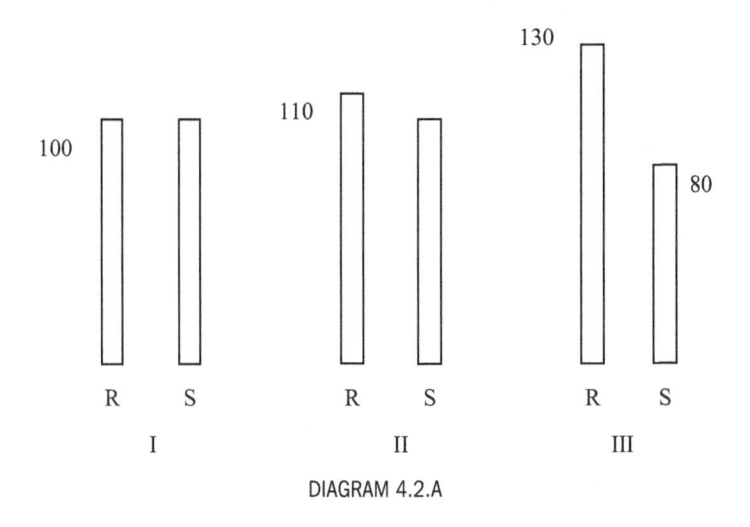

DIAGRAM 4.2.A

---

[14] Michael Slote has defended a *satisficing*, as opposed to a *maximizing*, conception of individual rationality, according to which it can be rational to choose an alternative in which one has "enough" or a "sufficient" degree of well-being even when an alternative in which one is even better off is readily available, in his excellent book *Beyond Optimizing* (Cambridge, MA: Harvard University Press, 1989).

[15] See especially pages 336–39.

[16] *Anarchy, State, and Utopia*, 32–33.

Suppose that in case *I*, *R* and *S* have 100 units of welfare each, and that one can provide someone with a benefit that would increase the quality of her life by 30 units, but only if one also imposed a burden on someone that would decrease the quality of her life by 20 units. Cases *II* and *III* represent two alternative ways one might distribute the benefit and burden. In case *II*, both the benefit and the burden go to the same person, *R*, so the net result is a benefit to her of 10 units. In case *III*, the benefit is given to *R*, but the burden is given to *S*. We might say that, in *II*, *R* has been *amply* compensated for the burdens imposed on her—that is, *more than fully* compensated—while, in *III*, *S* has not been compensated for the burdens imposed on her. What, if anything, is the moral relevance of these facts about compensation?

It is, I think, unclear. Compensation might be relevant to our assessment of both the outcomes' comparative goodness and the moral permissibility of bringing them about. But it is only *relevant* to these assessments, it doesn't *determine* them. Moreover, it is obscure to what extent compensation *itself* is relevant, as opposed to various related notions with which it may often be associated or conflated.

Consider first the issue of betterness, which is our main concern here. We may think that *II* is better than *I*, despite the burden of 20 imposed on *R*, because *R* was amply compensated with a benefit of 30. However, the fact that *II* involves a case of ample compensation is, seemingly, incidental to the judgment that *II* is better than *I*. Presumably, we might make the same judgment regarding *II*'s being better than *I* even if *R* hadn't been burdened at all, and had merely been benefited by 10. But, of course, in that case, there wouldn't be an issue of *compensation* underlying our judgment about the relative goodness of *II* and *I*.

Many people's judgment about the relative goodness of *II* and *I* would be based on their acceptance of a kind of pareto, or person-affecting, principle like John Broome's *principle of personal good*.[17] On this view, for any two outcomes involving the same people, if one outcome is at least as good as the other for everyone involved, then it is at least as good all things considered, and if one outcome is better than the other for some of the people and at least as good for everyone else, then it is better all things considered. On this view, the role of compensation may be as follows. Compensation is not *itself* intrinsically, or noninstrumentally, valuable, for there is *nothing* to be said, relating to the fact of compensation itself, for preferring a state involving burdens with compensating benefits to a state lacking those burdens with the same, or greater, overall net benefits. However, in situations where someone has been inappropriately burdened, it is better for benefits to accrue to that person so that they are compensated for their burden, than for such benefits to go to another, no more deserving, person. Moreover, for a large class of cases, the nature and extent of compensation will determine whether the principle of personal good can be

---

[17] See Broome's *Weighing Goods* (Oxford: Basil Blackwell, 1991), especially chapter 8.

appealed to in order to rank two outcomes, and if so what that ranking will be. Thus, the principle of personal good can be invoked for ranking outcomes in all cases where burdens are fully or amply compensated for by benefits accruing to the same people, and also in all cases where some people bear burdens that are not fully compensated and everyone else is unaffected. On the other hand, the principle of personal good will be silent in any case where some people receive net burdens while others receive net benefits.

Although many people are attracted by principles like the principle of personal good, as we will see in chapter 12, and as I have argued at length in other works,[18] there are reasons to doubt it. For example, if we had reason to believe that R and S were equally deserving, and that in fact both deserved to be at level 100, we might think that I was in one way better than II, and perhaps even all things considered better, because it was better regarding absolute justice, as well as equality, or comparative justice. More generally, we might think that our judgment regarding I and II wouldn't so much depend on whether II involved R's being fully compensated for a burden of 20 by a benefit of 30 but, rather, on how I and II compared in terms of all the ideals we deem relevant for assessing outcomes, giving each ideal its due weight. Relevant ideals might include utility, equality, priority, maximin, perfection, freedom, comparative justice, and absolute justice.

Consider next the relative goodness of I and III. Relative to I, in III R is benefited and S is burdened. Nozick is surely right that S's burden isn't *compensated* by R's benefits. But, as Parfit recognizes, this doesn't *settle* the question of whether there could be a moral *balancing* of the benefits and burdens so as to yield a ranking of the relative goodness of I and III. Although III involves an uncompensated burden on S, which counts in favor of I's being better than III, III also involves an unmitigated benefit to R, which presumably counts in favor of III's being better than I. Moreover, our judgment regarding I's and III's relative goodness won't just turn on whether there are unmitigated benefits or uncompensated burdens, or on whether the benefits are greater or less than the burdens, but on the *net* effect that the distribution of benefits and burdens has on *all* of the ideals that are relevant to the assessment of outcomes. Thus, we might favor III insofar as III was better regarding perfection, but I insofar as I was better regarding maximin. Likewise, we might favor I insofar as I was better regarding absolute or comparative justice, as it would be if R and S both deserved to be at level 100; yet we might favor III insofar as III was better regarding absolute or comparative justice, as it would be if R deserved to be at level 130, and S deserved to be at level 80. In sum, in assessing the relative goodness of two

---

[18] See, for example, chapter 9 of *Inequality* (New York: Oxford University Press, 1993); "Equality, Priority, and the Levelling Down Objection," in *The Ideal of Equality*, ed. Matthew Clayton and Andrew Williams (London: Macmillan; New York: St. Martin's Press, 2000), 126–61; "Personal versus Impersonal Principles: Reconsidering the Slogan," *Theoria* 69 (2003): 20–30; "Egalitarianism Defended," *Ethics* 113 (2003): 764–82; and "Equality, Priority, or What?" *Economics and Philosophy* 19 (2003): 61–88.

outcomes, the overall balancing of benefits and burdens must take account of much more than the brute fact of whether some people bear burdens that are not fully compensated. It must take account of the total impact that the benefits and burdens have on *all* of the ideals relevant to assessing the goodness of outcomes. As noted earlier, these might include utility, equality, priority, maximin, perfection, freedom, comparative justice, and absolute justice.

Return to Nozick's claim that when someone is used for the benefit of others "*He* does not get some overbalancing good from his sacrifice."[19] As noted earlier, this claim can be interpreted as a claim about *compensation*, to the effect that someone who is burdened so that others may benefit is not, herself, compensated by those benefits. So interpreted, Nozick's claim is a linguistic truth that is uncontroversial, but also trivial.

Suppose one interprets Nozick's claim to imply that any outcome where one person bears uncompensated burdens is, ipso facto, worse than any outcome where she does not. If all this means is that it is worse in *one* respect and, in particular, that there is someone for whom it is worse, then it is obviously true, but once again trivial. Anyone who believes in moral balancing would agree that if someone has an uncompensated burden that is a bad-making feature of the outcome; but she would insist that in some cases such bad-making features can be balanced, or outweighed, by other good-making features, including, for example, gains with respect to justice, equality, or benefits to others. Thus, those who believe in the possibility of moral balancing would contend that all things considered one outcome might be better than another even though it involves some people who have uncompensated burdens.

Suppose, however, that one interpreted Nozick's position more strongly. Suppose that one claimed that any outcome where one person bears uncompensated burdens is, ipso facto, *all things considered* worse than any other outcome where she does not. Such a view is decidedly not trivial. But it is also highly implausible. Indeed, arguably, it is incoherent in the sense of entailing inconsistent all things considered judgments.

For example, suppose that there is an outcome *I* in which John and Mary are both in the status quo position of being at level 100. Suppose that Henry is planning to do *x*, which will produce an outcome *III*, in which John has been raised to level 130, but Mary has been lowered to level 80, having had an uncompensated burden of 20 imposed on her. Suppose also that the only way I could prevent Henry from doing *x* would be by doing *y*, where this would produce outcome *IV*, where in *IV*, Mary would be at level 120, but John would be at level 95, having had an uncompensated burden of 5 imposed on him. Setting aside the question of whether or not we think it would be *wrong* for Henry to do *x*, or required, permissible, or wrong for me to do *y*, how do *III* and *IV* compare

---

[19] Nozick, *Anarchy, State, and Utopia*, 32–33.

regarding goodness? Here, it looks as if on the interpretation of Nozick's view currently under consideration, all things considered, *III* would be worse than *IV* and *IV* would be worse than *III*. This is because, in *III*, Mary would have an uncompensated burden relative both to the status quo outcome, *I*, and, more important, to the outcome I might produce, *IV*. Likewise, in *IV*, John would have an uncompensated burden relative both to the status quo outcome, *I*, and, more important, to the outcome that Henry might produce, *III*.

The view is also highly implausible for reasons unconnected with its being inconsistent. For example, suppose that among two equally deserving people, pure luck has determined that one is at level 1,000, and the other at level 500, though both *deserve* to be at level 900. Suppose also that by burdening the better-off person and benefiting the worse-off person, one could transform the outcome into one where both were at level 900. The resulting outcome would be better regarding utility, equality, maximin, priority, and absolute justice, and the case might be such that it was not worse, or even better, regarding freedom and perfection. Here, it seems clear that the second outcome would be better than the first all things considered. I conclude that one should reject the view that any outcome where one person bears uncompensated burdens is, ipso facto, all things considered worse than any outcome where she does not. There is, I think, nothing to be said in favor of it.

One might interpret Nozick's view as a claim about duties, rights, or obligations. In particular, one might interpret Nozick's view to imply that one has a *duty* to never impose an uncompensated burden on someone by *harming* them (unless they have done something to *deserve* that harm), and that this is so no matter how much good one might be able to achieve in other respects by harming the person in question. So stated, this position may remind one of Kant's famous claim that one ought never to *use* someone *merely* as a means to promoting the good.[20]

Since I am primarily concerned about the goodness and comparative ranking of different outcomes, I shan't labor all of the various interpretations of this kind of view that might be offered.[21] Still, a few observations are in order. First, one might hold the strong view that one had a duty or obligation

---

[20] See Kant's *Groundwork for the Metaphysics of Morals*, especially the second section. For an acute discussion of this principle and its limitations, see Derek Parfit's *On What Matters* (Oxford: Oxford University Press, 2011).

[21] I shall briefly comment on the difference and relations between the right and the good in section 7.4. For now, let me simply observe that as I use the term, roughly, an action is *right* for an agent if that agent ought, morally, to do that action. In some cases, at least, there may be factors that make an action right, such as deontological or agent-relative duties, that are distinct from those factors that make an outcome good or desirable. For example, it could be that I have agent-relative duties toward my mother which would make it *right* to save my mother rather than two strangers, even though saving the two strangers would produce a *better* outcome in terms of all of the factors that are relevant and significant for assessing the goodness of outcomes. Of course, in some cases, at least, factors may be

to never impose an uncompensated burden on someone—except, perhaps, to avoid a catastrophe (henceforth, this clause will be omitted but assumed)—unless the burden were a deserved punishment for a morally culpable action. Violations of this duty or obligation would be wrong. Analogously, one might hold that it was always a violation of someone's right, and therefore impermissible and wrong, to impose an uncompensated burden on someone, unless the burden were a deserved punishment for a morally culpable action. Such views may seem slightly more plausible than the previously discussed views about the desirability of outcomes, but I believe that they are still highly implausible. At least, I believe that they are highly implausible if we assume, as I do throughout this discussion, that the burden imposed is *nonviolent*, meaning that it involves something like a transfer of resources, or a reduction in opportunities, rather than violations of the right to be free from physical or psychological aggression.

In the case described earlier, I not only believe that the outcome produced by imposing a burden of 100 on the person at level 1,000 and bestowing a benefit of 400 on the person at level 500 would be *better* than the initial outcome, I believe that it need not be *wrong*, or impermissible, to produce such an outcome in the manner described. Correspondingly, I'm inclined to believe that the person who deserves to be at level 900, but in fact is lucky to be at level 1,000, doesn't have a *right* to be at level 1,000, and that there needn't be any rights violations if one imposes on him an uncompensated burden of 100. However, even if he has a right not to be so burdened, I believe that it is only a prima facie, defeasible right that is outweighed in this case by all the countervailing considerations that favor producing the better outcome.

A more plausible interpretation of Nozick's view might hold that it would be wrong to impose an uncompensated burden on anyone who has earned the right to be at or above the level they are at. But even this seems to me dubious. Setting aside the many qualifications that would have to be made to adequately handle cases where any choices we made would impose uncompensated burdens on some—where different numbers of people, different initial levels, and different levels of burden all might factor in our decision—I believe that even nonconsequentialists must regard uncompensated burdens that leave people

---

relevant to both the right and the good. For example, the fact that action *A*'s outcome would be just, and action *B*'s outcome unjust may be relevant both to the rightness of doing *A* rather than *B* and to the relative goodness of their resulting outcomes. So, justice can be both a *right-making* feature of actions and a *good-making* feature of outcomes, and the same is true of many other morally relevant factors and ideals. But, as indicated, I want to allow for the possibility that in some cases an action's right-making features are not simply reducible to the good-making features of the action's outcome (where for these purposes the doing of the action may itself be counted as part of the action's outcome).

As indicated in the text, my principal concern in this work is with questions about the goodness or relative desirability of outcomes, and not with the rightness of actions. So, insofar as Nozick's claims are construed as bearing on the latter issue they will be largely orthogonal to my claims.

worse off than they deserve to be as but one factor among many relevant to the permissibility of actions. And it is not plausible to think that that particular factor trumps, or should be given lexical priority over, all others.

So, consider a variation of our example. Suppose that the person at level 1,000 deserves to be at that level. We might then say that he has a right to be at that level, and that one violates that right if one imposes an uncompensated burden on him. Still, suppose that someone else has also earned the right to be at level 1,000, or perhaps has earned the right to be at an even higher level, say 1,500, but due to bad luck is at level 500. Would it be *wrong* to benefit such a person by 400 at the cost of an uncompensated (nonviolent) burden of 100 to the better-off person? I think not. Even if burdening the one person would be violating his right to be at level 1,000, I think such a right is a relatively weak, prima facie, or defeasible right that would be outweighed by the many competing considerations that obtain in this case. Nozick, of course, might not agree. And he would not be alone. But I believe that many, including many nonconsequentialists, would agree.

I conclude that the view that any outcome where one person bears uncompensated burdens is, ipso facto, all things considered worse than any alternative where she does not, should be rejected. It is inconsistent and deeply implausible. However, as implied earlier, I accept the much more modest claim that any outcome where one person bears uncompensated burdens is, ipso facto, worse *in one respect* than any outcome where she does not.[22] The weaker claim may seem too obvious to warrant mentioning, but as we will see in chapter 12, when we examine person-affecting principles, it is both important and controversial.

This section may be summed up as follows. Compensation is distinct from moral balancing. While in some cases compensation is *relevant* to the goodness of outcomes involving different distributions of benefits and burdens, facts about compensation *itself* don't determine the goodness of such outcomes. Rather, what matters is the net effect that the distribution of benefits and burdens has on

---

[22] Shelly Kagan notes that the notion of "uncompensated burdens" is hardly transparent. For example, are uncompensated burdens to be understood as relative to some actual or hypothetical status quo or as relative to any available or possible alternative? Each of these might generate very different answers as to whether or not any given individual was, in fact, bearing an uncompensated burden in any given outcome.

As I am employing this notion, one person bears uncompensated burdens in any given outcome A relative to any alternative outcome B, if and only if the person is worse off, all things considered, in A than in B. On this construal, every person in every outcome will bear some uncompensated burdens relative to some other *possible* outcome. However, one might argue that for purposes of evaluating the relative goodness of different outcomes, one should only consider whether or not the members of those outcomes have uncompensated burdens relative to each other and/or relative to any other *available* possible outcomes. The different versions of this view have different and significant implications, some of which I will explore in later chapters, especially chapters 11–13. But I shall not pursue this issue further here. Also, I am not denying that there might be alternative notions of "uncompensated burdens" that would be plausible and defensible.

all of the factors and ideals relevant to assessing outcomes. Thus, while in some cases compensation makes the difference between the goodness of the distributions of benefits and burdens, in other cases it does not, as the distributions of benefits and burdens will be good or not whether or not they befall the same or different people, and hence whether or not they involve compensation. Moreover, importantly, in some cases distributions of burdens and benefits will be better if they do *not* involve compensation than if they do. This might be so if the outcomes involving uncompensated burdens were sufficiently better than the outcomes involving compensated burdens regarding such ideals as freedom, perfection, maximin, absolute justice, and equality or comparative justice.

4.3 Compensation, Prudential Balancing, and Additivity

As noted earlier, Rawls and Nozick appeal to the separateness of individuals to challenge Sidgwick's argument for the utilitarian conclusion that the best outcome is the one with the greatest sum total of individual goods. But they don't challenge his assumption that the best achievable life is the one with the greatest sum total of "local" goods contained within the different moments of that life. This may be because compensation is possible within lives, but not between lives, and they assume that the plausibility of simple additive aggregation stands and falls with the possibility of compensation. But this, I believe, is a great mistake. As we have seen, moral balancing across lives is possible, even if compensation is not, and it is the full set of relevant ideals for assessing the goodness of outcomes, rather than the mere lack of possible compensation, that determines when, and why, a simple additive-aggregationist approach should be accepted, or rejected, in assessing outcomes. Likewise, the prudential balancing of different moments of a life will turn on the *full* set of relevant ideals for assessing the goodness of a life, and the correct method of combining the relevant ideals so as to aggregate across the moments of a life is *not* simply determined by the fact that compensation within a life is possible.

Specifically, while the possibility of compensation may *permit* the sort of simple additive-aggregationist approach associated with total utilitarianism, and may make such an approach seem more plausible within lives than between lives, it neither entails nor requires such a position. Indeed, as we shall see, notwithstanding their differences regarding the possibility of compensation, aggregation within lives parallels aggregation across lives, in that there may be many circumstances where the "correct" prudential balancing of different moments of a life involves rejecting additive aggregation (here, and in what follows, I mean by "additive aggregation" the kind of additive-aggregationist approach associated with total utilitarianism, where you determine the goodness of a "whole" by simply adding up the goodness of each "local" component of that whole, moment by moment).

If the preceding is right, we should reject the conception of individual self-interest advanced by Sidgwick (what he called Prudence, or Rational Self-Love) and left unchallenged by Rawls and Nozick. This, by itself, is not surprising. However, as we will see in the next chapter, it has surprising and important implications, as doing so raises troubling issues similar to those advanced in chapters 2 and 3.

To be sure, many people who attach great weight to anti-additive aggregationist principles, like equality or maximin, in assessing outcomes involving many people, nevertheless believe that it would be wrongheaded to give weight to such principles in assessing alternative lives for a single individual. They believe, for example, that it would be ludicrous to oppose students making great sacrifices during graduate school for the sake of significant benefits later in life, on the grounds that this would promote inequality between their lives' stages, or on the grounds that this would violate maximin if (contrary to fact!) their graduate student days were the worst period of their lives. Correspondingly, at first blush it may seem that a simple additive-aggregationist approach may be correct for determining the overall goodness of a *single* life, even if such an approach is *not* plausible for determining the overall goodness of an outcome involving *different* lives. Nevertheless, many objections can be raised to a simple additive-aggregationist approach for assessing lives. Most of these are familiar and can be stated briefly.

Consider a scale of well-being where someone with an average quality of life is at level 50, someone with an *extremely* high quality of life is at level 100, and someone whose life is *barely* worth living is at level 1. Now suppose one could live 50 years at level 100, or 100 years at level 50. On a simple additive approach to measuring the goodness of lives these two lives would be exactly equally as good; both would contain a total of 5,000 units of well-being. But it is dubious that these two lives are equally good. Perhaps, as long as one is living a "sufficiently" long life, where, let us suppose, 50 years counts as such, quality counts more than duration, so that for any given total of well-being to be experienced, it is more important that the years one lives be at a higher level than that one merely lives longer at a lower level. Or perhaps, as long as one is living a "sufficiently" high-quality life, where, let us suppose, level 50 counts as such, duration counts more than quality, so that for any given total of well-being to be experienced, it is more important that one lives a longer life at a lower level than a shorter life at a higher one. Either of these views, or more context-specific variations of them, might be correct. In either case, this would undermine a simple additive approach to aggregating the different moments of a life.

Or consider two different ways that one's life might sum to a total 50,000 units of goodness over the course of a 50-year life. In one, which I'll call the *drab life*, one would consistently experience a mildly pleasurable existence, of approximately 3 units of good per day, such that one was equally well off throughout one's life, and totaled 1,000 units of well-being per year. In a second, which I'll call the *wildly fluctuating life*, one's life would be filled with many highs, but also many lows. During the highs, one would experience great achievements and rich relationships, and would be as well off as is humanly possible, but the lows would involve great setbacks, pain, and suffering, so much so that during those periods one's life would be well below the level at which life ceases to be worth living. The positive periods might total well into the thousands of units of goodness per day, but the negative moments would likewise total to a large number of units of badness, or negative units of goodness, as it were, and would cancel out all but 50,000 units of goodness. On a simple additive approach to measuring the goodness of lives, these two lives would be equally good. But that seems deeply implausible. Depending on how the details of the case are fleshed out, I can imagine significant arguments for regarding the second alternative as much better, and also significant arguments for regarding it as much worse, but what I don't find plausible is the additive approach's claim that as long as there is the same *sum total* of goodness minus badness in the two lives, they would be *exactly equally as good*. The differences between the two lives are extremely significant, and their impact on the overall quality of the lives is not to be captured by simply adding up the goodness and badness within each life day by day, or moment by moment.

Here is another way to put the point. As indicated, depending on the details of the case, I think it likely that one of the two lives would be *much* better than the other. Correspondingly, I don't believe that a *slight* increase or decrease in the total benefits or burdens in the two lives would affect their relative rankings. In other words, I don't believe that it would make a difference to the ranking of the two lives whether for two days out of 50 years the drab life had reached level 4, so that the sum total of goodness in that life was actually 50,002, or whether for two days out of 50 years the drab life had only reached level 2, so that the sum total of goodness in that life was actually only 49,998. Likewise, I don't believe that it would make a difference to the ranking of the two lives whether for two days out of 50 years the wildly fluctuating life had reached level 2,076, rather than 2,074, so that the sum total of goodness in that life was actually 50,002, or whether for two days out of 50 years the wildly fluctuating life had "only" reached level 2,072, rather than 2,074, so that the sum total of goodness in that life was actually only 49,998. It seems to me clear that the differences between the two lives are so stark, and so significant, that a mere difference of a couple of extra units of good or bad during two days of a 50-year life span couldn't possibly alter the relative ranking of the two lives.[23]

---

[23] I am not claiming here that no two lives that differ starkly in certain respects could be equally good, all things considered. Rather, my view is that for the particular lives in question the difference between them is stark in ways that have significant implications for their overall goodness, such that it is implausible to believe they might, in fact, be equally good, or even almost equally good.

If the drab life would be better than the wildly fluctuating one in the case where the sum total of goodness happened to be 50,002, it would be better than the wildly fluctuating one if its sum total happened to be 49,998. Similarly, if the drab life would be worse than the wildly fluctuating one in the case where the sum total of goodness happened to be 49,998, it would be worse than the wildly fluctuating one if its sum total happened to be 50,002. Likewise, for the wildly fluctuating life.

There are many factors that seem relevant to the overall goodness of a life besides merely the sum total of local goodness or badness that obtains within that life. One such factor might be referred to as the "pattern," "direction," or "shape" of a life.[24] To illustrate this, consider two scenarios. In the first, one's life starts out poorly and steadily improves, so that at the end of one's life one is very well off. For simplicity, let's just divide the life into five twenty-year segments and say that as the life progresses, one's levels would be 10, 30, 50, 70, and 90, respectively. In the second scenario, the pattern is reversed. The life starts out very well off and steadily worsens, so that the life ends poorly. Specifically, as the life progresses, one's levels would be 90, 70, 50, 30, and 10, respectively. On the simple additive approach, the two lives are equally good, and if, in fact, the second life ended at level 12 instead of level 10, then that life would be better than the first all things considered. But I think relatively few people would actually choose a life plan for themselves, or a loved one, in accordance with this position.[25]

To be sure, here, as elsewhere, advocates of the simple additive approach can argue that we are being misled by our intuitions in such cases. They

---

[24] The idea that the "shape" of a life is relevant to its overall goodness is an old one in philosophy, and a position that is similar to it in important respects can already be found in Aristotle. For example, rejecting the notion that the happiness of a life simply depends on how much total happiness the life contained, moment by moment, Aristotle writes, "We cannot have happiness unless we have complete goodness in a complete lifetime. Life is full of chances and changes, and the most prosperous of men may in the evening of his days meet with great misfortunes, like Priam in the stories we read in the epic poets. A man who has encountered such blows of fate and suffered a tragic death is called happy by no one" (*Nicomachean Ethics*, book 1, chapter 1, trans. J. A. K. Thompson [London: George Allen and Unwin, 1953]). This passage is open to various interpretations, but one plausible one is that Aristotle attaches special importance to how our lives conclude in assessing the overall goodness of our lives, and all of them reject a simple additive-aggregationist approach to assessing the goodness, or happiness, of a life.

An important contemporary account defending the importance of the "shape" or narrative structure of a life is David Velleman's "Well-Being and Time," *Pacific Philosophical Quarterly* 71 (1991): 48–77. For an interesting analysis of why the "shape" of a life might matter, or at least might seem to matter, see Frances Kamm's appendix to chapter 2, "Inclines and Declines," of *Morality, Mortality, Vol. I: Death and Whom to Save from It* (New York: Oxford University Press, 1993), 67–71.

[25] Of course, some utilitarians and others *would* choose in the manner suggested, and others would insist that they *should* choose in such a manner even if, because of weakness of the will, they actually might not. But as discussed previously, in section 2.4, and as I shall return to below, Jake Ross has given us good reason to think that it would be a mistake to act on one's utilitarian beliefs in such cases, as long as one gave *some* reasonable credence to the possibility that the simple additive-aggregative approach to valuing lives should be rejected.

might claim that to be at level 10 after one has experienced the highs of level 90 is actually much worse than to be at level 10 with nothing better to compare it to. Similarly, they might note that one will appreciate being at level 90 a lot more if one has previously been at level 10, than if one has never known what it is like to be poorly off. Correspondingly, it is suggested that while people are *told* that in the first and second lives people's levels are, respectively, 10, 30, 50, 70 and 90, and 90, 70, 50, 30, and 10, *in fact* they are intuitively reacting *as if* the levels are really something like 10, 35, 60, 80, and 100, and 90, 65, 40, 20, and 5, respectively. And, *of course*, the argument concludes, if we are thinking about the lives that way, we will regard the first as much better than the second, since it will have a much greater sum of well-being.

I don't deny that there are kernels of psychological truth underlying such a position. But ultimately it amounts to the view that either people's judgments about such alternatives are unreflective, or even on reflection people can't accurately assess the alternatives presented. I find such a view both deprecating and dubious. When I think about such cases, I don't have to think that the people are dwelling on the past, anticipating the future, or otherwise experiencing the present through the prism of past and future. I can, instead, consider someone who basically lives life as it comes, appreciating where he currently is at in life, whether good or ill, simply for what it is. When I do this, I can imagine people's lives actually unfolding in the way described earlier. One life starts off poorly and ends very well. The other starts out very well and ends poorly. But both lives have the same *total amount* of "local" goods and bads occurring within them. Thinking about these alternatives as clearly and carefully as I can, I stand by my earlier claims. It seems evident that the former life is much better than the latter. While each life has the same total amount of well-being spread among its moments, each life has a pattern or direction that crucially matters.

The claim that the shape of a life can matter resonates with a basic insight common to the thinking of certain holists, Gestalt psychologists, and advocates of organic unity, namely, that sometimes the whole can be greater or less than the sum of its parts. While this insight is notoriously difficult to pin down, it seems neither mystifying nor implausible if it is understood "merely" as the rejection of a simple additive-aggregationist approach to understanding the goodness of certain "wholes." On reflection, it seems clear that this insight applies *within* lives as well as *between* lives.

In sum, given two lives with the same total amount of goodness and badness, as measured additively moment by moment, one of which began poorly, steadily improved, and ended well, and the other of which began well, steadily declined, and ended poorly, the first seems much better than the second, all things considered. It is the life I would wish for myself, and anyone I cared about. Moreover, I am confident that most people, even after careful deliberation, would agree.[26]

Next, let me suggest that an analogue of chapter 2's Disperse Additional Burdens View applies within lives as well as between lives. I'll begin with an example that illustrates the appeal of such analogue couched in terms of burdens, and then offer an example couched in terms of benefits.

Suppose that one is faced with a choice of living one of two lives. In the first, one will get to live at the exceptionally high level of 91 for 100 years, in the second, one will get to live at the slightly higher exceptionally high level of 93 for 99 years, but the cost of doing so is a year of *exceptionally* bad pain and suffering, where one's life is *much* lower than the level at which life ceases to be worth living, at a level of −90. (Here, and elsewhere, when I claim that one life is at a higher level than another, say at level 93 rather than at level 91, I am assuming that the former truly has higher *quality* than the latter, rather than that it merely contains a greater *quantity* of goods of similar or lower quality.) As

---

[26] I say "most." I certainly don't think everyone accepts this view. One person who is not convinced is Mikhail Valdman. He suggests, in correspondence, two cases where he doesn't share my intuitions. Case *I* involves a dog, Rufus, who has a poor memory and who lives for only a week. You can give Rufus very little attention or affection on day one, with increasing attention and affection each day, until the last day of its weeklong life you are lavishing him with love and attention. Or, you can lavish Rufus with love and attention on day one, but give him decreasing attention and love each subsequent day. If the *total* amount of love and attention that Rufus receives is the same in the two scenarios, Valdman isn't convinced that Rufus's life would be better on the first scenario than the second. Case *II* involves scientists injecting two people with a drug once a month. The drug causes pleasure for a day, but also causes its recipient to soon forget how intense the pleasure was. The first person gets a heavy dose the first month that causes really intense pleasure, but gets decreasing doses afterward so that each month he is getting less and less pleasure. The second person gets a really small dose to begin with that causes just a tiny bit of pleasure, but increasingly larger doses afterward so that each month he is getting greater and greater pleasure. If the two people receive the very same doses, only in reverse order, and their lives are equal in all other respects, Valdman sees little if anything to choose between them; he writes, "My intuition here is that neither life is clearly better than the other." Thinking about such cases, Valdman suggests that the claims I make about the relevance of a life's "shape" may reflect "our thoughts about a life's aesthetic value and not its prudential value."

Valdman's cases are instructive. I'm not sure I share Valdman's intuitions about his cases, but for those who do, let me note the following. First, we might think that the "shape" of a life is relevant for beings like us, with complicated hopes, projects, commitments, relationships, etc., but not necessarily for beings like dogs.

Second, we might think time scales matter, and that it also matters how significant the differences are between the "highs" and "lows" of a life. There is, for example, a big difference between going without food or attention for a day, as Rufus presumably does in Valdman's first case, and suffering starvation and utter neglect for a period of years. So, even if we were persuaded that the "shape" of Rufus's life mattered little in the case Valdman gave us, we might feel very differently about different cases. Suppose, for example, that Rufus was going to live one of two lives, each of which lasted ten *years* rather than seven *days*. In the first, Rufus's life begins absolutely *horribly*—for two years he is a stray who is *constantly* sick, injured, beaten, hungry and lonely. But afterward, his life steadily and significantly improves, as he moves first to a pound, and then to a series of increasingly caring and competent owners, so that with each passing year there is marked improvement in his diet, health, injuries, and the attention and affection he receives, until the final two years of his life are truly *wonderful*. Alternatively, Rufus's life

constructed, the simple additive-aggregationist approach would claim that the second life is *better*, since there would be 9,117 total units of good spread throughout the moments of one's life (here, the additive approach involves subtracting the total amount of bad from the total amount of good), as opposed to 9,100. But I reject this ranking as deeply implausible, and I believe that most people would strongly agree with me.

Here, it seems clear that reasoning similar to that underlying the Disperse Additional Burdens View applies. Specifically, in this case, where additional burdens are to be disbursed among the different periods of a life, it is preferable for a given total burden to be dispersed among many periods of that life, so that the additional burden the person has to bear at any given time is "relatively small," than for a smaller total burden to fall on just one period, or

---

might *start out* wonderfully for two years, but then steadily and significantly deteriorate, reaching its nadir in his final two years, as he suffers the horrible life of the abandoned stray described earlier. Here, I think Rufus's life goes better on the first scenario than the second.

Third, our overall assessment of lives is going to be mainly a function of the quality of the relationships within those lives, of the nature of their projects and commitments, of their mental and physical health, of the degree of respect, self-realization, and accomplishments attained, and so on. I agree that if we think two normal human lives are equal in all *those* respects, we might rightly judge that neither is "clearly better than the other" even *if*, as in Valdman's second case, one of them had some drug-induced pleasures that increased in intensity each month, while the other had the same kinds of drug-induced pleasures that decreased in intensity each month. But this hardly shows that the shape of a life as a whole doesn't matter for the overall quality of the life.

Fourth, it is noteworthy that Valdman's two cases focus mainly on hedonistic elements of a life. As just implied, for human lives, at least, our assessment of the overall quality of a life depends heavily on nonhedonistic elements, and it may well be that the relevance of "shape" to the overall goodness of a life is mostly related to the nonhedonistic elements that contribute to the goodness of a human life. Thus, even if the shape or pattern of hedonistic elements within a life didn't matter—which I doubt, but which would explain Valdman's intuitions about his cases—it wouldn't follow that the shape or pattern of *well-being* doesn't matter, since, for humans, at least, well-being includes so much more than mere hedonistic elements. I conclude that even if one shared Valdman's intuitions about the cases he presented, one would need much more to seriously challenge the view that the shape or pattern of a life may be relevant to its overall value.

Finally, I have worries about the suggestion that our intuitions about my cases may reflect our thoughts about a life's aesthetic value rather than a life's prudential value. I'm not sure why we should find a life that begins poorly but ends well more *aesthetically* pleasing or desirable than a life that begins well but ends poorly. I don't deny that we may make aesthetic judgments about a life, considered as a whole, but I suspect that in the cases I have described any aesthetic judgments we may have about them largely track our prudential judgments about those lives. That is, it is because we regard a life that begins poorly and ends well as *better for* the possessor of that life than one that begins well and ends poorly that we might be led to judge the former kind of life as aesthetically more desirable than the latter. This is, admittedly, speculative on my part. But, as indicated, I don't see any independent reason for thinking an "upward"-sloping life should be any more or less aesthetically pleasing than a "downward"-sloping life, especially if, as we are assuming, the slopes in question have the same shape and grade. In any event, I deny that my judgments about such lives are aesthetic rather than prudential. I would want my child's life to start poorly and end up well rather than vice versa *not* because when I contemplate the two alternatives I judge the former to be aesthetically more appealing, but because it would be better *for her*. Of course, I may be mistaken about this claim; but if so, I think I am making a substantive mistake about prudential value, rather than the very different mistake of conflating an aesthetic judgment with a prudential one.

just a few periods, of the life, such that the additional burden the person has to bear during that period, or those few periods, is substantial. Note, I don't need to claim that such reasoning will always be plausible. There are different cases, and perhaps in some cases one might plausibly reject the reasoning in question.[27] But in cases like the example noted, anti-additive-aggregationist reasoning of the sort underlying the Disperse Additional Burdens View seems both applicable and compelling. Though the *total amount* of burden imposed is greater in the first life described earlier than the second, 198 units of burden rather than 181, in the first life the burden is spread out so that no period is significantly affected adversely, while in the second the burden all falls on *one* period, with disastrous consequences for that period.[28] Surely, it is better to live a life *all* of which is at an exceptionally high level, than to live a life that is slightly better most of the time but includes a full year of terrible pain and suffering, during which time one's life is worth not living.[29]

Next, consider a choice between living a life at the exceptionally high level of 92 for 100 years, or living a life at the slightly less exceptionally high level of 91 for 99 years in order to reach the truly blissful level of 170 for one year. On the simple additive-aggregationist approach, the first life is better, since there would be 9,200 total units of good spread throughout one's life, as opposed to 9,179. But once again I reject this ranking, and I believe most others would as well. The life that includes a year of bliss seems clearly superior to its alternative. Here, as elsewhere, what matters is not merely the *sum total* of local goods and bads within the life, but the *way* those goods and bads are distributed.

---

[27] Oscar Horta has suggested, in correspondence, that he can think of a number of cases where he acts in accordance with the Disperse Additional Burdens View within his own life, but other cases where he acts contrary to it. I suspect that many others are like Horta in this respect. For my present purposes, I don't need the bolder claim that we are always influenced or guided by such a principle within our lives, merely the more cautious one that it is often reasonable to give such a principle weight in our normative deliberations.

[28] I am calculating the total amount of burden in each life as follows. In the first life, there are 99 years where the person is living at level 91, as opposed to the level 93 that he would be living at if the second life were instantiated, and there is 1 year where the person is living at level 91, as opposed to the level −90. It is *no* burden to be living at level 91 rather than level −90, but it *is* a burden of 2 to be living at level 91 rather than at level 93; hence, since there are 99 years of such a burden, we can calculate the *total* amount of burden of living life one rather than life two as 2 × 99 = 198. Similarly, in the second life, there are 99 years where the person is living at level 93, as opposed to the level 91 that he would be living at if the first life were instantiated, and there is 1 year where the person is living at level −90, as opposed to the level 91. It is *no* burden to be living at level 93 rather than level 91, but it *is* a burden of 181 to be living at level −90 rather than at level 91; hence, since there is one year of such a burden, we can calculate the *total* amount of burden of living life two rather than life one as 1 × 181 = 181.

[29] Interestingly, Oscar Horta has suggested that similar considerations might apply when considering different ways in which a given total amount of "burden" might be dispersed within a life at any given time, as well as over time. Horta reasons as follows. In assessing how good an individual's life is at any given time, we may pay heed to a host of factors. For example, we may pay attention to how fulfilling his job is, how good his relationship is with his family, his friends, his coworkers, etc., his level of self-respect, his level of respect from others, his level of accomplishments, how satisfying his sex life is

In this case, reasoning similar to that underlying the Disperse Additional Burdens View again seems applicable, bearing in mind that as I am using the notions of benefits and burdens, you benefit someone if you prevent him from having a burden, and you burden someone if you prevent him from having a benefit. Specifically, in this case, where additional benefits are to be disbursed among the different periods of a life, it is better for a given total benefit to be consolidated in just one period, such that the positive impact on that period is substantial, than for a larger total benefit to be disbursed among many periods of that life, so that the additional benefit to any single period of the life is "relatively small." Once again, I am not claiming that such reasoning will always seem plausible for all cases. But it does seem compelling in cases like the one in question.

At this point, let me partially address an issue that has so far been skirted.[30] Suppose that one is in a current, status quo state, outcome *I*, and one is contemplating transforming it into one of two alternative states, outcomes *II* or *III*. In deciding which, if either, of the alternative states one should bring about, should one compare each of those states with the status quo state, with each other, or in some other way? This is an important, nontrivial issue given views like chapter 2's Second Standard View and chapter 3's Disperse Additional Burdens View. To illustrate this, let me consider two different sets of cases.

In the first set of cases, the status quo outcome, *I*, involves 11 people at level 20. One can disperse a given total burden of −20 to the people in *I* in one of

---

his level of material comfort, his states of psychological and physical health, and so on. Suppose, for simplicity, that ten factors contribute to a person's overall well-being at any given time, and that for each factor one might construct a scale from 0 to 10 representing how well off someone was with respect to that factor, where 0 meant that they were faring *horribly* and 10 meant that they were faring extraordinarily well. Finally, imagine, simply for the sake of illustration, that each category was as important as every other, so that being at any given level with respect to any given factor would be equally important in terms of its contribution to one's well-being at any given moment. Horta then suggests that if someone was at level 8 with respect to all ten factors, and was told that they faced a total burden of 8, it would be reasonable for them to prefer a loss of 1 with respect to 8 different factors to a loss of 8 with respect to any single factor.

That is, Horta is suggesting that with respect to the ten factors that determined how well off one was at any given time, a life which scored 7, 7, 7, 7, 7, 7, 7, 7, 8, 8 would be more desirable than a life which scored 8, 8, 8, 8, 0, 8, 8, 8, 8, 8. Horta's suggestion, then, is that even though, in *one* sense, the *sum total* of benefits and burdens involving the different factors that are relevant to assessing how good an individual's life is at any give time might be the same, how good the life actually is at any given time depends in part on how those benefits and burdens are *distributed* among the different relevant factors.

Although I don't think my arguments *require* me to accept Horta's view, I think it is plausible and consistent with my arguments. That is, I think that in addition to there being reason to accept an analogue of the Disperse Additional Burdens View within lives over time as well as between lives, there might also be reason to accept another analogue of the Disperse Additional Burdens View within lives at any given time as well as over time. As should be apparent, pursuing Horta's suggestion very quickly raises the issue of holism and the Principle of Contextual Interaction, which I advert to at various points throughout this work. I am grateful to Horta for his intriguing suggestion.

[30] I am indebted to Shelly Kagan for impressing upon me the importance of clarifying and emphasizing the points made in this and the following six paragraphs. Even so, the issues raised in this paragraph are not fully addressed here. They receive more attention in chapters 11–13, in the context of my discussion of what I call Essentially Comparative Views.

two ways. One can give a burden of −2 to each of 10 different people, thereby bringing about outcome *II*, in which 10 people are at level 18 and 1 person is at level 20; or, alternatively, one can give all of the burden of −20 to a single person, thereby bringing about outcome *III*, in which 10 people are at level 20 and 1 person is at level 0. Assuming that a loss of only 2 is a relatively small burden that does not make a significant impact on someone's life, but that a loss of 20 is a relatively large burden that does make a significant impact on someone's life, this is the kind of case for which a principle like chapter 3's Disperse Additional Burdens View seems relevant. So, should we bring about *II*, or *III*, or neither, and how should we determine this?

If we compare *II* to *I*, we will note that 10 people are worse off by 2, and 1 person is not worse off by anything. If we compare *III* to *I*, we will note that 10 people are not worse off by anything, and 1 person is worse off by 20. This might seem to support the view that *III* is worse than *I*, in accordance with the Disperse Additional Burdens View. But what happens if we compare *II* and *III* directly? We note that in this case our calculation of how they compare (see note 28) will depend on who, exactly, gets the burdens in the different alternatives. Suppose, for example, that the very same person who would be at level 20 in *II* would be at level 0 in *III*. Then in that case our calculation of how *II* and *III* compare would directly parallel our calculation of how each would compare with *I*, and our judgment about them would be the same. That is, we would say that in *II*, 10 people are worse off by 2, and 1 person is not worse off by anything, while in *III*, 10 people are not worse off by anything, and 1 person is worse off by 20, and hence, in accordance with the Disperse Additional Burdens View, *III* is worse than *II*.

However, suppose that the person who would be at level 20 in *II* would be *different* than the person who would be at level 0 in *III*. In that case, our calculation to determine how *II* and *III* compare directly would be a little different. Specifically, we would determine that in *II*, 9 people are worse off by 2 (the 9 who are at level 18 rather than level 20), and 2 people are not worse off by anything (including the 1 person who is at level 20 in both cases, and the 1 person who is at level 18 in *II* but at level 0 in *III*); while in *III*, 10 people are not worse off by anything, and 1 person is worse off by 18. Now in this case, we may *still* judge that *III* is worse than *II*, just as we would have in the other case, and if we had based our judgment on how *II* and *III* each compared to *I*. Still, recognizing that our calculation of how *II* directly compares with *III* will vary depending on the details of those alternatives illustrates the importance of comparing them *directly*, and *not* simply inferring how they compare by noting how they compare with respect to some third alternative, such as the status quo, *I*. The importance of this lesson will be made vivid by considering my second set of examples.[31]

---

[31] The following is a variation of a set of cases suggested to me by Kagan.

Suppose, again, that the status quo outcome, *I*, involves 11 people each at level 20, and that the first alternative outcome, *II*, once again involves a dispersal of burdens of −20 in such a way that 10 people are at level 18 and 1 person is at level 20. But this time suppose that the second alternative outcome, *III*, would involve a dispersal of benefits of 100 units and burdens of −10, in such a way that the 10 people who would be at level 18 in *II* would all be at level 30 in *III*, while the 1 person who would be at level 20 in *II* would only be at level 10 in *III*. In this case, if we compared *II* with *I* in terms of burdens, we would say that 10 people have a burden of 2 (the burden of being at level 18 rather than 20), and 1 person has no burden (since he is at level 20 in both outcomes), while if we compared *III* with *I* we would say that 10 people have no burden (since it is no burden to be at level 30 rather than level 20), and 1 person has a burden of 10 (since he is at level 10 instead of level 20). Correspondingly, if we thought that a burden of 10 represented a significant impact on the overall quality of someone's life, but, as before, that a burden of only 2 didn't, then one *might* be tempted to assume that if one's status quo position was *I*, and one could bring about either alternative *II* or alternative *III*, then, in accordance with the Disperse Additional Burdens View, one should bring about alternative *II*! After all, this would involve just small burdens for 10 people rather than a large burden for 1 person.

But notice, the temptation in question completely disappears if one compares *II* and *III directly*. In doing so, one sees that in *II* 10 people would have burdens of 12 (the burden of being at level 18 rather than level 30), and 1 person would have no burden (since it is no burden to be at level 20 rather than level 10), while, conversely, in *III* 10 people would have no burdens (since it is no burden to be at level 30 rather than level 18), and 1 person would have a burden of 10 (the burden of being at level 10 rather than level 20). Once one compares *II* and *III* directly, one sees that the Disperse Additional Burdens View doesn't even *apply* to *that* comparison, and offers *no* support for the judgment that *II* is better than *III*.

We see, then, that if one wants to compare two alternatives with respect to principles like chapter 2's Second Standard View and chapter 3's Disperse Additional Burdens View, it is not enough to compare them with some third alternative, such as the status quo. One has to compare them *directly*. But this is not yet to imply that it is *sufficient* to compare them directly. For example it *might* be that if one wants to compare two alternatives with respect to principles like chapter 2's Second Standard View and chapter 3's Disperse Additional Burdens View, one has to compare them directly and *also* compare them with every *other* available alternative, including the status quo, assuming there is one. I shall return to this important and complex issue in chapters 11 through 13.

Next, let us consider in some detail an analogue of Parfit's Repugnant Conclusion, but for a single life. Paraphrasing Parfit, it might be put as follows:

The Single Life Repugnant Conclusion: For any possible life, no matter how long or how high the quality of that life might be, there must be some much longer imaginable life whose existence, if other things are equal, would be better, even though each period of that life would be barely worth living.

Interestingly, a version of the Single Life Repugnant Conclusion was first discussed by J. M. E. McTaggart, many years before Parfit presented his own Repugnant Conclusion. But McTaggart denies that the repugnance "in this case would be right."[32] Though lengthy, McTaggart's discussion is brilliant, and worth presenting in detail. He writes the following:

The values of states in time vary, caeteris paribus, with the time they occupy.

From this principle it follows that any value, which has only a finite intensity, and which only lasts a finite time, may be surpassed by a value of much less intensity which lasts for a longer time. Take a life which in respect of knowledge, virtue, love, pleasure, and intensity of consciousness, was unmixedly good, and possessed any finite degree of goodness you choose. Suppose this life prolonged—for a million years if you like—without its value in any way diminishing. Take a second life which had very little consciousness, and had a very little excess of pleasure over pain, and which was incapable of virtue or love. The value in each hour of its existence, though very small, would be good and not bad. And there would be some finite period of time in which its value would be greater than that of the first life, and another period in which it would be a million times greater [note omitted]. This conclusion would, I believe, be repugnant to certain moralists. But...I can see no reason for supposing that repugnance in this case would be right. So far as I can see, it rests on a conviction that quality is something which is inherently and immeasurably more important than quantity. And this seems to me neither self-evident nor capable of demonstration.

Nor is there any reason to doubt our conclusion because it is highly probable that many people, if offered the million years of brilliant life, followed by annihilation or by a state whose value should be neither good nor evil, but zero, would prefer it to any length of an oyster-like life which had a slight excess of good. For it must be remembered that men's choice in such cases is very much affected by their imagination. Now it is much easier to imagine the difference between the two sorts

---

[32] See J. M. E. McTaggart, *The Nature of Existence*, 2 vols. (Cambridge: Cambridge University Press, 1921), 2:452–53.

> of life which we have considered, than it is to imagine the difference between an enormously long time and another time which is enormously longer. And, again, we are generally affected more than is reasonable by the present or the near future in comparison with the far future. And a change which will only happen after the end of a million years is in a very far future.[33]

Here, McTaggart clearly recognizes the intuitively repugnant implications that additive aggregation can have for lives of sufficient length, perceptively sees much of what is at stake in the matter, and offers several sophisticated explanations for why we should not trust our intuitions about such cases. However, while McTaggart's remarks are deeply insightful, ultimately I find his deflationary account of our intuitions about such cases unconvincing. Let me next suggest why.

Consider first his contention that it is "much easier to imagine the difference between the two sorts of life which we have considered, than it is to imagine the difference between an enormously long time and another time which is enormously longer." I readily grant that we may have no clear intuitive grasp on numbers as large as a million, and so it might be argued that our intuitions about such cases don't accurately reflect the difference between a million years and some indefinitely much longer period of time. But though true, it isn't evident how much weight this observation bears.

First, it isn't as if we would have any trouble choosing between a million years in Heaven or Hell, and some indefinitely much longer period of time in Heaven or Hell. We would clearly, and rightly, prefer the longer time in Heaven and the million years in Hell. Here, our judgment readily guides us to "correct" for our intuitive shortcomings. But in the choice between the brilliant life and the oyster-like life our judgment doesn't similarly lead us to "correct" for our intuitive shortcomings; rather, for some of us at least, it leads us to reject additive aggregation and trust our intuitions about such cases.

Second, it isn't as if we can pretend to have an accurate intuitive grasp of the *real* difference between the brilliant life and the oyster-like life. Rather, we just have the firm conviction that the quality of the former life would be *much much* higher than that of the latter. Similarly, we can have the firm conviction that the indefinitely long life would be much much longer than the life of a million years. Moreover, while our judgment might lead us to think that the size of he gap in quality between the different lives must, for finite beings, be naturally limited, the gap in number of years could be as large as one likes, so our

---

[33] McTaggart, *The Nature of Existence*. The passage here is principally from sections 869–70 of book 7, chapter 7, "The Total Value in the Universe," but it begins with the end of the last sentence of section 868. I am grateful to Thomas Hurka for bringing McTaggart's brilliant discussion to my attention, and for sending me the quoted material.

judgment naturally leads us to recognize that the difference in duration between the two lives might be many many times greater in magnitude than the difference in their quality. Yet even as our judgment recognizes this truth, it doesn't cause us—or at least not me, anyway—to revise our judgment about which life would be better. Rather, it causes us to question the additive-aggregationist approach for comparing such alternatives, thereby confirming our intuitions rather than dismissing them as distorting.

Third, while the Single Life Repugnant Conclusion may seem *especially* repugnant in the case McTaggart imagines, where we are to forsake a *million* years of flourishing for an indefinitely long period of oyster-like life, I believe that most people would make the same judgment if the choice were between a mere *100* years and an indefinitely long period of oyster-like life. Consider *seriously* the difference between the two lives. The first would involve 100 years as rich and rewarding as any human life that has ever been lived, *filled* with great achievements of the highest order, serious and lasting loves, rewarding friendships, and so on. The second would involve eons of a life *barely* worth living; such a life would be *utterly devoid* of the achievements and relationships that contribute to human flourishing and would contain only the lowest and mildest of conscious pleasure. Surely, most people would choose the former life for themselves or a loved one. But in this case one can hardly explain away the choice as resulting from our inability to "imagine the difference between an enormously long time and another time which is enormously longer." We certainly can imagine that the difference between 100 years and many eons might be of such a magnitude, that in a sense the *total amount* of utility would be greater in the longer oyster-like life than in the shorter flourishing life. But what we cannot believe, on reflection, is that the *goodness* of the different lives is a simple additive function of the total amount of utility in those lives. While there would be *more* utility in the oyster-like life with each passing year, we don't believe that the different oyster-like pleasures spread out over many eons *add up* in the way they would need to to make the oyster-like life *better* than the flourishing life.

The truth is that we don't believe there would be a *significant* difference between the goodness of an oyster-like life that lasted 100 years, or 1,000 years, or 10,000 years. And these are numbers that we certainly can, I believe, intuitively grasp. Moreover, importantly, we don't see the difference between such lives as on a trajectory that, over time, would eventually amount to a great difference. Correspondingly, we *judge* that there wouldn't be a *significant* difference between the goodness of an oyster-like life that lasted 100 years and one that lasted a million years, or many eons. I suggest, then, that our view about such cases rests not on our intuitive inability to grasp large numbers, as McTaggart suggests, but on our reflective *judgment* that merely adding more years to an oyster-like life does not significantly increase the goodness, or desirability, of such a life.

To be sure, advocates of additive aggregation may continue to insist that our intuitions about such cases are not to be trusted, even for cases involving intuitively graspable numbers. So, for example, they might insist that the difference between oyster-like lives of 100, 1,000, and 10,000 years *is* on a trajectory that would *eventually* amount to a great difference, but that the slope of the trajectory is *so* slight that we don't intuitively notice it, or perceive its long-term implications. But though it is possible such a view is correct, it has the air of an untestable article of faith that advocates of additive aggregation are compelled to invoke to explain away our intuitions, and I doubt that many will find it sufficiently compelling to alter their judgments about such cases.

Consider next McTaggart's suggestion that our intuitions about such cases are not to be trusted because "we are generally affected more than is reasonable by the present or the near future in comparison with the far future. And a change which will only happen after the end of a million years is in a very far future." McTaggart is certainly right in his observation, but I seriously doubt that our "bias" toward the near accounts for our attitude about such cases. Suppose, for example, people were offered the following choice. In each of two outcomes, people would, starting today, live eons and eons, followed by annihilation. In the first outcome, they would live oyster-like lives the entire time. In the second outcome, they would live slightly less contented oyster like-lives for all but the last 100 years, during which time their lives would be as rich and rewarding as is humanly possible. Finally, supposed that each life began and ended at the same time, and contained the exact same *total* amount of utility. Confronted with such a choice, I have no doubt that most people would clearly prefer the latter, for themselves or a loved one. But if this is right, then the explanation of that choice would have nothing to do with our bias toward the present, or near, which in this case would favor the first outcome over the second, since by hypothesis the first outcome would be better for us in the present, and for eons to come.[34]

I submit, then, that McTaggart's attempt to explain away the preference most people would have for an extended flourishing life over a much longer oyster-like life in terms of our imaginative limitations regarding differences between large numbers and our bias toward the present and near is unconvincing. However, as should be evident, I believe he is very close to on target when he suggests that the repugnance "certain moralists" would feel about his view "rests on a conviction that quality is something which is inherently and immeasurably more important than quantity."[35] But the view is not simply that quality is *always* "inherently and immeasurably more important" than number or duration. There are plenty of instances where McTaggart's opponents would

---

[34] I am grateful to Mikhail Valdman for this example, which is an improvement on one that I originally presented to make this point.
[35] See note 33.

permit, and even insist on, certain trade-offs between quality and number or duration. I believe, for example, that most of McTaggart's opponents, including me, would readily accept an analogue of chapter 2's First Standard View like the following:

> *The Third Standard View (TSV)—Trade-offs between Quality and Duration Are Sometimes Desirable*: In general, it is better for an individual to receive a lower-quality benefit for a longer period of time than a higher-quality benefit for a shorter period of time, *if* the difference in the quality of the benefits and its impact on the person's life are not "too" great, and *if* the duration of the lower-quality benefit would be "sufficiently" longer than the duration of higher-quality benefit.

However, what McTaggart's opponents believe—which surely includes almost everyone, as McTaggart himself recognizes—is that *when* the differences in quality are *sufficiently* large, as they are between the most flourishing human life possible and an oyster-like life, then as long as the higher quality life persists for a "sufficient" period of time, it would be better, or more valuable, than any duration of the lower quality life. Of course, as McTaggart rightly observes, this view is neither "self-evident" nor capable of "demonstration." But despite the rhetorical flourish with which McTaggart made that observation, his opponents needn't think otherwise. Neither self-evidence nor demonstrability is necessary for truth, much less for reasonable belief or acceptance.

Comparing a flourishing human life of 100 years with an indefinitely long oyster-like life, we seem to have another example of what Jim Griffin described as "discontinuity between values" where "enough of *A* outranks any amount of *B*."[36] As Griffin put it in the passage previously cited in chapter 2, such cases involve "the suspension of addition;... we have a positive value that, no matter how often a certain amount is added to itself, cannot become greater than another positive value, and cannot, not because with piling up we get diminishing value or even disvalue...but because they are the sort of value that, even remaining constant, cannot add up to some other value."[37]

Together the preceding considerations suggest a position analogous to chapter 2's Second Standard View. It might be put as follows:

> *The Fourth Standard View (FoSV)—Even within Lives, Trade-offs between Quality and Duration Are Sometimes Undesirable Even When Vast Differences in Duration Are at Stake*: If the difference in the quality of benefits is "sufficiently" large, it would be preferable for someone to receive a larger (higher quality) benefit, as long as it persisted

---

[36] *Wellbeing: Its Meaning, Measurement, and Moral Importance* (Oxford: Clarendon Press, 1986), 85.
[37] *Wellbeing*, 85.

for a "sufficiently" long duration, than for that person to receive a smaller (lower quality) benefit for any period of finite duration.

As discussed in chapter 2, most people regard Parfit's Repugnant Conclusion as genuinely repugnant. Correspondingly, most people accept the kind of anti-additive-aggregationist position reflected in chapter 2's Second Standard View. Similarly, as McTaggart recognized, most people would regard the Single Life Repugnant Conclusion as genuinely repugnant. Correspondingly, I submit, most people accept the kind of anti-additive-aggregationist position reflected in the Fourth Standard View. On reflection, then, it appears that the overall goodness of a life is not just an additive function of the goodness of each moment of that life, considered separately from the others. Thus, a simple additive-aggregationist approach is dubious within lives as well as between lives.

Let us consider one final example, which combines several of the elements discussed in this chapter.[38] Consider diagram 4.3.A.

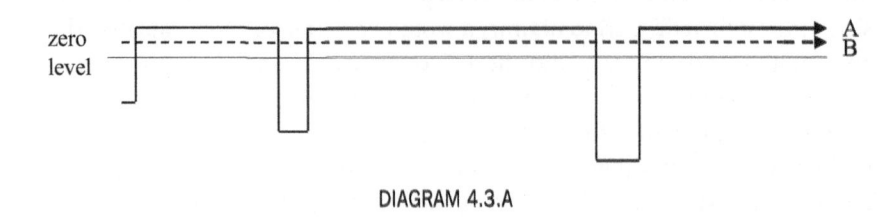

DIAGRAM 4.3.A

Diagram 4.3.A represents two possible lives that one might lead which are equally long and perhaps very lengthy. The dotted line represents a life, *B*, that is just above the zero level, the point at which a human life ceases to be worth living. The solid line represents a life, *A*, that starts out below the zero level for a period of time, say, and then moves just above the level of the *B* life for a longer period of time; it then moves farther below the zero level than it was originally, for twice as long, before returning to the level just above the level of the *B* life, for more than twice as long as it was originally at that level; it then again moves even *farther* below the zero level for three times as long as it was originally, before once again returning to a level just above the level of the *B* life, this time for a much longer time than it was originally at that level, and so on.

Since diagram 4.3.A is not drawn to scale, it is important to spell out exactly what it is intended to portray. We are imagining that *B* is a very long

---

[38] I am grateful to Oscar Horta for suggesting this example to me. Horta claims that he finds this example even more forceful than the case of the Single Life Repugnant Conclusion, in support of applying anti-additive-aggregationist considerations within a life. While I'm not sure whether I share Horta's comparative view of the two cases, I grant that there are some especially nice features of his case, that are not present in the other cases I have presented, that make it particularly compelling.

drab life, just barely worth living. *A* is an equally long life that vacillates between increasingly long and increasingly worse periods below the zero level, and increasingly long periods of drab existence during which time one would be *slightly* better off than one would be in *B*. Finally, crucially, we are imaging that each period in *A* that is at a slightly higher level than *B*'s level is sufficiently long to weigh off against each period in *A* that is below the zero level, so that the *sum total* of benefits and burdens is *equal* in lives *A* and *B*. Given these assumptions, we might ask which life, if either, would be better?

Total utilitarians would regard each life as equally good. But I suspect that few people would in fact be indifferent between *A* and *B* for themselves or a loved one. Bearing in mind that during the time that one's life was below the zero level one would be better off dead, and that in *A*, as one's life progressed, one would experience increasingly long and increasingly worse periods of such horrible existence, I believe that most people would regard life *B* as *better* than *A*, all things considered, notwithstanding the fact that there is the same total amount of utility, or well-being, within each life. This is because, as I have argued, people care about *more* than how *much* utility or well-being they have in their lives; they also care about how that utility or well-being is *distributed* within their lives.

The judgment that *B* would be a better life than *A* can be seen as reflecting a version of the Disperse Additional Burdens View for a single life. To see this, imagine that one is currently facing the prospect of a life *C*, where one would be at *A*'s higher level for the duration of one's life. One is then told that one faces a *significant* amount of total burden, but that one can choose how that burden will be dispersed throughout one's life. It can be dispersed evenly, so that each of the moments of one's life is *slightly* worse, resulting in one's living life *B*; or one can choose an uneven distribution of the burden, so that most of the moments of one's lengthy life will remain unaffected, but there will be increasingly long, and worse, periods where one's life will be worth not living, resulting in one's living life *A*. Here, I think a version of the Disperse Additional Burdens View applied within a life would support *B* over *A*, and, as indicated, I think many people would choose in accordance with such a principle.[39]

Let me conclude this section by observing that J. Ross's Principle (discussed in section 2.4) would be relevant to many of this section's cases. For example, consider the question of whether the shape of a life is relevant to its overall goodness. As we have discussed, faced with a choice between an "ascending" life (10, 30, 50, 70, and 90) or a "descending" life (90, 70, 50, 30, and

---

[39] This is not to deny that other elements might also influence people's choice of *B* over *A*. Also, to repeat the point of note 27, I am not committed to the view that if one thinks it would be reasonable to follow a Disperse Additional Burdens View for some cases, one is committed to following such a view in all cases to which it could be applied. This may or may not be the case.

10) simple additive aggregationists will regard them as equally good, while those who believe that the "shape" of a life matters, and, in particular, that it is better for someone if her life gets progressively better than if her life get progressively worse, will regard the first life as much better than the second. Given this, someone who had credence in both views, and who actually faced a choice between the two lives, would have powerful reason to choose the first life over the second, in accordance with the first clause of J. Ross's Principle. That is, she would have good reason to choose *as if* the "shape of life matters" view was true, even if in fact she had *greater* credence in the simple additive-aggregationist view, since in such a case she would have everything to gain and nothing to lose by choosing in such a manner.[40] Similarly, in accordance with the second clause of J. Ross's Principle, it would often be rational to choose between two alternative lives that were not equally good as if the "shape of life matters" view was true, as long as one had some significant credence in that view. This would typically be so when one life was judged *significantly* better than the other by the "shape of life matters" view, and only slightly worse by the simple additive-aggregationist view.

Similarly, consider two lives where one is equivalent or only slightly worse than the other in terms of the simple additive-aggregationist view, but vastly better in terms of the personal analogue of the Disperse Additional Burdens View—for example, the previously discussed case where one life involved living at the exceptionally high level of 91 for 100 years, while the second involved living at a slightly higher exceptionally high level of 93 for 99 years, but at the cost of living one year at −90, a level of exceptionally bad suffering well below the level at which life is worth living. Here, again, there would be powerful reason to choose between such lives in accordance with J. Ross's Principle, as long as one gave some credence to both of the noted views for assessing such lives. That is, confronted with the choice between two such lives, there would be powerful reason to choose as if the personal analogue of the Disperse Additional Burdens View were true, even if one gave greater credence to the simple additive-aggregationist view. After all, in such a case, what one stands to "gain" by following the simple additive-aggregationist view, if it is true, is insignificant in comparison with what one stands to lose by following it, if it is false; while the exact opposite is the case with respect to the personal analogue of the Disperse Additional Burdens View.

---

[40] This assumes that there isn't another principle that one also has credence in that would be relevant to such comparisons and that would make another choice equally or more rational. For example, if one had equal or greater credence in the view that, other things equal, a "descending" life was actually *better* than an "ascending" life that would change my result here. But I don't believe that many people do have equal or greater credence in the view that values a "descending" life over an "ascending" life—in fact I know of no one who actually holds such a position—whereas many people do have substantial credence in the opposite view. A similar qualification is relevant for each of the examples I discuss.

Lastly, consider a version of the Single Life Repugnant Conclusion, where the incredibly long-lasting oyster-like life would only be equal to or slightly better than the million-year life of extraordinary brilliance in terms of an additive-aggregationist approach, while it would be vastly worse in terms of an anti-additive-aggregationist approach; or the choice between *A* and *B* in diagram 4.3.A, where the two lives would be equally good in terms of an additive-aggregationist approach, while *A* would be much worse than *B* in terms of an anti-additive-aggregationist approach. Here, again, as long as we grant some credence of any significance to the anti-additive-aggregationist approach, J. Ross's Principle gives us powerful reason to choose between such lives as if that position were true, even if (contrary to fact for most of us!), we give greater credence to the additive-aggregationist approach for such comparisons.

As in section 2.4, it is worth emphasizing that J. Ross's Principle is *neutral* between the various theories and principles I have been discussing. There will be many cases where J. Ross's Principle gives us no reason to follow anti-additive-aggregationist reasoning rather than additive-aggregationist reasoning, and there will be some cases where it will give us reason to follow additive-aggregationist reasoning rather than anti-additive-aggregationist reasoning. Still, it is important to remember that in addition to the powerful considerations I have offered to accept various anti-additive-aggregationist positions,[41] it would often be rational to *follow* such positions *even if* one weren't convinced that they were correct. In some cases, where clause *1* of J. Ross's Principle comes into play, one will have something to gain and *nothing* to lose, if one follows this chapter's anti-additive-aggregationist views. And in other cases, where clause *2* of J. Ross's Principle comes into play, it will often be better and more rational to follow such principles, since, at worst, doing so will only involve taking a large chance of going slightly wrong, while not doing so will involve taking a small chance of going terribly wrong.

*****

This chapter argues that we should reject Sidwick's conception of individual self-interest. In particular, it argues that anti-additive-aggregationist principles of the sort presented in chapters 2 and 3 apply within lives, as well as between lives. Thus, we saw that even for ranking alternatives regarding a single life, in some cases the reasoning underlying the Disperse Additional Burdens View applies, and in some cases reasoning analogous to the Second Standard View, which I called the Fourth Standard View, applies.

---

[41] At least as relevant for comparing the kinds of alternatives discussed in this chapter.

Unfortunately, because of the important role played by the notions of compensation and the separateness of individuals in contemporary thought, the inadequacy of additive aggregation for assessing lives has not, perhaps, been as widely recognized as it has for assessing outcomes. Nevertheless, I suspect that most people, on reflection, will regard this chapter's results as unsurprising. But, "unsurprising" or not, such results are highly controversial. As we will see in the next chapter, combined with other positions that most people accept, they lead to grave worries similar to those raised in chapters 2 and 3. But this time, the worries concern trade-offs within a life, as opposed to trade-offs between lives.

5

Aggregation and Problems about Trade-offs within Lives

SINGLE-PERSON SPECTRUM ARGUMENTS

In chapter 4, I argued that we should reject Sidgwick's conception of individual self-interest because it assumes a simple additive-aggregationist approach for assessing the overall value of a life. Specifically, I argued that in some cases anti-additive aggregationist principles are applicable within lives, as well as between lives, including analogues of chapter 2's Second Standard View and chapter 3's Disperse Additional Burdens View. However, as should be evident, like the anti-additive aggregationist principles of chapters 2 and 3, chapter 4's analogues of those principles are *incomplete*. They are only applicable to, and generate rankings for, *certain* cases. In other cases, they are silent, and we must rely on other principles to rank alternative lives. However, as we will see, often the principles that are appropriate for ranking alternative lives generate judgments that are incompatible with the judgments generated by the anti-additive-aggregationist principles, if "all-things-considered better than" (in my wide reason-implying sense) is a transitive relation. Thus, in this chapter we will see that, as with rankings involving different lives, the relevance of different principles for ranking individual lives raises deep problems about aggregation and trade-offs within lives.

5.1 The Third Standard View

In chapter 2, I argued that most people accept:

> *The First Standard View (FSV)—Trade-offs between Quality and Number Are Sometimes Desirable*: In general, an outcome where a larger number

of people have a lower-quality benefit is better than an outcome where a smaller number of people have a higher-quality benefit, *if* the number receiving the lower-quality benefit is "sufficiently" greater than the number receiving the higher-quality benefit, and *if* the differences in the initial situations of the people benefited and the degrees to which they are benefited are not "too" great.

I also noted in chapter 4 that most people accept a similar view within lives, where within lives the trade-offs can be put, more aptly, in terms of quality versus duration. Specifically, I claimed that most people accept:

The Third Standard View (TSV)—Trade-offs between Quality and Duration Are Sometimes Desirable: In general, it is better for an individual to receive a lower-quality benefit for a longer period of time than a higher-quality benefit for a shorter period of time, *if* the difference in the quality of the benefits and its impact on the person's life are not "too" great, and *if* the duration of the lower-quality benefit would be "sufficiently" longer than the duration of higher-quality benefit.

One could give countless examples where the Third Standard View seems plausible. Given the relation I have previously noted between benefits and burdens, let me give several examples of this put in terms of benefits, and several put in terms of burdens. Here are three examples put in terms of benefits.

First, I must choose between two pleasurable experiences, a ten-minute back and neck massage followed by ten minutes of "nothing," or a twenty-minute back massage. Assuming that neither has any long-term effects, that a back and neck massage feels better than a back massage alone, but that the latter is *almost* as good as the former, the second choice seems clearly better than the first. Second, in exchange for a single week's work, I can be paid $100 for one week or, for the same single week's work, I can be paid $90 dollars for each of two weeks; but, let us suppose, I can't save my pay from week to week. Assuming that the difference in the quality of the benefits that I can buy with $90 dollars is not *too* much less than what I could buy with $100 dollars, the second option seems clearly better than the first. Surely it is better to have a slightly lower-quality benefit for *twice* as long, than a slightly higher-quality benefit for *half* as long. Third, suppose I could live a rich and rewarding life for twenty-five years, followed by seventy-five years of suspended animation, or a life that was *almost* as rich and rewarding for fifty years, followed by fifty years of suspended animation. Assuming the difference in the overall quality of the conscious life was not "too" great, the second seems better than the first. Of course, people will have different views about when the differences in conscious lives would be "too" great. Some would happily forgo a larger house, or fancier cars, for twice as many years of conscious life. Others would make trade-offs in their job satisfaction, health, or relationships. But virtually all would agree that *some* loss in the quality of one's conscious life, even in terms of things that matter, would be worth *sufficient* gain in the duration of one's conscious life, as long as the difference in quality between the two conscious lives was not *too* great.[1]

Consider the last example more closely. I suspect that even those who most love their jobs would readily accept a bit less satisfying one for an extra twenty-five years of pretty good life! And as much as people rightly value robust health, would it not be worth ongoing allergies, some loss of hearing, or perhaps a limp, for an extra twenty-five years of pretty good life? Likewise, as important as it is to have wonderful relationships with one's friends and family, mightn't it be worth a *few* less satisfying relationships—or even fewer friends or family members!—for an extra *twenty-five years* of pretty good life? Not sure? Make it an extra *fifty* years of life, or *seventy-five*! And suppose it isn't your *best* friend, or a member of your *immediate* family, but just a pretty good friend, and maybe a cousin, aunt, or uncle that you like, but don't see *all* that much.

Does this sound crass or cold-blooded? Perhaps it is, but it reflects an important truth. There are many sources of value in life, and as long as the quality of one's life remains positive, some losses in quality that are not "too" big can be more than made up for, overall, by *sufficient* gains in the duration of one's life.

The preceding examples range from the trivial (trade-offs involving different massages for less than an hour) to the substantial (trade-offs involving important components of well-being and significant differences in the length of one's conscious life). Together, they help indicate the robustness of the Third Standard View. In a wide range of cases involving alternatives for individuals, it would be better to receive a lesser benefit for a longer duration, than a greater benefit for a shorter duration, *if* the longer duration is "sufficiently" longer, and *if* the difference in the quality of the benefits is not "too" great.

Next, let me note three examples put in terms of burdens. Borrowing from alternatives presented in chapter 2, I can be brief. Let us suppose a given case of warts is worse than a given case of acne, but not "too" much so. Then, other

---

[1] Some people may wonder what role the years of suspended animation play in my argument. Basically, it is to forestall a possible objection that might otherwise arise, by ensuring that we can make a meaningful comparison between the two lives for each period where there is consciousness in one of the lives. In particular, some people who might balk at thinking that one could make a meaningful comparison between the second life and the first, during the second twenty-five-year period of that person's conscious life *if* the first person would *no longer exist* during that time period, would readily grant that it is better to have a positive state of consciousness for a twenty-five-year period than to be in a state of suspended animation during that time. As for why I add the "extra" fifty years of suspended animation in each life, this is in anticipation of some comparisons to be considered in the following paragraph.

things equal, most people would prefer *n* weeks of acne to *n* weeks of warts, but they'd rather suffer a given duration of warts than a "sufficiently" longer duration of acne. How much longer the duration of acne would have to be would, of course, depend on the details of the alternatives. This need not concern us here. The important point is simply that if the negative impact of the acne was close "enough" to that of the warts, the warts would be better than the acne, if the acne lasted two, or three, or five times as long. Moreover, this would be true whether the bouts of skin ailments were measured in months, years, or decades. Thus, in general, it would be better to suffer warts for a month, year, or decade, than acne for two (or three, or five) months, years, or decades, respectively.

Similar claims would hold for trade-offs between broken arms and broken legs, or bouts of psychosis versus bouts of depression. Even if, other things equal, a broken arm is worse than a broken leg, or psychosis is worse than depression, duration involving trade-offs between such illnesses makes a difference. Thus, while final judgments would, of course, depend on the details of the cases, in general, it would be better to suffer a broken arm for a month, a year, or a decade, than a broken leg for two (three, or five) months, years, or decades, respectively. Similarly, for trade-offs between psychosis and depression.

As with the examples put in terms of benefits, the preceding examples range from the trivial (trade-offs involving warts versus acne) to the substantial (trade-offs involving psychosis versus depression). They also range over different lengths of time, from months, to years, to decades. Thus, applying the Third Standard View to cases put in terms of burdens, for a wide range of cases it would be better for someone to receive a greater burden for a shorter duration, than a lesser burden for a longer duration, *if* the longer duration is "sufficiently" longer, and *if* the difference in the quality of the burdens is not "too" great.

5.2 Another Worry about Consistency

In section 2.5, we illustrated an inconsistency between the First Standard View, the Second Standard View, a plausible assumption, and the transitivity of the "all-things-considered better than" relation (in my wide reason-implying sense). As should be evident, similar worries arise about consistency for the Third Standard View, chapter 4's Fourth Standard View, a very plausible assumption, and the transitivity of the "all-things-considered better than" relation (in my wide reason-implying sense). This should not be surprising. Problems of consistency can arise for comparing alternatives involving a single life *for the very same reason* that they can arise for comparing alternatives involving different lives, namely, that for *some* such comparisons trade-offs between quality and duration seem appropriate, but for *others* they do not. Thus, in some cases one employs an additive-aggregationist approach when comparing alternatives, but in others one does not.

Let us spell out the purported inconsistency putting the case in terms of benefits, and then briefly note how the same point might have been put in terms of burdens.

To start, let me explicate the plausible assumption that underlies the purported inconsistency. It should look familiar, as it is analogous to the assumption underlying section 2.5's purported inconsistency. The assumption involves two elements. The first is just that there is, or at least could be, a spectrum of alternatives involving benefits that might accrue to an individual, such that at one end of the spectrum the alternative would involve the individual receiving a great benefit for a "sufficiently" long period of time, while at the other end the alternative would involve the individual receiving a minor benefit for a much longer period of time. The second is just that one could move from one end of the spectrum to the other in a finite series of small steps, such that the Third Standard View would apply to all pairwise comparisons involving alternatives that were "near" each other on the spectrum, while the Fourth Standard View would apply to all pairwise comparisons involving alternatives that were at opposite ends of the spectrum. Naturally, alternatives that were "near" each other on the spectrum might only be one small step, or perhaps a few small steps, apart, while alternatives at opposite ends of the spectrum would be more than a few small steps, and perhaps, in fact, a great many small steps, apart.

So, for example, one might set a scale ranging from 1, representing the quality of an oyster-like life that is barely worth living, to 1,000, representing the quality of life of the highest form of human existence. Then, one might believe that for differences in quality of life of, say, 3 or less, the Third Standard View would apply, while for differences in quality of life of, say, 900 or more the Fourth Standard View would apply. Intuitively, then, the idea is that the difference in the quality of lives between, say, 779 and 776, or 238 and 235, or 27 and 24, is "sufficiently" small that, in accordance with the Third Standard View, it would be better in a life that would last z years total, to live the slightly lower-quality life for n years, followed by $z - n$ years of suspended animation, rather than to live the slightly higher-quality of life for m years followed by $z - m$ years of suspended animation, *as long as n* is "sufficiently" greater than m, so that one's positive and nearly as good quality of life lasts for a "sufficiently" longer duration in the former alternative than in the latter alternative. But, intuitively, the difference in the quality of lives between, say, 950 and 50 is *so* significant that, in accordance with the Fourth Standard View, no matter how long one lived, say z years, it would be better to live a life of level 950 for a significant period of time, say 100 years, followed by $z - 100$ years of suspended animation, than to live all z years of one's life at level 50. But, of course, for familiar reasons, these two sets of views are incompatible with the transitivity of the "all-things-considered better than" relation, as the first view entails the rejection of the second *if* the "all-things-considered better than" relation (in my wide reason-implying sense) is transitive.[2]

It follows that we must reject at least one of the following positions: the Third Standard View, the Fourth Standard View, the transitivity of the "all-things-considered better than" relation (in my wide reason-implying sense), or the plausible assumption that there *could be* a spectrum of lives ranging from one involving the highest form of human existence for a significant number of years (followed by many years of suspended animation) to one involving an oyster-like quality that persisted for many years, such that the Third Standard View would apply to lives that were near each other on the spectrum, while the Fourth Standard View would apply to lives at opposite ends of the spectrum. Giving up any of these views will not be easy.

Naturally, this same point could have been put in terms of burdens, as follows. First, one observes that there is, or a least could be, a spectrum of alternatives involving burdens that might accrue to an individual, such that at one end of the spectrum the alternative would involve the individual receiving a great burden for a "sufficiently" long period of time, while at the other end the alternative would involve the individual receiving a minor burden for a much longer period of time. Second, one notes that one could move from one end of the spectrum to the other in a finite series of small steps, such that the Third Standard View would apply to all pairwise comparisons involving alternatives that were "near" each other on the spectrum, while the Fourth Standard View would apply to all pairwise comparisons involving alternatives that were at opposite ends of the spectrum. Finally, one notes that the judgments generated by the Third Standard View are incompatible with those generated by the Fourth Standard View if "all-things-considered better than" (in my wide reason-implying sense) is a transitive relation. Hence, one of the inconsistent positions must go. But here, as elsewhere, it is by no means evident which position(s) should be given up.

5.3 A Powerful Example: From Torture to Mosquito Bites

The discussion in section 5.2 is fairly abstract. This is particularly true of the discussion put in terms of burdens, where I merely presented a schema for

---

[2] On the role that the varying periods of suspended animation play in this argument see note 1. I am grateful to Shelly Kagan for pointing out a small error in my original formulation of this argument and how to easily correct it.

recognizing the inconsistency of our views. To aid in the exploration of this topic, let us consider in detail a powerful, more concrete example illustrating the kind of inconsistency identified in section 5.2.

The example I shall present is a variation of an example sent to me by Stuart Rachels. I have altered the details of Rachels's example in ways he objects to, and the discussion of it is my own. So, I shall refer to the following example as my own, and Rachels deserves no blame for it. Still, if the reader finds the following compelling, Rachels deserves the credit.

Rachels offered his example as a counterexample to the transitivity of the betterness relation, and in an earlier paper of mine I followed him in this regard.[3] Indeed, at the time, I thought Rachels's argument was the simplest, most powerful counterexample to the transitivity of the betterness relation that had yet been offered. And, I might add, I still think that's true to this day! But my aim here is not to argue for the intransitivity of the betterness relation, but rather to illustrate the incompatibility of four highly plausible views.

I begin with a rough statement of the four views.

> *View One*: For any unpleasant or "negative" experience, no matter what the intensity and duration of that experience, it would be better to have that experience than one that was only a "little" less intense but twice (or three or five times) as long.
>
> *View Two*: There is, or could be, a spectrum of unpleasant or "negative" experiences ranging in intensity, for example, from extreme forms of torture to the mild discomfort of a mosquito bite, such that one could move from the harsh end of the spectrum to the mild end in a finite series of steps, where each step would involve the transformation from one negative experience to another that was only a "little" less intense than the previous one.
>
> *View Three*: The mild discomfort of a mosquito bite would be better than two years of excruciating torture, no matter how long one lived and no matter how long the discomfort of a mosquito bite persisted.
>
> *View Four*: "All-things-considered better than" is a transitive relation. So, for any three outcomes, *A*, *B*, and *C*, which involve unpleasant experiences of varying intensities and durations, if, all things considered, *A* is better than *B*, and *B* is better than *C*, then *A* is better than *C*.

To avoid unnecessary complications, let me emphasize that the argument I am presenting does *not* turn on differences in intensity that are imperceptible, or on *least barely noticeable* differences. Specifically, I take it that one

---

[3] See my "A Continuum Argument for Intransitivity," *Philosophy and Public Affairs* 25 (1996): 175–210.

negative experience could count as only a "little" less intense than another, in the sense required by Views One and Two, even if, *at least when attended to*, it were more than "barely noticeably" less intense. So, while the logic of my argument does not require it, throughout this discussion when I speak of one negative experience as being only a "little" less intense than another, I shall assume that it is nevertheless true that the one is noticeably, and more than *barely* noticeably, less intense than the other.

Let me also note that I am supposing that the intensity of a pain reflects how it feels to us, phenomenologically, and that one could construct a scale of pain intensities such that someone could reasonably place any two pains on such a scale reflecting with a fair degree of accuracy how intense they were, and enabling us to plausibly say, in most cases at least, which of two qualitatively distinct pains was less intense, and whether it was less intense by a lot or only a little. In addition, the notion of intensity I am dealing with may also come apart from corresponding judgments of how good or bad it would be to experience a pain of a given intensity for a certain duration of time. This is important for reasons that will become clearer later, if they are not clear already.[4]

As should be apparent, View One reflects the Third Standard View, and View Three reflects the Fourth Standard View. Most people find both views intuitively compelling. Indeed, I have presented variations of the example to many hundreds of people in countless audiences over the years, and the *overwhelming*

---

[4] Derek Parfit has a notion of pain intensity according to which we determine the intensity of pains in part by asking about the trade-offs that we would make between different pains for different durations (conveyed to me in discussion). So, for Parfit, if someone would be indifferent between experiencing pain X for a week and pain Y for two weeks, this reveals that pain X is twice as intense, and twice as bad, as pain Y. I have in mind the possibility of arriving at an independent scale of pain intensity that does not require trade-offs of the sort Parfit has in mind.

So, to consider a crude analogy, we have an independent way of determining the weight of tomatoes, and employing it to determine, say, that one tomato is only half as heavy as another. Still, I might prefer to eat two five-ounce tomatoes over two days rather than one ten-ounce tomato on one day, or to be pelted with three five-ounce tomatoes rather than one ten-ounce tomato! As I say, the analogy is crude, but it conveys the sort of distinction I want to allow for. On my conception of pain intensity, it could make perfect sense to claim that pain X is only twice as intense as pain Y, yet to think it would be better to experience pain Y for three weeks rather than pain X for one week. It could also make sense to be indifferent between one week of pain X and two weeks of pain Y, yet to have a clear preference for four years of pain Y over two years of pain X. On Parfit's conception of pain intensity such claims are confused and mistaken. For Parfit, if it would be better to experience pain Y for three weeks rather than pain X for one week, then pain Y must be less than a third as intense as pain X; and likewise, if one should be indifferent between one week of pain X and two weeks of pain Y, then pain X is twice as intense as pain Y, and one should also be indifferent between four years of pain Y and two years of pain X.

I don't want to deny that there can be a conception of pain intensity of the sort Parfit has in mind, which intimately links pain intensity with the badness of having that pain for different durations of time; but his is not the only viable conception of pain intensity, and it is not the one I am working with in this book. Still, on the relations between quantity, quality, duration, and number, which perhaps lend some support to the kind of approach Parfit favors, see appendix B.

majority have accepted both Views One and Three. In fact, while I suspect that some people might have doubts about the general formulations of the Third and Fourth Standard Views, and hence might wonder about the full scope of those views, almost everyone regards Views One and Three as "obvious," "uncontroversial," or "undeniably true." View Two reflects the plausible assumption regarding a spectrum of burdens presented in section 5.2. It seems to assert a straightforward (modal) fact. View Four is a position widely assumed. Unfortunately, however, Views One, Two, and Three are incompatible with View Four.

The argument for this is straightforward. To see this, we will consider a large series of alternative lives, A_1 through A_{n+1}, each of which is lengthy—perhaps, indeed, *very* lengthy—and each of which includes, as a kind of steady background condition of low-level annoyance, fifteen mosquito bites per month. First, compare two lives, A_1 and A_2, and suppose that A_1 and A_2 are similar, except that A_1 contains two years of excruciating torture, and A_2 contains four years of torture whose intensity is almost, but not quite, as bad as A_1's. Think of the intensity of A_2's pain as clearly and noticeably less bad than A_1's, yet of roughly the same order of magnitude, so that it would be accurate to characterize A_2's pain as only a "little" less intense than A_1's. In accordance with View One, most would regard A_1 as clearly better than A_2, meaning that it would be better to live life A_1 than to live life A_2. Next, compare A_2 with A_3, where A_3 stands to A_2 as A_2 stands to A_1. Given the choice between two long lives which are otherwise similar, except that one contains four years of very intense pain, and one contains eight years of pain whose intensity is almost, but not quite, as bad, most would judge the former as clearly better than the latter. That is, most would judge A_2 better than A_3, in virtue of the same considerations that led them to judge A_1 better than A_2. Iterations of this reasoning imply that A_3 would be better than A_4, A_4 better than A_5, A_5 better than A_6, and so on, with the intensity of the unpleasant experiences slowly, but steadily, decreasing in each successive life. *Eventually*, in accordance with View Two, one would be comparing two alternatives, say, A_n and A_{n+1}, such that in addition to the fifteen mosquito bites per month present in each outcome, A_n involved a very minor discomfort for a *very* long time, while A_{n+1} involved a mild discomfort that was almost, though not quite, as unpleasant as A_n's, but that lasted twice (or three or five times) as long. (Recall that each life being compared is, perhaps, *very* lengthy.) Finally, we may assume that the extra mild discomfort that obtains in A_{n+1} is just *one extra* mosquito bite per month, so that for the duration of that discomfort A_{n+1} is bearing sixteen mosquito bites per month rather than the "usual" fifteen.[5]

---

[5] One might wonder why I have the background condition of fifteen mosquito bites per month. Basically, this is to avoid certain psychological distortions that might otherwise arise in thinking about this case. For example, due to the well-known psychological phenomenon of *salience*, people naturally tend to take more notice of, and hence give more consideration to, something which "sticks out" from

Summing up, View Two implies that there could be a gradual and finite spectrum of equally lengthy lives, from A_1 to A_{n+1}, such that A_1 contained two years of excruciating torture, together with a lifetime of fifteen mosquito bites per month, A_{n+1} contained *many* years of the mild discomfort of one extra mosquito per month, in addition to the "standard" fifteen mosquito bites per month, and each spectrum member after A_1 contained an unpleasant or "negative" experience that was a "little" less intense than its predecessor's but lasted

---

its surroundings—as it might if it is the *only* thing of its kind present. Thus, we tend to notice and attach much more significance to the presence of someone who is brunette, tall, or nonwhite in a room where everyone else is blond, short, or white, respectively, than we do to the presence of such a person in a room filled with people of different hair colors, heights, or races. Similarly, people often attach much more weight to the difference between zero and one than they do to the difference between any other two numbers, and in some contexts it may be perfectly plausible to do so. For example, there may be good reason to pay an exorbitant amount to acquire the *only* extant copy of an important historical document, but no reason to pay anywhere near that amount for the very same document, if there are fifteen other copies. Likewise, perhaps it is reasonable to pay virtually anything to increase one's chances of living from 0 percent to 1 percent, but not reasonable to pay anywhere near that same amount to increase one's chances of living from 15 percent to 16 percent. But given this, there may be a natural tendency to attach much more importance to the difference between zero instances of something and one instance of something *even in contexts where it is a mistake to do so*. For reasons of this sort, I think it is safer to consider the case that I have given, where we are ultimately choosing between sixteen or fifteen mosquito bites per month, rather than the simpler case I might have given, where we would be choosing between one mosquito bite per month and none.

Also, in my example, the difference between sixteen or fifteen mosquito bites per month over the course of a very long life is the difference between a life with *lots and lots* of mosquito bites or a life with fewer, but still *lots and lots* of mosquito bites, whereas the difference between one or zero mosquito bites per month over the course of a very long life is the difference between a life with *lots and lots* of mosquito bites or a life with *no* mosquito bites *ever*. Although the difference in the *total* number of mosquito bites between the two lives would be exactly the same given either scenario, some people may, understandably, react very differently to the two scenarios. But it is an interesting question as to whether people should, in fact, react very differently to the two scenarios, and one reason to think that they shouldn't is if one bears in mind that most people will experience lots and lots of small annoyances of *many* different kinds over the course of their lives, of which mosquito bites are just one type. So, even in the one or zero scenario, the choice isn't *actually* between a life filled with lots and lots of small annoyances and one that is totally free of small annoyances, it is *still* just a choice between a life filled with lots and lots of small annoyances and one filled with fewer, but still lots and lots of small annoyances, none of which, as it happens, are mosquito bites.

There are, then, various reasons to focus on the scenario I have given, where there is a steady background condition of fifteen mosquito bites no matter what, rather than to consider the simpler scenario where one's choice would be between one and zero mosquito bites. My example is a fair one, serves my purposes, and is less prone to misleading interpretations and mistaken judgments.

Having said all this, I'll note that *my* reaction to the example would not, in fact, be affected by considering the simpler scenario of one versus zero mosquito bites, and I think the same is true for most people. But it isn't important for my argument that everyone share the same judgment about both scenarios. Nor is it important for my argument that the two scenarios *should* be judged the same. If a justification could be given for judging the sixteen versus fifteen scenario differently than the one versus zero scenario, that wouldn't affect my argument one bit. All I need for my argument is that most people would make the considered judgments I attribute to them in the case as I have presented it. And there can be little doubt that that is the case.

For an important discussion of many of the points I have raised here, in the context of our intuitions about our obligations to the needy, see Peter Unger's *Living High and Letting Die: Our Illusion of Innocence* (New York: Oxford University Press, 1996). (cont.)

twice (or three or five times) as long. View One implies that for each pair of adjacent members of the spectrum the first is better than the second. Thus, A_1 is better than A_2, A_2 is better than A_3,...A_{n-1} is better than A_n, and A_n is better than A_{n+1}.

Given the foregoing, View Four implies that A_1 is better than A_{n+1}. But if View Three is right, A_1 is *not* better than A_{n+1}. To the contrary, in accordance with View Three, the real but mild discomfort of one extra mosquito bite per month would be better than two years of excruciating torture, no matter how long one lived, and no matter how long the discomfort of one extra mosquito bite per month persisted.

This completes my example. I believe it raises serious questions about the consistency of our views about aggregation *even within a life*. More important, I believe that the questions it raises are deeply problematic as I think it is highly implausible to deny *any* of the four views underlying the example. More accurately, even if there are reasons to question one or more of the Views *as stated*, and as we shall see later there may be, I think *some* version of this example will be compelling. And I am confident that I am not alone in thinking this. After discussing versions of this example with literally thousands of people over the years, it is apparent that almost everyone, at least initially, accepts some versions of Views One through Four that are incompatible.

5.4 Refining Views One through Four and Clarifying the Example

Before going on, it should be emphasized that, as indicated, I was only offering a *rough* characterization of Views One through Four. Likewise, as presented, the example is somewhat underdescribed, leaving it open to various uncharitable interpretations and objections. Correspondingly, I recognize that both the Views and the example may need to be tightened up and revised in various ways to avoid objections. In most cases, I think it is evident how the Views could be revised and the example spelled out to avoid possible objections, and rather than present all the necessary nuanced qualifications I shall simply trust the reader to recognize the refinements that might be in order. Still, it might be useful to give a few samples of what I have in mind, to

---

Finally, one might wonder if there is something worrisome about my example because it seemingly moves from a "continuous" negative experience of torture to an "intermittent" negative experience of a mosquito bite that lasts for only a couple of days each month. But there is no cause for concern here. First, the negative experience of torture may itself be "intermittent"; perhaps one would be subject to the torture for "only" an hour at a time every two hours around the clock. Second, I see no objection to the example even if it did gradually move from a continuous negative experience to an intermittent one. There could be a spectrum of high-intensity, continuous negative experiences to low-intensity, intermittent negative experiences, just as there could be a spectrum from a motor running at high speed continuously to its running at a low speed intermittently.

prevent unnecessary misunderstandings or premature rejection of my argument, as well as to indicate lines of refinement that are available.

Someone might assume that a life containing extreme torture is not worth living, while a life that is merely very painful is. Similarly, someone might claim that the most extreme forms of torture will result in a disintegration of the self—perhaps in the form of a psychotic breakdown—and that a tortured life with a nonintegrated self would be worse than a merely very painful life with an integrated self. On either of these views one might claim that long before one reaches A_{n+1} one will reach a point, say between A_{27} and A_{28}, where the slight decrease in intensity of pain transforms the case from one involving extreme torture, where one's life is not worth living, to one "merely" involving great pain, where one's life is worth living, or from one involving a tortured nonintegrated self to one involving a painful integrated self. Correspondingly, one might reject the judgment that A_{27} is better than A_{28}. This, in turn, might appear to undermine View One and allow one to argue that the transitivity of the "all-things-considered better than" relation (in my wide reason-implying sense) would only entail that A_1 is better than A_{27}, not that A_1 is better than A_{28}. Correspondingly, on either of the views in question one might be able to avoid the highly implausible claim that given the transitivity of the "all-things-considered better than" relation, A_1, the life involving two years of torture, is better than A_{n+1}, the life involving one extra mosquito bite per month, for many months.

I think one might challenge either of the positions in question. But I'm inclined to grant them. Even so, however, I don't think they undermine the example. More specifically, such positions suggest that View One may be limited in scope, and need to be revised accordingly; but the example can be spelled out in such a way that the problems still arise with the properly revised version of View One. Let me explain.

Both positions imply that there can be *some* abrupt transition points between one pain and another that is only a "little" less intense, where the slight difference in pain levels could, as it were, be like the proverbial straw that broke the camel's back, making the difference, literally, between whether the life is worth living or not, or whether the life was integrated or not. If we grant this, we should also grant that View One fails for such transition points. Clearly, it would *not* be better to have a more intense pain for a given duration, than a "little" less intense pain for two (or three, or five) times as long, if the latter life was worth living but the former life was not. And it is certainly arguable that an integrated life has value that is lacking in a nonintegrated life, so that a very painful integrated life might be better than a tortured nonintegrated life, even if the pain in the former lasted much longer than the torture in the latter. Still, this limitation of View One's scope is not especially restrictive. Even if we agree that View One does not apply to the transition points in question, we may continue to find it compelling for comparing relevant alternatives on each side of the dividing lines between the different kinds of lives. Correspondingly, my example might be spelled out in such a way that *all* of the lives being compared, from A_1 to A_{n+1}, are understood to be on the *same* side of each dividing line. Thus, all of the lives might be assumed to be integrated or not (presumably, lives can be nonintegrated for reasons not involving torture), and likewise all of the lives might be assumed to be worth living or not.

In my example, I was assuming that all of the lives were, on the whole, worth living. This can be a plausible assumption. For example, I believe that most survivors of the Nazi concentration camps probably had lives that were, on the whole, worth living, even if the portion of their lives when they were in the concentration camps may not have been. Similarly, lives that are sufficiently good for a sufficiently long period of time will, on the whole, be worth living, even if there are significant periods of those lives which are not themselves worth living, and I was assuming that such would be the case for each of the alternative lives in my example. Likewise, in my example I was assuming that A_1 involved two years of the most excruciating torture humanly endurable, *compatible with an integrated self*. So, as the example is to be understood, throughout the period in which someone would be enduring torture or significant pain, he would retain his sense of self, his awareness that the great pain he was experiencing was happening to *him*, his desperate hope that the torture would stop and that he would be returned to a life of normalcy, and so on. I conclude that while the scope of View One may need to be restricted in light of the positions noted earlier, those positions aren't relevant to my example as I intend it to be interpreted. That is, I submit that my example can be plausibly fleshed out such that View One *is* highly plausible for comparing alternatives A_1 through A_{n+1}. Our problems remain.

An opponent might persist. Even if one grants that each of the lives of my spectrum may be worth living *on the whole*, the crucial question is whether there might be some step from an intense pain to one which is only a little less intense, which, though small, nevertheless involves the move from a pain which is unbearable to one which is bearable. If there is, one might argue, then View One should be rejected for that transition point as well. So, for example, if the pain involved in life A_{27} was literally unbearable, while the pain involved in life A_{28} was, though only a little less intense, bearable, even if only barely so, it might seem that, contrary to View One, A_{28} would be better than A_{27}, as it would be better to have to suffer the bearable pain for two (or three or five) times as long as one would otherwise have to suffer the unbearable pain. In this case, the transitivity of the "all-things-considered better than" relation might yield the claim that A_1 was better than A_{27}, and that A_{28} was better than A_{n+1}, but since A_{27} would *not* be better than A_{28}, it would *not* imply the unpalatable conclusion that A_1, a life containing two years of intense torture, would be better than A_{n+1}, a life containing one extra mosquito bite per month for many years.

The preceding is a particular instance of a general line of argument that is powerfully seductive. Though I've introduced it here, it is sufficiently important to warrant a separate, detailed response. I believe the argument is mistaken and should be rejected. I will argue for this in section 9.1.

Here are some other ways one might attempt to resist the inconsistency I have argued for. One might assume that in A_1 the two years of torture takes place at the end of a long life, while in A_2 the four years takes place at the beginning. One might then reject View One, arguing that A_2 would be better than A_1, since it would enable one to avoid a lifetime of dreaded anticipation and since it is more tragic to end one's life in misery than to begin one's life that way. Alternatively, one might assume that year after year after year of an extra mosquito bite per month might eventually have the effect of the infamous "water torture"—where a steady drip of water, over time, ultimately drives one crazy, even though each drop, by itself, would be innocuous. With this assumption, one might deny View Three, arguing that A_1 would, in fact, be better than A_{n+1}. Or, echoing the first lines broached earlier, one might assume that even though there might be only a small decrease in the intensity of a pain, say, between A_{12} and A_{13}, these differences might be correlated with neurological differences that might have tremendously significant consequences. Perhaps, on the "straw that broke the camel's back" analogy suggested earlier, although A_{13}'s pain might be only a little less intense than A_{12}'s, the neurological consequences of the latter might involve permanent psychological scarring—say painful memories and terrifying nightmares for the duration of one's life—while those of the former might not. On such an assumption, of course, one could reject View One, and its implication that A_{12} would be better than A_{13}.

The foregoing illustrates that my example *could* be construed in ways that would render it innocuous. But this does not seriously threaten my argument. Rather, it illustrates that my example and the Views underlying it need to be refined and interpreted carefully, and that, among other things, they depend on appropriate "other things equal" clauses. In my example, I explicitly state that A_1 and A_2 are "similar" except for the small difference in the intensity of their unpleasant experiences, and the length of those experiences. And I claim that A_3 stands to A_2 as A_2 stands to A_1, and imply, more generally, that each alternative A_m is to be regarded as "similar" to A_{m+1}, except insofar as their pains differ in intensity and duration. Correspondingly, I was explicitly intending to rule out scenarios such as those suggested earlier. Similarly, I take it for granted that Views One through Three assume appropriate "other things equal" clauses. *Nobody* would deny that if A_{12} has horrendous consequences that A_{13} lacks, then A_{13} might be better than A_{12} even if it involved a pain that was almost as bad as A_{13}'s, but that lasted two (or three, or five) times as long. View One is offered as plausible *on the assumption* that the alternatives *don't* differ in significant ways *besides* the intensity and duration of the pains in question. Alternatively, one might insist that the example is to be understood so that *whatever* negative experiences obtain in A_m—including whatever negative consequences might ensue from any other negative experiences—A_{m+1} will have comparable negative experiences that are a little less intense but last two (or three, or five) times as long.

So, my example assumes that the timing of the unpleasant experiences will be comparable in each life. It also assumes that there are no unstated side effects, or "extrinsic" bads associated with the alternatives. A slight increase in the intensity of torture *might* lead to a lifetime of sleepless nights and painful memories. But suppose it didn't. Lots of tiny annoyances *could* drive one to permanent distraction, but embedded in a rich and fulfilling life, they needn't. And so on. I suggest, then, that while my example, and Views One through Three, *can* be interpreted, uncharitably, in all sorts of ways that would render my example innocuous, other interpretations are available. Properly spelled out, Views One through Three retain their plausibility, and my example retains its force. The inconsistency of our views is not easily avoided.

Some people acknowledge the general appeal of View One, but suggest that it no longer holds once an unpleasant experience becomes mild enough. Correspondingly, they deny that the transitivity of the "all-things-considered better than" relation implies that A must be better than A_{n+1}, because they deny that A_n is better than A_{n+1}. Frankly, I don't really understand this position. To be sure, a mosquito bite is pretty minor as far as unpleasant experiences go, but it is still annoying to have one. Surely, there is no doubt that, other things equal, it would be better to have fewer mosquito bites than more mosquito bites—better to have one extra mosquito bite per month for one year, a decade, or a hundred years, than to have one extra mosquito bite per month for two (or three, or five) times as long. But then, by the same token, it seems clear that it would be better to have an experience that was noticeably more bothersome than a mosquito bite, as long as it was only a *little* more bothersome (say, for the sake of argument, 10 percent worse, though this suggests a level of phenomenological precision that almost certainly doesn't exist), than to have a mosquito bite that lasted two (or three, or five) times as long.

The assumption underlying the preceding position seems to be that once an unpleasant experience becomes minor enough, its duration no longer matters. As indicated, I see no reason to accept this assumption. Thus, I think View One remains plausible *even at the level of mosquito bites*, and that A_n is, indeed, better than A_{n+1}, as View One implies. But even if one rejects this, a variation of my counterexample is easily constructed. Take the intensity of a negative experience that is *just above* the level where duration no longer matters. Suppose this is the level obtaining in A_p. Then we can rerun my argument from A_1 to A_p. View One will presumably apply to the lives from A_1 to A_p, so A_1 will be better than A_2, A_2 better than A_3,..., and A_{p-1} better than A_p. The transitivity of the "all-things-considered better than" relation would then imply that A_1 must be better than A_p. But I now deny this. If A_p's negative experience is *so* minor that if it were any less bad it wouldn't matter *how long it lasted*, then it is virtually insignificant. Given this, I believe View Three would apply. A_p would be better than A_1. Two years of excruciating torture would be worse than any amount of such virtually insignificant pain.

The preceding suggests that I could limit the scope of View One. I could grant that at the most extreme end of the spectrum of negative experiences, View One would no longer hold. Nevertheless, it seems clear that it would hold for a large enough portion of the spectrum to generate the problem I have highlighted. There will be a range of cases for which our views remain inconsistent.

A similar point might be made to those who have questioned whether View One is plausible for extremely short durations. Thus, for example, it might be claimed that a negative experience that lasted only a nanosecond *wouldn't be* better than a negative experience that was a little less intense, but lasted two (or three, or five) nanoseconds. Here, it might be claimed that it wouldn't matter which negative experience one had. Or it might even be claimed that for extremely negative experiences, like excruciating stabs of intense pain, it would always be better to experience a less intense pain than a more intense pain, as long as both events were extremely short.

I am not persuaded that we should accept the preceding suggestion, but I also don't think it matters. First, the *logic* of the argument I presented would allow View One to be revised so that the less intense negative experience might last *much* longer than the more intense one, even more than five times as long if necessary. And surely an extremely intense stab of pain that lasted only a nanosecond *would* be better than one that was only a *little* less intense, but that lasted for one second, or five seconds, or a minute! So View One might be revised to allow for longer lengths of the less intense negative experience for instances of short duration, and the problems of inconsistency would remain. But one might also simply limit View One's scope and grant that it doesn't apply for durations of nanoseconds, or perhaps not even for durations of less than a second, or even a minute. As before, though I think one needn't grant such a claim, it is enough if there is a spectrum of cases, and durations, for which it does apply. And as my example illustrates, I think there clearly is.

The preceding is related to a point that can be made about both View Three and the Fourth Standard View. The Views in question don't simply maintain that if the difference in quality of burdens is sufficiently high, then *any* duration of the smaller burden will be better than *any* duration of the greater burden; rather, they suggest that any duration of the smaller burden will be better than a "substantial" period of duration of the larger burden. This limitation in the scope of the two views is not ad hoc; rather, it is both necessary and appropriate. The truth is that if the duration of a significant burden becomes short enough, it ceases to be a significant burden. Indeed, it may even cease to be a burden. So, while it may well be true that two years of intense torture is worse than any duration of a mosquito bite, it needn't be true that two seconds or two nanoseconds of intense torture would be worse than any duration of a mosquito bite. In fact, it may not be meaningful to speak of only two seconds or two nanoseconds of pain as intense torture. Stabs of pain, even if willfully and maliciously inflicted, may have to persist for a "significant" duration before they might count as *torture*.

I have no particular view about how long the willful infliction of pain might have to persist before it should "properly" be counted as torture. Nor do I have a developed view about where the cutoff point, or range, might be, such that once intense torture persisted beyond that point, or range, it would be worse than one extra mosquito bite per month for any number of months. But it is perfectly plausible to believe that there is such a point, or range, and that two *years* of intense torture is well beyond it. This, of course, is all View Three contends, and all I need for my argument.

In sum, View Three and the Fourth Standard View are already formulated so as to recognize that their scope is limited. And perhaps they need to be further refined to recognize other limitations in their scope. Likewise, as we have seen, the other views I have presented may also need refinements to reflect ways in which they, too, are limited in scope. However, this does not affect my argument, as long as suitably revised versions of the views are compelling, as I believe they are, for *some* spectrum of cases like the one I presented.

I conclude that while my example is liable to interpretations that would render it innocuous, properly spelled out it remains deeply problematic. The example highlights a significant inconsistency in our thinking; an inconsistency that can only be avoided by giving up a highly plausible position.

5.5 An Objection to View Three: Invoking Principles of Decomposition and Recombination

In the preceding section, I suggested that a negative sensation might have to persist for a "significant" period of time before it could count as *torture*. Still, any duration of torture will be composed of a large number of nanoseconds of *something*, which we may, for lack of a better word, refer to as *prototorture*. Now I've granted that one nanosecond of prototorture might be better than n years of one extra mosquito bite per month, for some n. Suppose this is so. Some people might use that as a key premise in a "proof" against View Three. Their argument might run as follows.

There are approximately 63 quadrillion nanoseconds in two years. For simplicity, let us just say that there are q nanoseconds in two years. Then two years of intense torture is composed of q nanoseconds of prototorture. Now imagine a life with a duration of $q \times n$ years. By hypothesis, one nanosecond of prototorture is better than n years of one extra mosquito bite per month. So,

$q \times 1$ nanoseconds of prototorture must be better than $q \times n$ years of one extra mosquito bite per month. But $q \times 1$ nanoseconds of prototorture just is, as noted, two years of torture. So two years of torture is better than $q \times n$ years of one extra mosquito bite per month, contrary to what View Three says. Therefore, View Three should be rejected. It is not true that any number of years of one extra mosquito bite per month would be better than two years of intense torture.

This argument has two related components. It invokes a principle of *decomposition*, according to which a given whole can be meaningfully decomposed into a set of disjoint parts. In this case, a life of duration $q \times n$ years is regarded as decomposable into q segments of n years each, and two years of torture is regarded as decomposable into q segments of one nanosecond each. Additionally, the argument invokes a principle of simple additive aggregation, according to which the *value* of the whole is equal to the *sum* of the values of each part.

In other words, the argument supposes that two years of torture and a lengthy lifetime of mosquito bites can each be divided into q parts, and that the value of each whole is just equal to the sum of the values of its parts. So, the value of two years of torture will just be equal to q times the value of a nanosecond of prototorture, and the value of a life of $q \times n$ years of one extra mosquito bite per month will just be equal to q times the value of n years of one extra mosquito bite per month. Since, by assumption, a nanosecond of prototorture is better than n years of one extra mosquito bite per month, the value of the former must be greater than the value of the latter, and hence q times the value of the former must be greater than q times the value of the latter, given that q is a positive number. It follows, on this reasoning, that the value of two years of intense torture must be greater than $q \times n$ years of one extra mosquito bite per month, and hence that the former must be better than the latter. Therefore View Three should be rejected.

Many people are attracted to an argument like the preceding one. But I think it should be rejected. The first point to note is that it *assumes*, as a starting point, the legitimacy of a simple additive-aggregationist approach in assessing the value of outcomes. View Three obviously rejects such an approach. Hence, the objection in question does not, so much, *argue* against View Three, as *beg the question against it*. Of course, advocates of simple additive aggregation might retort that View Three is in the same boat—that View Three does not, in fact, provide an *argument* against simple additive aggregation, but simply begs the question against it. I accept this rejoinder. But it should be noted that View Three was never offered as an *argument* against additive aggregation. It was offered as a position that virtually everyone finds highly intuitive. This is important. If it comes down to choosing between two positions, each of which can be construed as begging the question against the other, typically the advantage will lie on the side with the greatest intuitive plausibility, and the burden of proof will lie on the other side.

But advocates of View Three can do much more than charge the objection with question begging. They can directly challenge the plausibility of the second assumption underlying the objection. I have, of course, already offered a series of examples illustrating the intuitive implausibility of applying a simple additive-aggregationist approach for assessing the value of individual lives, in section 4.3. But other considerations, some of which are more general and theoretical, can also be offered against the assumption in question. To do this, it will be useful to first take note of a domain where both of the argument's assumptions hold, the domain of arithmetic.

To facilitate discussion, let us say that in arithmetic, the value of a number is just equal to the number itself. For example, the value of the number 8 is just eight, which we will express as $V(8) = 8$. Now in arithmetic, the principle of decomposition holds. Any numerical "whole" can be decomposed into a set of disjoint "parts." In fact, any whole can be decomposed into many different sets of equal or unequal size. For example, 8 can be decomposed into two parts of equal size, four parts of equal size, two parts of unequal size, three parts of unequal size, and so on. That is, $8 = 4 + 4$, $8 = 2 + 2 + 2 + 2$, $8 = 5 + 3$, and $8 = 5 + 2 + 1$. Moreover, in arithmetic, additive aggregation holds. Specifically, the value of a whole *is* equal to the sum of the values of its parts. So, $V(8) = V(5 + 3 + 1) = V(5) + V(3) + V(1)$. We can further note that in virtue of the commutative property of arithmetic, according to which $x + y = y + x$, a view that incorporates both the principle of decomposition and the principle of additive aggregation will *also* entail a principle of *recombination*, according to which the parts of a whole can be "rearranged" in *any* order without affecting the value of the whole. So, for example, $V(8) = V(5 + 3 + 1) = V(3 + 5 + 1) = V(1 + 3 + 5)$, and so on, since $V(5) + V(3) + V(1) = V(3) + V(5) + V(1) = V(1) + V(3) + V(5) = 8$. All this is straightforward. The axioms of arithmetic entail principles of decomposition, additive aggregation, and recombination of the sort invoked by the objection to View Three.

Because of the familiarity of arithmetic, and the ubiquitous role that it plays in our understanding of both natural and social sciences, it may be natural to suppose that arithmetic and its underlying assumptions hold for all domains. But while no domain can be, strictly speaking, *incompatible* with arithmetic, there may be domains to which it doesn't apply, or, more important, cases within various domains for which it would be *mistaken* to directly apply the underlying assumptions of arithmetic. This is a point that has been recognized by philosophers and others throughout the ages. For example, it has been recognized wherever a version of holism has been defended, with its fundamental insight that in *some* cases the value of a whole, considered as a whole, is greater or less than the sum of the values of its parts, considered separately as parts.[6] More generally, it has long been recognized that the normative realm is rife with examples where the assumptions underlying the objection to View Three fail.

Holism is often regarded as a mysterious doctrine. But as I am employing the term here, it needn't entail anything more than ordinary facts of the sort that economists describe as *interaction effects*. Here is a standard example. Consider two meals, each composed of two parts. One meal combines a nice fish, F, with a fine white wine, WW, the other beef, B, with a fine red wine, RW.[7] It is widely accepted that the value of these two meals cannot be assessed along the lines assumed by the objection to View Three. That is, one cannot assess the value of the two meals by decomposing them into their separate parts, determining the value of each part separately, and then summing the resulting individual values. The idea is that the white wine and fish may complement or interact with each other in such a way that each enhances the taste of the other. As a result, the value of a meal which combines the white wine and the fish may be greater than the value of each partaken separately. That is, $V(WW + F) > V(WW) + V(F)$. Similar remarks might apply to the red wine and the beef, so that $V(RW + B) > V(RW) + V(B)$. By the same token, there may be negative interaction effects such that, when combined, the tastes of white wine and beef might detract from each other, and similarly for the tastes of red wine and fish. In such cases, $V(WW + B) < V(WW) + V(B)$, and $V(RW + F) < V(RW) + V(F)$. All this is commonplace. Similarly, you don't have to be a gourmand to know that the *order* of a seven-course meal is crucially important

---

[6] A defense of holism appears as far back as Plato. See, for example, Plato's *The Republic*, trans. Allan Bloom (New York: Basic Books, 1968); *Phaedrus*, trans. R. Hackforth (Cambridge: Cambridge University Press, 1952); *Gorgias*, trans. Eric Robertson Dodds (Oxford: Clarendon Press, 1959); *Protagoras*, in *Protagoras and Meno*, trans. William Keith Chambers Guthrie (London: Penguin Books, 1956); and Aristotle's *Poetics*, trans. N. G. L. Hammond (Copenhagen: Museum Tusculanum, 2001). The related notion of organic unity is famously presented and defended by G. E. Moore in *Principia Ethica* (Cambridge: Cambridge University Press, 1903). These notions, and related ones, have been widely discussed by contemporary theorists. See, for example, Franz Brentano's *The Origin of Our Knowledge of Right and Wrong*, trans. Roderick M. Chisholm and Elizabeth Schneewind (London: Routledge and Kegan Paul, 1969); William Frankena's *Ethics*, 2nd ed. (Englewood Cliffs, NJ: Prentice-Hall, 1973); Robert Nozick's *Philosophical Explanations* (Cambridge, MA: Harvard University Press, 1981); Christine Korsgaard's "Two Distinctions in Goodness," *Philosophical Review* 92 (1983): 169–95; Roderick M. Chisholm's *Brentano and Intrinsic Value* (Cambridge: Cambridge University Press, 1986); Noah M. Lemos's *Intrinsic Value: Concept and Warrant* (Cambridge: Cambridge University Press, 1994); Shelly Kagan's "Rethinking Intrinsic Value," *Journal of Ethics* 2 (1998): 277–97; Thomas Hurka's "Two Kinds of Organic Unity," *Journal of Ethics* 2 (1998): 299–320; and Jonathan Dancy's *Ethics without Principles* (Oxford: Clarendon Press, 2004).

[7] My apologies to those whose sensibilities are offended by this example, and other similar examples that appear in this book. I hope it is clear that I use such examples merely because they are familiar ones, and they usefully illustrate my point. I am certainly not endorsing the eating of fish, beef, or other animals. I am grateful to Oscar Horta for reminding me that some readers may find such examples objectionable. It would, perhaps, be better to dispense with such examples entirely, but I hope this apology suffices to alleviate their insensitivity.

to the success, or value, of that meal. So, as with the case just discussed, to determine the value that someone would receive from a meal, it is not enough to consider the value that they would receive from ingesting each item separately, and then add those values together. One needs to know the order in which the items would be consumed, how, if at all, they would combine, and the interaction effects, if any, between them. So, for the domain of gustatory value, at least, one must resist employing the principles of decomposition, additive aggregation, and recombination in the ways that work for arithmetic.

Another classic example of holism, or organic unity, for which combining the principles of decomposition, additive aggregation, and recombination evidently fails concerns beauty. Consider, for example, the beauty of a face.[8] It is widely accepted that the most beautiful face, overall, may not be composed of the most beautiful features as judged independently. Specifically, there may be two sets of features—say, eyes, nose, mouth, chin, and ears—such that each member of the first set might be judged more beautiful than the corresponding member of the second set, *when considered alone*, and yet the *combination* of more beautiful features might be considerably less beautiful than the combination of less beautiful features. That is, letting $V(Eyes_1) > V(Eyes_2)$ express the judgment that, considered alone, the eyes in the first set of features are more beautiful than the eyes in the second set of features, and using a similar notation for the other comparisons, it might well be that $V(Eyes_1) > V(Eyes_2)$, $V(Nose_1) > V(Nose_2)$, $V(Mouth_1) > V(Mouth_2)$, $V(Chin_1) > V(Chin_2)$, and $V(Ears_1) > V(Ears_2)$, and yet it may still be that $V(Eyes_1 + Nose_1 + Mouth_1 + Chin_1 + Ears_1) < V(Eyes_2 + Nose_2 + Mouth_2 + Chin_2 + Ears_2)$. Perhaps the most beautiful eyes would be too wide for the most beautiful nose, which might be petite, and neither might fit especially well with the most beautiful chin, which might be pronounced. Moreover, it is evident that nothing like a principle of recombination applies in the case of beauty. Order, in this case in the form of spatial arrangement, makes all the difference, as moving a pair of eyes two inches up, or to the left, or interchanging an eye with an ear might well result in a grotesque appearance that only Picasso and his fans could love! Again, all this is commonplace, but it serves to remind one that while the principles of decomposition, additive aggregation, and recombination apply in arithmetic, they often fail in other domains.

Here is a familiar example from the normative realm. Suppose we know four facts about a given outcome. We know that one person has been good, one person has been bad, one of the two people has fared well, and the other has fared poorly. These factors are insufficient to judge the overall goodness of the outcome, because the goodness of the outcome is *not* just an additive function of the value of those factors considered independently. It matters whether it is

---

[8] Plato discusses this example in the *Protagoras*.

the good person who fares well, and the bad person who fares poorly, or vice versa. In the former case the outcome is just, in the latter it is unjust, and this makes a significant difference to the overall goodness of the outcome. Here, too, principles of decomposition, additive aggregation, and recombination fail to apply.

Finally, consider two cases more directly analogous to the objection we are considering. In the first case, we know that there are *many* pieces of straw that have been placed on a camel's back and subsequently removed. In the second, we know that there are *many* snowflakes that have landed on the ground and then melted. What can we say about the effects in those two scenarios? Clearly, not much. Timing, here, can make a crucial difference to the interaction effects, if any, that obtain in these scenarios. For example, if each piece of straw that was placed on the camel's back was removed prior to another piece of straw's being similarly placed, it would be utterly inconsequential that the camel had *so much* straw placed on its back over the course of its life. Things would be markedly different, however, if all the straw were placed on its back *at once*, or each piece was added sequentially, but none were removed until *after* the camel's back was broken! Likewise, many snowflakes spread out over many winters might amount to nothing more than a series of inconsequential "dustings" of light snow, while the same *total amount* of snow occurring in a three-hour span might produce a devastatingly dangerous blizzard. This is, of course, perfectly obvious. But it is important. The value, or disvalue, of a given total amount of straw on a camel's back, or a given total number of snowflakes that fall, *cannot* be determined by simply decomposing the total amounts into individual components of single pieces of straw, or single snowflakes, assessing the value or impact of those components considered separately, and then simply summing the resulting values or impacts. In some cases there may be a dispersal or dissipation of components, so that there are no interaction effects between them, while in other cases there may be an accumulation of factors resulting in significant interaction effects. Given this, one cannot simply decompose or recombine the whole into any set of parts one wants, and then apply the principle of additive aggregation to those parts in order to determine the value of the whole.

Return now to the argument against View Three. It fails, because the relation between a nanosecond of prototorture and two years of severe torture is like the relation between a snowflake and a blizzard. Even if we agree that, considered by themselves, n years of one extra mosquito bite per month is worse than a nanosecond of prototorture, and that two years of torture consists of q nanoseconds of prototorture, we needn't agree that $q \times n$ years of mosquito bites is worse than two years of torture. One nanosecond of prototorture every n years for $q \times n$ years may be utterly inconsequential, just as one light dusting of snowflakes every winter might be. This is because each nanosecond of torture, or light dusting, and its effects would have *completely dissipated* before the next one occurred. But *q consecutive* nanoseconds of prototorture would be a very different matter, as would the accumulation of snowfall in a blizzard. In these cases there would be no dispersal or dissipation of individual effects, but instead an interaction, combination, and accumulation of factors and effects that would radically alter their normative significance. In sum, even though there might be the same *total* number of nanoseconds of prototorture in two straight years of unremitting torture, as in one nanosecond of prototorture every *n* years for *q* × *n* years, the former would be a human tragedy, while the latter would be inconsequential.

The preceding discussion reminds us that just because *A* would be better than *B*, and *C* better than *D*, it does *not* follow that *A* + *C* would necessarily be better than *B* + *D*. Similarly, just because *A* would be better than *B*, it doesn't follow that *n* instances of *A* would be better than *n* instances of *B*. The *key* question is *how* the different factors are related to each other and, in particular, the nature, if any, of the interaction effects between them. On the assumption that one nanosecond of prototorture would be better than *n* years of one extra mosquito bite per month, which I've granted, View Three expresses the view that there is a powerful accumulated effect of consecutive moments of prototorture, but not between consecutive periods of mosquito bites lasting *n* years each. This seems right. The effect of a mosquito bite on any given day will be completely dissipated long before the effect of a mosquito bite in later months arrives. Correspondingly, we don't believe that while a few years of one extra mosquito bite per month would merely be a nuisance, *lots* of years of one extra mosquito bite per month would rise to the level of a human tragedy. They would remain merely a nuisance. A *persisting* nuisance, to be sure, but still only a nuisance. This is why View Three seems so powerful. While one nanosecond of prototorture would be insignificant, and better than *n* years of one extra mosquito bite per month, *q* consecutive nanoseconds of prototorture would rise to the level of excruciating torture, while *q* periods of one extra mosquito bite per month, each lasting *n* years, would remain a mere nuisance. And as View Three rightly reflects, a nuisance is better than a tragedy.[9]

I conclude that we should reject the argument against View Three. It relies on a set of views that work fine together in the domain of arithmetic, but not in the normative realm generally, or in the pain sphere in particular. To be clear, one can, if one wants, point out that any given set of pain experiences could, in theory, be decomposed or recombined in any way one wants; but one cannot infer, as the argument against View Three presupposes, that the *value* of any resulting wholes would be the same, in accordance with a simple additive-aggregationist approach.

---

[9] One might question whether two years of torture would still be a tragedy in a life that lasted billions of years. I address this question in the following section.

5.6 A Proportionality Argument against View Three

Some people might offer the following argument against View Three. I have granted that a nanosecond of prototorture would be insignificant. This, it might be claimed, is because a nanosecond is a teeny tiny insignificant "blip" in a life span lasting seventy years. For beings such as us, who live as long as we do, anything that endures for such a *tiny* fraction of our lives must rightly be regarded by us as completely trivial. After all, in the absence of long-term side effects, surely, the overall assessment of our lives will be *utterly* unaffected by what goes on during a single nanosecond of our life, a period which is a mere 2,205 *quadrillionth* of a normal seventy-year life span.

Similarly, it might be argued, if we lived long *enough*, specifically, if we lived 4,410 *quadrillion* years, 2 years would be a teeny tiny insignificant "blip" in our life spans. Correspondingly, in the absence of long-term side effects, surely, the overall assessment of such lives would be *utterly* unaffected by what goes on during a single 2-year period, a duration which would be a mere 2,205 *quadrillionth* of the "normal" life span. Thus, anything that endured for such a *tiny* fraction of such lives would rightly be regarded as completely trivial. Therefore, View Three should be rejected, as an extra mosquito bite per month that lasted for *quadrillions* of years could easily outweigh something that was completely trivial.

We can call the preceding argument the *proportionality argument* against View Three. It asserts that since two years of torture within a sufficiently long life stands in the same proportion as one nanosecond of prototorture within a normal seventy-year life span, the former, within such a life, should have the same normative significance as the latter, within a normal life. At first blush, the proportionality argument has some intuitive appeal. However, on reflection, it is clear that it should be rejected. Let me explain why.

The proportionality argument claims that the *reason* a mere nanosecond of prototorture is completely trivial, within a normal life span, is that a nanosecond is but a tiny fraction of such a life span. If this were true, that would explain how two years of intense torture would also be completely trivial, if they were embedded within a life that was sufficiently long. But it isn't true. The reason that a nanosecond of prototorture is completely trivial is simply that it wouldn't even be noticed! A nanosecond of prototorture would almost certainly be imperceptible at the conscious level, and probably even at the subconscious level. Hence, a nanosecond of prototorture would remain completely trivial even if it occurred within a life that persisted only 7 years, or 7 months, or 7 days, or 7 seconds. So, the *proportion* of the life that is subject to a nanosecond of prototorture is simply *not* what accounts for its being trivial; facts about perceptibility and human psychology are.

Consider a normal human who is subjected to a nanosecond of prototorture. Such a person would presumably not even notice the event. Moreover, even if there were, at some level, some subconscious awareness of the instantaneous event, there would be no particular reason to even form the desire to be rid of the experience, since it takes time to formulate a desire, and the event would almost certainly have already passed before the desire was completely formulated. Thus, if the occurrence of a nanosecond of prototorture somehow succeeded in prompting the desire to be rid of the prototorture, there would be no moment at which that desire was frustrated, as the desire would have almost certainly already been fulfilled by the time it was fully formed. So there is, indeed, good reason to regard a nanosecond of prototorture as completely trivial, as it would have (virtually?) no negative impact on the quality of a person's conscious mental states, and would involve (virtually?) no frustration of a person's desires.

The situation is rather different in the case of two years of intense torture. Even within a life of extraordinary length, two years of intense torture would involve incredibly negative conscious mental states and give rise to the fervent and overriding desire to be rid of such states. That desire would, of course, persist and be horribly frustrated throughout the two years. The combination of agony suffered and the frustration of what would almost certainly be, at the time, one's deepest desire, accounts for why two years of intense torture would be a human tragedy, even within a life of extraordinary length.

The proportionality argument *requires* that the facts of human psychology would have to change, so that two years of intense torture within a sufficiently long life would have the same psychological impact as one nanosecond of prototorture would within a normal life. But there is no reason to grant this. Even if, as a matter of fact, human psychology would undoubtedly change in countless, unpredictable ways if we lived for quadrillions of years, one cannot assume that it would *have to*, as a matter of *logical necessity*, change in the way the proportionality argument requires. For the sake of my argument, it is enough if there is *some* possible world in which beings with psychologies sufficiently like ours persisted for quadrillions of years. Since such a world is possible, the proportionality argument should be rejected.

Finally, let me illustrate the preceding point with the following example. Suppose that while Hell is a place of intense torture, Heaven simply turns out to be an earthlike place, where people can experience normal earthlike lives indefinitely. On the proportionality argument, it would be *completely trivial* if God chose to send us to Hell for *billions and billions* of years, *as long as* He sent us to the earthly afterlife for the rest of eternity. Indeed, He needn't even send us to the earthly afterlife for an eternity. He merely needs to send us for a sufficiently long period, that the *proportion* between the time spent in Hell and that spent living the earthly existence would be equal to the proportion between a nanosecond and a normal life span. This view is absurd. If God were to send us to Hell for billions and billions of years it would be a great tragedy, and He could not avoid the charge of sadism, or inflicting grievous harm on us, merely by making sure that He *also* provided us with *many* years of an earthly existence. The proportionality argument should be rejected.

5.7 Trusting Our Intuitions Regarding Inordinate Lengths of Time

Some people offer a different challenge to View Three. Specifically, while they grant the intuitive plausibility of the claim that no matter how long the discomfort of one extra mosquito bite per month persisted, it would be better than two years of excruciating torture, they insist that our intuitions are *not to be trusted* in such matters. Such people offer numerous explanations for why we might naturally, but nonetheless wrongly, accept View Three—explanations that ultimately rest on the ground that our intuitions were not developed, and are poorly equipped, to adequately respond to the overall significance of small amounts spread out over innumerable years.[10]

The claim here is that to move from A_1, the state involving two years of excruciating torture, to A_{n+1}, the state involving one extra mosquito bite per month, would require *so* many intervening steps that we would have to imagine what it would be like to have one extra mosquito bite per month for *billions* or *trillions* of years. (Recall that each step involves a slightly less unpleasant experience, but one that lasts twice—or three or five times—as long as the previous one.) But, it is argued, we have *no* intuitive conception of what it would be like to live such a lengthy life, and in particular no intuitive conception of *how bad it would be* to experience one extra mosquito bite per month for *such* a long time. Correspondingly, it is argued, our intuitions about such wild science-fiction-type cases cannot be trusted. So, in cases involving inordinately large numbers of small amounts, we should trust the judgment of those theories which do the best job of capturing our intuitions in the ordinary cases for which it seems our intuitions *can* be trusted. And, it is claimed, the theories that do the best job of capturing our intuitions in the ordinary cases are maximizing ones like Sidgwick's Self-Interest Theory. But, it is contended, what such theories tell us is that no matter *how* slight a mosquito bite's discomfort may be, if only having one extra mosquito bite per month lasts *long enough*,

---

[10] Fred Feldman has sent me a long list of such explanations, many of which are quite ingenious and sophisticated. Still, I don't find these explanations ultimately convincing, in part for the reasons I will give in this section. It isn't just that I find myself with a set of "intuitions" that I can trace to some evolutionary or social process that once served, or continues to serve, some purpose, but which happens to lead us astray in the sorts of cases I am considering. Rather, there appear to be powerful *reasons* to hold the view in question. More particularly, at the end of the day I find the debunking explanations offered by Feldman less plausible and defensible than the view they are intended to debunk.

eventually the total amount of discomfort one experiences *will* outweigh, and then be worse than, the pain of two years of excruciating torture. On this view, then, our understanding supposedly leads us to recognize a truth that our imagination fails to appreciate, namely, that View Three should be rejected.

I have some sympathy for this *kind* of response. People often appeal to intuitions in cases where our intuitions cannot be trusted. Moreover, our intuitions *are* notoriously suspect in cases involving small amounts or large numbers.[11] Nevertheless, I do not find this response compelling. First, for the reasons given in chapter 4, there is ample reason to deny that maximizing theories of self-interest of the sort favored by Sidgwick and many economists *do* best capture our intuitions in ordinary cases that don't involve unimaginably large numbers; indeed, we have seen that for a number of such cases they do not. Second, it isn't clear that my present argument *turns on* our inability to grasp unimaginably large numbers. Let me suggest why.

First, the response turns on a dubious assumption, namely, that moving from A_1 to A_{n+1} would necessarily involve *so* many steps that the mosquito bite's duration would be unimaginably long—billions, or perhaps trillions, of years. This may be false. Consider the following example. A man who is 5′ 2″ is *very* short. A man who is 6′ 4″ is *very* tall. In this range, a difference of 2 inches is noticeable but relatively small—less than 3.3 percent for someone 5′ 2″, less than 2.6 percent for someone 6′ 4″. Yet, one can move from the very short to the very tall in just seven relatively small steps.[12] If, by analogy, one could move from the pain of torture to the discomfort of a mosquito bite in seven relatively small steps, the relevant trade-off would be between 2 years of torture and 256 years of the discomfort of a mosquito bite. Two hundred fifty-six years is a long time, but it is hardly unimaginable. And I am confident that were I fortunate enough to live 256 years, I would much prefer the discomfort of a mosquito bite throughout my life to two years of torture somewhere within it.

Moreover, if one seriously doubts whether one can vividly imagine 256 years of the discomfort of a mosquito bite, one might change the torture's length. If one starts with 1 year of torture instead of 2, the discomfort of having a mosquito bite might last only 128 years. If one starts with 1 day of torture, the discomfort of having a mosquito bite might last only 128 days! One day of torture is clearly imaginable; so, too, is 128 days of the discomfort of having a mosquito bite. When I vividly think of these possible experiences, I know which I prefer. The discomfort of having a mosquito bite would be *vastly* better than the torture. These are not cases where my imagination gives out. Nor do I think it fails me here. It rightly guides my judgment. All things considered, the

---

[11] See chapter 3 of Derek Parfit's *Reasons and Persons* (Oxford: Oxford University Press, 1984), also the striking results in Daniel Kahneman, Paul Slovic, and Amos Tversky's *Judgment under Uncertainty: Heuristics and Biases* (Cambridge: Cambridge University Press, 1982).

[12] I am grateful to Peter Unger for this example.

life with the torture would be much worse than the life with the discomfort of having a mosquito bite.[13]

A perceptual analogy might be useful here. The visual spectrum ranges across the seven colors of the rainbow: red, orange, yellow, green, blue, indigo, and violet. The differences between adjacent members of the spectrum are clearly perceptible, yet still relatively small. Phenomenologically, there is not *that* great a difference between red and orange, or indigo and violet. Hence, it appears that one can get from one end of the visual spectrum all the way to the opposite end in six relatively small steps.

Do the steps seem too big? Add intervening ones. Consider the following spectrum: red, reddish-orange, orange, orangish-yellow, yellow, yellowish-green, green, greenish-blue, blue, blue-indigo, indigo, indigo-violet, violet. It is hard to deny that, phenomenologically, the gaps between adjacent members of this spectrum are pretty small, though still clearly perceptible. Yet it would take only twelve steps to get from one extreme of the spectrum to the other.

The preceding suggests that although, phenomenologically, the pain of torture and the discomfort of a mosquito bite are at opposite ends of the pain spectrum, it may take a surprisingly small number of short steps to get from one to the other. To be sure, each step, though short, may involve differences that are clearly noticeable and of some significance. But there is no reason to deny this. Given the choice between a greater pain for a certain length of time and a lesser pain for *twice* as long, I prefer the former, unless the latter pain is *much* less intense. Clearly, my choice requires that the difference between the two pains not be *too* great, but it certainly does *not* require that it be either imperceptible or the least perceptible difference.

In sum, there is reason to doubt whether my example *depends* on having to imagine what it would be like to have an extra mosquito bite for billions, or perhaps even trillions, of years. The relevant trade-off *might be* between two years of torture and a few hundred, or maybe thousands, of years of a mosquito bite. Or, if we change the scale, between two months of torture and a few hundred, or maybe thousands, of months of a mosquito bite. Such trade-offs are not the sort typically made, but they are not unimaginable.

Let me acknowledge that the preceding considerations are purely suggestive. I certainly have not *established* that the case of pain is analogous to those

---

[13] Note, I do not believe that any amount of torture, no matter how short, must be worse than any amount of a mosquito bite, no matter how long. Nor does my argument commit me to this. It might well be that two *seconds* worth of torture would be better than *many* years of a mosquito bite, and it is almost certainly true that two *nanoseconds* of torture would be better than many years—or even a day!—of a mosquito bite. Correspondingly, there may be perfectly transitive orderings from outcomes involving *very* short amounts of torture to ones involving very long amounts of a mosquito bite. I don't deny this, nor do I need to. All I need to establish is one case of nontransitivity, and for this it is enough if torture that lasts long *enough* would be worse than a mosquito bite of *vastly* longer (and even perhaps any) duration.

of height and color. Although a small number of fairly small steps gets one from a very short to a very tall person, and from one end of the visual spectrum to the other, it remains *possible* that vastly many steps would be necessary to get from the pain of torture to the discomfort of a mosquito bite. Still, given facts about human evolution, and the roles our different sense modalities play in survival, one might not expect our phenomenological powers of discrimination to differ *radically* across our sense modalities. That is, it isn't clear that we should need *vastly* greater powers of discrimination among pains, than among colors. Indeed, from the perspective of armchair psychology, it might seem sufficient if we are able to distinguish between three kinds of pains: the innocuous, which we can safely ignore; the threatening, which we might want to avoid and should keep an eye on; and the dangerous, which we definitely need to avoid if possible, and otherwise remedy. Moreover, from an evolutionary standpoint the phenomenological differences between such signals might be slight, as long as the signals are clear, reliably detected, and accurately interpreted.

In any event, it seems an *empirical* fact whether our sensory apparatus for pain operates analogously to our sensory apparatus for color, and that may be all I need for my argument. After all, unless it is *metaphysically impossible* for the pain and color modalities to be analogous in the way suggested, there are some possible creatures for whom my argument would work—even if it does not, in fact, work for humans. This is all one needs to show the inconsistency between Views One, Two, Three, and Four.

But this is absurd, some will insist. Torture really is *very* bad. And the discomfort of a mosquito bite is *very* mild. Surely, it is *obvious* that one can't get from the *very* bad to the *very* mild in a small number of steps. But *is it* obvious? Or is it possible that *this* is a place where our intuitions lead us astray? After all, as we've seen, a 6′ 4″ man really is *very* tall, and a 5′ 2″ man really is *very* short, but we certainly *can* get from the one to the other in seven short steps!

So, I am not convinced that in moving from torture to mosquito bites we would necessarily end up comparing alternatives of such a massive humanly incomprehensible scale that our intuitions can't be trusted. And I find the example particularly gripping and compelling. Still, a second response to the objection in question is to change the example. So, let me present four cases where similar problems arise regarding the consistency of our judgments. I shall discuss the first case at length, and the three other cases minimally.

> *Case I.* Imagine a scale of uncomfortable experiences, ranging from a level of 1, the discomfort of a mosquito bite, to a level of 100, extreme torture. Suppose a moderately uncomfortable limp is an
> 11—significantly worse than a mosquito bite, but not nearly as bad as extreme torture. Start with a choice between *A*, level 100 discomfort for 2 days, or *B*, level 80 discomfort for 4 days. *B*'s discomfort is 20 percent

less than A's, but lasts twice as long. Many believe A is better than B. Next compare B to C, where C stands to B as B stands to A. C is 20 percent less intense, level 64, but lasts twice as long, 8 days. Again, many think B is better than C. The tenth choice would be between J, discomfort of level 13.4 for 1,024 days, and K, discomfort of level 11 for 2,048 days. Again, many would think J is better than K.

Given these rankings, the transitivity of "better than" (in my wide reason-implying sense) entails that A is better than K. Is it? Given our assumptions, A involves extreme torture for 2 days, K involves a moderately uncomfortable limp for 2,048 days, or 5.6 years. Which would you choose for your child—that for the next 5.6 years she suffers an uncomfortable limp, or for 2 days she suffers extreme torture? (Here, as always, I assume there are no relevant side effects. A pill, or hypnosis, removes all memories of the torture, other children do not mercilessly ridicule your child as a "gimp," etc.) I would choose the limp over the torture for someone I loved. And I would do so because I think it the better alternative. But I would also think A is better than B, B better than C, . . . and J better than K.

It might be claimed that the preceding necessarily involves some kind of conceptual confusion. Specifically, it might be claimed that if the discomfort of 5.6 *years* of a moderate limp seems better than a mere two *days* of intense torture, then the gap between the pain of torture and the discomfort of a moderate limp must be much greater than my example imagines it to be, such that one could never bridge it in only ten steps of the sort described. On this view, the pain of a moderate limp would have to receive a much lower score than 11 on our scale from 1 to 100, and the real trade-off we would have to imagine would be between two days of torture and a much longer period of a moderate limp. But I don't see why we should believe this. B's pain is 20 percent less intense than A's. That is quite a significant difference. And C's is 20 percent less intense than B's, also quite a significant difference. The combined result of *ten* such changes could be a *very* large gap indeed, as large as the phenomenological difference between torture and a moderate limp.

Think about it carefully. Imagine being in a state of intense torture, and then having the intensity of that pain reduced by 20 percent. The result would still be a *quite* painful state—painful enough, I think, to warrant the judgment that A, which is only *half* as long, would be better than B. Still, there is no denying that the move from A to B would involve *significant* improvement regarding the intensity of the pain. Next imagine the pain being reduced by *another* 20 percent. This, again, would involve *significant* improvement regarding the intensity of the pain, but not so much that we should prefer the latter alternative to the former if it lasted *twice* as long. But then imagine the intensity of the pain being reduced by another 20 percent. And then another. And another. And another. And another. And another. And another. And yet another. While each reduction is sufficiently small that a state involving the former pain might be better than a state involving the latter pain of *twice* the duration, each reduction would be quite significant, and the combined effect of *ten* such reductions would be to produce a state, such that the gap between the first state and the last might be *so* large that, intuitively at least, we would regard 5.6 years of the latter as better than only two days of the former.

To be sure, our intuitions about such a case might *still* be mistaken. I have not argued otherwise. But we certainly can imagine what it would be like to suffer extreme torture for two days. And likewise we can certainly imagine what it would be like to suffer a vastly reduced pain, 89 percent less intense, for 5.6 years. If, as I believe, we intuitively believe the latter would be better than the former, such intuitions cannot simply be dismissed by appeal to the fact that our intuitions cannot be trusted in cases involving inordinate lengths of time.

Next, let us consider cases *II* through *IV*.

> *Case II.*[14] *A* involves random interruption of one's electrical service 20 minutes per time, 9 times a day, for 24 months; *B* the same kind of interruptions 7 times a day for 42 months; *C* 5.66 times a day for 63 months; *D* 4.33 times a day for 94 months; *E* 3.33 times a day for 141 months; *F* 2.33 times a day for 210 months; *G* 1.6 times a day for 315 months; *H* 1.1 times a day for 473 months; *I* 0.76 times a day for 710 months; *J* 0.53 times a day for 1,065 months.
>
> *Case III. A* involves driving delays of 4.5 hours per day for 24 months; *B* delays of 3.5 hours per day for 42 months; *C* delays of 2.83 hours per day for 63 months; *D* delays of 2.17 hours per day for 94 months; *E* delays of 1.67 hours per day for 141 months; *F* delays of 1.17 hours per day for 210 months; *G* delays of 0.8 hours per day for 315 months; *H* delays of 0.55 hours per day 473 months; *I* delays of 0.33 hours per day for 710 months; *J* delays of 0.27 hours per day for 1,065 months.
>
> *Case IV. A* involves 48 garbage pickups missed per year (against the backdrop where garbage would normally be picked up once a week) for 24 months; *B* 40 missed pickups per year for 42 months; *C* 32 missed pickups per year for 63 months; *D* 25 missed pickups per year for 94 months; *E* 19 missed pickups per year for 141 months; *F* 13.5 missed pickups per year for 210 months; *G* 9.23 missed pickups per year for 315

---

[14] As with many of my examples, the *particular* numbers chosen for this case and the following two are completely arbitrary. There is no special reason why, for example, *H* involves an interruption of electrical service 1.1 times a day for 473 months, rather than once a day for 450 months or 500 months. There are lots of ways one could have come up with alternatives that involved simpler "round" numbers. But the key is that the numbers I employ in my example *work*. In fact, I constructed my examples by considering several variations until I came up with alternatives that did not involve unimaginably large numbers and about which it seems our intuitions could be trusted, which did, indeed, elicit the intuitions I claim they do from everyone to whom I presented them.

months; *H* 6.35 missed pickups per year for 473 months; *I* 4.42 missed pickups per year for 710 months; *J* 3.1 missed pickups per year for 1,065 months.

Cases *II*, *III*, and *IV* are obviously similar. They each present different sets of alternatives involving different kinds and degrees of frustration of different durations. Ranking the various alternatives involves making trade-offs between given levels of frustration for a given length of time, and decreased levels of frustration for longer periods of time. Having asked numerous people about such cases, I believe that for each of these cases many would judge *A* better than *B*, *B* better than *C*, *C* better than *D*, and so on. But many would also judge, for each of these cases, that *J* is better than *A*. Their reasoning appears to be straightforward. When comparing *A* with *B*, *B* with *C*, *C* with *D*, and so on, the degree of frustrations in the different alternatives is sufficiently similar that it seems reasonable to rank the alternatives merely on the basis of which has the greater *sum total* of frustrations. But when comparing *A* with *J*, the difference in the degree of individual frustrations is so great that the *distribution* of the frustrations and its overall effect on the quality of the lives seems more pertinent than the sum total of the frustrations.

Now my aim here is not to *defend* the intuitive judgments noted previously. It is, rather, to illustrate that the same kinds of worries I raise about the spectrum from torture to mosquito bites can arise in other cases that do *not* involve lives of inordinate lengths. I can certainly imagine what it would be like to have my garbage not picked up 48 weeks out of 52 (case *IV*'s *A*). Likewise, I can certainly imagine not having my garbage picked up approximately once every four months for the duration of an eighty-nine-year life (case *IV*'s *J*). And I can imagine all the intervening alternatives (case *IV*'s *B* through *I*). Such alternatives do not involve unimaginably large periods of billions or trillions of years, for which our intuitions were not developed. Hence, it does not appear that one can readily dismiss our intuitions about such alternatives as obviously suspect. But, for many, their intuitions about cases *I* through *IV* mirror the firm intuitions most have about my original example. I suggest, then, that the conflict in our views that my original example points to is real and must be squarely faced. Dismissing it as an artifact of wild science-fiction-type cases for which our intuitions cannot be trusted is, I think, a mistake.

View Three is an example of a particularly strong anti-additive-aggregationist position. In claiming that the mild discomfort of a mosquito bite would be better than two years of excruciating torture, no matter *how long* one lived and no matter *how long* the discomfort of a mosquito bite persisted, it naturally gives rise to the concern about large numbers and lives of inordinate length that we have been discussing. But it is worth emphasizing that one doesn't have to make such a bold claim for the problems I have been raising to arise. It is enough if one believes that there are some cases where alternatives can be rightly judged on the basis of sum totals, while there are other cases where sum totals are not all that matters, as the pattern of distribution is also relevant. The latter claim is a relatively weak anti-additive-aggregationist position, but it is enough to give rise to my concerns. One will either have to reject the first kind of view, that sometimes an additive-aggregationist approach is appropriate for ranking outcomes, the second kind of view, that sometimes distributions are relevant, the transitivity of the "all-things-considered better than" relation (in my wide reason-implying sense), or the empirical assumption that there can be spectrums of cases such that the first criterion is relevant for comparing the alternatives near each other on such spectrums, and the second is relevant for comparing alternatives at the opposite ends of such spectrums. I continue to believe that each of the views is extremely plausible, and that giving any of them up would require major revision in our thinking.

*****

Problems of aggregation arise within lives, as well as between lives. Specifically, within lives, as well as between lives, there is an inconsistency between two highly plausible and widely held views about how to compare alternative outcomes, an apparent empirical fact, and the transitivity of the "all-things-considered better than" relation (in my wide reason-implying sense). Something must be given up; but to this point, at least, it is by no means clear what that should be.

In this chapter, I have considered various possible responses to my Spectrum Arguments. Other important responses still need to be considered. One of the most important of these is the claim that my Spectrum Argument can be understood, and dismissed, as yet another example of the well-known, and fallacious, Sorites Paradox. Another important response challenges the transitivity of the "all-things-considered better than" relation (in my wide reason-implying sense). I consider these, and other responses, in later chapters. In doing so, a clearer understanding of the nature of Spectrum Arguments and their implications will emerge.[15]

---

[15] My arguments in this chapter and the preceding ones have been heavily theoretical; but as I have tried to indicate they may have great practical significance. One topic to which they may apply is the divisive topic of abortion. I believe that one conservative argument, which purports to show that the death of a newly fertilized egg is nearly as bad as the death of a newborn infant, has been misunderstood, and that the argument in question can be recast as a Spectrum Argument of the sort I have been considering. So recast, the argument has great appeal and cannot simply be dismissed, as it typically is, as a Standard Sorites Paradox (see chapter 9). In particular, I believe that a familiar conservative argument against abortion can be recast as a Spectrum Argument which demonstrates an inconsistency between several positions that most people, including most liberals on abortion, accept, and the assumption that "all-things-considered better than" (in my wide reason-implying sense) is a transitive relation. My argument for this is given in "An Abortion Argument and the Threat of Intransitivity," in *Well-being and Morality: Essays in Honour of James Griffin*, ed. Roger Crisp and Brad Hooker (Oxford: Oxford University Press, 2000), 336–56.

6

Exploring Transitivity

PART I

In chapters 2 through 5, I illustrated a deep tension between certain widely held views about aggregation, an empirical premise, and the assumption that the "all-things-considered better than" relation (in my wide reason-implying sense) is transitive. I subjected the First Standard View, the Fourth Standard View, and View One to some scrutiny, and claimed that it would be difficult to reject such views. Thus, so far, at least, it appears that additive-aggregationist reasoning is plausible for a wide range of cases, such that often, in comparing alternatives, both between lives and within lives, it would be better to trade off between quality and number, or quality and duration. Likewise, I subjected the Second Standard View, the Third Standard View, and View Three to some scrutiny, and claimed that it would also be difficult to reject such views. Hence, so far, at least, it appears that anti-additive-aggregationist reasoning is also plausible for a wide range of cases, such that often, in comparing alternatives, both between lives and within lives, it would not be better to trade off between quality and number, or quality and duration. As for the empirical premise, I expressed my conviction that it would be extremely difficult to refute. To this point, I have *not* subjected the transitivity of the "all-things-considered better than" relation (in my wide reason-implying sense) to scrutiny. Together, this chapter and the following one aim to rectify that.

Most people *assume* that "all-things-considered better than" is a transitive relation. Indeed, many probably assume that there is only *one* "all-things-considered better than" relation that *must* be transitive, or that even if there is more than one "all-things-considered better than" relation, *all* such relations *must* be transitive if the notions of "all-things-considered better than" are intelligible and not self-contradictory, and they couldn't imagine how it could be otherwise. I believe that the truth in this area is exceedingly complex, and will only be determined after much careful argument and thought.

Before considering the transitivity of the "all-things-considered better than" relation directly (in my wide reason-implying sense), it will be helpful to look at different examples of relations that are, or are not, transitive. Doing this will illuminate the nature and foundation of transitive relations and help clarify the conditions that would have to obtain for "all-things-considered better than" to be a nontransitive relation. It will also be useful to explore the notions of incommensurability, rough comparability, and the nontransitivity of the "not worse than" relation. In addition, I shall discuss the so-called *money pump*, and the importance of global and strategic reasoning as a practical response to money pump situations that do not arise from intransitive preferences.

In the following chapter I shall continue the exploration of transitivity by assessing the nature of two other normative relations, the *permissibility* relation "is permissible to do rather than," and the *obligatoriness* relation "ought to be done rather than." I shall then, finally, identify the factors that ultimately determine whether or not "all-things-considered better than" (in my wide reason-implying sense) is, in fact, a transitive relation.

6.1 Transitive and Nontransitive Relations

Recall that transitivity is a property of relations. Specifically, a relation, R, is transitive, if and only if whenever a stands in relation R to b, and b stands in relation R to c, then a stands in relation R to c. We can represent this by saying that R is a transitive relation if and only if for all a, b, and c, if aRb and bRc, then aRc.

Taller than is a classic example of a transitive relation, since for any three people, a, b, and c, if a is taller than b, and b is taller than c, a *must* be taller than c. Being the father of is a classic example of a nontransitive relation, since if a is the father of b, and b is the father of c, it does not follow that a is the father of c. Indeed, in the real world, if a is the father of b, and b the father of c, then a will be the *grand*father of c, but can't be the father of c. Consider the relation, L, "is in love with." It might be true that dad is in love with mom, mom in love with son, and dad also in love with son. So, in fact, dLm, mLs, and dLs. Even so, the relation L is not a transitive relation, since the fact that a is in love with b, and b is in love with c does not *entail* that a is in love with c. Clearly, Sam may be in love with Ann, and Ann in love with Jim, without it having to be the case that Sam is in love with Jim. Indeed, Sam may *hate* Jim, his successful rival for Ann's affection.

Can we say more about the circumstances, or underlying conditions, that account for when a relation will or will not be transitive? We can. Though here, as elsewhere, we must proceed carefully.

Paradigmatic examples of transitive relations are *comparative* relations like "is bigger than," "is heavier than," "is taller than," and "is faster than." Correspondingly, a first guess might be that all, and only, "...er than" relations are transitive. But this will not do.

Consider first the identity relation, *I*, "is identical to." Identity is a transitive relation, since for all *a*, *b*, and *c*, if *aIb* (*a* is identical to *b*), and *bIc*, then *aIc*. The sameness relation, *S*, "is the same with respect to property *q* as" is likewise a transitive relation, since for all a, *b*, and *c*, if *aSb* and *bSc*, then *aSc*. On a straight horizontal line, in a Euclidean plane, the right of relation, "is to the right of," is also a transitive relation, since for all *a*, *b*, and *c*, if *a* is to the right of *b*, and *b* is to the right of *c*, then *a* must be to the right of *c*. But the identity, sameness, and right of relations are not "...er than" relations. Clearly, then, it is not *only* "...er than" relations that are transitive.

But perhaps it remains true that *all* "...er than" relations are transitive. Unfortunately, this is trickier to assess. Consider the following example. Let us define the relation "larger than" as follows: for any two people, *a* and *b*, *a* is *larger than b* if *a* is heavier than *b* or if *a* is taller than *b*. Clearly, so defined, *a* might be larger than *b*, because heavier, and *b* might be larger than *c*, because taller, yet *a* might *not* be larger than *c*, as *c* might be both heavier and taller than *a*. So, it appears that one *could* have a "...er than" relation that is not transitive.

Now it might be argued that, as defined, "larger than" is an incoherent notion (henceforth, I shall assume, but generally omit, the qualification "as defined"). But is it? It seems well defined, at least in the sense that for any two people it tells you whether the one is larger than the other or vice versa. Of course, the relation "larger than" violates transitivity, but lots of relations violate transitivity, and that doesn't make them incoherent. Similarly, "larger than" allows for the possibility that *a* might be larger than *b*, yet *b* larger than *a*.[1] And, admittedly, this sounds odd, since for most familiar "...er than" relations it would be impossible both for *a* to stand in that relation to *b*, and for *b* to stand in that relation to *a*. So, for example it *couldn't* be true both that *a* is taller, or faster, than *b*, *and* that *b* is taller, or faster, than *a*. But this just shows that "larger than" isn't like other, more familiar "...er than" relations, not that it is incoherent. After all, *lots* of relations have the property that for some, but not all, *a* and *b*, *aRb* and *bRa*. We might call such relations *sometimes symmetrical*, in contrast to those (fully) symmetrical relations, *R*, where for *all a* and *b*, if *aRb* then *bRa*.

Consider the fondness relation, "is fond of." Like "larger than," "is fond of" is a nontransitive relation, since it might well be the case that *a* is fond of *b*, and *b* is fond of *c*, yet *a* isn't fond of *c*. Also like "larger than," it is sometimes true that *a* is fond of *b*, but *b* isn't fond of *a*, and sometimes true that *a* is fond of *b*

---

[1] A number of people have pointed this out to me over the years, including Toby Ord, who noted, in correspondence, that "even anti-symmetry fails in the case of 'larger than,'" where a relation, *R*, is antisymmetrical if, for any two alternatives, *a* and *b*, if *aRb*, then it is not the case that *bRa*.

and *b* is fond of *a*. But surely there is nothing *incoherent* about the fondness relation. Correspondingly, one can't conclude that "larger than" is incoherent on the basis of the claim that it is both intransitive and sometimes symmetrical.

One might claim that "larger than" is a useless concept, that there would never be any reason to invoke such a concept. But this is an empirical claim that could be false. There might be certain roles for which, other things equal, a casting director would want to hire the larger of two actors, in that for any two actors it wouldn't particularly matter if they hired the heavier actor or the taller actor, but it *would* matter if they hired an actor who was both lighter *and* shorter than his competitor. Similarly, a wealthy person might leave his entire fortune to a certain cause on the condition that one person is larger than another, and here it might be crucially important that the condition of the will is satisfiable in *either* of the two ways allowed by the larger than relation. Of course, I am not claiming that we couldn't dispense with the terminology of "larger than" as I've defined it. Clearly we could. Nor am I denying that there might be other, much more useful and intuitively satisfying, conceptions of "larger than" than the one I have proposed. There are. But the fact that "larger than," as defined, is not an especially useful or intuitive concept is not enough to render it incoherent, and if it *is* coherent, then it appears there *could* be a "...er than" relation that is not transitive, and that is the issue currently under consideration.

Next, one might argue that "larger than" is a suspect relation, in that it is clearly a human *construction* that combines two natural relations, "heavier than" and "taller than." But I suspect that many "...er than" relations are human "constructions" that perhaps track certain natural relations, and that that isn't sufficient to render them suspect or incoherent. For example, the relation "wiser than" may be "constructed" out of a combination of relations including "smarter than," "more judicious," and "more experienced," such that *a*'s being wiser than *b* is a complicated function, determined by humans, of how *a* and *b* compare in terms of intelligence, judgment, and experience.

Finally, one might press the preceding point in another way. Granting that in *some* sense "larger than" and "wiser than" are both human constructions, one might nevertheless insist that the *way* "heavier than" and "taller than" combine to form the relation "larger than" is distinctly different than the *way* "smarter than," "more judicious," and "more experienced" combine to form the relation "wiser than." Correspondingly, one might contend that in the relevant sense "larger than" is an *artificial*—mere-Cambridge or grue-like—relation which should be dismissed, whereas "wiser than" is a "natural" relation to which we can rightly appeal. This claim is hard to assess. It has some intuitive appeal, and if it could be defended it might show that "larger than," as I defined it, is not a *genuine* counterexample to the claim that all *natural* "...er than" relations are transitive. But the artificial/natural distinction is notoriously difficult to defend, and even if it could be defended *other* counterexamples to the claim in question might still be possible.

Leaving open, for now, the question of whether *some* "...er than" relations are both coherent and nontransitive, let us consider further whether there is something shared by those "...er than" relations that are transitive that might illuminate the ultimate grounds of transitivity when it obtains.

Consider the sentences "John is tall," "John is heavy," and "John is fast." In these sentences, "tall," "heavy," and "fast" are each one-place properties that are ascribed to John. More important, for our purposes, linguists have claimed that such properties are *gradable*, and that gradability is correlated with transitivity.[2] According to linguists, there are two main tests for whether a property is gradable. First, is there a *natural comparative* associated with it? That is, can one naturally and intelligibly move from "*P* is *x*" to "*P* is *x*er than *Q*" or to "*P* is more *x* than *Q*"? Second, can one naturally and intelligibly attach *intensifiers* to the property? That is, could one easily move from "*P* is *x*" to "*P* is very *x*," or "*P* is very very *x*," or "*P* is extremely *x*"? One can see, then, that "tall" is a gradable property, since one can naturally and intelligibly move from "*P* is tall" to "*P* is taller than *Q*," and also to "*P* is very tall" or "*P* is extremely tall." Similarly for "is heavy" and "is fast."

Since "is taller than," "is heavier than," and "is faster than" are paradigmatic instances of transitive relations, and each is correlated with gradable properties, one might wonder whether gradability underlies transitivity, and if so, whether this can give us further insight into the nature and grounds of transitive relations. Let us consider this next.

The first point to note is that for a relation, *R*, to be transitive, it is not *necessary* that there be an underlying property, *P*, that is gradable. This is easily seen by considering the same examples as undermined the hypothesis that all transitive relations are "...er than" relations. Consider the transitive relation, *I*, "is identical to." There is no underlying property *P*, "is identity" or "is identical" that can be ascribed to an object. That is, while we can say, intelligibly, that "John is identical to himself" or "John is identical to John," we can't say, intelligibly, that "John is identity" or "John is identical," without that being ungrammatical or elliptical for a sentence unrelated to the identity relation, such as "John has a secret identity" or "John is an identical twin." Moreover, even if we can come up with a property *P*, which we might ascribe to someone by saying something like "John is identity" or "John is identical," it is clear that the identity relation, "is identical to," is not a natural comparative of such a property. That is, there is no natural and intelligible move from "*a* is identity" or "*a* is identical" to "*a* is more identical than *b*" or "*a* is identicaler than *b*." Similarly,

---

[2] I am grateful to Jason Stanley for informing me of the linguists' views on this topic and for discussing them with me. I have followed Stanley's characterization of the linguists' position in what follows.

there is no property, P, say, "is identical," underlying the identity relation, I, such that one can naturally and intelligibly attach intensifiers to that property. That is, it doesn't make sense to say that "a is very identical" or "a is extremely identical with b." Identity is an all-or-nothing notion. It doesn't admit of degrees. So, two things are either identical or they are not, but no one object is ever "very" identical or "extremely" identical.

Analogous remarks apply to the sameness relation, discussed earlier, "is the same with respect to property q as," as well as the right of relation, discussed earlier, "is to the right of" on a straight horizontal line in a Euclidian plane. Neither relation can be plausibly understood as the natural comparative of an underlying property, P, nor could one imagine applying intensifiers to any candidate P whose meaning would track that of the relations in question. So, for example, one couldn't intelligibly say something like "John is very, or extremely, the same"; nor could one intelligibly say something like "John is very, or extremely, to the right of on a straight line."

As noted previously, identity, sameness, and being to the right of are all transitive relations. It follows that it is not a necessary condition for a relation R to be transitive, that there be a gradable property P that underlies that relation.

But we can ask another question. If a property P *is* gradable, is that a *sufficient* condition for the relation, R, that is the natural comparative of P, to be transitive? Is there a link between gradability and transitivity of that sort?

I think not. Consider again my earlier defined notion of "larger than," where a is larger than b if and only if a is heavier than b or a is taller than b. We might think that underlying the "larger than" relation is the property of "largeness," where we could correctly describe someone as being large if and only if they were heavy or tall. So understood, the property of "largeness" would appear to be gradable in the linguists' sense of that notion. That is, there is a "natural" comparative, "larger than," associated with it, in the sense that one could naturally and intelligibly move from "John is large" (meaning that John is heavy or tall) to "John is larger than Mary" (meaning that John is heavier or taller than Mary). In addition, one can naturally and intelligibly attach *intensifiers* to the property of "largeness," in the sense that one could easily move from "John is large" to "John is very large" or "John is extremely large"—meaning that John is very heavy or very tall, or that John is extremely heavy or extremely tall, respectively. But, as we saw previously, the defined notion of "larger than" is *not* a transitive relation. Thus, it appears that the fact that a property P is gradable, in the linguists' sense, is *not* a sufficient condition for the relation, R, that is the natural comparative of P, to be transitive.

But recall that earlier I granted that the notion of "largeness," as I defined it, may not be a "natural" property. So, perhaps what linguists have seen is that there is a correlation between gradability and transitivity for all *natural* properties; specifically, that for all natural properties, P, if P is gradable, then the natural comparative relation, R, for the property P—"is Per than" or "is more P than"—is a transitive relation. Maybe this is right. But, as earlier, when I raised the question of whether or not all *natural* "...er than" relations were transitive, let me not try to decide this here. Instead, let me observe that when one thinks of the paradigmatic examples of "natural" properties that are gradable in the linguists' sense—"heaviness," "tallness," "fastness" and so on—one notices that such properties are *also* "gradable" in another, straightforward, sense, namely, that objects possessing the properties can be assigned grades or scores representing the degrees to which the objects possess the properties in question. One further notices that such grades or scores can be placed on a common, linear, scale—with separate scales for each gradable property—such that each point (or range of points, henceforth, for simplicity, I'll omit this qualification) on the scale would represent the amount or degree to which any object possessed the property in question. Importantly, but unsurprisingly, it is then apparent that there is a correlation between a property's being gradable in *this* sense and transitivity. This is because a linear scale is one that can be represented by the real number line, and "being a larger number than" *is* a transitive relation.

Thus, for properties like "heaviness," "tallness," or "fastness" there will be separate linear scales ranging from zero to infinity, such that any object that possesses the properties in question, to any degree, can be represented by a particular point or number on the relevant scale that would accurately reflect the amount or degree to which the object possessed the property. Naturally, such representations would guarantee and preserve transitivity, since if one point or number represents a larger amount or degree of the property in question than another second point or number, which in turn represents a larger amount or degree of the property in question than a third point or number, then the first point or number *will* represent a larger amount or degree of the property in question than the third point or number.

For example, one could construct a common linear scale for heaviness, on which the heaviness of all objects could be accurately represented, such that any three material objects could be represented on that scale by particular fixed points or numbers reflecting how heavy each was. The lightest object would be represented by a point closer to the low end of the scale than the others, and the heaviest object would be represented by a point closer to the high end. Since the particular point representing an object's amount or degree of heaviness remains fixed on that scale *independently* of what alternatives that object might be compared with regarding heaviness,[3] it follows that if the

---

[3] This is compatible with the observation that one might need two objects to set the common linear scale on which all objects might be ranked with respect to heaviness. For example, one might arbitrarily set one's linear heaviness scale so that a given feather weighs 1 unit and a given bar of iron 1,000 units, or so that the given feather weighs 100 units and the given bar of iron 1 million units, and then the number used to represent the weight of any given object would obviously depend on which scale one

points representing the first and second objects accurately reflect the fact that the second is heavier than the first, and the points representing the second and third objects accurately reflect the fact that the third is heavier than the second, then the points representing first and third objects *will* accurately reflect the fact that the third is heavier than the first, as transitivity entails. That is, if the number representing the weight of the third object is larger than the number representing the weight of the second object, and if the number representing the weight of the second object is larger than the number representing the weight of the first object, then, by the transitivity of the "being a larger number than" relation, the number representing the weight of the third object will be larger than the number representing the weight of the first object; thus, the "heavier than" relation *is* transitive as we all believe.

In sum, for any property, P, that is gradable in the sense we have been discussing—namely, that one can construct a common linear scale, such that the amount or degree to which any object possesses the property in question can be accurately represented by a point or number on that scale—there will be a relation, R, which is the comparative of P—corresponding to the two-place relation "is Per than" or "is more P than"—such that R will be a transitive relation. It may also be that any *natural* property P which is gradable in the linguists' sense is also gradable in the sense I have been discussing. If so, this may help explain, or illuminate, why linguists have thought that there is a connection between gradability in their sense and transitivity.

Return, now, to my previously discussed example of the nontransitive relation "larger than," where "*a* is larger than *b*" means "*a* is heavier than *b* or *a* is taller than *b*." Clearly, there is no common linear scale whose points would accurately represent the degree to which someone was "large." Rather, to compare any two people, *a* and *b*, regarding largeness, one would need to consult *two* linear scales to determine if either or both were larger than the other. Correspondingly, to know that *a* is larger than *c*, it would *not* be enough to know that *a* is larger than *b*, and *b* is larger than *c*. One would have to compare *a* and *c directly* in terms of how they compare on the different scales. For, as we've seen earlier, *a* might be larger than *b* because heavier, and *b* larger than *c* because taller, and yet *a* might not be larger than *c*, because *a* might be both lighter *and* shorter than *c*.

Let us sum up our results so far. Some two-place relations, R, are the comparatives of underlying one-place properties, P, which are gradable in the sense

---

chose to use. But the key point I am gesturing toward in the text is that the number used to represent the weight of any given object would just depend on facts about that object and the scale one was employing, so that the score that was warranted for a pencil on one's chosen scale wouldn't vary depending on the weight of any alternative objects one might compare it with. Thus, for example, it wouldn't be that a given pencil should be given a score of 1,000, say, in comparison with a feather, but a score of 10, say, in comparison with a bar of iron; whatever score the pencil was given to represent its weight on a given heaviness scale should remain fixed as long as the pencil, itself, remained unchanged.

I have been describing; namely, each object, O, which possess property P can be given a score representing the amount or degree of P that O possesses, where this score doesn't vary depending on which, if any, alternative objects O is compared with, and where the score can be represented by a point on a common linear scale whose points accurately represent the different amounts or degrees of P that an object might possess. In that case, R will be a transitive relation.

On the other hand, some two-place relations, S, are such that to know whether or not a stands in the relation S to b cannot always be determined by referring to a common linear scale that ranks each possible alternative with respect to a single underlying one-place property Q, where S is the comparative of Q. In that case, as we have seen, S may be a nontransitive relation. This is the case with my defined notion of "larger than," which I contended is a coherent notion, but which I also admitted may be an "artificial" notion of limited practical use.

Finally, we saw that some relations, like identity, sameness, and rightness, are transitive, though they are not "...er than" relations, and though there does not appear to be any underlying properties associated with those relations that are gradable in either of the senses we have discussed.[4] So, even if a property P's being gradable in my sense is *sufficient* to guarantee that its comparative relation, R, is transitive, it is not *necessary* for a relation, R, to be transitive that it be the comparative of an underlying property P that is gradable in my sense.[5] This is why I want to say that discovering that there is no common linear scale on which we can rank, and hence compare, alternatives with respect to an underlying one-place property Q—in order to determine whether or not a stands in the relation S to b, for any two alternatives a and b capable of standing in the S relation—*opens up the possibility* that S is a nontransitive relation and may help (when combined with some further considerations developed later) to account for why S is a nontransitive relation, if, in fact, it is; but it doesn't, by itself, *ensure* that S will be nontransitive, as the "identity" relation reminds us.

---

[4] I presented some considerations to think this was so for the linguists' sense of "gradability," but I think it is also true for my sense of "gradability" (though I didn't actually argue for this claim).

[5] I might add that other notions of "gradability" are also plausible that would generate transitive rankings of alternatives, but where individual outcomes could not be represented by points on the real number line. This might be because the number of alternatives being compared is too *large* for each alternative to be represented by a real number line (that is, cases where there are not only an infinite number of alternatives, but a number of alternatives that involves a higher order of infinity than that of the real numbers), or cases involving lexical priority, where any amount, no matter how small, of one kind of factor is more valuable than any amount, no matter how large, of another kind of factor, but where appeals to the second factor can break ties between any two alternatives that are equally good with respect to the first factor (see note 10 of chapter 10). I am grateful to Toby Ord for calling my attention to these points. Thus, while it is sufficient and illuminating in *most* cases, and for my present purposes, to think about the relation between gradability and transitivity along the lines I have suggested here, I am aware that a more complicated discussion is needed to handle *all* transitive relations.

6.2 Incommensurability/Incomparability and Conditions Where Transitivity Either Fails to Apply or Fails

It is often claimed of two objects, alternatives, or concepts that they are *incommensurable*. Literally, this means that there is no common scale on which they can both be measured and no single system of units in virtue of which they can both be measured, such that one could say the one object is this much better than the other in terms of those units, say, n units better, or m times as many units better. The notion of incommensurability is often conflated, or used interchangeably, with the notion of incomparability. Thus, when someone says that two objects are incommensurable, he often just means that the two objects are *incomparable*, and vice versa. In addition, someone might assert that two alternatives are incomparable *because* he thinks that they are incommensurable in the formal sense just indicated, and he believes that for *those* alternatives, at least, comparability *depends* on there being a common scale or unit in terms of which the alternatives can be measured.

Strictly speaking, I believe there is reason to distinguish between the formal notion of incommensurability just suggested, which holds that there is no common scale or system of units for measuring two objects, and the broader notion of incomparability. For example, it is often claimed that God's intelligence is incommensurable with ours. But this claim is false if incommensurability is interpreted to mean that the two intelligences are incomparable. The two *are* comparable; Hers is *vastly* superior to ours, indeed infinitely superior. On the other hand, the claim may well be true if it means that there is no common scale or system of units in which Her intelligence and ours can both be measured, and hence no meaningful content to the claim that Her intelligence might be n units or m times as many units greater than ours. However, having indicated that the notions might be usefully distinguished, in the following discussion I shall mostly follow the fairly common practice of not distinguishing between them. This will simplify my presentation and enable me to put my points in the way that they would often be put by people making the claims I shall be discussing. Still, at one point, I shall make plain how some people's claims about the *incomparability* of certain alternatives may be expressing or reflecting the view that the alternatives are *incommensurable* in the formal sense noted earlier.

Oddly, it is often remarked of two objects that are supposedly incommensurable that comparing them would be like comparing apples and oranges. But apples and oranges *are* comparable, at least in many respects and many contexts. They are comparable—and measurable in terms of a common scale or units—regarding their size, weight, nutritional value, and so on. For any particular individual, they are also comparable in terms of their taste, desirability, and so on.

Often the claim that two objects are incommensurable just amounts to the claim that they are not *precisely* comparable. We shall discuss this further soon, but comparability does not require *precision*. It might be that we can certainly compare two objects, and rightly rank one as superior to another, even if we cannot say *precisely how much* greater the one is than the other, and even if this is not due to any ignorance on our part, but to the fact there *is* no precise fact of the matter as to how much greater the one is.

I'm not sure if there are ever cases when two entities or alternatives are completely incommensurable, in *all* contexts. Consider, for example, two concepts which some people might claim are incommensurable: justice and the number 2. Assuming that justice is relevant to our moral deliberations, but the number 2 is not, while the number 2 is relevant to our mathematical manipulations while justice is not, might one not reasonably contend that justice is better than the number 2—because relevant—for the purposes of moral deliberation, while the number 2 is better than justice—because relevant—for the purposes of mathematical manipulation? And isn't this enough to show that there are at least *some* contexts where even such diverse "entities" as justice and the number 2 are comparable?

But perhaps not. It might be claimed that for two entities to be truly comparable it is not enough that one is relevant for a certain purpose and the second irrelevant. Rather, it might be contended, in claiming that one "entity" is better than another for a certain purpose, it has to at least make sense to ask the *extent* to which the one is better. Could it be the case, for example, that the one is n units better, or m times as good as the other, or anywhere from just a little better to vastly better? Here, it might be claimed, it makes no sense to say that justice is n units better, or m times as good as the number 2 for the purposes of moral deliberation, or vastly better rather than only moderately better. Hence, it might be urged, there is no real *comparison* being made here; there is just a taxonomic division of "entities" into two disjoint sets, which stand in the all-or-nothing relations of being relevant or not relevant for a particular purpose.

My aim here is not to settle the issue in question. Nor do I have anything novel or significant to contribute to the debate about incommensurability/incomparability. But it is, I think, worth reflecting on the thinking which underlies the claims that two concepts or "entities" are incommensurable. Rightly or not, those who believe that the number 2 is incommensurable with the ideal of justice believe that the two cannot be put on a common scale. A fortiori, they believe that there is no intelligible, linear scale measuring the degree to which something possesses a given property or properties, such that there is a point on that scale accurately representing the number 2, and another point accurately representing justice, such that the relation between those points accurately reflects the way the number 2 and justice compare with respect to the property or properties in question.

Why might someone hold such a view? They *might* believe that the nature of numbers is so radically different than the nature of moral ideals that there are simply no genuinely significant properties or characteristics that they share, such that they might be meaningfully compared in terms of those characteristics or properties. In other words, those who believe that numbers and moral ideals are incommensurable might believe that the factors that are relevant and significant for identifying and evaluating numbers differ from those that are relevant and significant for identifying and evaluating moral ideals. This would explain why there is no common scale for the two different kinds of things, and why there is no basis for comparisons between them. Correspondingly, knowing how two numbers compare, and knowing how two moral ideals compare, would tell us *nothing* about how the numbers compare to the ideals. It would, for example, be utterly absurd to claim that the best ideal was better than the lowest number, or that the greatest number was better than the least valuable ideal. Likewise, it would be equally absurd to claim that the best ideal was greater than the lowest number, or that the greatest number was greater than the least valuable ideal. Nor is there any other respect in which they might be meaningfully compared. This is, to repeat, for the fundamental reason that the factors that are relevant and significant for assessing numbers are different from those that are relevant and significant for assessing ideals. Thus, the evaluative categories that apply to numbers are different than the evaluative categories that apply to ideals, and there is no basis for evaluatively comparing numbers with ideals.

Let me stress that the preceding is not offered as a defense of the claim that numbers and moral ideals are completely incommensurable. Rather, it is intended to illuminate the thinking of those who might believe that there are cases of complete incommensurability.

In at least some cases of complete incommensurability, if there are any, we would have radically different categories of entities. So, it might be claimed, numbers are numbers, ideals are ideals, and nothing is both a number and an ideal.

Often we have disparate categories, subject to different standards of evaluation, where a single entity might be a member of both categories. There is nothing mysterious about this. John might belong to the categories of human, husband, father, philosopher, tennis player, and people over five feet tall. Clearly, the factors that are relevant and significant for identifying and evaluating husbands are different from those that are relevant and significant for identifying and evaluating tennis players. So, John might be a great husband but poor tennis player, and vice versa.

Suppose we know that Tim is a better tennis player than John, and that John is a better husband than Ted. What does that tell us about how Tim and Ted compare? Nothing! Why not? Because the factors that are relevant and significant for comparing tennis players are different than those that are relevant and significant for comparing husbands. By hypothesis, Tim ranks higher on the tennis-playing ability scale than John, and John ranks higher on the good husband scale than Ted. But though John appears on both scales, this gives us no basis for comparing Tim and Ted in terms of tennis ability, their goodness as husbands, or anything else. To know how Tim and Ted compare in terms of tennis-playing ability we'd have to compare them in terms of the factors that are relevant and significant for making *that* comparison, and this would involve determining where Ted ranks on the tennis-playing ability scale. To know how Tim and Ted compare in terms of being good husbands, we'd have to compare them in terms of the factors that are relevant and significant for making *that* comparison, and this would involve determining where Tim ranks on the good husband scale. In both cases, the fact that John is a better husband than Ted but a worse tennis player than Tim is irrelevant.

Suppose someone claimed that since we know Tim is better than John, and John better than Ted, we *do* know that Tim is better than Ted, by transitivity. In this case, such a claim would seem to evidence a gross misunderstanding of the concept of transitivity. Transitivity obtains for any relation R, such that if aRb, and bRc, then aRc, but transitivity does not *apply* where *different* relations, R, are invoked. Specifically, as we have just seen, if the factors that are relevant and significant for comparing people in terms of R_1 are different than the factors that are relevant and significant for comparing people in terms of R_2, then from the fact that aR_1b and bR_2c, *nothing* follows about how a and c compare, with respect to R_1 or R_2. Moreover, importantly, this would not be a *failure* of transitivity; rather, it would be a case where transitivity simply didn't *apply*.

In the preceding example, there *isn't* a single "better than" relation, B, such that if Tim$B$John, and John$B$Ted, then Tim$B$Ted. Rather, there are *two distinct* relations: "better than with respect to tennis-playing ability," B_t, and "better than with respect to being a good husband," B_h. It is not surprising, then, that although TimB_tJohn, and JohnB_hTed, *nothing* follows about how Tim compares to Ted, either with respect to tennis-playing ability or being a good husband. Thus, as seen, transitivity simply doesn't apply in such scenarios. It only applies to comparisons involving *single* two-place relations, not to comparisons involving two or more distinct two-place relations.

But now suppose there is a *third* relation, B_n, such that aB_nb if and only if either aB_tb or aB_hb. Clearly, TimB_nJohn, since TimB_tJohn. Also, JohnB_nTed, since JohnB_hTed. But it doesn't follow that TimB_nTed, since it *might be* that neither TimB_tTed nor TimB_hTed. In this case, it would be a mistake to claim that transitivity doesn't *apply* to the relation B_n. B_n *is*, in the relevant sense, a single two-place relation; hence it makes perfect sense to ask whether B_n is a transitive relation. And since there can be some alternatives a, b, and c, such that aB_nb and bB_nc, but not aB_nc, there is a straightforward answer. Like the relations "is fond of," "is near to," and "is the father of," B_n is *not* a transitive relation.

Our previously defined notion of "is larger than" fits precisely this model. We said that *a* is larger than *b*, *aLb*, if and only if either *a* is heavier than *b*, *aHb*, or *a* is taller than *b*, *aTb*. Certainly, we can intelligibly ask if the relation "is larger than," so understood, is transitive. That is, since *L* is a single two-place relation, we can reasonably consider whether it is transitive. But, as we've seen, for perfectly clear reasons, it is not. This is because it could be the case that *aLb*, because *aHb*, and *bLc*, because *bTc*, yet it is not the case that *aLc*, because it *might* be that both *cHa* and *cTa*.

The preceding is important. In one sense, B_n is a nontransitive relation *for the very same reason* that transitivity *fails to apply* across comparisons involving different relations. But we should distinguish between those cases where transitivity simply fails to apply and those cases where a relation *R* is nontransitive for underlying reasons that mirror those cases in which transitivity doesn't apply. *If* the factors that are relevant and significant for comparing two alternatives *with respect to a given relation R* can *vary* depending on the alternatives being compared—so, for example, *a* will stand in the relation *R* to *b* if it stands in the relation R_1 to *b*, and *b* will stand in the relation *R* to *c* if it stands in the relation R_2 to *c*, where R_1 and R_2 are distinct relations—then *R will be* a nontransitive relation. But if we simply compare one set of alternatives in terms of one relation, R_1, and another set of alternatives in terms of a second relation, R_2, then there is no single relation *R* to be judged transitive or nontransitive, hence the notion of transitivity doesn't even apply to such comparisons.

The preceding considerations support the following general conclusions. For any three alternatives, *a*, *b*, and *c*, there will be a transitive relation *R* in terms of which they can be compared *if* there is a common linear scale on which each of the alternatives can be ranked, where this will be the case whenever *R* is the natural comparative of a gradable one-place property that *a*, *b*, and *c* each possess to a certain extent. On the other hand, for any three alternatives, *a*, *b*, and *c*, if two of the alternatives are compared in terms of a relation, R_1, based on their rankings on one scale, while other alternatives are compared in terms of a different relation, R_2, based on their rankings on another scale, transitivity will not *apply* to the resulting set of pairwise rankings. However, *if* there were a relation, *R*, such that the comparison of certain alternatives with respect to *R* depended on how those alternatives ranked on one scale, while the comparison of other alternatives with respect to *R* depended on how those alternatives ranked on a different scale, then *R* would be a nontransitive relation, and this would be so for the very same underlying reason that transitivity fails to apply across different relations. Ultimately, this will occur if the relevant and significant factors for making one of the pairwise comparisons with respect to *R* differ from the relevant and significant factors for making any of the other pairwise comparisons with respect to *R*.

6.3 Rough Comparability

Some people distinguish between the notions of *full* comparability and *rough* comparability. A notion admits of full comparability if, for any two entities, *a* and *b*, that can be compared in terms of that notion, *a* is better than *b*, *b* is better than *a*, or *a* and *b* are exactly equal. A notion admits of rough comparability if there is a fourth category reflecting how two alternatives compare in terms of the notion in question which is distinct from, and mutually exclusive of, the other three categories of "better than," "worse than," or "exactly equal to."[6] This fourth category is described in various ways as "rough comparability," "not worse than," "the same league," "on a par," or "imprecise equality."[7]

---

[6] The fact that the notion of "rough comparability" discussed in this section and elsewhere in this book is distinct from and mutually exclusive of the other three categories of "better than," "worse than," or "exactly equal to" is very important. See note 13.

[7] Derek Parfit now claims that there are *six* categories of comparison, three of which he calls *precisely equal to*, *precisely better than*, and *precisely worse than*, and three of which he calls *imprecisely equal to*, *imprecisely better than*, and *imprecisely worse than*. These categories reflect Parfit's current view that some alternatives might be better than, worse than, or equal to others and by a precise amount, while others might be better than, worse than, or equal to others but only imprecisely so, where this is a metaphysical and not merely conceptual or epistemological matter. The view that Parfit previously called *rough comparability* he now calls *imprecise equality*. I prefer, and so employ, Parfit's original terminology for the view in question. However important Parfit's other two categories of "imprecisely better than" and "imprecisely worse than" may be in their own right, they are not pertinent to the points I want to make in this book. Hence, I mention them here, but ignore them in the text.

The terminology of "on a par" is owing to Ruth Chang; see her masterful introduction to her edited volume *Incommensurability, Incomparability, and Practical Reason* (Cambridge, MA: Harvard University Press, 1997). Although her understanding of the "on a par" relation is distinct from Parfit's understanding of the "rough comparability" relation in certain important respects, they are both members of a family of views that I don't need to distinguish between for my present purposes. Moreover, the locution "on a par" seems an apt one for describing the fourth category I am discussing here, whether or not one accepts the particular understanding of the "on a par" relation that Chang has defended.

Shelly Kagan has suggested that one might understand the fourth category in a way that does not presuppose that it is mutually exclusive of the other three mutually exclusive categories of "better than," "worse than," or "equal to." I readily grant that it is intuitively plausible to say of two alternatives that they are roughly comparable, or in the same league, or on a par, where this would *not* rule out one of the alternatives being a bit better or worse than the other. But, as Kagan recognizes, interpreted in such a way the fourth category is *not* equivalent to the one I am discussing in the text.

The category I am discussing is much more interesting, though also much more problematic and controversial! Indeed, some people are convinced that the category I am discussing is incoherent and, as such, has zero members in it—meaning that *no* two alternatives can actually stand in the relation of "rough comparability" or "not worse than" as I am characterizing it. Nevertheless, it is crucial to the category I am discussing that it *is* exclusive of the other three normally accepted categories of "better than," "worse than," and "equal to." The idea is that it might be true of two alternatives that we *can* say how they compare, but that how they compare just *is* that they are they are roughly comparable, not worse than each other, in the same league, etc., where this *further* means that neither is better or worse than the other, nor is it is the case that they are exactly equally as good. So, whereas "not worse than" is *usually* interpreted as equivalent to "at least as good as," as it is employed here it is a *technical* term which *rules out* *a*'s being equal to, better than, or worse than *b*, if *a* is not worse than *b*. See note 13.

The notion of full comparability is a familiar one, and easily demonstrated. Tallness is an example of a notion that is fully comparable. There are, of course, some objects that cannot be compared in terms of tallness, because the concept of tallness does not apply to them. So, for example, it isn't true that the number 2 is taller than the ideal of justice, or that the ideal of justice is taller than the number 2, or that they are equally tall. Still, for any two objects, *a* and *b*, to which the concept of tallness does apply, *a* is taller than *b*, or *b* is taller than *a*, or *a* and *b* are equally tall.

The notion of rough comparability is much less familiar. Parfit presents and motivates this notion in an important passage that is worth quoting in full. He writes:

> Consider three candidates for some literary prize, one Novelist and two Poets. We might claim, of the Novelist and the first Poet, that neither is worse than the other. This would not be claiming that these two cannot be compared. It would be asserting rough comparability. There are many poets who would be worse candidates than this Novelist, and many novelists that would be worse candidates than the First Poet. We are claiming, of these two, that something important can be said about their respective merits. Neither is worse than the other. They are in the same league. Suppose next that we judge the *Second* Poet to be slightly better than the first. (When we are comparing two poets, our judgments can be less rough.) Does this judgment force us to conclude either that the Second Poet is better than the Novelist, or that the First is worse? It does not. We can claim that, though the Second Poet is better than the First, neither is worse than the Novelist, who is worse than neither....
>
> Rough comparability is, in some cases, merely the result of ignorance. When this is true, we believe that there is in principle precise or full comparability. This would be true, when we compare the Novelist and either Poet, if the only possibilities are that one is better, or that both are exactly equally as good. In such a case, this is not plausible. The rough comparability is here *intrinsic*, not the result of ignorance. Must it be true, of Proust or Keats, either that one was the greater writer, or that both were *exactly equally* as great? There could not be, even in principle, such precision. But some poets are greater writers than some novelists, and by more or less.[8]

On Parfit's view, then, when two people are roughly comparable in some respect, we *can* make true positive claims about how they compare. So it isn't that they aren't in fact comparable in that respect, or that there is no fact of the matter how they compare, or that while there is a fact of the matter we can't

---

[8] Derek Parfit, *Reasons and Persons* (Oxford: Oxford University Press), 431.

determine what it is; rather we can say, truly, that neither is *worse than the other*. This is a meaningful, and important, direct comparison which tells us that neither is better than the other and that they are *not* exactly equally as good; rather they are *roughly comparable*, in the same league, or on a par.

As Parfit explicitly acknowledges, the preceding directly implies that "when there is only rough comparability *not worse than* is not a transitive relation.... The First Poet is not worse than the Novelist, who is not worse than the Second Poet. This does not force us to change our view that the First Poet *is* worse than the Second."[9]

John Broome once argued for the same position.[10] Suppose one is choosing between two alternative career paths. One might choose to be a lawyer or an academic. Broome observed that while there might be some careers as a lawyer that would be clearly inferior to some academic careers, and vice versa, and some careers as a lawyer that would be clearly superior to some academic careers, and vice versa, there might be some careers as a lawyer that were not worse than some academic careers, where this meant that the different careers were in the same league, or on a par, and *not* that the careers were *exactly equally* as good, or that one was really somewhat better than the other, but that the differences between them were so small that we either couldn't detect them, or could safely ignore them in our deliberations.

Broome offered a helpful illustration of the scenario he had in mind. Consider diagram 6.3.A.[11]

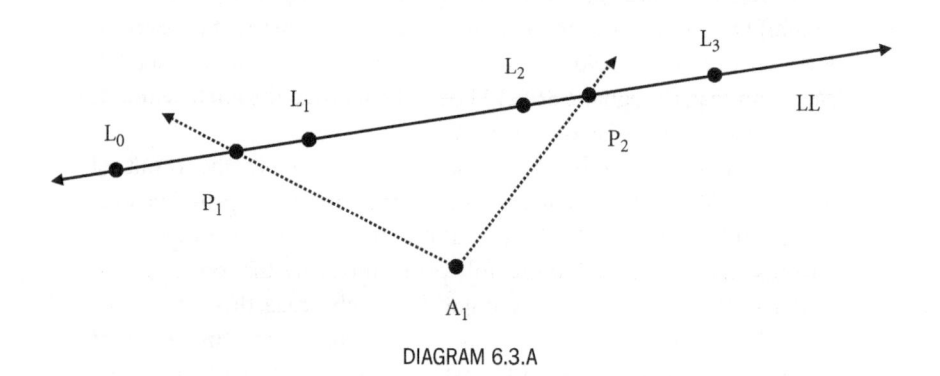

DIAGRAM 6.3.A

---

[9] Parfit, *Reasons and Persons*, 431.

[10] In a talk given at an Eastern Division meeting of the American Philosophical Association. The following presentation of Broome's view, including diagram 6.3.A, is taken from that talk, and although some of the details of my presentation may differ from Broome's original talk, I am confident that my presentation is faithful to the content of his talk. In particular, I pointed out to Broome during the question-and-answer period following his talk that his diagram and discussion implied that "not worse than" was not a transitive relation, and he explicitly recognized and accepted that that was the case. Unfortunately, Broome's talk was some years back, and neither he nor I recall its title, year, or location.

[11] Diagram 6.3.A is based on a diagram presented by Broome at his APA talk (see note 10), but Ruth Chang informs me that she has also used a diagram of this kind to illustrate her notion of "on a par," and Derek Parfit has also drawn similar diagrams with me to indicate what he thinks is going on

A_1 represents a pretty good, but not outstanding, academic life. The line, LL, containing L_0–L_3 represents a range of possible legal careers, such that each point on the scale represents a career that is better than those careers represented by those points to the left of it, but worse than those careers represented by those points to the right of it. Thus, as drawn, L_1 represents a legal career that is better than L_0, L_2 a career that is better than L_1, and L_3 a career that is better than L_2.

For Broome, diagram 6.3.A is intended to reflect the following. Some legal careers, such as the one represented by L_0, would clearly be worse than A_1. Perhaps L_0 involves 100 hours per week of thankless drudgery in a high-pressure environment with low pay. By the same token, some legal careers, such as the one represented by L_3, would clearly be better than A_1. Perhaps L_3 involves stimulating work, reasonable hours, tremendous pay, and an array of fantastic personal benefits. Still, there will be some legal careers that are neither better nor worse than A_1. L_1 and L_2 are two such lives. L_1 and L_2 offer an array of advantages and disadvantages that are quite different than the advantages and disadvantages offered by the academic life of A_1, but the lives are roughly comparable. As indicated earlier, this means that *those* legal lives are *not worse than* the academic life of A_1, and vice versa, but this does *not* mean that they are exactly equally as good. Rather they are in the same league, or on a par.

As drawn, diagram 6.3.A is slightly misleading. It suggests that there may be precise points, P_1 and P_2, such that every legal career represented by a point to the left of P_1 would be worse than A_1, every legal career represented by a point to the right of P_2 would be better than A_1, and every legal career represented by points between P_1 and P_2 would be not worse than A_1. But one needn't believe that there would be such precise delineations. Rather, one might believe that there would be a range of legal careers around P_1, where it would be indeterminate whether those careers were worse or not worse than A_1, and similarly a range of legal careers around P_2, where it would be indeterminate whether those careers were not worse or better than A_1. But it is true that at some point each of the legal careers to the left of the indeterminate range around P_1 would be worse than A_1, each of the careers to the right of the indeterminate range around P_2 would be better than A_1, and each of the careers between the two ranges would be not worse than A. That is all diagram 6.3.A is intended to convey, along with the fact that L_0 represents a life in the worse

---

with his notion of "not worse than." All agree that two alternatives that are "not worse than," "roughly comparable," or "on a par" with each other cannot be put on a common linear scale, which would enable one to judge that one of the alternatives was better than the other, or that they were equally good. Unfortunately, I don't know who deserves credit for first coming up with such a diagram to illustrate the view in question, or whether the idea originated with several people independently.

career group, L_3 a life in the better career group, and L_1 and L_2 careers in the not worse group.

Like Parfit, Broome believed that "not worse than" is a nontransitive relation. His diagram reveals this, since according to the diagram, L_1 is not worse than A_1, and A_1 is not worse than L_2, but L_1 *is* worse than L_2.

Why might someone hold such a position? Recall that when we say that a legal career that pays $180,000 per year might nonetheless be in the same league as or on a par with an academic career that pays $85,000 per year, we do not mean that they are *exactly equally* as good. Why not? Because nobody believes that if the law firm were to pay $4,000 per year less the law career would then be worse than the academic career, while if it were to pay $4,000 per year more it would then be better. The choice between careers is going to largely turn on considerations of stress, freedom, personal integrity, prestige, location, prospects of success, love of teaching or research, and so on. Of course, salary will certainly be relevant, in that the academic life might be better if the two salaries were equivalent, while the lawyer's life might clearly be better if it paid $1 million more per year. But if one didn't believe that one of the careers was better or worse than the other when the difference in salary was $95,000 per year, surely, one might think, $4,000 a year more or less wouldn't settle the issue one way or the other. But, and this is the key point, $4,000 a year *could* make the difference, and rightly so, between two legal careers that were otherwise equivalent. That is, if one presumed that L_1 and L_2 would be the same in all other respects, but that in L_1 one would make $180,000 per year, while in L_2 one would make $184,000 per year, it would make perfect sense to rank L_2 as better than L_1. Hence, one can see why Broome and Parfit have concluded that "not worse than" is not a transitive relation. On the preceding reasoning, it might well be that L_1 is not worse than A_1, and A_1 not worse than L_2, and yet L_1 *is* worse than L_2.

Diagram 6.3.A is, I think, highly illuminating. *LL* is a line that represents a common, linear scale ranking different legal careers. Now Broome needn't believe that *all* legal careers can be placed on such a scale; however, it is reasonable to believe that there could be such a scale enabling us to rank many legal careers as better or worse than each other. But, then, what Broome has recognized, and what diagram 6.3.A reveals, is that if there *is* a notion of rough comparability of the sort we have been discussing, those alternatives that are only roughly comparable to certain legal careers *can't be put on such a scale*. Such considerations suggest the following. We might have one linear scale that would enable us to fully compare, in the sense of ranking as better, worse, or equal to, certain legal careers. And we might have a different linear scale that would enable us to fully compare certain academic careers. But then we would require a third, nonlinear scale, to compare certain legal careers with certain academic careers, and this scale would often only generate rankings of rough comparability. Correspondingly, for all the reasons discussed in section 6.2, we shouldn't expect transitivity to obtain between different alternatives, if they cannot all be accurately represented by points on a single, linear scale.[12]

In "explaining" how it can be the case that "not worse than" is not a transitive relation, Parfit only offers one, parenthetical remark. As noted earlier, he writes, "When we are comparing two poets, our judgments can be less rough." So, his claim is that we might only have rough comparability between the First Poet and a Novelist, and we might only have rough comparability between the Novelist and the Second Poet, and yet we might have full comparability between the First Poet and the Second, because our judgments between two poets "can be less rough" than our judgments between poets and novelists. This, then, supposedly "explains" why not worse than may be nontransitive, since, by hypothesis, the First Poet is not worse than the Novelist, and the Novelist is not worse than the Second Poet, but it doesn't follow that the First Poet is not worse than the Second. Indeed, it might be that the First Poet is better than, worse than, or equal to the Second. But what still cries out for explanation is *why* our judgments can be "less rough" when comparing two poets.

Parfit rests his claim on its intuitive plausibility. But our discussion in this section and section 6.2 helps illuminate this issue. Why are there different scales for comparing fathers than for comparing tennis players? Because different factors are relevant and significant for being a good father than for being a good tennis player. Why are there different scales for comparing poets than for comparing novelists, or for comparing legal careers than for comparing academic careers? Because different factors can have different relevance and significance for being a good poet than for being a good novelist, or for being a desirable career as a lawyer or academic. Furthermore, the factors that come into play in comparing poets with novelists, or the careers of lawyers with the careers of

---

[12] I have put Broome's position here in terms of the notion of "not worse than," which is the way Parfit has put it and the way Broome put it in the lecture where he presented his original diagram. In recent correspondence, Broome put his claims in terms of "incommensurability" in the formal sense discussed in section 6.2. Putting the point in terms of incommensurability would require some minor revisions in my presentation, but no substantive changes in the content of my claims. The idea would be that there are certain academic lives, like A_1 that are incommensurate with certain legal lives, like L_1 and L_2, but this does not mean that L_1 and L_2 must be incommensurate. This is what diagram 6.3.A reflects. L_1 and L_2 can be put on a common linear scale enabling us to compare them and to determine that L_2 is better than L_1, but A_1 is incommensurate with them and hence cannot be put on the same linear scale. If one further adds that in the case in question, where A_1 is incommensurate with L_1 and L_2, there is no other, independent reason to judge A_1 as better than, worse than, or equal to L_1 and L_2 (which would be a slightly weaker claim than the one I made in the text, about having a third, nonlinear, scale, to compare certain legal careers with certain academic careers which would generate rankings of rough comparability), then, to anticipate our later discussion, Broome might claim that given the choice between L_2 and A_1 it would be rational to be indifferent between them, and similarly that given the choice between A_1 and L_1 it would be rational to be indifferent between them, but that given the choice between L_2 and L_1 it would *not* be rational to be indifferent between them. Here we have a position which is substantively similar to the position presented in the text, only it is put in terms of incommensurability rather than in terms of "not worse than."

academics, can vary, and vary in their significance, than those that come into play when just comparing alternatives of the same type. Thus, as we've seen, a factor that might have great significance when comparing two careers of the same kind, say, a salary difference of $4,000, might have different significance when comparing careers of markedly different kinds.

To sum up, we have seen that transitivity obtains among alternatives that can be ranked on a common linear scale. Also, that there is no reason to expect transitivity to obtain between alternatives that cannot be ranked on such a scale. But the key point is that whether or not alternatives can be ranked on the same linear scale will depend on whether the relevance and significance of the factors are the same for assessing and comparing the alternatives in question. If the factors for comparing a with b differ in their relevance or significance from those for comparing b with c, or a with c, then knowing how a compares to b in terms of the factors that are relevant and significant for making that comparison, and knowing how b compares to c in terms of the factors that are relevant and significant for making that comparison, will tell us nothing about how a compares to c in terms of the factors that are relevant and significant for making *that* comparison. This explains how it can be the case, and when it will be the case, that a relation is not transitive, or that transitivity does not even apply for certain sets of comparisons. Finally, we have seen that when the alternatives being compared are sufficiently different (for example, in certain contexts poets are sufficiently different than novelists, and the careers of lawyers sufficiently different than the careers of academics), then the relevance or significance of the factors for comparing such disparate alternatives may vary from the relevance or significance of the factors for comparing similar alternatives (like poets with poets, or legal careers with legal careers).

Not everyone accepts the category of rough comparability. Correspondingly, not everyone believes that "not worse than" (in my wide reason-implying sense) is not a transitive relation. My aim here has not been to defend this position, but to articulate it, and illustrate the reasoning underlying it. Even if one has doubts about the position espoused by Parfit and (at one time) Broome, understanding *why* someone might think that "not worse than" is not a transitive relation helps illuminate the underlying conditions that determine whether a relation is ultimately transitive or not.[13]

---

[13] It is perhaps worth emphasizing again a point already made in note 6 that the notion of "rough comparability" discussed in this section and elsewhere in this book is importantly different from another, "standard" notion of "rough comparability," according to which "rough comparability" simply means "roughly equal to" or "about as good as." This is a perfectly plausible notion of "rough comparability" that is widely used, and that also corresponds to an intransitive relation in a perfectly clear, straightforward, and innocent way. We might illustrate it as follows.

Suppose that, in fact, we could assign precise numbers, ranging between 0 and 100, to accurately represent how good any given career was. Suppose, further, that we thought that any two careers whose numbers were within 7 were "roughly comparable," meaning that they were "*roughly* equal to" or "*about*

6.4 Rational Decision Making and the Nontransitivity of Not Worse Than

Suppose that Parfit and Broome were right that "not worse than" is not a transitive relation. Specifically, suppose that as diagram 6.3.A illustrates, it could be that L_1 is not worse than A_1, which is not worse than L_2, but that L_1 is worse than L_2. This raises a problem analogous to the problem of iteration raised in sections 3.3 and 3.5. Specifically, it might well be that the result of our making a series of choices, each of which was rationally defensible, or perhaps even rationally required, might lead us from one alternative to another that was clearly inferior to it. Let me illustrate this.

Suppose one was given a choice between adopting one career and another that was clearly inferior to it, where, for the sake of the example, assume that there is a time delay between making one's choice and its realization. So, suppose one had a choice between L_2 and L_0 in diagram 6.3.A, where whichever alternative one chose would be realized three months from now. Clearly, one would rationally choose L_2, since, by hypothesis, L_2 is a far superior career to L_0.

---

as good as" each other, but that any two careers whose numbers differed by 7 or more were not "roughly comparable," meaning that we wouldn't say they were "*roughly* equal to" or "*about* as good as" each other. Clearly, the corresponding relation of "roughly comparable to" would be intransitive, as there could be three careers, A, B, and C, such that the scores representing how good those careers were would be 60, 55, and 50, respectively, in which case, A would be roughly comparable with B, and B would be roughly comparable with C, but A would not be roughly comparable with C.

As indicated, *this* notion of "rough comparability" is a perfectly plausible one that also generates intransitive "roughly comparable to" judgments in a perfectly straightforward way. And *this* notion does not raise the specter that "all-things-considered better than" might not be a transitive relation. However, as should be clear, *this* standard notion of "rough comparability" is *not* the one that Parfit, Broome, and Chang have in mind when they claim that there may be a fourth relation in which alternatives stand to one another other than the "better than," "equal to," or "worse than" relations. After all, on the standard notion of "rough comparability," any two alternatives that are roughly comparable will *also* stand in one of the other three relations of being better than, equal to, or worse than each other. So, for instance, in the preceding example, A would be roughly comparable with B, but it would *also* be *better* than B, and similarly, B would be roughly comparable with C, but it would *also* be *better* than C. But on the view that Parfit, Broome, and Chang have in mind this is *not* the case. On their view "being roughly comparable to" is distinct from and mutually incompatible with "being better than," "being equal to," or "being worse than"; so, *if* two alternatives are roughly comparable, they do *not* stand in one of the other three relations. This is why Broome, Parfit, and Chang would all appeal to a diagram like diagram 6.3.A to represent the relation of "rough comparability" or "not worse than" or "on a par" that they have in mind. On the standard notion of "rough comparability" each alternative could, in principle, be represented on a common linear scale like the real number line, and, correspondingly, that notion of "rough comparability" does not give rise to any worries about whether "all-things-considered better than" is a transitive relation.

So, my point in this section is to show how understanding the notion of "rough comparability" that Parfit, Broome, and Chang had in mind, and that many people accept, helps to illuminate certain conditions that would account for why a relation might be intransitive, and, as we will see later, helps to illuminate how it might be the case that "all-things-considered better than" (in my wide reason-implying sense) is not a transitive relation. But this is not to deny that there is also another standard notion of "roughly comparable to" that is also intransitive, but that does not give rise to any worries about the transitivity of the "all-things-considered better than" relation.

I am grateful to Geoffrey Ferrari for pressing me to clarify this point.

Next, suppose that after one has chosen L_2, but before it is realized, one is given a further option of choosing A_1. By hypothesis, neither alternative is worse than the other, all things considered, so one might rationally choose to decide between them on the basis of a fair coin flip.

Next, suppose that just as one is about to flip the coin, someone offers one $2,000 to select A_1. If, as seems reasonable, one was genuinely prepared to take either A_1 or L_2 on the basis of a coin flip—that is, if one might be rationally justified in accepting A_1 rather than L_2 without *any* inducement to do so—it seems it would be perfectly rational to choose A_1 if given $2,000 to do so. Indeed, though my argument does not depend on this, it might seem *irrational not* to take the $2,000 in that case, letting the extra money one would thereby receive be the basis for one's decision.

So suppose one does so. One then has $2,000 and will realize alternative A_1 in three months. But now, suppose that before A_1 is actually realized, one is given a further option of choosing L_1. Exactly similar considerations would apply to the choice between A_1 and L_1 as previously applied to the choice between L_2 and A_1. Since, *by hypothesis*, neither is worse than the other, all things considered, if given the choice between them one might rationally choose on the basis of a fair coin toss.

But then suppose, as before, that just as one is about to flip the coin, someone offers one $2,000 to select L_1. Once again, if one was genuinely prepared to take either on the basis of a coin flip—that is, if one would be rationally justified in accepting L_1 rather than A_1 without *any* inducement to do so—it seems it would be perfectly rational to choose L_1 if given $2,000 to do so. Indeed, it might again seem *irrational not* to take the $2,000 in that case, letting the extra money be the basis for one's decision (though, again, the argument here does not depend on this stronger claim).

Thus, it appears that it would be rational to choose A_1 rather than L_2 if given $2,000 to do so, and rational to choose L_1 rather than A_1 if given $2,000 to do so. But this means that if one makes both, *perfectly rational*, choices, one would end up at L_1 with $4,000 rather than L_2. But, by hypothesis, L_2 is just like L_1 except that it involves a higher salary of an extra $4,000 *per year*. Assuming, for simplicity, that one will hold one's job for twenty years, and that one's salary will remain constant throughout one's job, then clearly L_2 is a *much* better alternative than L_1 plus $4,000, as over the course of one's career one would earn an extra $80,000 in L_2. How much better of an alternative is L_2 than L_1? We don't need a precise answer to this question, but surely it would be rational to spend $6,000 to be able to have the career depicted by L_2 rather than the one depicted by L_1. Correspondingly, it would clearly be irrational to choose L_1 and $4,000 over L_2.[14] It appears, then, that this is another case where a series of

---

[14] Here, as elsewhere, my example assumes an "other things equal" clause. I am assuming, for example, that one doesn't have an immediate need or use for $4,000 which would make $4,000 now more valuable than $80,000 spread out in the coming years.

rational choices might lead us away from a clearly superior outcome to a clearly inferior one.

6.5 Rational Preferences and the Money Pump

Economists have long claimed that people with *intransitive preferences* were irrational. In partial support of their claim, they noted a worry connected with the problem of *cycling*, illustrated by examples like the "money pump." Suppose Sue has intransitive preferences between three outcomes, genuinely preferring A to B, and B to C, but C to A. And suppose Sue starts in C. Since, by hypothesis, Sue *genuinely* prefers B to C, presumably she would be willing to pay a small amount, say a nickel, to move to B. Similarly, she would also pay a small amount, say another nickel, to move from B to A. But then, given her intransitive preferences, Sue should also be willing to pay a nickel to move from A to C. The result is that Sue might pay fifteen cents to end up in the very place she started. Worse yet, unless she changes her intransitive preferences—or simply refuses to pay even a small amount to move from one outcome to another *genuinely* preferred one—then nothing prevents Sue from "cycling," and hence being "money pumped," again and again, until eventually she has spent *all* her money only to end up where she began.

Section 6.4 suggests that there may be some cases where one could be "money pumped" where the preferences which account for this are not *themselves* intransitive. There is no *intransitivity* between (1) starting at L_2, it is rational to accept \$2,000 to choose A_1 rather than to flip a coin between A_1 and L_2; (2) starting at A_1 with \$2,000, it is rational to accept \$2,000 to choose L_1 rather than to flip a coin between A_1 and L_1; and (3) starting at L_1 with \$4,000, it is rational to pay \$6,000 to move to L_2. That is, there is no way of understanding the three statements in terms of three distinct alternatives, *a*, *b*, and *c*, and a single relation, *R*, such that (1) is equivalent to the claim that *aRb*, (2) equivalent to the claim that *bRc*, and (3) equivalent to the claim that it is not the case that *aRc*.

Suppose, for example, that *R* is the "it is rational to prefer" relation, so that *aRb* means that it is rational to prefer *a* to *b*. Then (1) tells us that it is rational to prefer *a*, accepting \$2,000 to choose A_1 to *b*, flipping a coin between A_1 and L_2 when one is initially at L_2; (2) tells us that it is rational to prefer *c*, accepting \$2,000 to choose L_1, when one is initially at A_1 with \$2,000 to *d*, flipping a coin between L_1 and A_1 when one is initially at A_1 with \$2,000; and (3) tells us that it is rational to prefer *e*, L_2 less \$6,000 to *f*, L_1 with \$4,000. Here, we simply have *aRb*, *cRd*, and *eRf*, where *a*, *b*, *c*, *d*, *e*, and *f* are all *distinct* alternatives. Correspondingly, one cannot conclude that *R* is intransitive on the basis of (1), (2), and (3).

Yet, clearly, anyone who accepts (1), (2), and (3) can be money pumped. After all, starting at L_2, one would accept \$2,000 to move to A_1, accept an additional $2,000 to move to L_1, and then pay $6,000 to move to L_2. Thus, one would have suffered a net loss of $2,000 only to end up where one started, and unless one changes one of one's beliefs, and rejects at least one of (1), (2), and (3), or alternatively refuses to act on the basis of one of those beliefs when the relevant opportunity presents itself, nothing will prevent one from continually being money pumped until, as in the original money pump cases, one eventually ends up where one began, but broke.

Economists may be unimpressed by the preceding claim.[15] They may grant that our acceptance of (1), (2), and (3) does not *itself* involve a set of intransitive preferences, but they may nonetheless assert that it is *based* on a set of intransitive preferences reflecting our acceptance of an intransitive *indifference* relation. That is, it is only because our preferences are such that we are *indifferent* between L_2 and A_1, and *indifferent* between A_1 and L_1, but we are *not indifferent* between L_2 and L_1, that we accept each of (1), (2), and (3) and hence are susceptible of being money pumped. Thus, economists may continue to insist that the *root* of our being liable to being money pumped is having intransitive preferences, whether or not they underlie "better than" judgments or "indifference" judgments.

As indicated earlier, economists tend to claim that people with intransitive preferences are *irrational*, and they might now add that this is so whether or not the intransitive preferences involve "better than" judgments or merely "indifference" judgments. But though it may sound plausible to claim that someone who *prefers a* to *b* and *b* to *c* is irrational if they don't also prefer *a* to *c*, it is much less obvious that someone who is *indifferent* between *a* and *b* and *b* and *c* must also be indifferent between *a* and *c*, if they are not to be irrational. Indeed, as we have seen, both Parfit and Broome, who want to insist that "better than" is a transitive relation, once agreed that "not worse than" is not a transitive relation. But if "not worse than" *isn't* a transitive relation, then it would seem to be perfectly rational to be indifferent between *a* and *b* and indifferent between *b* and *c*, yet not be indifferent between *a* and *c*. Yet, as we have seen, someone with intransitive indifference judgments is susceptible to being money pumped, just as someone with intransitive better than judgments is. Thus, it is unclear that the possibility of being money pumped is really quite the mark of irrationality that some economists and others have taken it to be.

Indeed, even if economists are right that in *some* sense people with intransitive preferences are irrational, strictly speaking all the *money pump* shows is that in certain circumstances it would be irrational to both retain, and *repeatedly act on*, one's intransitive preferences. So, for example, it is assumed that part of the circumstances is that people have an overarching aim that their lives go well in ways that would be precluded if they allowed themselves to go

---

[15] I owe the following point to Shelly Kagan.

broke by being repeatedly money pumped. If people didn't have such an overarching preference, or didn't allow themselves to *act* on their intransitive preferences, it is hard to see how the mere possibility of being money pumped in virtue of their having intransitive preferences would be enough to make people irrational.

Economists tend to assert, often derisively, that people with intransitive preferences ought to "get their preferences in order." I have some sympathy with this assertion in many of the standard cases where intransitive preferences are presumed to obtain. But, importantly, this is because in such cases we often think that there is no *fact of the matter* about what preferences people *should* have. Suppose, for example, that in fact Jane prefers chocolate to vanilla, and vanilla to strawberry, but strawberry to chocolate. Here, one might claim that each of Jane's preferences is perfectly rational, considered *individually*, but that *collectively* they are irrational. Correspondingly, one might argue that if Jane wants to be rational she either has to refrain from *acting* on her individual preferences or has to *change* at least one of her preferences.

But notice, in this case it doesn't matter *which* individual preference she changes. More important, there is no rational objection to her changing *any* of her individual preferences. So, while there is nothing irrational about Jane's actual preference for chocolate over vanilla, there would also be nothing irrational about her preferring vanilla to chocolate. And similarly for her other particular individual preferences in this case. This is why, in such cases, it seems perfectly reasonable for economists and others to insist that if people want to avoid getting money pumped, they should "get their preferences in order." After all, in such cases there is no rational objection to getting them in order in any way they'd like if they are able to.

In the case I have been discussing the economists' solution to "standard" cases where one might be money pumped rings hollow. One can't just avoid being money pumped by "getting one's preferences in order" for the simple reason that the possibility of being money pumped does not rest on the intransitivity of some arbitrary or merely subjective set of preferences. Rather, it rests on the fact that "not worse than" is *not* a transitive relation. And given this fact, each of (1), (2), and (3) seems *true*. Moreover, and more important, if (1), (2), and (3) *are* true, it is not *up to us* to change their truth value, the way it *is* up to us to change our preferences if we are able.

Recall the person with the intransitive preferences regarding ice cream. As noted, there is *nothing* objectionable about her changing *any* of her three preferences, if she is able to. So, for example, if she previously preferred strawberry to chocolate but, to avoid being money pumped, is now willing and able to prefer chocolate to strawberry, there would be *nothing* odd or irrational about her changing her preference in that manner for that purpose. Contrast that case to the situation involving (1), (2), and (3). One can't simply *decide* to reject (3) to avoid being money pumped. After all, (3) tells us that it is rational to prefer L_2 less $6,000 to L_1 with $4,000, and it really *is* rational to prefer L_2 less $6,000 to L_1 with $4,000! The truth about this claim depends upon facts about L_1 and L_2, and it is not simply *up to us* to change those facts. Our rational desire to avoid being money pumped may give us reason to ignore the truths expressed by (1), (2), and (3), or to refuse to *act* on those truths, but it doesn't alter the fact, assuming it is a fact, that (1), (2), and (3) *are* true, and that we have most reason, theoretically or epistemically, to *believe* them.

To sum up. In section 6.4, we saw that if Parfit and Broome were right that "not worse than" is not a transitive relation, then a series of rational choices might lead one from a rationally superior outcome to a rationally inferior one. In this section, we saw how this fact could lead one to being money pumped in a way that was not merely based on a set of arbitrary or subjective intransitive preferences, and hence could not be avoided by simply getting one's preferences in order.

6.6 The Importance of Global and Strategic Reasoning

Jon Elster once characterized rationality as the ability to effectively engage in global reasoning.[16] More specifically, Elster distinguished between organisms or systems that were "local maximizers," and those that were "global maximizers." Focusing on agents, a local maximizer was someone who, when faced with a choice between two alternatives, always chose *as if* those alternatives were the only options he would ever have, and so he based his choice on whichever of those options would *itself* maximize his expected benefit. A global maximizer, on the other hand, looked beyond any currently available options and anticipated what other options might become available as a result of his choices. Among currently available options, he then chose whichever option was part of the sequence of present and future options that would maximize his expected benefit over the course of his life. So, in essence, the local maximizer chose among options as they came along and always maximized his local, or current, state of well-being. Whereas the global maximizer looked ahead, and planned ahead, and made some choices now not merely with an *eye* toward other choices that would later be available, but with the *purpose* of making some choices available that would otherwise be unavailable, and all so as to maximize his global level of well-being. So, the global maximizer was someone who committed himself to following the path, or sequence of options, that would make his (expected) life, as a whole, go as well as possible.

---

[16] See chapter 1 of Elster's illuminating book *Ulysses and the Sirens* (Cambridge: Cambridge University Press, 1979).

Elster suggests that the crucial difference between a local maximizer and a rational, global maximizer is that the latter, but not the former, is able to take "one step backwards for the sake of two steps forward." He illustrates this idea as follows. Suppose one has a strong desire to see as far as possible, and is halfway up a small hill. Given the choice between moving farther up the hill or down the hill, the local maximizer will always move up the hill, as this will enable him to see farther than he currently does. As the choice is faced repeatedly, the local maximizer will soon find himself at the top of the small hill, where he will remain, since any move away from the top will worsen his view and hence be "locally" worse for him. The global maximizer, on the other hand, takes a different perspective. He takes a broader, long-term, global perspective. The global maximizer would look around, and if he sees that there is a much taller mountain nearby, he will climb down the small hill in order to then be able to climb up the much taller mountain. In the short run, of course, his view will worsen, but in the long run he will have a much better view from the tall mountain than he ever would have had from the small hill. Here, Elster suggests, the global maximizer is better able to achieve his aim, overall, than the local maximizer because of his ability to take "one step backwards in order to take two steps forward."

As noted previously, the global maximizer is a planner. He looks ahead, he anticipates changes in circumstances, and he takes certain steps with the aim of affecting the future choices that will be available to him. Often, to do this is to engage in *strategic* planning involving others. In chess, for example, one might move a valuable piece to a vulnerable position, in hope and anticipation that one's opponent will take the piece in question, so that one might then make an effective move that would otherwise not be available. Similarly, to ensure that one's life, on the whole, go as well as possible, one might engage in strategic planning with one's own future self, making certain decisions now in anticipation of what one will later do, or want to do, or indeed to directly influence what one will later do or want to do.

Elster gives the classic example of Ulysses tying himself to the mast to exemplify such reasoning. Ulysses wants to hear the Sirens' song. But he knows that if he hears the Sirens' song he will desperately want to turn the ship toward the Sirens, where it will be dashed on the rocks, killing him and his men. Ulysses might avoid the Sirens' island altogether, but that would require frustrating his desire to hear the Sirens' song. So he has his men tie him to the mast, instructs them to row past the island and ignore any orders he might issue to turn the ship, and then puts cotton in his men's ears so *they* cannot hear the Sirens' song. Elster describes this as a case of *precommitment*. Anticipating an intense future desire to turn his ship toward the Sirens, but recognizing that acting on this desire would be worse for his life as a whole, Ulysses precommits to frustrating his future intense desire, in this case by literally binding himself, physically, so that he *cannot* act on his future desire.

Elster offers many examples of similar phenomena. For example, rather than prevent a desire from being acted upon, as Ulysses did, one might take steps to prevent a desire from arising in the first place. Thus, he notes, someone who is trying to quit smoking, but who is unable to resist the urge to smoke once it arises, may take steps to prevent the urge from arising, for example, by crossing the street so as to not pass by a tobacco shop or avoiding locations where smokers congregate.[17]

Here is an example from my own life. Sometimes, when I am trying to watch my weight, I nevertheless get a craving for junk food. I might think a hamburger would be better for me than a pizza, but a pizza would be better for me than a hamburger and onion rings. One restaurant serves a very good hamburger, an excellent pizza, and terrific onion rings. A second restaurant serves a decent, but certainly not excellent, pizza. I might go to the second restaurant. Why? In one sense it is clear that I have chosen an inferior outcome. I would be better off going to the first restaurant and ordering a pizza, or better still, just ordering a hamburger. But I know myself. I suffer *akrasia*—weakness of the will. I am a sucker for good onion rings, so I know that if I go to the first restaurant I won't be able to help myself. I'll order the hamburger *and* onion rings, which will, overall, be worse for me. So, in this case I anticipate my desires and weaknesses, and I plan a strategy that will be the best of my psychologically feasible options. Here, in essence, I take one step backward—settling for an option that is worse than two other better options that are clearly available to me—because I know that in fact if I don't take that one step backward I'll take two steps backward—I would, in fact, select the option that I would *most* want *at the time*, the hamburger and onion rings, but that would be worse for me overall.

Elster may be mistaken in believing that rationality is tied to *optimizing*. Perhaps it can be rational to be a *satisficer*, to choose any outcome that is *sufficiently* good, even if another available option would be better.[18] Elster may also be mistaken in assuming that the rational agent should ultimately be concerned about his overall well-being.[19] There are many goals that may be rationally

---

[17] *Ulysses and the Sirens*, 37.

[18] For an intriguing and important defense of this position, see Michael Slote's *Beyond Optimizing: A Study of Rational Choice* (Cambridge, MA: Harvard University Press, 1989).

[19] To be sure, this has probably been the dominant view of individual rationality from the time of Plato to the present. It is what gives Glaucon's challenge, "Why should I be moral?" much of its force (see Book II of Plato's *The Republic*, trans. Allan Bloom [New York: Basic Books, 1968]). Sidgwick accepted this view (see chapter 4) and devoted his masterpiece, *The Method of Ethics*, 7th ed. (London: Macmillan, 1907), to trying to adequately come to terms with it. It remains a standard assumption of many contemporary economists. For two important critiques of the view see part 2 of Derek Parfit's *Reasons and Persons* and Amartya Sen's seminal paper "Rational Fools: A Critique of the Behavioral Foundations of Economic Theory," *Philosophy and Public Affairs* 6 (1977): 317–44.

defensible other than how my life, as a whole, fares. Still, the general point that rationality often requires that we engage in global and strategic reasoning is important, and not to be lost sight of.

Return to the upshot of sections 6.4 and 6.5 that, given the intransitivity of not worse than (in my wide reason-implying sense), there is a set of truths, expressed by (1), (2), and (3), such that a series of pairwise choices might lead one from a rationally superior outcome to a rationally inferior one, and, correspondingly, this fact could lead one to being money pumped in a way that was not merely based on intransitive preferences. The truth of these claims is compatible with recognizing that a rational agent *might not allow himself to be money pumped*. As someone who takes a global perspective and engages in strategic reasoning, the rational agent could refuse to consider, and act on, the truths of (1), (2), and (3) *separately*. For the practically rational agent, perhaps the question is not whether each choice one makes is *locally* rational, but whether the sequence of choices one would make is *globally* rational, and then it would clearly not be practically rational to follow a sequence of choices that would lead one from L_2 to L_1 plus $4,000.

So, even if *in fact* the rational agent were only offered a series of pairwise comparisons one at a time, and each move, considered one at a time, would be rational, the rational agent can take a global perspective, plan ahead, and anticipate future choices that he might be offered. Doing this, he can see *in advance* that it would be irrational, given his overarching desire not to end up in a worse place than where he began, or to be money pumped, to allow himself to be guided by what would be most rational considering each pairwise comparison separately *as if* those were the only choices he would be facing. Correspondingly, he might find some way of precommitting himself not to do so—perhaps by simply firmly resolving *not* to move from L_2 to A_1, even if offered $2,000 to do so; or, alternatively, by allowing himself to make *that* move, but not the subsequent one.[20]

Suppose a rational agent were offered three alternatives all at once: L_2, A_1 with $2,000, or L_1 with $4,000. Since L_2 is just like L_1, except that it involves a

---

[20] As observed in note 15 of chapter 3, there has been a great deal of discussion in the literature of how one might rationally and strategically respond to the kinds of issues I am discussing here. To repeat the gist of that note, Elster's notion of *precommitment* (from *Ulysses and the Sirens*), Edward McLennen's notion of *bounded rationality* (from his *Rationality and Dynamic Choice: Foundational Explorations* [New York: Cambridge University Press, 1990]), and David Gauthier's notion of *constrained maximizing* (from his *Morals by Agreement* [Oxford: Oxford University Press, 1986]) are all presented as rational strategies for preventing ourselves from doing what we would most want to do or what the best theory of rationality would prescribe that we do at some points in the future, in the face of predictable changes in circumstances or desires, *in order to* give us the best chance, over time, of actually living the life that we (now) most value or that would be best according to that very theory of rationality. See, also, part 1 of Parfit's *Reasons and Persons*, and Thomas Nagel's *The Possibility of Altruism* (Oxford: Oxford University Press, 1970).

greater salary of an extra $4,000 *per year*, it seems clear that whatever one chooses, one should not select L_1 with $4,000. That is, there appears to be overpowering reason to remove L_1 with $4,000 from consideration *as long as L_2 is also* an option. There is no analogous reason to remove L_2 from consideration, or A_1 with $2,000 from consideration. It seems, then, that given all three alternatives at once, the rational agent might choose between either L_2 or A_1 and $2,000.

The preceding suggests the following. As someone who is capable of engaging in global and strategic reasoning, a rational agent should refuse to assess alternatives in the immediate context in which they are presented. Instead, he should consider, and indeed anticipate, the larger contexts of which he may become a part. If a rational agent does this, he will see that given the choice between L_2, and receiving $2,000 to move to A_1, he might rationally choose the latter, but if he does, it must be with the precommitted understanding that he wouldn't allow himself to make a similar choice between A_1 with $2,000 and receiving $2,000 to move to L_1 with $2,000. Only in this way can he avoid the practically undesirable outcome of moving from a rationally superior outcome to a rationally inferior outcome, or of being money pumped.

Borrowing from Elster, we might think of accepting $2,000 to move from L_2 to A_1 as a small step "forward." Similarly, we might think of accepting $2,000 to move from A_1 with $2,000 to L_1 with $2,000 as a small step forward. But moving from L_2 to L_1 with $4,000 would be a big step backward. So here, we have a case where the strategic global reasoner would recognize that you have to refuse to take two small steps forward to avoid taking one large step backward. Analogously, if one began at L_1, one might think it a small step "backward" to pay $2,000 to move to A_1, since, by hypothesis, L_1 is not worse than A_1. Likewise, one might think it a small step "backward" to pay $2,000 to move from A_1 less $2,000, to L_2 less $2,000, since again, by hypothesis, A_1 less $2,000 is not worse than L_2 less $2,000. Yet, one might think it a big step forward to pay $4,000 to move from L_1 to L_2. So, here it would be practically rational to take two steps backward, in order to take one big step forward.

It appears, then, that even if "not worse than" is not a transitive relation, a rational agent may be able to avoid being money pumped, or moving from a rationally superior outcome to a rationally inferior outcome. This will be so if she adopts certain strategies, such as the strategy of precommitment, recommended by a global perspective. However, it must be noted that sticking to one's strategy may require one to act *as if* a certain possibility is available *even if it isn't and won't ever be*. So, to avoid the possible slide from L_2 to A_1 with $2,000 to L_1 with $4,000, one might refuse to take even the first step, even if the second step never, in fact, became available, or one might refuse to take the second step, even though the initial state of L_2 might no longer be an option. Both of these positions might be *practically* defensible, as part of one's best, overall, *global* plan, but they are *theoretically* unsettling. This is so for the same reason that it is theoretically unsettling to abide by a rule even in those cases where doing so defeats the very purpose for which the rule was instituted, as, for example, may occur on certain multilevel versions of utilitarianism.[21]

There are many tensions between practical and theoretical reasoning. So, for example, while there are many practical solutions to Prisoner's Dilemmas, none resolve the deep theoretical issues that Prisoner's Dilemmas raise.[22] It is important to recognize when there are *practical* solutions to apparent problems of rationality. But by the same token, it is important to recognize that some problems of rationality are theoretical, not practical, and others may be both theoretical and practical. Theoretical problems require theoretical solutions, and the latter should not be conflated with any practical solutions on offer.

*****

In this chapter, I have explored the circumstances, or underlying conditions, that account for when a relation will or will not be transitive. In the following chapter, I will continue my exploration of transitivity, focusing on the transitivity or nontransitivity of several important normative relations, including the "better than" relation.

---

[21] There is a large literature on so-called two-tier versions of utilitarianism or indirect utilitarianism, which assess actions not in terms of whether those individual acts *themselves* maximize the good, but, roughly, whether the acts are in accordance with an "appropriate" rule or motive the following or having of which would maximize the good. A standard objection to such theories is that they are guilty of abstract "rule-worship" if they would approve of one following the "appropriate" rule or motive even in those cases where one knows, in advance, that doing so would not, in fact, maximize the good, given that maximization of the good is the very reason why the rule or motive is deemed "appropriate" in the first place. On multilevel versions of utilitarianism, see, for example, David Lyons's *Forms and Limits of Utilitarianism* (Oxford: Clarendon Press, 1965); Richard Brandt's "Toward a Credible Form of Utilitarianism," in *Morality and the Language of Conduct,* ed. H. N. Castañeda and G. Nakhnikian (Detroit: Wayne State University Press, 1963), 107–43; R. M. Hare's "Ethical Theory and Utilitarianism," in *Contemporary British Philosophy IV*, ed. H. D. Lewis (London: Allen and Unwin, 1976), 113–31; Robert Adams's "Motive Utilitarianism," *Journal of Philosophy* 73 (1976): 467–81; Derek Parfit's *Reasons and Persons*; Shelly Kagan's *The Limits of Morality* (Oxford: Oxford University Press, 1989); and Brad Hooker's Ideal Code, *Real World: A Rule-Consequentialist Theory of Morality* (Oxford: Oxford University Press, 2000).

[22] See part 1 of Parfit's *Reasons and Persons*, especially chap. 4.

7

Exploring Transitivity
PART II

In this chapter, we shall continue our exploration of transitivity. In chapter 6, we saw that one important normative relation, the "not worse than" relation, may be nontransitive. We also developed and explored a model for understanding why that relation, and others, would be nontransitive. In this chapter, I shall begin by discussing two other important normative relations that may be nontransitive, the "permissibility" relation and the "obligatoriness" relation. I shall then suggest that there is good reason to believe that if the "obligatoriness" relation is nontransitive, the "all-things-considered better than" relation will also be nontransitive. I shall next consider an important response to the claim that the "obligatoriness" relation is nontransitive. I will then directly take up the question of whether the "all-things-considered better than" relation (in my wide reason-implying sense) could be nontransitive. I shall spell out the conditions under which the relation would or would not be transitive and reexamine some of the arguments of earlier chapters in this light. Finally, I shall note some of the important theoretical commitments that accompany both the view that the "all-things-considered better than" relation (in my wide reason-implying sense) is transitive and the contrary view that it may not be, pointing out that the former view will hold if a position I call the *Internal Aspects View* is correct, while the latter view will hold if a position I call the *Essentially Comparative View* is correct. These commitments, together with their implications, will be further discussed and, I hope, illuminated, in later chapters.

7.1 The Nontransitivity of Permissibility

Francis Kamm has offered an argument for the nontransitivity of permissibility.[1] Her argument is both interesting and compelling. It will be instructive to examine it in some detail.

Kamm notes that given a choice between doing my duty, *D*, and performing an act of supererogation, *S*, it may be permissible to do *S*. For example, it might be permissible for me to risk my life trying to save someone from a burning building, rather than fulfill a promise I made to keep an important appointment. She also notes that given the choice between an act of supererogation, *S*, and a self-interested act, *SI*, it may be permissible to do *SI*. Thus, it may be permissible for me to go to the movies, rather than to risk my life trying to save someone from a burning building. But, given the choice between doing my duty, *D*, and acting self-interestedly, *SI*, it might not be permissible to do *SI*. Thus, it would not be permissible for me to go to the movies, rather than fulfill a promise I made to keep an important appointment. So, Kamm has shown that "permissible to do rather than" is a nontransitive relation, since there might be three actions *SI*, *S*, and *D*, such that it might be permissible to do *SI* rather than *S*, and *S* rather than *D*, and yet *not* be permissible to do *SI* rather than *D*.

Kamm's analysis of the nontransitivity of permissibility is particularly instructive. Kamm recognizes that different factors are relevant in determining the permissibility of an action, *depending not only on the nature of the action itself, but also on its alternatives*. Specifically, different factors are relevant to an action's permissibility, depending on whether the action and its alternatives involve self-interest, supererogation, or duty. In addition, Kamm realizes, rightly and importantly, that where different factors are relevant for comparing alternatives, transitivity can fail to hold, as it does in this case.

It is worth noting, however, that Kamm's nontransitivity is based on pairwise comparisons that *depend* on our considering the alternatives two at a time. There is no issue of nontransitivity if all the alternatives are confronted at once.[2] Let me explain.

---

[1] In "Supererogation and Obligation," *Journal of Philosophy* 82 (1985): 118–38. Actually, Kamm offered her argument in support of the conclusion that the "permissible to do rather than" relation is *intransitive*. For reasons given later, I think this is a mistake, but I think her argument *does* show that permissibility is a *nontransitive* relation as I employ that term. Recall that a relation can be nontransitive if the notion of transitivity *fails* or *fails to apply* across different sets of alternatives between which that relation obtains (though in the latter case it is disputable whether there is, in fact, a *single* relation that obtains between the different sets of alternatives).

[2] Because of this, Roger Crisp thinks it is confusing to talk about nontransitivity in Kamm's case, or in other similar cases. He suggests, in correspondence, that unless there is nontransitivity in any actual situation of choice, all we have is *apparent* nontransitivity. I have some sympathy with Crisp's claim here. The notion of nontransitivity, as I employ it, *is* somewhat confusing, as it reflects two distinct kinds of "failure": the failure of a relation to be transitive, and the failure of the relation of transitivity to *apply* across different sets of alternatives that stand in one or more relations generated by a given notion and to which we might have naturally expected the relation of transitivity to apply. But as I employ the notion of "nontransitivity," *apparent* cases of *intransitivity* can be *actual* cases of *nontransitivity*. This is so for Kamm's case and many of the others I discuss. Still, if Crisp and others find my usage of "nontransitivity" too confusing, it could be dispensed with. I think doing so would make my presentation considerably more cumbersome, but it would not affect the substantive points I want to make here or elsewhere in this work.

As noted, Kamm's nontransitivity arises because we think it permissible to do *SI* rather than *S*, and *S* rather than *D*, and yet *not* permissible to do *SI* rather than *D*. But, importantly, our judgment that it is permissible to do *SI* rather than *S depends* on our considering those alternatives *by themselves*. It would *not* be permissible to do *SI* rather than *S if* we had a duty to do *D*. Our duty to do *D* can be absolved by doing *S*, but it cannot be absolved by doing *SI*. Thus, if we do not do *S*, we must do *D*. We do *not* have the option to do *SI* rather than *S* or *D*, simply because it is permissible to do *S* rather than *D*, and it *would* have been permissible to do *SI* rather than *S* had we not had a duty to do *D*. So, faced with the *simultaneous* choice between going to the movies (*SI*), risking our life trying to save someone (*S*), and fulfilling our promise to keep an important appointment (*D*), it would not be permissible to go to the movies (*SI*); hence, the purported nontransitivity would not arise.

Similarly, it is instructive to note that Kamm's example does not involve cycling, or instability, of the sort that leads many to worry about intransitivity. Given the choice between *SI*, *S*, and *D*, we can permissibly choose *D* or *S*, and rest comfortably and securely with either choice. Since, given *D*, *SI* is not an option, there is no danger of being rationally propelled from *S* to *SI* to *D*, to *S* to *SI* to *D*, and so on. Indeed, since "permissible to do rather than" does not mean "must," "ought," or even "should do rather than," there is not even danger of our being rationally compelled to "move" from *D* to *S* or vice versa. Either choice is rationally permissible. Neither is rationally required. Hence, either choice can be stable and rationally defensible.

Finally, although Kamm's result is striking, on reflection it is not surprising. Transitivity is a property that holds of *orderings*.[3] It reflects the position that alternatives can be consistently *ranked* relative to each other. In saying that *A* is taller, heavier, or faster than *B*, we are ranking *A* and *B* with respect to height, weight, or speed. Correspondingly, with respect to any given property, we naturally suppose that if *A* is ranked higher than *B*, and *B* is ranked higher than *C*, then *A* must be ranked higher than *C*.

But notice, in saying that it is permissible to do *A* rather than *B*, we are *not* ranking *A* relative to *B*. Indeed, *A* may be significantly more or less worthwhile

---

[3] Technically, an *ordering* obtains for any set, *S*, that is *ranked* according to a transitive relation, *R*; that is, for any three members, *x*, *y*, and *z* of the set, *S*, if *xRy*, and *yRz*, then *xRz*. *R* is a *ranking relation* for the set if and only if *R* is transitive. So, technically, any relation that is intransitive is not a ranking relation, and does not yield an ordering of the set to which it applies. Thus, transitivity is a property of orderings or rankings, and intransitivity is not. (I mention these facts, because although the following discussion does not require a technical interpretation of the notion of *ranking*, someone unaware of these facts may find the following discussion needlessly confusing.) Incidentally, a ranking relation may be *complete*—if for all members of the set either *xRy*, or *yRx*, or both; or *incomplete*—if some members of the set cannot be ranked vis-à-vis each other, that is, if there are some members *x* and *y* of the set, *S*, where neither *xRy* nor *yRx*. If *R* is complete, it yields a *complete ordering* of the set; if *R* is incomplete, it yields a *partial* or *quasi ordering*.

than *B*. The claim is merely that there is no moral prohibition against doing *A* when the alternative is *B*. But, of course, if we are not ranking *A* and *B*, and *B* and *C*, in judging that it is permissible to do *A* rather than *B*, and *B* rather than *C*, then we cannot derive a ranking of *A* and *C* based on those judgments.

In Kamm's example, whether it is permissible to do *SI* rather than *D* depends on whether there is a moral prohibition against doing *SI* when the alternative is *D*. There is. Moreover, as Kamm has rightly recognized, this fact is perfectly consistent with there being no moral prohibition against doing *SI* when the alternative is *S*, and no moral prohibition against doing *S* when the alternative is *D*. Since judgments of permissibility do not reflect a ranking of alternatives, and since an action's permissibility clearly depends on its alternatives, it is not surprising that the notion of transitivity fails to apply in Kamm's example. Nor is it especially troubling. Still, it is instructive to recognize *why* "permissible to do rather than" is not a transitive relation, as well as why there would be no problem of nontransitivity or cycling were all three alternatives offered at once.

7.2 The Nontransitivity of Moral Obligatoriness

We have seen that the permissibility relation, "is permissible to do rather than," is nontransitive. The moral obligatoriness relation, "ought to be done rather than," may also be nontransitive. To see this, consider the following position regarding affirmative action.

Some believe that for certain positions in America a significant, but not overwhelming, preference should be given to African Americans over whites. That is, the preference should do more than break the mythical tie between otherwise "equally deserving candidates," though a white should still be selected if his qualifications are "sufficiently" greater than an African American's. However, preference should not be given to African Americans over Mexican Americans, nor to Mexican Americans over whites. According to this position, what *justifies* affirmative action regarding African Americans vis-à-vis whites is *the particular nature of the historical relationship between African Americans and whites* in American society, and, put crudely, Mexican Americans didn't enslave African Americans, nor were they enslaved by whites.

Whether such a position is ultimately defensible, many believe that *something* like it is, or at least might have been, correct. But, on this view, it could be that all things considered *A* ought to be hired rather than *B*, and *B* ought to be hired rather than *C*, yet *C* ought to be hired rather than *A*. This might be so if *A* were white, *B* were Mexican American, and *C* were African American; for then, a factor which was relevant and significant when comparing *A* with *C*—that is, the particular historical relationship between African Americans and whites in American society—and which might give *C* the edge over *A*, would *not apply* when comparing *A* with *B*, or *B* with *C*.

Some people may be uncomfortable with the example of affirmative action, relying as it does on a history of past wrongdoing. So let me note another example. In many societies, it is accepted that parents are owed the respect and obedience of their children; hence, it would be regarded as unseemly or inappropriate for parents to have to answer to or be subordinate to their children. Accordingly, many would accept that parents should be given preference over their offspring in certain situations, for example, in determining who should be the leader of a group project or the boss at work. This seems plausible, especially on the view that such preferences should be significant, but not overwhelming. But then, if *C* were the parent of *A*, and *B* were a stranger, it could be that, for certain purposes, all things considered it would be better if *A* were selected rather than *B*, and better if *B* were selected rather than *C*, yet it would be better if *C* were selected rather than *A*. By now, this should be unsurprising. After all, a relevant and significant factor which might make it better to select *C* rather than *A* would not apply when comparing *A* with *B*, or *B* with *C*.[4]

There might be many such examples. Many special relationships give rise to factors that seem to rightly influence our judgments about which of various outcomes would be better all things considered—were the relationships different, we would make different judgments. But then, in comparing alternatives affecting different individuals or groups, between whom different relationships obtain, the relevant and significant factors may vary with the alternatives being considered. Correspondingly, the moral obligatoriness relation may be nontransitive *for the same reason* that the permissibility and not worse than relations are; because for any given relation, *R*, if *different* factors are relevant and significant for comparing different alternatives with respect to *R*, or, alternatively, if the same factors can have different relevance or significance for comparing different alternatives with respect to *R*, then it can be true that even if *aRb* and *bRc*, given the relevance and significance of the factors for making *those* comparisons, it may *not* be the case that *aRc*, given the relevance and significance of the factors for making *that* comparison.

Some people believe that the nontransitivity of moral obligatoriness is like the nontransitivity of permissibility, in that it only arises when one considers each pairwise comparison in isolation from the others. On this view, there would be no issue of nontransitivity if all the alternatives were confronted at once. This may be right, but I find the situation less clear in the case of moral obligatoriness than in the case of permissibility. Let me explain why.

Suppose that we are hiring for a job for which affirmative action would be relevant. By hypothesis, if African American and White were the only two candidates

---

[4] I owe this parent/offspring example to an unpublished note which Ronald Dworkin sent to Parfit, and which Parfit showed me after reading an early draft of this work. F. M. Kamm presents two similar examples on page 137 of her "Supererogation and Obligation."

for the job we *ought* to hire African American, if White and Mexican American were the only two candidates we *ought* to hire White, and if African American and Mexican American were the only two candidates we *ought* to hire Mexican American. What should we do, then, if all three apply at once?

Some might argue that in this case it would be just as wrong to hire White given African American's candidacy, as in the case where White and African American were the only two candidates. In both cases, it might be claimed, hiring White would be an affront to the collective sense of moral outrage that we feel about the way African Americans were historically treated by whites, and so we ought *not* to hire White, as a way of expressing our collective acknowledgment and disapproval of those particular past injustices. On this view, it would always be wrong to hire a white to fill a position for which a "sufficiently" qualified African American had applied. So, it might be claimed, we should rule White out of contention, and then choose among the remaining candidates. Thus, it might be concluded, in the case where all three apply at once there is no nontransitivity, and the Mexican American should be hired.

The preceding has great plausibility, and perhaps it is right. But one can imagine White responding as follows. I *share* the sense of moral outrage about how African Americans were historically treated by whites, and agree that a policy of affirmative action might be the appropriate response to those past injustices. Correspondingly, I readily accept that *if it comes down to a choice between African American and me*, one ought to hire him rather than me. But the plain fact is that if I hadn't applied, African American wouldn't have gotten the job anyway. It would have gone to Mexican American. So hiring me would *not* express a failure to appreciate the past injustices perpetrated by whites against African Americans, but the simple recognition that those injustices are not relevant when comparing African Americans with Mexican Americans, or whites with Mexican Americans. Since African American wouldn't get the job anyway if you don't hire me, and everyone agrees that I am a better candidate than Mexican American, it is only fair that you hire me. It violates the equal opportunity/merit principle—according to which, absent special countervailing moral considerations, one ought to give everyone equal opportunity for each job, and simply hire the person who most merits the job, as determined solely by their job-related qualifications—to give Mexican American a job for which I am better qualified, given that there is no reason to accept an affirmative action policy giving preference to Mexican Americans over whites.

Naturally, one might imagine African American mounting a similar challenge. He might note, rightly, that if he hadn't applied for the job, Mexican American wouldn't have gotten it. It would have gone to White, since, by hypothesis, White is better qualified. In other words, African American agrees with White that it would be unfair to hire Mexican American rather than White, since doing so would violate the equal opportunity/merit principle, and there are no affirmative action reasons to favor Mexican Americans over whites. So Mexican American should be taken out of consideration. But he then notes that he is sufficiently qualified that he should be hired, rather than White, for affirmative action reasons. These are reasons that, by hypothesis, all agree are relevant in the comparison between African Americans and whites.

I think the preceding considerations have some force, and may point to an important difference between the nontransitivity of the permissibility relation and the apparent nontransitivity of the obligatoriness relation. When Kamm's three options are considered all at once, it is clear that one may permissibly do one's duty or act supererogatorily, and there is no lingering doubt that whatever one does perhaps one *ought* to have done something different. In the preceding case, even when all three options are considered at once, there seem to be powerful considerations in favor of choosing each of the options, and whichever option one chooses, there may be a lingering doubt that there was another available option that would have been fairer, and that one ought to have chosen instead.

So, it *may* be that the nontransitivity of moral obligatoriness does not only arise when pairwise comparisons are made separately, and can persist even when three alternatives are offered simultaneously. However, it *may* also be that the plausibility of the preceding positions depends on confusion in our thinking about what, exactly, the correct policy of affirmative action should be given the particular historical relationship between whites and African Americans in American society. If this is right, once we clear up the confusion and determine what the correct policy of affirmative action should be, it may be clear what we ought to do when we consider all three alternatives together.

So, if we decide that the correct policy of affirmative action "merely" generates the conclusion that it would always be wrong to have a white occupy a position for which a sufficiently qualified African American applied, then in fact we may go with the first answer noted earlier and decide that we ought to hire Mexican American. However, we may decide that the correct policy of affirmative action "merely" tells us to rank all candidates in terms of their job-related characteristics and then choose the top one, unless the top one is White, and the second one is a sufficiently qualified African American, in which case choose the second one. This view would support the second answer noted earlier, that we should hire White. Finally, we might decide that the correct policy of affirmative action tells us to rank all candidates in terms of their job-related characteristics and then choose the top one, unless the top one is white, in which case we should hire the top-ranked African American candidate, as long as he is sufficiently qualified relative to the top-ranked white. This would support the third answer noted earlier, that we should hire African American.

So, as indicated, it is *possible* that once we get clear on the correct policy of affirmative action, assuming there is one, the apparent nontransitivity of the obligatoriness relation will disappear, when all three alternatives are considered together. On the other hand, it may seem that there are significant moral considerations supporting *each* of the different positions. If this happens, several possibilities arise. First, we may decide the different moral considerations are equally important, so that any hire we make would be equally good. Second, we may decide the different moral considerations are roughly comparable, or on a par, in which case we may think that each possible choice would be "not worse than" the others, without thinking they are exactly equally as good. Third, we may decide that some of the moral considerations are weightier than others, so that all things considered there is a determinate answer to the question of what we ought to do. Finally, we may find the relation between the different moral considerations to be like the case of so-called moral blind alleys, where no matter what choice we make, it seems that in an important sense we have acted wrongly, since in making that choice we declined to make another available choice that seems fairer and morally superior.

I note the preceding possibilities, but shall not try to choose between them. For now, let me merely emphasize the following. It has long been recognized that whether or not we ought, morally, to do something will depend on its alternatives. This is both unsurprising and unimportant, if it merely reflects the truth that some alternatives are morally more compelling than others, and that one ought not to do a less compelling alternative, when a morally more compelling one is available. However, if one accepts that the *reason* that an option's obligatoriness depends on its alternatives is *sometimes* because the factors that are relevant and significant for an option's being obligatory themselves depend on the alternatives with which the option is being compared, then we have an interesting and significant result. In that case, the obligatoriness relation may be nontransitive for the same underlying reason that the "not worse than" and "permissibility" relations are.[5]

7.3 The Obligatoriness Relation and Another Possible Money Pump

As with a case explored in chapter 6, the preceding considerations raise the possibility of a money pump of sorts, even if one believes that the apparent nontransitivity of the obligatoriness relation only arises when separate pairwise comparisons are made, and disappears when all three options are considered at once. To see this, consider the following example.

Suppose that a position is open for which the affirmative action policy of giving preference to a sufficiently deserving African American over a white is

---

[5] The considerations I have been presenting raise a number of interesting issues relevant to another position that is often regarded as a fundamental principle of practical reasoning, which is often referred to as the *Independence of Irrelevant Alternatives Principle*. Roughly, this principle holds that the relative goodness of two outcomes, A and B, is determined solely on the basis of how they compare with each other, and cannot depend on how either or both of those outcomes compare with respect to some other outcome or set of outcomes. I discuss a number of issues raised for this principle in chapter 13, including the role this principle plays in practical reasoning, the conception of moral ideals that underlies this principle, and the implications of retaining or rejecting this principle in light of this book's considerations.

deemed appropriate. As before, assume that the *justification* for this policy is the particular historical relationship between African Americans and whites in American society, so that African Americans won't get preference over Mexican Americans, nor will Mexican Americans get preference over whites. Next, suppose there is a national search, with considerable costs arising for everyone involved, costs associated with carefully compiling and screening applications, interviewing candidates, and so on. To help cut down on wasted time, effort, and money, those doing the hiring make it clear *exactly* what their criteria are, including their intention to adhere to the preceding policy of affirmative action. In addition, while removing all personal identifying and contact information, the hirers put each applicant's qualifications, including race, online. That way, people can see in advance if there is any point in their applying for the position, or if it would just be a waste for them to do so. Moreover, to further prevent frivolous applications, they charge a $300 application fee, though $150 of that is returnable if one withdraws one's application before the interview stage. If, at some later point, one decides to reapply for the position, one needs to repay the $150, along with a $25 reactivation fee.

Suppose that White, who would dearly like the job, goes online and sees that no more qualified candidate than he has applied. He then decides, quite reasonably, to apply, sending in his application materials together with his $300 fee. Naturally, his qualifications are then posted online, for other potential applicants to consider before applying.

Next, suppose that African American, who would also dearly like the job, accurately recognizes that while his purely job-related skills are not quite up to the level of White's, he would be given the edge over White for affirmative action reasons. Correspondingly, he sends in his application, along with his $300 fee. Naturally, his qualifications are then posted, including his race.

At this point, White, who has been keeping track of the applications online, realizes that the job will go to African American. Disappointed, but realistic, he sees no reason to waste his time, effort, and resources flying to the interview, renting a car, spending a night in a hotel, and so on. Understandably, he decides to withdraw his application, and at least get $150 back from his initial fee. He does so, and his application information is therefore removed from the relevant website.

Now, Mexican American gets involved. He, too, would love the job. And he realizes he is more qualified than any of the other current candidates. So he sends in his application with his $300 fee, and his qualifications are put online.

African American now finds himself in the same boat that White previously was in. Disappointed, but realistic, he sees no reason to waste his time, effort, and resources flying to the interview, renting a car, spending a night in a hotel, and so on. So he, too, decides to withdraw his application, and at least get $150 back from his initial fee. Correspondingly, his application information is removed from the relevant web site.

White, who has continued to follow the web site, now realizes that he would once again be the top candidate. It is a very good job that he keenly wants. For the mere cost of the $25 reactivation fee, and the remittance of the refunded $150, he reapplies. His qualifications are then reposted.

At this point, of course, Mexican American is now in the same boat that White and African American previously were in. There is no point in wasting his time, effort, and money flying to an interview for a job that he won't get, so he might as well get his $150 back. He withdraws his application, and his qualifications are removed from the web site.

But, now, of course, African American might as well reapply, for a mere $25 reactivation fee and the remittance of the originally refunded $150! And the cycle will continue, indefinitely, with each of the three candidates being money pumped $25 at a time, unless one of them actually changes his preference for having such a desirable job, or refuses to act on that preference, or decides that he should keep his application active and not seek a refund of $150, and should spend the time, money, and effort necessary to fly out for the interview, *even when he realizes that if he does he still will not get the job.*

Here we see that, in essence, an unfortunate confluence of events might lead three individuals, each of whom seemingly has a perfectly coherent and rational set of preferences, to collectively, over time, be money pumped, due to a sequence of pairwise decisions that each, in turn, might rationally make. This would be due to the fact that the obligatoriness relation appears to be nontransitive over pairs of alternatives considered separately, even *if* it is not nontransitive over that same set of alternatives considered jointly.

7.4 From Obligatoriness to Better Than: On the Right and the Good, and the Inheritability of Nontransitivity

Many people believe that obligatoriness might be a nontransitive relation, but that the "all-things-considered better than" relation could not be. So, for example, they have no problem believing that perhaps what I ought to *do* is hire White over Mexican American, Mexican American over African American, and African American over White, but they find it difficult to believe that, in the case in which all three candidates apply, it could really be the case that hiring White is *better than* hiring Mexican American, hiring Mexican American is *better than* hiring African American, *and* that hiring African American is really *better than* hiring White. Derek Parfit has held such a position for many years.[6]

Underlying this position is the view that there might be reasons that are relevant to the question of what one ought to *do*, that are *not* relevant to the question of which of two outcomes would be *better*, and that it is only in virtue of *such* reasons that the nontransitivity of the "obligatoriness" relation arises.

---

[6] I base this claim on many discussions I have had with Parfit about this topic over the years.

In particular, just as one believes that there are *agent-relative* reasons that give different people reasons to act, so one might believe, more generally, that there are *context-relative* reasons that apply, perhaps with varying weights, in different circumstances, which make it true that whether one ought to *do X* depends on the alternatives with which it is compared. The claim, then, in essence, is that it is because of context-relative reasons that "obligatoriness" is nontransitive, and that neither such reasons, nor any other nontransitivity-generating factors of their ilk, will be relevant to the betterness of outcomes.

Such a view is perfectly coherent. But on reflection I find it dubious. It requires that there be strictly circumscribed limits on the manner and extent to which the realm of the obligatory might impact the realm of the good. But I believe there is good reason to deny that there are limits of the sort required by such a view, and hence that we should reject the view in question.

Consider the long-standing issue of the relation between the right and the good. Consequentialists, of course, believe that the right is subservient to the good, so that what we *ought* to do is always determined by considerations of goodness. Conceptually, one might also hold the reverse position, that the good is subservient to the right. On such a view, not only would one believe that whether one acted rightly or not depended on deontological factors that were independent of the goodness of one's alternatives, one would *further* believe that acting rightly *itself* makes the outcome of which it is a part better, in terms of *goodness*, than any alternative outcome in which one acted wrongly. Variations of such a view might hold that acting rightly is the only good, that acting rightly is a good that is lexically prior to all other goods, or simply that the value of acting rightly is so great that, in fact, it outweighs the value of all other goods combined.

Like most, I believe that the relation between the right and the good fits neither of the preceding models. Specifically, I believe that the right is often *relevant* to the good, and that the good is often *relevant* to the right, though neither is subservient to the other. Thus, in my judgment, the right and the good are distinct moral categories, in the sense that neither is wholly determined by the other. But, importantly, each can have a bearing on the other in the sense that each can both influence, and be influenced by, the other.

The distinctness of the two categories is easily highlighted by a familiar example. Suppose that I am confronted with a choice between saving my mother, doing A, or saving five strangers, doing B. One can believe that there are morally relevant agent-relative duties, or reasons, that make it the case that I ought, morally, to do A, without committing oneself to the view that the outcome I produce by doing A would be a *better* outcome than the outcome I would produce by doing B. Here, the right and the good are distinct, in that I may have a moral obligation to produce a less good outcome.

Still, as indicated earlier, one can believe that the right and the good are distinct, and yet believe that each is often relevant to the other. Thus, I believe that in some cases, what I ought, morally, to *do* is to produce the best outcome, and I ought to do this, at least in part, precisely because it *is* the best outcome. So, for example, perhaps I ought to save the lives of five strangers rather than prevent a different stranger from suffering a headache, and I ought to do this precisely because the former outcome would be a *much* better outcome than the latter and there is no countervailing agent-relative duty dictating that I act otherwise in such a circumstance.

By the same token, I believe that acting rightly is *itself* a good-making feature, and acting wrongly *itself* a bad-making feature, of the outcomes of which they are a part. So, for example, if, in saving my mother rather than five strangers, I am acting rightly, the fact that I have acted rightly makes that total outcome, of which my act is a part, better than the outcome that would have resulted from my mother's surviving by some chance circumstance. And likewise, if, in saving five strangers, I would be acting wrongly, my so acting would make the outcome of which it is a part worse than it would otherwise have been had the five strangers survived by chance circumstances. But, as it happens, the extent to which my acting rightly makes the one outcome better, and the extent to which my acting wrongly makes the other outcome worse, are not sufficient to offset the other respects in which the outcome where I save my mother is worse than the outcome in which I save the strangers. This is why, all things considered, the outcome in which I rightly do *A* is still worse than the outcome in which I wrongly do *B*, even though, as indicated, I *ought* to do *A*, rather than *B*.

To avoid misinterpretation, let me add that the preceding remarks are not intended to take a stand on whether we should give a buck-passing account of right and wrong.[7] Throughout my discussion, when I say something like "acting rightly is *itself* a good-making feature of the outcome of which it is a part," this is compatible with understanding such a claim as shorthand for the position that "a person's acting in accordance with the underlying reasons that make it the case that she ought to act in a certain way, and hence that her so acting is right, is itself a good-making feature of the outcome of which it is a part." So, for example, doing *X* might be right because it would save your life, and then, perhaps, the *ultimate* reason why I ought to do *X* is not that it is *right*, per se, but that it would *save your life*. My view is simply that my actually doing what I *ought* to do, in this case saving your life, is itself a good-making feature of the outcome. Thus, it is not merely good that your life has been preserved, it is good that I have responded appropriately to the reasons that there are for saving your life.

---

[7] There has been much discussion of "buck-passing" since Thomas Scanlon's seminal discussion of a buck-passing account of "goodness" in *What We Owe to Each Other* (Cambridge, MA: Harvard University Press, 1998). Philip Stratton-Lake offers a buck-passing account of "rightness" in the introduction to his edition of W. D. Ross's *The Right and the Good* (Oxford: Clarendon Press, 2002). I am grateful to Roger Crisp and Derek Parfit for bringing Stratton-Lake's view to my attention.

Before proceeding, let me consider two objections to my claim that acting rightly is itself a good-making feature of the outcome of which it is a part. Mikhail Valdman put the first objection as follows: "Suppose that two people are able to rescue my mother—myself, and some stranger. And suppose that my mother will not remember my rescue. Here I'm tempted to say that the goodness of the outcome in which my mother is saved does not depend in any way on who saves her, whether is it me or some stranger."[8]

Unfortunately, this objection is underdescribed. Suppose, first, that it is only my *mother's* life that is at stake. Although I have special obligations toward my mother that the stranger does not, that doesn't mean that it wouldn't be right for the stranger to save my mother if he could, or that it would be *more* "right" or valuable for me to save her than for a stranger to. Nor does it mean that I have a duty to make sure that she is saved by *me*, rather than a stranger. Rather, it means that I have a duty to save my mother in contexts where a stranger would not. Still, if I knew that a stranger could more safely and reliably save my mother, I would not be remiss regarding my special obligations toward my mother if I allowed the stranger to save her. So, whether my mother is saved by me or a stranger, someone may be acting rightly and no one need be acting wrongly. Thus, the example fails to provide an objection to the claim that right actions contribute to the goodness of outcomes.

Suppose, on the other hand, that either I or a stranger could save my mother by doing *A*, or save five other strangers by doing *B*. In that case, I'm not attracted to Valdman's view "that the goodness of the outcome in which my mother is saved does not depend in any way on who saves her." Rather, I believe each of the following might be true. First, as noted previously, it might be the case that because of my special obligations to my mom, it would be *right* for me to do *A*, even though, all things considered, my doing *B* might still produce a better outcome than my doing *A*. Second, lacking the special obligations that I have toward my mom, it would be right for a stranger to do *B*, and wrong for a stranger to do *A*. Third, all things considered, the outcome in which *I* did *A* would be *better* than the outcome in which a *stranger* did *A*, and the outcome in which *I* did *B* would be *worse* than the outcome in which a *stranger* did *B*. On my view, there is something *good* about the outcome in which I do *A*, where, having recognized and responded appropriately to all of the relevant normative considerations—including my special agent-relative obligations—I have acted *rightly*; and something *bad* about the outcome in which I do *B*, where, having failed to recognize and respond appropriately to all of the relevant normative considerations, I have acted *wrongly*. Similarly, there is something good about the outcome in which a stranger does *B*, where, having recognized and responded appropriately to all of the relevant (agent-neutral) considerations, he has acted rightly, and something bad about the outcome in

---

[8] From correspondence.

which a stranger does A, where, having failed to recognize and respond appropriately to all of the relevant (agent-neutral) considerations, he has acted wrongly.

Consider a different case. Suppose that my mother is drowning, and that due to a blow to her head, she will remember nothing of the next twenty-four hours if she survives. In accordance with my special obligations toward my mother, I can act rightly by jumping in and saving her, or, knowing that I ought morally to save her, I can callously calculate my expected inheritance and act wrongly by going to the movies and leaving her to her fate. I believe that in a very important way the outcome in which I do the latter is decidedly *worse* than the outcome in which I do the former, *even if*, per chance, a log floats by my mother, enabling her to save herself! Valdman implies that as long as my mother is saved either way, and won't remember the surrounding events, *how* she is saved is irrelevant to the comparative value of the different outcomes. But I see no reason to accept this. *Perhaps*, depending on one's conception of individual welfare, it doesn't matter *for her*. And *perhaps*, it would actually be better for *me* to have been able to see the movie than to have gotten all wet and dirty saving her. Still, the outcome in which I act rightly is an outcome in which a moral agent recognizes and responds appropriately to relevant normative considerations, while the outcome in which I act wrongly includes an outcome in which a moral agent willfully disregards relevant normative considerations. I regard the second outcome as *worse* than the first, in virtue of the factors I have been discussing.

I claim that an outcome in which rational agents act morally has value in it that is both relevant to how good it is all things considered and lacking in an outcome in which rational agents act amorally or immorally, and that this is so independently of any other ways in which the values of such outcomes differ. This is what I mean in contending that right actions are themselves good-making features of the outcomes of which they are a part, and Valdman's first objection doesn't shake my confidence in this view.

A second objection to claiming that right action is a good-making feature of outcomes is that it leads to an infinite regress, at least insofar as there can be cases where in order to act rightly I have to produce the most good.[9] This objection might be put as follows. Suppose I am initially choosing between two actions A and B, where I determine that A would produce a value of 200 and B a value of 180, and this is a context where I ought to produce the most good. It looks like I ought to do A, thereby producing 200 units of good. But, in doing so, I would be acting rightly, which contributes to the outcome's goodness, producing a greater total value, say, of 200 + n. But this gives me even *greater* reason than before to do A, the reason that

---

[9] A version of this objection has been put to me by both Mikhail Valdman (in correspondence) and Nick Beckstead (in discussion).

stems from the fact that in doing A I'll be acting rightly. So, it seems that in fact my acting rightly should contribute even *more* to the goodness of the outcome, so that I would then be producing a greater total value, say, of $200 + n + m$, and so on. Another way to put this is that if I am *fully* responsive to all the reasons that there are, then I will not only do A, I will act rightly in doing A, and I will see that I have an additional reason to act rightly in doing A provided by the goodness that my acting rightly produces, which in turn will make it right for me to act rightly in doing A, which will itself contribute further to the goodness of the outcome, thereby providing me with still further reason to act rightly, by acting rightly in acting rightly in doing A, and so on, without end. But this seems to make it too easy to add value to the world by simply attending to the increasingly strong reasons that I have for doing a given action, generated by the layers of right actions that become available to me on the view that acting rightly contributes to the goodness of outcomes.

This is an interesting but puzzling objection. Let me offer two main comments in response. First, it isn't clear that my view *is* open to a regress of the sort envisaged by the objection. Consider the following analogy. Suppose I go into a store, looking to buy the best present I can for my daughter. The store has already figured out which presents are best and has priced them accordingly. In addition, it has a large selection of bows, and I know that the more expensive the present, the larger and prettier the bow will be that goes with it. I also know that my daughter likes beautiful big bows, so I have *extra* incentive to be sure to buy her the best present, since she will then have the benefit of the better present *and* the better bow. But, interestingly, the store does not tell me which present is more expensive, nor, a fortiori, which bow will go with which present; I have to figure out which present is best on my own, by weighing up the various advantages and disadvantages of each, independently of the question of which present will go with which bow. Suppose I have narrowed down my choice to one of two presents, P or Q. I am confident that one of them is best, and so will get the biggest and prettiest bow (*BPB*, for short), and the other will get a smaller uglier bow (*SUB*, for short), but am still not sure which bow will go with which present. As much as I want my child to get *BPB*, that provides me with no basis for choosing between P and Q, since *BPB* will go with the best choice as determined by grounds that are independent of the fact that *BPB* will accompany the best choice. Thus, as indicated, the desirability of my daughter receiving *BPB* gives me extra incentive to choose carefully and wisely between P and Q, but that choice must be made on the grounds of which of those presents would itself be better for my daughter. Moreover, importantly, it is not the case that if I do choose wisely, aiming to get both the best present *and* the best bow, the store will throw in *another* bow for my daughter, making her overall gift even *better*. She simply gets *one* bow, whichever choice I make, reflecting how good of a choice I made.

The view that right action is a good-making feature of outcomes may be analogous to the preceding example, especially if one assumes a scalar model of rightness, according to which, roughly, actions can have different degrees of rightness, and hence contribute to the goodness of outcomes to different degrees, proportional to their degree of rightness. In some cases, I may have good reason to maximize the good in choosing between two alternatives P and Q, to believe that if I *do* maximize the good via my choice I will be acting rightly, and to *further* believe that my acting rightly will itself be a good-making feature of the outcome. But however much my acting rightly will contribute to the overall goodness of the outcome, and however much I want to be sure to promote the most possible good, that only gives me extra incentive to choose carefully and wisely between P and Q on the basis of the values that those alternatives would *themselves* contribute to the outcome, independently of the value that acting rightly will contribute. Because the value that my acting rightly will contribute will attach to *whichever* is best between P and Q on those independent grounds (though in a way that will vary with the degree of rightness of the choices in question), it cannot provide any reason for favoring P or Q. Moreover, on the preceding analogy, aiming to bring about the best outcome by choosing whichever of P or Q adds more value to the outcome, and thereby adding the extra value to the outcome that comes from having acted rightly, doesn't add even *further* value to the outcome. Thus, while one *can* have as one of one's aims in choosing carefully between P and Q that one will thereby add extra value to the outcome from having acted rightly, it may well be that the maximum extra value that one can add will simply be a function of the degree to which one has acted rightly in choosing between P and Q. I submit, then, that it isn't clear that there must be a regress of the sort the preceding objection imagines. Perhaps in acting rightly there is only one "bow per customer," as it were, the size of which is determined by criteria that are independent of the desirability that one's bow be as big and beautiful as possible.

Second, even if there is a possible infinite regress of the sort the objection imagines, it isn't clear that it need be a vicious one. This partly depends on how one thinks the value of the outcome is affected by each iterated layer of right action. Suppose one thought the following. In acting rightly by doing A, one increases the value of the outcome as a function of the value that is directly produced by the doing of A, say, for the sake of argument, by 1 percent. Then, in our earlier example, by *doing A* one would increase the value of the outcome by 200, and by acting *rightly* in doing A, call that R_1, for first-order rightness, one would increase the value of the outcome by 2. So, the overall value of acting *rightly* in doing A, and *doing A*, would be 202. Next, one might think that in acting rightly by *rightly* doing A, call that R_2, for second-order rightness, one increases the value of the outcome as a function of the value that is directly produced by *rightly* doing A. For the sake of argument, let us again suppose that the function is 1 percent, so that the value of R_2 is 1 percent of the value of R_1, which in this case would be .02. It would then be the case that the total value of acting rightly (.02) by acting rightly (2) by doing A (200) would be 202.02. Similarly, one might suppose that the value contributed to the outcome by third-order rightness would be a 1 percent function of the value contributed to the outcome by second-order rightness (.02), that the value contributed to the outcome by fourth-order rightness would be a 1 percent function of the value contributed to the outcome by third-order rightness (.0002), and so on. On such a model, it doesn't appear that the regress in question need be particularly vicious. For instance, we needn't worry that a set of appropriate responses to a single right action would spiral out of control, somehow filling the outcome with indefinitely large, or even infinite, value. Moreover, this model would reflect the plausible view that what *most* contributes to the goodness of the outcome is the actual doing of *A*; the fact that doing *A* would be right would *also* contribute to the goodness of the outcome, but much less so, while the fact that it would be right to do the right thing in doing *A* would contribute even less to the goodness of the outcome, and so on.[10]

In sum, I find the regress worry interesting but not compelling. As seen, I'm not convinced that the view that right actions are good-making features of outcomes *is* open to a regress; nor am I convinced that if there were a regress it would be vicious. For now, then, I stand by my claims about the relevant relations between the right and the good; that each may be relevant to, though not determinate of, the other.

---

[10] I have suggested but one model that might remove some of the sting from the objection that thinking of right actions as themselves good-making features of outcomes leads to a regress problem. Other models are also possible, as are variations of the model I have suggested.

Note, the view suggested here is similar in important ways, though also dissimilar in important ways, to the complex view of organic unity that Robert Nozick presented in *Philosophical Explanations* (Cambridge, MA: Harvard University Press, 1981). Nozick suggests that some reactions to another's good fortune or misfortune add value or disvalue to an outcome because they are the appropriate or inappropriate reactions to have to such fortune or misfortune, and not merely because of the quality of the reactions themselves. Hence, for Nozick, if I take happiness in the good fortune of a good person, that will itself be good in a certain respect, but if I take happiness in the misfortune of a good person, that will itself be bad in a certain respect, and this is so even if I am equally happy in the two cases. Similarly, if I feel pain at the good fortune of a good person, that will itself be bad in a certain respect, while if I feel pain at the misfortune of a good person, that will itself be good in a certain respect, even if the phenomenological quality of my pain is the same in the two cases. Furthermore, Nozick believes that reactions to reactions can be appropriate or inappropriate in such a way as to add value or disvalue to an outcome, as can reactions to reactions to reactions, and so on. So, for example, Nozick suggests that beyond the values of the various pleasures themselves, there is a(n organic) value that would be contributed to the goodness of an outcome by my taking pleasure in the pleasure of a good person, an *additional* (organic) value that would be contributed to the goodness of the outcome by my, or someone else's, taking pleasure in the pleasure I take in the pleasure of a good person, an *additional* (organic) value that would be contributed to the goodness of the outcome by my, or someone else's, taking pleasure in the pleasure that I, or someone else, takes in the pleasure I take in the pleasure of a good person, and so on. My point here is not to endorse Nozick's particular complex view about organic unities. It is, rather, to indicate another example where one might think responding "appropriately" to a situation may *itself* be a good-making feature of an outcome, that would, in turn, warrant its own "appropriate" response that would be a *further* good-making feature of the outcome, and so on, and that this may open up the possibility of a regress that need not be vicious and may actually be welcomed.

I cast the preceding discussion in terms of the relation between the right and the good, because this is familiar terrain. Indeed, I suspect that most people will not only recognize the view I have offered, but accept it as uncontroversial. But, given how I am understanding the notion of "better than," the same point might have been put in terms of the "obligatoriness" and "all-things-considered better than" relations (in my wide reason-implying sense). That is, the notions of the "obligatory" and the "good" are distinct, in that neither is subservient to the other. But, in general, if doing A is morally obligatory, my doing A will be a good-making feature of the outcome in which it occurs, and will be an important, though not conclusive, reason to regard the outcome where I do A—and thereby act rightly—as better than the outcome where I do not—and thereby act wrongly. By the same token, the fact that one outcome would be better than another will often be an important, though not conclusive, reason why one ought to bring about that outcome rather than the worse one.

If this view is right, as I believe, and I think most would accept, it has important implications for the view that while "obligatoriness" might be a nontransitive relation, the "all-things-considered better than" relation (in my wide reason-implying sense) could not be. This is because, given the relation between obligatoriness and all-things-considered better than, the nontransitivity of the former is likely to be *inherited* by the latter. This is, I think, a particular instance of a general truth that we will see again later, namely, *that if an important aspect of a notion is nontransitive, the notion itself is likely to be nontransitive*. Or, more precisely, if there is a relation R that is relevant to another relation R', such that how two alternatives compare regarding R will generally be relevant to how they compare regarding R', then, typically, if R is nontransitive, R' will be as well.

The reasoning underlying this view might be illustrated as follows. Suppose that how two outcomes, X and Y, compare with respect to a given notion, N, depends on how they compare with respect to three factors, A, B, and C. Often, there will be a positive correlation between the factors A, B, C, and N, which supports a kind of *Pareto Principle*, according to which if X is better than Y in one important respect, say A, and at least as good as Y in the other respects, then all things considered X is better than Y with respect to N. More generally, the positive correlation between A, B, C, and N will often be such that, *other things equal*, how X compares to Y with respect to A is how X will compare to Y with respect to N, and similarly for B and C. It follows that if R is the relation that reflects how X compares to Y in terms of A, and R' the relation that reflects how X compares to Y in terms of N, then if R is nontransitive R' is also likely to be nontransitive. I say likely, rather than necessarily, because the argument assumes that it is possible for there to be three alternatives, X, Y, and Z, that are *equally* good in terms of B and C, and yet that stand in the nontransitive relation R' in terms of A. But as long as this is possible, the nontransitivity of R' will be inherited by R, as suggested earlier.

This discussion has been abstract. Let us return to the concrete case of the relation between obligatoriness and all-things-considered better than. Suppose we assume that the "obligatoriness" relation is nontransitive for the reasons suggested in section 7.2. Taking the example presented there, let us assume that there is a factor that is relevant and significant for comparing white applicants vis-à-vis African American applicants for certain jobs in American society that is *not* relevant for comparing white applicants with Mexican American applicants, or Mexican American applicants with African American applicants, and which thus accounts for the nontransitivity of the "obligatoriness" relation concerning who we ought to hire. Suppose, first, that White, Mexican American, and African American all have *identical* job-related skills. Then, we might think we ought to give White and Mexican American an equal chance at being hired, and we ought to give Mexican American and African American an equal chance at being hired, but it is not the case—for affirmative action reasons—that we ought to give White and African American an equal chance at being hired. So far, of course, we merely have a by now familiar example of nontransitivity governing what we ought to *do*.

But next consider the comparative goodness of the different alternatives. Given their equal job-related skills, the outcome in which White is hired and the outcome in which Mexican American is hired would be *equally* good. Similarly, the outcome in which Mexican American is hired and the outcome in which African American is hired would be *equally* good. It follows that if the "equally good" relation were transitive then it must be the case that the outcome in which White is hired and the outcome in which African American is hired would be *equally* good. But this I now deny.

Why? Because on the assumption of the example we *ought* to hire African American in such a case, and ought *not* to hire White. That is, for affirmative action reasons, hiring African American would be *right*, and hiring White would be *wrong*. Thus, on the view expressed earlier—according to which acting rightly is a good-making feature, and acting wrongly a bad-making feature of the outcomes of which they are a part—the fact that hiring African American would be right and hiring White wrong not only provides me with reason to *act* one way rather than another, it provides me with an important reason to regard the outcome where I act rightly as *better than* the outcome where I act wrongly. Moreover, since the outcome where I act rightly is *as good as* the one in which I act wrongly in all *other* respects relevant to the comparative goodness of the two outcomes, it seems clear that, all things considered, the outcome where I hire African American is better than the outcome where I hire White, for Pareto-type reasons of the sort suggested earlier. I conclude that if, as most believe, right and wrong actions are themselves *relevant* to, though not determinate of, the comparative goodness of outcomes, then the nontransitivity of the obligatoriness relation will be "inherited" by the "equally as good as" relation. If, indeed, the former relation is nontransitive, as many seem willing to grant, the latter is likely to be nontransitive as well.

Once one accepts that the "equally as good as" relation is nontransitive, there is little reason to resist the view that the "all-things-considered better than" relation (in my wide reason-implying sense) would also be nontransitive. Indeed, one might argue for such a position by slightly modifying our previous argument.

In the previous argument, we assumed that White, Mexican American, and African American were all *equally* qualified for a job, and that generated—via a policy of affirmative action, the intransitivity of the obligatoriness relation, and the relevance of right action to the comparative goodness of outcomes—the conclusion that the outcome where White is hired would be equally as good as the one where Mexican American is hired, that the outcome where Mexican American is hired would be equally as good as the one where African American is hired, and yet that the outcome where African American is hired would be better than the outcome where White is hired. We can then ask how *much* better the outcome in which African American is hired is than the outcome in which White is hired.

I don't have a precise answer to that question, but we don't need it for our argument. It is sufficient if we know that the one outcome *is* better than the other by some finite amount, say, P. Then let us change our example just a bit. Let us assume that White and Mexican American are no longer *exactly* equal in their job-related qualifications, but that in fact White is *slightly* more qualified than Mexican American. If White is slightly more qualified than Mexican American, then the outcome in which White is hired will be better than the outcome in which Mexican American is hired, though presumably only slightly. Indeed, we can safely assume that that there must be *some* possible world in which the extent to which White is more qualified than Mexican American is *sufficiently* slight that the outcome in which White is hired would be better than the outcome in which Mexican American is hired by a finite amount less than P. This is enough to ensure that the outcome in which we hire African American would still be better than the outcome in which we hire White, all things considered. This is because our policy of affirmative action still tells us that we ought to hire African American rather than White, since it does more than break ties between equally qualified candidates, and since White will be only *slightly* more qualified than African American. Moreover, though there will now be a *slight* respect in which the outcome where White is hired would be better than the outcome where African American is hired, it will remain the case that there is an important respect in which the outcome where African American is hired is better than the outcome where White is hired and, given the assumptions of our example, the latter respect will outweigh the former one.

But, then, the preceding considerations imply that the outcome where African American is hired is better than the outcome where White is hired, and the outcome where White is hired is better than the outcome where Mexican American is hired. It follows that if the "all-things-considered better than" relation is transitive the outcome where African American is hired *must* be better than the outcome where Mexican American is hired. But this would not be the case. Since Mexican American and African American are *equally* qualified candidates, and there is no affirmative action reason to favor African Americans over Mexican Americans, the outcome where African American is hired and the outcome where Mexican American is hired would be *equally* good. Thus, the "all-things-considered better than" relation, as well as the "equally as good as" relation, would be nontransitive.

There are many steps in the preceding argument that might be disputed. Indeed, many opposed to policies of affirmative action will want to object to the argument from the very start. But I hope it is clear that the appeal to the policy of affirmative action, and most of my example's details, are merely for illustrative purposes. Whatever one thinks about the ultimate defensibility of my argument, I believe the logical relations articulated in this section are correct.

In sum, many believe that the "obligatoriness" relation may be nontransitive, but that the "all-things-considered better than" relation could not be. This is, I think, an unstable position. Specifically, *if* one accepts that the "obligatoriness" relation is nontransitive, and if one *also* accepts that whether or not one acts rightly or wrongly is itself relevant to, even if not determinate of, the comparative goodness of the outcomes of which they are a part, then there is good reason to believe that the "all-things-considered better than" relation (in my wide reason-implying sense) will *also* be nontransitive. This is because, in general, nontransitivity is an "inheritable" trait, in the sense that if the comparative relation corresponding to an important aspect of a complex notion is nontransitive, the comparative relation of the complex notion will itself be nontransitive. That is, where A is an important aspect of complex notion N, R is the comparative relation with respect to A, and R' is the comparative relation with respect to N, then if R is nontransitive, R' will also, typically, be nontransitive. In particular, this will be so when (but not necessarily only when) there is a positive correlation between A and N, such that *other things equal* how two alternatives compare regarding A will determine how they compare regarding N, *and* if there can be three alternatives X, Y, and Z, such that X, Y, and Z stand in a nontransitive comparative relation with respect to A, and are equally good (or *almost* equally good) with respect to the other aspects relevant to N.

7.5 Defending the Transitivity of the Obligatoriness Relation: A Fine-Grained Solution

At this point we must consider an important rejoinder to the claim that the obligatoriness relation is nontransitive. If this argument succeeds, one could avoid the problem of the "all-things-considered better than" relation "inheriting" the nontransitivity of the "obligatoriness" relation.

In section 7.2, I offered an argument purporting to show that obligatoriness is a nontransitive relation. In response, it might be claimed that all my argument showed is the need for a subtler, more sophisticated, finer-grained understanding of the different alternatives that I was considering.[11] Once we have that understanding, it could be argued, it will be clear that the notion of transitivity doesn't even *apply* to the case I was considering.

Consider again the apparent threat to transitivity offered by the affirmative action case. It is agreed that as the example was presented in section 7.2, given the pairwise choice between White and Mexican American, one ought to hire White because his job related qualifications are better, and that for similar reasons one ought to hire Mexican American over African American given the pairwise choice between them. But, it is held that given the pairwise choice between White and African American, one should hire African American, because there is a relevant factor that applies in that case and gives African American the edge over White—namely, the particular historical relationship between whites and African Americans in American society—that didn't apply in making the other pairwise comparisons.

But this means that in a fundamentally important way the alternative of hiring White is a *very different alternative* when his fellow candidate is Mexican American, than when his fellow candidate is African American. In the first case, call it alternative A_1, the hiring of White simply expresses a commitment to hiring the best candidate where affirmative action considerations are not relevant. In the second case, call it alternative A_2, the hiring of White expresses a failure to sufficiently appreciate and respond to the deep injustices that were historically perpetrated by whites against African Americans. (Here, of course, I am retaining section 7.2's assumption that the relevant policy of affirmative action *is* the appropriate response to such injustices. This is, of course, a controversial substantive assumption, but it is the hypothesis of my example.)

Now, in fact, a similar fine-grained distinction would be in order regarding the hiring of African American, where such a hiring would have a different meaning, and hence, from a moral perspective, be a significantly different alternative, in the case where the only rival candidate was White than in the case where the only rival candidate was Mexican American. But for our present purposes we can ignore this and simply pretend that hiring Mexican American is one alternative, *B*, and hiring African American another alternative, *C*. Still, it is evident that once we acknowledge the fine-grained distinction between A_1 and A_2, there *is* no failure of transitivity for the obligatoriness relation in the affirmative action case. After all, there would only be a failure of transitivity if there were three alternatives, *A*, *B*, and *C*, such that *A* ought to be done rather than *B*, and *B*

---

[11] John Broome first introduced me to the strategy of invoking a fine-grained individuation of outcomes in the face of apparent counterexamples to the transitivity of "better than" in a note he sent me in response to my earliest draft on the topic of intransitivity back in 1984. For an appreciation of the power and appeal of such a strategy, see Broome's *Weighing Goods* (Oxford: Basil Blackwell, 1991), especially sections 5.3 and 5.4. I should perhaps add that Broome is fully aware of, and rightly acknowledges, the limitations of such a strategy, which I shall later present in chapter 13.

ought to be done rather than C, but C ought to be done rather than A. But, in fact, all the affirmative action case illustrates is that A_1 ought to be done rather than B, and B ought to be done rather than C, but C ought to be done rather than A_2!

Note, by the way, that as transitivity implies, A_1 *ought* to be done rather than C. That is, one *ought* to hire a more qualified white over a less qualified African American, when doing so expresses a commitment to the equal opportunity/merit principle *without thereby* failing to express condemnation of past injustices when it is merited. But it happens that in American society, unlike other societies, A_1 and C are not rival options. So, while A_1 ought to be done rather than C, *when those are the alternatives*—as transitivity entails, given that A_1 ought to be done rather than B, and B ought to be done rather than C—in *our* society, where the *actual* alternatives are A_2 and C, C ought to be done.

Thus, it might be concluded, we need not grant, as many have, that the "obligatoriness" relation is nontransitive. Rather, if we are careful to make the necessary fine-grained distinctions, we will recognize that different alternatives are actually being compared in the cases considered. Thus, rather than having an example where transitivity *fails*, we simply have yet another example where it doesn't even *apply*.

The preceding response would have great appeal against the claim that the obligatory relation is *in*transitive. Moreover, the general strategy of looking for finer-grained individuations of alternatives can be a powerful and effective weapon in the arsenal of those seeking to defend the transitivity of certain important normative relations in the face of apparent counterexamples. But, as should be clear, such a response doesn't even *engage* my claims regarding the "obligatoriness" relation and the implication of those claims for the "all-things-considered better than" relation, nor, importantly, is it clear that one gains much in the face of my arguments by appealing to such a move.

I claimed that the "obligatoriness" relation is *non*transitive. I *didn't* commit myself to the view that it is actually *in*transitive, though it might be. Recall that as I am employing the notion, a *non*transitive relation is one where transitivity either *fails*, or *fails to apply* across sets of alternatives to which we might have thought it should apply. If we naturally think of the hiring of White, African American, and Mexican American as three alternatives, we might have thought that the transitivity of "ought to hire rather than" should apply across those three alternatives; so that if we ought to hire White rather than African American, and African American rather than Mexican American, then we ought to hire White rather than Mexican American. When we learn that this isn't so, for the reasons suggested earlier, we are, in essence, acknowledging that the obligatoriness relation is nontransitive, *not* because it is *in*transitive, meaning that transitivity *fails* for that relation, but rather because the relation *fails to apply* across different sets of alternatives to which we might have expected it to apply. Hence, my claim stands, and we still have reason to believe that the nontransitivity of the "obligatoriness" relation would be carried over into the "better than" relation.

The point wouldn't be that we have learned that the "better than" relation (in my wide reason-implying sense) is *in*transitive, but it would still be *non*transitive in that it would fail to apply across certain sets of alternatives to which we might have thought it should apply. In particular, we might have assumed that if we could know that the outcome in which White was hired would be *better than* the outcome in which Mexican American was hired, when those were our alternatives, and we could know that the outcome in which Mexican American was hired would be *better than* the outcome in which African American was hired, when those were our alternatives, then we could correctly infer, via the transitivity of "better than," that the outcome in which White was hired would be *better than* the outcome in which African American was hired, *without having to consider those outcomes directly*. But, on the fine-grained solution, we couldn't properly infer this, because the outcome in which White was hired would be a different outcome when the alternative was hiring Mexican American than when the alternative was hiring African American. This is the kind of scenario where it seems appropriate to claim, as I did, that "better than" would be a *non*transitive relation, even if it wasn't an *in*transitive relation.

I shall explore this important issue further in chapter 13. As we will see then, however successful the fine-grained solution may be in defending transitivity as a *technical* feature of certain relations, including the "better than" relation, such a move has high costs. In particular, on such a move much of the *practical significance* of transitivity may be lost.

7.6 "All-Things-Considered Better Than": The Underlying Conditions That Might Make It a Transitive or Nontransitive Relation

Combining the results of this chapter and the preceding one, we can now articulate the conditions under which "all-things-considered better than" (in my wide reason-implying sense) is, or is not, likely to be a transitive relation. I begin by returning to the linguists' view that there is a correlation between transitivity and gradability such that the "all-things-considered better than" relation will be transitive if it is the natural comparative of a one-place property that readily admits of intensifiers.

Appealing to my notion of "larger than," I argued that a one-place property may be gradable in the linguists' sense *without* its being the case that its natural comparative is transitive. Still, it is interesting to note that, linguistically, "all-things-considered better than" doesn't *sound* like a natural comparative of a one-place property. So, whereas linguists are correct in noting that we can move naturally to the comparative claims that "P is taller than Q" or "P is heavier than Q" from the claims that "P is tall" or "P is heavy," respectively, one *can't* naturally move to the comparative claim that "P is better than Q, all things considered" from the claim that "P is bett, all things considered," since there *is* no property of "being bett, all things considered" or "all-things-considered bettness" in the English language. Putting the point differently, we *can't* naturally move from the claim that "*P* is good, all things considered" to the comparative claim that "*P* is gooder than *Q*, all things considered" or that "*P* is more good than *Q*, all things considered"; instead, we move to the claim that "*P* is *better than Q*, all things considered" to express the comparative of *all-things-considered goodness*. So, insofar as one thinks that there is *often*, even if not always, a connection between transitivity and gradability in the linguists' sense, and hence is *tempted* to be moved by linguistic evidence in this area, one might suspect that "all-things-considered better than" is not, in fact, a transitive relation.

However, on reflection, one might worry that it is merely an artifact of English that the natural comparative of "goodness" is "better than" rather than "gooder than" or "more good than." Suppose, for example, that we used the words "is desirable" as equivalent in meaning to the words "is good," and similarly that we used the words "more desirable than" as equivalent in meaning to the words "all-things-considered better than." Here, *desirableness* would be understood as a property of people, objects, or states of affairs (where, as noted previously, whether or not something was desirable would not depend on whether it was *actually* desired by anyone, though if something was desirable it would be desired by an "ideal observer" or an appropriately situated "rational impartial spectator"). Now it looks like the property of being desirable *is* gradable in the linguists' sense, in that one could move from "*P* is desirable" to the natural comparative "*P* is more desirable than *Q*," and similarly one could naturally attach intensifiers to the property, moving from "*P* is desirable" to "*P* is very desirable or extremely desirable." So, here, the linguists' criteria of gradability would lead us to expect that "more desirable than" would be a transitive relation.

But now we seem to have a problem. The linguists' view about the relation between gradability in their sense and transitivity would lead us to expect that "all-things-considered better than" is *not* a transitive relation, but that "more desirable than" *is* a transitive relation. Yet, by hypothesis, the expression "all-things-considered better than" picks out the *very same* relation as the expression "more desirable than." Hence, if we want to know whether or not a relation is transitive, we should look beyond the mere linguistic evidence of whether or not the relation is the natural comparative of an underlying one-place property which is gradable in the linguists' sense.

Fortunately, our previous discussion suggests a good place to look. We should look to see if the relation represents how alternatives compare in terms of an underlying property that is gradable in my sense of there being a common linear scale which accurately represents the degree or extent to which an alternative possesses the property in question. Moreover, for those who continue to find the linguists' position intuitively attractive, it is worth observing that in those paradigmatic cases where the linguists' criteria seems to get the right answer, we can, in fact, construct a common linear scale to measure and compare the extent to which any two alternatives possess the one-place property that is gradable in the linguists' sense. So, for example, we can construct common linear scales to measure the extent to which an alternative possesses the property of being tall, being heavy, or being fast, and thus the relations of "being taller than," "being heavier than," or "being faster than" are transitive. Hence, we can explain the transitivity of the comparative relations in question by appeal to the fact that the underlying properties are gradable in my sense of the term, and do not have to appeal to their being gradable in the linguists' sense.

We see, then, that for any comparative relation, R, that indicates how two alternatives compare in terms of some underlying property, P, R will be transitive if it tracks how any two alternatives compare on a common linear scale that accurately reflects the extent to which alternatives possess the property of P. If, however, there is no common linear scale that we can use to measure and compare how each alternative compares with every other in terms of some underlying property, P, then there is no guarantee that any relation, R, expressing such comparisons will be transitive.

Return, then, to the question of whether or not "all-things-considered better than" is a transitive relation. One way of establishing that "all-things-considered better than" is a transitive relation would be to identify a given set of factors with fixed weights relative to each other that together constitute a meaningful notion of goodness or desirableness that is a gradable one-place property in my sense of gradability. If one could do this, then the extent to which outcomes possessed those factors would determine their degree of goodness or desirability, and hence their placement on a common linear scale measuring goodness or desirability. This information would, in turn, determine how any two alternatives compared all things considered, and more generally, for any three alternatives A, B, and C, if their placements on the common linear scale for desirability determined that A was better than B all things considered, and that B was better than C all things considered, then they would also determine that A was better than C all things considered. Hence, "all-things-considered better than" (in my wide reason-implying sense) would, indeed, be a transitive relation.

By contrast, it should now be clear that if *different* factors might be relevant for determining how two alternatives compare all things considered, depending on the alternatives being compared, or if the *significance* of the factors for determining how two alternatives compare all things considered might vary depending on the alternatives that are being compared (so that the very same factors might be given different weights), then we have no reason to expect that the "all-things-considered better than" relation (in my wide reason-implying sense) will be transitive. After all, how two alternatives compare all things considered depends on how they compare in terms of *all* of the relevant factors for making that comparison, taking into account the relative significance of each of those factors. This point is crucial, so let me spell it out in some detail.

If *different* factors were relevant for comparing different outcomes, it could be true that even if A were better than B, and B better than C, in terms of the relevant factors for comparing *those* alternatives, A might *not* be better than C, in terms of the relevant factors for making *that* comparison. Notice, further, that even if there is *substantial* overlap in the factors for comparing alternatives, as long as there is *some* difference, intransitivity may arise. For example, suppose that factors X and Y are each relevant when comparing A, B, and C, but that another factor, Z, is relevant *only* when comparing A and C. Then it might be that, *all things considered*, A is better than B (because it is better taking into account *all* of the factors relevant for making *that* comparison, namely, X and Y), and B is better than C (because it is better taking into account *all* of the factors relevant for making *that* comparison, again, X and Y), but C is better than A. This could be so, if C was *sufficiently* better than A regarding Z, to outweigh the extent to which it was worse than A regarding X and Y.

Similarly, even if the *same* factors are always relevant for comparing A, B, and C, if the *significance* of those factors can vary with the alternatives being compared, intransitivity can arise. For example, suppose factors X and Y are both relevant for comparing A, B, and C, but X is more significant than Y when comparing A with B, and B with C, but less significant than Y when comparing A with C. Then it might be that, *all things considered*—that is, taking account of *both* the factors that are relevant to making each comparison *and* their relative significance—A is better than B, and B is better than C, but C is better than A. This could be so if A were better than B, and B better than C, regarding X, but C were better than B, and B better than A, regarding Y.[12]

As should be evident, our point here might have been put in terms of the proper scales that need to be employed to compare different outcomes. For any

---

[12] I shall spare the reader further details of this example. I trust it is clear how the example should be filled out given the relevant assumptions.

Ironically, one reader for *Philosophy and Public Affairs* worried about my schematic explanation of intransitivity because it seemingly works a bit *too* well! As the reader observed, "If this explanation is accepted, it no longer seems so clear why intransitivity should seem troubling in the way that it does."

I agree that *once my explanation is accepted*, it is no longer clear why the intransitivity or nontransitivity of "all-things-considered better than" (in my wide reason-implying sense) should seem so puzzling. Moreover, I am pleased to note that many readers of my work on intransitivity *do* no longer find the idea puzzling. Still, ultimately my explanation relies on a conception of moral ideals that is opposed by an alternative conception that is natural, plausible, and extremely powerful (I introduce the two conceptions later, in section 7.7, and discuss them at length in chapters 11 through 13). Since the alternative conception is widely held, and entails that the "all-things-considered better than" relation must be transitive, this helps to explain why most people initially find my claims about intransitivity perplexing, and why it may take a while to convince some people that they should accept my explanation. Finally, even if one accepts my account of intransitivity—so that the notion is no longer difficult to *understand*—there remain a host of reasons to find the issue deeply troubling, many of which I will discuss in later chapters. This may help to account for the negative reaction most have to the claim that "all-things-considered better than" may not be a transitive relation.

three alternatives, *A*, *B*, and *C*, if it could be the case that the relevance and significance of the factors for comparing *A* and *B* all things considered differ from the relevance and significance of the factors for comparing *B* with *C* all things considered, then, in essence, we will ultimately be comparing *A* with *B* according to *one* scale, and *B* with *C* according to *another* scale. From this, of course, nothing follows about how *A* and *C* would compare according to either scale. Indeed, nothing follows about what scale would need to be employed to compare *A* with *C* all things considered, whether it might be the same scale as the one for comparing *A* with *B*, the same scale as the one for comparing *B* with *C*, or a different scale entirely. A fortiori, knowing that *A* is better than *B*, and *B* better than *C*, would tell us nothing about how *A* and *C* compare all things considered. Hence, "all-things-considered better than" would be a nontransitive relation.

So, a key question regarding whether "all-things-considered better than" (in my wide reason-implying sense) is a transitive or nontransitive relation is simple and straightforward. *Is* there a given set of factors with fixed weights that ultimately determine how any two alternatives compare all things considered? Or is it sometimes the case that the relevance or significance of the factors for comparing alternatives all things considered vary, depending on the alternatives being compared? If the former, "all-things-considered better than" (in my wide reason-implying sense) will be a transitive relation. If the latter, there is no reason to expect that it will be a transitive relation, and one shouldn't be at all surprised if, in fact, it is a nontransitive one.[13]

Thinking about the various spectrum cases presented in chapters 2 through 5, and the plausibility of the First Standard View, the Third Standard View, and View One, it appears that there is a wide range of cases for which additive-aggregationist reasoning seems plausible. Specifically, for a host of alternatives that are similar to each other in terms of how the quality of individual lives would be impacted, we should trade off between quality and number or quality and duration both between lives and within lives. However, the Second Standard View, the Fourth Standard View, and View Three also seem quite plausible, which is to say that for a wide range of cases anti-additive-aggregationist reasoning seems plausible. Specifically, for a host of alternatives that are significantly different from each other in terms of how the quality of individual lives would be impacted, it seems that we should not trade off between quality and number or quality and

---

[13] As I emphasized in section 1.5, this is compatible with there being some senses of "all-things-considered better than" where the "all-things-considered better than" relation is transitive. This may be so, for example, of an *internal aspect* reason-implying sense of "all-things-considered better than," as well as various other senses of "all-things-considered better than," including some that might be properly regarded as *essentially comparative* in a way that is different from the main way that I shall be using that notion later (on the notions of "internal aspect" and "essentially comparative," see chapters 11 and 12). But as this work suggests, these senses of "all-things-considered better than" may be less central and important for practical reasoning than the wide reason-implying sense with which I am mainly concerned here and throughout this work.

duration whether between lives or within lives. Thus, thinking about the spectrum cases discussed earlier, it appears that we *do* appeal to different criteria depending on the alternatives being compared. If we are right to do so, then "all-things-considered better than" (in my wide reason-implying sense) *will* be a nontransitive relation, and hence we cannot appeal to the transitivity of "all-things considered better than" when comparing (all) outcomes.

It remains possible that, despite their intuitive plausibility, we must ultimately reject either the additive-aggregationist reasoning underlying the First Standard View, the Third Standard View, and View One, or the anti-additive-aggregationist reasoning underlying the Second Standard View, the Fourth Standard View, and View Three. But our discussion has revealed good reason to wonder whether the transitivity of the "all-things-considered better than" relation can be preserved in a practically satisfying way.

For one, though it is merely suggestive, there is the general consideration that if three other significant normative relations may be nontransitive—the "not worse than" relation, the "permissibility" relation, and the "obligatoriness" relation—perhaps the "all-things-considered better than" relation will also be nontransitive. Or, to put this point with a bit more rhetorical flourish: *if* we are prepared to accept that transitivity fails, or fails to apply, for the important normative relation of "permissible to do rather than" (as Frances Kamm has argued we should be) and *if* we are prepared to accept that transitivity either fails, or fails to apply, for the important normative relation of "ought to do rather than" (as I have argued we should), and *if* we are prepared to accept that transitivity either fails, or fails to apply, for the important normative relation of "not worse than" (as Parfit, Broome, and Chang have all argued we should)—and, in fact, I believe that many people *are* prepared to accept *all three* of the positions in question—then shouldn't we at least be *open* to the real possibility that transitivity may *also* fail or fail to apply for the important normative relation of "all-things-considered better than" (in my wide reason-implying sense, which may be the sense that has most practical significance)? Indeed, it might seem rather *odd* if "all-things-considered better than" in the wide *reason-implying* sense *were* to be transitive, if these other central normative relations are not.

But setting the rhetorical point aside, there is the more concrete issue of the logical relationship between different normative relations. Given the relation between the right and the good, and the corresponding relation between the "obligatoriness" and "all-things-considered better than" relations—namely, that each is relevant to, though not determinate of, the other—there is good reason to believe that if, indeed, the "obligatoriness" relation is nontransitive, then the "all-things-considered better than" relation will be as well. This is because, as we saw, in general, if there are two relations, R and R', related in such a way that *other things equal* if aRb then $aR'b$, then if R is nontransitive R' will also be nontransitive.

Now, as I have indicated, many people *are* willing to grant that the "obligatoriness" relation could be nontransitive. In particular, it seems perfectly plausible that the factors that are relevant and significant for determining whether we ought to *do* one of two alternatives could vary with the particular alternatives being compared. But if this is so, and if, indeed, whether or not one acts rightly or wrongly is itself relevant to the goodness of the outcome of which it is a part, then, a fortiori, the relevance and significance of the factors for comparing alternatives all things considered could vary with the particular alternatives being compared. Thus, given the relationship between the "obligatoriness" and "all-things-considered better than" relations, there is good reason to believe that the nontransitivity of the former would be inherited by the latter. So, ultimately, the transitivity or nontransitivity of the "obligatoriness" and "all-things-considered better than" relations may stand or fall together.

Next, we might focus on the logical relation between the "not worse than" and "all-things-considered better than" relations. Though Broome and Parfit both have doubts about whether "all-things-considered better than" could be nontransitive, both have previously argued that "not worse than" is nontransitive.[14] But when one examines the diagram that Broome offered to illuminate his position (chapter 6's diagram 6.3.A), and the examples and considerations he and Parfit adduced in support of their claim, it seems clear that on their view there will be certain sets of alternatives for which there is no common linear scale that we can employ to determine how each of the alternatives compare with each other. So, for example, we saw that we might be able to rank all applicants for a fellowship vis-à-vis each other, but that we might need to use one scale to compare two poets with each other, and another scale or some different basis to compare a poet with a novelist. Similarly, while we might be able to compare different kinds of careers, we might need one scale to compare two legal careers, and a different one or some other basis to compare a legal career with an academic one.

But "not worse than" is a relation that purportedly indicates how two alternatives compare *all things considered*. So it appears that Broome and Parfit have both given us a model for comparing alternatives according to which the relevance and significance of the factors for determining how alternatives compared all things considered might depend on the alternatives being compared. As noted, a factor relevant to our ranking of two poets, or two legal careers, might not be relevant, or might have a different weight, when comparing a poet with a novelist, or a legal career with an academic one. But *once one accepts this model*, there seems little reason to believe that its implications will extend only so far as to the "not worse than" relation. To the contrary, as we have seen, once one recognizes that different factors may be relevant or have different significance for comparing two outcomes, depending on the alternatives being considered, then there is no reason to expect

---

[14] Recall that here "not worse than" is being used in the sense of *rough comparability* presented in chapter 6. Both Parfit and Broome readily grant that there is a *different* sense of "not worse than," where "not worse than" is equivalent to "at least as good as," such that "not worse than" in *that* sense *is* a transitive relation.

that the "all-things-considered better than" relation will be transitive, and every reason to expect that it will be nontransitive. After all, on such a view it certainly *could* be that *A* is *better than*, and not merely "not worse than," *B*, in terms of the factors relevant and significant for making *that* comparison, and *B* is *better than*, and not merely "not worse than," *C*, in terms of the factors relevant and significant for making *that* comparison, and yet we'd have no basis for saying how *A* compared to *C* all things considered. It appears, then, that the model and reasoning that underlie the plausibility of Broome's and Parfit's claims about "not worse than" also apply to the "all-things-considered better than" relation. If one accepts that "not worse than" is not a transitive relation, for the reasons suggested by Broome's and Parfit's claims, then one should also accept that the "all-things-considered better than" relation (in my wide reason-implying sense) is also likely to be nontransitive.

Return to the kinds of examples discussed in chapters 2 through 5. Many people think there is something fishy about my examples because they trade on the fact that an illness like very severe depression is a very different *kind* of condition than a condition of merely being "pretty down" once a month, or on the fact that the pain of intense torture seems to be of an entirely different *kind* than the mild discomfort of a mosquito bite. This is why, they claim, that *no* number of people being "down" occasionally, or months of having one extra mosquito bite, could outweigh someone having a lifetime of severe depression, or undergoing a significant period of intense torture. This observation is, I think, revealing. But it does not undermine my argument; rather, it illuminates it.

If we grant the claim in question, then the spectrums from severe depression to being "down," and from intense torture to a mosquito bite, would exemplify the fact that *together* a sufficient number of differences in degree can sometimes amount to a difference in kind. But, then, it shouldn't be surprising that transitivity fails along this spectrum, since the relevant factors for comparing alternatives that merely differ in degree, may differ from those for comparing alternatives that differ in kind; or, at least, the relative significance of factors relevant for comparing alternatives that merely differ in degree, may differ from the relative significance of those factors for comparing alternatives that differ in kind. Correspondingly, as we have just seen, if there is a continuum from *A* to *Y*, such that *A* and *B*, *B* and *C*, ... , and *X* and *Y* merely differ in degree, while *A* and *Y* differ in kind, then there may be good reasons for ranking *A* better than *B*, *B* better than *C*, *C* better than *D*, and so on, yet for not ranking *A* better than *Y*. After all, the relevant factors, or the significance of those factors, for comparing "distant" alternatives *A* and *Y*, may differ from the relevant factors, or the significance of those factors, for comparing the intervening "adjacent" alternatives.

In comparing pains that merely differ in degree, duration clearly plays a significant role. This is why we think a shorter intense pain might clearly be better than a much longer less intense pain. But in comparing pains that differ in kind, duration seems to play a very different role. *In comparison with torture of sufficient duration*, a mosquito bite's duration basically doesn't matter. So, a factor that is clearly relevant and significant in comparing some outcomes seems not relevant—or at least to have a very different significance—in comparing different outcomes. Thus, transitivity would seemingly fail for reasons that are clear, straightforward, and perfectly appropriate.

But notice, we don't actually have to hold the extreme view that the opposing ends of my spectrums are of entirely different *kinds* in order to maintain our position. It is enough if, following Broome and Parfit, we recognize that alternatives can vary in degrees of similarity and dissimilarity, and that the relevant and significant factors for comparing largely similar alternatives may differ from those for comparing largely dissimilar alternatives.

When I consider alternatives involving illness or pains that are different, but still quite similar, it is like considering two poets for a fellowship, or two legal careers for a way of life. Given the close similarity between the different alternatives, I'll compare them on the basis of a certain set of relevant factors that will correspond to a given scale that measures such factors. But when I consider alternatives involving illnesses or pains that are quite *dis*similar—indeed, as far apart as a lifetime of very severe depression versus being pretty "down" once a month, or a lifetime including a significant period of torture versus one extra mosquito bite a month—while I can still *compare* such alternatives, I may have to invoke different criteria, or give my criteria different weight, just as I have to invoke different criteria when I compare a poet with a novelist, or a legal career with an academic one. Surely, if there is reason to believe that the relevance and significance of the factors for comparing a poet with a novelist might be different from the relevance and significance of the factors for comparing two poets, it is reasonable to believe that the relevance and significance of the factors for comparing very severe depression with occasionally being "down" might be different from the relevance and significance of the factors for comparing two depressions which are different, but of the same order of magnitude.

On reflection, then, the same kinds of considerations that support the limited, though plausible, conclusion that "not worse than" is nontransitive, also support the stronger conclusion that "all-things-considered better than" (in my wide reason-implying sense) is nontransitive. Ultimately, I submit, the two positions stand, or fall, together.

In light of the preceding, many are attracted to the following view.[15] "Better than" *is* a transitive relation, whenever it is elliptical for "better than with respect to *x*," where *x* is a fixed, determinate feature or property which an alternative will possess to a given degree that can be accurately represented on a linear scale. However, when we compare how two alternatives compare all things considered, we are *not* comparing them in terms of a fixed, determinate property of the sort

---

[15] This view has been expressed to me by many people over the years, including John Doris, after a talk I gave at Washington University in St. Louis.

in question. Thus, once we see what the notion of "all-things-considered better than" involves, it is not surprising that "all-things-considered better than" (in my wide reason-implying sense) is not a transitive relation.

Let me next revisit a natural response to these considerations, briefly alluded to earlier. One might argue that there is no issue of nontransitivity in some of these various relations. Instead, there is merely a confusion or ambiguity of terms that needs to be sorted out, and once it is sorted out it will be clear that rather than a *failure* of transitivity in these cases, we merely have a set of instances where transitivity doesn't *apply*.

For example, it might be argued that we must distinguish different senses of "all-things-considered better than." Sometimes when we say that "A is better than B," we mean that "A is better than B in terms of both quality and quantity of pleasure or pain." We might call this the "all-things-considered better than$_1$," or P_1, relation. There will be a scale ranking all alternatives according to P_1, and P_1 will be a perfectly transitive relation. On the other hand, sometimes when we say that "A is better than B," all we actually mean is something like "A is significantly better than B in terms of the quality of pleasure or pain."[16] We might call this the "all-things-considered better than$_2$," or P_2, relation. Again, there will be a scale ranking all alternatives according to P_2, and P_2 will be a perfectly transitive relation. On this view, it is a mistake to think that "all-things-considered better than" might be a nontransitive relation. There are just two distinct all-things-considered better than relations, P_1 and P_2, both of which are *perfectly* transitive. But, unfortunately, we use the same *words*, "all-things-considered better than," to express each relation, so we are sometimes *confused* as to what we are actually claiming. If we were sufficiently careful and precise, we would see that chapter 2 through 5's apparent counterexamples to the transitivity of the "all-things-considered better than" relation are all simple instances where we *rightly* observe that aP_1b, and bP_1c, but cP_2a. This, of course, is not a *counterexample* to transitivity, but an instance where the notion of transitivity *fails to apply*.

If this strategy worked, it might be similarly applied to Parfit's and Broome's claims about the nontransitivity of "not worse than." Thus, it might be argued that we must be careful to distinguish between different senses of "attractive fellowship candidate" or "attractive career." So, for example, there might be "attractive career$_1$," corresponding to a relation R_1, which would apply the criteria relevant for comparing legal careers, and "attractive career$_2$," corresponding to a relation R_2, which would apply the criteria relevant for comparing white-collar careers (including both legal and academic), and

---

[16] The "something like" in this sentence is important. In fact, for ease of this discussion I have oversimplified the actual view that many of us find attractive, which, as I emphasized in my discussion of the torture to mosquito bites spectrum case, permits us to focus on the quality of pleasures or pains in comparing outcomes only if the relevant pleasures and pains are of sufficiently long duration in the first place.

there would be no instance of nontransitivity. R_1 and R_2 might both be perfectly transitive, and in essence our conviction that "not worse than" is nontransitive would have arisen from our failure to recognize that we were shifting criteria in making different comparisons. In fact, we would simply be judging, correctly, that in comparing one legal career with an academic career, aR_1b, in comparing that same academic career with a different legal career, bR_1c, and in comparing the two legal careers with each other, cR_2a. As before, there would be no *failure* of transitivity involved in such judgments, just an instance where the notion of transitivity *failed to apply*.

There are several responses to be made to such a move, one of which is that it is dubious that we are actually just confusing different senses of our notions. For example, Parfit and Broome might deny that they are confusing "attractive career$_1$" with "attractive career$_2$" in claiming that "not worse than" is nontransitive. Instead, they might assert that they are employing a *single* sense of "attractive career" in making their claims, a sense according to which the relative attractiveness of two careers is determined by comparing them directly in terms of *all* of the factors that are relevant and significant to choosing between them. This sense of "attractive career" might be perfectly clear and unambiguous, and if one supposes that it is correlated with the relation R, then as long as it could be the case that *different* factors could be relevant or vary in their significance for comparing careers, depending on the alternatives involved, it could be the case that R will be nontransitive.

Clearly, similar claims might be made regarding the "all-things-considered better than" relation (in my wide reason-implying sense). One might deny that we are confused about two different senses of the words "all-things-considered better than." Rather, it might be claimed, we are using a single, unambiguous sense, according to which, roughly, A is better than B if and only if, given *all* of the factors that are relevant and significant for choosing between them, there is most reason to choose A rather than B from an impartial perspective. As we've seen, this notion of "all-things-considered better than" may be nontransitive, as long as it could be the case that the factors that *are* relevant and significant for comparing two alternatives can vary depending on the alternatives being compared.

I think, then, that we should reject the notion that there must be a confusion of different senses underlying the claims that "not worse than" or "all-things-considered better than" are nontransitive. But I grant that we might accept the prescriptive recommendation that we not *use* such notions. Certainly, we could dispense with such notions, and focus merely on the underlying relations that they express. If we did this, our examples would no longer raise worries about *transitivity*, as we'd simply have a host of cases where aR_1b, and bR_1c, but cR_2a. But, as should be evident by now, while such a move would ensure that the notions we allow ourselves to employ when comparing alternatives are all transitive, it would do *nothing* to alleviate the deep worries raised by the examples. If we really think that from the impartial perspective

R_1 is the *relevant* relation in terms of which to compare A and B, and also B and C, but that R_2 is the *relevant* relation in terms of which to compare A and C, then we are no better off *practically* than if there were a nontransitive all-things-considered better than relation ranking A, B, and C.

As should be clear by now, this would be another case where a perfectly transitive set of relations might give rise to a money-pump situation. More important, this would be a case where knowing how A compared to B, and B compared to C, would be of no use to us in determining how A compared to C. In particular, though we might know that aR_1b, and bR_1c, and so could correctly infer that aR_1c, this information would be irrelevant to knowing how A compares to C all things considered. After all, we would still need to know how A and C compared in terms of the factors relevant to making *that* comparison, namely, those relevant to R_2.

I have argued that if the relevance and significance of the factors for comparing two alternatives can vary depending on the alternatives being compared, then the "all-things-considered better than" relation will be nontransitive. But let me now qualify that claim. If one assumes that the relevance and significance of the factors for comparing A with B will depend *solely* on features of A and B, and the relations between them, then my claim will stand. However, if one believes that how two situations A and B compare all things considered can also depend on features of *other* alternatives, including, perhaps, how A or B might compare with other alternatives besides each other, there is a possibility that the "all-things-considered better than" relation (in my wide reason-implying sense) will be transitive even though the relevance and significance of the factors for comparing A with B *directly* may differ from the relevance and significance of the factors that would be relevant and significant for comparing other alternatives directly. This is an important position that I will return to in chapter 13. Unfortunately, as we will see, this possible way of preserving the transitivity of the "all-things-considered better than" relation (in my wide reason-implying sense) also has significant practical costs, costs comparable to those of forsaking transitivity itself.

7.7 Introducing the Internal Aspects and Essentially Comparative Views

In this section, I want to briefly present a new point which involves a fundamentally important distinction.[17] I will discuss the point in depth in chapters 11 through 13, where it will be the central focus. But it is appropriate to introduce the point here, as it naturally grows out of what has come before, but extends those ideas in an important and, I hope, illuminating way.

---

[17] I am grateful to Shelly Kagan for suggesting that this point is sufficiently new and important to warrant a section of its own.

The point is just this. Ultimately, whether the "all-things-considered better than" relation (in my wide reason-implying sense) is transitive or nontransitive will be correlated with two entirely different ways of thinking about the assessment of outcomes. On one way, each outcome is composed of a multitude of features. Together, these features and the relations between them will determine the value of that outcome from an impartial perspective. This value, which could (perhaps) be accurately represented on a linear scale measuring the value of outcomes, is *fixed solely by the outcome's internal features*, and hence will be unchanged as long as the outcome's internal features are themselves unchanged. This value has a special significance—it is, as it were, the real value or true value or, perhaps, the intrinsic value of the outcome. Correspondingly, this value will be the key feature determining how the outcome compares to other outcomes, whose values will likewise be determined solely by *their* internal features and will also be accurately representable on the same linear scale. Clearly, on this way of thinking about the assessment of outcomes, which I now call the *Internal Aspects View*, the relevance and significance of the factors for determining an outcome's value will *not* vary depending on the alternative with which the outcome is compared, and the "all-things-considered better than" relation will be transitive.[18]

On the other way of thinking about the assessment of outcomes, though each outcome is composed of a multitude of features, the value of an outcome depends not merely on those features, and the relations between them, but *also* on the relations between those features and the features of *other* outcomes with which they might be compared. On this view, though one *might* be able to determine the value of an outcome considered by itself, that value will have no special primacy or normative significance. On this view, the relevance and significance of the factors for determining an outcome's value will vary depending on the alternatives with which it is compared, so that the value of an outcome X might be n, when considered by itself, o, when its alternative is Y, p, when its alternatives are Y and Z, and so on. On this view, there is no single fact of the matter representing how valuable an outcome *really* is. But, importantly, this does not imply that values are relative, subjective, humanly determined, or anything of this sort. On this view, values may still be objective, in that it may be an objective *fact* that X's value is n when consid-

---

[18] In previous publications I called this position the *intrinsic aspect view*, and it naturally reflects the view that the goodness of an outcome is its intrinsic value, and that outcome A will be better than outcome B, if A's intrinsic value is greater than B's (see my "Intransitivity and the Mere Addition Paradox," *Philosophy and Public Affairs* 16 [1987]: 138–87, and "Rethinking the Good, Moral Ideals and the Nature of Practical Reasoning," in *Reading Parfit*, ed. Jonathan Dancy [Oxford: Basil Blackwell, 1997], 290–344). However, I have come to the view that since the term "intrinsic value" is used in so many different ways in the literature, my position will be less liable to misinterpretation or confusion if I call it the "Internal Aspects View." In addition to avoiding the different and often conflicting connotations and commitments that come with the term "intrinsic value," there are various other advantages to my new terminology that I won't bother to detail here.

ered by itself, *o* when its alternative is *Y*, and so on. As we have seen, on this way of thinking about the value of outcomes, what I call the *Essentially Comparative View*, the "all-things-considered better than" relation (in my wide reason-implying sense) may be nontransitive. And even if transitivity can be defended on such a view—for example, by appeal to a fine-grained individuation of alternatives—the practical significance of transitivity may have been lost.

Clearly, it is of the utmost consequence for practical reasoning which, if either, of these ways of understanding the value of outcomes is correct. But having now introduced the Internal Aspects View and Essentially Comparative View, and illustrated some of the considerations relevant to deciding between them, I shall leave further exploration of this important topic to chapters 11 through 13.

*****

In this chapter, I have completed my exploration of the notion of transitivity. Between this chapter and the preceding one, we now have a better understanding of when we should expect the comparative of a given property to be a transitive relation. If the property is gradable, in the sense that there is a common linear scale which can be used to accurately measure and compare the extent to which any given alternative possesses the property, then the relation, *R*, that compares alternatives in terms of that property based on that scale will be transitive. If, however, how two alternatives compare with respect to a given relation *R* depends on how they compare in terms of one scale for some alternatives, but in terms of how they compare on another scale for other alternatives, then there is no reason to expect *R* to be a transitive relation.

We have seen that several important normative notions are nontransitive, including the "permissible to do rather than," "ought to do rather than," and "not worse than" relations. This naturally raised the thought that if those three important normative relations are all nontransitive, then perhaps the "all-things-considered better than" relation (in my wide reason-implying sense) should also be nontransitive; and I presented some considerations in support of the claim that the transitivity or nontransitivity of some of these relations should stand or fall together.

More particularly, we saw that whether or not "all-things-considered better than" is a transitive relation will ultimately depend on which of two very different ways of thinking about the value of outcomes is correct. If an Internal Aspects View is correct, so that the relevance and significance of the factors for determining an outcome's value will not vary depending on the alternatives with which it is compared, and each alternative's degree of goodness can be ranked on a common linear scale, then the "all-things-considered better than" relation will be a transitive relation. But if an Essentially Comparative View is correct, where the relevance or significance of the factors for assessing an outcome may vary depending on the alternatives with which it is compared, and hence where there is no common linear scale which can be employed to accurately compare each set of alternatives, then "all-things-considered better than" (in my wide reason-implying sense) is likely to be a nontransitive relation. As we will see later, both of the competing views about how to think about the comparative value of outcomes have great plausibility and significant advantages, but both have significant disadvantages, as well.

Some people may believe that there is a compelling reason to reject the Essentially Comparative View and the possibility that "all-things-considered better than" might not be a transitive relation that I have not yet considered, namely, that those positions are incompatible with Expected Utility Theory. I address this view, and raise some worries about an important variation of Expected Utility Theory, in the following chapter.

8

Expected Utility Theory/Expected Value Theory

In previous chapters, I have offered a number of "impossibility" results. I have argued that certain deeply held views are incompatible, so that, seemingly, at least one of the views in question must be rejected. I have noted that among the views that might be rejected is the view that "all-things-considered better than" (in my wide reason-implying sense) is a transitive relation. Among those who accept my impossibility results, some are convinced that the transitivity of "better than" *cannot* be the position we should reject, because of the role that it plays in Expected Utility Theory as such a theory might be applied to the domain of value, a position that we might call *Expected Value Theory*. In this chapter, I want to cast doubt on whether we can confidently insist that "all-things-considered better than" must be a transitive relation, because of the role that such a position plays in Expected Value Theory.

8.1 Clarifying My Target

The view I want to challenge can be stated briefly as follows. Expected Utility Theory is an enormously attractive theory that underlies game theory, decision theory, and much of modern economics. Although Expected Utility Theory has been the subject of much scrutiny and criticism, the power and successes of the theories relying on it give us good reason to believe that Expected Utility Theory is *essentially* correct, even if it requires some "tinkering with" to handle certain problems to which it gives rise. A fortiori, there is compelling reason to accept the *premises* that underlie Expected Utility Theory; since forsaking those premises would undermine the theory, leaving us unable to account for the power and successes of the theories it underlies. But *one* of the premises of Expected Utility Theory is an Axiom of Transitivity, which holds that if one prefers A to

B, and B to C, then one is rationally *required* to prefer A to C (or change one of one's other preferences).

Now, strictly speaking, Expected Utility Theory and its Axiom of Transitivity apply to *preferences* about *utilities*, not to *values*, and so it tells us nothing, directly, about the "all-things-considered better than" relation (in my wide reason-implying sense). But if one believes, as many do, that Expected Utility Theory can be plausibly *extended* to apply to claims about *values*, producing a variation of Expected Utility Theory which might be called Expected Value Theory, then one of the premises of the theory in question will be the familiar axiom of transitivity for "better than"; namely, that if, all things considered, A is better than B, and all things considered B is better than C, then, all things considered, A is better than C. Hence, the centrality of the role that Expected Utility Theory plays in other theories, the power and success of those other theories, and the ease and appropriateness of extending Expected Utility Theory to the realm of values, should make us confident that "all-things-considered better than" is, indeed, a transitive relation. In sum, in the face of my various impossibility results we must choose one of my arguments' *other* premises to reject, as the transitivity of the "all-things-considered better than" relation is unassailable, given the role that it plays in Expected Value Theory, and that its close cousin plays in Expected Utility Theory.

I have some sympathy with the argument just offered.[1] But ultimately, I can't attach the same weight to it as its advocates would. To see why, I want to look more closely at the premises and implications of Expected Utility Theory as it might be extended beyond the realm of preferences to the realm of value.

8.2 A Brief Characterization of Expected Utility Theory and Expected Value Theory

John Broome characterizes Expected Utility Theory roughly as follows.[2] There are *alternatives* or *prospects* that individuals might face or choose, and ways the world might be or *states of nature*.[3] Corresponding to each prospect and state of nature is an *occurrence* or *outcome*. "Each alternative is a vector $(x_1, x_2, \ldots x_s)$ of occurrences, one for each state."[4] For example, one might face two prospects,

---

[1] John Broome has put such an argument to me in conversation, and over the years I have found that a number of people are attracted to a view of this sort.

[2] The characterization I provide is taken from sections 2.1, 4.2, and 5.1 of *Weighing Goods* (Oxford: Basil Blackwell, 1991); see, especially, pp. 22, 65, and 90–91. Broome refers to this version as *axiomatic* Expected Utility Theory, to distinguish it from other versions of Expected Utility Theory. In this work, whenever I refer to Expected Utility Theory, it is the version presented here that I have in mind. For simplicity, I have omitted the qualifier "axiomatic" that Broome scrupulously adds.

[3] For Broome, "states of nature are *locations* of good" (*Weighing Goods*, 23).

[4] *Weighing Goods*, 90.

visiting London or sailboarding. For each prospect there may be two states of nature, say, fine weather or bad weather, and an outcome corresponding to each state of nature. For example, if one chooses to visit London, one might have an enjoyable trip regardless of the weather, while if one chooses sailboarding, one might have thrills and achievement if the weather is fine, but boredom if the weather is bad. Expected Utility Theory tells one which prospect it would be rational to choose, depending on one's *preferences* over the different outcomes and on the *probability* of each state of nature.

Expected Utility Theory is a theory about rational preferences. As Broome puts it:

> What expected utility theory says about rational preferences is no more nor less than this: that they can be represented by a utility function U having the form
>
> $$U(x_1, x_2, \ldots x_s) = p_1 u(x_1) + p_2 u(x_2) + \ldots + p_s u(x_s), \quad (5.1.1)$$
>
> where p_1, p_2, and so on are non-negative numbers that sum to one.... U is such that one prospect is preferred or indifferent to another if and only if it has as least as great a value of U. Let us call the function u a "subutility function," and its values "subutilities" or, loosely, "utilities." Let us call the numbers p_1, p_2 and so on "probabilities." Then the right hand side of (5.1.1) is the expectation of utility, or expected utility. Equation (5.1.1) says, in brief, that one alternative is preferred or indifferent to another if and only if it has as least as great an expected utility. To put it another way, expected utility theory says that rational preferences maximize expected utility.[5]

Now, Expected Utility Theory was originally developed as a view connecting *utilities* and *rational preferences*. In particular, on Expected Utility Theory, the utility function, U, assigns a real number to each alternative in such a way that $U(A)$ (the expected *utility* of A) is greater or equal to $U(B)$ if and only if A is rationally preferred or indifferent to B.[6] But, as implied previously, Expected Utility Theory can easily be extended or interpreted as a theory connecting *value* or *goodness* and rational preferences, by reinterpreting (replacing) the utility function U as (with) a *value* function V, and reinterpreting (replacing) the subutility function u as (with) a *subvalue* function v, so that instead of (5.1.1) one has:

$$V(x_1, x_2, \ldots x_s) = p_1 v(x_1) + p_2 v(x_2) + \ldots + p_s v(x_s). \quad (5.1.1^*)$$

Here, the subvalue function, v, assigns a real number to each possible outcome, x, representing the value or goodness of outcome x, and the value function V

---

[5] *Weighing Goods*, 91.
[6] *Weighing Goods*, 65.

assigns a real number to each prospect, A, representing the expected value of prospect A (recall that prospect A is a vector of possible outcomes $(x_1, x_2, \ldots x_s)$) in such a way that the value function V represents the *betterness relation*. That is, $V(A)$ is greater than or equal to $V(B)$ if and only if prospect A is *at least as good as* prospect B.[7] So interpreted, Expected Utility Theory, which might now be called Expected Value Theory, says that rational preferences maximize expected value.

Since this book is largely concerned with the related notions of value, goodness, better than, and the like, my discussion will focus on Expected Utility Theory as it applies to such notions. Thus, henceforth, I shall be focusing on Expected Value Theory. But the key point to note is that Expected Value Theory will have the very same premises and implications as Expected Utility Theory, except that everything will be put in terms of value rather than utility.

To illustrate, consider a simple case involving two possible prospects, A and B. Suppose that if one chooses prospect A, either outcome w_1 will occur with probability .8 or outcome w_2 will occur with probability .2, whereas if one chooses prospect B, either outcome x_1 will occur with probability .6 or outcome x_2 will occur with probability .4. Suppose that the values of w_1, w_2, x_1, and x_2, are 100, 300, 150, and 200, respectively. Then, according to Expected Value Theory, $V(A) = V(w_1, w_2) = .8(100) + .2(300) = 80 + 60 = 140$, and $V(B) = V(x_1, x_2) = .6(150) + .4(200) = 90 + 80 = 170$. So, Expected Value Theory tells us that the expected value of prospect A is 140, and the expected value of prospect B is 170; hence, prospect B is better than prospect A, and it would be rational to prefer B to A, as choosing B rather than A maximizes expected value.

Expected Value Theory embodies numerous axioms or assumptions. Among these are various *Axioms of Transitivity*, of which I shall distinguish three. First, "all-things-considered better than" (henceforth, represented as >) is a transitive relation, so, if A is all-things-considered better than B ($A > B$), and B is all-things-considered better than C ($B > C$), then A is all-things-considered better than C ($A > C$). Second, "equal to" or "equally as good as" (henceforth, represented as =) is a transitive relation, so, if A is equally as good as B ($A = B$), and B is equally as good as C ($B = C$), then A is equally as good as C ($A = C$). (Here, and later, I often drop the qualifier "all things considered"; all value judgments are assumed to be all-things-considered value judgments unless indicated otherwise.) Third, "at least as good as" (henceforth, represented as ≥) is a transitive relation, so, if A is at least as good as B ($A \geq B$), and B is at least as good as C ($B \geq C$), then A is at least as good as C ($A \geq C$).[8]

---

[7] See Broome, *Weighing Goods*, 65.

[8] Expected Utility Theory is usually characterized in terms of the transitivity of the "at least as good as" relation. However, the different relations are obviously related. Indeed, they can be defined in terms of each other given the assumption of Completeness (defined later) and the logical connectives of "and," "or," and "not." So, given Completeness, $A = B$ if and only if $A \geq B$ and it is not the case that

Another assumption that will come under scrutiny later in this chapter is the *Principle of Continuity*. On this assumption, for any three outcomes A, B, and C, such that A is better than B and B is better than C, there must be some probability, p, between 0 and 1, such that one should be rationally indifferent between having B occur for sure and having A occur with probability p or C occur with probability $(1 - p)$.[9] Here is a way to represent that. Suppose that if one chooses prospect X, outcome B will occur for sure. Then $V(X) = V(B) = 1v(B)$. In this case, the value of choosing X is just equal to the value of choosing B, which is simply determined by the subvalue function, v, which assigns a real number to B representing its value. Suppose that if one chooses prospect Y, then either A will occur with some probability p, between 0 and 1, or C will occur with some probability $(1 - p)$. Then $V(Y) = V(A,C) = pv(A) + (1 - p)v(C)$. Here, the subvalue function v assigns a real number to A representing its value and a real number to C representing its value, and the value of choosing prospect Y is just equal to the sum of A's value weighted by the probability, p, of its occurring if Y is chosen and C's value weighted by the probability, $(1 - p)$, of its occurring if Y is chosen. Then what the Principle of Continuity says is that for all outcomes A, B, and C, if $v(A) > v(B) > v(C)$, then there must be some probability p, such that $V(X) = V(Y)$, so that we should be rationally indifferent between the prospect of X and the prospect of Y. And since $V(X) = V(B) = 1v(B)$ and $V(Y) = V(A,C) = pv(A) + (1 - p)v(C)$, we can represent this as saying that for all outcomes A, B, and C, if $v(A) > v(B) > v(C)$, then there must be some probability p, such that $v(B) = pv(A) + (1 - p)v(C)$.

Another assumption of Expected Value Theory involves *Completeness*. Specifically, it is assumed that, for every outcome, x_i, the subvalue function v assigns a real number representing the value or goodness of x_i, and for every prospect A_i, the value function V assigns a real number representing the expected value of that prospect. Accordingly, for any two outcomes, x_i and x_j, one and only one of the following is true, $v(x_i) > v(x_j)$, $v(x_i) = v(x_j)$, or $v(x_j) > v(x_i)$. This means that the value of x_i is one and only one of the following: greater than, equal to, or less than the value of x_j. From this it follows, on Expected Value Theory, that outcome x_i must be one and only one of the

---

$A > B$. Similarly, $A \geq B$ if and only if $A = B$ or $A > B$. And $A > B$ if and only if $A \geq B$ and it is not the case that $A = B$. While much of this book's discussion has focused on the transitivity of the "better than" relation, since, by definition, if A is better than B, then A is at least as good as B, if the "better than" relation is not transitive, neither is the "at least as good as" relation. Similarly, since, by definition, if A is as good as B, then A is at least as good as B, if the "as good as" relation is not transitive, neither is the "at least as good as" relation.

[9] I am grateful to Preston Green for pointing out that in my original presentation of the Principle of Continuity I had inadvertently neglected to state that the probability, p, must be between 0 and 1. This qualification is important, because otherwise some of my later claims where I state the Principle of Continuity in terms of the "better than" or "at least as good as" relations become trivially true.

following: better than, equal to, or worse than outcome x_j. Likewise, for any two prospects A and B, one and only one of the following is true, $V(A) > V(B)$, $V(A) = V(B)$, or $V(B) > V(A)$, which means that the expected value of prospect A is one and only one of the following: greater than, equal to, or less than the value of prospect B. Again, on Expected Value Theory this in turn means that prospect A must be one and only one of the following: better than, equal to, or worse than prospect B.

There are other important assumptions of Expected Value Theory, the most important of which is the assumption of *strong separability*. These further assumptions will be characterized, as needed, later.

Finally, I note that Expected Value Theory is assumed to be compatible with the basic principles of logic and arithmetic. So, any formulas whose constants or variables represent real numbers, as the formulas representing the values of different prospects are assumed to do, can be manipulated in accordance with the rules of math or logic without change in the truth values of those formulas. One such rule I shall invoke later may be called the *Principle of Substitution of Equivalents* (PSE). Roughly, this principle requires that for any x and y, where x and y are numbers or mathematical formulas, if $x = y$, then x and y are interchangeable in any formulas where they occur. It is worth emphasizing that PSE holds for *any* x and y, whether simple or complex. A principle similar to, and perhaps implied by, PSE in the context of Expected Value Theory might be called the *Principle of Like Comparability for Equivalents* (PLCE). According to this principle, if two outcomes or prospects are equivalent (meaning equally good) in some respect, then however the first of those outcomes or prospects compares to a third outcome or prospect in that respect, that is how the second of those outcomes or prospects compares to the third outcome or prospect in that respect. So, for example, if A and B are equally good regarding equality, then if A is better than C regarding equality, B is better than C regarding equality, and to the same extent; similarly, if A and B are equally good all things considered, then if A is better than C all things considered, B is better than C all things considered, and to the same extent.

8.3 On the Relation between Rough Comparability and Expected Value Theory

In chapter 6, I introduced and explored the notion of rough comparability, according to which one outcome or prospect may be roughly comparable to another, where this is a *distinct* relation from the "better than," "worse than," or "equal to" relations. A fortiori, anyone who accepts the view that two outcomes or alternatives could be roughly comparable (that is, not worse than or on a par with each other) is *committed* to rejecting the Completeness assumption of Expected Value Theory. This is a familiar point that has long been recognized. Moreover, many people accept the idea that Completeness is a questionable assumption of Expected Value Theory that will ultimately have to be jettisoned. But I suspect that most who hold such a view have assumed that Expected Value Theory could be easily revised to handle the possibility of *Incompleteness*, or that in any event the problems that arise from Incompleteness are not too damaging.[10] Let us explore if this sanguine attitude is appropriate.

Here is one Principle of Equivalence that holds for Expected Value Theory given Completeness:

> *First Principle of Equivalence*: For any two prospects A and B, if for every possible outcome, w_i, that might arise with a given probability, p_i, if A is chosen, the same outcome, w_i, might arise with the same probability, p_i, if B is chosen, and vice versa, then prospects A and B are equally good (that is, $V(A) = V(B)$).

The First Principle of Equivalence has great plausibility. I believe it is a principle one should accept even if one rejects Completeness. That is, even if one allows for rough comparability, it seems one will want one's theory of rational preferences to reflect the First Principle of Equivalence.

Here is another Principle of Equivalence that holds for Expected Value Theory given Completeness:

> *Second Principle of Equivalence*: For any two prospects A and B, if for every possible state of nature, s_i, the very same outcome, w_i, will occur if A is chosen or if B is chosen,[11] then prospects A and B are equally good ($V(A) = V(B)$).

The Second Principle of Equivalence is implied by the First. But the reverse is not true, and I believe the Second Principle of Equivalence has independent

---

[10] John Broome writes the following:

> Completeness is dubious.... It seems plausible that the reasons in favour of one alternative may sometimes be *incommensurable* with the reasons in favour of another. It may be that neither side dominates the other but that they do not exactly balance either.... If this is so, it seems it would be rational to prefer neither of the alternatives to the other, and not to be indifferent either. So it seems that rational preferences need not be complete.
>
> This is a problem for expected utility theory, but I am sorry to say that I am going to ignore it.... Incommensurability is a well-recognized problem, and this book is about other problems. Simply for the sake of moving on, I shall assume that rational preferences are indeed complete. (*Weighing Goods*, 92–93)

Broome's attitude is understandable. Not everyone needs to address every problem, especially problems that have been "well-recognized." Still, to a large extent Broome's work depends on and defends Expected Utility Theory. (This is so not only in *Weighing Goods*, but in his more recent book *Weighing Lives* [Oxford: Oxford University Press, 2004]). Given this, simply ignoring the issue of Incompleteness would be rather curious and cavalier, perhaps even indefensible, if one really thought that Incompleteness was *seriously* damaging to Expected Utility Theory.

[11] Note, a state of nature's probability fixes the probability of the outcome that obtains if that state of nature occurs.

plausibility. Moreover, I believe that the Second Principle of Equivalence can be seen as a particular application of a more generalized principle:

> *The State-by-State Comparison Principle*: For any two prospects A and B, if the value of A's outcome stands in a particular comparative relation, R, to the value of B's outcome for *each* possible state of nature, then prospect A stands in relation R to B. More specifically, for any two prospects A and B, if the value of A's outcome is, respectively, greater than (>), equal to (=), at least as good as (≥), or roughly comparable to (~) the value of B's outcome for *each* possible state of nature, then prospect A will be, respectively, better than, as good as, at least as good as, or roughly comparable to prospect B. That is, if there are n states of nature, s_1 through s_n, and A's outcomes in s_1 through s_n are w_1 through w_n, respectively, while B's outcomes in s_1 through s_n are x_1 through x_n, respectively, then if, for each state of nature s_j, $v(w_j) > v(x_j)$, $v(w_j) = v(x_j)$, $v(w_j) \geq v(x_j)$, or $v(w_j) \sim v(x_j)$, respectively, then $V(A) > V(B)$, $V(A) = V(B)$, $V(A) \geq V(B)$, or $V(A) \sim V(B)$, respectively.

Expected Value Theory entails the State-by-State Comparison Principle for the relations of "better than," "equal to," and "at least as good as" given its Completeness assumptions. But I think the principle is plausible for the relation of "roughly comparable to" as well, so that if one wanted to revise Expected Value Theory to accommodate Incompleteness, one would want to revise it in such a way as to reflect the State-by-State Comparison Principle. There are several reasons for this. Let me indicate two.

John Broome has argued that at the heart of Expected Value Theory is a condition variously known as strong separability, strong independence, or the *Sure-Thing Principle*.[12] The technical definition of strong separability is a bit complex, but roughly it holds that the value of a prospect depends in an additive way on the values of the prospect's outcomes in each possible state of nature, where, crucially, the value of a prospect's outcome in a state of nature is wholly independent of the prospect's outcomes in any other state of nature.

Paul Samuelson once considered a simple case of a prospect involving two states of nature, "heads" or "tails" depending on the result of a fair coin flip. In advocating the strong separability of Expected Value Theory, Samuelson remarked, "Either heads *or* tails must come up: if one comes up the other cannot."[13] Broome explicates this remark as follows:

---

[12] The argument extends throughout much of *Weighing Goods*, but see, especially, chapters 4 and 5.

[13] I have taken this quotation from *Weighing Goods*, 96. Broome cites Samuelson's "Probability, Utility, and the Independence Axiom," *Econometrica* 20 (1952): 670–78, as his source. Broome adds (in note 11 of *Weighing Goods*, 118) that "von Neumann and Morgenstern make the same point in *The Theory of Games and Economic Behavior*, p. 18" (2nd ed., Princeton, NJ: Princeton University Press, 1944). (Samuelson won the Nobel Prize in Economics in 1970, while John van Neumann and Oskar Morgenstern are widely regarded as the fathers of modern game theory.)

The value you assign to what happens in one state of nature should depend on what it will be like if that state occurs. But if that state occurs, no other does. So what would have happened in other states should make no difference to the value. For a rational person there should be no complementarity... [between] states of nature... because two states never exist together."[14]

But if the value of prospect A's outcome, w_i, in state of nature, s_i, can't depend in any way on the value of prospect A's outcome, w_j, in any *other* state of nature, s_j, since if s_i obtains s_j does not, then surely the value of prospect A's outcome, w_i, in state of nature, s_i, can't depend in any way on the value of some other prospect B's outcome, x_j, in any *other* state of nature, s_j; and similarly for the values of prospect B's outcomes. Such reasoning entails that how two prospects, A and B, compare for any state of nature will depend *solely* on the values of the prospects' consequences in that state of nature. And this *suggests* (though does not strictly entail) that in comparing any two prospects, it is reasonable to focus on how those prospects compare at *each* state of nature, knowing that *whichever* state of nature ultimately obtains, *no other will*. Accordingly, if I *know* that *whatever* happens (i.e., *whichever* state of nature, s_j, obtains) the value of the outcome ($v(w_j)$) that will result if I choose prospect A will be greater than, equal to, at least as good as, or roughly comparable to, respectively, the value of the outcome ($v(x_j)$) that will result if I choose prospect B, then I have good reason to judge the value of prospect A, $V(A)$, as greater than, equal to, at least as good as, or roughly comparable to, respectively, the value of prospect B, $V(B)$; hence, it would be rational for me to regard A as better than, as good as, at least as good as, or roughly comparable to, respectively, B for purposes of practical reasoning. In sum, it appears that the reasoning that makes the strong separability of Expected Value Theory plausible also makes the State-by-State Comparison Principle plausible. So, if one wants to revise Expected Value Theory to allow for rough comparability, there is reason to do so in such a way as to capture the State-by-State Comparison Principle.

Here is a second reason for wanting one's theory to capture the State-by-State Comparison Principle. Consider:

A Reflection Principle: If, on reflection, I know that at some point in the future I'll have more knowledge than I currently have, and I now know that given that future *knowledge* it will be reasonable to assess two prospects in a certain way, then it is *now* reasonable for me to assess the two prospects in that way.

---

[14] *Weighing Goods*, 96.

This Reflection Principle has great plausibility, and many would accept it as a condition of rationality. Clearly, however, it entails the State-by-State Comparison Principle. After all, in conditions of uncertainty I don't now know which state of nature, s_j, will occur. But I do know that *whatever* state of nature obtains, *no other will*, and I also know that at some point I will know which state of nature obtains. If, by hypothesis, I *already* know that *whatever* state of nature occurs, prospect A will be better than, equal to, at least as good as, or roughly comparable to, respectively, B, then I *already* know that in the future, when I have the further knowledge of knowing what state of nature obtains, it will be reasonable for me to assess A as better than, equal to, at least as good as, or roughly comparable to, respectively, B. But then, according to the Reflection Principle, it is *now* reasonable for me to assess them in that way. But that is precisely what the State-by-State Comparison Principle holds.

We are now in a position, *finally*, to raise an important issue. I have suggested that once we agree to reject Completeness, to make room in our understanding of the good for the notion of rough comparability, we will want to capture *both* the First Principle of Equivalence and the State-by-State Comparison Principle. But it is easy to see that, as stated, these two principles are incompatible.

Suppose I am facing two prospects, A and B. Suppose that if I pick A, a fair coin will be flipped, and if it comes up heads I will have a particular career as a lawyer, L_2, while if it comes up tails I will have a particular career as an academic, A_1, where these correspond to the careers represented in diagram 6.3.A and discussed in sections 6.3 through 6.5. In particular, by hypothesis, L_2 and A_1 are neither better nor worse than each other, nor are they exactly equal; rather, they are roughly comparable. Suppose, on the other hand, that if I pick B, the same coin will be tossed, but in this case, if heads comes up I will have career A_1, while if tails comes up I will have career L_2.

In accordance with the First Principle of Equivalence, prospects A and B will be equally good, since prospects A and B involve the very same possible outcomes with the very same probabilities. However, in accordance with the State-by-State Comparison Principle, prospects A and B will be roughly comparable. After all, there are only two states of nature, "heads" and "tails," only one of which will occur. Either A's outcome will be L_2 and B's outcome will be A_1, if heads occurs, or A's outcome will be A_1 and B's outcome will be L_2, if tails occurs. Either way, A's outcome will be roughly comparable to B's, since, by hypothesis, A_1 is roughly comparable to L_2. Thus, as noted, prospect A is roughly comparable to prospect B, according to the State-by-State Comparison Principle. But, of course, it cannot be the case both that A is *equal* to B and that A is *roughly comparable* to B; hence, as stated, the First Principle of Equivalence and the State-by-State Comparison Principle are incompatible.

There are powerful reasons to accept the First Principle of Equivalence. But, as we saw, there are also powerful reasons to accept the State-by-State

Comparison Principle. So what should we do when they conflict? Ultimately, we may decide that the two principles are *fundamentally* incompatible, and that we shall have to reject at least one of them. But rather than simply *rejecting* one of the two principles, one *might* try to amend one or both of them. One plausible suggestion would be to accept *both* principles, provisionally, and then to give priority to one over the other in cases of conflict.

When I think about the particular example in question, I incline toward the view that we should regard the alternative prospects as *equally* good, in accordance with the First Principle of Equivalence, and reject the implication of the State-by-State Comparison Principle that such prospects might be only roughly comparable. So, for *such* cases, at least, I'm prepared to accept the judgment of the First Principle of Equivalence. But, this doesn't lead me to reject the State-by-State Comparison Principle entirely. There are countless cases where the reasoning underlying the State-by-State Comparison Principle seems compelling, and where I would want to accept its judgments. So, I'm inclined to say that we should amend the State-by-State Comparison Principle just enough so as to accommodate the First Principle of Equivalence, at least in cases like the one discussed. Perhaps the most natural way to do that would be to limit the scope of the State-by-State Comparison Principle to all and only those cases where it would not directly conflict with the First Principle of Equivalence. I leave open, for now, whether there is a plausible non–ad hoc method of *justifying* the precise restriction in question.

Suppose, then, we accept both the First Principle of Equivalence and the amended version of the State-by-State Comparison Principle. A new problem arises. Expected Value Theory entails, and most people accept:

> *The Pareto Principle*: For any two prospects A and B, if the value of A's outcome is at least as good as the value of B's outcome for *each* possible state of nature, and, in addition, there is at least one state of nature where the value of A's outcome is greater than the value of B's outcome, then prospect A is better than prospect B. That is, if there are n states of nature, s_1 through s_n, and A's outcomes in s_1 through s_n are w_1 through w_n, respectively, while B's outcomes in s_1 through s_n are x_1 through x_n, respectively, then if, for each state of nature s_j, $v(w_j) \geq v(x_j)$, and, in addition, there is at least one state of nature s_k such that $v(w_k) > v(x_k)$, then $V(A) > V(B)$.

But, then, consider next a third prospect, C, along with the two prospects, A and B, considered earlier. Like A and B, C involves two states of nature, "heads" and "tails," determined by a fair coin flip. If I pick C, and the coin comes up heads, I will have career L_2; but if the coin comes up tails, I will have career A_1 *plus* $2,000. We are retaining the assumptions from sections 6.3 to 6.5 that A_1 plus $2,000 is *roughly comparable* to L_2; though A_1 plus $2,000 is *better* than A_1 alone. Comparing prospects A and C, we know that if heads comes up, I would get *exactly* the same outcome with prospect A or C, namely, career L_2, while if tails comes up I'll get a *better* outcome with C than A, since the academic life, A_1, *plus* $2,000, is a *better* outcome than the *very same* academic life, A_1, alone. It follows from the Pareto Principle that C is a *better* prospect than A.

So, we've seen that C is a *better* prospect than A, and we've accepted that A and B are *equally good* prospects. It follows from the Principle of Like Comparability for Equivalents that C is a *better* prospect than B; likewise, it follows from the transitivity of "at least as good as" that C is at least as good as B.[15] But, it follows from the amended State-by-State Comparison Principle that C is *not* a better prospect than B, nor is C at least as good as B. Rather, C and B are *roughly comparable*. After all, by hypothesis, there are only two states of nature relevant to C and B. If *heads* comes up, s_1, C's outcome will be L_2, B's outcome will be A_1, and, by hypothesis, L_2 and A_1 are roughly comparable. By the same token, if *tails* comes up, s_2, C's outcome will be A_1 plus $2,000, and B's outcome will be L_2, and once again, by hypothesis, C and B will be roughly comparable. Thus, *whatever* state of nature obtains, C's and B's outcomes will be roughly comparable; hence, C and B are roughly comparable.

So, it appears both that C is greater than or equal to B (in fact greater than B) and that C is roughly comparable to B. But, by definition, if C is roughly comparable to B, then it is *not* greater than or equal to B. So we have a contradiction.

The preceding suggests that accepting the notion of rough comparability requires *more* than simply acknowledging that Expected Value Theory has to be revised to recognize Incompleteness. For adequately *dealing* with the problem of Incompleteness will involve coming to terms with an inconsistency between a number of plausible positions. Among the positions in play are the initial assumption that some prospects or outcomes are roughly comparable, the First Principle of Equivalence, the original or amended State-by-State Comparison Principle, the Principle of Like Comparability for Equivalents, the Pareto Principle, and the transitivity of "at least as good as."

There are numerous moves available to advocates of Expected Value Theory. One option would be to dig in one's heals and insist that there *must* be Completeness in the value functions for outcomes and prospects—and hence to dismiss the notion of rough comparability as intuitively attractive but illusory and ultimately incoherent. Another option would be to claim that the value function, v, is not well-defined for outcomes that are roughly comparable,

---

[15] By definition, "at least as good as" means "equal to or better than." So, if C is better than A, then C is at least as good as A, and if A is equal to B, then A is at least as good as B. Thus, $C > A$ and $A = B$ entails that $C \geq A$ and $A \geq B$, respectively, from which it follows by the transitivity of "at least as good as" that $C \geq B$.

and, correspondingly, that the value function V is not well-defined for any prospects, A and B, where there is at least one state of nature, s_i, such that A's outcome at s_j is roughly comparable with B's outcome at s_j. On this view, it might be an open question whether and what the rationally appropriate attitude should be between prospects whose values are not well-defined. A third option would be to argue that once one recognizes the need to amend the State-by-State Comparison Principle when it conflicts with the First Principle of Equivalence, one should further amend it, or reject it entirely, so as to accommodate the view that C really *is* better than B in the outcome given earlier. Plausible and important arguments can be given in support of the latter position, but, as I have indicated, they come at the cost of denying the Reflection Principle and calling into question the significance of Samuelson's claim that "either heads *or* tails must come up: if one comes up the other cannot." Ultimately, then, the same arguments that might be invoked against the original or amended State-by-State Comparison Principle may support a holistic evaluation of prospects that is anathema to the strong separability of Expected Value Theory. I raise these options, but shall not pursue them. Suffice it to say, I think much more work remains to be done to fully understand the implications of the view that some outcomes or prospects are roughly comparable.[16]

Completeness is not the only dubious assumption of Expected Value Theory that may be harder to come to terms with than many people realize.

---

[16] I am grateful to many people for their influence and feedback on this section, including Fiona Macpherson, Nick Beckstead, Tim Campbell, Jake Ross, and Evan Williams. My biggest debt is to Fiona, who spent two days discussing these issues with me when our time overlapped at the Australian National University in the spring of 2008. In response to an earlier version of sections 6.3 and 6.4, Fiona argued that it was not merely rationally *permissible* to take $2,000 and allow someone else to choose for me whether I would have L_2 or A_1 as a career, but that it would be rationally *required* for me to take the money. Thus, Fiona argued that in fact I am liable to a *strong* money pump argument if I accept sections 6.3 and 6.4's claims about rough comparability. Although Fiona offered her argument as a friendly amendment in support of my claims, I wasn't sure that advocates of rough comparability were committed to the view in question, because Fiona's argument employed premises of Expected Utility Theory that advocates of rough comparability might ultimately deny. I developed this section's key claims in response to Fiona's argument. So, I am grateful to Fiona for both sparking, and helping me to develop, my thoughts on this topic.

I should note that the argument Fiona suggested to me was almost identical in substance to the main argument subsequently published by Caspar Hare in his article "Take the Sugar," *Analysis* 70 (2010): 237–47. I didn't see Hare's article until several years after Fiona and I discussed the issues in question, and I presume that Hare and Macpherson developed their arguments independently. It is also worth noting that Nick Beckstead, who had read both drafts of my early version of sections 6.3 and 6.4 and Hare's article, but had not learned of my response to Fiona, wrote a short paper of his own in which he made many of the same claims and arguments that I make in this section. Nick's treatment of the topic is more technical than my own, and in some ways more elegant, and I have benefited from reading his paper and discussing the issues with him.

Finally, I'd like to thank Evan Williams, who sharpened my thinking about this topic, and who helped me to see that some of my arguments regarding the plausibility of the State-by-State Comparison Principle could be best put in terms of its connection to the Reflection Principle.

The same is true of the Principle of Continuity. Let me turn to a discussion of that principle, next.

8.4 The Principle of Continuity

In section 8.3, we saw that one of the fundamental axioms of Expected Utility Theory is the Principle of Continuity, which holds that for any three outcomes A, B, and C, such that A is better than B and B is better than C, there must be some probability, p, between 0 and 1, such that one should be rationally indifferent between having B occur for sure and having A occur with probability p or C occur with probability $(1 - p)$. We saw that this could be represented as saying that for all A, B, and C, if $v(A) > v(B) > v(C)$, then there must be some probability p, between 0 and 1, such that $v(B) = pv(A) + (1 - p)v(C)$, where v is a subvalue function that assigns a real number to each possible outcome representing its value (or, we might add, its degree of goodness). For simplicity, in the ensuing discussion, let us say that for each possible outcome X, $v(X) = x$; here, x is a constant representing the real number that is assigned by the value function, v, to the outcome X, representing X's value or degree of goodness. Then, the Principle of Continuity holds that for all outcomes A, B, and C, if $a > b > c$, then there must be some probability p, between 0 and 1, such that $b = pa + (1 - p)c$.

Note, the Principle of Continuity could also be formulated in terms of the ">" or "≥" relations. That is, we might have said that for all outcomes A, B, and C, if $a > b > c$, then there must be some probability p, between 0 and 1, such that $pa + (1 - p)c > b$, or that for all outcomes A, B, and C, if $a > b > c$, then there must be some probability p, between 0 and 1, such that $pa + (1 - p)c \geq b$. In other words, the Principle of Continuity can be formulated in terms of the "greater than" or "at least as good as" relations, as well as the "equal to" relation. Formulated in terms of "greater than," the Principle of Continuity holds that for any three outcomes A, B, and C, such that A is better than B and B is better than C, there must be some probability, p, between 0 and 1, such that one should rationally prefer the prospect where A occurs with probability p or C occurs with probability $(1 - p)$ to the prospect where B occurs for sure; while formulated in terms of "at least as good as," the Principle of Continuity holds that for any three outcomes A, B, and C, such that A is better than B and B is better than C, there must be some probability, p, between 0 and 1, such that one should rationally regard the prospect where A occurs with probability p or C occurs with probability $(1 - p)$ as at least as good as the prospect where B occurs for sure. In the following discussion I shall sometimes employ one characterization of the Principle of Continuity and sometimes another, as suits my purposes at the time.

8.4.1 EXAMINING CONTINUITY: "EASY" CASES VERSUS "EXTREME" CASES

The Principle of Continuity has many supporters.[17] But it has detractors as well, and lacks the transparency and intuitive plausibility of some of Expected Value Theory's other axioms, such as its various Axioms of Transitivity. Moreover, unlike the Principle of Substitution of Equivalents, to which advocates of Expected Value Theory are also committed, the Principle of Continuity's appeal rests not on mathematics or logic, but on a particular normative conception of rationality. It is thus open to challenge, and, as we shall see in a moment, many reject it. Still, there are cases and there are cases, and it is useful to distinguish between cases where the Principle of Continuity is questionable and cases where it is difficult to deny. For the purposes of argument, I shall distinguish between four kinds of case:

> *Case I*: Outcomes A, B, and C differ little in value. So, what we stand to gain if we get A, rather than B, is relatively insignificant, though so, too, is what we stand to lose if we get C, rather than B.
>
> *Case II*: Outcomes B and C differ little in value, but outcomes A and B differ greatly. So, what we stand to gain if we get A, rather than B, is very significant, while what we stand to lose if we get C, rather than B, is relatively insignificant.
>
> *Case III*: Outcomes A, B, and C differ greatly in value. So, what we stand to gain if we get A, rather than B, is very significant, but so, too, is what we stand to lose if we get C, rather than B.
>
> *Case IV*: Outcomes B and C differ greatly in value, but outcomes A and B differ little. So, what we stand to gain if we get A, rather than B, is insignificant, while what we stand to lose if we get C, rather than B, is very significant.

The Principle of Continuity is plausible for instances of case *I*. For example, let A = having $1,000,001 per year throughout a long life, B = having $1,000,000 per year throughout a long life, and C = having $999,999 per year throughout a long life. (Henceforth, I drop the tag "throughout a long life." Unless noted otherwise, each example discussed involves a long life *for which a once-and-for-all-time decision must be made*.)[18] Here, outcomes A, B, and C differ little in

---

[17] Much of the material in this subsection, as well as the following two (8.4.2 and 8.4.3), originally appeared in my "Worries about Continuity, Transitivity, Expected Utility Theory, and Practical Reasoning," in *Exploring Practical Philosophy*, ed. Dan Egonsson, Jonas Josefsson, Björn Petersson, and Toni Rønnow-Rasmussen (Burlington: Ashgate, 2001), 95–108. However, I am grateful to Shelly Kagan for pointing out various points in my original presentation that were sloppy, unclear, or misleading, and I have revised my presentation and discussion of this topic in light of Kagan's concerns.

[18] The importance of this emphasized clause will be discussed later.

value,[19] and it seems clear that there would be *some p*, between 0 and 1, such that one should rationally regard the prospect of getting A with probability p or C with probability $(1 - p)$ as at least as good as the prospect of getting B for sure. (In fact, in my own case, this would be so for any $p \geq .5$. Here, and later, I employ the version of the Principle of Continuity framed in terms of "at least as good as.")

The Principle of Continuity is even *more* plausible for instances of case *II*. For example, if A = having \$1,000,001 per year, B = having \$2 per year, and C = having \$1 per year, there is *surely* some p, between 0 and 1, where one should rationally regard the prospect of getting A with probability p or C with probability $(1 - p)$ as at least as good as the prospect of getting B for sure.[20] (In my own case, this would be so for almost any p! But for those attracted to a maximin strategy, consider your reaction to the different outcomes if $p = .5$, or perhaps .9.)

I shall call cases *I* and *II* the *easy* cases for the Principle of Continuity. There is widespread agreement that the Principle of Continuity holds as a requirement of rationality for the easy cases.

The Principle of Continuity is more dubious for instances of case *III*. For example, let A = having \$2,000,000 per year, B = having \$1,000,000 per year, and C = having \$0 per year. Many would accept the Principle of Continuity here, too, maintaining that surely there must be *some p*, between 0 and 1, such that I should rationally regard the prospect of getting A with probability p or C with probability $(1 - p)$ as at least as good as the prospect of getting B for

---

[19] Jim Griffin would argue that A, B, and C don't differ in value at all. More carefully, Griffin rejects what he calls the "totting up" model for evaluating individual lives, according to which the overall value of a life is a simple additive function of the positive and negative experiences that occur locally within that life. On Griffin's view, there would be *nothing* to choose between two lives that would otherwise be equal, except that one life has a few more positive "local" experiences than the other, say, a few tastier meals, a few more enjoyable trips to the theater, a few more ice cream cones or lollipop licks, and so on. See Griffin's *Well-Being: Its Meaning, Measurement, and Moral Importance* (Oxford: Clarendon Press, 1986).

Many people reject Griffin's position. They think that even the *tiniest* of extra positive experiences would be enough to improve the overall quality of a life, even if only by the *tiniest* of amounts. For the purposes of this discussion, I am assuming that even *one* extra dollar a year (presumably used to buy a small positive experience), or *one* extra lick of a lollipop, and so on, could be enough to make one life or outcome *ever-so-slightly* better than an otherwise identical life or outcome. Most advocates of Expected Utility Theory and Expected Value Theory would accept this, so this assumption is certainly not unfair to their position. But for those who share Griffin's view of the matter, one should adjust the details of my argument accordingly. The *key* point is simply that according to Expected Utility Theory and Expected Value Theory, the Principle of Continuity is supposed to hold no matter *how* small, or large, the differences between A, B, and C are supposed to be, as long as A is preferred to or better than B, and B is preferred to or better than C.

[20] This example assumes the value of \$2 is not significantly different from the value of \$1. If we imagine a scenario where the difference of \$1 meant the difference between life and death, then this wouldn't be an example of case *II*.

sure. And they would point out that if p is close enough to 1, the expected value of the former prospect might be nearly twice that of the latter.[21] Still, some people, most notably satisficers[22] or risk avoiders, would reject this view. They would argue that a bird in the hand—especially a fine bird—is not only worth two in the bush, it is worth two fine birds that are *almost* in hand. They might urge that a million dollars per year is "enough," and that rationality doesn't *require* that one maximize expected value. On their view, it is not worth taking even the *tiniest* chance of losing a *certain* $1,000,000 per year, even for the sake of a *substantial* gain that is almost—but not quite—certain to be realized.

For many, instances of case *III* are enough to raise doubts about the Principle of Continuity. But the strongest objection to the Principle of Continuity arises with instances of case *IV*. Peter Vallentyne offers an example of the following sort.[23] Consider three possible outcomes. In *B*, one has $1,000,000 per year and, indeed, a full, rich life. In *A*, one has $1,000,001 per year and an *ever-so-slightly* fuller, and richer, life. In *C*, one has a life of poverty, pain, and misery that ends with a torturous, lingering death. Vallentyne denies that there is *any* p between 0 and 1 such that rationality *requires* him to regard the prospect of receiving either outcome *A* with probability p or outcome *C* with probability $(1 - p)$, as at least as good as the prospect of having *B* with certainty. Put differently, Vallentyne denies that it would be *irrational* not to be indifferent between the two prospects or to be unwilling to trade the latter prospect for the former one, but this is what is implied by Expected Value Theory's Principle of Continuity.

Many share Vallentyne's intuition about such examples, and the common assumption is that the intuition trades on our attitudes toward risk versus certainty. But, clearly, the issue isn't merely one of certainty versus risk; rather, it is one of certainty of a great outcome versus risk of a much worse outcome, especially when there is little to be gained by taking the risk. That is, in general, people have no objection to risking a certain outcome in hopes of significant gain if the downside risk is relatively small (case *II*); what they balk at is risking a certain outcome for a *slightly* better one if the downside risk is *huge* (case *IV*). What seems crazy, in Vallentyne's example, is the idea that rationality should *require* a willingness to trade the *certainty* of a *full, rich life* for the prospect of

---

[21] For the sake of discussion, I assume, contrary to fact, that there is no significant diminishing marginal utility of income between $1,000,000 per year and $2,000,000 per year.

[22] Satisficers are people who believe there is a point where "enough is enough," after which they eschew a maximizing strategy in decision making. For an interesting discussion of the attractions of satisficing, see Michael Slote's *Beyond Optimizing: A Study of Rational Choice* (Cambridge, MA: Harvard University Press, 1989).

[23] Vallentyne's example is contained in his illuminating review of John Broome's *Weighing Goods*, "The Connection between Prudential and Moral Goodness," *Journal of Social Philosophy* 24 (1993): 105–28.

an *ever-so-slightly* better one, when doing so means taking some risk—no matter how small—that we would end up with an *entire life of pain and misery*.

Advocates of Expected Value Theory may regard Vallentyne's position as incoherent. But it isn't incoherent. Rather, it denies the central tenet of Expected Value Theory, that the *rationality* of choosing a prospect is always determined by the *expected value* of that prospect, *as defined by* Expected Value Theory. Put differently, Vallentyne drives a wedge between two notions that Expected Value Theorists see as equivalent, namely, the rational desirability of a prospect for an agent, and the *expected value* of that prospect. Suppose, in the earlier example, that if I choose prospect X, I get outcome B for sure, while if I choose prospect Y, I get outcome A with probability p or outcome C with probability $(1 - p)$. Vallentyne isn't denying the truth that, as Expected Value Theorists have defined the notion, there is some p, between 0 and 1, such that $pa + (1 - p)c \geq b$ so that $V(Y) \geq V(X)$. That truth is a simple, straightforward, mathematical fact. What he is denying is that rationality *requires* me to regard alternative Y as *at least as good as* alternative X. That is, Vallentyne accepts that for a given subject, S, the value, or rational desirability, of Y might *not* be at least as good as X, even though its *expected value*, as that notion is defined, is at least as great.

Vallentyne offers his example as an objection to the Principle of Continuity, and hence as a threat to Expected Value Theory. Yet many would deny that the example poses a *serious* threat to Expected Value Theory. They might readily accept that the Principle of Continuity fails in "extreme" cases of the sort Vallentyne imagines, yet they might insist that the Principle of Continuity holds for the vast majority of cases. Minimally, they might urge that the Principle of Continuity holds for the so-called easy cases—cases *I* and *II*—and hence that Expected Value Theory works fine for at least those cases. Moreover, they might urge, these are in fact the kinds of cases we are mainly worried about when invoking game theory, decision theory, or economics.

This reaction to Vallentyne's example is natural, and intuitively appealing. It grants that Expected Value Theory is problematic "at the edges," but insists that it works fine "at its core," and so can be safely relied on for the central, paradigmatic cases for which it is typically employed. But this response to Vallentyne's example is inadequate and must be rejected. As we will see next, examples like Vallentyne's pose a much greater challenge to Expected Value Theory than is normally recognized.

8.4.2 FROM SAFE BETS TO HIGH-STAKES BETS: THE CHALLENGE

The problem facing Expected Value Theory can be stated simply. *If* we agree, as many do, that the Principle of Continuity fails in "extreme" cases of the sort Vallentyne describes, then one can generate a contradiction between the

Principle of Substitution of Equivalents and the Principle of Continuity even for the "easy" cases for which it supposedly holds. Correspondingly, we must accept continuity for *all* cases, reject it even for easy ones, or reject the Principle of Substitution of Equivalents. An important fourth option is to reject Expected Value Theory's fundamental assumption about how to determine the value of a prospect, as represented by section 8.2's formula 5.1.1*. I shall discuss this option later. (Of course, a fifth possibility, accepting an inconsistent set of views, always remains as a final, unpalatable, option. However, I confess that *all* of the options in this area are unpalatable, though perhaps to varying degrees!)

To illustrate the contradiction in question, let us start with a simple "extreme" example where many would reject the Principle of Continuity.

Let B be an outcome where I receive \$1,000,000 per year, A an outcome where I receive \$1,000,001 per year, and Z an outcome where I receive \$0 per year. According to the Principle of Continuity, here put in terms of "equally as good as," there *must* be some probability p, between 0 and 1, such that $b = pa + (1 - p)z$, where this means that rationality *requires* me to regard the prospect of receiving A, with probability p, or Z, with probability $(1 - p)$, as equally as good as the prospect of receiving B for sure. But many deny this. So, let us assume that this represents the kind of "extreme" example for which many agree that the Principle of Continuity should be rejected.

But consider examples where the gap between the *certain* alternative and the worst *risky* alternative is small. For such cases, most people would readily, and plausibly, accept the Principle of Continuity. For example, if B is an outcome where I receive \$1,000,000 per year, A an outcome where I receive \$1,000,001 per year, and C an outcome where I receive \$999,999 per year, most people would readily grant that there must be some p, between 0 and 1, such that I should rationally regard as equally good the prospect of receiving outcome B with certainty and the prospect of receiving either outcome A with probability p or outcome C with probability $(1 - p)$. That is, there must be some p such that (1) $b = pa + (1 - p)c$. But then, consider outcomes B, C, and D, where B and C are as previously, and D is an outcome where I receive \$999,998 per year. Surely, most will accept that there is some probability q, between 0 and 1, such that (2) $c = qb + (1 - q)d$. But then, by the Principle of Substitution of Equivalents, one can replace c in (1) with $qb + (1 - q)d$ (from (2)), at which point one can show via basic, though rather messy algebraic manipulation that there is a probability r between 0 and 1 (where $r = p/(1 - q + pq)$) such that (3) $b = ra + (1 - r)d$.[24] Thus, from (1) and (2) one can conclude that there *must* be some

---

[24] For those readers who are interested, here is the messy calculation, all of whose steps are licensed by basic principles of arithmetic, given that a, b, and c are real numbers, and p and q are real numbers between 0 and 1.

probability r such that, according to Expected Value Theory, one is rationally required to regard as equally good the prospect where one receives $1,000,000 per year for sure, and the prospect where one either receives $1,000,001 per year, with probability r, or $999,998 per year, with probability $(1 - r)$.

But then, next consider B, D, and E, where E is an outcome where one receives $999,997 per year. Since the gap between D and E is small, most would readily admit that the Principle of Continuity holds for B, D, and E, and hence that there must be some probability s, between 0 and 1, such that (4) $d = sb + (1 - s)e$. But then, if one replaces d in (3) with $sb + (1 - s)e$ (from (4) by Principle of Substitution of Equivalents) one can then show that there must be some probability t, between 0 and 1, such that (5) $b = ta + (1 - t)e$.[25] Iterations of this reasoning lead to the conclusion that there must be some probability x, between 0 and 1, such that (N) $b = xa + (1 - x)z$, where z is the real number that represents the value of outcome Z where, as noted earlier, one receives $0 per year. But, by hypothesis, those who reject continuity in "extreme" cases deny what (N) implies according to Expected Value Theory. That is, they deny that given the three outcomes, A, B, and Z, where A is an outcome where one receives $1,000,001 per year, B an outcome where one receives $1,000,000 per year, and Z an outcome where one receives $0 per year, there must be some probability x, such that rationality *requires* one to regard the prospect of receiving A, with probability x, or Z, with probability $(1 - x)$, as equally as good as the prospect of receiving B for sure.

Hence, we seem to have shown that *if* we want to continue to reject the Principle of Continuity for "extreme" cases, like (N), then we must *also* reject it for "easy" cases *or* reject the Principle of Substitution of Equivalents. But the Principle of Substitution of Equivalents is a basic principle of arithmetic, so rejecting that principle does not seem to be an option. Thus, at first blush, it appears that we don't have the option of accepting the Principle of Continuity for "easy" cases and rejecting it for "extreme" ones; rather, we must accept it for both cases or neither. But, for many people, neither of these options will be palatable.

$b = pa + (1 - p)c$ by assumption of the Principle of Continuity for "easy" cases
$c = qb + (1 - q)d$ by assumption of the Principle of Continuity for "easy" cases
$b = pa + (1 - p)(qb + (1 - q)d)$ from 1 and 2 via Principle of Substitution of Equivalents
$b = pa + (1 - p)(qb) + (1 - p)(1 - q)d$ from 3 via Distributive Property of Arithmetic
$b = pa + (1qb) - pqb + (1(1 - q)d - p(1 - q)d$ from 4 via Distributive Property
$b = pa + qb - pqb + d - qd - pd + pqd$ from 5 via Distributive Property
$b - qb + pqb = pa + d - qd - pd + pqd$ from 6 subtracting qb from, and adding pqb to, both sides
$b(1 - q + pq) = pa + d - qd + pqd - pd$ from 7 via Distributive Property on the left side and Commutative Property of Arithmetic on the right side
$b(1 - q + pq) = pa + (1 - q + pq)d - pd$ from 8 via Distributive Property
$b = (p/(1 - q + pq))a + 1d - (p/(1 - q + pq))d$ from 9 dividing each side by $(1 - q + pq)$
$b = (p/(1 - q + pq))a + (1 - (p/(1 - q + pq)))d$ from 10 via Distributive Property
$b = ra + (1 - r)d$ from 11, where $r = (p/(1 - q + pq))$ QED.

[25] The proof of this will follow the same steps as the one presented in the preceding note, mutatis mutandis.

Is there another possible way out of this dilemma? As indicated earlier, there is, and by now it should be familiar. One *might* contend that Expected Value Theory provides the right way of assessing *certain* prospects in comparison with each other, but not others. Let us detail what this contention amounts to.

One might believe, as Expected Value Theory holds, that for any given prospect, P, there is a value function V that will assign a real number to that prospect, which corresponds to the *expected value* of that prospect as that notion is defined by Expected Value Theory. Naturally, such numbers can be represented on a common linear scale, the real number line, and one could compare any two prospects in terms of their expected value, by seeing how they compare along the scale in question, which we may, for simplicity, simply call the *expected value scale*. One might then further hold that for any two prospects, P_1 and P_2, how they compare *all things considered* will be determined by how they compare along the expected value scale *if* P_1 and P_2 are related to each other in the way that the different prospects in the so-called easy cases for the Principle of Continuity are related to each other, in cases *I* and *II* noted earlier. However, one might *also* believe that if two prospects, P_1 and P_n, are related to each other in the way that the different prospects in the so-called extreme cases for the Principle of Continuity are related to each other, as in case *IV* noted earlier, then how P_1 and P_n compare all things considered will *not* be determined by how they compare on the expected value scale; thus, one must appeal to some *other* scale or method to determine how *such* prospects compare.

On such a view, the relevance and significance of the factors for assessing a prospect will *not* simply depend on the internal features of that prospect; they will also partly depend on what alternative prospects, if any, the prospect is compared with. That is, in the terminology introduced at the end of chapter 7, such a view embodies an Essentially Comparative View rather than an Internal Aspects View. But then, for the reasons presented in chapters 6 and 7, this opens up the possibility that the "better than," "at least as good as," and "equally as good as" relations (in my wide reason-implying sense) will not be transitive (or, in the terminology I introduced previously, will be nontransitive).

In sum, we can't reject the Principle of Continuity in "extreme" cases but assume that this has no significant bearing elsewhere regarding the plausibility of Expected Value Theory and its implications. For the following four positions are inconsistent: (1) the Principle of Continuity fails for "extreme" cases, (2) the Principle of Continuity works for "easy" cases, (3) the Principle of Substitution of Equivalents, and (4) the Axioms of Transitivity for the "equally as good as," "at least as good as," and (almost certainly) "better than" relations.

To be sure, most economists, game theorists, and decision theorists will deny that the Principle of Continuity should be rejected in "extreme" cases of the sort

Vallentyne imagines. Moreover, they will take the preceding considerations as a reductio of the intuition in question, rather than as a serious threat to the Axioms of Transitivity, to the Principle of Substitution of Equivalents, or to the Principle of Continuity even in so-called easy cases. Nevertheless, I believe that many people will continue to find it very hard to believe that rationality *requires* them to be willing to trade the *certainty* of a *full, rich life* for the prospect of a *slightly* better one, when doing so means taking *some* risk—no matter how small—of ending up with a life of unremitting pain and misery. Moreover, I believe there is strong reason to resist such a conclusion, even if this requires substantial revision in our understanding and assessment of Expected Value Theory and its role in practical reasoning.

8.4.3 OBJECTIONS AND RESPONSES

In response to the preceding argument, some people may worry that my argument depends on employing rules that work in the realm of mathematics, but are illegitimate in the realm of objects of value.[26] This worry may arise especially for those who looked at the details of my argument presented in note 24. For example, when dealing with numbers, it is true that $2 + (5 + 3) = (2 + 5) + 3$, but a similar "commutative property" doesn't apply when dealing with objects of value; for example, it isn't the case that the value of the combination fish + (red wine + beef) is the same as the value of the combination (fish + red wine) + beef. Similarly, when dealing with numbers, it is true that if $a = b$ then $2a = 2b$, but when dealing with objects of value it isn't true that if one object would have the same value to someone as another object, then two of the former objects would have the same value to the person as two of the latter objects. For example, it could be that one pill would merely be very tasty, but that two pills would save my life, while if I'm full, two ice cream cones may be little, if any, better than one. Accordingly, one pill may have the same value for me as a single ice cream cone, but two pills may be much more valuable for me than two ice cream cones.

The observed disanalogy between the realm of numbers and the realm of objects of value is undoubtedly correct and important, but it is *irrelevant* to my argument. In my argument, I never employ rules of math to the realm of *objects* of value. I only employ rules of math to formulas which contain nothing but constants and mathematical symbols, which represent real numbers and functions (like addition and multiplication) that apply to those numbers. These are precisely the kinds of formulas to which the mathematical rules I employ can be properly applied. Accordingly, the only way for this objection to my argument to gain any traction would be as an objection to the way in which the

---

[26] Shelly Kagan raised this worry, for one.

formulas that I manipulate are derived from, and supposed to represent, the goodness, value, or rational desirability of the outcomes or prospects that are being evaluated. But this amounts to an objection to the way in which Expected Value Theory assigns values to outcomes and prospects, and its claim that how two prospects compare, all things considered, is a function of the expected values they are assigned by Expected Value Theory, since the formulas I manipulate, and the conclusions I draw from them, are derived from a straightforward application of Expected Value Theory to the prospects I consider.

One might, for example, deny that the subvalue function, v, that assigns a value to the outcome that obtains in each state of nature should ignore what outcomes will occur in other states of nature in assigning such values; or, similarly, one might deny that the value function, V, that assigns values to prospects should do so as a simple additive function of the values of the different outcomes that would occur in the different possible states of nature multiplied by the probabilities of those states of nature occurring. But such claims would amount to rejecting the principle of strong separability that Broome recognizes as lying at the heart of Expected Value Theory. Thus, such claims do not *defend* Expected Value Theory against my argument; rather, they *abandon* Expected Value Theory in the face of my argument.

In sum, my argument does not rely on an illegitimate application of math rules to the realm of objects of value, and succeeds given the assumptions of Expected Value Theory. Hence, one must look elsewhere if one hopes to limit the worries raised by my argument for Expected Value Theory.

Another response to the worries I have raised is to argue that the Principle of Continuity holds even for so-called extreme cases of the sort Vallentyne imagines. For example, one common response to my argument runs as follows.

Many of us believe that we currently have full, rich lives. Yet we will make a left turn across a busy street to save one dollar in filling our car with gas. Likewise, we'll leave a hotel and cross busy intersections to save a few dollars on the cost of a meal. These actions, and countless similar ones that we routinely make, seem perfectly rational. Yet, in such cases, we seem perfectly willing to risk a full, rich life for the sake of a slight gain. Moreover, though small, the probability of risk to life and limb is still *much* greater in such cases than the probability of risk that the Principle of Continuity would require us to accept in "extreme" cases, since that probability can be as small as one likes, as long as it is still finite. Thus, it is argued, if, as most believe, our actions in such cases are not irrational, one cannot criticize the Principle of Continuity for requiring us to be willing to take *vastly smaller* risks in cases where the potential gains are similarly slight.

This response is initially plausible, but it should, I think, be questioned. First, it might be claimed that our actions in such cases are not, in fact, rational, if the cases are truly as described, that is, if the best way of understanding them truly is in terms of our putting full, rich lives at risk merely for the sake of insignificant gains. But setting such a response aside, one might note that it is one thing to grant that such actions might be rationally *permissible*, quite another to maintain that they must be rationally *required*. Thus, it is one thing to maintain that it is not irrational to risk great personal harm for the sake of a slight gain if that is what one most wants to do; it is quite another to maintain, as Expected Value Theory does given the Principle of Continuity, that rationality *requires* a willingness to accept *some* small probability of great harm (no matter how great) for the possibility of a slight gain (no matter how slight). The former may seem plausible for reasons that do not support the latter.

Second, the real-world cases this response appeals to are not analogous to the possible-world "extreme" case where, I claimed, the Principle of Continuity fails. In my "extreme" case, I am supposed to trade off the *certainty* of a full, rich life for the prospect of a *slightly* better one, when doing so means taking some risk—no matter how small—that I would end up with a life of pain and misery. In the real-world cases there is no certainty of a full, rich life if we don't adopt the more risky alternative. If I turn into the gas station on my right, instead of the one on my left, I may be hit by a car foolishly passing on the right. If I stay in the hotel, I may break my neck tumbling down the escalator, or die of a heart attack from the "sticker shock" of the overpriced meal! It is one thing to trade off between different pairs of risky alternatives, preferring one risky alternative with a slightly higher payoff to another less risky alternative with a slightly lower payoff. It is another matter, altogether, to trade the *certainty* of a high payoff for the probability of an ever-so-slightly higher one, if there is also a probability, however small, of a *vastly* worse outcome.

Third, and most important, my example involves a unique, once-in-a-lifetime opportunity to *guarantee* a full, rich, lengthy life with $1,000,000 per year. The decision whether to risk turning left across a busy street, or crossing several busy intersections to save a few dollars, is not analogous. We are constantly confronted by such decisions where, at best, adoption of the cautious alternative merely increases the probability of *temporarily* preserving the status quo. Moreover, and this is the key point, because of the pervasive contingencies of human existence, in general, an inability or unwillingness to expose oneself to slight increases in risk will result in a crimped, impoverished life.

In saying that one is not being irrational in crossing a busy street for the sake of a few dollars, one is acknowledging the rationality of a certain kind of desire, disposition, or lifestyle. Our judgment reflects a global judgment of the actor, and of the kind of life he has chosen to live. We view the act as the kind of act that rational agents typically do, and precisely because they have good reason to be disposed to do such acts. One *could* minimize one's risks by never venturing out, never meeting others, never eating foods that one has not grown oneself, and so on. But such a life would be lacking in much of what makes human life valuable. We judge the life of someone who *engages* the world as more valuable,[27] even if more risky. Correspondingly, we regard someone as rational in developing and acting in accordance with those desires and dispositions that promote the more valuable life. Crossing busy streets is the kind of activity that rational people do. It involves some increase of risk to the status quo, but the alternative to taking such risks is to preserve a status quo that is not nearly so worth preserving.

In sum, in my example, one has a momentous once-in-a-lifetime choice where a risk avoider can guarantee a tremendously valuable life. In the apparent counterexamples, one's choice is of a kind frequently confronted, where to be a risk avoider regarding such actions is almost certain to lead a crimped existence. The examples are not analogous. Our judgment that a rational person *might* choose the riskier alternative in the latter case does not support the judgment that a rational person *must* choose the riskier alternative in the former case.

There is another objection to apparent counterexamples to the Principle of Continuity in "extreme" cases. Recall that the Principle of Continuity merely requires that for any three outcomes, A, B, and C, where A is better than B, and B better than C, there must be *some* probability p, between 0 and 1, such that we should be indifferent between prospect X, where B occurs for sure, and prospect Y, where A occurs with probability p, or C occurs with probability $(1-p)$. In particular, p can be as close to 1 as one likes, so the probability of the undesirable outcome $(1-p)$ can be as close to 0 as one likes. For example, as Derek Parfit likes to colorfully put it, the probability of C could be as small as .000...001, where the total number of zeros equaled the number of atoms in the universe.[28] But, it is argued, we can't *possibly* accurately imagine probabilities this small. Correspondingly, for "extreme" cases we should trust theory over intuitions. Since our theory—Expected Value Theory in general, and the Principle of Continuity in particular—seems acceptable for the "easy" cases, where our intuitions seem well grounded, we should also accept it for the "extreme" cases, where its judgments may seem counterintuitive, but our intuitions cannot be trusted.

The idea here might be illustrated as follows. Imagine that there is an urn containing some number of white and red balls. Outcome A will obtain if a white ball is randomly selected from the urn, outcome C will obtain if a red ball is selected. If we know there are five white balls and five red balls, we may be

---

[27] Or at least as not less valuable, which is all one really needs to defend this position.

[28] Indeed, as Chris Meacham pointed out to me, Parfit's colorful description doesn't even *begin* to convey just *how* small the probability of C could actually be. For example, the number of zeros might be 10 raised to the nth power, raised to the nth power, raised to the nth power, and so on as many times as one would like, say, n times, where n was equal to the number of particles in the universe. Such a number would be incomprehensibly larger than the mere number of atoms in the universe! Though Meacham is undoubtedly correct, I suspect that for our purposes any unimaginably large number is as good as any other, and hence Parfit's description will do just fine.

fairly good at intuitively judging the probability that we shall select a red ball. Similarly, if there are nine white balls and one red ball, or perhaps even ninety-nine white balls and one red ball. But if we are told that while there is only one red ball, the number of white balls is a billion, or a trillion, or equal to the number of atoms in the universe, there is no way we can accurately "intuit" our probability of randomly selecting a red ball. Thus, we cannot trust our intuitions about such cases—which are precisely the kind of "extreme" cases where the Principle of Continuity allegedly fails.

This objection raises a legitimate worry. Our intuitions are *not* finely calibrated to reflect extremely small, or large, probabilities. Thus, in "extreme" cases, we will inevitably attach either greater or less intuitive weight than we should to the likelihood of the worst outcome occurring. It is, however, slightly ironic that one might turn to this kind of defense to defuse our strong intuitive reactions to such cases, since, typically, the greater danger lies in people *underestimating* the probability of a terrible outcome occurring, rather than in their overestimating the probability of such an outcome. Humans are notorious for treating a very small chance of a bad event happening as if there were *no* chance of it happening. This is a grave mistake. Of course, it is a mistake that most individuals will get away with most of the time. Still, as Derek Parfit writes, for reasons he amply presents, "When the stakes are high, no chance, however small, should be ignored."[29]

In the "extreme" case of the offered counterexample to the Principle of Continuity, an inflated estimate of the probability of the worst outcome may lead me to choose prospect X, where B will obtain for sure, rather than prospect Y, where A will obtain with probability p or C will obtain with probability $(1 - p)$. As the example was described, this would *almost* certainly cost me an extra dollar a year, and an *ever-so-slightly* fuller and richer life than I would have led had I chosen prospect Y. This slight difference in the quality of my life, caused, let us now suppose, by our inflated estimate of C's probability, may be a source of rational regret, but it won't be of much significance.

Suppose, on the other hand, that we underestimate C's probability. Impressed by C's *extreme* unlikelihood, we decide as if there were *no* chance of C's occurring and, on this basis, we choose prospect Y rather than prospect X. Unfortunately, we are the victims of bad luck of truly cosmic proportions, and we end up with a life of pain and misery rather than the full, rich life with

---

[29] *Reasons and Persons* (Oxford: Oxford University Press, 1984), 75. In writing this paragraph, I am not denying that many people are also prone, on occasion, to treat a very small chance of a bad event happening as if it were a very big chance of a bad event happening, and that that, too, can be a grave mistake. But when we overinflate the possibility of a terrible outcome happening, the result is typically that we take extra undue precautions to prevent it from happening, and the result of our doing this will often (though not always) pose less danger to us than the result of our failing to take sufficient steps to prevent a terrible outcome from occurring.

$1,000,000 per year that we would have been *guaranteed* had we chosen prospect X. Here, it seems, our underestimation of C's probability could be the source of tremendous rational regret.

Of course, defenders of the Principle of Continuity even for "extreme" cases might deny this. They might insist that we can only *rationally* regret our miscalculation of C's probability, and the corresponding difference in *expected value* between prospects X and Y, *not* the tremendous difference in the *actual* outcome that our miscalculation led to because of horrendous bad luck. But this is precisely what some opponents of the Principle of Continuity in "extreme" cases will deny. They may insist that if we can effectively guard against horrendous bad luck at *very* little cost to our well-being, and we fail to do so, then our choice is open to serious rational regret. Indeed, strong opponents of the Principle of Continuity in "extreme" cases might even claim that in such circumstances our choice would be open to serious rational *criticism*. On such a view, not only wouldn't rationality *require* us to choose in accordance with expected value, in such circumstances, it would *preclude* us from doing so. On the stronger position, one couldn't avoid rational criticism, if the disastrous outcome ensued, merely by correctly pointing out that the bad outcome only occurred because of *horrendous* bad luck. Though true, the horrendous bad luck with its disastrous result could have been *completely* guarded against *at virtually no cost*.

So, acknowledging that we are intuitively incapable of accurately assessing extremely small, or large, probabilities does not yet support the conclusion that we must accept the Principle of Continuity for "extreme" cases as well as "easy" cases. We may *judge* that the dangers of underestimating the probability of the worst outcome far exceed the dangers of overestimating its probability. Such a judgment would provide direct grounds for rejecting the Principle of Continuity in "extreme" cases, one not based on our intuitive calculation of the expected values of prospects X and Y.

Note, by the axioms of Expected Value Theory, our intuitive calculation of the expected values of prospects X and Y *must* either support the Principle of Continuity or be mistaken. But this is not an *argument* against our intuitions about "extreme" cases, since those cases are being offered as a *challenge* to the axioms of Expected Value Theory. Appealing to the axioms of Expected Value Theory doesn't refute such a challenge; it merely begs the question against it.

In thinking about the rationality of one's choice where probabilities are involved, it is, I think, useful to consider cases where that choice would be made repeatedly. Imagine, for example, that I am a benevolent leader of a large population. I am going to urge on my fellow citizens a principle of choice that each will follow. If they choose prospect X, they will each receive outcome B ($1,000,000 per year and a full, rich life). If they choose prospect Y, they will receive either outcome A ($1,000,001 per year and an ever-so-slightly fuller, richer life) or outcome C (a life of unremitting pain and misery). Suppose, first, that if they choose prospect Y, the odds of C are only one in a million. If there are a million people who will follow my advice, I would urge each to choose prospect X. I know that with a million people choosing, the odds are great that *one* of them would end up with outcome C if each chose prospect Y. Thinking of my fellow citizens as I might members of my own family—remember, I am a benevolent leader—I *much* prefer the situation where each of them has outcome B, to the situation where virtually every one has outcome A, but one ends up with outcome C. In accordance with the kinds of reasoning evidenced in chapters 2 through 5 (by, for example, the Second Standard View, the Fourth Standard View, View Three, and the Disperse Additional Burdens View), it won't seem worth it to me to trade off an incredibly huge loss for one, for the sake of tiny gains for many others, even for almost a million others.

What if instead of one in a million, the odds are one in a billion, or one in a zillion, or one in the number of atoms in the universe? To be sure, these are inconceivably large numbers. But if I imagine the size of the population increasing proportionally, so that the number of my fellow citizens who will follow my advice is a billion, or a zillion, or equal to the number of atoms in the universe, then my advice would be the same. I would urge each to choose prospect X, knowing that if each chose prospect Y, the odds would be high that *one* of them would end up with a life of unremitting pain and misery.

In considering this position, it may help to recall section 2.3's discussion of the Repugnant Conclusion and the Lollipops for Life case. I believe that the response people make against trusting our intuitions about the Principle of Continuity in "extreme" cases is the same kind of response total utilitarians make to the problem of additive aggregation.[30] But few people are willing to "bite the bullet" and accept the total utilitarian's response to the Repugnant Conclusion and the Lollipops for Life case. And I believe they are right not to do so. Similarly, I believe one should reject such a response to my claims about the Principle of Continuity for "extreme" cases.

Just as I think one cannot trade off between extra lollipop licks and lives, so I think one cannot trade off between tiny increases in well-being for many, and an *immense* loss in well-being for one. On my view, the goodness of outcomes is not an additive-aggregative function of well-being in the way it would need to be for me to urge my fellow citizens to choose prospect Y. Just as I think the moral value of a human life exceeds the value of one extra lollipop lick for *any* number of people, so I think that no matter *how* large a population might be, the outcome in which *everyone* has outcome B ($1,000,000 per year and a full, rich life) is better than the outcome in which *almost* everyone has outcome A ($1,000,001 per year and an ever-so-slightly fuller, richer life)

---

[30] See section 2.3.

except, regrettably, for one person who has outcome C (a life of unremitting pain and misery).

Similarly, imagine that I am to live a large number of lives successively. Each life will be confronted with the choice between prospects X and Y, and I must adopt a principle of choice for each of my future selves. If the number of my future selves was large enough, so that the odds were high that even *one* of them would end up with outcome C if they each chose prospect Y, then I would want each of my future selves to choose prospect X. I realize that this would cost each of an innumerably large number of my future selves a small amount of well-being (equal to the difference between outcomes A and B), but I believe that that would be a cost well worth innumerable future selves bearing, to prevent one of my future selves having to endure outcome C rather than outcome B. Here, as before, I think the tiny differences between outcomes A and B that would be borne by many of my future selves don't aggregate in the way that they would need to to outweigh the difference between outcomes B and C that would be borne by one of my future selves.

So we find ourselves in familiar territory. Unless one is willing to bite the bullet regarding the problem of additive aggregation, one has good reason to recommend prospect X rather than prospect Y to innumerable citizens, or future selves, confronting that choice. But this suggests (though does not entail) that it may be rational to choose prospect X rather than prospect Y for oneself. Though the risk of ruining one's life might be astonishingly small, it may not be worth taking, for the rough equivalent of a few extra licks of a lollipop.

In sum, there remains reason to doubt the Principle of Continuity for "extreme" cases. But, as we have seen, *if* one rejects the Principle of Continuity in certain "extreme" cases, then Expected Value Theory is deeply problematic. One cannot simply assume that Expected Value Theory may fail only in rare "extreme" cases, but will work fine for the vast majority of "normal" cases. To the contrary, *if* one rejects the Principle of Continuity in "extreme" cases, then one must reject the Principle of Continuity even in the "easy" cases for which it seems *most* plausible, reject the Principle of Substitution of Equivalents, or open oneself up to rejecting the Axiom of Transitivity for the "better than," "at least as good as," and "equally as good as" relations.

To give up the Principle of Continuity even for easy cases would have radical implications for practical reasoning. But so, too, would giving up the Principle of Substitution of Equivalents or the various Axioms of Transitivity. Indeed, I suspect the implications of any of these moves would be so great that many people will be tempted to reject the position causing all the trouble—namely, the view that the Principle of Continuity should be rejected in certain "extreme" cases. I am tempted by this view myself, but for reasons indicated here, and in previous chapters, this, too, I find deeply problematic.

8.4.4 J. ROSS'S PRINCIPLE REVISITED

Let me conclude my discussion of the Principle of Continuity with a refrain that will now be familiar. Unsurprisingly, given our discussion to this point, this may be another instance where J. Ross's Principle is relevant.[31]

I have said that it is hard to believe that it is rationally *required* that we accept the Principle of Continuity even in "extreme" cases. But my discussion has left open the possibility that it is at least rationally *permissible* to always act in accordance with the Principle of Continuity. However, some may find even this hard to accept. Just as Rawls famously argued that in certain choice conditions, it would be rationally *required* to adopt a *maximin* strategy,[32] so, it might be argued that in the conditions present in "extreme" cases, it would be seriously irrational *not* to take the prospect that *guarantees* a truly *wonderful* outcome, rather than a prospect with the same or only *slightly* higher expected value, if the *most* one stands to gain by taking the latter prospect with a nonguaranteed result is only an *ever-so-slightly* better outcome, while the cost of taking the latter prospect is to open oneself up to the chance, however small, of an utterly *disastrous* outcome.

We can up the ante of accepting the Principle of Continuity for all cases, by imagining an even *more* "extreme" case than those given to this point. We might call this the *Super Extreme Case*. Let outcome B involve the guarantee of a full, rich, billion-year life for *each* person who ever lives for billions and billions of years to come; let outcome A be just like B, except that *one* person gets *one* extra lick of a lollipop over the course of her billion-year life, making her life, and hence the outcome as a whole, *ever-so-slightly* better; and let C be an outcome where *each* person who ever lives endures unimaginably bad pain, suffering, frustration, and disappointment for a billion years, and where this continues for billions and billions of years to come. Surely, many would contend, confronted with the choice between prospect X, where outcome B would obtain *for sure*, or prospect Y, where outcome A would obtain with probability p or outcome C would obtain with probability $(1 - p)$, it would be *deeply irrational* and *wrong* not to choose prospect X for *any* finite probability p less than 1. Let us assume that underlying the judgment in question is a theory which I shall call, tendentiously, the *Sane Theory*.

Now suppose that one actually confronted a choice like the one just imagined. According to Expected Value Theory, there must be some probability p approaching, but less than, 1, according to which one should rationally regard prospects X and Y as *equally good*. That is, there *must* be some probability p,

---

[31] J. Ross's Principle was first introduced in section 2.4 and then invoked again in section 4.3. See Jacob Ross, "Rejecting Ethical Deflationism," *Ethics* 116 (2006): 742–68.

[32] See chapter 3 of John Rawls, *A Theory of Justice* (Cambridge, MA: Harvard University Press, 1971), especially section 26.

such that we should rationally regard the prospect of outcome A obtaining with probability p or outcome C obtaining with probability $(1 - p)$ as *just as good* as the prospect of outcome B obtaining for sure. Still, on Expected Value Theory, the prospect of outcome B obtaining for sure is *no worse* than the prospect of outcome A obtaining with probability p or outcome C obtaining with probability $(1 - p)$. On the other hand, as we just implied, there is a *huge* difference in the desirability of the various prospects according to the Sane Theory. It follows, in accordance with J. Ross's Principle, that if we ever actually confronted an "extreme" choice like the one envisaged, it would be *practically* rational to choose *as if* the Sane Theory is true as long as we attach *some* credence to it, *even if* we attach *more* credence, and even vastly more credence, to Expected Value Theory. By making such a choice, there is a *lot* to be (potentially) gained, and *nothing* to lose.

In sum, wherever Expected Value Theory tells us that we should be indifferent between two prospects, and another theory that we attach some credence to favors one prospect over the other, it will be *practically* rational to follow the other theory, in accordance with the first clause of J. Ross's Principle.[33] Similarly, if Expected Value Theory tells us that there is very little to choose between two prospects, while another theory we attach some credence to *strongly* favors one alternative over the other, it will often be practically rational to follow the other theory, in accordance with the second clause of J. Ross's Principle. Thus, even if one *believes* that Expected Value Theory is probably the correct theory for rational decision making, it would typically be practically rational *not* to *follow* it in so-called extreme cases.

8.5 Concluding Remarks

The main point of this chapter may be summed up as follows. Many people grant the intuitive force of my arguments that seemingly put pressure on the view that "all-things-considered better than" (in my wide reason-implying sense) must be a transitive relation. But some people believe that it is a mistake to trust their intuitions about my arguments, in large part because they fly in the face of Expected Value Theory. Such people typically have unswerving confidence in Expected Value Theory, because of the intimate connection between it and Expected Utility Theory, and the central and successful role that the latter theory plays in underlying game theory, decision theory, and much of modern economics.

---

[33] As in our earlier discussions of J. Ross's Principle, this assumes that there isn't another competing theory that we attach similar credence to that points in the opposite direction of the original rival to Expected Value Theory. But that assumption seems right for the cases we have been discussing. So, for example, there is no rival to the Sane Theory that we have any credence in that implies that in the Super Extreme Case we would be *seriously irrational* if we chose the prospect that *guaranteed* the extraordinarily fantastic outcome for *everyone* if the expected value of the two prospects was the same.

To be sure, many people grant that some of the premises of Expected Value Theory and Expected Utility Theory are problematic in certain respects; for example, that Completeness is dubious, and that the Principle of Continuity is implausible in "extreme" cases. Nevertheless, it is commonly assumed that such problems lie at the "periphery" of such theories, not at their core, so that eventually one will be able to revise such theories to accommodate such problems without affecting their central tenets, plausibility, or implications. More generally, it is commonly assumed that we will eventually be able to "explain away" any apparent problems for Expected Value Theory and Expected Utility Theory or lightly revise such theories to accommodate the problems without doing significant damage to any of our core assumptions about rationality. Given this, some people feel that they may confidently reject any steps in my arguments that conflict with Expected Value Theory and Expected Utility Theory, even if they share the intuitions or judgments that underlie or are reflected by those steps. This chapter's discussion shows that this attitude is questionable.

As we saw, adequately dealing with Incompleteness will involve coming to terms with an inconsistency between a number of deeply plausible positions, including the assumption that some prospects or outcomes are only roughly comparable; the First Principle of Equivalence; the original or amended State-by-State Comparison Principle; the Principle of Substitution of Equivalents; the Pareto Principle; the Reflection Principle; and the transitivity of the "at least as good as" relation (in my wide reason-implying sense). Likewise, adequately dealing with the Principle of Continuity for "extreme" cases will involve coming to terms with an inconsistency between the following: the view that the Principle of Continuity should be rejected for "extreme" cases; the view that the Principle of Continuity should be accepted for "easy" cases; the Principle of Substitution of Equivalents; and the view (the Internal Aspects View) that would ensure that the "better than," "at least as good as" and "equally as good as" relations are transitive.

Finally, let me say a bit more about how we should think about Expected Value Theory and, mutatis mutandis, Expected Utility Theory, in light of this book's arguments. I agree that Expected Value Theory is an extremely useful and illuminating tool. But it is only that, a useful tool that humans have constructed to help model, explain, and in some cases guide rational behavior. I am not convinced that Expected Value Theory has to endorse a simple additive-aggregative-approach for assessing and comparing all prospects or outcomes. If it doesn't, then it obviously can't be invoked to rule out our anti-additive-aggregationist judgments, like those expressed in the Second Standard View, the Fourth Standard View, View Three, and the Disperse Additional Burdens View. But if it does, then it must face all of the objections and worries that have been raised in this book against a simple additive-aggregationist approach for comparing all alternatives.

If the Repugnant Conclusion really *is* repugnant, no appeal to Expected Value Theory can remove that repugnance. Similarly, if it really wouldn't be a better outcome to give each of innumerable people *one* lick of a lollipop, if this unavoidably involved one person suffering unbearable agony for countless years, it is no use pretending otherwise because Expected Value Theory would supposedly judge it so. And if Expected Value Theory cannot reflect the view that the goodness of a life is determined, in part, not just by *how much* pain occurs in that life, but by the quality of the pain and the way it is distributed, then so much the worse for Expected Value Theory.

I am, in fact, a fan of Expected Value Theory. But the problems I have been raising in this book require a response. They cannot, I think, simply be rejected because they are claimed to be incompatible with Expected Value Theory. Decisions need to be made about which of our views should be rejected, and why. And in making those decisions, the costs of doing so must be fully realized. When this is done, we may see that Expected Value Theory needs revision or is limited in scope. Or we may see that it remains intact. But even if it remains intact, we will have a much better understanding of why this is so, including a much deeper understanding of the nature of moral ideals and practical reasoning, if we confront the issues I am raising head-on, than if we simply sweep them under the rug as "obviously" misguided, because incompatible with Expected Value Theory. Ultimately, the issues raised in this book challenge some of the foundations of Expected Value Theory, including, but by no means limited to, the assumption that "all-things-considered better than" (in my wide reason-implying sense) is a transitive relation. Correspondingly, one cannot respond to such issues simply by appealing to the very theory that they challenge.

At the end of the day, Expected Value Theory may be the best theory going. This chapter and this book are not intended to show otherwise. But the best theory going may still be flawed, wrong, or deeply problematic. In any event, here, as throughout this book, I am mainly concerned to illuminate various positions that stand or fall together and the true costs of adopting one position or another.[34]

---

[34] Mikhail Valdman observes the following (in correspondence): "To a large extent, your book is a critique of expected utility theory, but one wonders how serious of a critique it is if, as you say [at the end of chapter 10] ... 'there is no plausible coherent account that adequately captures all of our deepest beliefs about the nature of the good, moral ideals, and practical reasoning.' No doubt you've shown that there are deep and interesting problems with expected utility theory. And that is a significant accomplishment. But I can see a defender of expected utility theory insisting that you haven't yet given him a reason to *abandon* his theory unless you can show that a rival theory does a better job of capturing the aforementioned deepest beliefs." Interestingly, Nick Beckstead made a similar claim (in discussion) regarding utilitarianism. In particular, Beckstead suggested that while this book highlights various powerful objections to utilitarian reasoning, utilitarians may see no reason to abandon their view in light of such objections, given my book's result that there is *no* coherent view that captures *all* of our deepest normative beliefs.

As I've tried to make plain, and as I shall briefly address in my conclusion, I think it is a serious and open question what the best overall theory must look like given this book's results. But I grant that in light of my arguments it would not be unreasonable for a defender of Expected Utility Theory or utilitarianism to respond to my results in the manner suggested by Valdman and Beckstead. Instead of trying to refute or deflate every possible objection, defenders of such theories can take comfort in the fact that every other view must also face deep objections, and then focus on the *overall* advantages of their theories relative to rival theories.

9

Spectrum Arguments
OBJECTIONS AND REPLIES

In chapters 2 through 5, I presented various Spectrum Arguments. These arguments reveal an inconsistency between certain standard views regarding how to make trade-offs between different alternatives along a spectrum, certain factual premises, and the transitivity of the "better than" relation (in my wide reason-implying sense). Many people are suspicious of Spectrum Arguments, and many objections have been raised to my arguments. Some of these have already been addressed. But others have not. In this chapter, I present and respond to the most serious of the remaining objections, of which there are three main types. I shall consider a representative example of each type.

Type one responds to my arguments by appealing to the significance of there being different *kinds* of alternatives along my spectrums. Type two claims that my arguments are versions of the *Standard Sorites Paradox*. Type three suggests that my arguments elicit well-known heuristics and similarity-based reasoning schemes that are leading our intuitions astray. I argue that none of these objections is compelling.

In appendix D, I address three further, less worrisome, objections that have been raised to my Spectrum Arguments.

9.1 Different Kinds, Different Criteria

In earlier work,[1] I attempted to explain the possibility of intransitivity obtaining across a spectrum of alternatives by reasoning along the following lines. First, I noted that one could move from one end of a spectrum to another via

---

[1] "A Continuum Argument for Intransitivity," *Philosophy and Public Affairs* 25 (1996): 175–210.

a series of short steps, such that the difference between any member of the spectrum and any adjacent one a "short step away" was merely one of degree. I next noted that, together, a large number of small differences in degree could amount to a difference in kind. I then pointed out that the factors that were relevant and significant for comparing alternatives that differed merely in *degree* might be different from the factors that were relevant and significant for comparing alternatives that differed in *kind*. Finally, I showed that for any set of alternatives, if the relevant and significant factors for comparing some alternatives differed from the relevant and significant factors for comparing other alternatives, then there was no reason to expect transitivity to hold for the "all-things-considered better than" relation (in my wide reason-implying sense). This explained the possibility of transitivity either failing, or failing to apply, across spectrums of the sort I considered.

Some people have thought that instead of explaining the possibility of transitivity failing to hold in some cases, such reasoning provides a way of defending transitivity, by rejecting one of the key premises that purportedly helps threaten it. The thinking underlying this position can be usefully illuminated in terms of chapter 5's spectrum from torture to mosquito bites. It might be put as follows.

Suppose we think that there is a difference in *kind* between the pain of intense torture, P_{IT}, and the "pain" of one extra mosquito bite per month, P_{MB}, where, for simplicity, let us temporarily say that the pain of P_{IT} corresponds to P_n, the pain of P_{MB} to P_3, and that one could move from P_n (P_{IT}) to P_3 (P_{MB}), via a series of $n - 3$ equal short steps. Here, I have arbitrarily chosen P_3 to represent the mosquito bite's "pain" level, to highlight the fact that though it is a *very* mild pain, there might be a few pains, corresponding to P_2 or P_1, that were even *milder*. Then we can legitimately ask: Is $P_{(n-1)}$ of the same *kind* of pain as P_3? Presumably not. It is more likely of the same kind as P_n. What about $P_{(n-2)}$? Once again, it seems likely that this, too, will be of the same kind as P_n. Still, on reflection, it seems that there must be *some* step in the spectrum of pains between P_n and P_3, which is the *last* step where we have a pain of the same kind as P_n.[2] Let us arbitrarily suppose that this is P_k (where $n > k > 3$). It doesn't matter for the purposes of this argument which step it is. On this assumption, P_k differs not merely in degree, but also in *kind*, from $P_{(k-1)}$.

But, so the argument then goes, given their difference in kind, we can't expect the same factors to be relevant and significant for comparing P_k with $P_{(k-1)}$, as we would for comparing any of the alternatives P_n to P_k. Indeed, if we assume that $P_{(k-1)}$ is the same kind of pain as P_3, then just as we believe that no number of years of P_3 would be worse than two years of P_n, so we can believe that no number of years of $P_{(k-1)}$ would be worse than q years of P_k. So, in essence, we should deny that chapter 5's View One—for any unpleasant or "negative" experience, no matter the intensity and duration of that experience, it would be better to have that experience than one that was only a "little" less

---

[2] This might be denied because of worries about vagueness. But I want to grant it for the sake of the argument currently under discussion.

intense but twice (or three or five times) as long—applies when comparing P_k and $P_{(k-1)}$. That is, we can deny that View One applies for *each* pair of adjacent alternatives in the pain spectrum from $P_{IT}(P_n)$ to $P_{MB}(P_3)$.

On this view, we might have good reason to judge that transitivity holds for all pains of the same kind as P_{IT}, and so we might grant that 2 years of P_n is better than 4 years of $P_{(n-1)}$, 4 years of $P_{(n-1)}$ better than 8 years of $P_{(n-2)}$, all the way to $2^{(n-k)}$ years of $P_{(k+1)}$ is better than $2^{(n-k)+1}$ years of P_k, and hence that 2 years of P_n is better than $2^{(n-k)+1}$ years of P_k.[3] Similarly, we might have good reason to judge that transitivity holds for all pains of the same kind as P_3, and so we might grant that $2^{(n-(k-1))+1}$ years of $P_{(k-1)}$ is better than $2^{(n-(k-2))+1}$ years of $P_{(k-2)}$, $2^{(n-(k-2))+1}$ years of $P_{(k-2)}$ is better than $2^{(n-(k-3))+1}$ years of $P_{(k-3)}$, all the way to $2^{(n-4)}$ years of P_2 is better than $2^{(n-3)}$ years of P_3, and hence that $2^{(n-(k-1))+1}$ years of $P_{(k-1)}$ is better than $2^{(n-3)}$ years of P_3. However, since P_k and $P_{(k-1)}$ are different *kinds* of pains, we can *deny* that there is a chain of transitive judgments entailing that two years of intense torture would be better than many years of one extra mosquito bite per month. As seen, on this view the chain will be broken at *some* point—in this case we have assumed that point to be between P_k and $P_{(k-1)}$—when a small difference in degree *in fact* corresponds with a difference in kind.[4]

Note, advocates of this view need not claim that we can easily identify the precise point in question. To the contrary, they may claim that different people might intensely dispute about where, exactly, the point in question is, or they might even claim that the point might be epistemologically inaccessible to us. Nevertheless, they might insist that we know there must *be* such a point, since we know that the pain spectrum involves *one* kind of pain at one end, and a *different* kind of pain at the other, and hence that *somewhere* along the spectrum the transformation *must* take place between the one kind of pain and the other.

This objection is seductive, but it should be rejected. To see why, it will be helpful if we start by looking closer at the nature of the pain spectrum, and other spectrums, where one end of the spectrum seems to be radically different in kind than the other.

First, even if we grant that the pain of intense torture is different in kind than the pain of a mosquito bite, and further grant that there must be some precise point along the spectrum of pains where pain first becomes different in

---

[3] Here, we are assuming that for each pair of adjacent pain intensities, P_k and $P_{(k-1)}$, the slightly less intense pain is lasting twice as long, and since the initial pain intensity P_n is assumed to last for two years, the length of any subsequent pain intensity P_k is determined by the formula $2^{(n-k)+1}$. The reader will note that in this paragraph I have simplified some of the expressions, but not all. So, for example, I have simplified $2^{(n-(k+1))+1}$ to 2^{n-k}, $2^{(n-2)+1}$ to 2^{n-1}, and $2^{(n-1)+1}$ to 2^n, but I have not bothered to simplify expressions like $2^{(n-(k-2))+1}$ to $2^{(n-k)+3}$.

[4] This response is taken directly from an anonymous reviewer of my article "A Continuum Argument for Intransitivity" for *Philosophy and Public Affairs*. It is not clear whether the reviewer was actually endorsing this response or merely offering it as worthy of consideration. Regardless, I am grateful that the reviewer brought this response to my attention. In discussing these issues over the years, I have found that many are tempted to some version of this response.

kind from that of intense torture, and also some precise point at which pain first becomes the same kind as that of a mosquito bite, there is *no* reason to believe that these points will be the same. Indeed, there is very good reason to believe that they will be different. Thus, in terms of the foregoing, one might grant that all pains from P_n to P_k are of the same kind, and that pain $P_{(k-1)}$ is the first pain that is *not* of *that* kind; yet this *doesn't* commit one to thinking that this means that $P_{(k-1)}$ must be the same kind of pain as P_3. The point is that there may be any number of distinguishable "kinds" of pain along the pain spectrum from P_n (the pain of intense torture) to P_3 (the pain of a mosquito bite).

Consider a simple analogy. One might agree that someone with a complete head full of hair is extremely hairy. One might also agree that someone with but a few wisps of hair, or less, is bald. But that doesn't mean that one believes that there must be a precise point along the spectrum from extremely hairy to bald heads such that the loss of *one* hair will suddenly transform one from being *extremely* hairy to being *bald*. That is a silly, and obviously false, position. What *may* be true is that there *must* be a precise point at which one would go from being extremely hairy to *not* being extremely hairy, and a precise point at which one would go from not being bald to being bald.[5] But there is no reason to believe, and every reason to deny, that those two points must be the same point.[6] Instead, we should acknowledge that along the spectrum of hairiness, there will be at least *three* kinds of hairiness. There is the kind of hairiness that involves being extremely hairy, the kind of hairiness that involves being *neither* extremely hairy *nor* bald, and the kind of hairiness that involves being bald.

Let me be clear. One might, if one wants, plausibly divide the hairiness spectrum into just two kinds—the extremely hairy and the not extremely

---

[5] Or, alternatively, there might be a precise point at which the situation would go from there being a determinate fact that one was extremely hairy (or bald), to its being indeterminate whether one was extremely hairy (or bald), where, in the cases of indeterminacy, it would be neither true nor false that one was extremely hairy (or bald). This kind of view is controversial, but I am granting it, temporarily, for the sake of argument. Timothy Williamson offers a defense of this kind of view in his important book *Vagueness* (New York: Routledge, 1994).

[6] My point here is reminiscent of Aristotle's distinction between *contrary* notions and *contradictory* notions. For Aristotle, "black" and "not black" are contradictories, which means that it would be a contradiction to assert both that "x is black" and "x is not black." "White" and "black" are *primary* contraries, which means that one, in this case black, is the *privation* of the other. "Green" and "red" are intermediaries, and may also be called contraries of "white," though they are not primary contraries. Aristotle recognized that in changing from white to black an object would go through intermediate contrary colors like green before it reached the color black, and that in doing so it would go from white to not white before it had actually become black. This is analogous to my claim that taking away one hair at a time, one would go from being extremely hairy to not being extremely hairy, before one had become bald. One would first reach an intermediate position between extreme hairiness and baldness. I am not committed to Aristotle's particular metaphysical conception of privation, though it is, of course, natural to think of baldness as involving a privation of hair in some sense. See Aristotle's *Metaphysics*, trans. Hippocrates G. Apostle (Bloomington: Indiana University Press, 1966), book 10, especially chapters 3, 4, and 7. I am grateful to Alan Code for informing me of where Aristotle makes these distinctions, and for clarifying some of the details of Aristotle's view.

hairy. Similarly, one might, if one wants, plausibly divide the hairiness spectrum into just two different kinds—the bald and the not bald. But each of these approaches would be dividing the hairiness spectrum at *different* points, since being not extremely hairy is *not* the same as being bald, and since being not bald is *not* the same as being extremely hairy. Correspondingly, *if* one chooses to distinguish between being extremely hairy and being bald as involving different kinds of hairiness, then (at least if one means by those terms what is generally meant by them) one should also recognize that there is at least *one* further kind of hairiness, the kind that involves being neither extremely hairy nor bald.

Indeed, once one recognizes this, one might recognize a multitude of possible *kinds* of hairiness, corresponding to different degrees of hairiness. Moreover, one might have finer- or coarser-grained distinctions between different kinds of hairiness, and these may or may not track different proportions of the hairiness spectrum. So, for example, for certain purposes one might distinguish between three different kinds of hairiness: the "quite" hairy, the neither "quite" hairy nor "quite" bald, and the "quite" bald. Perhaps each kind might represent an equal proportion of the hairiness spectrum, one-third. Alternatively, one might prefer to distinguish between the "really" hairy and the "really" bald, corresponding, say, to the top and bottom 15 percent of positions along the hairiness spectrum, and just regard the other 70 percent as falling within the category "moderately" hairy/bald. Or perhaps one has a broader category for the "really" hairy, including the top 20 percent in terms of hairiness, a narrower category for the "really" bald, including only the bottom 5 percent in terms of hairiness, and just regards the intervening 75 percent as "moderately" hairy/bald. Kinds of hairiness, so understood, do not correspond to natural kinds, and there may be as many different kinds of hairiness as there may be different purposes for making finer or coarser distinctions along the hairiness spectrum.

I have been discussing different ways in which one might divide the hairiness spectrum into three "kinds" of hairiness. But, of course, there is nothing special about the number three, or the particular divisions suggested. For certain purposes it might be particularly plausible and suitable to employ a relatively fine-grained set of distinctions, distinguishing between people who are extremely hairy, very hairy, quite hairy, moderately hairy, slightly hairy, barely hairy, barely bald, slightly bald, moderately bald, quite bald, very bald, and extremely bald. Similarly, for other purposes it might be appropriate and sufficient to employ a relatively coarse-grained set of distinctions—that is still much finer grained than any simple three-kind partition—distinguishing between people who are very hairy, moderately hairy, barely hairy, barely bald, moderately bald, and very bald. For simplicity, let us assume that people who are very hairy according to the coarser-grained analysis will include all and only those who are very hairy or extremely hairy according to the finer-grained analysis, and that there are similar correlations between the other kinds of hairiness distinguished by the coarser- and finer-grained analyses. Note, on the kind of view currently under consideration, there *will* be various precise points along the hairiness spectrum—even if we cannot identify them—where having one less hair would determine what kind of hairiness one possessed. So, for example, at a precise point, one less hair would make the difference between being extremely hairy and very hairy on the finer-grained approach, and similarly, at some other precise point one less hair would make the difference between being very hairy and moderately hairy on the coarse-grained approach. Note, given our simplifying assumption, the single hair whose loss would account for a change in kind from "very" hairy to "quite" hairy, according to the finer-grained division of hairiness, would account for a change in kind from "very" hairy to "moderately" hairy, according to the coarser-grained division of hairiness.

Return now to the case of pain. Analogous considerations to those just presented will apply to the pain spectrum. We may believe that intense torture involves a significantly different kind of pain than that of a mosquito bite, and hence that one extra mosquito bite per month for any number of years would be better than two years of intense torture. We may further accept that there must be a precise point along the pain spectrum such that the slightest decrease in intensity of pain would transform one from being in the kind of pain that intense torture produces to another kind of pain. But there is *no* reason to believe, and every reason to *disbelieve*, that there is a precise point at which the slightest decrease in intensity of pain would transform one from being in the kind of pain that intense torture produces to the kind of pain that one extra mosquito bite per month produces. Minimally, one should recognize that the pain spectrum can be divided into at least three different kinds, such that at one end of the spectrum pains are extremely intense, at the other end they are extremely mild, and in between they are neither extremely intense nor extremely mild.

Indeed, as with hairiness, for different purposes one might plausibly and appropriately distinguish between numerous different kinds of pains. A fairly fine-grained set of distinctions might divide the pain spectrum along the following lines: extremely intense, very intense, quite intense, moderately intense, slightly intense, barely intense, barely mild, slightly mild, moderately mild, quite mild, very mild, and extremely mild. Alternatively, a coarser-grained set of distinctions might distinguish only half as many kinds of pains: very intense, moderately intense, barely intense, barely mild, moderately mild, and very mild. As earlier, for simplicity, let us suppose a correlation between the finer- and coarser-grained distinctions, such that each kind of pain that is distinguished on the coarser-grained analysis encompasses two and only two of the kinds of pain that are distinguished on the finer-grained analysis. So, for example, the kind of pain that is recognized as very intense on the coarse-grained analysis will include both the kind of pain that is recognized as extremely intense and the kind of pain that is recognized as very intense on the fine-grained analysis. Also, for simplicity, let us further suppose that for each set of distinctions each kind recognized represents an equal proportion of the pain spectrum. So, on the finer-grained analysis, which divides the pain spectrum into twelve kinds of equal "bandwidth," the top 8.33 percent of pains in terms of their intensity will be "extremely" intense, the next 8.33 percent will be "very" intense, and so on. Similarly, on the coarser-grained analysis, which divides the pain spectrum into six different kinds, the top 16.66 percent of pains in terms of their intensity will be "very" intense, the next 16.66 percent will be "moderately" intense, and so on.[7]

Next, let us arbitrarily suppose that there are 600 evenly spaced gradations of pain intensity, so that the mildest possible pain gets a score of 1, and the most intense possible pain gets a score of 600. Then we can suppose that there will be 50 even gradations of pain within each of the twelve kinds of pain distinguished by the fine-grained analysis, and 100 even gradations of pain within each of the six kinds of pain distinguished by the coarse-grained analysis. Finally, we assume that the pain of intense torture is near one end of the pain spectrum, and the pain of a mosquito bite near the other. Specifically, let us arbitrarily assume that the pain of intense torture is 597, and that of a mosquito bite is, as before, 3.

In light of the foregoing, we are now in a position to respond to the argument offered earlier against my Pain Spectrum Argument.

First, invoking the fine-grained analysis offered earlier, we could plausibly claim that the kind of pain produced by intense torture is "extremely" intense, while that produced by a mosquito bite is "extremely" mild. Second, in accordance with chapter 5's View Three, we believe that, given the mild discomfort of a mosquito bite and the extreme pain of intense torture, other things equal, no matter *how* long one lived, a life containing *one* extra mosquito bite per month (from fifteen to sixteen) for the duration of one's life would be better than a life containing two (consecutive) years of excruciating torture and fifteen mosquito bites per month. But, of course, our current opponent isn't disputing chapter 5's View Three; he is disputing chapter 5's View One, the view that for any unpleasant or "negative" experience, no matter what its intensity and duration, it would be better to have that experience than one that was only a "little" less intense but twice (or three or five times) as long.

But how, exactly, was our opponent's objection supposed to work? We readily grant, at least for the sake of argument, that if the pain of a mosquito bite really *is* of a different kind than the pain of intense torture, then there must be some *first* point along the pain continuum, call it $P_{(k-1)}$, where $P_{(k-1)}$'s pain would be only a "little" less intense than that of its nearby point, P_k, and where P_k would be the same kind of pain as intense torture, while $P_{(k-1)}$ would be a *different* kind of pain than intense torture. But that, surely, is not enough to get

---

[7] Strictly speaking, for this model to work one has to assume both an upper and a lower limit to how intense a pain could be. So, here, and elsewhere, I shall make the simplifying assumption that for beings with our psychologies, there are both upper and lower limits to the intensities of pain that we are capable of distinguishing experientially. This assumption may not be true, but it doesn't affect the substance of my claims, just the ease of presentation.

our opponent what he needs. For our opponent's argument to work, he needs the difference between P_k and $P_{(k-1)}$'s pain to be *akin to the difference between the pain of intense torture and the pain of a mosquito bite*. If there *were* such a difference, then, indeed, we would agree that View Three applied to the two "nearby" pains P_k and $P_{(k-1)}$; correspondingly, we would reject View One, and the threat to the transitivity of "better than" would evaporate.

But there is *not* such a difference. Using the fine-grained scale of pains suggested earlier, P_k will be the same *kind* of pain as intense torture; specifically, it will have an intensity of 551, and hence be the first of the pains that count as an "extremely" intense pain in the range from 551 to 600. But $P_{(k-1)}$ is decidedly *not* the same kind of pain as a mosquito bite! To the contrary, on the scale of pains currently employed, $P_{(k-1)}$ will have an intensity of 550, and hence be the *most* intense of the pains that count as a "very" intense pain in the range from 501 to 550. Such a pain is *very* painful and *vastly* worse than the kind of "extremely" mild pain of a mosquito bite. Indeed, if it were only a *little* worse it would have an intensity of 551 and be the same *kind* of pain as intense torture!

P_k is more like intense torture than $P_{(k-1)}$ is. And $P_{(k-1)}$ is more like a mosquito bite than P_k is. But this doesn't mean that the criterion appropriate for comparing alternatives involving P_k with alternatives involving $P_{(k-1)}$ should be the same as the criterion for comparing alternatives involving intense torture with alternatives involving mosquito bites. In fact, P_k and $P_{(k-1)}$ are much more like each other than either of them is like P_{597} or P_3. View Three is the right criterion for comparing P_{597}-type alternatives with P_3-type alternatives. But it is the wrong criterion for comparing P_k-type alternatives with $P_{(k-1)}$-type alternatives.

Presumably, my opponent grants that View One might be appropriate for comparing alternatives of the *same* kind. So, we allow trade-offs between intensity and duration among any two pains that are both "extremely" painful, or both "extremely" mild. For example, View One would be plausible when comparing alternatives involving intense torture—pains of intensity 597—with alternatives involving P_k—pains of intensity 551. But clearly the difference in intensity between P_k (551) and $P_{(k-1)}$ (550), namely, 1, is much smaller than the difference in intensity between intense torture P_{597} (597) and P_k (551), namely, 46. Given this (and, we might add, given that it is fairly clear that it is merely a matter of convention whether or not P_k and $P_{(k-1)}$ happen to be classified as the same, or different, kinds of pain), and given the vast difference in kind and intensity between $P_{(k-1)}$ and mosquito bites ("very" intense 550 versus "extremely" mild 3), it seems ludicrous to suppose that we should employ View Three rather than View One in comparing alternatives involving P_k and $P_{(k-1)}$.

As noted previously, in explaining how transitivity might fail, or fail to apply, across different alternatives involving the pain spectrum, I once observed that tiny differences in degree can, if added together, amount to a difference in kind, and that we shouldn't expect the same factors that are relevant and significant for comparing alternatives that differ merely in degree to be relevant and significant for comparing alternatives that differed in kind. And, of course, I argued that if different factors are relevant and significant for comparing different alternatives, then we shouldn't expect transitivity to hold, or apply, across those alternatives.

I thought my remark about the relation between degrees and kinds helped illuminate what was going on in my spectrum cases, and I still do. But the preceding discussion suggests that my remark may have also been seriously misleading. The crucial question is *not* whether two alternatives are of the same, or different kind, but whether the two alternatives are "sufficiently" similar or "sufficiently" dissimilar. Sometimes tiny differences in degree—if enough of them are taken together—amount to a difference in kind that is relevantly significant, and sometimes they do not. Likewise, sometimes a difference in kind may be relevantly significant, and sometimes not.

Although, by hypothesis, the tiny difference in degree between P_k and $P_{(k-1)}$ amounts to a difference in kind—in our example, between being an "extremely" intense pain and "merely" a "very" intense pain, in fact, the relation between P_k and $P_{(k-1)}$ is not relevantly different than the relation between P_m and $P_{(m-1)}$ for any m. Correspondingly, just as View One is appropriate for comparing any two alternatives P_m and $P_{(m-1)}$ if they are the *same* kind of pain, so it is appropriate for comparing any two alternatives P_m and $P_{(m-1)}$ if they "happen" to be *different* kinds of pains. The crucial point is that the *relevant* relations for comparing P_m with $P_{(m-1)}$ are the same, whether or not they happen to be pains of the same kind. Accordingly, the same criterion is relevant for comparing P_m with $P_{(m-1)}$, for any m, namely View One.[8]

Similarly, what *ultimately* matters in comparing intense torture with mosquito bites is not whether they are, in some sense, the same or different in

---

[8] In chapter 5, I granted, for the sake of argument, that View One may not actually apply across the *full* pain spectrum. Perhaps it fails to apply, for different reasons, at the *very* extremes of the pain spectrum. Still, I contended that there will be a spectrum of pains, sufficient for my purposes, ranging from very horrendous pains at one end, to very mild pains at the other, such that for all pains, P_m and $P_{(m-1)}$, that are members of *that* (slightly truncated) spectrum, View One applies for comparing them. In the discussion here, I am simply ignoring this complication for ease of presentation.

It might be argued that if there could be radical breaks between adjacent alternatives at the very ends of the pain continuum, there could also be radical breaks at other points along the continuum. Perhaps, but it seems to me that the considerations that might move one to grant the possibility of such breaks at the extreme ends of the spectrum simply don't apply elsewhere along the continuum. For example, the thought that a slight increase in pain intensity might cause a disintegration of the self *might* be plausible at the most intense end of the spectrum, but will not be plausible for lesser levels of pain. Likewise, the thought that if a pain is slight enough, it just won't matter whether it is reduced at all, or how long it lasts, *might* be plausible for a few pains at the *least* intense end of the spectrum, but won't be plausible for pains with intensities of any significance.

The challenge for my opponent is to come up with an area toward the middle of the pain spectrum where it is plausible to believe that there is a break of the kind needed for his argument. I have yet to see a concrete suggestion of this sort that people find remotely plausible. Instead, I mainly see the assertion, as a matter of theoretical faith and commitment, that there *must* be such a point, because otherwise we face the (impossible!) failure of the transitivity of "all things considered better than" (in my wide reason-implying sense).

kind. Presumably there are *some* categories according to which they will count as *different* kinds—as, for example, when intense torture counts as being of the kind "extremely" intense and mosquito bites count as being of the kind "extremely" mild—while there are *other* categories where they will count as being of the *same* kind—as, for example, they would both count as being of the kind "unpleasant experience," or "experience there is reason to avoid." Clearly, what *really* matters here is that the intensity of the pain of torture is *so* different from that of mosquito bites that it seems appropriate to employ different criteria when comparing alternatives involving such diverse pains, from those that are appropriate for comparing alternatives involving pains of "sufficiently" similar intensities.

In sum, though it may have helped illuminate how it could be the case that different factors could be relevant and significant for comparing different alternatives, the issue of different *kinds* is a red herring, and I ought not to have put some of my earlier discussions in those terms. The point is simply that when the difference between two pains is "sufficiently" great, View Three is appropriate for comparing them, whereas when the difference between two pains is "sufficiently" small, View One is appropriate.[9]

It may seem that I have been unfair to my opponent. After all, my opponent needn't insist on the implausible claim that there must be a precise point where a tiny difference in degree would suddenly transform a situation from one involving a kind of pain like that of intense torture into one involving a kind of pain like that of a mosquito bite. All my opponent needs for his argument is that there must be a precise point where a tiny difference in degree makes the difference between whether trade-offs between quality and duration are, or are not, permissible. So, to take our earlier scale between 1 and 600, where the pain of torture is 597 and that of a mosquito bite 3, our opponent might claim the following. There must be a precise point, P_k, where P_k represents a pain of intensity k, such that trade-offs regarding intensity and duration are permissible between P_{597} and P_k (here, and in what follows, I omit the more cumbersome locution "alternatives involving P_{597} and alternatives involving P_k," but I trust my meaning is plain enough), but not permissible between P_{597} and $P_{(k-1)}$. Likewise, my opponent might add, there must be some point g, such that trade-offs are impermissible between P_{597} and P_g, but not impermissible between P_{597} and $P_{(g-1)}$. Acknowledging the preceding discussion, my opponent might add that P_k and P_g may be different points, and that being "not permissible" is not the same as being *impermissible*, and likewise that being "not impermissible" is not the same as being *permissible*. Hence, my opponent might admit that for pains from P_g through P_k, trade-offs in terms of quality and duration with P_{597} are neither permissible nor impermissible. But the key

---

[9] I am grateful to Dan Hausman for a conversation that convinced me that it was misleading to emphasize the fact that tiny differences in degree could amount to a difference in kind, in explaining why transitivity may fail, or fail to apply, across certain spectrums.

point is that my opponent can insist that it is enough to undermine my challenge to transitivity if one can show that there is at least one "break" in the continuum between P_{597} and P_3, such that View One is appropriate for comparing alternatives on one side of the break but not across the break.

I readily grant most of the preceding points. But my earlier arguments against my opponent are just as telling against this revised version of his argument. Even more so. *If* one could plausibly maintain that there must be a break in the continuum between P_{597} and P_3 such that on one side of the break the pain would be like that of intense torture, while on the other side it would be like that of a mosquito bite, then it is obvious that any advocate of View Three must reject the applicability of View One for at least one pair of "nearby" points along the pain spectrum. But if the revised argument simply amounts to the claim that there must be some point P_k, such that trade-offs are permitted between P_{597} and P_k, but not between P_{597} and $P_{(k-1)}$ (though the latter are not necessarily *im*permissible, either), then it is clear that the challenge to View One's scope is woefully inadequate.

In essence, View One tells us that for any two pains that are "sufficiently" close in intensity, it would be better to have the more intense one than the one that is only a "little" less intense, if the less intense one lasted much longer. But View One is not committed to the position that if trade-offs in intensity and duration are permissible between P_{597} and P_k, and $P_{(k-1)}$ is only a "little" less intense than P_k, then trade-offs must *also* be permissible between P_{597} and $P_{(k-1)}$. Such reasoning would be fallacious and should be rejected. After all, P_k may be the *last* pain whose intensity is "sufficiently" close to P_{597}'s that View One applies to them. In that case, no matter how close $P_{(k-1)}$'s intensity may be to P_k's, it may still be *too* much less intense than P_{597}'s—even if only barely—for View One to plausibly apply in comparing them. But all I need for my argument is the claim that View One is appropriate for comparing P_k and $P_{(k-1)}$, *not* the claim that it is appropriate for comparing P_{597} and $P_{(k-1)}$, and the former claim seems clearly true.

In sum, my opponent starts by noting that advocates of View Three must admit that there must be *some* point, P_k, such that while View One would be applicable for comparing P_{597} and P_k, it would not be applicable for comparing P_{597} and $P_{(k-1)}$. I grant this point, at least for the sake of argument. But for my opponent's argument to work, he needs to insist that this entails that the break between P_k and $P_{(k-1)}$ is so sharp and significant that View One is not applicable for comparing *them* either. But I see *no* reason to accept this claim, and every reason to reject it. View One *is* plausible and relevant for comparing all pains whose intensities are "sufficiently" close. We can, if we like, let the gap in intensity between P_k and $P_{(k-1)}$ be as small as we like. A fortiori, the gap between P_k and $P_{(k-1)}$ will be sufficiently close for View One to be plausible and relevant in comparing them. This is true *even if* the gap between P_{597} and $P_{(k-1)}$ is *not* sufficiently close for View One to be plausible in comparing alternatives involving pains of *those* intensities. That point is simply *irrelevant* to the plausibility and applicability of View One for comparing alternatives involving pains that are "sufficiently" close in intensity.

Consider the following analogy. Imagine a long, straight line of adjacent houses, A through N, such that John lives in A and Mary lives in N. I may believe that neighbors should be friendly with each other, but not believe that John must be friendly with Mary. This commits me to the view that John and Mary are not neighbors, and hence commits me to the view that there must be some house, between A and N, which counts as the last house that is still in John's neighborhood.[10] Let us assume that house is K, so that the first house that is not in John's neighborhood is L. Given my views, I would be committed to claiming that the people in K should be friendly with John, but not committed to the view that the people in L must be. But this does *not* mean that the "break" between K and L must be so sharp and significant that I deny that the people in K should be friendly with those in L. I can retain my view that neighbors should be friendly, and *rightly* recognize that this applies to the people in K and L. After all, the people in K and L *are* neighbors, even if those in A and L are not. Patently, the fact that the people in A and K are neighbors, but those in A and L are not, does not entail that the people in K and L are not neighbors. A fortiori, a principle that applies to all neighbors would have implications for how the people in A and K must treat each other, and also have implications for how the people in K and L must treat each other, even if it does not have implications for how the people in A and L must treat each other.

Likewise, my View One applies to "neighbors" along the pain spectrum. And the fact that P_{597} and P_k are "neighbors," but P_{597} and $P_{(k-1)}$ are not "neighbors," does not entail that P_k and $P_{(k-1)}$ are not "neighbors." A fortiori, a principle may plausibly apply to all neighbors along the spectrum, and hence apply to P_m and $P_{(m-1)}$ for any m, even if it doesn't apply to any two alternatives across the spectrum, and in particular doesn't apply for comparing P_{597} (intense torture) with P_3 (mosquito bites), or, more generally, for some P_k, doesn't apply for comparing P_{597} with $P_{(k-1)}$ through P_3. View One is just such a principle for the pain spectrum.

Of course, nobody believes that the relation "being the neighbor of" is transitive, while most have thought that the relation "all things considered better than" must be transitive; so the fallacy I have been pointing out in my opponent's argument is more readily recognized and accepted in the one case than the other. But I submit that the reasoning is equally fallacious in both cases. The argument in question should be rejected.

In light of the foregoing, let me end this section as follows. The objection I have been considering would have us reject View One. It accepts the plausibility of View Three, but insists that if, indeed, torture's pain is sufficiently different than a mosquito bite's that no amount of the latter would be worse than the former, then there *must* be some pain whose intensity lies between that of torture and that of a mosquito bite, such that it would be *worse* to have a pain of that intensity for some duration, than to have a pain that was only *a little less intense* for twice (or three, or five times)

---

[10] Recall that I am granting that I would be committed to this position for the sake of my opponent's argument. Depending on one's views about vagueness, one might deny this claim.

as long. I find this *deeply* implausible. And I am hardly alone. Faced with the prospect of experiencing pains whose intensities differ only slightly, people *rightly* want to know how *long* they will last. Given *such* alternatives, duration clearly matters. If the slightly less intense pain will last *twice* or *three* or *five* times as long, we want the shorter, more intense pain. Moreover, we want it because it is the better alternative, all things considered. Thus, I reject the objection. Perhaps it is a mistake to accept View Three, but View One retains its deep plausibility.

9.2 Sorites Paradoxes

Many are dubious of my arguments because they think that they are variations of the *Standard Sorites Paradox*: a much-discussed and rightly rejected form of argument which also appeals to spectrums. In this section, I briefly detail the purported analogy between my arguments and the Standard Sorites Paradoxes. I then show that the analogy fails, by pointing out some crucial differences between the two arguments. I then consider the claim that some Standard Sorites Paradoxes might be *revised* so as to make them genuinely analogous to my argument. I suggest that if this claim is correct, such *Revised Sorites Paradoxes* would be importantly distinct from the Standard Sorites Paradoxes and would raise the same deep and puzzling issues with which this book is consumed.

9.2.1 THE PURPORTED ANALOGY

Among the most famous examples of the Standard Sorites Paradox are those purporting to show that heaps of sand are the same as grains, or that hairiness is the same as baldness. Notoriously, these are ingenious but unsound arguments for obviously false conclusions, and they are universally, and rightly, rejected. However, there is dispute as to exactly *how* the arguments go astray, and this helps account for the persistent air of paradox surrounding these arguments.

Let us focus on one example, the argument purportedly showing that someone can be both hairy and bald at the same time. Intuitively, the key premise in the argument is that one hair, more or less, will not make a difference to whether or not one is hairy or bald. Call this the *Crucial Premise* of the standard Hairiness/Baldness Sorites Paradox, or *CP* for short. One then considers a spectrum of cases where someone is extremely hairy on one end and bald on the other. The thought is that if a person starts at the extremely hairy end of the spectrum, and you take away a *single* hair, then, in accordance with *CP*, the person will *still* be hairy. This seems undeniably true. But then this thought is iterated. If the person *is* still hairy after removing a single hair, then, in accordance with *CP*, he will *still* be hairy after another hair is removed. And so on. As one iterates, one steadily moves along the spectrum of hairiness until one eventually ends up with someone who is clearly bald. The key, of course, is that one moves from one end of the spectrum to the other via a series of short steps, where one continually applies *CP* to adjacent members of the spectrum. And *CP seems* obviously true. But, of course, iterated applications of *CP* seem to lead to the conclusion that someone who is bald is also hairy. And that is obviously false. Hence the argument should be rejected.

This argument may *seem* analogous to my Spectrum Arguments. Take, for example, the pain spectrum. We have the thought that for each pair of adjacent members of the pain spectrum, the slightly less intense pain seems worse than the slightly more intense one, if it lasts two, or three, or five times as long. Call this the Pain Argument's *Important Additive-Aggregationist Premise*, or *IAAP*, for short. Like *CP*, *IAAP* seems obviously true. But like *CP*, *IAAP* seems to lead to an absurd conclusion. In particular, iterated across the pain spectrum via a series of short steps, *IAAP* seems to lead to the conclusion that a long life containing one extra mosquito bite a month could be worse than a long life containing two years of torture, given transitivity. But this conclusion seems obviously false. So, it may be concluded, in each case something has clearly gone awry, and it may be *assumed* that the *same* thing has gone awry in my argument as in the standard Hairiness/Baldness Sorites Paradox. Hence, it may be assumed that both arguments can be readily rejected, and presumably for the same reason—whatever that reason may turn out to be! (I say this because, as implied earlier, the best explanation for *why* the Standard Sorites Paradox fails remains in dispute, even if there is no dispute that it does, obviously, fail, since baldness is *not* the same as hairiness.)

9.2.2 DISANALOGIES

There is, in fact, an important difference between my argument and a Standard Sorites Paradox. Because of such factors as the vagueness, elasticity, and context relativity of our notion of hairiness, ordinary usage permits us to say that if someone is hairy, and you simply remove one hair from his head, he will *still* be hairy. As noted, the Standard Sorites Paradox trades on this fact in generating its absurd conclusion. But the Standard Sorites Paradox does *not* claim that if someone is hairy, and you remove a single hair from his head, he will then be clearly *hairier* than before. In particular, the Standard Sorites Paradox argues that the person starts out hairy and then *remains* hairy throughout the steady removal of one hair at a time, though at the end he has become bald. For the argument to parallel mine, it would have to be arguing that the person is clearly getting hairier with *each* hair removal, though at the end he has become much *less* hairy than he was initially.

My argument claims that as one moves along the pain spectrum, each "nearby" pain is clearly *worse* than the preceding one, as it is only a *little* less intense, yet persists *much* longer. So I *am* in the position of arguing that with each step the situation is clearly getting *worse* than the preceding one, though the end situation is clearly *better* than the initial one! The Standard Sorites Paradox, as normally presented, makes no such claims. And for good reason. It is plausible to think that, other things equal, one less hair will not turn a person who is hairy into someone who is

Spectrum Arguments: Objections and Replies   279

not hairy, but there is *no* plausibility to the claim that, other things equal, one *less* hair will turn someone who is hairy into someone who is *clearly hairier*![11]

The Standard Sorites Paradox *turns* on the vagueness and elasticity of the concept of "hairiness," a vagueness that *permits* the claim that one hair, more or less, will not make the difference between whether someone is hairy or not, but which decidedly does *not permit* the claim that *removing* a hair from someone's head will render him *clearly hairier*. *Without* vagueness, there *would be* a precise point along the spectrum of hairiness where one less hair would make the difference between whether someone was hairy or not, and the Crucial Premise underlying the Standard Sorites Paradox regarding hairiness would be rejected. Although the notion of pain is *also* vague and elastic, my Pain Spectrum Argument in no way *turns* on this vagueness. If, counterfactually, we could measure the intensity of pains precisely, so that we could say, definitively, *exactly* how much less intense one pain was than another, and we knew exactly how long different pains might last, this would not affect my argument. The crucial premise underlying my argument would remain just as plausible as before, as we would still readily hold that it would be worse to have a pain that was less intense than another by some precisely small amount if it lasted two or three or five times as long.

One way of illuminating the difference between my Spectrum Arguments and those involving a Standard Sorites Paradox is to compare two cases that might represent what we actually think is going on in the two arguments. Consider, for example, diagram 9.2.2.A.

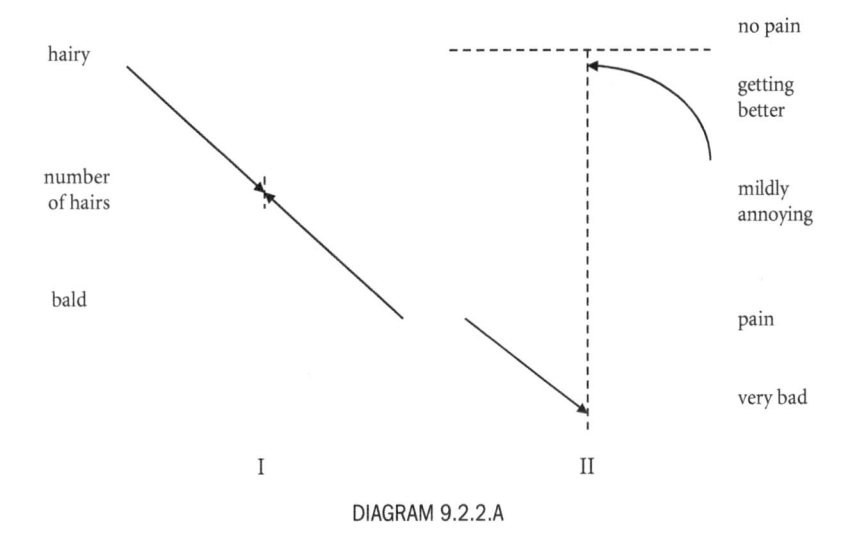

DIAGRAM 9.2.2.A

---

[11] I am indebted to Stuart Rachels for this point. In my original article on intransitivity, "Intransitivity and the Mere Addition Paradox," *Philosophy and Public Affairs* 16 (1987): 138–87, I noted how we could have sequences that were seemingly getting *better and better*, but whose last member was clearly worse than the first. But it is Rachels who first emphasized, in correspondence, that this is a feature that clearly distinguishes our Spectrum Arguments from Standard Sorites Paradoxes.

Case *I* represents what we think is going on in a standard Hairiness/Baldness Sorites Paradox. The top arrow, pointing downward, represents one progression. Starting at the top left point, someone has a full head of hair, say, 300,000 hairs, and the downward direction of the arrow indicates what we think will actually happen as we remove more and more hairs, one at a time, namely, that he will have fewer and fewer hairs! Similarly, starting at the bottom right point, someone is bald, having, say, only a *single* hair, and the upward direction of the arrow indicates what we think will actually happen as we add more and more hairs, one at a time, namely, that he will have more and more hairs! The tip of the point of the top arrow represents how many hairs a person would have after 149,999 hairs had been removed, one at a time—by hypothesis, 150,001. Similarly, the tip of the point of the bottom arrow represents how many hairs a person would have after 149,999 hairs had been added, one at a time—by hypothesis, 150,000.

According to the Standard Sorites Paradox, from the fact that the person with 300,000 hairs is hairy, we can infer, via iterations of the Crucial Premise of the Paradox, *CP*, that the person represented by the tip of the downward arrow is *also* hairy. Similarly, from the fact that the person with one hair is bald, we can infer, via iterations of *CP*, that the person represented by the tip of the upward arrow is *also* bald. This makes it the case that by removing just a *single* hair from someone at the tip of the downward arrow he would *suddenly* go from being hairy to being bald, or, seemingly even worse, he would then be *both* hairy *and* bald. This is, indeed, a puzzle!

But notice, as we look at case *I* and what it represents, there is *no* puzzle in our understanding of how it could be the case that with the removal of a *single* hair one could "suddenly" jump from a position on the downward arrow (an arrow supposedly representing hairiness) to a position on the upward arrow (an arrow supposedly representing baldness). This is because in fact there is *no sharp discontinuity* between the two arrows at the point where they meet. Hence, there is hardly any "jump" involved at all!

We easily and naturally recognize the downward arrow as representing not merely whether one is hairy, but the *degree* to which one is hairy, and we see that as one moves farther and farther down the arrow, one is *in fact* becoming *less and less* hairy. Similarly, we easily and naturally recognize the upward arrow as representing not merely whether one is bald, but the *degree* to which one is bald, and we see that as one moves farther and farther up the arrow, one is *in fact* becoming *less and less* bald. Therefore, it is *no* surprise to us that the two arrows meet in the middle, and that a *single* hair can make the difference between whether one is on the "hairy" arrow or the "bald" arrow. The difference between the "least hairy" person on the "hairy" arrow and the "least bald" person on the "bald" arrow is in fact *one* hair. It is, by hypothesis, the difference between having 150,001 hairs and having 150,000 hairs.

Of course, the downward arrow can be extended all the way down to the lowest right point, and the upward arrow can be extended all the way up to the highest left point. And this seemingly licenses the paradoxical conclusion that among those whose number of hairs range from 300,000 to 1, even the hairiest person (who is clearly hairy!) is bald, and even the baldest person (who is clearly bald!) is hairy. But as puzzling as this is, we know that the puzzle clearly revolves around questions of vagueness. As case *I* illustrates, fully extended, the two arrows would completely overlap, as there is a single spectrum representing how *many* hairs someone has, with no sharp discontinuities along the spectrum. Given this, there is no puzzle about how one could move from any one point on the spectrum to any other, via a series of small steps involving nothing but the addition or subtraction of one hair at a time.

Next, consider case *II* of diagram 9.2.2.A. Case *II* represents what we think is going on in one of my pain spectrums. The top left point of the bottom arrow represents our judgment about the badness of the pain of two years of intense torture—we think such a pain is very bad. The downward direction of the bottom arrow indicates what we think will happen to the badness of a pain if we make it only a *little* less intense, but *much* longer—we think it will get worse. The bottom right point of the top arrow represents our judgment about the badness of the pain of one extra mosquito bite a month for the duration of a very long life. Most of us think such a pain would be only mildly annoying, and I have labeled the diagram to reflect this. But the *key* point, for my present purposes, is not our *absolute* judgments of the two starting points of B's arrows—namely, that two years of intense torture would be "very bad," while one extra mosquito bite a month would be only "mildly annoying"—but rather our *relative* judgment about those starting points. The point representing the badness of the pain of one extra mosquito bite per month is located "higher" in the diagram than the point representing two years of intense torture, to reflect our considered judgment that the former pain is *much better* than the latter. The upward direction of the top arrow indicates what we think will happen to the badness of a pain if we make it only a *little* more intense, but *much* shorter—we think it will get *better*. Finally, I have curved the upward arrow to reflect the judgment that, as a series of pains gets better and better, it will asymptotically approach the "no pain" level.[12]

Let us suppose that it takes $2n + 1$ steps to move from a situation involving two years of intense torture to many years of one extra mosquito bite per month, where each step involves making the previous pain only a "little" less intense, but having it last two, or three, or five times as long, and similarly, that it takes $2n + 1$ steps to move from a situation involving many years of one extra mosquito bite per month to two years of intense torture, where each step involves making the previous pain only a "little" more intense, but having it last only half, or a third, or a fifth as long Then the tip of the point on the bottom arrow represents how bad

---

[12] Since it is a series of *pains*, none of its members are *pleasures*; hence it will never cross the "no-pain" threshold. However, a series of pains may reach the no-pain threshold *at the limit*.

the pain would be after *n* steps, starting with the pain of two years of intense torture and moving toward the pain of many years of one extra mosquito bite per month; and the tip of the point of the top arrow represents how bad the pain would be after *n* steps, starting with the pain of many years of one extra mosquito bite per month and moving toward the pain of two years of intense torture. By hypothesis, only *one* step separates the tips of the two arrows, but *unlike* in case *I*, there is a *huge* puzzle as to how, with but *one* more step in either direction, one could *suddenly jump* from a position on the bottom arrow to a position on the top arrow, or vice versa. The problem, of course, is that there is a *sharp discontinuity* between the two arrows representing what we believe about the pain spectrum, whereas there is *no* sharp discontinuity between the two arrows representing what we believe about the hairiness spectrum. Indeed, as noted previously, if one extended the two arrows in case *I*, they would *completely* overlap, whereas if one extended the two arrows in case *II*, there would be *no* overlap between them. Accordingly, though we know (or at least assume in our arguments) that there is a single pain spectrum, there is a *deep* puzzle as to how one could move from any point on the bottom arrow to any point on the top arrow (or vice versa), via a series of small steps each of which involves lessening (or increasing) a pain's intensity by a little, while greatly increasing (or decreasing) the pain's duration by a lot. Indeed, looking at case *II*, it seems clear that it should be *impossible* to do this!

This last point is worth special emphasis. Looking at case *II*, one might think that there is a sharp discontinuity between the two pains represented by the tip of the bottom arrow and the tip of the top arrow. However, the fact that the discontinuity appears there is just an artifact of the diagram. If we lengthened the bottom arrow and shortened the top arrow proportionally, or vice versa, the discontinuity would appear to obtain between *any* two points along the pain spectrum corresponding to the tips of the altered arrows. But, importantly, as I have noted previously, most of us *don't* believe that there is a discontinuity between any two points along the pain spectrum. Bearing this in mind, and imagining the top and bottom arrows "extended" so that all of the points along the relevant pain spectrum are represented by each arrow, we see that our actual beliefs about the pain spectrum are clearly inconsistent or incompatible. Moreover, looking at cases *I* and *II*, we see that our actual beliefs about what is going on in the standard Hairiness/Baldness Sorites Paradox are *very* different than our actual beliefs about what is going on regarding the pain spectrum.

In diagram 9.2.2.A, case *I* reminds us that it isn't really a puzzle that as we remove one hair at a time from someone who is hairy, he or she eventually becomes bald. However, case *II* reminds us that it really is a *deep* puzzle how a sequence of pains could start out very bad and eventually end up much better, if each member of the sequence was *worse* than the preceding one. As noted previously, and as is widely recognized, the standard Hairiness/Baldness Sorites Paradox revolves around the vagueness of the terms "hairiness" and "bald," which (seemingly) licenses the claim that *one* hair, more or less, won't make a difference to whether or not one is hairy or bald. But, as I have shown, my argument about the pain spectrum revolves around the fact that we use additive-aggregationist reasoning for comparing points that are "near" each other on the spectrum, but anti-additive-aggregationist reasoning for comparing points that are "far apart" on the pain spectrum. Both the Standard Sorites Paradox and my arguments about the pain spectrum raise problems of consistency, but they are distinct problems with different roots and different implications. My argument challenges the transitivity of the "all-things-considered better than" relation (in my wide reason-implying sense). The Standard Sorites Paradox does not.

Finally, it is worth noting that people's responses to the Pain Spectrum Argument are often very different from people's responses to the Standard Sorites Paradox. This is important because, if the arguments were, in fact, analogous, one would expect people's responses to them to also be analogous. Faced with an argument purporting to show that a sufficiently long life containing one extra mosquito bite per month for the duration of the life is worse than a life that contains two years of excruciating torture rather than the extra mosquito bites, some people have argued that we should *accept* the relative ranking in question, however unintuitive it may seem. In particular, as we saw in chapter 5, some people have claimed that while two years of torture would be very bad, countless years of one extra mosquito bite would be even worse, while others have claimed that while many years of one extra mosquito bite per month wouldn't be bad, neither would two years of torture in a sufficiently long life. But in the Standard Sorites Paradox, *no one* claims that we should actually *accept* the relative ranking of the two ends of the hairiness spectrum, with some contending that everyone is bald, and others contending that everyone is hairy.

Let us expand on the preceding point.[13] In the Standard Sorites Paradox, *no one* is tempted to deny that someone with a full head of hair is hairy. Likewise, *no one* is tempted to hold that someone who has a bald head is hairy. Likewise, *no one* is tempted to deny that there could be a spectrum of heads ranging from the hairy to the bald, such that one could gradually move from one end of the spectrum to the other in a series of small and similar-sized steps, namely, steps that involve the removal or addition of a single hair. Rather, virtually *everyone* agrees that there must be *something* wrong with the Crucial Premise, CP, that one hair, more or less, will not make a difference to whether or not one is hairy or bald, even if it is not clear *where* that premise goes wrong or how it, or the Sorites Paradox, could be mistaken.

In my argument, on the other hand, there are *several* crucial premises, not just one, and there is absolutely *no* agreement about which premise should be given up. To be sure, *some* people are inclined to reject the Important Additive Aggregationist Premise, that a slightly less intense pain will be worse than a

---

[13] This paragraph and the following two are indebted to some remarks of Shelly Kagan's.

slightly more intense one, if it lasts two, or three, or five times as long—at least for *some* cases, even if they aren't sure exactly which cases those are. But, this is not the reaction of *most* people to my argument, let alone the reaction of virtually *everyone*. Indeed, I don't believe it is even the most *common* reaction to my argument. *Some* people are inclined to reject the claim that a really long life containing two years of torture would be worse than an equally long and otherwise similar life that was free of torture but contained one extra mosquito bite per month. Moreover, *some* people are inclined to reject the claim that "all-things-considered better than" (in my wide reason-implying sense) is a transitive relation. Finally, some people are inclined to reject the claim that there is a spectrum of pains ranging from the pain of intense torture to the pain of a mosquito bite, such that one could gradually move from one end of the spectrum to the other in a series of small and similar-sized steps; that is, some are inclined to insist that there *must* be sharp discontinuities along the pain spectrum of a sort that don't exist along the hairiness spectrum.

The fact that my argument generates so many different responses as to which of its premises must be mistaken, while the Standard Sorites Paradoxes do not, is further evidence that my argument really is very different than a Standard Sorites Paradox. Indeed, the fact that someone *could* rebut my argument, but *not* the Standard Sorites Paradox, by rejecting the assumption that "better than" is a transitive relation shows that the two arguments really *are* distinct. Why? Because it reflects the fact that the transitivity of "better than" is a *key* premise on which my argument *turns*, whereas it plays *no role at all* in the Standard Sorites Paradox.

I conclude that my Spectrum Arguments are not merely versions of the Standard Sorites Paradoxes.

9.2.3 NONNORMATIVE SPECTRUM ARGUMENTS

Ryan Wasserman has argued that many Standard Sorites Paradoxes could be revised, so that they had the same structure as my Spectrum Arguments.[14] Since my Spectrum Arguments have different premises, a different structure, and a different kind of conclusion than the Standard Sorites Paradox, I think there is good reason to claim that what he has actually shown us is not how to "revise" Sorites Paradoxes so that they have the same structure as my arguments, but, rather, how to *construct* Spectrum Arguments dealing with many of the same subjects—for example, hairiness or heaps—that Standard Sorites Paradoxes deal with.[15] I shall return to this point later; but however we ultimately choose to categorize or name Wasserman's arguments, what is important about them is that they show how Spectrum Argu-

---

[14] In an unpublished paper, "Paradoxes of Transitivity," December 2004.

[15] I am grateful to Shelly Kagan for suggesting that I emphasize this point, and the following one, right at the beginning of this section, rather than wait until after I presented Wasserman's arguments, as I originally did.

ments can seemingly be constructed for *nonnormative* as well as normative domains. Since my examples all involve normative domains, some moral skeptics may have assumed that they are just further evidence for the "oddness," "incoherence," or "unintelligibility" of normative claims, and hence for why one should be a skeptic about normativity. But, if Wasserman is right, my Spectrum Arguments provide no special comfort to skeptics about normativity, since they apply in nonnormative cases as well. Indeed, if Wasserman is right, *everyone* must come to terms with my Spectrum Arguments, whatever their views about normativity.

Consider, again, the Sorites Paradox regarding hairiness and baldness. Wasserman points out that *in fact*, our criterion for baldness is multidimensional. In determining whether or not someone is bald, we pay attention to several factors, including both the *number* of hairs on the head and the *distributional pattern* of the hairs. For example, there are several distinctive characteristic patterns of male baldness. One is something like a U-shaped pattern, where there are virtually no hairs running from the top of the forehead, over the top of the head, to the back of the head. Another is a roughly circular bald spot, which tends to center itself on the back of a man's head and spread out onto the top of the head, the sides of the head, and down toward the nape of the neck. If a man has a large enough area of U-shaped baldness on his head, or a large enough bald spot, we will say that he is bald, even if he has hair, and even quite a lot of hair, on the remainder of his head.

As suggested, then, there are several ways of being bald. One might have a prominent U-shaped patch of baldness, or a large circular bald spot, or one might simply have *so* few hairs that one is bald, even if one's hairs are distributed evenly over one's scalp. Of course, we might readily agree that someone who is *completely* bald is, in an important sense, *balder* than someone who is "merely" bald in one of these other ways. Still, it remains true that such people *are* bald, by criteria commonly accepted for what counts as being bald. Here, as elsewhere, meaning is use. People systematically *use* the term "bald" to refer to people with such patterns or distributions of hairs on their head, and hence what it *means* to be bald, and *is* to be bald, is (largely) dictated by such usage.

Let us focus on the person with the bald spot, and let us assume that anyone with a pronounced male bald spot (which we'll henceforth stipulate to involve a bald spot of six inches or more in diameter) counts as bald. This assumption resonates with the thought that those who hate the idea of being bald would dread having a six-inch-diameter bald spot, and that hair growth and toupee advertisers are pitching their products at such people, among others, when they proffer a solution to male baldness.

Wasserman then suggests the following. For any two heads of hair, the question of whether one is hairier than the other will depend on *two* factors: the *number* of hairs on the two heads, and the *pattern* or distribution of those hairs. But, the relation between these is not simple, and the two factors may be given different weights in different circumstances. In particular, Wasserman suggests that *if* two heads of hair are "sufficiently" similar in their *pattern* of hair distribution, then one head of hair will be hairier than the other if it has a "sufficiently" greater number of hairs. On the other hand, if two heads of hair have sufficiently dissimilar patterns of hair, and in particular, if the one head has an even distribution of hair, while the other has a pronounced male bald spot, then as long as the head with the even distribution has *enough* hair, it will be hairier than the head with the large bald spot, no matter *how* many hairs are in the areas around the bald spot (here, and in what follows, "even distribution" simply means "roughly evenly distributed over the top, sides, and back of the head"). Intuitively, the thought is that a head with "enough" hairs evenly distributed is hairy, a head with a large enough bald spot is bald, and a head that is hairy is hairier than a head that is bald!

The preceding claims should look familiar. They closely track the kinds of claims that I make in offering my various Spectrum Arguments. The idea is simply that for comparisons between certain pairs of heads both the *pattern* and the *number* of hairs will seem relevant in determining which head is hairier. Call this Wasserman's *Premise One*. This is like View One in my pain argument. But for comparisons between different pairs of heads—specifically, where one head has an even distribution, while the other has a pronounced bald spot—then as long as both have a "sufficiently" large number of hairs, the comparative hairiness of the heads turns *only* on their respective patterns of hair distribution, and not on the number of hairs on the two heads, so that the head with the even distribution will be hairier than the head with the pronounced bald spot. For symmetry, call this Wasserman's *Premise Three*, as it is like View Three in my pain argument. Premises One and Three can be stated, more precisely, as follows:

> *Premise One* (PO): For any two heads of hair, H_1 and H_2, whose number of hairs are n and j, respectively, if the *pattern* of hair distribution is "sufficiently" similar in H_1 and H_2, then H_1 will be hairier than H_2 if and only if n is "sufficiently" larger than j.

> *Premise Three* (PTh): For any two heads of hair, H_1 and H_2, if H_1 has a pronounced bald spot and H_2's hair is evenly distributed, then as long as H_2 has a "sufficiently" large number of hairs, H_2 will be hairier than H_1.

Note, it is important on *PTh* that the head with even distribution have "enough" hairs on its head, before the number of hairs is no longer relevant for the comparison in question. But this is just like my claim that it is important that intense torture last long "enough," before it would no longer matter how many extra months one might otherwise have to endure one extra mosquito bite. It was not my view that no number of extra months of one extra mosquito bite could be worse than a *nanosecond* of intense torture, or even, perhaps, a *second* of torture: only that it wouldn't be worse than *two years* of intense torture. Similarly, it needn't be Wasserman's view that a head with just a handful of hairs evenly distributed across its scalp will be hairier than a head with a pronounced bald spot surrounded by an incredibly thick mat of hair. In that case we may judge *both* heads bald, but acknowledge that the second is hairier than the first (just as one person may be faster or taller than a second, even though *both* are slow or short). It is simply that someone with "enough" evenly distributed hairs will be hairy, and someone with a large enough bald spot will be bald, and a hairy person is hairier than a bald person.

It should be clear how Wasserman's Premises One and Three would combine with a plausible empirical claim to generate a threat to the transitivity of "hairier than" analogous to my threats to the transitivity of "better than." Analogous to View Two of my pain argument, we can name and state the relevant empirical claim as follows:

Premise Two (PT): There is, or could be, a spectrum of heads ranging from one with a fairly large number of evenly distributed hairs, to one with a much larger number of hairs distributed in such a way that there was a pronounced bald spot, such that one could move from one end of the spectrum to the other, via a finite series of steps where each succeeding head would have "significantly" more hairs that were distributed only a "little" less evenly than the preceding one (so as to meet Premise One's relevant criteria for comparing heads, namely, that the *pattern* of distribution of hairs in the two heads is "sufficiently" similar, while the *number* of hairs is "sufficiently" larger in the succeeding head than in the preceding head).

The idea here should be familiar. Consider a spectrum of heads that meets the criteria of Premise Two. Let $Head_1$ be the first member of the spectrum which, by hypothesis, has a fairly large number of evenly distributed hairs. If there are "enough" such hairs, $Head_1$ will clearly be hairy. Now compare $Head_1$ with $Head_2$. Given Premise Two, $Head_2$ will have a pattern of distribution that is only a "little" less even than $Head_1$'s, but it will have "significantly" more hairs. Accordingly, Premise One will apply to the comparison and tell us that $Head_2$ is hairier than $Head_1$. Next compare $Head_3$ with $Head_2$. Once again, Premise Two tells us that the relationship between $Head_2$ and $Head_3$ is such that Premise One will be applicable for comparing them, and that $Head_3$ will be hairier than $Head_2$. Continue such pairwise comparisons across the spectrum. For every two "adjacent" heads along the spectrum, $Head_k$ and $Head_{(k+1)}$, Premise Two ensures that Premise One will be appropriate for comparing them and will yield the judgment that $Head_{(k+1)}$ is hairier than $Head_k$. So, if we suppose, for the sake of argument, that there are twenty-five heads in the spectrum, Premises One and Two will generate the judgments that $Head_2$ is hairier than $Head_1$, $Head_3$ is hairier than $Head_2$, $Head_4$ is hairier than $Head_3$, and so on, all the way to $Head_{25}$ is hairier than $Head_{24}$. It follows that if "hairier than" is a transitive relation, $Head_{25}$ must be hairier than $Head_1$.

But, according to Premise Two, there is a huge difference in the pattern of hair distribution between $Head_1$ and $Head_{25}$. In fact, $Head_{25}$ has a pronounced bald spot (which is a sufficient condition for being bald!) while $Head_1$ has a fairly large number of evenly distributed hairs (which is a sufficient condition for being hairy!). By hypothesis, Premise Three will be applicable for comparing

Head$_1$ with Head$_{25}$, and we will judge Head$_1$ hairier than Head$_{25}$. So, on this argument of Wasserman's, we find ourselves in the same kind of position we are in with my Spectrum Arguments. We must reject Premise One, Premise Two, Premise Three, or the transitivity of the hairiness relation. Indeed, as long as we retain the transitivity of "hairier than," Premises One and Two entail that we can start with a hairy head and undergo a steady transformation whereby the head is getting hairier and hairier, though at the end of a long series of such "improvements" the head has become bald!

There are many possible responses to Wasserman's argument. Rejecting Premise Two is, I believe, a nonstarter, as there clearly *could* be a spectrum of heads of the sort Premise Two describes. So, the real choices are to reject Premise One, Premise Three, or the transitivity of the "hairier than" relation. I shall not canvass all of the possible responses that might be offered in support of these different options. But let me comment on two lines of thought that might be raised against Premises One and Three, respectively.

Consider a spectrum of heads of the sort assumed earlier. Presumably, we might agree that the heads on one end of the spectrum are hairy, that the heads on the other end are bald, and that in between there might be heads that are neither hairy nor bald. For the sake of argument, let us make the controversial assumption that if this is the case, then there *must* be one precise point at which one goes from a head that is still hairy to one that is neither hairy nor bald, and another precise point at which one goes from a head that is neither hairy nor bald to one that is bald. It may then seem clear that we *must* reject Premise One. After all, suppose that the first transition occurs between Head$_7$ and Head$_8$. According to Premise One, Head$_8$ is hairier than Head$_7$. But, by hypothesis, Head$_7$ is hairy. Surely, if one head is hairier than another that is hairy, the former *must* be hairy. But, Head$_8$ is *not* hairy; it is, by hypothesis, neither hairy nor bald. It follows that we must reject Premise One. However plausible Premise One may sound, it *must* be false.

This argument against Premise One has great intuitive plausibility. But it should sound familiar. It is analogous to the argument presented, and rejected, in section 9.1. I shall not rehash the considerations presented in section 9.1, but let me note the following. *If* one has a concept whose instantiations vary along a *single* dimension, then considerations of the preceding sort are compelling. For example, if John is taller than Mary, and Mary is tall, then John *must* be tall. Similarly for other relations that vary along a single dimension, like "faster than," or "heavier than." But *if* one has a concept whose instantiations vary along multiple dimensions, and if, more important, they can vary *in the way* that baldness is purported to in Wasserman's argument, then one *must* reject the view in question.

This response sounds question begging, and in a way it is. But the charge of question begging can be levied in each direction, and the question is which position ultimately seems most plausible. Consider the difference between Head$_7$ and Head$_8$. By hypothesis, we have assumed that Head$_7$ is hairy and Head$_8$ is neither hairy nor bald. But our question isn't whether Head$_8$ is *hairy*, it is whether it is *hairier* than Head$_7$, and while this notion would be unintelligible if hairiness varied along a single dimension, it is not unintelligible if hairiness varies along different dimensions that can be given different weights for different comparisons. The key to recognizing this possibility is to recognize that while our criteria for being "hairy" and our criteria for being "hairier than" are intimately related to each other, we actually have *different* criteria for the two notions. So, while we might be willing to countenance the possibility that even a tiny difference in the pattern of hair distribution can make *all* the difference in terms of whether someone counts as hairy or not, we *don't* believe that such a tiny difference *alone* can settle the question of whether one head is hairier than another.

Here is the litmus test. Imagine someone who wants to have as full and rich a head of hair as possible. He is given the choice between two heads of hair. He can have Head$_7$ or Head$_8$. He is shown many slides of the two heads, from every angle, and many times. After poring over the pictures, he realizes that Head$_8$ has a *slightly* less even pattern of hair distribution than Head$_7$, in particular, that the hairs at the back of Head$_8$ seem to be slightly more spread out, or thinner, than those on Head$_7$. Nevertheless, it is *clear* that Head$_8$ is bushier *everywhere else* than Head$_7$, and that, overall, it is a fuller, thicker head of hair than Head$_7$. After full and careful deliberation of the matter, he chooses to have Head$_8$. Given our assumptions, this seems like an entirely reasonable choice for him to make. Indeed, given what he is looking for, it seems that it is his only reasonable choice. Head$_7$ is *slightly* better than Head$_8$ in *one* respect that matters to him (the overall pattern of hair distribution), but Head$_8$ is clearly *much* better than Head$_7$ in another respect that matters to him (the number of hairs on the head), and together it seems clear that in *this* case the trade-off between them is such that, all things considered, Head$_8$ is hairier than Head$_7$.

Suppose he then learns of a logical/philosophical *proof* that while Head$_7$ *is* hairy, Head$_8$ is "merely" neither hairy nor bald. Would that cause him to change his mind about which head of hair he would prefer? I think not. Nor should it. He is likely to be suspicious of such a proof. But even if, after fully understanding it, he comes to agree that Head$_7$ should be categorized as of the *kind* "hairy," while Head$_8$ should be categorized as of the *kind* "neither hairy nor bald," he might rightly conclude that in *this* case, where the difference between the instantiations of the two kinds is *so* slight in terms of the *pattern* of hair distribution, but *clearly* favors Head$_8$ in terms of the *number* of hairs, Head$_8$ would be preferable to Head$_7$. If asked why he opted for a head that was neither hairy nor bald over one that was hairy, he might simply reply: "Well, because it is clearly *hairier*."

Someone might, at first, think the preceding considerations merely show that we have drawn the line between the "hairy" and the "neither hairy nor bald" in the wrong place on the spectrum. They might conclude that Head$_8$ must also be hairy, and then seek to repeat the argument elsewhere along the spectrum. But that strategy will clearly fail because the *same* considerations will be available for *any* two adjacent points along the spectrum. For any two heads, $Head_k$ and $Head_{(k+1)}$, $Head_k$ and $Head_{(k+1)}$ will stand in the same relations to each other as $Head_7$ and $Head_8$. It seems, then, that at some point we must admit that someone who is neither hairy nor bald *could* be hairier than someone who is hairy, or we must admit that *every* head along the spectrum is hairy after all. I shall consider the latter alternative shortly.

In sum, it may initially sound absurd to claim that a head that was not hairy[16] could nevertheless be hairier than one that was hairy. And this, combined with the assumption that at *some* point along the spectrum one *must* go from being hairy to being neither hairy nor bald, seems to provide good reason to reject Premise One. But when one thinks hard about what Premise One asserts, and the actual relations between adjacent members of the spectrum dictated by Premise Two, it may seem hard to deny that Premise One yields the right judgment for adjacent members of the spectrum. Each $Head_{(k+1)}$ really *does* seem hairier than each $Head_k$. Moreover, on reflection, it seems that one can plausibly defend this position, once one recognizes that the "hairier than" relation is not based on a single dimension, like other "...er than" relations for which the reasoning in question *would* be cogent. In particular, *if* we are prepared to recognize that several dimensions are relevant for determining how alternatives compare with respect to hairiness, and, more important, *if* we are prepared to recognize that the relative importance of the dimensions can vary depending on the alternatives being compared—as the plausibility of Premises One and Three suggests we might be regarding hairiness, since we may think the number of hairs is crucially relevant for comparing heads with similar patterns of distribution, but not similarly relevant for comparing patterns of even distribution with those that involve a pronounced bald spot—then we have the conceptual apparatus necessary to deny the objection in question. Given such conceptions, it *could* be that one head is hairier than another, even though the hairier head is not hairy, and the less hairy head is! But, of course, as we have long since established, given such conceptions we can retain both Premise One *and* Premise Three, for on such conceptions it is clear that transitivity will either fail, or fail to apply, for the "hairier than" relation.

One may offer a more direct objection to Premise One. One might claim that once an area has become "sufficiently" thick with hairs, there is no advantage to adding even more hairs to that area. On this view, one might reach a stage where there is a balding area on the top of one's head, and an already "sufficiently" thick mat of hair everywhere else on one's scalp. In this case, one might decline to remove even *one* more hair from one's balding area, no matter *how*

---

[16] Throughout my discussion, I have been granting my opponent the position that there might be a point where one less hair transformed one from being hairy, to being neither hairy nor bald, where someone who is neither hairy nor bald is not hairy. That assumption makes my opponent's position as strong as possible. In fact, it is arguable that we should instead think that one less hair could only make it *indeterminate* whether the head was hairy, in which case it might be neither true nor false that the head was hairy. However, the claim about indeterminacy does not affect my arguments for the reasons given in section 9.1 and appendix D.

many extra hairs might be squeezed into the already saturated remainder of one's scalp. In doing this, one might claim that although there may be far *more* hairs in the one case than the other, the way in which number and distribution relate to each other to generate the "hairier than" relation is such that the head with fewer hairs more evenly distributed *is* hairier than the head with far more hairs with an *ever-so-slightly* more pronounced bald patch.

On this view, one rejects Premise One because one can reach a point where even though two alternatives *do* stand in relation to each other in the way Premise One supposes, it seems plausible to grant *lexical priority* to the pattern of distribution over the number of hairs *if* the area surrounding a balding area has already become *sufficiently* thick with hair. In that case, the thought is, there isn't *any* advantage to squeezing in *even more* hairs in the nonbalding area, while there will be a disadvantage to increasing the bald spot even by a tiny amount.

Without trying to settle this line's ultimate defensibility, let me grant that it is plausible, and may show that Premise One is restricted in scope. But even so, this may not be enough to completely undermine Wasserman's argument. Perhaps there is a spectrum of heads of the sort envisaged by Premise Two where the bald end point hasn't yet reached the relevant saturation point outside of the bald spot. Additionally, there might be a more complicated scenario, involving a temporal dimension, where the worry in question wouldn't arise.

Suppose, for example, that one faces two prospects: in case *I*, one has a fairly even distribution of hairs for fifty years, with *just enough* total hairs to count as hairy; in case *II*, one has a *little* less hair in the six-inch-diameter circle associated with the male bald spot—henceforth, *the balding region*—but case *II* is *just like* case *I* in the nonbalding region for the last forty-eight years, and *much* thicker and richer in the nonbalding region for the first two years. Here, one might think that something analogous to Premise One would apply, and that one might regard case *II* as hairier than case *I*, all things considered. After all, the difference between case *I* and case *II* may be barely noticeable for the last forty-eight years, while case *II* may be clearly and vastly better than case *I* for the first two years. Now compare case *III* to case *II*. Case *III* will be a little bit worse than case *II* in the balding region for all fifty years. But case *III* will be *just like* case *II* in the nonbalding region for the first two and last forty-six years, but *much* thicker and richer in the nonbalding region for years 3 and 4. Again, one might think that something analogous to Premise One would apply, and regard case *III* as hairier than case *II*, all things considered. As before, the difference between cases *II* and *III* may be barely noticeable for most of the fifty years, while case *III* may be clearly and vastly better than case *II* for years 3 and 4. Iterated, this reasoning would seem to imply that we should judge case *II* hairier than case *I*, case *III* hairier than case *II*, case *IV* hairier than case *III*, and so on, all the way to the last case, case *XXV* being hairier than case *XXIV*. And in this temporal case, we seemingly avoid the worries about "oversaturation" that might cast Premise One into doubt. But, of course, case *I* involves someone who is hairy, perhaps with 100,000 hairs scattered evenly over their scalp for fifty years, while case *XXV* might involve someone who is clearly bald, since, we may suppose, although he might have 200,000 hairs in his nonbalding area, he might also have a completely bare, six-inch-diameter bald spot!

To be sure, one might still insist that the version of Premise One appealed to in the preceding argument should be rejected. But one can see why Wasserman might think the same kinds of considerations presented elsewhere in this book could be relevant to the case of the hairiness/baldness spectrum. Having argued previously that both within and between lives it can be plausible to adopt positions like the Disperse Additional Burdens View (see chapters 3 and 4), it may seem perfectly possible that someone who is a *little* less hairy for a number of years, but a *lot* hairier for several, might be hairier, overall, than someone who is a *little* hairier for many years, but a *lot* less hairy for several. The key, of course, is how, if at all, the little differences of hairiness add up, across time, and their relative importance to the much larger difference in hairiness for a shorter period. It is compatible with much of this book's reasoning to think that there may be *some* spectrum of cases such that a version of Premise One will seem plausible for each pair of adjacent cases across the spectrum, even if the scope of Premise One is more restricted than one might initially think. This is what Wasserman has seen, and relied on, in developing his argument.

Let me next consider a response to Premise Three. One might accept that there is a spectrum of the sort dictated by Premise Two, for which Premise One is plausible when comparing each adjacent pair of cases. If this is so, and one is convinced that "hairier than" must be a transitive relation, one might then argue that Premise Three *must* be rejected.

In moving from $Head_1$ to $Head_{25}$, we have held that in *each* comparative judgment the hairier head was the one with *significantly* more hair. Well, it might be claimed, this is the judgment we should make *whenever* we are comparing two heads, and that the issue of whether the two heads are "sufficiently similar" in terms of their pattern of distribution is irrelevant. More carefully, one might argue that if, as we have supposed, in moving from $Head_1$ to $Head_{25}$ each slight worsening in the pattern of hair distribution was *sufficiently* offset by the increase in the number of hairs, so as to make each $Head_{(k+1)}$ hairier than each $Head_k$, then *surely* the *cumulative* effect of all of these changes should be such as to make the extent to which $Head_{25}$ has more hairs than $Head_1$ *more than sufficient* to outweigh the extent to which $Head_{25}$ has a worse pattern of distribution than $Head_1$. This *has* to be true, it might be claimed. Hence we should rightly conclude that $Head_{25}$ really *is* hairier than $Head_1$, notwithstanding the fact that $Head_1$ has a large number of hairs evenly distributed over its scalp, and $Head_{25}$ has a six-inch-diameter bald spot!

The advocate of this move then has several options. First option: following the kind of suggestion noted earlier, he can point out that our criteria for the relation "hairier than" *differ* from our criteria for "baldness," so that he can grant that $Head_{25}$ *is* bald, but is nevertheless *hairier* than $Head_1$, and not vice versa. Second option: he can maintain that since Head$_1$ is hairy, and Head$_{25}$ is hairier than Head$_1$, Head$_{25}$ must also be hairy, and hence he can *deny* that Head$_{25}$ is bald, contrary to what we have been assuming all along. In defense of this option, he might insist that although in *most* cases when someone has a six-inch-diameter bald spot they will, in fact, be bald, in a case where the area surrounding the bald spot is thickly matted with hair the person is not, in fact, bald, and should rightly be regarded as hairy. Third option: he might maintain that we have several conflicting criteria, some of which support the conclusion that Head$_{25}$ is bald, and some of which support the conclusion that Head$_{25}$ is hairier than Head$_1$ and (hence) hairy, and that we should just accept that both are, in a sense, true. This view yields the upshot of the original Sorites Paradox, namely, that the same head can be both hairy and bald at the same time. But it will seem less puzzling if the criteria for being hairy simply turn out to be different from, and not necessarily in conflict with, the criteria for being bald. Finally, fourth option: he might explicitly add to the preceding considerations the claim that there are different senses of "hairier than." In one sense—the sense entailed by accepting Premise One, Premise Two, and the transitivity of "hairier than"—Head$_{25}$ will be hairier than Head$_1$. In another sense—the sense entailed by the view that Head$_{25}$ is, in fact, bald, that Head$_1$ is hairy, and that a head that is bald is not hairier than a head that is hairy—Head$_{25}$ will not be hairier than Head$_1$.

I believe the first and second options will be hard to maintain. Consider the case of someone who is still hairy, with a decent amount of hair spread evenly over his head, but is deeply worried that his hair is thinning. He is desperate to remain hairy and wants, other things equal, to be as hairy as possible. If a salesman sells him a bottle of Miracle Hair Growth *guaranteed* to make him hairier, should he be happy or satisfied if, after a month of regular usage, he has developed a pronounced six-inch-diameter bald spot and lost *all* his hair within that bald spot? Would it be enough if the salesman rightly pointed out that he now had a *really* thick mat of hair around the bald spot? Would he be convinced by the arguments of philosophers that purported to *prove* to him that in fact he was *not* bald, or that in fact he *must* be hairier than before, since he would have readily agreed that he had gotten hairier *each* day that he had used the product?

Even if the salesman and philosophers were acting in good faith, I believe the person would, and would have good reason to, reject their claims. Indeed, I have little doubt that he would regret his decision to use the product, and that if he had it to do over again he would refrain from using the product. Whatever proofs or clever arguments might be offered, we all know that someone with a six-inch-diameter bald spot *is* bald, and *in the sense that matters most*, we think that someone with a six-inch-diameter bald spot is *not* hairier than someone with a *full* head of hair. This is not to deny that we can agree that the former person might have lots *more* hair than the latter. But in terms of what we actually care about, when we say we want to be *hairier*, we pay attention not only to the sum *total* of hairs on our head, but to the *distribution* of those hairs.

Indeed, as claimed previously, as long as there are "enough" hairs on our head, we may give a *lot* of weight to avoiding a substantial bald spot and having an even distribution of hair, and virtually no weight to our total number of hairs.

So, given how we use the notions of "bald," and "hairier than," it is hard to deny that $Head_{25}$ is, in fact, bald, and that in an important sense, and probably the most important sense, $Head_1$ is hairier than $Head_{25}$. Thus, as indicated, I think the first two options are not tenable.

What about the second two options? They are, I think, defensible. But they don't actually undermine Premise Three. Rather, they show that Premise Three could, in fact, be compatible with Premises One and Two and the transitivity of *a* "hairier than" relation. Indeed, they support the view that Premise Three's sense of "hairier than" *differs* from Premise One's, and that different criteria for "hairier than" underlie the comparative judgments based on the different premises. On this view, the "hairier than" relation expressed by Premise One may be perfectly transitive. And so, too, may be the "hairier than" relation expressed by Premise Three. Thus, so far, there would be no question of the transitivity of "hairier than" actually failing.

Still, even if we acknowledge that there are different senses of "hairier than," that hardly settles the question we are interested in. Specifically, giving full weight to *each* of the different senses of "hairier than," we can ask, insofar as we care about hairiness, which of the different heads of hair along the spectrum from $Head_1$ through $Head_{25}$ should one choose *all things considered*. And here, alas, the second two options, even if defensible, are of no help. We know that in terms of the "hairier than" relation underlying Premise One, we should choose $Head_{25}$. We also know that in terms of the "hairier than" relation underlying Premise Three, we should choose $Head_1$ over $Head_{25}$. But what then? The problem, of course, is that if we are confronted with all twenty-five options at once, Premise One will seem most relevant and significant when comparing the "nearby" options, Premise Three will seem most relevant and significant when comparing the "distant" options, and we have no obvious way of combining these facts in a way that generates a plausible, stable, and coherent ranking of the different alternatives. In fact, it is not at all clear what head one *should* choose given such a spectrum of options, since for any option one might choose there appears to be another available option that would be hairier.

These considerations are familiar. By invoking the claim that there are different *senses* of "hairier than," one can deny that any particular notion of "hairier than" is intransitive. But this immediately raises the possibility that transitivity doesn't actually apply across the hairiness spectrum, and hence that we can't actually appeal to transitivity in choosing among different alternatives along such a spectrum, precisely because different factors are relevant and significant for making different comparisons along the hairiness spectrum. Thus, we may find ourselves stymied in trying to choose among the different options along the hairiness spectrum. This result would not be surprising if one of the second two options is adopted, and is analogous to the conclusions that many think follow from my Spectrum Arguments.

I have presented Ryan Wasserman's reconstruction of the Standard Sorites Paradox regarding hairiness and baldness. In fact, Wasserman suggests that his result might be quite general, and that many Standard Sorites Paradoxes could be reconstructed along similar lines. Having examined the hairiness/baldness argument in some detail, I sketch how the argument is supposed to go for another famous Standard Sorites Paradox, the Paradox of the Heap, in appendix C.

As noted earlier, the main point of Wasserman's argument is to show that my worries arise in nonnormative as well as normative contexts. Thus, people shouldn't be too quick to welcome my arguments as supporting skepticism in the moral domain. After all, if Wasserman is right, similar worries can be raised about the nonnormative notion of "hairiness," yet surely this doesn't show that we should be skeptics about the nonnormative domain. A fortiori, it is a mistake to be dismissive about the normative realm, simply because of the worries I have raised and the difficulty of quelling them.

I think Wasserman makes an important point, and there is a lot more that could be said about this issue. But for my present purposes, I will limit myself to three main points.

First, nothing I or Wasserman have said commits one to the view that *all* Standard Sorites Paradoxes could be plausibly reformulated along the lines in question. It is arguable, for example, that the Standard Sorites Paradox purporting to show that acorns are oaks is not readily amenable to such a reinterpretation.

The *key* question is whether the notions being appealed to vary along several dimensions and, in particular, whether it is plausible to believe either that *different* dimensions are plausible for different comparisons, or that different *weights* to the different dimensions will be plausible for different comparisons. So, as we have seen, if a *slight* variation along one dimension can be outweighed by a sufficient gain along another dimension, but a radical difference along one dimension makes appeal to another dimension inappropriate (at least for some cases), then an argument of the sort I have presented will be in the offing.

Second, although I find Wasserman's arguments plausible and intriguing, and welcome any support they offer regarding the scope and importance of my overall project, my arguments do not depend on Standard Sorites Paradoxes being reformulable in the way Wasserman suggests. If, in fact, certain notions like "hairiness" operate in the way Wasserman has pointed out, and if the upshot of their doing so is that we should be worried about the transitivity of "…er than" relations either failing, or failing to apply, in the nonnormative as well as the normative realm, that is interesting and important. But I, for one, am not a moral skeptic, and I will be deeply worried about my results whether or not I find analogues of them in the nonnormative realm.

Finally, as we have seen, Wasserman's "revision" of the Sorites Paradox turns on premises analogous to mine, including a key premise about the transitivity of "hairier than," and *not* on the Crucial Premise of the standard Hairiness/Baldness Sorites Paradox that "if I remove a single hair from someone who is hairy, she will still be hairy." So this raises the question, noted earlier, of whether what Wasserman has offered really *is* a kind of Sorites Paradox, or whether it is simply a Spectrum Argument that happens to discuss the same subject matter as a well-known Sorites Paradox. Although I, myself, would reserve the name *Sorites Paradox* for the sort of *Standard* Sorites Paradox presented earlier—since the two kinds of arguments depend on different premises and lead to different conclusions—here, as elsewhere, I'm not very concerned about the terminological issue. If we decide to call Wasserman's argument a "Sorites Paradox" or perhaps a "Revised Sorites Paradox," then my examples should also be counted as such. But this doesn't change the fact that my arguments, as well as Wasserman's, raise serious questions about the nature and scope of the transitivity of certain "…er than" relations. The Standard Sorites Paradox does not do this.

The important point is not what we *call* the Rachels/Temkin/Wasserman Spectrum Arguments, but how we should *respond* to them. If the arguments are mistaken, we need to understand where they go wrong. If they are correct, we need to explore their scope and implications. Either way, I think my Spectrum Arguments require a different analysis and response than is appropriate for the Standard Sorites Paradoxes. However, thanks to Wasserman, I welcome the thought that my arguments may lead us to revise some familiar Sorites Paradoxes, and then, perhaps, to view the revised paradoxes as, in some respects, even more important and problematic than their predecessors.

9.3 Heuristics and Similarity-Based Arguments

In "Transitivity, the Sorites Paradox, and Similarity-Based Decision-Making,"[17] Alex Voorhoeve and Ken Binmore raise an objection to the argument for intransitivity contained in Warren Quinn's paper "The Puzzle of the Self-Torturer."[18] If successful, Voorhoeve and Binmore's argument against Quinn would threaten to undermine other Spectrum Arguments that I, and Stuart Rachels, have offered. Voorhoeve recognizes and argues for this in a subsequent paper, "Heuristics and Biases in a Purported Counterexample to the Acyclicity of 'Better Than.'"[19]

The key element of Voorhoeve and Binmore's objection to Spectrum Arguments involves an appeal to what has been called "similarity-based decision-making." Studied by Amos Tversky and Ariel Rubenstein, among others, it has been speculated that people often follow similarity-based decision making as

---

[17] *Erkenntnis* 64 (2006): 101–14.
[18] *Philosophical Studies* 59 (1990): 79–90.
[19] *Politics, Philosophy, and Economics* 7 (2008): 285–99.

a way of simplifying their choice between multidimensional alternatives.[20] Voorhoeve and Binmore present Rubinstein's characterization of this form of decision making as follows:

> When deciding between multi-dimensional alternatives, say bundles of (expected) pain and money (p_i, m_i) and (p_j, m_j), a decision-maker goes through the following three-stage procedure.
> **Stage 1:** The decision-maker looks for dominance. If $p_i > p_j$ and $m_i > m_j$, then bundle (p_i, m_i) is preferred over bundle (p_j, m_j).
> **Stage 2:** The decision-maker looks for similarities between p_i and p_j and between m_i and m_j. If she finds similarity in one dimension only, she disregards this dimension, and determines her preference between the two pairs using only the dimension in which there is no similarity. For example, if p_i is similar to p_j but m_i is not similar to m_j, and $m_j > m_i$, then bundle (p_j, m_j) is preferred over bundle (p_i, m_i).
> **Stage 3:** If the first two stages were not decisive, the choice is made using a different criterion.[21]

Voorhoeve and Binmore note some of the cases where Tversky and Rubenstein find evidence that people make decisions in this way. They also note that there are numerous reasons that it might be *rational* for people to adopt such a decision procedure. Specifically, Voorhoeve and Binmore recognize that it may be a *useful heuristic* to follow such a decision procedure for choosing among numerous multidimensional alternatives, especially when it is often unclear how to weight the numerous different dimensions relative to each other. But, as has long been known, useful heuristics can often lead us to trouble when employed in cases for which they are not well suited, and *one* troublesome heuristics notoriously lead to is intransitive judgments.[22] This is the case for similarity-based decision making, as many have pointed out.

Here is a variation of an example that Voorhoeve and Binmore use to illustrate how similarity-based decision making generates intransitivity. Suppose one judges job candidates along two dimensions, intelligence, as measured by IQ, and years of experience. Suppose that it is thought that two candidates are similar in intelligence if their difference in IQ points is less than or equal to 5,

---

[20] As cited by Binmore and Voorhoeve, see, for example, Amos Tversky's, "Intransitivity of Preferences," *Psychological Review* 84 (1967): 31–48, as well as his "Features of Similarity," *Psychological Review* 84 (1977): 327–52; Ariel Rubinstein's "Similarity and Decision-Making under Risk (Is There a Utility Theory Resolution of the Allais Paradox?)," *Journal of Economic Theory* 46 (1988): 145–53, as well as his "Economics and Psychology? The Case of Hyperbolic Discounting," *International Economic Review* 44 (2003): 1207–16.

[21] "Transitivity, the Sorites Paradox, and Similarity-Based Decision-Making," 107.

[22] This has been known ever since Tversky's original, and now classic, article, "Intransitivity of Preferences." Countless articles have since corroborated Tversky's original claims, too many to bother citing here.

and that they are similar in experience if their difference in experience is less than or equal to one year. Suppose, further, that if one candidate isn't superior on both dimensions (so stage-one reasoning doesn't apply), and the candidates aren't similar on either dimension (so stage-two reasoning doesn't apply), then stage-three reasoning says to pick the candidate with the highest intelligence, since significant differences in intelligence are regarded as more important than significant differences in experience, for the job in question. Finally, suppose that there are three candidates with the following qualifications: candidate A has an IQ of 115 and six years' experience, candidate B has an IQ of 120 and four years' experience, and candidate C has an IQ of 125 and two years' experience.

Following the similarity-based decision-making procedure suggested, stage-one reasoning wouldn't apply in comparing any of the candidates, since none of the candidates are superior to any of the others on both relevant criteria. Stage-two reasoning would apply for comparing candidates A and B, and similarly for comparing candidates B and C, since A and B are similar in terms of intelligence, but not in terms of experience, and likewise for B and C. In this case, A would be judged better than B (in virtue of his similar intelligence but dissimilar and greater experience) and B would be judged better than C (again, in virtue of his similar intelligence but dissimilar and greater experience). But, stage-three reasoning would apply for comparing A with C, and it would yield the judgment that C is a better candidate than A, since C's being significantly better qualified than A in terms of intelligence would be thought to carry the day against A's being significantly better qualified than C in terms of experience. Thus, similarity-based decision making can violate transitivity, as in accordance with the procedure in question, A is judged a better candidate than B, and B a better candidate than C, but C a better candidate than A.

Similarity-based decision making may be a useful *heuristic*; it is fast, easy to apply, and *generally* reliable *in certain contexts*. But, as Voorhoeve and Binmore point out, following Tversky and Rubenstein, it can lead us astray, and we have to abandon it when it does so. I agree.

Let us examine similarity-based decision making a bit further. In doing this, we will see that its shortcomings can be made apparent even with simple pairwise comparisons, where the issue of transitivity doesn't arise.

Often, we have to make difficult multidimensional choices where far more than two dimensions are involved. Suppose alternatives vary along *six* dimensions, and that $A = (2, 3, 2, 2, 4, 5)$ means that alternative A has a "score" of 2 along the first dimension, three along the second, two along the third, and so on. Suppose, further, that for any given dimension a difference of 1 or less between two alternatives counts as their being similar along that dimension, while a difference of greater than 1 counts as their being dissimilar. How should we compare A with B, where $B = (3, 2, 2, 1, 5, 8)$? Note, B is better than A according to the first, fifth, and sixth dimensions, worse according to the second and fourth, and equal according to the third. Given how many different dimensions are involved, and given that it may be very difficult to judge exactly how much to value each dimension, both in absolute terms and relative to the others, this is the kind of complex decision that may seem, at first blush, intractable. By the same token, it may seem like the kind of complex decision for which similarity-based decision making is especially helpful and appropriate. After all, by hypothesis, A and B are similar according to the first five dimensions, and only dissimilar according to the sixth. That may naturally tempt us to adopt similarity-based decision making and judge B better than A.

In a case like the preceding one, we may, in fact, feel fairly confident about the judgment yielded by similarity-based decision making. But if we do, our confidence is misplaced. To see this, compare A with another alternative, C, where $C = (1, 2, 1, 1, 3, 7)$. As with B, C is similar to A along the first five dimensions, and only dissimilar along the sixth, where it is better. Thus, similarity-based decision making would yield the judgment that C is better than A, in accordance with the same stage-two reasoning that yielded the judgment that B is better than A. But in *this* case there should be little confidence in the judgment yielded by similarity-based decision making. After all, C is *worse* than A along *five* relevant dimensions, and only *better* (and perhaps not by all *that* much) according to one. Clearly, we should only think that C is better than A if we think that the sixth dimension is *much* more important than the first, second, third, fourth, and fifth dimensions—so much so, in fact, that being *two* points better along the sixth dimension *alone* counts more than being *five* points worse along the other five dimensions *combined*. But note, while it is *possible* that the sixth dimension is so much more important than all the other dimensions, it is also possible, for anything that has been said *so far*, that the sixth dimension is actually the *least* important of the six relevant dimensions. Clearly, then, it is only in very special, and narrowly circumscribed, contexts that we can be confident of the judgments yielded by similarity-based decision making.

Similarity-based decision making seemingly offers us a way of finessing the tricky question of coming up with accurate measures of each of the dimensions comprising multidimensional alternatives. Likewise, it seemingly finesses the tricky question of determining how much we need to weigh the different dimensions vis-à-vis each other. But, except in those dominance cases where stage-one reasoning is involved, it does so only at considerable risk to the reliability of the judgments yielded by such reasoning. In totally "disregarding," for decision-making purposes, any dimensions with respect to which two alternatives are "similar," similarity-based decision making treats *small* differences as if they were *no* differences. But small differences are *not* no differences. Small differences along a single dimension can add up to a *significant* difference over a sequence of alternatives, and small differences along *many* dimensions can add up to a significant difference even with respect to a single pair of alternatives. This is especially so when the dimensions in question are of great significance. Indeed, a small difference along one dimension (such that two alternatives would be regarded as "similar" with respect to that dimension) might well outweigh a large difference along a different dimension (such that two alternatives would be regarded as "dissimilar" with respect to that dimension) if the first dimension were sufficiently more important than the second.

Before going on, let me note that similar considerations might be adduced against another common heuristic for choosing among complex multidimensional alternatives. The heuristic in question is to follow a kind of "majority rule" reasoning, applied to the different dimensions of the alternatives. This heuristic may be illustrated as follows. Suppose that instead of considering just two dimensions in comparing certain job applicants, one considers three: intelligence, educational background, and experience. Since it may seem difficult to know how much to count each of the different dimensions relative to each other, one *might* adopt the simple heuristic of ranking candidates in terms of the number of dimensions they score higher on. On such reasoning, A will be ranked higher than B if A has a higher score on at least two of the three relevant dimensions. So, for example, if A = (130, 2, PhD)—meaning he has an IQ of 130, two years' work experience, and a PhD—he will be ranked higher than B, if B = (120, 6, master's), because A does better than B in terms of two of the three relevant dimensions, intelligence and education.

Like similarity-based decision making, "majority rule" reasoning is a natural procedure for ranking multidimensional alternatives that is easy to apply and has a fair amount of initial intuitive appeal. But majority-rule reasoning faces difficulties analogous to those faced by similarity-based decision making. Majority-rule reasoning is susceptible to a multitude of well-known voter's paradoxes, and straightforwardly generates intransitive rankings. Consider, for example, the two preceding candidates, A and B, and an additional candidate C, where C = (140, 4, bachelor's). As noted earlier, applied to the three relevant dimensions, the majority-rule reasoning generates the ranking that A is better than B. Likewise, B is better than C, because he is better with respect to two of the three relevant rankings: experience and education. But, in violation of the transitivity of "better than," C is better than A, because he is better with respect to two of the three relevant rankings: intelligence and experience.

Like similarity-based decision making, majority-rule reasoning finesses the notoriously difficult question of determining exactly how much the different dimensions matter in absolute terms. Although this is part of what makes it attractive, as an easy-to-apply heuristic, it is also a serious weakness, as indicated earlier. Suppose that for a particular job, work experience is, in fact, *much* more important than intelligence or education. It may, indeed, be *so* much more important that we should prefer a candidate with two years of work experience to a candidate with no work experience, *even if* the first candidate had a lower IQ and less education. Specifically, it could well be that for two candidates D and E, where D = (110, 2, bachelor's) and E = (120, 0, master's), D is a better candidate than E, even though E is a stronger candidate on two of the three relevant dimensions, and hence would be judged as the better candidate by the majority-rule heuristic. Not all *relevant* dimensions are equally *important*, and this fact is ignored by the majority-rule heuristic.

Another shortcoming of the majority-rule heuristic is that it ignores the *extent* to which alternatives are better or worse than another along the different dimensions. So, whereas similarity-based decision making treats *small* differences as if they were *no* differences, the majority-rule heuristic treats large differences the same as it treats small differences. Just as the former is a mistake, so is the latter. If candidate *F* is barely worse than candidate *G* along two relevant dimensions, but *much* better along a third, *F* may clearly be the better candidate, even if all of the dimensions are equally important, and *perhaps* even if the third dimension is the least important of the three. So, for example, for certain jobs it might well be the case that *F*, who has a PhD and did a postdoc, eighteen years of experience, and an IQ of 160, is a much stronger candidate than *G*, who has a PhD, did a post doc and an extra master's, nineteen years of experience, and an IQ of 115, even though *G* is a stronger candidate on two of the three relevant dimensions.

Bearing the preceding in mind, let us now return to Voorhoeve and Binmore's response to my Spectrum Arguments. It is arguable that similarity-based decision making has the same *structure* as my arguments. Like my arguments, such reasoning appeals to different criteria for making different comparisons, and this accounts for the intransitivity that arises when employing such reasoning. Moreover, my arguments emphasize the importance of differences between "adjacent" alternatives along a spectrum being "sufficiently small," and differences between alternatives at the opposite ends of a spectrum being "sufficiently large," and this naturally resonates with the notions of similarity and dissimilarity that play a significant role on similarity-based decision making. So, I can certainly see how it might be *tempting* to try, as Voorhoeve and Binmore do, to both explain, and explain away, our intuitive responses to my Spectrum Arguments as yet further manifestations of our intuitive reliance on similarity-based decision making.

Still, other than the resemblances between the form and wording of the two positions, we can ask what *grounds* Voorhoeve and Binmore have given us to believe that the *reasoning* underlying my arguments is actually the *same* as the *reasoning* underlying similarity-based decision making. The answer, I'm afraid, is precious little. At most, by pointing out the resemblances noted, they have given us weak, prima facie cause to *wonder* if my Spectrum Arguments might be reflecting similarity-based decision making. But in the absence of any strong supporting evidence, which Voorhoeve and Binmore haven't given us, I think there is good reason to be suspicious of the deflationary "explanation" of my Spectrum Arguments which they have given. Moreover, on reflection, I don't believe that *my* intuitive judgments about Spectrum Arguments *are* based on similarity-based decision making, and I don't believe that most other people's are, either. More important, I think there are good reasons to doubt that my Spectrum Arguments *do* involve similarity-based decision making. Let me present those next.

At the end of "Heuristics and Biases," Voorhoeve writes the following:

> Interestingly, psychological research indicates that even if we are persuaded by this argument about the unreliability of our initial preferences in Rachels' and Temkin's example, this may not modify our gut feelings about this example. As Kahneman notes, the operation of intuitive methods of decision-making is typically "fast, automatic, effortless, associative, and difficult to control or modify," and the judgments that these methods generate may therefore be hard to shake off. The pull of our initial preferences in this case may therefore be strong and persistent.[23]

This is an important observation, and it is worth bearing in mind in trying to assess how much weight to give to the firm intuitions that many have about examples of the sort that Rachels and I present. But I think it actually cuts *against* Voorhoeve and Binmore's contention that similarity-based decision making underlies the plausibility of our examples, because it is not clear that Kahneman's claims generally apply to such reasoning.

Consistent with Kahneman's contention, many believe that we may have some intuitive illusions that are akin to various perceptual illusions. Even if we *know* that the stick in the water is straight, or that the brim of the hat is just as wide as the hat is tall, our visual apparatus is such that we can't *help* "seeing" the stick as bent, or the hat as taller than its brim is wide. Similarly, many suggest that our cognitive apparatus may be such that we can't *help* having a certain intuitive reaction to certain situations, even if we know that that intuitive reaction is unwarranted. This may be the case with our "gut" "visceral" reaction to the contemplation of incest or cannibalism. Even if we *convince* ourselves that our intuitive reactions to such matters are just the remnants of some ancient prehistorical superstition, or perhaps just an odd by-product of our evolutionary development, the intuitive *feelings* that we have in response to such cases may remain strong, persistent, and perhaps even unshakeable.

Perhaps there *is* a deep, unshakable, intuitive illusion underlying our judgments about Spectrum Arguments. But if this is so, that is reason to think that such judgments are *not* based on similarity-based decision making. As we have seen, the shortcomings of similarity-based decision making are easily identified and readily accepted. So are the shortcomings of majority-rule reasoning. In fact, once the various shortcomings are pointed out, there is little or no temptation to hang on to the mistaken judgments generated by such heuristics, however intuitively plausible those judgments might, at least initially, have seemed. Thus, as noted earlier, *if* my quick, initial, intuitive assessment that A is better than B is based on similarity-based decision making, I will

---

[23] Page 296. Voorhoeve appends a note to the quoted remarks citing Daniel Kahneman's "Maps of Bounded Rationality: A Perspective on Intuitive Judgment and Choice," *Nobel Prize Lecture* (2002): 449–89.

readily change that assessment when it is pointed out to me that the dimension along which *B* is dissimilar to, and better than, *A* is much less important than the dimensions along which *B* is similar to, though slightly worse than, *A*, or perhaps simply that there are *many* dimensions along which *A* is similar to, but still better than, *B*, while there is only *one* (not overwhelmingly important) dimension along which *B* is dissimilar to, and not *all* that much better than, *A*.

As Voorhoeve's preceding remarks implicitly acknowledge, the situation is otherwise with my Spectrum Arguments. People's intuitive judgments about my cases are extremely strong and not easily dislodged. More specifically, they are not easily undermined by considerations of the sort that lead us to readily and rightly reject many of the judgments generated by similarity-based decision making or other heuristics like majority-rule reasoning. This suggests that the intuitive judgments I appeal to are not, ultimately, based on similarity-based decision making.

I might add that most people retain their intuitive judgments about my cases even *after* they have subjected their judgments to careful, deliberate reflection. This, of course, does not guarantee that they are not caught in the grip of an especially powerful cognitive illusion, but it does suggest that most people's responses don't merely rest on heuristic-generated reasoning, or at least not on what Kahneman called "fast, automatic, effortless, associative" intuitive methods of decision making.

Let me next challenge Voorhoeve and Binmore's position more directly. I take it that similarity-based decision making is most plausible, and most likely to be invoked, when the value of the different dimensions are independent of each other. Often we implicitly assume this is the case. For example, one might implicitly assume that the different dimensions along which a prospective partner might vary are independent of each other. On this assumption, how valuable it is for someone to be humorous wouldn't depend on how valuable it is for that person to be physically beautiful, and in comparison with other prospective partners it will always be better if someone is more humorous, more physically beautiful, and so on.[24] The importance of this assumption for similarity-based decision making is easily illustrated.

Suppose people can vary along two dimensions that are measured on a scale from −20 to 20, where we regard two people as similar along a given dimension if

---

[24] The thought here is that if we knew how humorous someone was, we could give a "score" representing the "objective" value of being humorous to that degree, which would not depend on the "score" that person would receive reflecting the "objective" value of how physically beautiful he was. I don't deny, of course, that *subjectively* many people's assessments of how humorous someone is will be influenced by how attractive that person is; hence the sad, but well-known, phenomenon of people laughing hysterically at the lame jokes of a beautiful person, but being bored by virtually any remarks— no matter how witty—when they are uttered by someone homely. I should also add that I am not, myself, committed to the picture of attributes suggested here. In fact, I think it is probably implausible, and that a holistic account works better in this domain as well as many others. I am merely making this assumption to illustrate the following point about similarity-based decision making.

their scores for that dimension differ by 1 or less, and as dissimilar along that dimension otherwise. Let $X = (-4, 12)$ and $Y = (-3, 6)$, where X is an outcome in which someone would have a score of -4 along the first dimension and a score of 12 along the second dimension, and similarly, Y is an outcome in which someone would have a score of -3 along the first dimension and a score of 6 along the second dimension. Suppose we want to know which outcome was better, X or Y. On similarity-based decision making we disregard the first dimension and simply compare them in terms of the second. But if we do this we may be *completely* mistaken about how X and Y compare, or about the *extent* to which one is better than the other—which may be crucially important to know in certain decision-making contexts—if, in fact, the values of the two dimensions are interrelated.

Suppose that the second dimension that is reflected in X and Y is how much *pleasure* someone has in her life. Then, on similarity-based decision making we would judge X as better than Y, since X's score is twice as high as Y's along the dissimilar dimension, namely, pleasure, and if pleasure *were* our only concern, it would always be better to have a high score regarding pleasure than a low score regarding pleasure. But suppose that the first dimension that is reflected in X and Y is how *evil* someone is, where a score of -4 indicates that someone is more evil than a score of -3. Many believe that evil and pleasure are related in such a way that the more evil someone is, the *worse* it is for him to receive pleasure. Such people might suggest that one determine the value of outcomes like X and Y by *multiplying* the score along the first dimension by the score along the second dimension. On this way of reckoning, the value of $X = -48$, and the value of $Y = -18$, reflecting the way in which evil and pleasure are related, and the fact that a situation where a more evil person receives twice as much pleasure is in fact much *worse* than one where a similarly, but still less, evil person receives only half as much pleasure.

Clearly, then, similarity-based decision making is particularly ill suited for comparing multidimensional alternatives where the value of one dimension affects the value of another. Given this, one might have some reason to think that, on reflection at least, people would not appeal to similarity-based decision making for comparing such alternatives. But, as should be clear, the value of *duration*, which is a key element of many of my Spectrum Arguments, is *not* independent of the value of the experience to which it applies. Duration itself is neither good nor bad. Duration is good when applied to positive experiences, and bad when applied to negative experiences. And arguably, at least, the more positive an experience, the more valuable it is for it to last longer, and hence the more positively duration counts in that situation. Likewise, arguably, the more negative an experience, the more disvaluable it is for it to last longer, and hence the more negatively duration counts in that situation.

Let $X = (e, d)$ represent the extent to which an outcome, X, involves an experience of quality e, and duration, d, as measured in years. Let us arbitrarily suppose that for any two experiences, if the values of those experiences are within 10, then they count as similar for the purposes of similarity-based decision making, and likewise for any two durations whose values are within 1.

Then consider four alternatives, *P*, *Q*, *R*, and *S*, where *P* = (85, 12), *Q* = (90, 8), *R* = (−85, 12), and *S* = (−80, 8). Here, we are assuming that 90 and 85 represent very positive experiences, with the former being better than the latter, while −85 and −80 represent very negative experiences, with the former being worse than the latter. Using similarity-based decision making, as Voorhoeve and Binmore characterize it, we should say that *P* stands to *Q* as *R* stands to *S*. After all, since *P* and *Q* are similar regarding the first dimension, and *R* and *S* are also similar on that dimension, we would *disregard* the *first* dimension in making the comparisons in question, and make our comparisons *solely* on the basis of the second dimension, along which the alternatives are dissimilar. But *P* and *R* are *exactly the same* on the second dimension, as are *Q* and *S*. So, presumably, *however P compares with Q, that is how R should compare to S*, on similarity-based decision making. But virtually *nobody* would judge that *P* and *R* are better than *Q* and *S*, respectively. To the contrary, virtually everyone would agree that *P* would be *better* than *Q*, since more years of positive experiences are better than fewer years of similarly (slightly better) positive experiences, and *everyone* would agree that *R* would be *worse* than *S*, since more years of negative experiences are worse than fewer years of similarly (and even milder) negative experiences.

But the fact that this is so is enough to show that people would not *simply* use similarity-based decision making in comparing alternatives involving experiences of different value and duration. This is because people will *rightly* see that in valuing different experiences of different durations, the values of the intensity of the experience and the duration of the experience are *not* independent of each other, in the way one might assume (perhaps mistakenly!) that the value of being humorous is independent of the value of being physically beautiful in a prospective partner.

It may seem that I have been unfair to Voorhoeve and Binmore in offering such a strict interpretation of similarity-based decision making. Perhaps one shouldn't *completely* ignore a dimension along which two alternatives are similar, but one should only let the value of the first dimension affect whether increases along another dimension count positively or negatively. Thus, it might be agreed that for all negative experiences, such as pains, longer durations count negatively (as worse than shorter ones), while for all positive experiences, such as pleasures, longer durations count positively. Combined with that assumption, it might be claimed that people implicitly rely on similarity-based decision making in comparing alternatives involving different pains of different durations.

But this doesn't seem right either. Consider four new alternatives, *P*, *Q*, *R*, and *S*, where *P* = (−597, 2), *Q* = (−592, 4), *R* = (−3, 2), and *S* = (−2, 4). *P* represents our familiar alternative involving a pain (intense torture) of intensity −597, lasting two years; *Q* represents a similar pain of intensity −592, lasting four years; *R* represents our familiar alternative involving a pain (mosquito bite) of intensity −3, lasting two years; and *S* represents a similar pain of intensity −2, lasting four years. If we were invoking similarity-based decision making in comparing such alternatives, we should think that *P* stands to *Q* as *R* stands to *S*. The fact that we are dealing with pains would tell us that longer duration is worse, rather than better, but other than that we would ignore the similar first dimensions in comparing P with Q, and R with S, and simply judge that Q is worse than P for the same reason and to the same extent as we would judge that S is worse than R. In both cases, our judgments would simply be based on how they compared with respect to duration, and we would note that Q and S involve two more, or twice as many, years of pain as P and R, respectively. But, after years of discussing these issues with people, I am confident that most believe that the extent to which Q is worse than P is *much* greater than the extent to which S is worse than R. Specifically, many express the view that while S *is* worse than R, it isn't *much* worse, but they are confident that Q is, indeed, *much* worse than P.

These judgments, which virtually everyone makes, are not easily accounted for on the assumption that underlying our intuitions is an implicit appeal to similarity-based decision making. But it is easily accounted for if, as I have suggested, people are implicitly adopting an additive-aggregationist approach for comparing alternatives involving intensities that are "near" each other on the pain spectrum. On an additive-aggregationist approach, the value of P is determined by adding together each moment of intensity -597. This amounts to multiplying the first dimension, intensity, by the second, duration, and it generates an overall value score of $-1,194$ (where, for all value scores, m and n, $-n$ is worse than $-m$, if and only if $n > m$, and negative value scores correspond to *dis*value). By the same token, on this approach the value of Q is $-592 \times 4 = -2,368$, the value of R is $-3 \times 2 = -6$, and the value of S is $-2 \times 4 = -8$.

This way of comparing "near" alternatives on the pain spectrum readily explains people's intuitive reactions to the different pairs of alternatives. Q is rightly judged as *much* worse than P, involving $-1,174$ more units of value (which is to say much more *dis*value), whereas S is rightly judged as only a *little* worse than R, involving a mere -2 units more of value (which is to say only a little more disvalue). Indeed, this is why I often talk in terms of durations that are two or three or five times as long. For some people, the difference between R and S is so small that they don't feel it matters much one way or the other which outcome they might face. I think this is a mistake, but it is a fairly minor one; so I might ask them to compare R with an alternative, S', where a pain of intensity -2 lasts for *ten* years, which is five times as long as the duration of R's pain. In this case people calculate the value of S' as $-2 \times 10 = -20$, and while they may still rightly think that a value of -20 isn't *all* that bad, they typically readily admit that it would still be worse than R's value of -6. Suffice it to say, people are not relatively indifferent between P and Q; hence, I don't need to worry about appealing to durations of ten years, rather than four, when comparing a situation involving a pain of intensity -592 with P.

There would be *strong* reason to fight the move from a P-like situation to a Q-like situation, while there would only be a *minor* reason to fight the move from a R-like situation to an S-like situation. People intuitively feel, and have clearly recognized, this in thinking about my Spectrum Arguments. This is further support that underlying their intuitive judgments about alternatives involving intensities that are "near" each other on the pain spectrum is not the stage-two reasoning of similarity-based decision making, as Voorhoeve and Binmore have suggested, but the additive-aggregationist approach that I have suggested.

Finally, while I emphasize the fact that as one moves along my spectrum of alternatives one is comparing pains that are very similar in their intensities, but the durations of the less intense pains are *twice* (or three or five times) as long, there is an important *sense* in which what people clearly do in thinking about these situations is compare alternative *lives* of the *same* duration. Specifically, they reason in the following way. Suppose my choice is between a pain of intensity −200 for two years, and a pain of intensity −195 for four years. That is akin to a life that is the same in other respects, except that for *four* years there is a crucial difference. One way, two of the four years will involve a pain of −200, while the other two years will involve a pain of 0. The other way, two of the four years will involve a pain of −195, while the other two years will *also* involve a pain of −195.

In thinking about these alternatives, I do *not ignore* the dimension of pain intensity—since the pains on the two scenarios are similar—and simply focus on duration, with the thought that longer pains are worse than shorter ones. Rather, I am acutely aware that while the first alternative will be *worse* than the second for two years, it will also be *better* than the second for two years, and the extent to which it *will* be better is *directly* relevant to the *differences* in the levels of pain intensity being experienced in the two alternatives over the crucial four-year period. Specifically, thanks to a relevant difference in pain intensity that I do *not* ignore, I judge the first life as consistently worse than the second for two years—but only by 5 units per moment. On the other hand, thanks to another difference in pain intensity that I also do not ignore, I judge the first life as consistently *better* than the second for two years—and the extent to which it is better is *much* better than the extent to which it is worse, −195 units per moment, as opposed to merely −5. Since the durations of these differences in pain intensities are *equal*, this gives me *strong* reason to prefer the first life over the second. It is a reason provided by the fact that I will experience a much greater *total amount* of pain in the second life—together with the fact that the intensity of the pain experienced in the second life will be almost as bad as the intensity of the pain experienced in the first life.

Similarly, when I consider some disease of, say, utility −500 that will affect 1 million people, or some disease of utility −490 that will affect 2 million people, I do *not* simply disregard the differences between the two diseases, on the grounds that they are similar, and just focus on the number of people who are sick in the two scenarios, with the thought that it is worse for 2 million to be sick rather than 1 million. Rather, I am clearly aware that one situation will be *better* than the other, insofar as it involves 1 million only having utility of −490, rather than 1 million people having utility of −500. But, by the same token, I am also acutely aware that the extent to which the situation is better is relatively small, and *far* outweighed by the extent to which it is *worse*, insofar as it involves 1 million *others* also having a utility of −490, rather than 1 million others having a utility of 0. Here, as earlier, my judgment is based on the fact that the one situation involves so much more *total* negative utility due to disease—in a context where the difference between having the more severe disease in the one outcome and the less severe disease in the other is relatively minor.

Speaking for myself, I am confident that it is reasoning of the preceding sort that I am engaging in when considering my Spectrum Arguments for alternatives that are "near" each other along my spectrums. And having spoken with countless others about the rationale underlying their judgments about my cases, I am confident that many others are also relying on such reasoning. Such reasoning involves an additive-aggregationist approach that seems especially plausible for *such* comparisons. It does not rely on a similarity-based decision-making heuristic, as Voorhoeve and Binmore contend.

Let me sum up the argument to this point.[25] I *agree* that similarity-based decision making is fallacious and can lead us astray. But the suggestion that this is what lies behind the judgments in my Spectrum Arguments is implausible. There is little reason to be sympathetic to it, beyond the bare fact that my cases, like those where similarity-based decision making is involved, also involve small differences for certain comparisons. And we have now seen that there are strong reasons to believe that similarity-based reasoning is *not* what underlies my arguments. So, for anything Voorhoeve and Binmore have said to this point, we should continue to embrace the various premises of my Spectrum Arguments. Unfortunately, the pressure such arguments put on us remains—*including* the pressure to reconsider the truth or applicability of the premise that "all-things-considered better than" (in my wide reason-implying sense) is a transitive relation.

It is worth adding that if Voorhoeve and Binmore really believed that my arguments were based on similarity-based decision making, then they must reject View One of my Pain Spectrum Argument, since that is the only premise that involves alternatives that are "sufficiently" similar in certain respects as to possibly evoke similarity-based reasoning. But do they actually reject View One, or the analogous First Standard View from chapter 2? Nowhere do they tell us that they *do* reject those views. And for good reason. It is *deeply* implausible to do so!

Given the *real* choice between a pain of −597 for two years and a pain of −596 for four years, would they *really* take the latter? Can they honestly tell us—or themselves for that matter!—that our preference for the former is just a *mistake* based on a misapplied heuristic? And if *that* wouldn't be a mistake, why would it be a mistake to choose a pain of −596 for four years rather than a pain of −595 for eight years? And so on. Voorhoeve and Binmore need to tell us *where* in the spectrum from torture to mosquito bites we would be misapplying the heuristic of similarity-based decision making if we followed View One in choosing between adjacent alternatives. Or, at the very least, they need to claim that at *some* point—though they don't know where—it *would* be a mistake to choose a more

---

[25] Shelly Kagan suggested that I provide the following summary. He also suggested that I add the point I make in the following paragraph. Both this paragraph and the following one lightly paraphrase Kagan's suggestions.

intense pain over a *slightly* less intense pain that lasted two, or three, or five times as long! Could they really make such a claim with a straight face? Do they have an *argument* to offer in support of such a claim? Until they are prepared to make that claim and offer such an argument, the suggestion that my argument turns on fallacious similarity-based reasoning rings hollow.

I have discussed Voorhoeve and Binmore's claim that my Spectrum Arguments involve fallacious similarity-based decision making. As we have seen, this claim entails that we should reject the First View of my Pain Spectrum Argument. In his later article, "Heuristics and Biases," Voorhoeve also suggests that there is good reason to doubt the Third View of my Pain Spectrum Argument, and in particular our strong intuitive judgment that a long life with two years of torture would be worse than a long life with one extra mosquito bite per month. Let me end this section by examining the considerations Voorhoeve offers in support of his suggestion.

Voorhoeve begins his discussion by canvassing some pain research showing that in certain circumstances people's intuitive evaluations of pain episodes are unreliable. For example, Voorhoeve notes that in certain experiments:

> subjects displayed a phenomenon known as "duration neglect": the duration of experiences had little or no independent effect on the way they were evaluated. Instead, subjects appeared to evaluate these episodes by a constructed "representative moment": a collage of the intensity of pain at several singular instants, including the peak and end of the episode.[26]

He also notes that in other experiments:

> subjects appeared to rely on a kind of "anchoring and adjustment" heuristic in evaluating episodes: they took the aforementioned representative moment [of pain] as a base for their evaluation, and then made significant, but relatively small adjustments to this base to account for the episodes' duration.[27]

As Voorhoeve observes, one consequence of people's tendency to focus on the "peak" and "end" in evaluating a pain episode is that many subjects "will judge a shorter episode of pain as *worse* than a longer episode of pain which contains all the painful experiences of the shorter episode with some additional painful

---

[26] "Heuristics and Biases," 292. In support of these claims Voorhoeve cites Daniel Redelmeier and Daniel Kahneman, "Patients' Memories of Painful Medical Treatments: Real-Time and Retrospective Evaluations of Two Minimally Invasive Procedures," *Pain* 66 (1996): 3–8; also Carol Varey and Daniel Kahneman, "Experiences Extended across Time: Evaluation of Moments and Episodes," *Journal of Behavioral Decision Making* 5 (1992): 169–85. He also refers his reader to the literature cited in Daniel Kahneman, Peter Wakker, and Rakesh Sarin, "Back to Bentham? Explorations of Experienced Utility," *Quarterly Journal of Economics* 112 (1997): 375–405.

[27] "Heuristics and Biases," 293. In support of this claim Voorhoeve cites Charles Schreiber and Daniel Kahneman, "Determinants of the Remembered Utility of Aversive Sounds," *Journal of Experimental Psychology: General* 129 (2000): 27–42; and Kahneman, "Maps of Bounded Rationality," 477–78.

experiences, but which ends on a less unpleasant note."[28] This seems to patently involve some kind of cognitive failure or illusion. Understandably, then, Voorhoeve suggests that "preferences expressed in contexts that elicit duration neglect or the use of the anchoring and adjustment heuristic should be regarded with suspicion."[29]

Voorhoeve offers these observations as part of a possible explanation for why we might be suspicious of our firm intuition that two years of torture would be worse than any finite duration of a mosquito bite. Perhaps my presentation of these alternatives elicits duration neglect or the anchoring and adjustment heuristic. If this is the case—if, in fact, we aren't *really* taking the extreme duration of the mosquito bite adequately into account—then it won't be surprising if we judge the intense torture scenario as much worse than the mosquito bite scenario. But this, Voorhoeve implies, might just be another cognitive failure or illusion, like when we evaluate pain episodes in accordance with the "peak-end rule."

Voorhoeve's speculative claim here is interesting, and also a bit ironic. As we have seen, many respond to my torture to mosquito bite example by claiming that since humans don't live lives of extraordinary length, we can't accurately imagine how bad it really would be to experience one extra mosquito bite per month for countless years. Hence, they argue, having never actually experienced such a possibility, we can't trust any intuitions we might have about it. Voorhoeve, on the other hand, seems to accept that if we *did* live lives of extraordinary length, and our psychological mechanisms didn't change, then we might very well judge the extraordinarily long mosquito/pain alternative as much better than its two-year-long torture/pain alternative. But his point is that even if our intuitions remained firm were we to experience the two episodes, we should regard them as unreliable, and likely due to inappropriate duration neglect or the use of the anchoring and adjustment heuristic.

Voorhoeve is certainly right that even if people who *experienced* both alternatives uniformly agreed that two years of torture was worse than countless years of a mosquito bite, that wouldn't be enough to *establish* that their evaluative judgments were correct. But, of course, the fact that people are, under certain circumstances, susceptible to duration neglect and the anchoring and adjustment heuristic is not enough to prove that such cognitive mistakes are underlying the judgments they make about my hypothetical alternatives.

Consider the peak-end rule. Although some people seem to employ the peak-end rule to evaluate pain episodes they have *actually experienced*, I trust that few, if any, would employ the rule when judging between two hypothetical alternatives. That is, if you ask people which would be worse, alternative *A*, where they suffered great pain for a given duration, or alternative *B*, where they suffered the *very same* pain for the *very same* duration, and then suffered *further* pain, though of less intensity, for an additional period, I venture that no

---

[28] "Heuristics and Biases," 293. Here, again, Voorhoeve refers his reader to the literature cited in Kahneman, Wakker, and Sarin, "Back to Bentham?" and Schreiber and Kahneman, "Determinants."
[29] "Heuristics and Biases," 293.

one would judge A as *worse* than B, if the two pains episodes were considered abstractly just by themselves.

So, the mere fact that certain perceptual or cognitive mistakes or illusions arise when we reflect on our actual experiences hardly establishes that they are in play, and responsible for our judgments, about hypothetical cases. Perhaps, in some cases, they are. But perhaps in other cases, including mine, they are not.

In considering my alternatives, I am not making any claims about how people would psychologically react if they actually lived a life containing two years of intense torture, or how they would actually psychologically evaluate such a lived experience in comparison with the lived experience, were it possible, of *countless* years of a mosquito bite. I am asking how we *should*, normatively, evaluate the two pain episodes. I don't believe that the firm judgments most people make about such comparisons can easily be explained away by appeal to our tendency, in some cases, to neglect duration, or employ an anchoring and adjustment heuristic. People make the judgments they do because they believe that for *such* comparisons it is *appropriate* to employ an anti-additive-aggregationist approach. They believe that lots of moments of mosquito bites, spread out over time, or lives, do not *add up* in the way they would need to, in order to license the judgment that the lengthy mosquito pain episode would be worse than the two-year-long torture episode. Voorhoeve has to do much more than point out our psychological tendency to sometimes fail to adequately take duration into account. He has to actually argue for the theoretical claim that an additive-aggregationist approach is, in fact, appropriate even for comparisons of the kind in question. He hasn't offered us anything like such an argument.

Consider a variation of one of chapter 8's examples. Suppose that I were the benevolent leader of a planet with billions of people. Suppose, further, that I were actually capable of loving all of my fellow humans as I now love my children. Finally, suppose that a powerful alien comes and demands that I give it a nine-year-old girl, Ann, to use as its slave, including as a sex slave, for the following ten years. If I don't accede to its demand, one of two alternatives will ensue. *A*, it will take a nine-year-old boy, Bruce, and torture him mercilessly for two years. *B*, it will inflict on each of the billions of earthlings one mosquito bite that will itch for a month. To decide which alternative would be better, do I really have to "do the math" to determine if the *sum total* of negative experiences in B outweigh those in A, perhaps by a lot? I think not. Indeed, even if I *stipulate* that in accordance with an additive-aggregationist approach there will be a much greater *total* amount of suffering in B than in A, I am confident that B would be better. I am also confident that most others would agree with me.

In choosing between Ann and Bruce, I would be facing a Sophie's Choice scenario.[30] *Whatever* I decide, I may be destined to regret my decision, or to suffer

---

[30] In William Styron's book *Sophie's Choice* (New York: Random House, 1979), the main character, Sophie Zawistowska, was forced by a sadistic doctor at Auschwitz to choose which of her two young

from having made it, for the rest of my life. Choosing between Ann's slavery, and everyone getting a single mosquito bite for a month, would be *nothing like that*. It would be a no-brainer! I would immediately choose the mosquito bite option and never doubt, regret, or suffer from my decision, even for a moment. Can we explain away our intuitions about this kind of case by appeal to a psychological mechanism akin to duration neglect or the use of an anchoring and adjustment heuristic? This is dubious. Indeed, it isn't clear how such psychological factors would come into play or have any bearing on an example of this kind. What drives our judgment about this case has nothing to do with our actual felt experience of the alternatives in question, or some heuristic or faulty psychological mechanism that leads us to misremember, misinterpret, or misevaluate that felt experience. Rather, our judgment is driven by the fact that we have *reflectively* rejected an additive-aggregationist approach for comparing alternatives of the sort in question.

But if, as many believe, we can rationally reject an additive-aggregationist approach for determining the badness of pains across *different* people, then, as I have argued, we can *also* rationally reject an additive-aggregationist approach for determining the badness of pains across different times, *within* a single life. I conclude that while Voorhoeve is right that "preferences expressed in contexts that elicit duration neglect or the use of the anchoring and adjustment heuristic should be regarded with suspicion," this isn't enough to undermine the convictions that most people have regarding my alternatives. Although I can't rule out that our judgments ultimately rest on a cognitive mistake or illusion, I seriously doubt that our rejection of an additive-aggregationist approach in comparing alternatives at the opposite ends of my various spectrums ultimately rests on the kind of psychological mistakes or illusions to which Voorhoeve has pointed.

*****

I have now considered each of the main objections that have been raised to my Spectrum Arguments. I have argued that none of them is compelling. I conclude that the Spectrum Arguments raise deep problems that are not easily evaded. However, as much attention as I have devoted to these issues, it would still be premature to try to decide how best to respond to my Spectrum Arguments. Before doing that, one must consider many other issues, including how best to capture moral ideals in arriving at all-things-considered judgments (in my wide reason-implying sense), and how best to understand the nature of moral ideals. I turn to these issues in the following chapters.

---

children would die immediately by gassing, and which might continue to live. Failure to make the choice would have resulted in both dying immediately. The expression a "Sophie's Choice" has now come to be synonymous with a tragic choice between two utterly horrible and unbearable options. I discuss this kind of tragic choice further in section 14.7.

10

On the Value of Utility and Two Models for Combining Ideals

In previous chapters, I argued that we have a number of important beliefs that are inconsistent, and explored numerous objections, responses, and implications of my arguments. Among other things, I pointed out that often, in comparing outcomes, we adopt an additive-aggregationist approach, but often we adopt an anti-additive-aggregationist approach, and I noted that each approach seems plausible depending on the context. In this chapter, I turn to important new issues, considering how such approaches fit with our understanding of the value of utility, and the relation between utility and other ideals. I will explore a different way of understanding the value of utility and two different models for combining ideals, one of which (seemingly) fits our additive-aggregationist views and the other of which (seemingly) fits our anti-additive-aggregationist views. Exploring the value of utility and the different models for combining ideals will shed significant new light on the nature of the good, and the relations, scope, and structure of ideals. Unfortunately, however, each of the views I shall present is fraught with difficulties, only some of which will be broached here.

Like much of this book, this chapter raises far more questions than it answers. Indeed, the main conclusion we may ultimately draw is that none of the positions discussed are adequate or defensible, and that here, as elsewhere, our capacity to recognize serious problems considerably outstrips our current ability to solve them.

10.1 Preliminary Remarks

I don't know what the complete list of ideals is. Nor do I know how much different ideals matter relative to each other in different contexts and for different comparisons. But it is commonly supposed that *utility* is *one* ideal that is relevant for making certain comparisons, where *utility* is used as a term to represent the welfare, well-being, or quality of life of sentient beings. In particular, it is commonly held that there are many cases in which there are two outcomes, A and B, such that A's being better than B regarding utility—that is, A's being better than B in terms of the welfare, well-being, or quality of life of the sentient beings in those outcomes—provides some reason to judge A as a better outcome than B. In the following sections, I will consider several ways of thinking about the value of utility, and its relation to other ideals, in light of my discussion in previous chapters.

For the purposes of discussion, I shall assume that in addition to utility, only three other ideals are relevant for comparing the outcomes that I shall consider: equality, maximin, and perfectionism. Thus, I assume there is nothing to choose between the relevant outcomes in terms of other ideals such as virtue, duty, desert, autonomy, rights, and so on. This assumption is, of course, controversial—for what it both includes and excludes—so it is worth stressing that I make this assumption only for ease of presentation, and that none of my substantive claims hinge on it.

Also, I won't be providing anything like adequate characterizations, analyses, or measures of the different ideals I shall be considering. Fortunately, I don't need to do so for this chapter's purposes. It will be enough to give a rough idea of what the different ideals are concerned with and how they will be correlated with the outcomes I shall be considering. So, vastly simplifying for the purposes of discussion, I assume the following. *Equality* is concerned with how equally deserving people fare relative to each other. If the people in a given outcome are equally deserving and equally well off, that outcome is perfect regarding equality; if, among equally deserving people, some are worse off than others, that is bad, and the larger the gaps, the worse the outcome is regarding equality. *Maximin* aims for the worst-off group to fare as well as possible, so the worse off an outcome's worst-off group is, the worse the outcome is according to maximin. Accordingly, if the worst-off group in outcome A fares better than the worst-off group in outcome B, A would be ranked better than B according to maximin, and this would be so in proportion to the degree to which A's worst-off were better off than B's. Finally, *Perfectionism* is concerned with promoting that which is "best" or "highest" in human or global achievements. As noted in chapter 3, on different versions of perfectionism, the best outcome might be the one with the "greatest" achievements in social, political, moral, cultural, intellectual, or individual development. In what follows, I shall assume—again, this is *only* a simplifying assumption—that improvements in the best-off group's level are directly correlated with improvements regarding perfectionism. So, A will be ranked higher than B regarding perfection if its best-off group is better off than B's.

This concludes my preliminary comments. Let us now turn to a consideration of how to understand the value of utility, and two different models for understanding the value of utility, and the relation between utility and other ideals.

10.2 A Standard Model for Utility and a Standard Model for Combining Ideals

In thinking about utility, I believe many people implicitly accept six basic assumptions which I shall call:

The Standard Model for Utility:

1. Utility is noninstrumentally valuable—meaning that there is some value to utility over and above the extent to which it promotes other valuable ideals.
2. Utility is intrinsically valuable—meaning that each unit of utility contributes to the value of an outcome, and each unit contributes the same amount of value as every other, so that two units of utility add twice as much value to the goodness of an outcome as one, three units of utility add three times as much value to the goodness of an outcome as one unit and 50 percent more value to the goodness of an outcome as two units, and so on.
3. The ideal of utility is strictly neutral with respect to sentient beings, places, and times—meaning that a given amount of utility will count just as much no matter who experiences it, where it is experienced, or when it is experienced.
4. The ideal of utility is strictly impartial—meaning that each sentient being's utility counts as much as any other's.
5. Insofar as one cares about utility, one should care about total utility.
6. How good an outcome is regarding utility is a simple additive function of how much utility sentient beings have in that outcome.

I do not mean to imply that the preceding assumptions are wholly distinct. Perhaps 2 and 3 are equivalent, and 4, 5, and 6 are derivable from them, but whatever the precise logical relations between them, surely 2 through 6 are intimately related. I am mainly spelling out some widely shared assumptions about the ideal of utility, and how we understand the value of utility.

In thinking about how to assess the goodness of outcomes, I believe that most people also implicitly accept a position which I shall call:

The Standard Model for Combining Ideals: How good an outcome is all things considered is an additive function of how good it is regarding each ideal, so that insofar as an outcome gets better regarding any particular ideal it will, to that extent, be getting better all things considered.

The Standard Model for Combining Ideals assumes a numerical model for judging outcomes, according to which for each ideal relevant to assessing outcomes, each outcome will merit a (rough) numerical "score" representing how good that outcome is with respect to that ideal, and how good the outcome is all things considered will be represented by the numerical score arrived at by summing the individual scores of each relevant ideal.

In calling the preceding views "Standard Models" I do not mean to imply that everyone accepts them. For example, average utilitarians would reject assumption 5 of the Standard Model for Utility, and strict Kantians would reject most of the assumptions of the Standard Model for Utility, as well as the Standard Model for Combining Ideals. Nevertheless, the two Standard Models have great appeal. In fact, though rarely explicitly formulated, I believe that, together, they represent perhaps the most natural and prevalent way of thinking about utility and how it combines with other ideals to generate all-things-considered judgments about the goodness of outcomes.

The Standard Models reflect an additive-aggregationist approach in several separate ways. First, the Standard Model for Utility adds up utility within lives, to determine how good each individual life is regarding utility. Second, it adds up utility across lives, to determine how good each outcome is regarding utility. However, it is worth noting that, importantly, the Standard Model for Utility *needn't* focus on the value of utility within and across lives to determine how good an outcome is regarding utility. One could arrive at the same ranking of outcomes regarding utility by adding up all of the utility occurring at every space-time point (or every space-time region) in the outcome. Third, the Standard Model for Combining Ideals assumes that each outcome has a distinct value representing how good that outcome is with respect to each ideal, and it adds up the values of each ideal to determine how good the outcome is all things considered.

Throughout this work, I have suggested that there are many cases, and contexts, where an additive-aggregationist approach seems plausible. Given this, it shouldn't be surprising if many people have implicitly adopted the Standard Models for thinking about the value of utility and how it combines with other ideals to generate all-things-considered judgments about the goodness of outcomes. For such cases, and contexts, such models will seem plausible, and they capture our intuitive judgments. But I have also argued that there are many cases where an anti-additive-aggregationist approach seems plausible. I have argued that this is so both within and between lives. For such cases, we need an alternative model for thinking about the value of utility and how it combines with other ideals. I will sketch one such model later, noting that there are various ways of fleshing it out. But before doing that, let me discuss two features of the Standard Model for Utility that some may question in addition to its additive assumptions.

10.3 Is *All* Utility Noninstrumentally or Intrinsically Valuable?

Some people will reject assumptions 1 through 4 of the Standard Model for Utility. Specifically, some will deny that utility is always noninstrumentally valuable, will claim that not all utility is intrinsically valuable, or will argue that whether or not utility is valuable can depend on who receives it. Believing that utility consists, at least partially, in pleasure, or preference satisfaction, their view reflects the following positions: some pleasures or preference satisfactions are *not* valuable, indeed, some are positively *dis*valuable, and whether some pleasures or preference satisfactions are valuable depends, in part, on who is experiencing them. The thinking underlying these positions is familiar and can be stated briefly. I shall illustrate it in terms of pleasure, but similar points can be made in terms of preference satisfaction, or other plausible candidates for utility.

Some believe that there are some things one should not take pleasure in, and that if one does take pleasure in them that is a bad thing, not a good thing. For example, this is the case, some think, about the pleasure a sadist receives from watching an innocent person suffer. Holders of this view need not deny that the sadist's pleasure is genuine *pleasure* and that the sadist's utility has increased. But they insist that while the sadist's pleasure may be *subjectively* good, it is not *objectively* good. I shall return to the distinction between subjective and objective good later, but the key thought is simply that while the sadist's pleasure may be good *for him*, there is *no* respect in which it makes the *outcome* better. Advocates of this view challenge assumptions 1 and 2 of the Standard Model for Utility. Perhaps utility is noninstrumentally valuable or intrinsically valuable, subjectively, for the possessors of that value, but not *all* utility is noninstrumentally valuable or intrinsically valuable, objectively, for the goodness of outcomes.

Similarly, just as some believe that the objective value of pleasure depends on the *kind* of pleasure it is, some believe that the objective value of pleasure can depend on the nature of the agent experiencing it.[1] For example, some believe that there is nothing objectively valuable about an evil person receiving great pleasure and, more generally, that there is no objective value to the pleasure that a bad person receives beyond that which he *deserves*.[2] So, for example,

---

[1] Kant held this kind of view. Recall his claim at the end of the first section (Ak. 4:393) of the *Grounding of the Metaphysics of Morals* that "the sight of a being who is not graced by any touch of a pure and good will but who yet enjoys an uninterrupted prosperity can never delight a rational and impartial spectator" (trans. James W. Ellington [Indianapolis: Hackett, 1981], 7).

[2] Some may hold the even more general view that there is no objective value to *anyone* receiving more pleasure than they deserve, whether they are good or evil. But for many there seems to be an asymmetry in their attitudes toward people who are good and bad in this respect. They believe that if an evil sentient being receives utility beyond what he deserves, that utility is not objectively valuable and does not

while there may be nothing intrinsically *dis*valuable about the pleasures of enjoying perfect health, or the pleasures of good food, good company, or financial success, some believe that there is no respect in which an outcome is made better when an evil person experiences such pleasures, assuming that such pleasures contribute to his being better off than he deserves to be. As before, those who hold such a view need not deny that the evil person is experiencing pleasure in such cases and that he has greater utility. Likewise, they can admit that the greater utility is *subjectively* good *for* the evil person experiencing it. What they deny is that such utility makes the *outcome* in any way objectively better. This view denies assumptions 3 and 4 of the Standard Model for Utility—we shouldn't be neutral or impartial between an evil person receiving a certain amount of utility and a good person receiving such utility.

A variation of this position would admit *some* value to an evil person's utility beyond what he deserves, but deny that it is *as* valuable as the comparable utility of the innocent or good person. So, for example, on the assumption that both an evil person and an innocent or good person would get ten units of utility from activity x, the evil person's utility would have some objective value, contributing to the goodness of the outcome, but the innocent or good person's utility would have even more. Here, utility is understood in a way that corresponds to a *descriptive* measure of the *amount* of pleasure that someone receives, rather than an *evaluative* measure of the objective *value* of that pleasure. I shall return to the importance of this kind of distinction later.

The preceding views are controversial. Arguably, the sadist's or evil person's utility is just as valuable, *qua utility*, as that of the innocent or good person, but the former is (perhaps) *outweighed* by other bad features of the situation, for example, the suffering of the innocent person in which the sadist is taking delight, or the injustice of the evil person getting more than he deserves. Still, it is worth noting that even those who hold the views in question might accept revised versions of assumptions 1 through 4. Specifically, they might grant that 1 through 4 are plausible for so-called innocent pleasures, and as long as they are coming to sentient beings that are themselves good, innocent, or not undeserving of them.

I suggest, then, that while some might want to restrict the scope of utility to accommodate the concerns in question, this could be done if necessary. Accordingly, even those who worry about the unqualified versions of assumptions 1 through 4 might agree that suitably modified versions of 1 through 4 have great plausibility.

---

make the outcome better in any respect, while if an innocent or good sentient being receives utility beyond what he deserves, that utility is objectively valuable and helps make the outcome better. It is unclear whether this asymmetry is ultimately defensible, but I shall not pursue this here. Shelly Kagan explores these issues in his pathbreaking work *The Geometry of Desert* (Oxford University Press, forthcoming).

10.4 Total versus Average Utility

Some people reject assumption 5 of the Standard Model for Utility, because they think that we should be concerned about *average* rather than *total* utility. More particularly, some people believe that focusing on average utility provides a plausible way of capturing both our concern that utility matters and our anti-additive-aggregationist intuitions. As we will see soon, for some comparisons, at least, there may be good reason to reject assumption 5, but even if there is, I don't believe that insofar as we care about utility we should be concerned with average utility.

Average views are dubious for familiar reasons. Consider, for example, diagram 10.4.A, which illustrates an example of Derek Parfit's.[3]

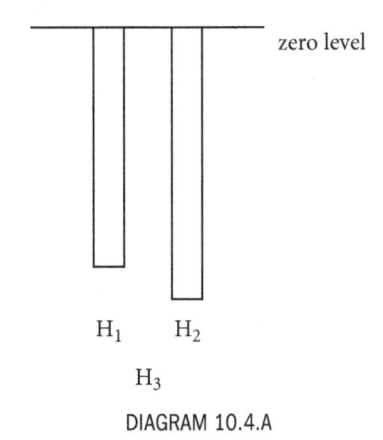

DIAGRAM 10.4.A

H_1 represents *Hell One*. It is populated by millions of completely innocent beings suffering excruciating pain of unimaginable proportions. Their lives are *far* worse than any lives ever lived on earth, well below the point at which life ceases to be worth living. If they could, everyone in Hell One would rationally choose to immediately kill themselves. Unfortunately, they can't: everyone in Hell One is doomed to remain there for billions of years. *Surely*, insofar as we care about *utility*, we should think that Hell One is an unbelievably horrible outcome and do everything we possibly could to prevent such an outcome from obtaining.

H_2 represents *Hell Two*. It is like Hell One, with the same size population of millions of innocent beings suffering excruciatingly for the same billions of years as those in Hell One, except that, somehow, everyone in Hell Two is even *worse* off than those in Hell One, though not by much. Clearly, insofar as we care about utility, we should regard Hell Two as even *more* horrible than Hell One.

Next, consider *Hell Three*. Hell Three includes *both* Hell One and Hell Two. In Hell Three there are twice as many innocent people suffering unbelievable

---

[3] See part 4 of Derek Parfit's *Reasons and Persons* (Oxford: Oxford University Press, 1984), 422.

torments as there are in either Hell One or Hell Two alone. Surely, if anything in the world is clear, it is that Hell Three is much worse than either Hell One or Hell Two alone. Surely, insofar as we care about *utility*, we should find Hell Three the most objectionable of the three hells, and the one we have *most* reason to prevent from obtaining.

Now suppose the devil has created Hell Two. He tells us that we can improve the outcome by pushing a button labeled H_1. When we ask him what will happen if we push the button, he smiles and informs us that doing so will create an equal number of innocent people to those who are already in Hell Two, and that they will be tormented mercilessly, though not *quite* as badly as those in Hell Two! Specifically, by pushing the H_1 button we will be bringing about Hell One, and *adding* it to the previously existing Hell Two, thereby transforming the outcome from Hell Two into Hell Three. *Surely*, we ought *not* to push the button! More to the point, *insofar as we care about utility*, we ought not to push the button. There is simply *no* respect in which one *improves* an outcome regarding *utility*, by creating millions of innocent people and subjecting them to the excruciating pain of unimaginable proportions that obtains in Hell One.

But notice, Hell Three has a higher *average* level of utility than Hell Two! Still, the *only* reason that adding Hell One to Hell Two increases the average level of utility in the outcome is that the unfortunate innocents in Hell Two are even *worse* off than those in Hell One. Adding Hell One to Hell Two does absolutely *nothing* to lessen the horribleness of Hell Two's situation regarding utility. Likewise, the presence of Hell Two does absolutely nothing to lessen the horribleness of Hell One's situation regarding utility. Given this, there is absolutely *no* reason to believe that Hell Three is better than Hell Two regarding utility. As indicated, one does *not* improve a situation regarding utility in *any* respect, merely by adding millions of excruciatingly tormented people to an already horrific situation.[4] Thus, I submit that while average utility may often be *correlated* with other morally relevant factors, it is not *itself* morally relevant.

Here is another example, regarding perfection, rather than utility. Consider the three following works: Michelangelo's 1499 *Pietà*, Rembrandt's 1658 *Self-Portrait*, and da Vinci's *Mona Lisa*.[5] There is general agreement that these

---

[4] My claim here concerns the ideal of *utility*. On my view there are *certain* respects in which adding millions of tormented people to an already horrific situation *could* improve an outcome regarding the ideal of *equality*, but this is because on my view the ideal of equality is concerned with how people fare *relative to others* in a way that utility is not. I hasten to add that on my view such a change would not be an *all-things-considered* improvement even regarding equality, let alone taking account of all relevant ideals. For further discussion of these issues, see *Inequality* (New York: Oxford University Press, 1993) especially chapter 7.

[5] For those readers who are curious, da Vinci created only one *Mona Lisa*, while Michelangelo created several important pietàs, and Rembrandt created a number of self-portraits. Hence, I include dates to fix the reference to what are, in my judgment, Michelangelo's best *Pietà* and Rembrandt's best *Self-Portrait*, whereas a date is unnecessary to fix the reference of da Vinci's *Mona Lisa*.

are three masterpieces, among the greatest artistic works produced within Western civilization. Suppose, ridiculously of course, that we could precisely rank all three works in terms of their perfection, on a scale of 1 through 100, and that the *Pietà* ranked 98, the *Self-Portrait* 94, and the *Mona Lisa* 91, where any ranking in the 90s reflected true genius, and the *vast* majority of artworks didn't rank above 50.

Next, suppose that I decided to become an art collector and that I wanted to acquire the most perfect masterpieces I could get my hands on, where my sole criterion in assembling my collection was that it, and the works within it, be as close to perfect as possible. Suppose that I could acquire, as the very first piece in my collection, the *Pietà*. Alternatively, for the very same amount of money, I could acquire the *Pietà and* both the *Self-Portrait* and the *Mona Lisa*. Specifically, suppose that the latter two masterpieces would be thrown in *for free*, if I wanted, as long as I promised to include them in my collection. Surely, it would be *ludicrous* for me to turn down two of the greatest masterpieces in the history of Western civilization *merely* because if I did so it would lower the *average* level of perfection in my collection!

I can understand the view that it would be a mistake to add a lot of schlock to my collection, even if it were given to me for free. That seems to me clearly true. I can also understand the view that it would be a mistake to add a lot of genuinely important art to my collection, if it weren't a work of true genius. That seems to me less clearly true, but still a plausible position. I can *even* understand the view that adding the *Self-Portrait* and the *Mona Lisa* wouldn't *improve* my collection, relative to my just owning the *Pietà*. Perhaps, insofar as one cares about perfection, one should be *solely* concerned about the quality of the *very* best work in one's collection. While I find such a view deeply implausible, I don't find it completely absurd. But what I can't understand, and *do* find absurd, is the idea that adding two of the greatest works in the history of Western civilization would actually make my collection *worse* regarding perfectionism, simply because doing so would lower the *average* level of perfection of my collection's pieces. As earlier, I think there are many cases where a collection's average level of perfection may correlate with underlying factors that one *should* care about, but I see absolutely *no* reason to believe that insofar as one cares about an outcome's perfection, one should care about the outcome's *average* level of perfection. As with average utility, *average* perfection is not *itself* significant.[6]

---

[6] Parfit once used an example of this sort in his seminars to argue against average views in general, and not just average views regarding perfection. He noted that the Louvre's Reserve Collection was not as good as its Main Collection, but that by itself the Reserve Collection would probably be one of the ten greatest art museums in the world. Parfit would then ask, rhetorically, whether it was really plausible to believe that the Louvre's entire collection was actually made *worse* because it *included* a collection of works that on its own would be one of the world's ten best. Parfit thought not, but he pointed out,

Consider one final example, to illustrate the weakness of focusing on averages. Suppose, contrary to fact, that members of families with 3 children were very happy, members of families with 2 or 4 children were *almost* as happy, members of families with 1 or 5 children were pretty unhappy, and members of families with 0 or 6 children were miserable. Suppose, next, that one knew that in community A, the average number of children was 3, while in community B, the average number of children was 2.5. Based on that information, one would have *no* idea whether the people in A were happier than those in B, or even whether those in A were "on average" happier than those in B. The problem, of course, is that even though the "average" family size in A is "ideal," and the average family size in B is less than ideal, that tells us *nothing* important about the actual sizes of the families in A and B. For all we know, half the families in A have 0 children, and the other half have 6; while half the families in B have 3 children, while the other half have 2. In that case, *everyone* in B would be *much* happier than *everyone* in A, and B would rightly be regarded as the much happier society. Here again, we see the danger of focusing on averages, rather than on the underlying factors that generate those averages.

There may be some conventional cases where averages are particularly salient and significant. For example, the batting title may go to the hitter with the highest average, and the team bowling championship may go to the team with the highest average scores. Here, one may not care *at all* about the underlying scores that produce those averages; all that matters is the averages themselves. Still, I suggest that in most morally important cases averages are only significant when they are fortuitously correlated with underlying factors that are themselves morally significant, and hence that the significance of the former is derivative from the significance of the latter. Thus, it is generally mistaken and can be seriously misleading to focus on the average level of an outcome with respect to a given ideal, in assessing how good that outcome is regarding that ideal.

I think, then, that insofar as one cares about utility, one ought not to care about average utility. More generally, I believe that an outcome's average level, with respect to a given ideal, is not *itself* of moral significance. Having said that, let me make three qualifying remarks about these considerations.

First, it is all too common in moral philosophy for someone to argue against a moral ideal by showing that that ideal, considered alone, has deeply implausible consequences. But as I have argued in many other works,[7] such arguments are weak. For each ideal, it may be easy to construct examples

---

correctly, that the *average* quality of the Louvre's collection was lower, as a result of its having the Reserve Collection *in addition* to its even greater Main Collection. My example is even harder to resist, since it involves only works of true genius, whereas the Louvre's Reserve Collection includes many pieces that, though outstanding in their own right, don't rise to the level of genius.

[7] I make this point in many places. See, for example, "Egalitarianism Defended," *Ethics* 113 (2003): 764–82; "Equality, Priority, or What?" *Economics and Philosophy* 19 (2003): 61–88; "Egalitarianism:

where that ideal, considered alone, has deeply implausible consequences. This wouldn't show that we should reject every putative moral ideal. All it would show is that morality is very complex, and that no moral ideal, alone, can capture *all* of our all-things-considered judgments.

Still, we should distinguish between cases which merely reveal that an ideal would have implausible implications if we acted as if it were the only ideal that mattered, and cases where a purported ideal seemingly lacks force altogether. In the former cases, we still feel the force of a moral ideal, but recognize that the ideal is *outweighed* by other ideals that we also value. In the latter cases, it *isn't* that the reasons a purported ideal provides for preferring one outcome to another are *outweighed* by competing reasons but, rather, that the purported ideal provides *no* reasons for preferring one outcome to another.

This distinction is crucially important. We *might* think that insofar as one cares about utility one should care about *average* utility, but agree that Hell Three is much worse than Hell Two *all things considered*. Here, one would be holding that Hell Three is better in *one* important respect—namely, with respect to average utility—but recognizing that there are *other* important respects in which Hell Three is worse, and that these far outweigh the respect in which it is better. But when I think about the cases in question, that isn't my reaction. I see, of course, that Hell Three has a higher *average* level of utility than Hell Two, but I don't see that that makes Hell Three normatively *better* than Hell Two in *any* respect. That is, on reflection, it seems clear that insofar as I care about *utility*, I should regard Hell Three as unequivocally *worse* than Hell Two, and that Hell Three's higher average of utility provides one with absolutely *no* reason to regard Hell Three as a better outcome than Hell Two.

Second, even if I am correct regarding the foregoing considerations, I readily grant that this does not, and cannot, conclusively establish that average views have *no* role to play in our best understanding of moral ideals. After all, as indicated in section 7.3, like many, I accept the kind of view that Frances Kamm called the *Principle of Contextual Interaction*.[8] In accordance with this, it is possible that an ideal might have *no* weight in certain contexts, and yet still have weight in other contexts. This is like the possibility discussed in section 10.3, that certain pleasures might have no weight if experienced by an evil person, and yet have positive weight if experienced by an "innocent" or good person. Thus, even if average utility has no weight or significance in cases like Hell Three and Hell Two, it might have weight in other scenarios.

A Complex, Individualistic, and Comparative Notion," in *Philosophical Issues*, vol. 11, ed. Ernie Sosa and Enrique Villanueva (Boston: Blackwell, 2001), 327–52; "Equality, Priority, and the Levelling Down Objection," in *The Ideal of Equality*, ed. Matthew Clayton and Andrew Williams (London: Macmillan; New York: St. Martin's Press, 2000), 126–61; and also *Inequality*.

[8] On the Principle of Contextual Interaction, see, for example, Kamm's *Intricate Ethics* (New York: Oxford University Press, 2007), 17, 45, 348, and 412.

So, I am open to the possibility that someone will offer a convincing argument for the significance of average utility, or the average of some other ideal, in certain cases. But I haven't seen such an argument yet, and am doubtful whether one will be produced. Given the previous considerations, I think the onus is on average-view advocates to present some cases where we need to rely on average views to adequately capture our moral views.

Finally, let me emphasize that my remarks have no bearing on the question of whether average utilitarianism might be more plausible than total utilitarianism as a complete moral theory—where *average utilitarianism* holds that one action or outcome is better than another if and only if it has a higher *average* level of utility, while *total utilitarianism* holds that one action or outcome is better than another if and only if it has a greater *total* amount of utility. It might. Utilitarians believe that utility is *all* that matters. So they need a principle of utility that captures *all* of our moral judgments by *itself*. Since total utilitarianism notoriously ignores distributional considerations in ranking outcomes, and average utilitarianism often seems to reflect distributional considerations in its rankings, the latter may do a better job of tracking our all-things-considered judgments than the former. After all, most of us believe that distributional considerations *do* matter.

Still, if one is a pluralist, as I am, the question to be addressed is not whether average or total utilitarianism is more plausible as a complete moral theory, but whether either or both reflect moral ideals that need to be incorporated into our full moral theory. As indicated, I think average utility does not plausibly reflect our concern for utility. I also think it is not the best way of capturing our distributive concerns. Such concerns are better captured, more directly, through principles like equality, maximin, or the Disperse Additional Burdens View. I suspect, then, that we won't have to make room for average utility in our complete moral theory.

Total utility is another matter. There are many cases where it seems that *insofar as we care about utility*, we care about *total* utility. And for many of these cases, the Standard Model for Utility together with the Standard Model for Combining Ideals seem plausible. However, there are many cases where the Standard Models don't seem plausible, and where the total view seems dubious *even* insofar as our concern is with *utility*. Unsurprisingly, these are the cases for which an anti-additive-aggregationist approach seems right. I shall illustrate this, and suggest some possible ways of responding to it, in the following sections.

10.5 Revisiting the Repugnant Conclusion

In chapter 2, I discussed Derek Parfit's Repugnant Conclusion, which is illustrated with the aid of diagram 10.5.A.

According to the Repugnant Conclusion, if only there are *enough* people in Z, Z will be better than A, and this is so no matter *how* large A's population

On the Value of Utility   **325**

DIAGRAM 10.5.A

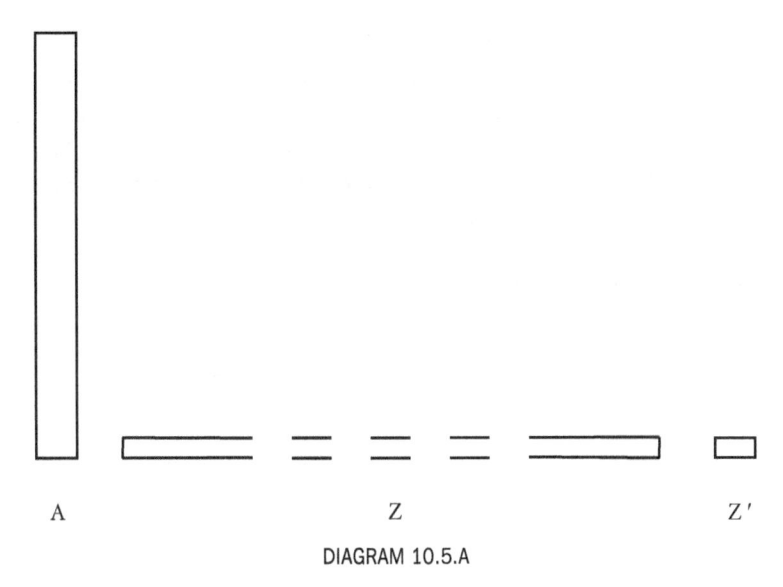

is, and even if those in A are as well off as anyone who has ever lived, while those in Z have lives barely worth living. As Parfit writes, "This conclusion [is] very hard to accept."[9]

In initially presenting the Repugnant Conclusion, I observed that most people agree with Parfit that the Repugnant Conclusion is, indeed, repugnant. I offered it as one of several examples where people intuitively reject a simple additive-aggregationist approach to assessing outcomes. We can now understand better to what that rejection commits us. It commits us to rejecting the combination of the Standard Model for Utility and the Standard Model for Combining Ideals, when comparing outcomes like A with outcomes like Z. This is because, together, the Standard Models entail the Repugnant Conclusion, given certain plausible assumptions about how to value A and Z with respect to other relevant ideals.

Recall that for the purposes of this discussion we are assuming that the only ideals relevant for comparing A with Z are utility (U), equality (E), maximin (M), and perfectionism (P). Also recall that for our present purposes, we are assuming a correlation between how good an outcome is regarding the levels of the best-off people, and how good it is regarding perfectionism.

On these assumptions, if we first imagined a world, Z', that had the same size population as A but where everyone was at the level of the people in Z, we would judge that A was as good as Z' regarding E—since, in each outcome, each person is as well off as everyone else in that outcome, each outcome is perfect regarding equality—but we would judge that A was much better than Z' regarding U, M, and P.

---

[9] *Reasons and Persons*, 388.

The Standard Models would rightly yield this judgment. In accordance with the Standard Model for Combining Ideals, a numerical "score" would be given to A and Z' for each ideal that mattered, and those individual scores would then be added together to yield the total scores for each outcome, representing how good they were "all things considered." As indicated, A and Z' would receive the same numerical score for equality, but A would receive much higher scores for U, M, and P. For illustrative purposes, let's suppose that, regarding each relevant ideal, A's scores are $E = 100$, $U = 90$, $M = 90$, and $P = 90$, while the scores for Z' are $E = 100$, $U = 10$, $M = 10$, and $P = 10$. Since A's total score would be 370, while the total score for Z' would be 130, A would clearly, and plausibly, be ranked higher than Z' on the Standard Model for Combining Ideals.

Next, suppose that other people at the very same level are added to those in Z', so as to gradually transform Z' into Z. Since maximin focuses on the expectations of the representative member of society's worst-off group, and merely *adding* more people to Z' at the very same level neither increases nor decreases the expectations of the representative member of the outcome's worst-off group, it is plausible to contend that there will be no significant difference between the scores for Z and Z' regarding M.[10] Similarly, it is plausible to believe that while merely adding more people to an outcome, with lives worth living, may not *improve* the outcome regarding perfection, it won't *worsen* it either.[11] It appears, then, that Z will get the same score as Z' for E,

---

[10] One might think that since the expectations of the representative member of the worst-off group are the same in Z and Z', they should be exactly equally as good regarding maximin. But, on some views, it is arguable that numbers should serve as a possible tiebreaker. That is, maximin may be construed as dictating that we first maximize the expectations of the representative member of the worst-off group, and then seek to minimize the number of people in that group. But if numbers only serve in this way as a possible *tiebreaker* between outcomes, then it is plausible to say that there is no "significant" difference between any two outcomes whose representative members of the worst-off group are equally well off. Hence, my claim as to the relation between Z and Z'—that there will be no significant difference between them regarding maximin—allows for the possible tie-breaking role of numbers. Still, in chapter 12, I will suggest that maximin's tie-breaking clause will only be plausible, if ever, in certain contexts, and in particular that the most plausible version of maximin would not rank Z as worse than Z' regarding maximin.

Interestingly, to make sense of the view that the number of people in the worst-off group may count for maximin, but only in a tie-breaking role, may require that one resort to infinitesimals if one wants to continue to employ a numerical model for ranking outcomes regarding maximin. But infinitesimals are not real numbers, so one won't be able to assign a score representing how good an outcome is regarding maximin on a real number line. Correspondingly, on both the Standard Model for Combining Ideals and the Capped Model for Ideals that I shall consider shortly, one wouldn't be able to assign a score representing how good an outcome is all things considered on a real number line. This is a complicating feature about how best to understand or interpret tie-breaking clauses that is, I think, quite general, but having mentioned it, I won't pursue it further. I am grateful to Shelly Kagan for bringing this point to my attention.

[11] Later in this chapter, I will argue that ideals share certain structural or formal features. In particular, I will argue that if numbers count for utility, as many believe, they may also count for equality. Given this, it may also be that numbers count for other ideals as well, including perfection. In that case,

basically the same score as Z' for M, and at least as good a score as Z' for P. So, it is safe to say that Z's scores will be $E = 100$, $M = {\sim}10$, and $P > 10$. So, on the Standard Model for Combining Ideals, Z's overall score will be approximately equal to, or greater than, 120, *plus* whatever score it receives for utility.

But, on assumptions 2 through 6 of the Standard Model for Utility, even if there is only a *tiny* bit of utility in each person's life in Z, each bit of utility will have the same intrinsic value, and will contribute to how good the outcome is regarding utility by the same, constant amount. In particular, how good Z is regarding utility will be a simple additive function of how much *total* utility there is in each of Z's many lives. So, as long as there are *enough* people in Z, Z's score for utility will exceed 250. Thus, given the Standard Model for Utility together with the Standard Model for Combining Ideals, if only Z is large enough its overall score will exceed 370, and it will be ranked as better than A all things considered.

We see, then, that together the Standard Models entail the Repugnant Conclusion.[12] This is not surprising, but it is important. The Standard Models reflect an additive-aggregationist approach to the assessment of outcomes. But the Repugnant Conclusion is one of many examples about which people have strong anti-additive-aggregationist intuitions. Correspondingly, if we want to avoid the Repugnant Conclusion, and capture our other anti-additive-aggregationist intuitions, we must develop an alternative model to the Standard Models for understanding utility and the role that it plays in our all-things-considered judgments. More carefully, even if we think the Standard Models are appropriate for *certain* comparisons (namely, those for which an additive-aggrega-

---

adding more people to an outcome whose lives have positive value regarding perfection should *improve* the outcome regarding perfection, and this would make the outcome better, overall, on the Standard Model for Combining Ideals. This would strengthen my current argument. But I don't want to rely on this position here. For now, I want to allow for the possibility that merely adding more people to an outcome whose lives, individually, have positive value regarding perfection may not make the *outcome* better regarding that ideal. This is a view that many people will, at least initially, find intuitively plausible, so it is worth considering.

I should add that it *is* important to my argument that I am assuming that the individual lives in Z' do not have *negative* value regarding perfection. That is, I am assuming that the level of perfection in Z is much *less* than that in A, but that it isn't *bad*; thus, if anything, it adds positive value to the outcome, not negative value. We may, if we like, think of the people in Z as living lives similar to those of cats. Cats don't have nearly the opportunities to achieve perfection that humans have, but we wouldn't be inclined to think that merely adding lots more cats to an outcome, living their limited cat lives, would make the outcome *worse* regarding perfection. That is the kind of thought I have in mind in claiming that merely adding more people at the level of those in Z would not itself make the outcome *worse* regarding perfection.

[12] Given the key assumption, implied earlier, that the mere addition of extra people whose lives were both worth living and as good as everyone else's would not (significantly) *worsen* an outcome with respect to those ideals relevant to assessing the goodness of outcomes. Note, even if one thought that adding extra people made an outcome worse to some extent, for certain ideals, as long as the extent to which the outcome was made better by adding extra people regarding utility outweighed the extent to which it was made worse regarding other ideals, the Repugnant Conclusion would follow on the Standard Models.

tionist approach are appropriate), we need to develop an *alternative* model for certain other comparisons (namely, those for which an anti-additive-aggregationist approach is appropriate). Let us consider one such model next.

10.6 The Capped Model for Ideals

Reflecting on the Repugnant Conclusion, most of us are reminded that we are not strict total utilitarians.[13] After all, if we were strict total utilitarians, we wouldn't find the Repugnant Conclusion repugnant! For most, this reminder hardly comes as a revelation. While utility matters a lot, virtually everyone agrees—including virtually all modern consequentialists—that it is not *all* that matters. If this "reminder" were all there were to be gleaned from considering the Repugnant Conclusion, it would not be particularly interesting. But it is not. In thinking about the Repugnant Conclusion, and other similar cases, we learn a further, deeper lesson. We learn that mere increases in *quantity* of utility are not sufficient—or so we think—to outweigh significant losses regarding other ideals. *This* is why Z is worse than A. Even if we think Z is better regarding utility, it is not better regarding equality, and it is much *worse* regarding other ideals, like maximin and perfectionism.

The importance of the further lesson cannot be exaggerated. As seen earlier, it implies that for certain comparisons, at least, we need to reject the combination of the Standard Model for Utility and the Standard Model for Combining Ideals. Additionally, it *suggests* that for certain comparisons there may be an upper limit to how *good* situations can be regarding utility. Moreover, if this is so for utility, it is probably also so for the other ideals, and hence, for certain comparisons there may also be an upper limit to how good situations can be all things considered (in my wide reason-implying sense).

Consider an analogy from sports. In gymnastics competition, the best all-around gymnast is determined by adding together each person's score in each event. For women, there are four events, and on the scoring system that was in place until 2005, each event had a maximum score of 10, so, the maximum total score one could attain was 40.[14] While one could approach,

---

[13] Here, and in what follows, when I refer to "total utilitarianism" or "strict total utilitarianism," it is classical versions of utilitarianism that I have in mind. As espoused by such proponents as Bentham, Mill, and Sidgwick, classical utilitarianism was a version of total utilitarianism that involved a deep commitment to additive aggregation, partly in virtue of its conception of the good. As Roger Crisp pointed out (in correspondence), depending on their conceptions of the good, there could be some versions of total utilitarianism that rejected additive aggregation.

[14] As indicated, this scoring system is no longer in use, but since I have been using this example for many years now, and it nicely illustrates the point I want to make, I shall continue to use it. As should be evident, the fact that women's gymnastics has moved to a much more complicated scoring system is irrelevant to my claims and arguments.

and even attain, a perfect performance, one could never exceed the maximum score. So, to be the best all-around gymnast, it wasn't enough to near, or even attain, perfection in the floor exercises. One also had to excel on the balance beam, the vault, and the uneven parallel bars. For example, suppose that Olga was *perfect* in the floor exercises, earning a 10, but dreadful in the other events, earning a 3 in each, whereas Nadia was consistently very strong, though not perfect, in all of the events, earning a 9 in each. Nadia's total score would have been 36, Olga's would have been 19, and Nadia would rightly have been judged a *much* better all-around gymnast than Olga.

On reflection, it seems something like this may also hold for certain of our all-things-considered judgments (in my wide reason-implying sense). Perhaps, in comparing certain situations, all things considered, we must compare them in terms of each ideal, where there is a maximum score they can get for each ideal, determined by how much the ideals matter vis-à-vis each other. And perhaps, having already taken account of how much the ideals matter vis-à-vis each other in setting their upper limits, we can arrive at an outcome's all-things-considered score by simply adding up the scores it gets for each relevant ideal. Suppose, for example, that in assessing certain outcomes, U, E, M, and P were equally important and all we cared about. Then we might assign numbers to outcomes such that the highest score an outcome could get for each ideal would be, say, 100 and the perfect outcome—were it possible—would score 400. Similarly, to note a more complicated example, if we thought that P and E were equally important, but twice as important as M, and half as important as U, then we might assign numbers to outcomes such that the highest score an outcome could get would be, say, 150 for P and E, 75 for M, and 300 for U. In that case, the perfect outcome would score 675. Clearly, the highest score for each ideal sets an upper limit to the score that an outcome can receive for that ideal. Outcomes will receive the highest score for an ideal if they are perfect regarding that ideal; to the extent that they are less than perfect, they will receive appropriately lower scores. Also clearly, on this view there will be an upper limit on how good an outcome can be all things considered. Let us call such a position the *Capped Model for Ideals*.

As presented, the Capped Model is compatible with the Standard Model for Combining Ideals. That is, like the Standard Model for Combining Ideals, the Capped Model can endorse a numerical model for judging outcomes, according to which (1) for each ideal relevant to assessing outcomes, each outcome will merit a (rough) numerical "score" representing how good that outcome is with respect to that ideal, and (2) how good the outcome is all things considered will be represented by the numerical score arrived at by summing the individual scores of each relevant ideal. But the Capped Model *supplements* the Standard Model for Combining Ideals with a crucial third clause, namely, (3) that there is an upper limit on how much *better* any individual ideal can make an outcome, all things considered, and hence an upper limit on the maximum score that can be given for any ideal, representing how good an outcome is regarding that ideal. Together, the second and third clauses imply (4) that there is an upper limit on the total score that an outcome can get, and hence an upper limit on how good an outcome can be all things considered. As we will see later, important variations of these four clauses are consistent with what might be reasonably called a Capped Model, but for now, I shall assume that the Capped Model includes a commitment to each of the four clauses just noted.

On one version of the Capped Model, a "perfect" outcome regarding U—one that could not be improved upon and would merit the highest possible score regarding U—would have infinite total utility. On this view, no finite world will be perfect regarding utility. So, on this Capped Model, a finite world may approach the maximum score for utility, but it can never attain that score or go beyond it. Note, on the Capped Model, there is no limit on how *much* utility can be added to an outcome. In addition, for any finite outcome, it may always be possible to improve that outcome regarding utility—even if only slightly. However, as there is an upper limit on how good an outcome can be regarding utility, there is also an upper limit on how much an outcome can be improved—that is, be made normatively *better*—regarding utility. So, after a point, mere increases in the *amount* of utility will not substantially increase the *value* of an outcome, even regarding utility. It follows that, on the Capped Model, mere increases in utility alone, however great, will not generally be sufficient to outweigh significant losses in other respects.

To illustrate this position, let us again make the simplifying assumption that each ideal matters equally, and let us arbitrarily assign scores to A and Z of up to 100 for U, E, M, and P. A is perfect regarding E, and, by hypothesis, very good for U, M, and P. So let us suppose that $E = 100$, $U = 90$, $M = 90$, and $P = 90$. A would then have an all-things-considered score of 370. Z is also perfect regarding E, and, on the version of the Capped Model we are currently supposing, we may suppose that it is also nearly perfect[15] regarding U, but it is much worse regarding M and P. For Z, then, let us suppose $E = 100$ and $U = 99$, but $M = 10$ and $P = 10$. Z would then have an all-things-considered score of 219—a full 151 points lower than A's on a scale of only 400!

Notice, even if one thought that utility was the *most* important ideal, the Capped Model could capture our intuition that the Repugnant Conclusion

---

[15] As Parfit originally presents the Repugnant Conclusion, there is no reason to suppose that Z is "nearly perfect" regarding U, only that it is better than A. So, if $U = 90$ for A, we know $U > 90$ for Z, for example, it might be that $U = 91$ for Z. But on the position we are now discussing there will be some population size such that if Z were that size it would not merely be better than A, it would be nearly perfect regarding U. Though we could just as easily make our point using the "weaker" assumption that Z is (merely) better than A regarding U, the assumption that Z is "nearly perfect" strengthens the force of our example and better illustrates the position under discussion.

really is repugnant. Suppose, for example, that we thought utility was three times more important than any other ideal, so that the maximum score for utility was 300, while that for the other ideals was 100. Presumably, A, which has billions of people all of whom are incredibly well off, would have a really high score for utility, while we are supposing that Z, which has countless people with lives barely worth living, would nearly have the maximum score regarding utility. It might then be that A's scores would be $E = 100$, $U = 275$, $M = 90$, and $P = 90$, for an all-things-considered score of 555, while Z's scores would be $E = 100$, $U = 299$, $M = 10$, and $P = 10$, for an all-things-considered score of 419. We see that counting utility for much more than the other ideals would reduce the significance of the difference between A and Z—making the Repugnant Conclusion somewhat *less* repugnant—relative to when U was no more important than the other ideals, but there would still be a gap of 136 on a scale of only 600.

One can see, then, how a Capped Model could account for the genuine repugnancy of the Repugnant Conclusion. To be a *really* good outcome, overall, one must be good with respect to all, or most, of the ideals that significantly matter. A is, but Z, decidedly, is not.

Does the Capped Model entail the controversial claim that there is a diminishing marginal utility of utility? No, at least not in a way that is obviously objectionable. Unfortunately, there is an ambiguity in the usage of "utility," an ambiguity fostered by a rich philosophical tradition. "Utility" is often used interchangeably with such notions as "happiness," "welfare," and "quality of life." Moreover, given the influence of classical utilitarianism and its followers—according to which something is valuable to the extent, and only to the extent, that it promotes increases in happiness, welfare, or quality of life—"utility" is also often used interchangeably with the notion of "value." The Capped Model does *not* imply that there is a diminishing marginal utility (happiness) of utility (happiness)—that is, that the better off someone is, the less their happiness would be increased by each extra unit of happiness. I share the view that such a position is unintelligible. However, the Capped Model does imply that there is a diminishing marginal utility (value) of utility (happiness)—that is, that the objective *value* of increasing a situation's happiness by a certain amount is less if the situation already has a lot of happiness than if it doesn't. Such a position is not unintelligible; it merely requires that one break the particular intimate connection between value and happiness prescribed by utilitarianism. Here, the difference between the subjective and objective perspective of these matters is important, about which I shall say a bit more later.[16]

---

[16] This kind of position is integral to *prioritarianism*, which holds that it is important to increase each person's utility, happiness, or welfare, as much as possible, but that extra weight should be given to increasing the utility, happiness, or welfare of someone the worse off they are in absolute terms. On this view, increasing someone's utility by n units improves the objective value of an outcome by more if the

Let us next consider an example where one outcome is much better than another with respect to an ideal other than utility, but much worse in other respects. Take, for example, the outcome described by Kurt Vonnegut Jr. in his antiegalitarian diatribe "Harrison Bergeron."[17] Vonnegut describes a totalitarian regime blinded by the ideal of equality. In its zeal to promote the perfectly equal society, it weeds out all independence, creativity, and talent: disfiguring the beautiful, burdening the strong, crippling the intelligent, and so on. In doing this, it drastically limits people's options, destroys the bonds of friendship, loyalty, and love, and levels everyone down to a drab, soulless existence. As Vonnegut expects, most people react with horror to the scenario he describes. The Capped Model can easily account for why we think such an outcome would be very bad, even if it *were* perfect regarding equality (a rather dubious claim, in fact, given the significant inequalities of power and such that presumably obtain between the totalitarian leaders and their sheep-like citizens/victims).

Vonnegut has described an outcome that would be *much* worse in terms of every other significant ideal than the free society with which he implicitly compares it. Thus, adding an important fifth ideal, freedom (F), that is relevant for assessing the outcomes Vonnegut asks us to consider, in essence, Vonnegut has asked us to compare a supposedly equal, tyrannical society, whose scores for each ideal might be $E = 100$, $U = 10$, $M = 10$, $P = 0$, and $F = 0$, with an unequal free society whose scores might be $E = 10$, $U = 90$, $M = 10$, $P = 95$, and $F = 95$.[18] Unsurprisingly, we rank the free unequal society, whose all-things-

---

person is badly off than if they are well off, and the worse off someone is in absolute terms, the more it matters, and the more the outcome's utility would be made *better*, if her utility were increased by n units. Prioritarianism is a view that I originally characterized and discussed under the name "extended humanitarianism" in the late 1970s (in early drafts of my PhD dissertation, *Inequality*). It was later defended and made famous under the name "the Priority View" by Derek Parfit in his article "Equality or Priority?" (Lindley Lecture, University of Kansas, 1991, reprinted in *The Ideal of Equality*, ed. Matthew Clayton and Andrew Williams [London: Macmillan; New York: St. Martin's Press, 2000], 81–125). I have discussed the view at length in many places, including "Egalitarianism Defended," "Equality, Priority, or What?," "Equality, Priority, and the Levelling Down Objection," and chapter 9 of *Inequality*. I coined the term "prioritarianism" (from my "extended humanitarianism" and Parfit's "the Priority View") and first introduced it and its various cognates (such as "prioritarians") in my "Equality, Priority, and the Levelling Down Objection."

[17] "Harrison Bergeron" appears in Vonnegut's *Welcome to the Monkey House* (New York: Dell, 1970), 7–13.

[18] There are lots of other morally relevant factors that would also pertain to the situation Vonnegut describes which would help explain the strength of our reactions to Vonnegut's situation, including rights violations, deontological obligations, love for one's children, and agent-relative duties. In terms of each of these factors, as well as others, we assume that a free society would be vastly better than the tyrannical one Vonnegut describes. For simplicity, I am sticking to the five in the text to illustrate the point. Also, Vonnegut might well claim that the worse off would fare *better*, and hence the score for maximin should actually be *higher*, in the free society than in the totalitarian equal society. There is much plausibility to this claim, which would only strengthen the argument of the text, giving the free society an even higher score than the totalitarian one on the Capped Model.

considered score might be 300, as vastly better than the unfree equal society, whose all-things-considered score might be 120. Here, as earlier, the Capped Model provides a plausible way of thinking about the relations between ideals and how they combine to yield an all-things-considered judgment.

There is a logical limit to how much one can reduce a situation's inequality, but no logical limit to how *much* utility obtains. Because of this, it is natural to suppose that there is a limit to how much one can improve a situation regarding equality, but none regarding utility. Nevertheless, for certain comparisons, at least, this supposition seems mistaken. However much more we may care about one ideal relative to another, they play similar roles in our all-things-considered judgments. No one ideal matters more than all, or most of, the others put together. So, no matter how good an outcome is with respect to one ideal—even if it is *perfect* with respect to that ideal—it may still be poor, overall, if it is sufficiently poor with respect to other important ideals.

The Capped Model can similarly account for our anti-additive-aggregationist intuitions involving comparisons of lives rather than outcomes. But, of course, some of the morally relevant factors for comparing lives may be different from those relevant for comparing outcomes. Consider, for example, McTaggart's Single Life Repugnant Conclusion, discussed in chapter 4.

Among the many factors that seem relevant for assessing the overall quality of a life are utility (U), autonomy (AU), virtue (V), friendship (FR), achievements (ACH), family (F), and respect (R). This is a very rough and truncated list, but it is sufficient for my purposes. McTaggart asks us to imagine two lives, a paragon life, P, of as high a quality as one might like persisting for millions of years, or, alternatively, an oyster-like life, O, devoid of everything but the lowest level of sentient awareness and contentment, lasting vastly longer. As we saw, McTaggart suggests that while most moralists would find O repugnant in comparison with P, he suggests that this intuition is not to be trusted, and can be explained away by appeal to several natural cognitive distortions and errors. In fact, McTaggart insists, as long as O would persist *sufficiently* long, eventually it would *have* to be better than P, since it would have *so* much total utility.

Here, McTaggart assumes an additive-aggregationist approach for assessing lives. And if we accept something like the Standard Model for Utility and the Standard Model for Combining Ideals for comparing lives like O and P, we shall have to concur with McTaggart's judgment. But, as McTaggart recognizes, most of us reject his judgment, and in so doing we are rejecting a simple additive-aggregationist approach for comparing lives like O and P. We don't believe that a really good life, overall, could be one that was good in only one respect—no matter *how* good it might be in that one respect. Rather, in accordance with the Capped Model, we believe that for a life to be really good, overall, it must be good in most of the ways that are relevant to making a life good.

For simplicity, let's assume that on the Capped Model for comparing lives, the only factors that are relevant for comparing lives are the ones noted earlier, that each is as valuable as the others, and that there is an upper limit on how good a life can be with respect to a given factor, so that the highest score a life can achieve for any single ideal is 100. Then the paragon life's scores might be something like $U = 95$, $AU = 95$, $V = 95$, $FR = 95$, $ACH = 95$, $F = 95$, and $R = 95$, for an all-things-considered score of 665, while the oyster-like life's scores might be something like $U = 98$, $AU = 0$, $V = 0$, $FR = 0$, $ACH = 0$, $F = 0$, and $R = 0$, for an all-things-considered score of 98. Although our selection of ideals, scores, and relative weightings is arbitrary, it is clear how a Capped Model could account for our intuition that the paragon life is much better than the oyster-like life. No matter *how much* utility might be contained in the oyster-like life, we simply don't believe that a life which was devoid of *every other* factor that was relevant to life's goodness could be better, all things considered, than a life that was brimming with all of the factors that make for a flourishing life.

Let me mention just one other case where something like a Capped Model comes into play in our assessment of individuals: when we assess the moral virtuousness or viciousness of individuals. Suppose, for the sake of argument, that we regard the following as moral virtues: honesty, trustworthiness, loyalty, courage, kindness, friendship, fidelity, generosity, beneficence, and love. I submit that to be morally virtuous, overall, it is not enough for someone to highly possess one or two of the moral virtues.

Suppose, for example, that Attila the Hun was extremely courageous. Suppose also that he loved his mother a *lot*. But suppose that he was utterly vicious in every other respect. Surely, we would not say that Attila would be morally virtuous if only he were courageous *enough*, or if only he loved his mother *enough*. Even if we thought that Attila could somehow increase his courage without end, or increase his love for his mother without end, his doing so would not be the path to moral virtue. If he wanted to become virtuous, he would also have to become honest, trustworthy, loyal, and so on. This suggests that there is an upper limit to how much any particular virtue can contribute to someone's being morally virtuous, overall. Even if one could become increasingly virtuous regarding one or two virtues, being nearly or even perfect with respect to those virtues would not be enough to make up for significant deficiencies with respect to all of the other virtues. This thought can be captured by the anti-additive-aggregationist approach of a Capped Model for ideals, but not by the kind of additive-aggregationist approach embodied by an uncapped version of the Standard Model for Combining Ideals (that is, one that would reject clauses 3 and 4 of the Capped Model).

Notice, the preceding is distinct from the Aristotelian point about the unity (or reciprocity) of virtues. Aristotle thought that you couldn't truly possess *any* of the virtues, unless you possessed all of them.[19] So, Aristotle would have to deny that Attila truly possessed the virtue of courage, or the virtue of loving of his mother, in the absence of his possessing the other virtues as well. I think this is a mistake. It seems to me that one could be virtuous in some respects, without being virtuous in all. But what Aristotle has rightly seen is that one cannot be truly virtuous, overall, if one is virtuous in only one or two respects. Nor can someone who is virtuous in only one or two areas be more commendable regarding virtue than someone who is virtuous in all (or most) respects, no matter *how* much they excel in the respects in which they are virtuous. This latter point implies that we must reject a simple additive-aggregationist approach for thinking about moral virtues.

It is worth emphasizing that the Standard Model for Combining Ideals is not *itself* incompatible with our anti-additive-aggregationist intuitions, for we have seen that when supplemented with clauses 3 and 4 it can capture such intuitions. The problem arises when one has an *uncapped* version of the Standard Model for Combining Ideals and *combines* it with a conception of individual ideals analogous to the Standard Model for Utility. More particularly, if one believes that there are some moral ideals that are best captured along the lines that utility should be captured according to the Standard Model for Utility, such that positions analogous to clauses 2, 3, 5, and 6 of the Standard Model for Utility would apply to those ideals, then the possibility of a single ideal swamping every other will arise on the additive-aggregative approach of the Standard Model for Combining Ideals, and, as we have seen, this can lead to implications incompatible with our anti-additive-aggregationist intuitions. We see, then, that the Capped Model doesn't merely have implications for how best to understand the Standard Model for Combining Ideals; it has implications for how best to understand the individual ideals that underlie our all-things-considered judgments about the goodness of outcomes. This will become clearer in the ensuing discussion.

10.7 Upper and Lower Limits for Different Kinds of Utility

We have seen how a Capped Model for ideals could capture the anti-additive-aggregationist judgment that even unlimited gains with respect to a single ideal may not be sufficient to outweigh large losses with respect to many other ideals. But it is important to recognize that anti-additive-aggregationist reasoning might apply to comparisons involving single ideals, as well as comparisons involving multiple ideals. So, for example, just as the Capped Model implies that for certain comparisons, at least, there is an upper limit to how good an outcome is with respect to utility, it can accommodate the

---

[19] See *Nicomachean Ethics* VI, 13, 1144b30–45a2. I am grateful to Alan Code for this citation.

view that for certain comparisons there is an upper limit to how good an outcome is with respect to any particular kind of utility.

Consider, again, the Repugnant Conclusion. Assume that the people in A each experience the "highest" kinds of utility available to humans, while those in Z each experience the "lowest" kinds of utility available to any sentient beings. Since, by assumption, there are *so* many people in Z, relative to A, that the sum total of utility is greater in Z, on the Capped Model we *could* say that Z is better than A regarding utility, but that it is worse all things considered. As we saw earlier, since, on the Capped Model, there is an upper limit on how good an outcome can be with respect to utility, and, by assumption, A is already near that limit, no matter how much *greater* the sum total of utility is in Z than in A, Z will be only a little bit *better* than A regarding utility, while it will be much worse than A regarding many other important ideals. However, the Capped Model is also compatible with the view that Z is not only worse than A all things considered, it is even worse *regarding utility*. Having already recognized that there may be an upper limit to how good an outcome may be regarding utility, the Capped Model could also recognize that, for certain comparisons, there may be *different* upper limits to how good an outcome can be with respect to different *kinds* of utility. To echo a thought of Jim Griffin's, noted previously in section 2.3, intuitively, the idea would be that no amount of utility of one kind would be more valuable than a sufficient amount of utility of another kind.

So, even someone who thought that utility was the *only* ideal that mattered for assessing outcomes *could* find the Repugnant Conclusion genuinely repugnant. Such a person would care not merely about total utility (nor, for the reasons noted in section 10.4, about average utility), but about the different kinds of utility that obtain and the way they are distributed in different outcomes. This would involve an anti-additive-aggregationist approach to evaluating certain outcomes regarding utility, and it might be captured by something like the Capped Model applied directly to the ideal of utility and the different kinds of utilities encompassed by that ideal.

Consider again the Single Life Repugnant Conclusion. Many believe that an ongoing oyster-like life is not only worse than a flourishing eighty-year life in terms of factors like autonomy, virtue, friendship, achievements, family, and respect, but that it is even worse regarding utility. Specifically, they believe that the trivial pleasures available to an oyster don't *add up* in the way they would need to in order to make the utility of such a life more *valuable* than the utility obtaining in a truly flourishing human life of eighty years. They can grant that if the oyster-like life persists long enough, there will be *more total* utility in that life than in the flourishing one, but they deny that that is enough to make the former life *better* than the latter *even regarding utility*. As noted, they think that insofar as one cares about utility, one should care about the kinds of utility that obtain and the way that they are distributed in an outcome.

This is analogous to some of our earlier claims about the pain spectrum. Many believe that a long life containing two years of intense torture would be worse than a long life containing one extra mosquito bite per month, no matter how many extra months of mosquito bites may be involved. Moreover, this needn't be because they assume that the former life would be worse than the latter in terms of all sorts of other morally relevant factors besides the pain occurring in the lives. Rather, as noted previously, they may simply believe that the pains or disutilities of mosquito bites don't *add up* in the way they would need to in order to make the extra-mosquito-bite-filled life worse than the life involving two years of torture, *even regarding pain or disutility*. Thus, even insofar as one *only* cared about pain, one might regard the life involving less total pain (in the form of two years of torture) as *worse* than the one involving more total pain (in the form of one extra mosquito bite per month).

Finally, to note but one more of our earlier cases (from section 2.7), many would agree that the sum total of disutility might be greater in an outcome where billions of people had a short mild headache, than in an outcome where only fifty people were quadriplegic, but that the latter outcome would be *worse* than the former *even regarding utility*. Here, as elsewhere, the thought is that the disutilities of mild headaches don't add up across people in the way they would need to in order to make the former outcome *worse* than the latter regarding utility.

Before going on, let me reemphasize a point made at the end of section 10.2.[20] I have been claiming that we may need or want to employ something like a Capped Model to capture certain of our anti-additive-aggregationist intuitions. But I have *not* claimed, nor do I believe, that a Capped Model can plausibly capture *all* of our intuitions. As I have argued in previous chapters, in many contexts and for many comparisons we have powerful additive-aggregationist intuitions, and while the Capped Model will be able to capture some of these, it won't be able to plausibly capture all of them.

One way to see this point is to note the following. Both the Capped Model and the uncapped Standard Model for Combining Ideals will assign real numbers to each outcome representing how good that outcome is all things considered, as well as real numbers, for each ideal, representing how good each outcome is with respect to that ideal.[21] So, for both the Capped Model and the uncapped Standard Model for Combining Ideals, "all-things-considered better than" (in my wide reason-implying sense) will be a transitive relation. It follows that neither the Capped Model nor the uncapped Standard Model for

---

[20] Shelly Kagan alerted me to the importance of reemphasizing this point here to avoid confusion about the scope of my remarks.

[21] Here, I ignore the possible complication regarding infinitesimals and maximin's tie-breaking clause (if it has one) identified in note 10.

Combining Ideals will by itself capture the views that most people actually have regarding this book's various Spectrum Arguments, since, as we saw, most people's all-things-considered judgments (in my wide reason-implying sense) are nontransitive for such spectrums. So, importantly, my claim is not that for a spectrum of cases, from A to Z, we can employ a Capped Model for assessing A, B, C, and so on, and then infer how any two cases along the spectrum compare. Rather, my claim is that we may need or want to employ something like a Capped Model for determining how cases like A or B compare to cases like Y or Z, but *not* for determining how cases like A and B compare with each other, or how cases like Y and Z compare with each other. Analogously, to capture what most people actually believe about such spectrums, we may need or want to employ something like the uncapped Standard Model for Combining Ideals for determining how cases like A and B compare or how cases like Y and Z compare, but *not* for determining how cases like A or B compare to cases like Y or Z.

Thus, my claims about the Capped Model are limited in scope. Such a view may seem plausible for capturing our anti-additive-aggregationist views, but not our additive-aggregationist views (or not all of them, anyway; see section 10.8). Accordingly, it may seem relevant for making *certain* comparisons but not others. So, returning to the kind of claim that Jim Griffin made about discontinuity between values, applied to the value of utility, the thought is that no amount of utility of one kind would be more valuable than a sufficient amount of utility of another "sufficiently different" kind; but this does not entail that no amount of utility of one kind could be more valuable than a sufficient amount of utility of another "sufficiently similar" kind. Of course, as we know by now, there is no *coherent* account that captures these various views, if the test of coherence is that "all-things-considered better than" (in my wide reason-implying sense) is a transitive relation. Unfortunately, that is the unavoidable lesson that we learned in chapters 2 through 5.

10.8 Complications to Consider for a Capped Model of Utility

The thought that we may need to adopt a Capped Model for certain comparisons involving utility is compatible with several different ways of thinking.[22] Let me distinguish some of these, without assessing or choosing between them. Similar remarks may apply to a Capped Model for other ideals besides utility.

One might think that each kind of utility has its own limit. Specifically, one might think that for each kind of positive utility there is an upper limit on

---

[22] Much of the pioneering work on this topic was done by Derek Parfit in part 4 of *Reasons and Persons*. See, especially, chapter 18.

how much an outcome can be made better by the presence of instances of that kind of utility, and likewise for each kind of negative utility there is a lower limit on how much an outcome can be made worse by the presence of instances of that kind of utility. Alternatively, one may think that there is an asymmetry between positive and negative utilities. So, for example, one may think there is an upper limit on how good an outcome can be with respect to the presence of any particular kind of positive utility, but no lower limit on how bad an outcome can be with respect to any particular kind of negative utility.

Yet another view is that there are upper and lower limits for *some* kinds of positive and negative utilities, but not all. In particular, one might believe in different thresholds of experiences. Perhaps for very positive experiences above a certain threshold, there is no upper limit on how much further instances of such experiences would improve an outcome regarding utility, while for relatively mild positive experiences below a certain threshold there is an upper limit. Likewise, perhaps for very negative experiences below a certain threshold, there is no lower limit on how much further instances of such experiences would worsen an outcome regarding utility, while for relatively mild negative experiences above a certain threshold there is a lower limit. Additionally, one may or may not believe that there is an asymmetry between certain kinds of positive or negative experiences and whether there are upper or lower limits to the value that such experiences can contribute to an outcome, depending on whether those kinds of experiences obtain within a single life or within different lives. Moreover, one might think that there are *different* upper and lower limits to the value that any particular kind of experience can contribute to the goodness of an outcome with respect to utility, depending on whether that kind of experience occurs within a single life or within different lives.

I shall not detail each of these positions, but let me illustrate the thinking underlying a few of them. Recalling the Lollipops for Life case discussed in chapter 2, one might believe that even if the positive experience of licking a lollipop were, phenomenologically, exactly the same each time, there is an upper limit on how good an outcome could be regarding utility as a result of the presence of positive experiences of that sort. So, for example, one might think that a single instance of a lollipop lick might contribute to an outcome's value regarding utility by one unit, and that a single instance of watching one's child being born into the world might contribute to an outcome's value regarding utility by 10,000 units, but one might think that no number of lollipop licks would contribute more to the value of an outcome regarding utility than a single instance of watching one's child being born. Specifically, one might think there is an upper limit to how much one can improve an outcome regarding utility merely by adding more lollipop licks to that outcome. Drawing on our earlier distinction, one might hold that even if, *subjectively*, each lollipop lick were just as valuable to its experiencer as every prior lollipop lick was to its experiencer (an assumption that might not hold, but that we now grant for the purposes of argument), nevertheless the *objective* value of the outcome's utility can only be improved so much by the presence of additional lollipop licks. But note, we might think that the upper limit of the value of lollipop licks may vary depending on whether they are experienced by the same, or different, people. So, even if we thought that, *subjectively*, John would get just as much out of each lick of a lollipop as each of 10,000 people would get out of a single lollipop lick, we might think the objective value of John getting 10,000 licks of a lollipop would be much less than the objective value of each of 10,000 people getting one lick of a lollipop, and that both objective values would be less—and perhaps far less—than the objective value of a single person observing his child being born.

On the other hand, for really great positive experiences we may or may not feel similarly. Perhaps there is no upper limit on the value that can be contributed to an outcome's utility via experiences of watching one's child being born, or listening to Mozart's *Requiem*. Or perhaps there is an upper limit to such value if such experiences occur within a single life, but not within separate lives. Or perhaps, even with the highest positive experiences, we think there is an upper limit in both cases, but that the level of the limit varies in such a way that the same number of experiences will matter less, objectively, if they obtain within a single life than if they are dispersed among many lives.

Similar possibilities arise regarding negative experiences. For example, it may be plausible to think that there are limits on how bad an outcome can be made, objectively, regarding utility via the presence of many mild negative experiences, such as mosquito bites or mild headaches. Further, as with positive experiences, we may think the limits on how much certain kinds of negative experiences can worsen an outcome depends on whether those experiences obtain within a single life or are distributed over many lives. Perhaps as one person suffers more and more mosquito bites in her life, the outcome approaches a level of objective badness that might be represented as $-n$, but it is never *worse* than that, while in the many-person case, where more and more people each suffer one mosquito bite in their lives, the outcome approaches a level of objective badness that might be represented as $-k$, but it is never worse than that. Moreover, perhaps an outcome with $-n$ badness would be worse than an outcome with $-k$ badness, implying that it is worse for a single person to suffer innumerable mosquito bites than for innumerable people to suffer one mosquito bite each, though there is a limit in both cases on how much worse such a situation could make an outcome regarding utility.

Many views are possible in this area, but of course not all are equally plausible. For example, as Derek Parfit has observed,[23] there may be important asymmetries in our views about positive and negative experiences. Thus, while

---

[23] Parfit, *Reasons and Persons*, part 4.

it may be plausible to think that there is an upper limit on how objectively good an outcome can be made regarding utility via the presence of many wonderful positive experiences of a certain kind, it may not be equally plausible to think that there is a lower limit on how objectively bad an outcome can be made regarding utility via the presence of many terrible negative experiences of a certain kind. For instance, it is hard to believe that while *subjectively* each year of torture may be just as terrible for its possessor as any other, once someone has been tortured *long* enough, or once *enough* people have been tortured for a year, *objectively* it doesn't (much) matter anymore whether the one person is tortured for many more years, or whether many others are also tortured for a year.

As indicated, the notion that there may be upper limits to how objectively good or bad an outcome is with respect to different ideals, or different components of different ideals, is one that can be accommodated by a Capped Model for ideals. But, as presented here, the Capped Model is little more than a sketch of an approach that one might adopt for incorporating anti-additive-aggregationist intuitions. The details of such a model remain to be worked out, and here, as elsewhere, the devil is in the details.

One familiar way of reaching a limit runs as follows: the first instance of a certain kind of experience, k, adds a marginal value of n to the goodness of an outcome, the second instance k adds a marginal value of $½(n)$ to the goodness of an outcome, the third instance of k adds a marginal value of $¼(n)$, and so on. In this case, the limit of all possible k experiences would be $2(n)$. Clearly, any limit is possible for experiences of kind k. For example, the limit would be $1,000(n)$ if one assigned a value of $500(n)$ to the marginal value of the first instance of k, a value of $250(n)$ to the marginal value of the second instance of k, a value of $125(n)$ to the marginal value of the third instance of k, and so on. But one could also reach the limit of $1,000(n)$ in any number of different ways that involved decreasing marginal values for additional k experiences.

Another way of reaching a limit would be to have the marginal value of each subsequent k experience matter less than the previous one by a small finite amount, until eventually one reached a point where additional instances of k added *no* marginal value to the outcome. For example, suppose the first instance of k added a marginal value of 1 to the goodness of an outcome, and that each subsequent instance of k added a marginal value to the goodness of the outcome that was one millionth less than the marginal value added to the outcome by the preceding instance of k. So, the second instance of k would add a marginal value to the goodness of the outcome of .999999, the third instance of k would add a marginal value to the goodness of the outcome of .999998, the fourth instance of k would add a marginal value to the goodness of the outcome of .999997, and so on. In this case, even if each k experience had the same subjective value to its possessor as every other, the one million and first k experience, together with all subsequent k experiences, would add no additional marginal value to the goodness of the outcome, and the limit of the value that k experiences could contribute to an outcome's goodness would be 500,000.5.

Notice, one could approach a limit at a constant rate, as in the case just considered, or at a slower and slower rate, as in the case previously considered, or at a faster and faster rate. An example of the latter would be if the first extra k experience added one millionth less marginal value to the goodness of the outcome than the previous one, the second added three millionths less marginal value to the goodness of the outcome than the previous one, the third extra k experience added five millionths less marginal value to the goodness of the outcome than the previous one, and so on.

Another possibility would be for each subsequent k experience to add just as much marginal value to the goodness of an outcome as the previous one up to some finite number of k experiences, after which subsequent k experiences would begin to add less and less marginal value to the goodness of the outcome. Still another possibility would be for each additional k experience to add more marginal value to the goodness of an outcome than the previous one up to some point, after which each subsequent k experience would add less marginal value to the goodness of the outcome than the previous one.

Finally, variations in the rate of increases and decreases might also be possible along a number of lines. Perhaps decreases in the marginal value of k experiences might start out at a constant rate, but then begin speeding up or slowing down. Or perhaps they might start out at an increasing rate, before changing to a constant or decreasing rate. Or perhaps the rates of decrease in the marginal value of additional k experiences may vacillate in a regular or irregular pattern between constant, increasing, or decreasing rates.

As indicated earlier, the devil is in the details, and I shall not enumerate all the possible positions here or the considerations that might support some rather than others. Suffice it to say, if one believes in upper or lower limits that different kinds of experiences can contribute to an outcome's objective value, a great deal of thought has to go into determining what those limits might be for the different kinds of experiences in question, how they are related to each other, and how best to capture them in a plausible non–ad hoc manner. This is no easy task. Indeed, such a task is fraught with complexities that may be unsolvable, and every purported solution may have implications that are both unavoidable and unacceptable. But, for certain comparisons, at least, there are powerful reasons to pursue such a task. Accordingly, while the Capped Model for Ideals is currently little more than a sketch, it is, I think, worth further consideration and development. While other models may also be worth considering, the Capped Model offers one possible approach for capturing the notion of limits and certain of our powerful anti-additive-aggregationist views.

10.9 Contrasting the Capped Model with the Standard Model for Utility

Let us contrast the Capped Model with the Standard Model for Utility presented in section 10.2.

First, the Capped Model can accept the first assumption of the Standard Model for Utility that utility is noninstrumentally valuable. According to this assumption, utility represents a genuine ideal that there is some reason to promote over and above the extent to which promoting utility also promotes other valuable ideals. Of course, what counts as promoting the ideal of utility will vary on the Capped Model depending on how the ideal of utility is fleshed out. But, in general—subject to the caveats expressed in section 10.3, regarding, for example, a sadist's pleasure, or an evil person's undeserved pleasure or deserved suffering—positive utility will be a good-making feature of outcomes and negative utility a bad-making feature of outcomes.

Second, the Capped Model rejects the second assumption of the Standard Model for Utility that utility is intrinsically valuable. On the Standard Model, each unit of utility—or, given section 10.3's caveats, each unit of innocent or deserved utility—has a fixed objective value that it contributes to an outcome independently of any other features of that outcome, so that the marginal value that each additional unit of utility adds to the goodness of the outcome is the same. On the Capped Model, the marginal value that a unit of utility adds to the goodness of an outcome can vary depending on how many other units of utility (perhaps of that kind) obtain in the outcome. In particular, as more units of utility are added to an outcome, at some point each additional unit will tend to contribute less marginal value to the goodness of the outcome. Moreover, once an outcome contains so much utility that the objective value of the outcome's utility is already at, or near, its upper limit—as implied previously, the details of the Capped Model will be fleshed out differently depending on whether one believes that an outcome can actually reach, or only approach, its upper limit for the value of utility—additional units of utility will contribute vanishingly little or no marginal value to the outcome's goodness.

Third, the Capped Model can accept versions of the Standard Model for Utility's third and fourth assumptions, that the ideal of utility is strictly neutral with respect to sentient beings, places, and times, and is also strictly impartial between sentient beings with respect to utility. However, given its different view about the intrinsic value of utility, the implications of these requirements are markedly different on the Capped Model than on the Standard Model for Utility. Like the Standard Model for Utility, the Capped Model is neutral and impartial in the sense of not allowing any biases or prejudices to favor one sentient being over another for reasons of race, gender, religion, sexual orientation, nationality, or species. Nor can any preference be given to one place over another merely because it is "here" rather than "there," or a place where we or a loved one happen to abide rather than elsewhere. Likewise, no preference can be given to one time over another merely because it is "now" rather than "past" or "future," or a period during which we or a loved one exist rather than one where we or our loved ones don't exist. But since, on the Capped Model, the extent to which a given amount of utility contributes to an outcome's objective value will depend on how much other utility already exists, or perhaps has existed, in the outcome, it won't be true that neutrality means that a given amount of utility will count just as much no matter who experiences it, where it is experienced, or when it is experienced, nor that impartiality means that each sentient being's utility counts as much as any other's.

For example, if John would be one of a million well-off people in one possible outcome, and Susan would be one of a trillion well-off people in a different possible outcome, on the Capped Model it might be much less important to improve Susan's utility if that outcome obtained, than it would be to improve John's utility if that outcome obtained, given that so much more utility would already exist in Susan's outcome than John's. Likewise, Susan's possessing n units of utility might contribute significantly less to the overall goodness of her outcome than John's possessing n units of utility contributes to the overall goodness of his outcome.

An interesting question concerns the scope of the Capped Model: Are all places and times considered together regarding the upper limits for utility, or other ideals, or are different regions of space or time considered separately? The difference between these positions can be illustrated as follows. One might think that if there are already 100 billion units of utility in a given spatial or temporal region, one will already have reached, or approached very near to, the upper limit for how good that spatial or temporal region can be objectively regarding utility. In that case, one might think that merely adding more utility to that spatial or temporal region would make little or no difference to how objectively good the outcome was regarding utility, or all things considered. But this leaves open the question whether it might be significantly desirable to add utility to some other spatial or temporal regions. This is an important question for moral philosophy generally, which merits much more consideration than it has been given, but for now, let me simply make several observations.

If one treats all spatial and temporal regions together, then obviously adding more utility to another region or time period will be of no more significance than adding more utility to the region and time period already containing the 100 billion units of utility. Alternatively, one might treat spatial and temporal regions separately. This raises familiar line-drawing-type questions as to whether one can demarcate different spatial or temporal regions in a way that avoids arbitrary and implausible implications. So, for example, one would like to avoid the implication that adding n units of utility to one place or time wouldn't count much at all, objectively, but adding the same amount of utility one millimeter away or one nanosecond later, would have great objective significance. Still, there is a fair amount of intuitive appeal to the notion that once a planet, or century, has already attained, say, 100 billion units of utility, there is little objective value to be gained merely by adding even *more* units of utility to that planet or century, but there might be significant objective value to be gained by adding units of utility to some other planet or century that would otherwise be barren regarding utility.

This plausible intuitive position raises unsettling questions about whether our judgments in these domains are unduly calibrated to a human scale that is morally arbitrary. Perhaps from a drastically different perspective of space and time, our own planet or century is riddled with voids that could, in principle, be filled by sentient beings radically different in kind than us. Presumably, such voids might be every bit as objectionable from an objective perspective as the voids we humans are capable of comprehending in the distant reaches of space and time that are accessible to our human sensibilities. Still, such considerations might speak in favor of filling each type of void to an appropriate degree, yet not support adding even more utility to the "human" realm once a sufficient level of utility in that realm has already been reached. This might be so if, as we might suppose (though how could we possibly know?!), simply adding more utility to the human realm would not affect the voids that may surround us.

Suppose, for example, contrary to fact, that there were subatomic-sized voids within each atom that were capable of being filled by subatomic-sized sentient beings we have yet to meet. If so, adding more utility to the world by adding more humans to the surface of the earth presumably wouldn't help fill *those* voids. On the other hand, however intuitive it may seem, there remains a puzzle as to *why*, exactly, it should matter more to add utility to pockets of space and time that are currently devoid of it than to add equal amounts and quality of utility to neighborhoods of space and time that already contain utility and are perhaps even teeming with it.

If the subjective value of the utility in an additional human's life would be as good *for* that human as the subjective value of the utility from adding a subatomic-sized sentient being to a subatomic-sized space would be *for* that subatomic-sized sentient being, why should it be *objectively* better for the goodness of the outcome to do the latter rather than the former? Even if the surface of the earth is heavily populated by sentient human beings, while the subatomic spaces that pervade our world are currently devoid of sentient beings, it is, on reflection, hard to see how that, by itself, could be morally *relevant* to the desirability of adding a sentient being to one level or the other. But, of course, if it isn't relevant, then that raises questions about the initial intuition we started with, that many people, including me, find plausible: namely, that there may be little objective value to be gained merely by adding even *more* units of utility to a planet or century that already contains 100 billion units of utility, but there might be significant objective value to be gained by adding units of utility to some other planet or century that would otherwise be barren regarding utility. But let me not pursue these wild speculations and the questions they prompt.

Importantly, contrary to what most moral theorists commonly assume, one needn't necessarily treat space and time the same. Perhaps spatial regions should be treated together, but temporal regions separately, or vice versa. For example, intuitively, one might think that once there is enough utility in a given time period, it doesn't matter much, objectively, whether even more utility is added to that time period, and that this is so wherever in space that utility might be added. On the other hand, no matter how much utility exists during some time periods, one might think there is always objective value to adding utility to other time periods if those periods would otherwise be lacking in utility. Further variations of these views are also possible. For example, one might think that until at least one spatial region in a given time period is "saturated" with utility, there is always reason to add more utility to that time period in any spatial location, but that once even one region is "saturated," there is no longer significant objective reason to add more utility to any region in that time period.

I shall return to some related issues in chapter 12, and so shall not pursue these issues further here. But, as should be evident, whether or not spatial or temporal regions are treated together or separately, it will not be the case on the Capped Model, as it is on the Standard Model for Utility, that a given amount of utility will have the same value, and contribute the same amount of marginal value to its outcome, no matter where or when it is experienced. On the Capped Model, if spatial or temporal regions are treated together, then how much value a given amount of utility has at a given time or place and how much marginal value it adds to the outcome will vary depending on how much utility obtains at other times and places. So, for example, in one outcome, O_1, where other times or places are already filled with a lot of utility, adding a given amount of utility, p, to a given time, T_1, or space, S_1, may add only a small amount of marginal value, x, to the outcome, and if the total amount of utility in O_1 was n, and the total value of the utility was i, then the value of p in O_1 would be $p(i)/n$. On the other hand, in another outcome, O_2, where other times or places do not have a lot of utility, adding the very same given amount of utility, p, to the same or different time, T_1 or T_2, or the same or different space, S_1 or S_2, may add a much larger amount of marginal value, y, to the outcome, and if the total amount of utility in O_2 was k, where k is much less than n, and the total value of the utility was j, where $j < i$, then the value of p in O_2 would be $p(j)/k$, where this would be greater than $p(i)/n$. Thus, the very same amount of utility, p, would have different value and add a different amount of marginal value in O_1 and O_2, because of the differences in the amounts of utility that occur in other times and places in O_1 and O_2. On the other hand, if spatial or temporal regions are treated separately, then both the marginal and objective values of a given amount of utility, p, would be different, and indeed greater, in an "unsaturated" time or place than in a "saturated" time or place.

On the Value of Utility 347

Let me make one more observation regarding how best to interpret the neutrality and impartiality of the Capped Model for Ideals. Suppose we have an outcome A that is already near, or at, the limit of how good an outcome can be regarding utility. By hypothesis, on the Capped Model, adding more people to A with lots of utility would add little or no value to A's objective value regarding utility. But how should we understand the impact that adding such people would have on the objective value of the lives of the other people already in A? Throughout this section and the preceding one, I have been assuming that the requirement of neutrality and impartiality implies that A's total amount of objective value would be distributed between A's members proportionally to the amount of utility that each person possesses. It is perhaps worth spelling out the model I have in mind, and that has been underlying some of my preceding claims and calculations.

Suppose that that A has 10 billion members, each of whom is equally well off, with k units of the same kind of utility, and that A's total objective value regarding utility is m. In that case, I suggest that we should count the objective value of each individual person's utility as $m/10,000,000,000$. That is, since, by hypothesis, each person has the same amount of the same kind of utility, each person is counted as contributing an equal share to the outcome's objective value. Next, suppose that 10 billion extra people are added to A, each of whom has the same amount, k, of the same kind of utility as everyone else. And suppose that the value of utility was already near its upper limit before the extra people were added, so that A's objective value regarding utility was increased only by g, where g is much less than m, and $m + g$ is not much greater than m. One *might* think that, regarding utility, the objective value attributable to each person in the original group would remain what it was, namely, $m/10,000,000,000$, while the objective value attributable to each person in the new group would be much less; specifically, an equal share of the total additional objective value that the new group adds to the outcome regarding utility, namely, $g/10,000,000,000$. However, I believe that on the Capped Model one should revise the values contributed by the original members to reflect the view that once the new group has been added, each person's contribution to the outcome's objective value would be $(m + g)/20,000,000,000$ regarding utility.

By the same token, suppose that each of the 10 billion additional people actually has twice as much of the same kind of utility in their lives as each of the original 10 billion people, but that, as before, since A was already near the limit for how good it could be, objectively, regarding utility, this increased A's objective value only by g, regarding utility. In that case, I think the Capped Model would revise the objective value of each original person's contribution to only $(1/3)(m + g)/10,000,000,000$, regarding utility, while the value of each new person's contribution would be twice as large, namely, $(2/3)(m + g)/10,000,000,000$.

Similar remarks would apply, mutatis mutandis, for versions of the Capped Model which held that one could actually reach an upper limit regarding utility, after which additional units of utility would have zero marginal value, and so the outcome's objective value regarding utility would remain unchanged. In this case, we may suppose, if A's objective value regarding utility was m with its original population of 10 billion people, it would still be m after an additional 10 billion equally well-off people were added. A fortiori, I suggest that on the Capped Model we would say that the objective value of the utility of each of A's original 10 billion members would go from $m/10,000,000,000$ before the extra people were added to $m/20,000,000,000$ afterward.

Measuring the objective value of people's utility in this manner would capture the following views. For any two people, P_1 and P_2, in a given outcome O, if P_1 and P_2 experience the same amounts and kinds of utility, so that the *subjective* values of P_1 and P_2 are the same regarding utility, then the *objective* values of P_1 and P_2's utility would also be the same, meaning that the extent to which P_1 and P_2 affect O's objective value regarding utility would be the same. Accordingly, insofar as one was concerned with O's objective value regarding utility, one should be indifferent between increasing or decreasing P_1's utility in a certain way and increasing or decreasing P_2's utility in that way. In this way, the Capped Model would require that P_1 and P_2 be treated the same in O, regarding utility, reflecting an important sense in which the ideal of utility should be neutral and impartial.

Fourth, on most interpretations the Capped Model rejects the fourth assumption of the Standard Model for Utility, that insofar as one cares about utility, one should care about total utility, and on all interpretations it rejects the spirit of that assumption. But on one interpretation of the Capped Model the fourth assumption would reflect an important truth, and on another it would approximate an important truth. Let me elucidate these claims.

I take the spirit of the fourth assumption to imply that if A has much *more* utility than B, A will be much *better* than B regarding utility. Clearly, the Capped Model rejects this implication on all of its interpretations regarding the objective value of utility. After all, if B is already at or near the limit for how good an outcome can be, objectively, regarding utility, then, on the Capped Model, no matter *how* much *more* utility A may have than B, A *cannot* be *much* better than B, objectively, regarding utility.

Next, consider the version of the Capped Model that assigns different upper limits to how good different kinds of utility can make an outcome, objectively. Clearly, this version rejects the fourth assumption outright, since, as we have seen, on this version even if there is more total utility in a large number of lollipop licks than in a small number of experiences of watching one's child being born, the objective value of the latter can be greater than the objective value of the former, regarding utility.

Similarly, consider the versions of the Capped Model that treat different spatial or temporal regions separately. On these versions, if *A* involves a spatial or temporal region that is "supersaturated" with utility while all its other regions are barren regarding utility—so that, in effect, the vast majority of *A*'s utility is "wasted" in the sense of obtaining in a region that would already be at or near its upper limit even if it weren't there—while *B* involves a number of regions each of which has a fair amount of utility, but none of which has reached or neared the upper limit on how good a region can be objectively regarding utility, *B* can be objectively better than *A* regarding utility, even if there is more total utility in *A* than *B*. So, on such interpretations, as well, the Capped Model clearly rejects the fourth assumption of the Standard Model for Utility.

Consider, however, a version of the Capped Model that treats all spatial and temporal regions together, that puts only a single upper limit on how good an outcome can be, objectively, regarding utility regardless of the different *kinds* of utility that obtain, and where this limit is approached, but never reached, as an outcome contains more and more utility. I suspect some may find this a particularly attractive version of the Capped Model for capturing the relation between utility and its relation to other ideals, and while this version, too, rejects the spirit of the fourth assumption as articulated earlier, on this version it would be true that one outcome would be objectively *better* than another regarding utility if and only if it had *more* total utility. On this view, total utility would track the ordinal ranking of all outcomes regarding the objective value of utility. Hence, in an important respect it would be true that insofar as one cared about utility, one should care about total utility.

Finally, consider the version of the Capped Model where one could not only approach but actually reach an upper limit on how good an outcome was, objectively, regarding utility. On such a version, once the upper limit had been reached, any additional units of utility would be wasted, in the sense of adding no additional objective value to the goodness of the outcome regarding utility. Hence, on this version *A* might have more total utility than *B* and yet not be better, objectively, regarding utility. This would be so if *A* and *B* were both sufficiently "saturated" with utility as to be at the limit of how good an outcome could be, objectively, regarding utility. Clearly, then, this version rejects the fourth assumption, since *beyond* a certain point one wouldn't care about total utility. Still, the fourth assumption could be seen as approximating an important truth, since, regarding utility, more utility would never be worse, objectively, than less utility, objectively; indeed, until the upper limit had been reached—including, perhaps, all real-world cases—more utility *would* always be better than less.

Fifth, the Capped Model rejects the sixth assumption of the Standard Model for Utility that how good a situation is regarding utility is a simple additive function of how much utility sentient beings have in that situation. So, for example, depending on the version of the Capped Model, the fact that one outcome has twice as much utility as another may not make the outcome objectively better, regarding utility, depending on the kinds of utility involved in the different outcomes or how the utility is distributed across people, places, or times. Moreover, even if the outcome with twice as much utility is, objectively, better, it will not generally be *twice* as good as is implied by the simple additive approach. Indeed, as noted, if an outcome is already near or at the limit on how good it can be objectively regarding utility, doubling its utility will have little or no impact on how good it is, objectively, on the Capped Model.

Finally, as noted previously, I have presented the Capped Model as supplementing, and hence being compatible with, the Standard Model for Combining Ideals. So, as presented, the Capped Model assumes a numerical model for judging outcomes, according to which for each ideal relevant to assessing outcomes, each outcome will merit a (rough) numerical "score" representing how good that outcome is with respect to that ideal, and how good the outcome is all things considered will be represented by the numerical score arrived at by summing the individual scores of each relevant ideal. This is a controversial feature of the Capped Model that warrants further consideration. For now, let me just make two comments regarding it.

First, one might think that if one is moved to something like a Capped Model for ideals by anti-additive-aggregationist views, then one should adopt an anti-additive approach "all the way down," as it were. On this view, there may be a holistic relationship between different ideals that requires a nonadditive approach for understanding how morally relevant ideals combine to determine how good an outcome is all things considered. Following the holistic insight that the whole may be greater or less than the sum of its parts, one might believe that one outcome could be better than another all things considered, even if it was genuinely worse with respect to each relevant ideal considered individually. A more modest version of this view would maintain that one outcome could be better than another all things considered, even if it were no better with respect to any particular ideal, considered individually, and was positively worse with respect to at least one ideal, considered individually. If one did ultimately believe that ideals could combine to generate all-things-considered judgments in such ways, one would need to revise the Capped Model accordingly so as to reject the Standard Model for Combining Ideals. Alternatively, one might ultimately conclude that one should reject the Capped Model entirely, and seek another approach for more fully and accurately capturing our anti-additive-aggregationist views.

Second, I have noted that the Capped Model assumes a numerical model for judging outcomes, according to which for each ideal relevant to assessing outcomes, each outcome will merit a (rough) numerical "score" representing how good that outcome is with respect to that ideal. I should emphasize that this approach is compatible with both of the following views: (1) the score assigned to an outcome for any given ideal depends *solely* on features of the outcome itself, or (2) the score assigned to an outcome for any given ideal depends partly on the alternatives with which that outcome is compared. Thus, the Capped Model is compatible with either of the two very different views of ideals introduced at the end of chapter 7, the Internal Aspects View or the Essentially Comparative View. I shall return to these views, and their significance, in the following chapters.

10.10 Shared Formal or Structural Features of Ideals

The Capped Model reflects the view that different ideals play similar roles in our all-things-considered judgments. More particularly, it reflects the view that however much more we may care about one ideal relative to another, we don't believe that any one ideal swamps every other ideal in its importance. Accordingly, we deny that losses with respect to every other ideal, no matter how great, could always be offset by sufficient gains with respect to a single ideal. Working out this view led to the recognition that, for certain comparisons at least, each ideal may be limited in how much it could improve an outcome.

This lesson comes as something of a surprise. We are used to thinking that there may be an upper limit on how good an outcome can be regarding equality—a limit that would be reached as soon as the outcome was perfectly equal—but we are not used to thinking that there may be an upper limit on how good an outcome could be with respect to other ideals, like utility or perfection, since it may seem that there is no end to the further gains that might be possible regarding such ideals. Nevertheless, in thinking about problems like the Repugnant Conclusion, and how best to respond to them, we are led to recognize that, for certain comparisons at least, every ideal may be like the ideal of equality and share the formal or structural feature of being bounded, or capped, in terms of how much of a contribution it can make to an outcome's overall goodness.

Since this is a book that tries, among other things, to shed light on the nature of moral ideals, and the way they combine to generate all-things-considered judgments, it is important to see that different ideals may have to share certain formal or structural features in the way entailed by the Capped Model.[24] In this section, I want to suggest a further way in which this may be so for the ideals of utility and equality. Specifically, I shall argue for the unexpected conclusion that in certain contexts, at least, if numbers count regarding utility, they may also have to count regarding equality. Consider diagram 10.10.A.

---

[24] The philosopher who has perhaps done the most to shed light on the importance of recognizing the formal or structural features of the good is John Broome, in his wonderful books *Weighing Goods* (Oxford: Basil Blackwell, 1991) and *Weighing Lives* (Oxford: Oxford University Press, 2004). Although I don't always agree with Broome regarding the particular formal or structural features that he thinks the good possesses, I do agree with his crucial insight that the good—and the ideals which constitute it—have certain formal or structural features and that it is important to explore what they are.

352 Rethinking the Good

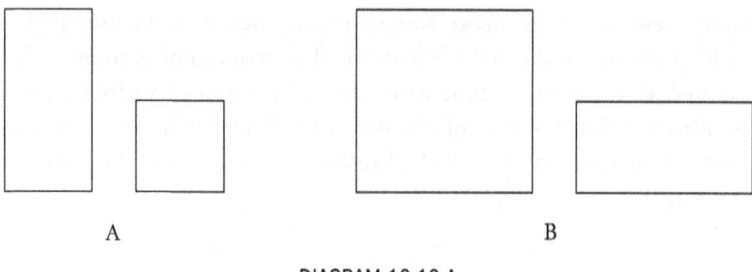

DIAGRAM 10.10.A

As drawn, *A*'s and *B*'s better- and worse-off groups are at the same levels, but *B*'s groups are twice as large as *A*'s. Regarding *inequality*, many would judge *A* and *B* equivalent. As they might put it, since the *pattern* of inequality is identical in *A* and *B*, there is nothing to choose between them; the "mere" fact that *B* is larger than *A* is irrelevant to how they compare regarding inequality.

The judgment that *A* and *B* are equivalent expresses the following view:

(*PV*) Proportional variations in the number of better- and worse-off do not affect inequality.

According to *PV*, size is not *itself* relevant to inequality. Size variations will only matter insofar as they affect inequality's *pattern*, for example, by altering the better- and worse-off's levels or the ratios between them.

PV is widely accepted and has great plausibility. It is, for example, implied by each of the economists' statistical measures of inequality, and they have not, to my knowledge, been criticized for that feature.[25] Yet, despite its appeal, and the fact that numerous considerations can be offered supporting it, ultimately *PV* may be incompatible with our views about other ideals and the role they play in our all-things-considered judgments.

Consider diagram 10.10.B.

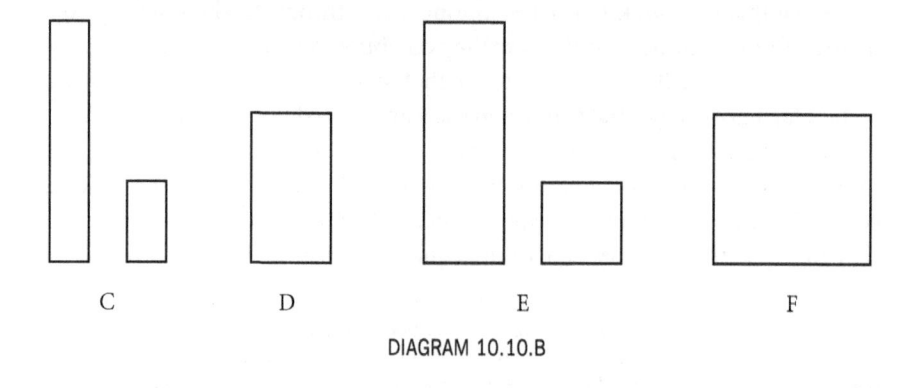

DIAGRAM 10.10.B

---

[25] Except by me, in chapter 7 of *Inequality*. The statistical measures that implicitly reflect *PV* include the *range*, the *relative mean deviation*, the *variance*, the *coefficient of variation*, the *standard*

As drawn, *C* represents an unequal society, *D* a perfectly equal society with less total utility. *E* and *F* are just like *C* and *D*, respectively, except that they are twice as large. Assume, for purposes of argument, that none of the alternatives would be at, or near, the limit of how good an outcome could be, objectively, regarding utility on a Capped Model. So, *C*, *D*, *E*, and *F* represent alternatives where gains and losses of utility would be objectively significant on both the Capped Model and the uncapped Standard Model for Combining Ideals.

Looking at *C* and *D*, many would judge that *D* is better than *C* all things considered. They would judge the loss of utility in moving from *C* to *D* regrettable, but outweighed by the substantial gain in equality. Similarly, looking at *E* and *F*, many would judge that *F* is better than *E* all things considered. Again, they would judge the loss of utility in moving from *E* to *F* regrettable, but outweighed by the gain in equality. More important, few, if any, would approve redistribution between the better- and worse-off in *C* so as to bring about *D*, yet oppose redistribution between the better- and worse-off in *E* so as to bring about *F*. That is, most would agree that *if* moving from *C* to *D* were desirable, moving from *E* to *F* would *also* be desirable.

Why might they think this? Here is one reason. Imagine a divided society, like *C*, where the better-off are whites and the worse-off are blacks. Next, imagine a second divided society exactly like the first. Surely, if equalizing between the whites and blacks would be desirable in the first society, where this involved transforming the situation from a *C*-like one into a *D*-like one, then equalizing between the whites and blacks would also be desirable in the second society, if this once again involved transforming the situation from a *C*-like one into a *D*-like one.[26] Given this, if it really would be desirable to bring about equality in *one* of the societies, it seems plausible to believe that it should also be desirable to bring about equality in *both* societies. The latter is not *logically* entailed by the former, but the claim nonetheless seems right.[27] But, then, it *also* seems reasonable to believe, though again it is not logically entailed by anything said so far, that *if* it would be desirable to equalize between the different groups of whites and blacks if they were members of *different* societies, it would *also* be

---

deviation of the logarithm, and the *Gini coefficient*. A useful discussion of these measures is contained in Amartya Sen's *On Economic Inequality* (Oxford: Clarendon Press, 1973). See also sections 5.1, 5.2, 6.8, and 7.11 of *Inequality*.

[26] This argument assumes that there are no other morally relevant factors present in the different situations that are not represented in diagram 10.10.B.

[27] There may well be some cases where if one outcome occurs alone, it would be good, and if a second outcome occurs alone, it would be good, but if the two outcomes occur *together*, it would be bad. Such cases normally involve some kind of complementarity between the two outcomes that would account for why two goods, together, make a bad (see section 5.5). But the case being described in the text doesn't seem to be one where complementarity would come into play and lead us to reject the view that the two outcomes, each of which would be good if they occurred separately, would be bad if they were combined and occurred together.

desirable to equalize between the whites and blacks if they were members of the *same* society, as long as the extent to which the various people gained or lost would be *exactly* the same in either case.

So, let *E* represent the case where the various groups are, in fact, members of a single society, where the whites are in *E*'s better-off group and the blacks are in *E*'s worse-off group. Together, our previous considerations suggest that if, as before, it would have been desirable to transform a *C*-like situation into a *D*-like situation by equalizing between *C*'s better- and worse-off groups, then it would also be desirable to transform an *E*-like situation into an *F*-like situation by equalizing between *E*'s better- and worse-off groups. Moreover, as should be evident, basic consideration of impartiality and neutrality entails that our judgments about this should be unaffected by the demographic membership of the different groups. It doesn't matter who is in *C* or *E*'s better- or worse-off groups; if, all things considered, it would be desirable to transform a *C*-like situation into a *D*-like situation, then, all things considered, it should also be desirable to transform an *E*-like situation into an *F*-like situation.

The foregoing claims may seem obvious and uninteresting, and hardly worth all the argument I have given them. However, they have important implications. Depending on how one thinks ideals combine to yield all-things-considered judgments, they imply that *if* numbers count for utility, they must *also* count for equality.[28]

---

[28] Not everyone accepts the view that numbers count in the moral realm. But most do. And I think they are right in doing so, even though, for the reasons I have been discussing, I also think that for certain comparisons, at least, numbers probably do not count in any simple additive way.

John Taurek explicitly denies that numbers should count in his rich and widely discussed article "Should the Numbers Count?" *Philosophy and Public Affairs* 6 (1977): 293–316. Other authors who raise serious questions about whether numbers count in all cases include Bernard Williams and Elizabeth Anscombe. See the concluding comments of "2. The Structure of Consequentialism," in Williams's "A Critique of Utilitarianism," in *Utilitarianism: For and Against*, with J. J. C. Smart (Cambridge: Cambridge University Press, 1973), and also Anscombe's "Modern Moral Philosophy," *Philosophy* 33 (1958): 1–19.

Shelly Kagan challenges a number of widely held assumptions about additivity in his fascinating article "The Additive Fallacy," *Ethics* 99 (1988): 5–31. Kagan's worries about additivity mirror many of the worries about additivity raised in this book. I first broached worries about simple additivity, implicitly, in my "Intransitivity and the Mere Addition Paradox," *Philosophy and Public Affairs* 16 (1987): 138–87, and, explicitly, in *Inequality*. It is perhaps worth emphasizing that *some* reasons people are drawn to the view that numbers don't count, or that additivity should be rejected, are in fact compatible with an additive model for ideals but not with a *simple* additive model. As we have seen, we might retain the view that two pains or deaths are worse than one, that three are worse than two, and so on, and yet reject the view that two pains or deaths are necessarily *twice* as bad as one, that three are three times as bad, and so on. So, even if utilitarians and others are right to insist that massacring 7 million plus 1 is worse than massacring 7 million, perhaps Anscombe and Williams are correct in thinking that the *objective* difference between those cases may not be nearly as great as the objective difference between murdering 2 people and murdering 1. Indeed, it could even be that the difference between such alternatives was objectively insignificant, though whether or not this is so would depend on our ultimate answers as to whether limits even applied to such cases, and if so, how quickly one approached them. Remember, we may think that limits apply to some factors, like headaches or mild pleasures, but not to others, like torture, sublime experiences, or massacres.

Consider. Suppose one thinks that the move from C to D is only a *slight* improvement all things considered, because the gain in equality is just *barely* enough to outweigh the attendant loss in utility.[29] Then it looks as if F would be *worse* than E if numbers count for utility but not for equality. After all, E and F are twice as large as C and D. This means that the loss in utility in moving from E to F will be twice that of the loss in utility in moving from C to D. Since, by hypothesis, the outcomes are ones for which gains and losses in utility are objectively significant, on the view that numbers count for utility, the move from E to F will be significantly worse than the move from C to D regarding utility. Yet, if numbers don't count for equality, or, more specifically, if we accept *PV*—the view that proportional increases do not affect inequality—then the gain in equality in moving from F to E will be *exactly* the same as the gain in equality in moving from D to C. But then it looks as if the gain in equality in moving from F to E won't be sufficient to outweigh the attendant loss in utility, since, by hypothesis, the gain in question is *barely* enough to outweigh a loss in utility which is only *half* as large. In sum, if moving from E to F is significantly worse than moving from C to D regarding utility, and no better regarding equality, then it is easy to see that, all things considered, moving from E to F could be undesirable even if moving from C to D were desirable. But this, of course, is contrary to the "obvious and uninteresting" view noted earlier.

The foregoing result may be surprising. But on reflection it is not, I think, perplexing or disturbing. Suffice it to say, I accept the view that if moving from C to D were desirable, so too would be moving from E to F. I also accept the view that in an important sense the latter move would be worse than the former regarding utility. This leads me to believe there is an important sense in which the latter move would be better than the former regarding equality. But, of course, this implies that E is worse than C regarding equality, which in turn implies that there is reason to reject *PV*.[30]

This argument is powerful, but not conclusive. It seems to depend on the kind of additive assumption accepted by both the uncapped Standard Model for Combining Ideals and the Capped Model as presented earlier, namely, that how good an outcome is all things considered is an additive function of how good it is regarding each ideal, so that insofar as an outcome gets better or worse regarding any particular ideal, it will, to that extent, be getting better or worse all things considered. But, as noted at the end of section 10.9, holistic

---

[29] If this doesn't seem plausible for C and D as drawn, imagine them redrawn (along with E and F) such that it *does* seem plausible. I presume, of course, that someone who genuinely cares about both equality and utility will want to permit *some* losses regarding either of the ideals for "sufficient" gains regarding the other.

[30] The argument presented here is only one of several supporting the conclusion that *PV* should be rejected. Others are presented in my article "Intergenerational Inequality," in *Philosophy, Politics, and Society*, 6th ser., ed. Peter Laslett and James Fishkin (New Haven, CT: Yale University Press, 1992), 169–205, as well as *Inequality*.

considerations may ultimately lead us to reject that additive assumption, and to adopt another way of understanding the relations between ideals and the way they combine to determine the goodness of outcomes.

Suppose, for example, that we adopted a multiplicative function for certain ideals, rather than an additive one. David Aman and John Broome have claimed that this would enable us to resist the foregoing argument.[31] Their reasoning is simple. If, instead of adding together numbers representing how good situations are regarding utility and equality in arriving at all-things-considered judgments, one multiplied the relevant numbers, this would seemingly enable one to maintain that while moving from E to F is worse than moving from C to D regarding utility, and no better regarding equality, the move from E to F will be desirable if the move from C to D is.

The math is plain enough. Suppose, for purposes of illustration, that with respect to equality, we assign scores of 70, 100, 70, and 100, and with respect to utility we assign scores of 100, 80, 200, and 160, to C, D, E, and F, respectively. Then, it looks like the gain in equality would be the same, 30 points, in moving from C to D as in moving from E to F, but the loss in utility would be different, 20 in moving from C to D, but 40 in moving from E to F. Accordingly, if one simply *added* the values of equality and utility, the move from C to D would be desirable, as the gain in equality would outweigh the loss in utility, 30 to 20, but the move from E to F would be undesirable, as the gain in equality would be outweighed by the loss in utility, 30 to 40. On the other hand, if we *multiplied* the values of equality and utility, then the overall values of C, D, E, and F, measured as a function of equality and utility, would be 7,000, 8,000, 14,000, and 16,000, respectively. Accordingly, both of the moves, from C to D and E to F, would be desirable regarding the trade-offs between equality and utility, and this is so even though the gain in equality would seemingly be the same in the two cases, while the loss in utility would seemingly be greater—and in fact twice as great given the numbers we are assuming—in the move from E to F than in the move from C to D.[32]

---

[31] In correspondence. David Aman is a former student of mine.

[32] A general proof that a multiplicative function could accommodate both PV and the view that if the move from C to D is desirable, then so is the move from E to F is straightforward for the Standard Model for Utility and the uncapped Standard Model for Combining Ideals. Assume that the overall goodness of an outcome is a multiplicative function of how good that outcome is regarding utility times how good it is regarding equality. Suppose that C's value is u_1 for utility and e_1 for equality, and that D's value is u_2 for utility and e_2 for equality. If D is better than C, this means that $u_2 \times e_2 > u_1 \times e_1$. E and F have twice as much utility as D and E, respectively, and on the Standard Model for Utility and the uncapped Standard Model for Combining Ideals this entails that E and F are twice as good as D and E, respectively, regarding utility, while, according to PV, the equality in E and F will be exactly as good as the equality in D and E, respectively. It follows on the simple multiplicative function we are currently assuming that the overall value of E will be $(2u_1) \times e_1$, while the overall value of F will be $(2u_2) \times e_2$. From this it follows that if D is better than C, then F is better than E, since, by the basic rules of arithmetic, if $u_2 \times e_2 > u_1 \times e_1$, then $(2u_2) \times e_2 > (2u_1) \times e_1$. (cont.)

Let me offer several comments regarding Aman and Broome's claim. First, although I have already acknowledged that we may ultimately want to reject the view that how good a situation is all things considered is a simple additive function of how good it is with respect to each individual ideal, it is not clear that we should replace the additive function with one that is wholly or even partly multiplicative. Though such a move could accommodate our initial intuition that if the move from C to D were desirable, so, too, would be the move from E to F, I am not sure that it can be independently motivated or ultimately defended. Prima facie, at least, it seems odd, implausible, and ad hoc to contend that how good a situation is all things considered will depend on, among other things, how good it is regarding utility *times* how good it is regarding equality. Can we think, for example, of any other ideals that might be related in a multiplicative manner? Would we, for example, think it plausible that how good an outcome is all things considered might be partly a function of how good it was regarding perfection *times* how good it was regarding freedom? For that matter, why multiply equality by utility, rather than equality by

---

A proof can also be given for the Capped Model, but the proof is more complicated, since on the Capped Model it won't be the case that doubling on outcome's utility will make it twice as bad regarding utility. The key to the proof is to recognize that, on the Capped Model, the more utility there is in an outcome, the less value will be added to the outcome, regarding utility, for each extra unit of utility that is added to the outcome (since the more utility there is, the closer the outcome already is to the maximin score, or value, for utility.) So if, as earlier, we assume that C's value for utility is u_1, and D's value for utility is u_2, then we know that on the Capped Model E's value for utility will be u_3 and F's will be u_4 where u_3 will be greater than u_1 but less than $2u_1$, and u_4 will be greater than u_2 but less than $2u_2$. But then, since, by hypothesis, there is more utility in C than in D, we know that each extra unit of utility that would be added to C to bring about E would add more value to the outcome than each extra unit of utility that would be added to D to bring about F, which entails that (1) $u_4/u_3 > u_2/u_1$. Since u_1, u_2, u_3 and u_4 are all positive real numbers, this implies that (2) $u_4 > u_3 u_2/u_1$ (just multiply both sides by u_3). This, in turn, entails that (3) $u_4 = (u_3 u_2/u_1) + k$, where k is a positive real number. Now we are assuming, as earlier, that if one accepts PV, then if C's value for equality is e_1, and D's value for equality is e_2, then the value of equality for E and F will also be e_1 and e_2, respectively. And what we are trying to show, recall, is how the multiplicative model could accommodate both PV and the intuition that if the move from C to D is desirable, then so is the move from E to F. That is, we are trying to show that if D is better than C, which means that (4) $u_2 e_2 > u_1 e_1$ (by hypothesis), then F is better than E, which means that (5) $u_4 e_2 > u_3 e_1$. Now we know that (6) $u_4 e_2 = ((u_3 u_2/u_1) + k)e_2$ (from (3), via the Principle of Substitution of Equivalents). We also know that (7) $e_2 > u_1 e_1/u_2$ (from (4) dividing both sides by the positive real number u_2, which entails that (8) $e_2 = (u_1 e_1/u_2) + l$ (where l is a positive real number). So (9) $u_4 e_2 = ((u_3 u_2/u_1) + k)((u_1 e_1/u_2) + l)$ (from (3) and (8) by the Principle of Substitution of Equivalents). So (10) $u_4 e_2 = (u_3 u_2/u_1)(u_1 e_1/u_2) + (k)(u_1 e_1/u_2) + (u_3 u_2/u_1)(l) + (k)(l)$ (from (9) by the Distributive Property of arithmetic). So (11) $u_4 e_2 = u_3 e_1 + (k)(u_1 e_1/u_2) + (u_3 u_2/u_1)(l) + (k)(l)$ (from (10), reducing the first term of the right-hand part of the equation). Since u_1, u_2, u_3, e_1, k, and l are all positive real numbers, (12) $((k)(u_1 e_1/u_2), (u_3 u_2/u_1)(l))$, and $((k)(l))$ are all positive real numbers. Thus, (5) $u_4 e_2 > u_3 e_1$ (from (11) and (12)). QED.

So, we have shown that, as Broome and Aman claimed, a multiplicative function could accommodate both PV and the view that if the move from C to D is desirable, then so is the move from E to F on both the Standard Model for Utility and the uncapped Standard Model for Combining Ideals, as well as the Capped Model (given the key assumption that, on the Capped Model, at some point each extra unit of utility would add less value to the outcome than the previous one). As should be clear, if one thought that each extra unit of utility contributed *more* value to the outcome than the previous one, then combined with PV, a multiplicative model could allow for the possibility that even if the move from C to D was desirable, the move from E to F might not be.

freedom, or utility by perfection, or some other combination of ideals including, perhaps, every ideal times every other?

Additionally, there are absurd implications of a multiplicative model if one allows negative numbers to represent disutility, or bad outcomes regarding equality. For example, suppose, that scores for equality could range from negative numbers to positive numbers, such that −1,000 represented a *terribly* unequal situation and 1,000 represented an almost perfectly equal situation. Similarly, suppose that scores for utility could range from negative numbers to positive numbers, such that −1,000 represented a *terrible* situation regarding utility (one filled with pain and suffering) while 1,000 represented a wonderful situation regarding utility (one filled with happiness and flourishing). On a multiplicative model, a situation that was horrible in terms of both equality and utility would be just as good as one that was wonderful in terms of both equality and utility, and it would be much better than countless outcomes that were very good regarding both equality and utility. After all, (−1,000 × −1,000) = (1,000 × 1,000) = 1,000,000 and (−1,000 × −1,000) > (900 × 900) as 1,000,000 > 810,000. Indeed, on a multiplicative model, it would be better if the pain and suffering in the outcome *doubled* than if it were cut in *half* as (−2,000 × −1,000) = 2,000,000 > (−500 × −1,000) = 500,000!

Likewise, suppose that one outcome was only slightly good regarding equality, receiving the fairly low, but still positive, score of 10 for equality, but that it was quite bad regarding utility, receiving a fairly poor score of −500 for utility. On a multiplicative model, improving the equality significantly would actually worsen the outcome's overall score. So, for example, if the equality score went from 10 to 1,000, the overall score would go from (10 × −500) = −5,000 to (1,000 × −500) = −500,000. Similarly, the multiplicative model will have deeply implausible implications if the values of utility or equality are allowed to approach, or equal, 0. For example, a tiny change in the value of equality, say from ½ to ¼ would have as dramatic an effect on the overall value of the outcome as a massive change in the value of utility, say from 10,000,000 to 5,000,000, since (10,000,000 × ¼) = (5,000,000 × ½). Likewise, if the value of either equality or utility were 0, then it wouldn't matter *at all* whether one *vastly* improved or worsened the outcome regarding the other ideal, since 0 times anything is still 0.

These observations hardly constitute a conclusive refutation of a multiplicative approach. Perhaps one needs a more nuanced and sophisticated model; for example, one that employs only positive scales for measuring equality or utility, or one that deals with negative numbers in a special manner. But isn't it most natural and plausible to use positive numbers to represent positive utility, zero to represent neutral utility, and negative numbers to represent negative utility or disutility? And if we find ourselves treating negative numbers in a "special" manner to avoid unpalatable implications, doesn't that smack of fiddling with our numbers in an ad hoc manner to ensure that we get the desired results?

Given the many problems with additive approaches which this work has highlighted, it is worth canvassing a wide range of alternative models for understanding how different ideals combine to determine the goodness of outcomes, including ones involving multiplicative elements. But I think much more work needs to be done exploring the possible foundations and implications of alternative models, and I have doubts whether the most plausible and defensible model will include a multiplicative element of the sort suggested by Aman and Broome.

Finally, although the math certainly works out in the way Aman and Broome noted, for the case I was considering, I'm not sure that such a move really undermines this section's main point, namely, that different ideals may share certain formal or structural features, and, in particular, that if numbers count regarding utility, they may also have to count regarding equality. To suggest that how good an outcome is regarding utility and equality is a function of how good it is regarding utility *times* how good it is regarding equality is to see utility and equality as intimately bound together in a way that ensures a kind of formal or structural unity in the way that equality and utility work together to influence the goodness of outcomes.

Consider the following example. Suppose an employer promises to match an employee's contributions one-for-one to some charitable cause. One way of looking at this, mathematically, is to say that the employer is doubling the contribution, so that the charity is receiving twice the amount that the individual employee contributes. This might be represented as follows: $IC \times 2 = TCCR$, where IC stands for the individual contribution, and $TCCR$ stands for the total contribution the charity receives. If the individual employee's contribution increases by 50 percent, say, from \$1,000 to \$1,500, the total amount that the charity receives will also increase by 50 percent, from \$2,000 to \$3,000. Notice, although it is only the number for IC that doubles, while the number representing the extent to which the individual contribution is multiplied remains constant, namely, 2, it would be a mistake to think that the increase in the total contribution was due only to the increase in the individual contribution. In fact, in this scenario the employer's contribution will have increased by just as much as the employee's, and it will have contributed just as much to the change in the total contribution received by the charity.

Reflection on the preceding suggests the following. Where two terms are *added* together, one can increase the value of one without affecting the impact that the value of the other has on the overall total, but where two terms are *multiplied* together, one cannot increase the value of one without increasing the impact that the value of the other has on the overall total. Thus, while on an additive model a number representing the extent of equality or utility in an outcome may also represent the impact that the equality or utility has on the outcome's overall value, this will decidedly not be the case on a multiplicative model of the sort suggested by Aman and Broome. So, on such a model, the fact that the same number can accurately represent the degree to which inequality has changed in the move from C to D as in the move from E to F does not yet mean anything about the extent to which the change in inequality has affected the outcome's objective overall goodness.

Recognizing this, we can see that if one adopts a multiplicative approach for determining the way in which equality and utility combine to affect an outcome's overall objective goodness, the ideals of equality and utility will share certain formal or structural features. In particular, it will remain true that in a fundamentally important sense, if numbers count for utility, they will also count for equality. After all, given the tight reciprocal relation that obtains between elements in a multiplicative relation, if increases or decreases in an outcome's numbers affect the impact that the ideal of utility has on the outcome's objective overall goodness, then it will simultaneously and invariably affect the impact that the ideal of equality has on the outcome's objective overall goodness.

Some will insist that inequality is not bad in the same way that disutility is. More generally, they will insist that equality and utility are different *kinds* of ideals and that the two ideals must be treated differently. So, for example, some will insist that while utility is essentially additive, equality is essentially distributive—that is, that while utilitarians are essentially concerned with how much there is, egalitarians are essentially concerned *not* with how much there is, but with the way or *pattern* in which what there is is distributed. On this view, the fact that numbers count regarding utility should be completely irrelevant to whether numbers count regarding equality.

Such thinking is powerfully seductive, but as we have seen, it is not clear that our ideals can be fully and adequately characterized in isolation from each other. Specifically, a plausible and coherent account of the role ideals play in relation to each other and our all-things-considered judgments may require at least some ideals to share certain formal or structural features. Thus, as the Repugnant Conclusion reveals, for certain comparisons, at least, there may be a limit to how much improvement regarding one ideal can offset significant losses regarding other ideals, and this in turn suggests that just as there may be an upper limit regarding how good a situation can be regarding equality, there may be an upper limit regarding how good a situation can be regarding each of our ideals. So, too, as we have seen, if one holds that numbers count regarding utility, one may also have to hold that numbers count regarding equality.

10.11 Concluding Remark

Let me conclude this chapter by returning to the issue framed in its introductory paragraph, and commented upon at the end of sections 10.2 and 10.8. Throughout this book, I have been arguing that in comparing some outcomes we often adopt an additive-aggregationist approach, whereas in comparing others we often adopt an anti-additive-aggregationist approach. I have suggested that a combination of the Standard Model for Utility and the Standard Model for Combining Ideals could capture the former, but that we need a Capped Model for ideals, or some other model, to capture the latter. But it might be thought that we could dispense with the Standard Model for Utility and the uncapped Standard Model for Combining Ideals, and simply go with some version of the Capped Model, since a Capped Model can also capture our additive-aggregationist intuitions in *most* cases about which we have firm intuitions. This is because in most cases for which we have firm intuitions, it is arguable that we won't yet have reached, or even approached, the limits set by a Capped Model, so that the rankings generated by such a model will in fact track the rankings set by the Standard Models. Thus, the Capped Model can also claim to adequately capture most of our additive-aggregationist intuitions, even if it does not, itself, embody the simple additive-aggregationist elements involved in the Standard Model for Utility.

If this is right, then it looks as if the Capped Model may provide us with a way of capturing *most* of our additive-aggregationist intuitions, as well as our anti-additive aggregationist intuitions. So, the Capped Model provides a way of avoiding the Repugnant Conclusion, and, as noted previously, by itself, the Capped Model will generate a ranking of alternatives that is perfectly transitive. Thus, it may seem that a Capped Model will give us everything we want regarding how best to understand ideals and the way they combine to generate all-things-considered rankings of outcomes.

Unfortunately, however, matters are not quite so simple. There will remain cases, involving "super" large numbers, about which most people seemingly have *very* firm *considered* judgments, which can be accounted for only by appealing to a genuinely additive-aggregationist account of the sort represented by the combination of the Standard Model for Utility and the uncapped Standard Model for Combining Ideals. That is, the very features that enable the Capped Model to reject the Repugnant Conclusion will ensure that it is unable to capture our intuitions about *such* cases. Were this the only problem with exclusive reliance on the Capped Model, perhaps we could persuade ourselves that our seemingly firm considered judgments about such cases are not to be trusted after all, especially given that "super" large numbers are notoriously difficult to intuitively grasp or understand. Unfortunately, however, there are other deeply counterintuitive and controversial implications of any version of the Capped Model,[33] or any other model for that matter, that avoids intransi-

---

[33] Nick Beckstead has written a short paper, "Problems for Capped Models of Moral Ideals" (December 2009, unpublished), that elegantly and succinctly shows that all of the most obvious contenders for a Capped Model have wildly counterintuitive implications—indeed, implications that are at least as counterintuitive as those facing the Standard Model for Utility and the Standard Model for

tivity, some of which we will illustrate in the following chapters. Ultimately, then, it remains true that there is no easy solution to the problems highlighted in this book. There are many different moves one can make in response to such problems, but there is no plausible coherent account that adequately captures all of our deepest beliefs about the nature of the good, moral ideals, and practical reasoning.

Combining Ideals, including, for example, additive-aggregationist positions like the Repugnant Conclusion. Of course, Beckstead's arguments do not show that Capped Models should be jettisoned entirely, but they do show that they need to be carefully limited in scope, and in conjunction with this book's other arguments, they support the general conclusion reiterated in this chapter's final sentences.

11

On the Nature of Moral Ideals

PART I

We have considered various arguments challenging the widely held assumption that "all-things-considered better than" *must* be a transitive relation. Though many regard the assumption as a fundamental principle of practical rationality, and it serves as one of the principle axioms of Expected Value Theory, our arguments raise doubts as to whether, in the many kinds of cases that we have considered, the relevant "all-things-considered better than" relation is transitive or applies to certain sets of alternatives for which we might have thought it should apply. Specifically, we have seen that the transitivity or applicability of the "better than" relation (in my wide reason-implying sense) is incompatible with certain other deeply held views reflecting the plausibility and relevance of additive-aggregationist reasoning for certain comparisons, and anti-additive-aggregationist reasoning for other comparisons. Since, so far, my worries about the "all-things-considered better than" relation appeal to Spectrum Arguments—involving comparisons between different alternatives across a spectrum of cases—many assume that they are versions of the Standard Sorites Paradox. But I have argued that this is not the case. Spectrum Arguments are particularly powerful examples where we appeal to different considerations in assessing different alternatives. However, the fact that my arguments involve a spectrum is, I believe, a red herring. The *key* question, I claim, is whether or not the factors that are relevant for making different all-things-considered judgments can vary, or vary in their significance, depending on what alternatives are compared.

This key question is intimately related to the nature of the goodness of outcomes, which in turn is likely to be related to the nature of moral ideals. If the goodness of outcomes and moral ideals must be understood one way, in accordance with a position I call the *Internal Aspects View*, then the "all-things-considered better than" relation will, indeed, be transitive. But if the goodness of outcomes and at least some moral ideals should be understood another way, in accordance with a position I call the *Essentially Comparative View*, then for at least some outcomes "all-things-considered better than" (in my wide reason-implying sense) either may not be a transitive relation or may fail to apply across certain sets of alternatives.

Thus, a fundamentally important question for practical reasoning is how best to understand the goodness of outcomes and the nature of moral ideals: Is the Internal Aspects View correct, is the Essentially Comparative View correct, or is, perhaps, some other view correct? In this chapter, and the following one, I shall distinguish between the Internal Aspects View and the Essentially Comparative View and illustrate some of the implications of adopting one or the other. In doing this, I will begin by exploring an important example that illuminates the appeal of the Essentially Comparative View, Derek Parfit's *Mere Addition Paradox*.[1] In analyzing the Mere Addition Paradox, its implications, and various possible responses to it, we will develop a much better understanding of a number of important views that stand or fall together. One of these views, which I shall call the *Independence of Irrelevant Alternatives Principle*, is also, along with the transitivity of "better than," widely regarded as a fundamental principle of practical rationality. In these chapters, we will see that both the Internal Aspects View and the Essentially Comparative View have great plausibility. Unfortunately, each also has deeply unintuitive implications.

11.1 The Mere Addition Paradox

In part 4 of *Reasons and Persons*, Derek Parfit presents the Mere Addition Paradox. Some regard it as an arcane esoteric puzzle involving hypothetical future generations that has little to do with the central problems of moral philosophy. Nothing could be further from the truth. I believe the Mere Addition Paradox is one of the most interesting and important—though least well-understood—problems in contemporary moral philosophy. As we will see, on close examination the Mere Addition Paradox may rest on a powerful conception of moral ideals that is both deeply attractive and extremely controversial. This conception is what I call the *Essentially Comparative View of Moral Ideals*, and it raises profound questions about our understanding of the nature of moral ideals and practical reasoning. Before articulating the Essentially Comparative View and illustrating how it may underlie the Mere Addition Paradox, let me begin by presenting the Mere Addition Paradox itself.

Parfit offers several versions of the Mere Addition Paradox. For our purposes, it will be sufficient to consider a slightly simplified form of his first version.[2] Consider diagram 11.1.A.

---

[1] See part 4, chapter 19 of his *Reasons and Persons* (Oxford: Oxford University Press, 1984).

[2] It is simplified in omitting Parfit's "Divided B," which does not affect my argument. Parfit's first version of the Mere Addition Paradox appears in part 4 of *Reasons and Persons*, sections 142–47 (pp. 419–33).

DIAGRAM 11.1.A

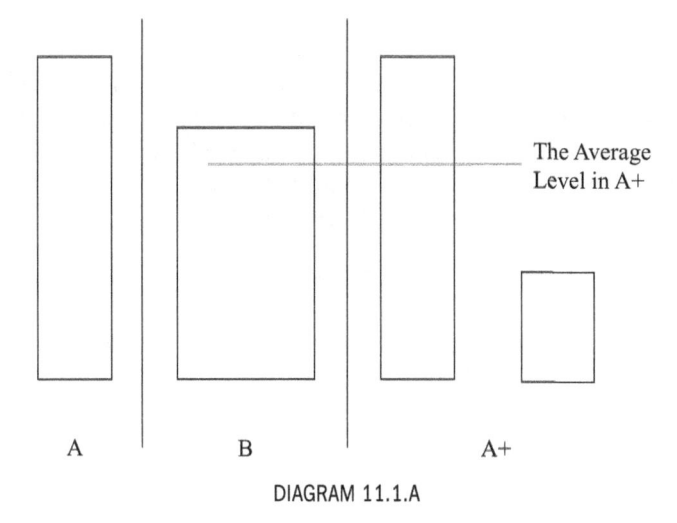

A represents an outcome with a large population, say, 10 billion people, all of whose members are equal and very well off. *A+* represents an outcome with two groups of people. The first group is the same group of well-off people that would be in *A*; the second group is the same size as the first group, and everyone in that group has a life that is well worth living, but they are much less well off than the members of the first group. *B* represents an outcome containing the same two groups as *A+*, where everyone is equally well off and better off than the average level of *A+*. So, *A+*'s better-off group is worse off in *B*, while *A+*'s worse-off group is better off in *B*, and the extent to which the worse-off group is better off is greater than the extent to which the better-off group is worse off.

Parfit claims that all things considered most would judge that *B* is worse than *A*. After all, by hypothesis, *A* is already a large population of 10 billion, and *everyone* in *A* is better off than *everyone* in *B*. Parfit also argues that all things considered most would judge that *B* is better than *A+*. Though *B* is worse than *A+* regarding perfection, it is better regarding maximin, equality, and utility;[3] so, though perfectionists might deny that *B* is better than *A+*, or *elitists* who judged outcomes on the basis of how the *best*-off people fared, most would not. Finally, Parfit contends that all things considered most would judge that *A+* is not worse than *A*. Parfit's lengthy argument for this[4] will be discussed later, but the key point is that *A+* involves *Mere Addition*, where, according to Parfit, there is

> Mere Addition when, in one of two outcomes, there exist extra people (1) who have lives worth living, (2) who affect no one else, and (3) whose existence does not involve social injustice.[5]

---

[3] Parfit puts his discussion in terms of beneficence; for simplicity, I have recast it in terms of utility. The shift in terminology does not affect my arguments.
[4] See *Reasons and Persons*, 419–26.
[5] *Reasons and Persons*, 420.

As Parfit puts it in a passage from "Future Generations: Further Problems,"

> Let us compare A with A+. The only difference is that A+ contains an extra group, who have lives worth living, and who affect no one else…it seems [hard]…to believe that A+ is *worse* than A. This implies that it would have been better if the extra group had never existed. If their lives are worth living, and they affect no one else, why is it bad that these people are alive?[6]

According to Parfit, then, most believe that A+ is not worse than A and that B is better than A+. Parfit writes, "These beliefs together imply that B is not worse than A. B cannot be worse than A if it is better than something—A+—which is not worse than A."[7] But, Parfit contends, most also believe that "*B is* worse than A. [Hence] we have three beliefs that are inconsistent and imply contradictions.... this [is] the *Mere Addition Paradox*."[8]

Parfit insists that the Mere Addition Paradox does *not* merely illustrate a tension between different moral principles, which may often conflict and cloud our all-things-considered judgments. Such cases needn't reflect any inconsistency. "In the Mere Addition Paradox," Parfit claims, "things are different. We are here inclined to believe, *all things considered*, that B is worse than A, though B is better than A+, which is not worse than A. These three judgments cannot all be consistently believed, since they imply contradictions. One of these beliefs must go."[9]

In sum, Parfit believes that rationality requires us to give up one of the three claims, and the paradox is that, considered alone, each claim seems (far) more plausible than its denial.

11.2 Illuminating the Mere Addition Paradox: Parfit's Implicit Appeal to an Essentially Comparative View of Moral Ideals

Unfortunately, Parfit's discussion of the Mere Addition Paradox is misleading. Believing that the Mere Addition Paradox would be dissolved if one of Parfit's three main claims were rejected, many spend time questioning whether B really *is* worse than A all things considered, and whether the judgment that B is better than A commits one to the Repugnant Conclusion.[10] Similarly, some people wonder if

---

[6] *Philosophy and Public Affairs* 11 (1982): 158–59.
[7] *Reasons and Persons*, 426.
[8] *Reasons and Persons*, 426.
[9] *Reasons and Persons*, 427.
[10] Some people do not find the Mere Addition Paradox problematic; what they find problematic is iterations of the Paradox which seemingly lead to the Repugnant Conclusion. Specifically, some would accept that A+ is not worse than A, and is perhaps even better, that B is better than A+, and that B is better than A. They might also grant that B+ would be better than B, C better than B+, and C better than B, where B+, C, and B roughly stood to B, B+, and C, respectively, as A+, B, and A stood to A, A+, and B, respectively, in Parfit's original example. But they are confident that *somewhere* between A and Z the line should be drawn, even if they are not sure exactly where, so as to resist our being led from A to Z. (cont.)

B really is better than $A+$, and whether one could deny this without being an elitist.[11] Also, as we will see shortly, some people argue that $A+$ really is worse than A, since, for example, it is much worse regarding equality or maximin.

As it happens, I think Parfit is right—though his arguments are not conclusive—regarding the most plausible pairwise judgments of A, $A+$, and B. But even if Parfit is wrong, and we can resolve the Mere Addition Paradox by plausibly rejecting the claim that A is better than B, or the claim that B is better than $A+$,

---

I believe this line is defensible, and not merely because, as Parfit suggests in section 146 of *Reasons and Persons*, "not worse than" is not a transitive relation. Parfit writes, "It is true that, by the same reasoning [underlying the Paradox], C cannot be worse than B, D cannot be worse than C, and so on. But since 'not worse than' is not transitive, we can claim that, while C is not worse than B, which is not worse than A, C *is* worse than A" (*Reasons and Persons*, 432). Suppose, however, we think $A+$ is *better* than A, and B better than $A+$, then since, according to Parfit, "better than" *is* a transitive relation, B would be better than A, and it *looks* as if iterations of the Paradox would entail the Repugnant Conclusion. After all, "by the same reasoning" C would be better than B, D would be better than C, and so on. Hence, given the transitivity of the "better-than" relation, C would be better than A, and Z would be best.

Such reasoning is appealing, but it can, I think, be resisted. Specifically, it is not clear that "the same reasoning" which underlies our judgments regarding A, $A+$, and B would apply to situations closer to Z. For example, even if $A+$ is better than A, and $B+$ is better than B, $F+$ might be worse than F. This might be so if, as many believe, and as I argued in *Inequality*, inequality matters more at low levels than at high levels, or if, analogously, maximin matters more at low levels (after all, given that maximin expresses our special concern for how the worst-off fare, this concern may be reasonably heightened the worse off the worst-off are). On such views, the move from F to $F+$ may be worse regarding equality or maximin than the move from A to $A+$. Similarly, if one adopts something like chapter 10's Capped Model for understanding utility, then the extent to which $F+$ is greater than F regarding utility may be less than the extent to which $A+$ is better than A. Any of these factors alone could prevent the slide from A to Z. Combined, they make it quite plausible that $F+$ could be worse than F, even if $A+$ is better than A.

In sum, critics of the Mere Addition Paradox could not only reject the claim that B is worse than A, they could insist that $A+$ is better than A, B is better than $A+$, and B better than A without accepting the Repugnant Conclusion. I might add that this position corresponds to some people's actual reactions to the Mere Addition Paradox and iterations of it.

[11] Parfit questions whether one could deny that B is better than $A+$ without being an elitist. He writes, "Can we honestly claim to believe that a change from $A+$ to B would not be a change for the better? If we claim [this]..., we would be saying that what matters most is the quality of life of the best-off people. Call this the *Elitist View*. On this view, what happens to the best-off people matters *more* than what happens to the worst-off people" (*Reasons and Persons*, 427).

Parfit's remarks here are, perhaps, misleading. Someone might care about perfection, as one ideal among others, and might assume that B is sufficiently worse than $A+$, regarding perfection, to outweigh the respects in which B is better than $A+$ with respect to other ideals like equality, maximin, or utility. Parfit may be assuming that this can't be the case with his example, as *he* is imagining it, but his description of his case does not rule out this possibility as it currently stands. Hence, depending on how the details of the case are fleshed out, it is certainly possible for someone to believe that an $A+$-like outcome might be better than a B-like outcome on perfectionist grounds. Clearly, such a person need not be an elitist; indeed, she might vehemently deny that "what matters most is the quality of life of the best-off people," or that "what happens to the best-off people matters *more* than what happens to the worst-off people."

Notice, if we thought that B was as good as $A+$ on perfectionist grounds, as it *could* be depending on how the details of the case were spelled out, then it seems that Parfit's charge would be more defensible. In that case, B would be better than $A+$ in terms of equality, maximin, and utility, and at least as good in terms of perfection; hence, absent an appeal to some *other* difference between the outcomes not previously discussed (for example, perhaps one might think that $A+$ was vastly better than A regarding autonomy, for some reason), it is difficult to see how one could deny that B was better than A, unless one was an elitist in Parfit's sense.

the most *fundamental* insights and implications of Parfit's argument would remain unaffected. The *crucial* question Parfit raises is whether the fact that A+ involves Mere Addition is *relevant* to our assessment of outcomes. As we shall see, the answer to this question has profound implications about the nature of moral ideals, implications that challenge some of our deepest assumptions about practical and moral reasoning, and hence our understanding of rationality itself.

Consider the difference between A and A+. One natural response to the Mere Addition Paradox, that some are attracted to, is to claim A+ *is* worse than A, in part because it is worse regarding equality. Against such a response one might reason as follows. Typically, when we say one outcome's inequality is worse than another's, the same people exist in both outcomes and the worse-off fare worse in the one outcome than the other. This, we may agree, is bad. However, comparing A+ to A, the choice *isn't* between an outcome where the worse-off fare poorly relative to the better-off and one where they fare better; rather, it is between one where they exist—with lives worth living—and one where they don't. Here, it may seem, the inequality is not morally regrettable.

Parfit explicitly adopted this line. His argument is worth giving in some detail. He wrote:

> Whether inequality makes...[an] outcome worse depends on how it comes about. It might be true either... that some existing people are worse off than others, or...that there are extra people living who, though their lives are worth living, are worse off than some existing people. Only...[the former] makes the outcome worse....When inequality is produced by Mere Addition, it does not make the outcome worse....It would not be better if there was no inequality because the extra people do not exist. It would be better only if the extra people do exist and are as well off as everyone else....Since the inequality in A+ is produced by Mere Addition, this inequality does not make A+ worse than A. We cannot plausibly claim that the extra people should never have existed, *merely because, unknown to them, there are other people who are even better off.*[12]

Here, Parfit was *not* denying the obvious fact that A is perfectly equal while A+ is not. Nor was he denying that A+'s inequality is morally regrettable *when compared with B's*. Parfit's contention was that A+'s inequality is not regrettable *if the alternative is A*. As we shall see next, it is hard to overstate the importance of this view.

On Parfit's view, *equality is essentially comparative*, not merely in the ordinary sense—that it involves judgments about how some fare relative to others—but in the sense that our judgment about an outcome's inequality depends on the alternative to which it is being compared. An advocate of the view that equality is essentially comparative believes that inequality is not objectionable when it involves the mere addition of extra people all of whom have lives worth living and who

---

[12] *Reasons and Persons*, 425.

affect no one else, and where the alternative is *not* an outcome where those people are better off, but one where they *don't exist*. As we have seen, this underlies Parfit's view that A+'s inequality *is* morally regrettable when A+ is compared to B, but *not* when A+ is compared to A. So, on the view that equality is essentially comparative, the *relevance or significance* of the factors for comparing A+ and A regarding equality differ from the *relevance or significance* of the factors for comparing A+ and B regarding equality. In the one case, the fact of Mere Addition is present and is both relevant and greatly significant; in the other it is not.

By now, the implications of this are well known. If, indeed, equality is essentially comparative, then transitivity will either fail, or fail to apply, across Parfit's alternatives A, A+, and B. This would provide us with a way of responding to Parfit's Mere Addition Paradox without rejecting *any* of the three judgments that supposedly constitute the paradox.

I shall spell this out shortly, but before doing so, it will be useful to provide a general characterization of the view that some moral ideals are essentially comparative. To do this, it will help to first introduce and characterize a rival conception of moral ideals that I will discuss in more detail in section 11.3. As I shall characterize both the Essentially Comparative View and its rival conception, a cardinal scale is assumed to be available for ranking outcomes both in terms of how good they are with respect to individual moral ideals and in terms of how good they are all things considered. In addition, the notion of goodness is assumed to be the fundamental notion from which the notion of betterness is derived. I am aware that these assumptions are controversial and rejected by some. Still, I think most will find such assumptions natural and plausible, and I make them in part because they simplify my presentation, and in part because they reflect my own views about the normative domain. Having said that, my presentation of alternative conceptions of moral ideals *could* be revised in complicated ways to reflect the views that only ordinal rankings of outcomes are available with respect to individual ideals or all-things-considered judgments, and that the notion of "better than" is the fundamental notion from which the notion of goodness is derived. Thus, this chapter's substantive claims could be defended on "ordinal/better than" versions of the conceptions of moral ideals I discuss, as well as the "cardinal/goodness" versions I actually consider. Bearing this in mind, I note that one might hold the following position.

The Internal Aspects View of Moral Ideals (IAVMI):[13] Roughly, for each outcome, O, and each moral ideal, F, there is an extent to which outcome

---

[13] Here, and in what follows, I use the notion of "moral ideal" as equivalent to the notion of "true moral ideal" or "morally relevant ideal." Later, we will see that similar claims about the structure of ideals to those that I am making about moral ideals might be made about other ideals of practical reasoning that are not, strictly speaking, *moral* ideals. For example, one might advocate an Internal Aspects View or an Essentially Comparative View of *Prudential Ideals* or *Prudential Goodness*. Similarly, one might advocate an Internal Aspects View or an Essentially Comparative View of *Practical Ideals* or *Practical Goodness* generally.

O is good with respect to F which depends solely on O's internal features.[14] Moreover, for any two outcomes, O_1 and O_2, and any moral ideal F_1, O_1 will be better than O_2 regarding F_1, if and only if the extent to which O_1 is good regarding F_1, as determined solely on the basis of O_1's internal features, is greater than the extent to which O_2 is good regarding F_1, as determined solely on the basis of O_2's internal features. In addition, if O_1 is better than O_2 regarding any moral ideal F_1, the extent to which this is so will depend solely on the extent to which O_1 is good regarding F_1 is greater than the extent to which O_2 is good regarding F_1.[15]

In addition to the Internal Aspects View of Moral Ideals one might hold the following.

The Internal Aspects View of Outcome Goodness (*IAVOG*): Roughly, for each outcome, O, how good that outcome is *all things considered* depends solely on how good it is with respect to each moral ideal that is relevant for assessing the goodness of outcomes, and on how much all of the relevant ideals matter vis-à-vis each other, where these depend solely on O's internal features. Moreover, for any two outcomes, O_1 and O_2, O_1 will be better than O_2 *all things considered* if and only if the extent to which O_1 is good all things considered, as determined solely on the basis of O_1's internal features, is greater than the extent to which O_2 is good all things considered, as determined solely on the basis of O_2's internal features. In addition, if O_1 is better than O_2 all things considered, the extent to which this is so will depend solely on the extent to which O_1 is good, all things considered, is greater than the extent to which O_2 is good, all things considered.

There is, I believe, room in conceptual space for someone to accept the Internal Aspects View of Moral Ideals but not the Internal Aspects View of Outcome Goodness, and vice versa. But, in fact, I believe most people who accept the one also accept the other. Accordingly, for ease of presentation, in what follows I will not always distinguish between the two positions, and will use the expression "the Internal Aspects View" (*IAV*) to refer to each of the positions, whether considered separately or together. In most cases, I hope that context will make

---

[14] In making this claim, I am *not* claiming that the extent to which O is good regarding F is precise. Goodness may or may not admit of precision. The claim is simply that whether precise or not, the extent to which O is good with respect to F depends solely on O's internal features.

[15] Note, this view is compatible with the kind of view now favored by Derek Parfit, according to which most comparisons between outcomes are imprecise, since, if Parfit is right, the extent to which some outcome is good with respect to any given moral ideal may itself be imprecise and, similarly, the extent to which one outcome may be better than, worse than, or equal to another with respect to any given ideal may be imprecise. Similar remarks apply to the *Internal Aspects View of Outcome Goodness* presented next, since that view, like this one, does not require us to assume that there is precision, even in principle, in ranking outcomes with respect to goodness.

plain whether I am referring to the Internal Aspects View of Moral Ideals, the Internal Aspects View of Outcome Goodness, or both, and that in any event there will be no significant danger to my conflating the positions in this way.

We are now in a position to characterize

The Essentially Comparative View of Moral Ideals (ECVMI): Roughly, there is at least one moral ideal, F, and at least one outcome, O, such that there is no answer to the question of how good O is regarding F, based solely on F's internal features; or, even if, for each moral ideal, F, and each outcome, O, there is an answer to the question of how good O is regarding F based solely on O's internal features, there is at least one ideal, F, and two outcomes O_1 and O_2, such that how O_1 compares with O_2 regarding F is not simply a function of the extent to which O_1 is good with respect to F based solely on O_1's internal features and the extent to which O_2 is good with respect to F based solely on O_2's internal features.

As the reader may recognize, in essence I have characterized the Essentially Comparative View of Moral Ideals as the *denial* of the Internal Aspects View of Moral Ideals. On the Essentially Comparative View of Moral Ideals, matters are more complicated than the Internal Aspects View recognizes when it comes to assessing the relative goodness of outcomes regarding at least some moral ideals.[16]

Paralleling the Essentially Comparative View of Moral Ideals is

The Essentially Comparative View of Outcome Goodness (ECVOG): Roughly, there is at least one outcome, O, such that there is no answer to the question of how good O is all things considered based solely on O's internal features; or, even if, for each outcome, O, there is an answer to the question of how good O is all things considered based solely on O's internal features, there are at least two outcomes, O_1 and O_2, such that how O_1 compares with O_2 all things considered is not simply a function of the extent to which O_1 is good, all things considered, based solely on O_1's internal features and the extent to which O_2 is good, all things considered, based solely on O_2's internal features.

As with the two Internal Aspects Views, there is room in conceptual space for someone to accept the Essentially Comparative View of Moral Ideals but not the Essentially Comparative View of Outcome Goodness, and vice versa. But here,

---

[16] I am grateful to Jake Ross for suggesting (in correspondence) that I characterize the Essentially Comparative View of Moral Ideals in this way. As Ross notes, this is analogous to the way in which deontology is often characterized as the denial of consequentialism in maintaining that, in some cases at least, matters are more complicated than consequentialism allows regarding what makes an action right. I say "more complicated" here, because most deontologists will grant that in some cases consequences are relevant to, and may even determine, the rightness of actions, but they deny that it is always true that *only* consequences matter for the rightness of actions.

too, I believe that most who accept one of the Essentially Comparative Views also accept the other. So, for simplicity, I shall often use the locution "Essentially Comparative View" (*ECV*) to refer to either or both of the two views. Again, I hope that in most contexts my meaning will be plain enough, and that there is no significant danger to my conflating the positions in this way.

It should now be clearer what I mean in saying that on Parfit's view, as he presented it in discussing the Mere Addition Paradox, equality is essentially comparative. For on his view, there may be no answer to the question of how bad $A+$'s inequality is based solely on $A+$'s internal features; moreover, even if there is an answer to that question, when considering $A+$ *by itself*, how bad $A+$'s inequality is in comparison with A or B is not merely a function of how bad each outcome's inequality is based solely on its internal features. More generally, we may say of any particular ideal that it is essentially comparative if we assess the goodness of outcomes with respect to that ideal in a manner that is incompatible with the Internal Aspects View of Moral Ideals.

Before proceeding, let me reiterate and emphasize some of the key points regarding essentially comparative moral ideals and note some of their implications. First, on an Essentially Comparative View, it may not even make sense to consider how good an outcome is considered *just by itself*. All judgments about how good an outcome is regarding an essentially comparative moral ideal may necessarily involve an alternative or set of alternative outcomes with which the outcome is explicitly or implicitly being compared. But even if this is not the case, and there is some meaningful sense in which we might appropriately judge how good an outcome is regarding an essentially comparative moral ideal, *considered just by itself*, that judgment will have no primacy or special role to play when it comes to judging how good that outcome is regarding that ideal *in comparison with other outcomes*. So, for example, even if we had a meaningful "score" representing how good outcome A was considered just by itself, regarding an essentially comparative moral ideal, F, and also had a meaningful "score" for how good outcome B was considered just by itself, regarding F, that would not tell us how A and B compared regarding F *if they were alternatives*. So, for example, if the relevance and significance of the factors for assessing A with respect to F vary depending on the alternatives, if any, with which it is compared, as may be the case if F is an essentially comparative ideal, then A might receive one score regarding F when it is considered alone, and yet receive a different score regarding F when B is an alternative. Thus, for example, in terms of the significance of *all* of the factors relevant for making each assessment, A could rightly receive a higher score regarding F if there were no alternative to A (and so if it were considered alone) than B would receive regarding F if there were no alternative to B (and so if *it* were considered alone), and yet A might receive a lower score than B regarding F if A and B were alternatives that were considered and compared together.

Similarly, knowing how good an outcome is regarding an essentially comparative moral ideal in comparison with *one* alternative may have no special bearing on how good it is regarding that ideal in comparison with a *different* alternative, or a different *set* of alternatives. So, for example, even if outcome A had one meaningful "score" for how good it was regarding F given an alternative outcome B (based on the significance of all of the factors relevant for F given *those* alternatives), A might have a completely different "score" for how good it was regarding F given a different alternative outcome C (based on the significance of all of the factors that were relevant for F given *those* alternatives). Thus, as we saw in discussing the Mere Addition Paradox (see diagram 11.1.A), on the view that equality is essentially comparative, $A+$'s inequality is bad when B is an alternative to $A+$, but not bad when A is an alterative to $A+$. Moreover, importantly, on the view that equality is essentially comparative, what we should say about $A+$'s inequality in the context where A and B are *both* alternatives to $A+$ is not yet determined by what we should say in the contexts where just one of them is an alternative, for we don't yet know which factors are relevant, or their significance, for assessing $A+$'s inequality in the wider context based on which factors are relevant and their significance for assessing $A+$'s inequality in the two narrower contexts. All of these possibilities open up with an essentially comparative moral ideal,[17] but are closed on an Internal Aspects View of Moral Ideals, where the goodness or badness of an outcome with respect to any ideal depends solely on the outcome's internal features. The significance of this point will become clearer later.

Before proceeding, let me emphasize that the issue here is not one of objectivity versus subjectivity. There may be no fact of the matter about how good an outcome is regarding an essentially comparative moral ideal *simpliciter*. But this does not mean that it is merely a subjective matter how we assess outcomes regarding essentially comparative moral ideals. The point is that for each essentially comparative moral ideal there may be an objective fact regarding which factors are relevant and how significant they are for comparing any given outcome with any given set of alternatives. This may not be simply "up to us," as it were. Thus, given any specified set of alternatives, there may well be an objective fact as to how the different alternatives compare regarding an essentially comparative moral ideal, but with different alternatives there may be different objective rankings.

In Parfit's Mere Addition Paradox, we are asked to compare different outcomes that are represented by abstract diagrams. Abstract diagrams may usefully convey certain bits of information, such as whether one outcome has more

---

[17] And others, as well. Evan Williams notes (in correspondence) that my discussion here focuses on one particular category of essentially comparative ideals, to the exclusion of others. He is right. I have focused on the category of essentially comparative ideals that is most relevant to my later discussion. But nothing I say here is intended to preclude other categories of essentially comparative ideals that may be worth developing and exploring. Recall that I have defined essentially comparative ideals in terms of their incompatibility with the Internal Aspects View of Ideals. Clearly, there may be more than one way of denying the Internal Aspects View of Ideals.

utility than another, whether the worst-off group is better off in one outcome or another, and, in some cases and given certain simplifying assumptions, whether one outcome is better than another regarding perfection or equality. But abstract diagrams also leave important information out, information that needs to be supplied by adding further details to the diagrams or by spelling out in more detail the alternatives represented by the diagrams. This point is uncontroversial, but it is important not to lose sight of it. To illustrate it, consider diagram 11.2.A.

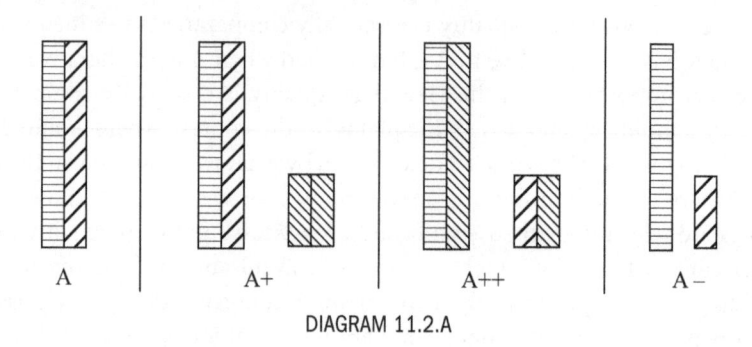

DIAGRAM 11.2.A

How do $A+$ and $A++$ compare all things considered? Ignore, for the moment, the different shadings in the various boxes, which are relevant for a later example. Considered purely abstractly, they are identical. Both involve two groups of equal size, and in each there is a better-off group at the same high level, and a worse-off group at the same low level. Does this mean that $A+$ and $A++$ are equally good, all things considered? At first blush, one might think this, but this *assumes* certain background conditions that may not hold. It assumes, for example, that either proportional justice doesn't matter, or that the people in the two better-off groups are equally deserving, and the people in the two worse-off groups are also equally, and less, deserving. As W. D. Ross made clear,[18] if we drop this assumption, then we can't know how $A+$ and $A++$ compare based solely on the information conveyed by the abstract diagram 11.2.A. After all, if the people in $A+$'s better-off group were saints, and the people in $A+$'s worse-off group were sinners, while the people in $A++$'s better-off group were sinners, and the people in $A++$'s worse-off group were saints, then those people who cared about proportional justice would rightly regard $A+$ as *better* than $A++$. If, on the other hand, it were the other way around, then $A++$ would be better than $A+$. We see, then, that any account of moral ideals that gives weight to proportional justice will be unable to judge how two outcomes compare based solely on the kind of abstract information conveyed by a diagram like 11.2.A. Further information will need to be provided, before an all-things-considered judgment is possible.

---

[18] In *The Right and the Good* (Oxford: Clarendon Press, 1930).

Both an Internal Aspects View and an Essentially Comparative View will need more information than is conveyed by diagram 11.2.A in order to assess how $A+$ compares to $A++$. But, importantly, in order to assess how two alternatives compare, an Essentially Comparative View may require *further* information that is lacking in diagram 11.2.A that would *not* be relevant on any Internal Aspects View. For example, on some Essentially Comparative Views one would need to know if the same or different people existed in the different alternatives, and if some of the same people existed in the different alternatives, how they compared in the different alternatives. Such information is irrelevant on an Internal Aspects View, where the goodness of an outcome depends *solely* on the internal features of *that* outcome. On an Internal Aspects View, it can be relevant to the goodness of an outcome how people fare in absolute terms, or relative to what they deserve, or relative to others *in that outcome*, but an outcome's goodness *cannot* depend in any way on whether some of its people would or would not exist, or would be better or worse off, in some *other* outcome. To illustrate this point consider again diagram 11.2.A, and now it may be helpful to pay attention to the shadings in the various boxes.[19]

How does $A+$ compare to A regarding equality? Parfit argued that $A+$ is not worse than A, *on the assumption* that $A+$ involves Mere Addition, where this means that $A+$ contains an extra group of people who are well off in addition to the very same group of well-off people that exist in A, and where the additional group of people in $A+$ in no way adversely affect the lives of those people who would exist in both A and $A+$. Relying on the view that equality is essentially comparative, Parfit suggested that even if $A+$'s inequality *is* bad when the alternative is B (see diagram 11.1.A), it is *not* bad when it involves Mere Addition and the alternative is A. Consider, however, $A++$. Suppose that $A++$ involved the following. First, half of the people who exist in A also exist in $A++$ and are in $A++$'s better-off group, and the other half of the people who exist in A also exist in $A++$ and are in $A++$'s worse-off group. So, considered just by themselves, the people who exist in both A and $A++$ stand in the relation depicted by $A-$. Clearly, if we assume that everyone is equally deserving, $A-$'s inequality would be very bad in comparison with A's. However, $A++$ also contains a second group of people who don't exist in A but who are the same size as the A group and who stand in the relation depicted by $A-$. So, in effect, $A++$ just involves a proportional increase of $A-$'s population, so the total population is the same size as that of $A+$, where half of the people in the better- and worse-off groups also exist in A, and half of the people in the better- and worse-off groups don't exist in A. Now, as we noted in chapter 10, all of the economists' standard measures of inequality support the view that

---

[19] My characterization of the Internal Aspects View and the Essentially Comparative View in this paragraph and the following ones has been significantly influenced by worries raised by Jake Ross, Tim Campbell, and Shelly Kagan regarding an earlier draft of this chapter.

mere proportional increases in a population do not affect an outcome's inequality, while my own view, defended in *Inequality*, and suggested previously in section 10.10, is that proportional increases in population size actually *worsen* an outcome's inequality.[20] There is, then, good reason to believe that $A++$'s inequality would be at least as bad as $A-$'s, which would be clearly worse than A's. But even if one thought that proportional increases in a population might mitigate an outcome's inequality,[21] there is good reason to believe that given the relation between A and $A-$, and the relation between $A-$ and $A++$, $A++$ *will* be worse than A regarding equality. After all, A is perfect regarding equality, while $A++$ not only involves inequality but involves inequality between those who were perfectly equal in A. Thus, there is clearly a bad-making feature of $A++$ in comparison with A regarding equality, while there is no bad-making feature of A in comparison with $A++$ regarding equality.

It appears, then, that to even make the kind of judgments Parfit asked us to make regarding alternatives like A and $A+$, it is not enough to simply consider the internal features of diagrams like 11.1.A and 11.2.A. On the view that equality is essentially comparative, we have to know the relations, if any, between them. That is, if Parfit was right, it makes a difference whether, in comparison with A, a particular alternative involves Mere Addition, like $A+$ does, or whether it involves a situation like $A++$, which, in essence, combines significant adverse effects for some but not all equally deserving people, with a proportional increase in population size. Parfit implicitly recognized this, which is why, in asking us to compare A and $A+$, he *emphasized* the fact that $A+$ involves Mere Addition. Indeed, the centrality of this fact to Parfit's claims explains why he called his larger argument the *Mere Addition* Paradox.

The preceding result may initially seem puzzling, but it has a straightforward explanation. On the view that equality is essentially comparative, how good an outcome is regarding equality will depend on with which alternative it is compared. But, in terms of the relevance and significance of the factors that come into play on the view that equality is essentially comparative, which alternative is the

---

[20] However, as I will observe later, my own view is that equality is best captured by an Internal Aspects View, not by an Essentially Comparative View, and my judgment about proportional increases reflects this. On an Essentially Comparative View, it is arguable that proportional increases in a population would produce an outcome that was neither worse nor better than the original outcome, regarding equality, and hence that the economists' view about proportional increases fits better with the Essentially Comparative View than my own. But the key point I need for my current argument is simply that there is good reason to believe that proportional increases in $A-$'s population to bring about $A++$ would do nothing to cancel or outweigh the factors that make $A-$ worse than A regarding equality, so that on an Essentially Comparative View there would be good reason to regard $A++$ as worse than A regarding equality, given how the two outcomes are related.

[21] Wlodek Rabinowicz offers an interesting argument in support of this position in "The Size of Inequality and Its Badness: Some Reflections around Temkin's *Inequality*," *Theoria* 69 (2003): 60–84. I respond to Rabinowicz's argument in "Measuring Inequality's Badness: Does Size Matter? If So, How, If Not, What Does?" and "Exploring the Roots of Egalitarian Concerns," *Theoria* 69 (2003): 85–107, 124–50.

one it is being compared with may itself partly depend on whether the same people exist in the different alternatives, and if so, how their lives are affected by the different alternatives. In other words, despite their internal structural similarities, A and $A+$, and A and $A++$, are *different* pairs of alternatives in the cases imagined. More particularly, *they are different in a way that is both relevant and of significance* on an Essentially Comparative View of Equality; this explains why our judgments can vary about those cases, on such a view.

The last point is worth special emphasis. An Internal Aspects View of Moral Ideals can *also* grant that $A+$ and $A++$ would be different alternatives. After all, in $A+$, all of the people who would also exist in A are in the better-off group, while in $A++$, half of the people who would also exist in A are in the better-off group while the other half are in the worse-off group. But, the key point is that on any plausible version of the Internal Aspects View such differences, by themselves, won't have relevance or significance for assessing how such alternatives compare vis-à-vis each other, or any other alternatives. This is because plausible versions of the Internal Aspects View will be wedded to a kind of neutrality that will rule out the relevance or significance of such differences. In other words, unless we think that some people's well-being is, by itself, more important than others, which is implausible, there is no room on the Internal Aspects View for judging the values of $A+$ and $A++$ differently.

Consider the following example. Suppose there were a population of people who were equal in all morally relevant respects; thus they were all equally hardworking, virtuous, talented, and so on—equally deserving, for short. Suppose that I arbitrarily divided the population into two equal groups, the X group and the Y group, and that the members of each group had no more in common with the other members of "their" group than they had in common with the members of the "other" group. If we were unrelated to them in any way, then from a moral perspective, we ought to be impartial or neutral between them. Accordingly, if there were an outcome in which half of the people were well off and half of the people were less well off, on an Internal Aspects View of Outcome Goodness the goodness of that outcome would depend solely on its internal features, and so, given the requirement of impartiality, an outcome in which all of the Xs were in the better-off group and all of the Ys were in the worse-off group would be exactly as good as one in which the positions were reversed. Similarly, on an Internal Aspects View of Moral Ideals, any distribution of Xs and Ys in the two groups would be exactly as good as any other with respect to any moral ideal; so, for example, if the better-off group had 1 percent Xs and 99 percent Ys (and, accordingly, the worse-off group had 99 percent Xs and 1 percent Ys), on the Internal Aspects View that would be no better or worse regarding equality than if the better-off group had 25 percent Xs and 75 percent Ys, or 50 percent Xs and 50 percent Ys, or 63 percent Xs and 37 percent Ys, and so on. Clearly, each of these possible distributions would represent different alternatives, but, assuming a plausible view about impartiality, the ways in which they are different would play no role in the assessment of the goodness of the different alternatives on an Internal Aspects View. Accordingly, assuming that the people in $A+$ and $A++$ who would also exist in A are equally deserving as those in $A+$ and $A++$ who would not exist in A, this implies, on the Internal Aspects View, that $A+$ would be as good as $A++$ regarding equality, and that however $A+$ compares to A, that is how $A++$ must compare to A regarding equality. Thus, we see that abstract diagrams of the sort Parfit asked us to consider fail to reveal certain factors that may have relevance and significance when comparing alternatives on an Essentially Comparative View, but which do not have relevance and significance when comparing alternatives on an Internal Aspects View.

We are now in a position to see why Parfit's arguments regarding the Mere Addition Paradox are so interesting and important. If, in fact, we should accept the view that equality is essentially comparative, then many patterns of inference generally regarded as valid for all concepts will in fact be invalid for inequality, with the result that "all-things-considered better than" (in my wide reason-implying sense) either will *not* be a transitive relation or will fail to apply to the set of alternatives that Parfit presents in the Mere Addition Paradox.

Consider. Most people accept what I have called:

The Principle of Like Comparability for Equivalents: If two outcomes or prospects are equivalent (meaning equally good) in some respect, then however the first of those outcomes or prospects compares to a third outcome or prospect in that respect, that is how the second of those outcomes or prospects compares to the third outcome or prospect in that respect. So, given any concept c, for all x, y, and z to which c is appropriately applied, then *regarding* c, if x and y are equally good, however x compares to z, that is precisely how y compares to z.[22]

Clearly, on the view that equality is essentially comparative, the Principle of Like Comparability for Equivalents is not valid. After all, in the Mere Addition Paradox, A and B are equally good regarding equality—both are perfect—and B is better than $A+$; yet, on the view that equality is essentially comparative, A is *not* better than $A+$, as $A+$ is not worse than A.[23] Thus, on the view that equality is essentially comparative, even knowing precisely how two situations compare to a third will not necessarily be

---

[22] In "Intransitivity and the Mere Addition Paradox," *Philosophy and Public Affairs* 16 (1987): 138–87, and also in "Rethinking the Good, Moral Ideals and the Nature of Practical Reasoning," in *Reading Parfit*, ed. Jonathan Dancy (Oxford: Basil Blackwell, 1997), 290–344, I called this the *Principle of Substitution for Equivalence*; I have changed my terminology to avoid confusion with the Principle of Substitution of Equivalents discussed in chapter 8.

[23] Shelly Kagan has pointed out that there is a different sense of "equivalence" than the one I have in mind here, where A and B would not be equivalent regarding equality. This is the sense in which A and B differ in certain respects that can be relevant to how they compare to different alternatives regarding equality. It follows that one could advocate a kind of Principle of Like Comparability of Equivalents, where "equivalents" are understood in the manner just suggested, that would be valid for both the Internal Aspects View and the Essentially Comparative View. The relevant point to note is that on the Internal Aspects View *both* principles will hold, whereas on the Essentially Comparative View *only* the second

helpful in determining how *they* compare. More generally, where a concept is essentially comparative, it can be true that even *precise* comparisons between A and B, and B and C, do not reflect how A and C compare. Thus, I may know that A+ is worse than B by some exact amount (if they are my two alternatives), and I may know that B and A are equally good (if they are my two alternatives), but I can't infer from that, as I could on an Internal Aspects View, that A+ is worse than A by the exact amount that B is, or even that it is worse at all (if they are my two alternatives). Similarly, whereas on an Internal Aspects View, if I knew that A was better than B by some precise amount, and I knew that C was better than B by a precise amount, I could infer from that whether A was better than, worse than, or equal to C, and by precisely how much; no such inference is valid on the Essentially Comparative View.

In Parfit's Mere Addition Paradox, the Principle of Like Comparability for Equivalents clearly fails to hold for equality, given Parfit's assumption that A+'s inequality is not a bad feature of that outcome *in comparison with A*, as long as A+ involves Mere Addition, that is, on the Parfitian view that equality is essentially comparative. But, as should be clear by now, on the view that equality is essentially comparative, transitivity will also fail or fail to apply across different sets of alternatives, for the ideal of equality.

Consider diagram 11.2.B.

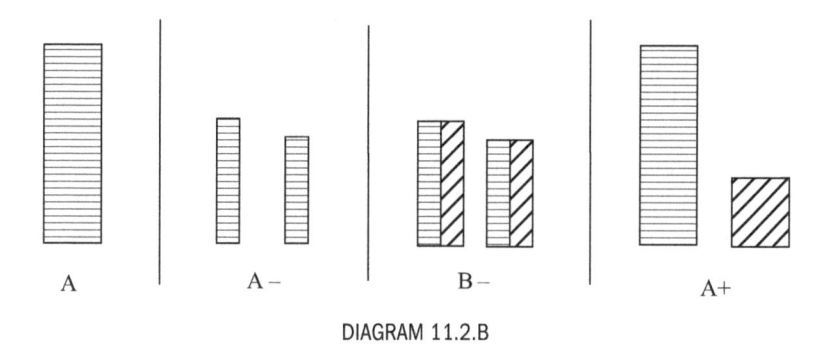

| A | A− | B− | A+ |

DIAGRAM 11.2.B

Assume that A− contains the same people as those in A, and that everyone is equally deserving in both A and A−. A− is clearly worse than A regarding equality. Next, suppose that B− includes A− and another equally deserving population just like it. Suppose, for example, that B− resulted from A− via mere proportional growth in the better- and worse-off groups—where each

---

principle will hold. We typically assume that if, in comparison with each other, two alternatives would be equally good in the sense of meriting the same "score" for any ideal, then each of those alternatives would merit that *same* score for that ideal in comparison with any *other* alternatives as well, and this is what underlies the plausibility of the Principle of Like Comparability for Equivalents in the sense I am intending in this discussion. But, as should be evident, this assumption presupposes an Internal Aspects View. On an Essentially Comparative View the assumption in question fails, and hence there is no reason to accept the Principle of Like Comparability for Equivalents in the sense I have in mind.

group doubled in size. On the view that equality is essentially comparative, we might think that the inequality between the new people in $B-$ is not bad when the alternative is A, since the new people between whom there is inequality have lives worth living and affect no one else. Still, although the additional people in $B-$ may not *worsen* $A-$'s inequality, the same factors that make $A-$ worse than A regarding equality should make $B-$ worse than A, namely, that there is undeserved inequality in $B-$ among a group of people who are equally well off in A. So, on the view that equality is essentially comparative, there is good reason to believe that A is better than $B-$ regarding equality. Next, compare $B-$ with $A+$. Suppose that $B-$ and $A+$ involve the very same people, with the better-off group in $A+$ containing all of the people who were originally in A, and the worse-off group containing all of the additional new people who were added when the population of $A-$ was doubled to produce $B-$. Since the same people exist in both $A+$ and $B-$, and the gaps between the better- and worse-off groups are much larger in $A+$ than in $B-$, if we assume that everyone in the two outcomes is equally deserving, then even though the composition of the better- and worse-off groups is different in $A+$ than in $B-$, it is pretty clear that all things considered we should judge $A+$'s inequality as worse than $B-$'s. That is, given the choice between $A+$ and $B-$, it is clear that if equality was *all* that mattered, $B-$ would be better than $A+$. It appears, then, that on the view that equality is essentially comparative, we should judge that A is better than $B-$ regarding equality, and also that $B-$ is better than $A+$. It follows that, if transitivity holds for the "better than regarding equality" relation, A must be better than $A+$ regarding equality. But, as Parfit has argued, on the view that equality is essentially comparative, A is *not* better than $A+$ regarding equality. On Parfit's view, $A+$ is *not* worse than A, since, in comparison with A, it involves the mere addition of extra people all of whom have lives worth living and who affect no one else. Thus, it appears that on the view that equality is essentially comparative, not only would the Principle of Like Comparability for Equivalents fail, the transitivity of "better than with respect to equality" would also fail, or at least fail to apply, across the alternatives A, $B-$, and $A+$.

The foregoing results are important, but by now they should not be surprising. Recall an earlier analogy from chapter 6. If A is a better tennis player than B, and B a better husband than C, *nothing* follows about how A and C compare either as tennis players or as husbands. The simple reason for this is that the relevance and significance of the factors for comparing tennis players are *different* from the relevance and significance of the factors for comparing husbands. Similarly, if a moral ideal F *is* essentially comparative, then by hypothesis the relevance and significance of the factors for comparing A and B regarding F may be different from the relevance and significance of the factors for comparing B and C, or A and C regarding F. Consequently, knowing how A and B, and B and C compare regarding F will not, by itself, be enough to know how A and C compare regarding F. This explains why there can be a failure of the Principle of Like Comparability for Equivalents, and also why the transitivity of "better than" may fail or fail to apply across different pairs of alternatives for an Essentially Comparative View.

Notice, in an important sense the advocate of the view that equality is essentially comparative could insist that the nature and extent of her concern regarding equality remain the same in each comparison. It is not as if she cares about equality when comparing $A+$ and $B-$, but not when comparing $A+$ with A. Nor, she might claim, is it that she really cares about $equality_1$ when comparing $A+$ and A, but an entirely different $equality_2$ when comparing $A+$ and $B-$. Arguably, she has an unchanging commitment to a *single* ideal of equality, but one that involves an Essentially Comparative View of Equality. Accordingly, the impact that an outcome's inequality has on her assessment of that outcome varies with the alternatives being compared. To be sure, at one level the relevance and significance of the factors appealed to by the view that equality is essentially comparative change with the alternatives being compared, but there needn't be anything inconstant or inconsistent about this. Instead, the advocate of the view that equality is essentially comparative could contend, this merely expresses what we really are, and should be, concerned about regarding inequality—including the conditions under which that concern is properly evoked.

Let us say that a concept is *nonsubstitutable* if the Principle of Like Comparability for Equivalents does not hold across different comparisons involving that concept. For simplicity, let us also say that a concept is *nontransitive* if transitivity either fails to hold, or fails to apply, across different comparisons involving that concept (this, of course, echoes our previously established usage of nontransitivity as applied to relations). Then it is easy to see that if F is an essentially comparative moral ideal that plays an important role in our all-things-considered judgments, the nonsubstitutability or nontransitivity of F may carry over into our all-things-considered judgments. The reasoning for this has already been given in chapter 7.

Suppose, for example, that an important moral ideal is both relevant and of genuine significance for assessing the goodness of outcomes all things considered, and that the ideal in question is an essentially comparative one. Then, the relevance and significance of the factors for comparing alternatives all things considered will, to at least some extent, depend on the alternatives being compared.[24] Correspondingly, there is no reason to expect the Principle of Like Comparability for Equiva-

---

[24] This follows from the particular concerns that I am focusing on in discussing the notion of an essentially comparative ideal. In saying this, I don't mean to suggest that there couldn't be *other* useful senses of "essentially comparative" that would not automatically have this implication. Suppose, for example, that we claimed that the *best team* was the one that beat the most other teams in head-to-head matches, a position I will discuss in more detail later in chapter 13. Such a view could be plausibly called an "essentially comparative view," since to determine how good a team was one would have to compare

lents or transitivity to hold or apply. After all, how any two situations compare *all things considered* will depend on how they compare in terms of the relevance and significance of *all* factors for making *that* comparison. But then, where *different* factors are relevant or vary in their significance for comparing different alternatives, as can happen with an essentially comparative ideal, it can be true that even if *A* is equivalent to or better than *B*, and *B* is better than *C* in terms of the relevance and significance of the factors for comparing *those* alternatives, *A* may *not* be better than *C* in terms of the relevance and significance of the factors for making *that* comparison. Hence, it appears that in *some* cases at least, the Principle of Like Comparability for Equivalents could fail, and similarly that transitivity could also either fail, or fail to apply across certain alternatives, for the "all-things-considered better than" relation (in my wide reason-implying sense).[25]

In sum, *if* Parfit was right regarding the nature of inequality—if the fact that *A*+ involves Mere Addition is, in an important sense, morally relevant and significant in assessing *A*+ when the alternative is *A* but not when the alternative is *B*− or *B*—then we are faced with a far graver problem than how to reject one of the particular judgments of Parfit's Mere Addition Paradox, that *A* is better than *B*, that *B* is better than *A*+, or that *A*+ is not worse than *A*. We are faced with rejecting the Principle of Like Comparability for Equivalents, and either the transitivity of "all-things-considered better than" (in my wide reason-implying sense) or its applicability to the cases that Parfit discusses. Clearly, this has enormous implications extending far beyond the topic of future generations.

It should now be clearer why I think the deepest questions raised in this book are distinct from the problems raised by the Standard Sorites Paradoxes discussed in chapter 9. Although many of my earlier arguments challenging transitivity involved Spectrum Arguments of sorts, the spectrum aspect of those arguments is a red herring. The *key* question, as I have emphasized, concerns the nature of

---

it with other teams, in terms of their overall winning percentages against all of the other teams. As we will see in chapter 13, this view will not have the implications I am discussing here, nor will it open up the possibility that "all-things-considered better than" (in my reason-implying sense) may be nontransitive. So here, as elsewhere, it is important to bear in mind that my discussion is focused on concepts or relations that are essentially comparative in the way that I have focused on in this chapter, according to which the relevance and significance of the factors for assessing and comparing an outcome will itself vary depending on the alternatives with which that outcome is compared. The sense in which "best team," as characterized earlier, is essentially comparative is distinct from, and hence has importantly different implications than, the sense in which an ideal may essentially be comparative as I have been employing that notion.

[25] Evan Williams asks (in correspondence) whether my argument here is intended to show that "if a morally significant ideal is essentially comparative, all-things-considered goodness is probably also essentially comparative. And if all-things-considered goodness is essentially comparative it could easily be non-transitive"? Or if it is intended to show that "if a morally significant ideal is non-transitive, all-things-considered goodness could easily inherit this non-transitivity"? Williams presents me with a false dichotomy here. My argument is intended to show both! Although the positions Williams distinguishes are, in principle, separable, because of the relations between Essentially Comparative Views and nontransitivity (as well as nonsubstitutability), the considerations I offer in support of the former position also support, and are intended to support, the latter position as well.

moral ideals. Is it the case that different factors can be relevant or vary in their significance for comparing different alternatives or not? If so, then our standard assumptions about the Principle of Like Comparability for Equivalents and the scope of the transitivity of the "betterness" relation have to be reconsidered. This is the most significant lesson to be learned from Parfit's Mere Addition Paradox.

Parfit's Mere Addition Paradox does not involve a spectrum. There is not a long series of alternatives each of which is just slightly different from its predecessor, but the last of which is vastly different from the first. Rather, it involves three simple, and clearly distinct, alternatives. But, what Parfit's three alternatives clearly illustrate is how natural and plausible it is to invoke different factors in comparing different alternatives all things considered. The fact that A+ involves Mere Addition weighs heavily in our assessment of how A+ compares to A, but is seemingly irrelevant in our comparison of A+ with B. This fact, we now see, is what lies at the heart of the Mere Addition Paradox, and what gives it its force.

So the ultimate challenge posed by Parfit's Paradox concerns the nature of moral ideals. Is Parfit's implicit appeal to an Essentially Comparative View of Moral Ideals ultimately defensible or not? If it is, all the worries raised about the transitivity of the "betterness" relation and its scope come to the fore, as well as a worry about the Principle of Like Comparability for Equivalents. If it is not, other worries arise. Our task, as throughout, is to get as clear as we can about the considerations on each side, including their full costs, benefits, and implications, so as to have a better idea of how to proceed in this incredibly difficult terrain.

11.3 The Internal Aspects View of Moral Ideals

Derek Parfit now claims that his argument for the view that equality is essentially comparative was, perhaps, his worst mistake in philosophy.[26] This is compatible, of course, with its being a brilliant mistake, if it was a mistake![27]

---

[26] In correspondence and personal conversation. Parfit attributes his making this mistake to me. In early versions of his Mere Addition Paradox, Parfit claimed that the inequality in A+ made A+ *in one way* worse than A because it involved inequality, but he insisted that A+ was not worse than A all things considered. I pointed out that this view seemed incoherent if one thought, as Parfit then did, that merely adding an extra group of worse-off people to a large and very well-off population in *no way* made the outcome *better*. I claimed that if adding the extra people was in *one* way worse, and in *no* way better, then we *should* conclude that A+ was worse than A, all things considered, contrary to Parfit's contention. It was in response to this argument that Parfit made what he now regards as his "worst mistake" in philosophy, contending that inequality that results from Mere Addition is not bad *at all, in comparison with the original situation*, since being worse off than another group is not bad for that group when their lives are well worth living and the alternative is *not* one where they are better off, but one where *they don't exist*!

[27] In typically modest fashion, Parfit wonders (in correspondence) whether he deserves credit for his brilliant mistake or whether, for the reasons conveyed in note 26, I do. I'm happy to share billing in this matter with Parfit, all the more so since I disagree with Parfit's current view that his brilliant move, in response to my worries about his original argument was, in fact, a *mistake*!

Seeing that Essentially Comparative Views raise deep problems about the transitivity of "better than" or its scope, as well as the Principle of Like Comparability for Equivalents, Parfit now thinks such views should be rejected.

I, too, think the view that equality is essentially comparative should be rejected. Indeed, while in previous publications I have emphasized the intuitive attractiveness of Parfit's contention regarding A+'s inequality,[28] *in fact*, I have *always* believed that the most plausible view of *equality* is *not* an essentially comparative one. As we will see in chapter 12, Essentially Comparative Views are often person-affecting views; they assess outcomes with respect to certain ideals in terms of how sentient beings are *affected* for better or worse in those outcomes with respect to those ideals. But I believe that the most plausible way of understanding *equality* is as an *impersonal* ideal.[29] On my view, inequality is bad when it involves *comparative unfairness*, and I believe that if the members of A+ are assumed to be equally deserving, then it *is* comparatively *unfair*, and hence bad, that A+'s worse-off members are so through no fault or choice of their own. In particular, I think this even though I'm willing to accept, in accordance with Parfit's claims about Mere Addition, that A+'s inequality is not bad *for* A+'s worse-off members, in terms of their individual good, welfare, or self-interest. That is, I grant that in comparison with an outcome where they don't exist at all, namely, A, it is not bad *for* the extra people in A+ to be alive and have lives well worth living, even though this involves their being worse off than A+'s better-off members.[30] Still, to my mind, this doesn't change the fact that A+'s undeserved inequality involves comparative unfairness, and that this is a bad-making feature of A+.

So, on reflection, both Parfit and I agree that the view that equality is essentially comparative should be rejected. The most general way of doing this is to reject the Essentially Comparative View of Moral Ideals in favor of the Internal Aspects View of Moral Ideals. Moreover, and most important, if, correspondingly, one also rejects the Essentially Comparative View of Outcome Goodness in favor of the Internal Aspects View of Outcome Goodness, this will enable us to avoid nonsubstitutability and nontransitivity in our all-things-considered judgments.

---

[28] In my "Intransitivity" and "Rethinking the Good" articles.

[29] I defend this view in "Equality, Priority, and the Levelling Down Objection," in *The Ideal of Equality*, ed. Matthew Clayton and Andrew Williams (London: Macmillan; New York: St. Martin's Press, 2000), 126–61; in "Personal versus Impersonal Principles: Reconsidering the Slogan," *Theoria* 69 (2003): 20–30; and in "Egalitarianism Defended," *Ethics* 113 (2003): 764–82.

[30] John Broome has an alternative view of these matters. He believes that comparative unfairness *is* bad *for* those who are worse off than others no more deserving than they. Accordingly, he would contend that if A+ genuinely involves comparative unfairness, then A+'s inequality *is* bad for A+'s worse-off members, even though they have lives worth living and wouldn't exist in the alternative outcome, A. See Broome's *Weighing Goods* (Oxford: Basil Blackwell, 1991) and also his *Weighing Lives* (Oxford: Oxford University Press, 2004). I respond to Broome's view in my articles "Equality, Priority, and the Levelling Down Objection," and "Weighing Goods: Some Questions and Comments," *Philosophy and Public Affairs* 23 (1994): 350–80.

The Internal Aspects Views of Moral Ideals and Outcome Goodness were presented previously, but they are worth restating for the purposes of our present discussion.

The Internal Aspects View of Moral Ideals (IAVMI): Roughly, for each outcome, O, and each moral ideal, F, there is an extent to which outcome O is good with respect to F which depends solely on O's internal features. Moreover, for any two outcomes, O_1 and O_2, and any moral ideal F_1, O_1 will be better than O_2 regarding F_1, if and only if the extent to which O_1 is good regarding F_1, as determined solely on the basis of O_1's internal features is greater than the extent to which O_2 is good regarding F_1, as determined solely on the basis of O_2's internal features. In addition, if O_1 is better than O_2 regarding any moral ideal F_1, the extent to which this is so will depend solely on the extent to which O_1 is good regarding F_1 is greater than the extent to which O_2 is good regarding F_1.

The Internal Aspects View of Outcome Goodness (IAVOG): Roughly, for each outcome, O, how good that outcome is all things considered depends solely on how good it is with respect to each moral ideal that is relevant for assessing the goodness of outcomes, and on how much all of the relevant ideals matter vis-à-vis each other, where these depend solely on O's internal features. Moreover, for any two outcomes, O_1 and O_2, O_1 will be better than O_2 all things considered if and only if the extent to which O_1 is good all things considered, as determined solely on the basis of O_1's internal features, is greater than the extent to which O_2 is good all things considered, as determined solely on the basis of O_2's internal features. In addition, if O_1 is better than O_2 all things considered, the extent to which this is so will depend solely on the extent to which O_1 is good, all things considered, is greater than the extent to which O_2 is good, all things considered.

The Internal Aspects Views can be fleshed out in various ways. In accordance with the assumption I made about cardinality in first presenting them, I will flesh them out in terms of the kind of numerical model discussed in chapter 10. As implied previously, I think this is a natural and intuitively attractive way of understanding the Internal Aspects Views. On a numerical model—or at least a simplified version sufficient for our purposes—for any moral ideal F, one can assign a number to represent how good an outcome is regarding F.[31] On the Internal Aspects View of Moral Ideals, the number assigned will depend *solely* on the

---

[31] In reality, of course, we might never be able to assign a precise number that would meaningfully reflect exactly how good a situation is regarding F. At best one could assign a rough range of numbers that would give us a partial, rather than complete, ordering of outcomes regarding F, but even that may not be possible. For simplicity our discussion ignores such complications. Though important in some contexts, they do not affect our central claims.

internal features of the outcome relevant to F. Thus, any alternatives with the same internal features will be assigned the same number representing how good that alternative will be regarding F.

As should be clear, on the numerical model of the Internal Aspects View of Moral Ideals, the Principle of Like Comparability for Equivalents will hold for each moral ideal. This is because for any two outcomes, O_1 and O_2, if O_1 is equivalent to O_2 regarding F, then O_1 and O_2 will each receive the same number representing how good they are regarding F, with O_1 receiving that number based solely on *its* internal features, and O_2 receiving that number based solely on *its* internal features. Likewise, for any third outcome, O_3, O_3 will receive a number representing how good it is regarding F, based solely on *its* internal features. Since the numbers representing how good O_1, O_2, and O_3 are regarding F are based solely on the internal features of those outcomes, respectively, they will remain fixed in any comparisons involving those outcomes. Thus, since the numbers representing how good O_1 and O_2 are regarding F are the same, it follows from basic math that on the Internal Aspects View, however O_1 compares to O_3 regarding F is the same as how O_2 compares to O_3 regarding F, exactly as the Principle of Like Comparability for Equivalents prescribes.

Analogously, on the numerical model of the Internal Aspects View of Moral Ideals, "better than regarding F" will be a transitive relation for each moral ideal F. This is because for any moral ideal F and any three outcomes O_1, O_2, and O_3, O_1, O_2, and O_3 will be assigned numbers representing how good they are regarding F based *solely* on their internal features, respectively. Correspondingly, if, regarding some moral ideal, A is better than B, and B is better than C, then A has to be better than C regarding that ideal, since if one number is higher than a second, which in turn is higher than a third, the first must be higher than the third. (As noted previously, "being a higher number than" *is* a transitive relation.)

As should be evident, similar remarks apply to the Internal Aspects View of Outcome Goodness. On a numerical model of the Internal Aspects View of Outcome Goodness, a number representing how good an outcome is all things considered will be assigned to each outcome based solely on the internal features of *that* outcome. Accordingly, basic truths of math reveal that on such a view the Principle of Like Comparability for Equivalents and the transitivity of the "all-things-considered better than" relation hold regarding the all-things-considered goodness of outcomes.

In sum, one way of defending the Principle of Like Comparability for Equivalents and the transitivity of the "betterness" relation for both individual moral ideals and all-things-considered goodness would be to reject Essentially Comparative Views in favor of Internal Aspects Views.[32]

---

[32] Shelly Kagan asks whether there could be some kind of Internal Aspects View, perhaps even combined with some kind of numerical model, where the Principle of Like Comparability for Equivalents and the transitivity of the "all-things-considered better than" relation (in my wide reason-implying sense) did not hold. There might be room in conceptual space for such a position, where the Internal Aspects View and the numerical model it was combined with would obviously be different

11.4 An Independence of Irrelevant Alternatives Principle

We have seen that a numerical model for the Internal Aspects View of Moral Ideals would support both the Principle of Like Comparability for Equivalents and the view that "better than with respect to F" is a transitive relation, for all moral ideals, F. We have also seen that a numerical model for the Internal Aspects View of Outcome Goodness would support both the Principle of Like Comparability for Equivalents and the view that "all-things-considered better than" is a transitive relation with respect to the value of outcomes. For the purpose of later discussion in chapter 13, let me add that an Internal Aspects View of Outcome Goodness would also support another deeply held belief.

Kenneth Arrow's famous Impossibility Theorem invokes an *Independence of Irrelevant Alternatives Principle (IIAP)*, which has been the subject of much scrutiny and criticism.[33] Whatever the merits of the principle as Arrow presents it, one version of such a principle seems almost overwhelmingly compelling. It might be put as follows. For any two outcomes, A and B, to know how A compares to B all things considered it is, at least in principle, sufficient to compare them directly in terms of each of the ideals about which we care. More particularly, if one accurately knew how A compared to B in terms of each ideal relevant to our all-things-considered judgments, and if one granted each ideal its due weight, then one would be in a position to know how A compared to B all things considered. In such circumstances, knowing how A or B compared to some third alternative, C, either regarding some particular ideal, like equality or utility, or all things considered, would be unnecessary and indeed *completely irrelevant* to knowing how A and B compared. More generally, the Independence of Irrelevant Alternatives Principle tells us that however we should rank A and B in comparison with each other if they were our only two alternatives, that is how we should rank A and B in comparison with each other if they were among a set with any number of alterna-

---

than I have characterized them here. Nothing I have said rules out such a possibility. I have been developing a conception of the Internal Aspects View which I think is both natural and powerful, and which reflects many views that people hold about the nature of, and relations between, goodness, ideals, and "better than" judgments. The conception I have developed, which reflects those views, is closely tied to the way of thinking embodied by the particular numerical model employed in the text (though some variations in the details of that model might still be consistent with the views my model aims to capture). So, in essence, I am trying to illuminate a way of thinking about goodness, ideals, and "better than" judgments that I believe is widely shared, and which *does* entail the Principle of Like Comparability for Equivalents and the transitivity of the "all-things-considered better than" relation. This way of thinking is, I think, nicely represented by the version of the Internal Aspects View and the numerical model I have employed. So, even if, as Kagan wonders, alternative versions of an Internal Aspects View or the numerical model for representing it are possible, if they don't entail the Principle of Like Comparability for Equivalents and the transitivity of the "all-things-considered better than" relation, they will not represent the way of thinking that I am currently discussing and trying to capture.

[33] Arrow's revolutionary Impossibility Theorem is presented in his book *Social Choice and Individual Values* (New York: Wiley, 1951).

tives, and vice versa. In other words, neither adding to nor subtracting from a set of alternatives whose members include *A* and *B* will affect how *A* compares to *B*.

Understood in such a way, the Independence of Irrelevant Alternatives Principle has great plausibility. Clearly, that plausibility is warranted if one accepts the Internal Aspects View. The point is that *any* alternative will be irrelevant to how *A* and *B* compare, because how they compare will depend solely on how good *they* are all things considered, and, on the Internal Aspects View, this will depend *solely* on *A*'s and *B*'s internal features.[34] More specifically, on the Internal Aspects View, *A* will receive a score representing how good it is all things considered. That score will be a function of how good it is with respect to *each* ideal relevant to assessing outcomes, giving each ideal its due weight; crucially, the scores for those ideals and the function combining them into an all-things-considered score will depend *solely* on *A*'s internal features. A fortiori, on the Internal Aspects View, how good *A* is all things considered will be wholly independent of whether *A* is compared with alternative *B*, alternative *C*, or any other alternative or set of alternatives. Similarly for *B*. Accordingly, once we know *A*'s all-things-considered score and *B*'s all-things-considered score, we'll know how they compare all things considered; clearly this ranking, determined as it is solely by *A*'s and *B*'s internal features, will be independent of whether or not *A* and/or *B* are compared with any other alternative or set of alternatives.

The intuitive appeal of the Independence of Irrelevant Alternatives Principle can be partly illustrated via an analysis of the following joke.[35] John goes into an ice cream store and tells the server, "I'll have strawberry, unless you have vanilla—in which case I'll have chocolate!" The joke, of course, is supposed to lie in the oddity of John's behavior. John's order makes him sound silly or stupid. More important, for our purposes, to many it makes him sound downright irrational. It makes sense, we think, for John to want to know whether the store has vanilla, if he would prefer vanilla to strawberry. That is, it would make perfect sense for John to say, "I'll have strawberry, unless you have vanilla, in which case I'll have that." But if John *really* prefers chocolate to strawberry, he should just order chocolate! If he isn't going to order vanilla in any event, why bother asking if the store has it? It seems odd, to say the least, that John should prefer strawberry to chocolate if vanilla isn't available, but chocolate to strawberry if vanilla *is* available.

---

[34] To avoid confusion, let me emphasize that this *isn't* Arrow's view. Arrow believed that no meaningful evaluation of an alternative was possible, except relative to, or in comparison with, other alternatives. Specifically, he would have denied that a meaningful comparison between *A* and *B* could be achieved by combining evaluations of *A* and *B* that were arrived at independently of comparisons with each other or other alternatives. But Arrow also thought comparisons with other alternatives would be irrelevant to the comparison between *A* and *B*. Hence, for Arrow, to know how *A* compared to *B* it was sufficient to compare them directly. My claim is that there is a version of the Independence of Irrelevant Alternatives Principle, different from Arrow's, which has great plausibility and is based on the Internal Aspects View of Outcome Goodness.

[35] This is a variation of a joke I first heard attributed to Sidney Morgenbesser; as I originally heard it, Morgenbesser's version involved choosing between different deli sandwiches.

In the preceding example, we aren't dealing with a *moral* assessment of two alternatives, so strictly speaking the Internal Aspects View of Outcome Goodness wouldn't be relevant. But a wider analogue of that principle might still be in play, which we might call the *Internal Aspects View of Practical Reasoning*. On this view, one could give a meaningful assessment and ranking of any two outcomes based solely on the internal features of those outcomes.

In the ice cream example, the assumption is that John's choice should depend solely on how, at that moment, strawberry and chocolate would each *taste* to him, and how much he would *enjoy* those tastes, and that these are determined by facts about the nature of the shop's ice creams, together with facts about John's taste buds, preferences, and psychological characteristics. *Given that assumption*, it seems that the value of the outcome where John eats the strawberry should depend solely on the internal features of that outcome, and similarly, that the value of the outcome where John eats the chocolate should depend solely on the internal features of that outcome, and thus that the ranking of those two outcomes should depend solely on those two values, and hence be independent of the availability of, or comparison with, some other outcome or outcomes, such as the eating of vanilla ice cream.

Notice, it is easy to imagine scenarios where it would make perfect sense for John to say, "I'll have strawberry, unless you have vanilla, in which case I'll have chocolate." It will be useful to explore one such scenario.

Suppose that John knew the following to be true. Some ice cream stores buy only from a high-quality company, while others buy from both high- and low-quality companies. The former carry only strawberry and chocolate, since those are the only flavors sold by the high-quality company. The latter carry strawberry, chocolate, and vanilla, in which case the chocolate is always provided by the high-quality company, while the strawberry and vanilla are provided by the low-quality company. Assuming that taste is directly correlated with quality, it would make perfect sense for epicurean John to say "I'll have strawberry, unless you have vanilla, in which case I'll have chocolate." Clearly, however, this would not challenge the Independence of Irrelevant Alternatives Principle or an Internal Aspects View of Practical Reasoning, since in this case vanilla is *not* an "irrelevant" alternative. Specifically, vanilla is an *epistemologically* relevant alternative, accurately indicating whether John is actually choosing between *one* set of alternatives, involving both high-quality strawberry and high-quality chocolate, or a significantly *different* set of alternatives, involving high-quality chocolate and low-quality strawberry. After all, it could be perfectly rational for epicurean John to prefer high-quality strawberry to high-quality chocolate, but to prefer high-quality chocolate to low-quality strawberry.

Importantly, on an Internal Aspects View of Practical Reasoning, the vanilla *is* an irrelevant alternative *metaphysically*. Even if John doesn't know it, there *is* a fact of the matter as to whether the strawberry is high or low quality. Given this, together with John's preferences, there is also a fact of the matter as to whether the strawberry or the chocolate is the better alternative for John. Accordingly, if John knew everything there was to know about the two relevant alternatives, including whether the strawberry was of high quality or not, and how each would taste to him, he would be able to rank the outcome of eating strawberry in comparison with the outcome of eating chocolate, and this ranking would *not* depend, in any way, on comparing either or both of those outcomes with any other outcome or set of outcomes, including the outcome of eating vanilla. So, in the relevant sense, vanilla will remain a metaphysically irrelevant outcome, and both the Internal Aspects View of Practical Reasoning and the Independence of Irrelevant Alternatives Principle will retain their plausibility.

We see, then, that an Internal Aspects View of Outcome Goodness, or, more broadly, an Internal Aspects View of Practical Reasoning, supports the widely held Independence of Irrelevant Alternatives Principle. We shall return to the significance of this point in chapter 13.

11.5 On the Relevance of Mere Addition

I have been explicating what is involved in rejecting the view that moral ideals, like equality, can be essentially comparative. It follows from what has been said that, on the Internal Aspects View, we are likely to be misled if, in considering the Mere Addition Paradox, we allow our comparative judgments about A, $A+$, and B to be influenced by Parfit's claim that $A+$ involves Mere Addition. What Parfit and we are presumably interested in is our considered judgments about how such outcomes compare all things considered. But, on the Internal Aspects View, *those* judgments should be based *only* on the outcome's *internal* features. The fact that $A+$'s better-off group is composed of the same people who are in A, and that $A+$'s worse-off group does not adversely affect the better-off group relative to how it would have been *in A* is not solely an *internal* feature of $A+$. One can only recognize such factors by directly comparing $A+$ with A. Accordingly, on an Internal Aspects View, such information should be irrelevant to our assessment of how good $A+$ is all things considered, and irrelevant to our assessment of how good $A+$ is in comparison with any other alternatives.

Consider diagram 11.5.A.

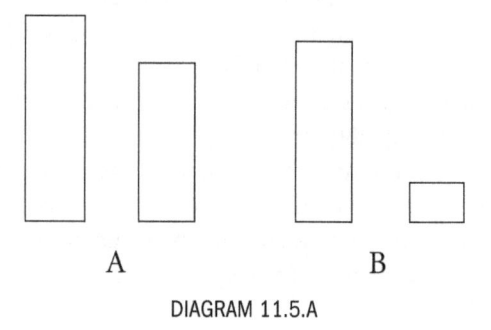

DIAGRAM 11.5.A

Assuming that those in *A* and *B* are equally deserving, and that *B* is no better than *A* regarding other moral factors like virtue or rights, *A* would be better than *B* all things considered, as it is better regarding utility, equality, perfection, and maximin. Of course, if one's *mother* would be in *A*'s worse-off group, but *B*'s better-off group, this might give one reason to *prefer B* to *A*, or perhaps even a *duty* to promote *B* rather than *A*, depending on one's agent-relative duties, if any.[36] But this would not make *B better* than *A* from the standpoint in which Parfit is interested. Similarly, if the only way to bring about *A* would be to lie or cheat, that might be relevant to what ought to be *done*, and even to whether *A together with its history* would be better than *B* together with *its* history. But it would not be relevant to how *A* and *B themselves* compare, and it is *such* judgments Parfit is presumably asking us to make regarding his alternatives in the Mere Addition Paradox.

The possibility of distinguishing between whether one outcome is better than another considering the two outcomes just by themselves, and whether one outcome together with its history or future would be better than another together with its history or future is intuitively plausible and both theoretically and practically important. Although the desirability of an end doesn't always justify the necessary means to achieving that end, the desirability of an end is often relevant to the permissibility of its means. For example, in just war theory or self-defense, the costs of a military or defensive action must be proportional to the goodness of the ends the actions seek to promote. Thus, I might be permitted to kill many enemy soldiers or an unjust aggressor, if doing so were necessary to save countless innocent citizens or to preserve my life, respectively, but such actions would be impermissible if they merely served to forestall a temporary occupation of a barren territory or the scratching of my little finger (to echo Hume), respectively. Intuitively, then, we often need to assess how good an outcome would be, considered by itself, in order to determine what actions, if any, might be permissibly done to achieve that outcome. Correspondingly, we may often find that while one outcome would be clearly better than another, there is no morally permissible path to the better outcome. Likewise, it might be that while *A* is better than *B*, if they are considered just by themselves, *A* would inevitably lead to further outcomes far worse than those to which *B*

---

[36] *Agent-relative duties*, as their name implies, are duties that are relative to particular agents; typically, they depend on the prior existence of special relations between the agent and the others to whom they have such duties. So, for example, it is often held that parents have agent-relative duties to *their* children (because of the special relations between parents and their own children) that they don't have toward other people's children. Similarly, teachers, doctors, and priests may all have agent-relative duties to their students, patients, and parishioners, respectively, which they don't have to people generally, including other people's students, patients, and parishioners. Agent-relative duties are often contrasted with *agent-neutral duties*, which are the duties that any moral agent is presumed to have to any other sentient being, independently of there being a special relationship between them. Thus, it might be claimed that while *I* have a special agent-relative duty to provide food, shelter, and clothing to *my* children, *everyone* has an agent-neutral duty to prevent the needless suffering of *any* innocent sentient being if she can do so at no cost or risk to herself.

would lead. As indicated, then, we really need and want to distinguish between how two outcomes might compare considered just by themselves, with how those outcomes together with their histories and/or futures might compare.

In the Mere Addition Paradox, Parfit asks us to judge how A, $A+$, and B compare. If, in making such judgments, we are supposed to be making the judgments about how *those* outcomes compare considered *just by themselves*, then, *if* we accept the Internal Aspects View, we open ourselves up to being seriously misled insofar as we allow our judgment about A and $A+$ to be influenced—as many of us surely did—by Parfit's claim, indeed emphasis, that $A+$ involves Mere Addition in comparison with A.[37] In thinking about Parfit's Mere Addition Paradox, it is tempting to think of $A+$ as an outcome that doesn't merely *involve* an extra group of people with lives worth living who affect no one else, relative to A, but as one that *resulted* from *adding* an extra group of people who have lives worth living and who affect no one else *to* A. That is, it is tempting to compare A and $A+$ by thinking about what would be involved in *transforming* an outcome like A into one like $A+$. But on the Internal Aspects View, it is imperative that we simply focus on the *internal* features of $A+$ that are relevant to assessing how good it is all things considered, if we want to know how good $A+$ *itself* is. We must close our ears to any information about how an outcome's internal features have been produced. Such information may be relevant to the *permissibility* of such a move, and to whether $A+$ together with its history might be better than A together with its history, but it is not relevant to how A and $A+$ *themselves* compare. And, of course, if $A+$ merely *involves* Mere Addition, as Parfit defines that notion, and was not literally *produced* by the mere addition of an extra group of people to A, then it is particularly dangerous to assess how A and $A+$ compare, by thinking in terms of whether we think *transforming* A into $A+$ would or would not be desirable or permissible.

Here is another way of thinking about this issue. An Internal Aspects View can take account of history in evaluating outcomes, in the sense that the entire "history" of an outcome (past, present, and future) is "internal" to that outcome and can be taken into account for the purposes of evaluating the overall goodness of that outcome taken as a complete whole. But, in Parfit's Mere Addition Paradox, A, $A+$, and B are assumed to represent the *complete* outcomes we are being asked to assess. So, were we to add a temporal dimension to our diagrams, there is a big difference between how we would represent an outcome that looked like $A+$ *throughout* its history, and how we would represent *the very different* outcome that looked like A for *part* of its history and $A+$ for the *rest* of its history. We might call the second outcome the $A/A+$ outcome. The point is that Parfit wants to know how A and $A+$ compare, and that is a very different question than how A and $A/A+$

---

[37] It does not follow that Parfit was mistaken in emphasizing the Mere Addition, since his original argument, in essence, challenges the Internal Aspects View. But if, on reflection, one accepts the Internal Aspects View, as Parfit himself is now inclined to, one cannot be influenced by such information.

compare, however interesting and important the latter question might be in its own right. Accordingly, Parfit's emphasis that A+ involves Mere Addition will be misleading if, in essence, it leads us to think of A+ as having been produced from A, and so inadvertently leads us, in thinking about the Mere Addition Paradox, to be comparing A with A/A+, rather than A with A+ as Parfit wants us to.

Moreover, since, according to Parfit, the fact that A+ involves Mere Addition is relevant for comparing A with A+, but not for comparing B with A+, we may, in thinking about Parfit's alternatives, actually be comparing A with B, and B with A+, but A with A/A+, in terms of what the outcomes are supposed to be like over their entire histories. In that case, it wouldn't be surprising if, as Parfit has seen, we would judge that, all things considered, A is better than B, and B is better than A+, but it is not the case that A is better than A/A+. But such judgments would not involve the troubling intransitivity of our "all-things-considered better than" judgments (in my wide reason-implying sense) that Parfit thought arises from the Mere Addition Paradox.

For Parfit, the crucial facts that he was pointing to in emphasizing that A+ involves Mere Addition are that the very same people who exist in A also exist in A+ where they are just as well off, and that the extra people living in A+ have lives that are well worth living, so that it is in no way bad for them that A+ obtains rather than A. But, as Parfit clearly saw, these facts, which are seemingly relevant for comparing A+ with A, don't come into play in comparing A+ with B. Clearly, then, Parfit's point about Mere Addition involved tracking the identities and fates of different individuals across outcomes, in order to assess the goodness of different outcomes, and this is illegitimate on an Internal Aspects View.

Put differently, the fact that A+ involves Mere Addition *in comparison with A*, but *not* in comparison with B, is only relevant for comparing the different alternatives on an Essentially Comparative View. If one rejects such a view in favor of the Internal Aspects View, as Parfit is now inclined to, we should ignore the fact that A+ involves Mere Addition in comparison with A, and instead focus *solely* on A+'s internal features in assessing its overall goodness, features whose relevance and significance will *not* change depending on whether A+ is compared with A, B, or any other alternative. Accordingly, on the Internal Aspects View, it is deeply misleading to refer to Parfit's problem as the Mere Addition Paradox. More particularly, what many, including Parfit, have regarded as a *crucial* factor in generating the Paradox must now be seen as fundamentally irrelevant, namely, the fact that we are to assume that A+ involves Mere Addition *in comparison with A*. On the Internal Aspects View of Moral Ideals, *all* that matters for evaluating A+ are A+'s internal features, including, for example, how well off the people are in A+, how well off the worse-off are, how much perfection or inequality there is, and so on; whether or not A+'s members would exist in some *other* alternative, or how they might fare *in* those alternatives, has *no* bearing on A+'s value.

Clearly, then, the relevance and importance of the fact that A+ involves Mere Addition in comparison with A, but not in comparison with B, depends on the correct view of moral ideals. The significance of this will become clearer in the remainder of this chapter, and in chapters 12 and 13.

11.6 Reconsidering the Mere Addition Paradox on the Internal Aspects View

Suppose we accepted the Internal Aspects View. What effect, if any, would that have on our understanding of the Mere Addition Paradox? I believe that the Mere Addition Paradox would then lose much of its air of intractability, and that insofar as it remained problematic, it would illustrate familiar problems, rather than new ones previously unrecognized.

On the Essentially Comparative View it would be extremely implausible to give up any of the three judgments that give rise to the Mere Addition Paradox.[38] However, as we have seen in earlier chapters, on the Essentially Comparative View transitivity would either fail, or fail to apply, for the "all-things-considered better than" relation (in my wide reason-implying sense). Accordingly, on the Essentially Comparative View, there would be no paradox in maintaining all three of the Mere Addition Paradox's judgments.

On the Internal Aspects View, matters are considerably different. As we have seen, on the Internal Aspects View "all-things-considered better than" *would* be transitive; so, as Parfit first thought, one could not consistently maintain that all things considered, A+ is not worse than A, though it is worse than B, which is worse than A. On the other hand, *once* one accepts the Internal Aspects View, it seems there would be much less difficulty giving up one of the judgments. In particular, while accepting the Internal Aspects View probably would not affect our judgment about A+ and B (though it might), it could easily cause revision in one of the other judgments.

Consider, for example, the judgment that A+ is not worse than A. Presumably, A+ is neither significantly better nor significantly worse than A regarding perfection, P.[39] However, on the Internal Aspects View of Moral Ideals, A+ would be worse than A regarding equality, E, and also worse regarding maximin, M. Now, admittedly, on the Internal Aspects View of Moral Ideals, A+ would pre-

---

[38] I give a detailed argument in support of this claim in part 1 of "Intransitivity and the Mere Addition Paradox."

[39] Recall that for the purposes of my examples, I am assuming that how good an outcome is regarding perfection tracks how well off the best-off people in that outcome are. My double use of the qualifying word "significantly" is intended to respond to the following observation made by Evan Williams (in correspondence): "I have generally-perfectionism-friendly intuitions which include: 'Any world containing Nietzsche is better than any world containing only figure skaters and office workers, no matter how many figure skaters and office workers are in the latter. Any world containing both Nietzsche and a figure skater is better than a world containing only Nietzsche and office workers, no matter how many office workers are in the latter. And any world containing both Nietzsche and a figure skater is better than a world containing only Nietzsche.' If you accept that this is a perfectionist intuition, it suggests that A+ is better than A regarding perfection." (cont.)

sumably be better than A regarding utility, U. Still, one can see how the Internal Aspects View of Moral Ideals leaves plenty of room for the judgment that $A+$ is worse than A. This would be so if the extent to which $A+$ is better than A regarding U is outweighed by the extent to which it is worse regarding E and M.

Similarly, the Internal Aspects View leaves room for the judgment that B is better than A. After all, on the Internal Aspects View of Moral Ideals, though B would only be the same as A regarding E, and worse regarding P and M, it would be better regarding U. Hence, one could judge B better than A all things considered, if one thought the extent to which it was better regarding U outweighed the extent to which it was worse regarding P and M.[40]

Although the Internal Aspects View of Moral Ideals rules out the consistency of the three judgments in the Mere Addition Paradox, it is misleading to think it *forces* us, by logic alone as it were, to give up one of three judgments we find deeply plausible. To the contrary, someone who accepts the Internal Aspects View may no longer find all three judgments deeply plausible.

Consider, for example, someone who accepts the Internal Aspects View of Moral Ideals, but retains the view that $A+$ is not worse than A. Unless she grants no weight to equality or maximin, she probably thinks $A+$ is *better* than A regarding utility. And, since it is unlikely that the extent to which $A+$ is better than A regarding U will be exactly equal to the extent to which it is worse regarding E and M, such a person may well believe the former outweighs the latter, so that $A+$ is actually better than A. In other words, on reflection, someone who accepts the Internal Aspects View of Moral Ideals may well come to believe that, all things considered, it is *good* the extra people are alive, rather than merely being not bad. This assumption corresponds to many people's actual reactions to $A+$ and A. But if she finds this plausible, why should she find it implausible that B is better than A? Why *shouldn't* she believe that the extent to which B is better than A regarding U outweighs the extent to which it is worse regarding P and M? Indeed, given that there is even *more* utility in B than in $A+$, and that B is *better* than $A+$ regarding equality and maximin, it would only be plausible to suppose that B was worse than A if one thought that the extent to which B was worse than A (and $A+$) regarding perfection outweighed the extent to which B was better than $A+$

I'm not sure whether this kind of reasoning does reflect perfectionist intuitions, particularly if it is generalized. But clearly Williams is only attaching tie-breaking significance to the figure skaters, or extra people in $A+$, relative to the presence of Nietzsche, or the A people in $A+$. So, for Williams, if Nietzsche or the people in A were even a *little* better off in terms of perfection in the outcome where they were alone, that outcome would be better, in terms of perfection, than the one in which they were less well off in terms of perfection, but they were accompanied by a figure skater or the extra people in $A+$. So, I think it is fair to say that even on Williams's view $A+$ isn't *significantly* better than A in terms of perfection.

[40] Recall that someone who judges B better than A need not necessarily be committed to the Repugnant Conclusion. As one moves from A toward Z, conditions may sufficiently change so as to block iteration of one's judgments regarding A, $A+$, and B. So, for example, it might be the case that all things considered B is better than A, and C is better than B, but G is not better than F. See note 10.

regarding U, E, and M. But, of course, if one thought *this*, there would be no paradox, as it would *not* seem that B was better than $A+$.

Similar considerations could be offered if one thought that A and $A+$ were merely "on a par." On the Internal Aspects View of Moral Ideals, if the internal features of A and B were such that A was ranked better than B, and the internal features of B and $A+$ were such that B was ranked better than $A+$, then the internal features of A and $A+$ *would* be such that A was ranked better than $A+$. Accordingly, we *know* that if the internal features of A and $A+$ were such that they should be ranked as on a par, then the internal features of B would *have* to be such that either A was not better than B, or B was not better than $A+$. And, again, the point to stress here is that we wouldn't be *forced* to this conclusion as a matter of logic, as it were. Rather, this is how we would actually respond to the different alternatives if we really accepted the Internal Aspects View and were really clear on the internal features of the different alternatives, and how much the various ideals mattered relative to each other on the Internal Aspects View.

I believe, then, that *if* one accepts the Internal Aspects View, the Mere Addition Paradox should lose its air of intractability. No longer must it seem deeply implausible to give up one of the three judgments. To the contrary, on the Internal Aspects View, the very factors convincing one of the plausibility of two of the judgments will serve to convince one of the implausibility of the third.

These considerations fit well with the reactions many have to variations of the Mere Addition Paradox. Consider diagram 11.6.A, where in each case $A+$ involves, relative to A, the existence of extra people all of whom have lives worth living and who affect no one else, and B stands to $A+$ in the manner Parfit described.

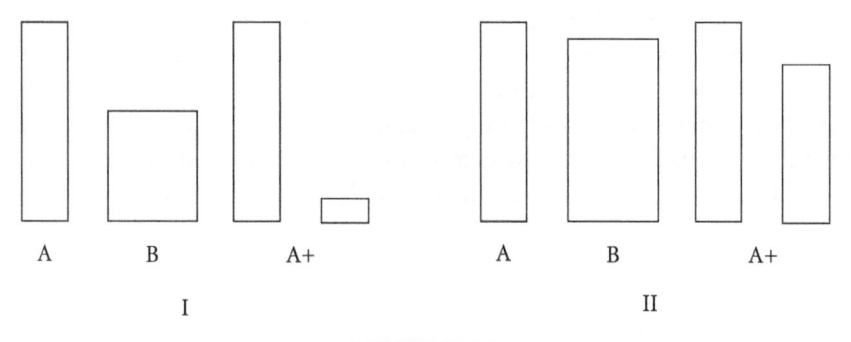

DIAGRAM 11.6.A

The difference between Parfit's original case and the preceding variations is that $A+$'s worse-off group fares much worse in case I, and much better in case II, than it does in Parfit's original case. Similarly for the B group.

Examining case I, most would agree that A is better than B. And many, though not all, would judge B better than $A+$. However, on the Internal Aspects

View, there is good reason to reject the claim that $A+$ is not worse than A. $A+$ is better than A regarding U, but not by much. On the other hand, $A+$ is *much* worse than A regarding E and M. So, unless one believes that utility matters *so* much more than equality and maximin that even *small* increases in the one can outweigh *large* decreases in the others—in which case one would not only have to, but want to, revise one of the other judgments—the judgment that $A+$ is not worse than A will be implausible.

In case *II*, I think many, though not all, would continue to judge that B is better than $A+$. But I also think many would alter their other two judgments. Unlike case *I*, the extra people in $A+$ are *very* well off, almost as well off as the very best-off. That may seem like a significant improvement regarding U. On the other hand, while $A+$ is worse than A regarding E and M, it is not much worse, especially on the plausible view that equality and maximin matter less at high levels than at low levels. Thus, in case *II*, it seems quite plausible that, all things considered, $A+$ is *better* than A. Similarly, in case *II*, it no longer seems implausible that B is better than A. To the contrary, it seems that the small difference between A and B regarding P and M would be outweighed by there being twice as many in B all of whom are *almost* as well off as those in A. Specifically, in case *II*, B may seem better than A, since *significant* gains in utility might well seem to outweigh *small* losses in perfection and maximin.

Cases *I* and *II* suggest the following. The Internal Aspects View provides a way of avoiding the Mere Addition Paradox because, on that view, there is always a way of rejecting one of the three judgments constituting the paradox. But this does not mean that in all cases of the sort Parfit has imagined the same judgment must be rejected. Which judgment should be rejected will depend on how the situations actually compare regarding the ideals we value, together with how much these ideals matter in relation to each other. This, of course, is precisely as it should be.

Now in some cases, like cases *I* and *II* perhaps, it may be obvious which judgments should be rejected. However, in other cases it may not be possible to simply look at a diagram and "read off" which judgment or judgments should be rejected. Perhaps, by drawing his diagram the way he did, Parfit, in essence, presented such a case. That is, even accepting the Internal Aspects View, it may not be evident for Parfit's case which of the three judgments should be given up. But, on the Internal Aspects View, there need be nothing surprising about this, much less deeply inconsistent. Rather, what Parfit would have given us, despite his protestations to the contrary, is an illustration of a case where our different moral principles so conflict that our all-things-considered view is clouded. More specifically, Parfit's case would simply be one where we are unsure of how the outcomes actually compare regarding U, E, P, and M, or of how much these different ideals matter in relation to each other.

There are, of course, many problems in deciding how outcomes compare regarding ideals, and how to weigh ideals against one another. Moreover, some of these may strike at the very intelligibility of the Internal Aspects View. But these problems are not new with the Mere Addition Paradox. They can arise in comparing just two outcomes.

11.7 Is the Mere Addition Paradox Genuinely Paradoxical?

I believe that we face a genuine *paradox* when we find ourselves with a set of beliefs, none of which can be abandoned, but which are irreconcilable. More weakly, I believe that a position is *paradoxical* if it involves two or more incompatible views, each of which seems, even on reflection, intuitively obvious, certain, or (virtually) undeniable. Parfit thought the Mere Addition Paradox was paradoxical, because he thought it would be extremely difficult to deny any of the three judgments that A is better than B, that B is better than $A+$, or that $A+$ is not worse than A, *and* he thought that together these three judgments were incompatible, given the intuitively "obvious" view that "all-things-considered better than" is a transitive relation. *If* one accepts an Essentially Comparative View, Parfit's three judgments regarding A, $A+$, and B may well be undeniable, but they will no longer be incompatible, since, as we have seen, given an Essentially Comparative View, either transitivity may fail for the "all-things-considered better than" relation (in my reason-implying sense), or the "all-things-considered better than" relation may fail to apply across different sets of alternatives, including, as it turns out, Parfit's alternatives. On the other hand, *if* one accepts an Internal Aspects View, the transitivity of "all-things-considered better than" will be undeniable, but it will no longer seem intuitively obvious, certain, or (virtually) undeniable that A is better than B, B is better than $A+$, and $A+$ is not worse than A. To the contrary, as we have seen, *once* one accepts the Internal Aspects View, it will be clear that various ideals oppose each judgment, and the question of which should ultimately be rejected will be a matter of determining how Parfit's outcomes actually compare regarding our ideals, together with how much weight each ideal should be given.

Now my own view is that once one accepts the Internal Aspects View, one is likely to feel little difficulty deciding these issues, at least sufficiently to resolve the "paradox." However, even if this is not the case, and one is unsure which judgment to give up, this need not reflect inconsistency in one's thinking. More likely, it will merely reflect the deep difficulties involved in measuring and balancing the ideals that matter. This is an important but familiar issue, one which might make Parfit's example problematic, but not a paradox, or even paradoxical.

I have suggested that *if* one accepts an Essentially Comparative View, then the Mere Addition Paradox will no longer be paradoxical. In addition, I have suggested that *if* one accepts an Internal Aspects View, then the Mere Addition Paradox may be problematic, but not paradoxical. Assuming that one or the other of these views of moral ideals is (roughly) right, then it may appear that the Mere Addition Paradox is not, in fact, paradoxical. After all, if one believes that *X* or *Y* is true, and one knows that both *X* and *Y* imply *Z*, then shouldn't one believe that *Z* is true, even if one doesn't know *which* of *X* or *Y* is true?

So, should we conclude that the "Mere Addition Paradox" was misnamed? Was Parfit mistaken in describing his results as paradoxical? Not necessarily. As we have seen, many believe that "all-things-considered better than" *must* be a transitive relation and that it should apply to all sets of different outcomes. Believing this, they may find it virtually undeniable that something like the Internal Aspects View must be right. By the same token, many may find it deeply implausible that in comparing *A* and *A*+ they should ignore the fact that *A*+ involves Mere Addition relative to *A*. More generally, it may seem intuitively clear that we cannot simply "close our ears" to considerations of the sort Parfit has adduced, that our judgments about different outcomes do, and should, depend on such considerations. Thus, on reflection, it may seem virtually undeniable that certain moral ideals are essentially comparative and that we should adopt an Essentially Comparative View of Outcome Goodness. (We shall return to this in chapter 12.) I submit that if, indeed, the Mere Addition Paradox is genuinely paradoxical, herein lies its source. It is not that we cannot decide between three seemingly incompatible judgments regarding *A*, *A*+, and *B*; rather, it is that the Mere Addition Paradox compels us toward an Essentially Comparative View which is incompatible with another view to which many seem committed,[41] namely, the Internal Aspects View.

The Mere Addition Paradox should lose its air of paradox when, and if, there are compelling reasons to either accept an Internal Aspects View and reject an Essentially Comparative View, or vice versa. But, until then, the Mere Addition Paradox will remain paradoxical for many.

*****

In section 11.3, I noted that Parfit now claims that his argument for the view that equality is essentially comparative was, perhaps, his worst mistake in philosophy. I think Parfit is wrong about this. First, even if Parfit was mistaken to claim that *equality* is essentially comparative, the *kinds* of considerations he offered in support of that claim may well support the conclusion that *other* moral ideals are essentially comparative, even if equality is not. Second, and more important, even if the view that some ideals can be essentially comparative *is* a mistake, far from being his "worst" mistake, I would argue that it is probably Parfit's *best*, most *brilliant*, mistake. As this work reveals, properly understood, it illuminates deep inconsistencies in our thinking, and forces us to seriously reconsider and revise our understanding of the good, moral ideals, and the nature of practical reasoning.

---

[41] This qualification is important. Some people may only be committed to an Internal Aspects View insofar as that seems necessary to preserve the transitivity of "all-things-considered better than," and, as we will see later, there is a way of reconciling an Essentially Comparative View with the transitivity of "all-things-considered better than." But, as we will also see, the move in question involves significant costs of its own.

In reading this chapter, some may be tempted to the following position. Some arguments, like Parfit's Mere Addition Paradox, may derive much of their appeal from an Essentially Comparative View of Morality or Practical Reasoning. But we should reject such a view, and any arguments that depend on it. This may be correct. However, as we shall see next, in chapter 12, for many, accepting such a position will not be easy. This is because, at the end of the day, some of the ideals that people value most *are* best understood as essentially comparative.

12

On the Nature of Moral Ideals
PART II

In chapter 11, we saw that Parfit appealed to an Essentially Comparative View of Equality in presenting his Mere Addition Paradox, and that Parfit now believes that his doing so was a big mistake. More generally, Parfit now thinks that we should reject any Essentially Comparative View about the goodness of outcomes, which means that we must reject the Essentially Comparative View for *all* moral ideals relevant to assessing the goodness of outcomes. I noted my agreement with Parfit that we should reject an Essentially Comparative View of Equality. But should we take the further step of rejecting an Essentially Comparative View for *all* moral ideals, in favor of the Internal Aspects View of Moral Ideals? Do we, in fact, open ourselves up to serious error if we allow our judgment about alternatives like A and $A+$ to be influenced by whether or not $A+$ involves Mere Addition?

It may seem the answers to these questions must surely be "Yes!" After all, as we saw in chapter 11, adopting the Internal Aspects View would give us a way of rejecting the Mere Addition Paradox. More important, it would enable us to avoid intransitivity in our all-things-considered judgments (in my wide reason-implying sense), allow the "all-things-considered better than" relation to apply to all sets of comparable outcomes, and license the Principle of Like Comparability for Equivalents. Moreover, in addition to the unwanted implications of its denial, the Internal Aspects View has great appeal in its own right. Unfortunately, however, as with many of this book's topics, the issue here is deeply complicated and fraught with difficulties.

In this chapter, I shall explore further the Essentially Comparative View. I shall argue that the Essentially Comparative View has great plausibility and that, for many, adopting the Internal Aspects View for all moral ideals will not be easy. In the following chapter, I will examine various ways of responding to an Essentially Comparative View and explore some of the implications of those responses. As we will see, there will be deeply implausible implications whether or not one rejects the Essentially Comparative View.

12.1 Reconsidering the Essentially Comparative View

I believe that some of the principles people attach most value to in arriving at their all-things-considered judgments are essentially comparative in nature, even if equality, in fact, is not. Let me next present some considerations supporting this view.

Consider first a principle like the following one:

Maximin (*M*): The best outcome is the one in which the worst-off people are best off.

Many people believe *M*, or something like it, represents a fundamentally important moral ideal relevant to the assessment of outcomes.[1] They may not believe that maximin is the *only* ideal on the basis of which outcomes should be ranked, but they believe that it is *one* important ideal, among others, relevant to assessing outcomes. Specifically, they believe that in many cases, the fact that the worst-off people fare better in one outcome than another makes the one outcome better than the other in a morally significant respect and provides an important reason to rank the one outcome as better than the other, though one that might be outweighed by competing reasons. But, as with equality, Parfit has offered considerations in support of an Essentially Comparative View of Maximin. And, unlike the case of equality, these reasons will strike many as especially powerful and compelling.

Consider, again, Parfit's Mere Addition Paradox, where *A*+ involves Mere Addition in relation to *A*. On the Internal Aspects View of Moral Ideals, *A*+ would be *worse* than *A* regarding maximin, since *A* is the outcome in which the worst-off group is best off.[2] Parfit denied this. Parfit distinguished two ways in which, in one of two outcomes, the worst-off group might be better off and contends that only one of these ways makes an outcome better. So, for

---

[1] Rawls's own version of maximin differs from *M* in important respects. But many people are attracted to *M* and, importantly for our purposes, it is probably the version of maximin most naturally adopted on the Internal Aspects View. I directly argue for the essentially comparative nature of Rawls's own version of maximin in "Intransitivity and the Mere Addition Paradox," *Philosophy and Public Affairs* 16 (1987): 138–87, and "Rethinking the Good, Moral Ideals and the Nature of Practical Reasoning," in *Reading Parfit*, ed. Jonathan Dancy (Oxford: Basil Blackwell, 1997), 290–344.

[2] This is, I think, both the most natural and most plausible way of thinking about maximin on an Internal Aspects View. Shelly Kagan has pointed out, in discussion, that on one interpretation of maximin, *A*+ would actually be *better* than *A* regarding maximin on an Internal Aspects View. On the interpretation Kagan has in mind, maximin would reflect an impersonal view of utility according to which one assessed outcomes by adding up the outcome's total utility, where one gave extra weight to the utility of those who were worst-off, such that the worse off the members of the worst-off group were, the more one counted each unit of utility that they possessed. One implication of this view is that if one had a situation like *A*+, where, say, the better-off group was at level 200 and the worse-off group was at level 100, it would be much *better regarding maximin* to *lower* the members of *A*+'s worse-off group to level 1 than to *raise* them to level 200, as long as one added 199 *new* people at level 1 for each member of *A*+'s worse-off group that one harmed instead of helped. Similarly, this version of maximin provides an "express" route to an especially repugnant version of the Repugnant Conclusion, since on

Parfit, while *A+ is* worse than *B* regarding maximin, *A+* is *not* worse than *A* regarding maximin, despite *A*'s worst-off group being better off than both *B*'s and *A+*'s. In particular, Parfit pointed out that the only reason *A*'s worst-off group is better off than *A+*'s is that in *A* the extra people who exist in *A+* and have lives worth living *do not exist*. This, Parfit insisted, does not make *A*'s outcome better than *A+*'s *even regarding maximin*.

Parfit's argument in support of his position is confusing.[3] But his crucial insight—though he does not put it in these terms—is that maximin is essentially comparative. This insight seems right on the mark. For many, an Internal Aspects View is *not* plausible for an ideal like maximin.

Consider diagram 12.1.A.

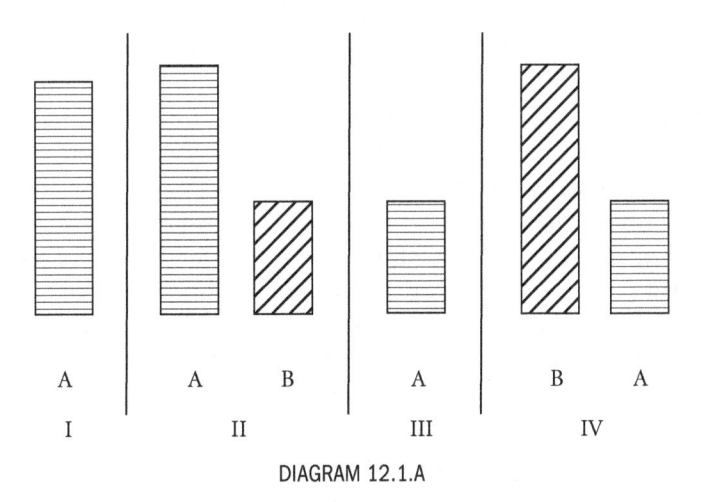

DIAGRAM 12.1.A

Assume that the very same people exist in the *A* group, in each of cases *I*, *II*, *III* and *IV*, and similarly that the very same people exist in the *B* group in cases *II* and *IV*. As drawn, the *A* group in case *II* and the *B* group in case *IV* are the very best-off, and equally so, the *A* group in case *I* is the next best-off, and the *B* group in case *II*, and the *A* groups in cases *III* and *IV* are the least well-off, and equally so, but let us assume that even they have lives that are *well* worth living.

---

this view outcome *Z* (where there are *lots* of people who have lives that are *barely* worth living) could be better than outcome *A* (where 10 billion people have lives that are *incredibly* well off) even though the total utility in *Z* might be considerably *less* than the total utility in *A*. Moreover, importantly, *Z* would not only be better than *A* regarding *utility*, it would be better regarding *maximin*. These implications are hard to accept.

So, as Kagan recognizes, while there is a place in conceptual space for such a version of maximin, no one who *actually* cares about maximin would be attracted to such a view. Hence, throughout the ensuing discussion, I'll continue to assume that on an Internal Aspects View, *A+* would be worse than *A* regarding maximin, and, more generally, if the members of the worst-off group in outcome *X* are worse off than the (possibly different) members of the worst-off group in outcome *Y*, then *X* will be judged worse than *Y* regarding maximin on the Internal Aspects View.

[3] The argument is given in section 144 of Derek Parfit's *Reasons and Persons* (Oxford: Oxford University Press), especially 423–24. Parfit himself now regards the argument in question as "opaque."

On the Internal Aspects View of Moral Ideals, *I* would be better than *II* regarding maximin since, considering solely their internal features, *I*'s worst-off are better off than *II*'s. Is this plausible? I think not.

Suppose that one were in a God-like position where one could create either outcome *I* or outcome *II*. In *I*, there will be a group of people, the *A* group, with lives that are well worth living, but no one else. In *II*, there will be the very *same A* group; *in addition*, there will be another group of people, the *B* people, who are not as well off, but *all* of whom have lives that are *well* worth living. Moreover, unlike Parfit's original case of Mere Addition, let us assume that it is not the case that the extra *B* group affects no one else; to the contrary, let us assume that it is their presence that makes the *A* group *better off*. Perhaps this is because the *B* group produces goods and services that benefit the *A* group. Following Parfit, we might suppose that the *A* people would be the French, in which case we might call this version of the example "How More Than France Exists."[4]

Now, I have already noted, in chapter 11, that there would be *one* consideration against producing *II* rather than *I*, since *II* involves the comparative unfairness of inequality between people none of whom, we are assuming, are less deserving than anyone else. But our current question is whether we should regard *II* as worse than *I*, at least to some extent, because it is worse regarding *maximin*.[5] *Does* the fact that the worse-off group in *II*, the *B* group, is worse off than the worse-off group in *I*, the *A* group, give us a reason to oppose bringing about *II* rather than *I*? As Parfit has rightly recognized, it seems not.

Why not? Because *maximin reflects our special concern for those worst off*, and this concern is addressed by *improving* the lives of those who are worst off, or perhaps by choosing the outcome in which the worst-off group is best off, among outcomes involving *different* people, but it is *not* addressed by failing to bring into existence people who *would* have had lives that were *well* worth living had they

---

[4] My thinking about this topic was heavily influenced by Parfit's rich and suggestive example, "How Only France Survives" (*Reasons and Persons*, 421). However, as numerous people have impressed upon me, including Tim Campbell, Jake Ross, Mikhail Valdman, Oscar Horta, and Shelly Kagan, Parfit's discussion of his example is problematic (see section 12.6). Hence, I have simplified his original example and revised my presentation and analysis of it in order to retain its insights while avoiding its problems.

[5] Here, it is important to distinguish between *maximin*, as a principle which focuses on the utility or well-being of those who are worst off, and a *maximin principle of equality*, which focuses on the size of egalitarian complaints of those who are worst off. As just noted, and discussed in chapter 11, I have claimed that *equality* is best understood in terms of the Internal Aspects View; accordingly, I am perfectly willing to accept, as Oscar Horta has claimed (in correspondence), that there is good reason to judge A+ as worse than A in accordance with a maximin principle of *equality*. But a maximin principle of *equality* is not the same as the principle of *maximin* as it is being considered here, and my current question is whether it is plausible to believe that A+ is worse than A regarding *maximin*, *not* whether A+ is worse than A regarding *equality* nor, a fortiori, whether it is worse regarding a maximin principle of equality. On the maximin principle of equality, see my *Inequality* (New York: Oxford University Press, 1993), especially chapter 2.

existed. The worse-off group in case *I*, namely, the *A* group, is even *better off* in case *II*, while the worse-off group in case *II*, namely, the *B* group, has members whose lives are well worth living and who wouldn't exist in case *I*. Hence, our special concern for those who would be worst off in case *I*, the *A* group, would *support* our bringing about case *II* rather than case *I*, since that *would* be better for those we would be so concerned to help, whereas our special concern for those who would be worst off in case *II*, the *B* group, would *not* support our bringing about case *I* rather than case *II*, since that would *not* be better for those we would be so concerned to help. I submit, then, that the mere fact that the worst-off group in *I*, namely, the *A* people, is better off than the worst-off group in *II*, namely, the *B* people, is not itself a reason to regard *I* as better than *II* regarding maximin. Thus, as Parfit rightly saw, our special concern for the worst-off, which maximin expresses, is not best captured by an Internal Aspects View.

Notice, our judgment about how cases *I* and *II* compare regarding maximin is predicated on identifying the particular people who exist in each outcome and comparing how those particular people fare across the outcomes being considered. This is precisely the sort of move that an Essentially Comparative View can capture, but which is ruled out as impermissible on an Internal Aspects View. This is also what accounts for the fact that on an Essentially Comparative View our evaluation of an alternative can depend on the other alternatives with which it is compared, whereas this is not the case on an Internal Aspects View.

Notice, also, how our judgment about how the cases compare might be very different if the positions of case *II*'s *A* and *B* groups were reversed, as in case *IV*. While I've argued that our special concern for the worst-off would provide *no* reason to prefer case *I* to case *II*, I think it would provide a powerful reason to prefer case *I* to case *IV*. After all, the worst-off in case *I* are much *worse* off in case *IV*, providing us with a maximin-based reason to prefer case *I* to case *IV*; likewise, the worst-off in case *IV* are much *better* off in case *I*, again providing us with a maximin-based reason to prefer case *I* to case *IV*. Indeed, *regarding maximin*— that is, insofar as we are concerned about how the worst-off fare—we might well agree that while the addition of extra groups of people with lives worth living may not, in itself, make an outcome *worse*, it won't make it *better*, either. Accordingly, since case *III* is *clearly* worse than case *I* regarding maximin, and case *IV* is no better for the *A* group than case *III*—it simply has an additional group of people, the *B* group, who are even better off—our special concern for the worst-off may well lead us to judge that case *I* is better than case *IV* regarding maximin.

But, note, cases *II* and *IV* are identical in terms of their internal aspects; the only respect in which they differ is in the *identities* of the different members of the better- and worse-off groups. Accordingly, case *II* would be judged equivalent to case *IV* regarding maximin on the Internal Aspects View. In addition, though I haven't argued for this, I think it is plain that case *II* would be judged equivalent to case *IV* regarding maximin on the Essentially Comparative View as well. Hence, we have a violation of the Principle of Like Comparability for Equivalents, since, regarding maximin, cases

II and *IV* are equivalent, but, as we have seen, they compare differently to case *I*. But this implies that our understanding of maximin is, indeed, essentially comparative, since, as we have seen, the Principle of Like Comparability for Equivalents is entailed by the Internal Aspects View, but not by the Essentially Comparative View.[6]

---

[6] Parfit has claimed that maximin is not appropriately applied in different number cases of the sort I have been considering (see *Reasons and Persons*, section 144). So, he has argued that we can't appeal to maximin in comparing outcomes like case *I* and case *III*, with outcomes like case *II* and case *IV* in diagram 12.1.A. Parfit's claim reflects the crucial insight that we need an Essentially Comparative View to capture our views about maximin, since, if Parfit is right, the factors that are relevant and significant for assessing *A* in comparison with *B* will be different from those that are relevant and significant for assessing *A* in comparison with *C*, if *A* and *B* are same number cases, but *A* and *C* are different number cases of the sort we have been discussing.

Parfit's suggestion involves restricting the scope of maximin, a controversial move that I discuss further in section 12.5, and which, for reasons that should be clear by now, opens the possibility that "all-things-considered better than" (in my wide reason-implying sense) will be a nontransitive relation. However, I think that Parfit's claim about numbers in this context is a red herring. To see why, consider diagram 12.1.B.

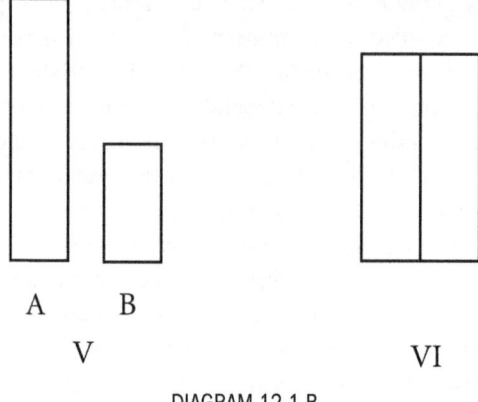

DIAGRAM 12.1.B

If cases *V* and *VI* have the same number of people, most would agree that case *VI* would be better than case *V* regarding maximin, *if* cases *V* and *VI* had entirely different populations, or *if* cases *V* and *VI* had the very same populations. But suppose case *VI* contained case *V*'s *A* group, and an altogether different group of people, the *P* group, equal in size to case *V*'s *B* group. Our discussion of diagram 12.1.A. implied that if *VI* contained *only* the *A* group at their lower level, it would not be better than *V* regarding maximin, and our discussion also claimed that simply adding extra people to an outcome does not make an outcome *better* regarding maximin, even if, as long as their lives are well worth living, it does not make it worse. Together, this suggests that outcome *VI wouldn't* be *better* than *V* regarding maximin *if* it were made up of groups *A* and *P*. But, on any plausible version of the Internal Aspects View, *VI* should have the same overall score, regarding maximin, whether or not it contained the *A* and *P* groups, the *A* and *B* groups, or an entirely different set of people. Thus, even where *same* numbers are involved, judgments about how different outcomes compare regarding maximin will not depend solely on an outcome's internal features in the way required by any plausible version of the Internal Aspects View.

By the same token, suppose that we could bring about an outcome with 8 billion people, or a second outcome with 10 billion people all of whose members were much better off, and so, a fortiori, where the worst-off group would be significantly better off. I think there is good reason to think that the second outcome would be better than the first regarding maximin, whether the second outcome contained none, some, or all of the people contained in the first group. More particularly, in such a

In sum, the Internal Aspects View is unable to capture what many people actually care about, insofar as they value maximin.[7] Accordingly, for many who value maximin, it won't be easy to avoid our worries about the nontransitivity of "all-things-considered better than" (in my wide reason-implying sense) by simply adopting the Internal Aspects View.[8]

---

scenario, I think the fact that the second outcome's worst-off group would be significantly better off than the first outcome's worst-off group would be *one* reason to think it was better. Thus, I think that the manner and extent to which maximin applies to different alternatives depends not on whether or not they have the same number of people, but on the details about how the different alternatives are related. But whether I am right about this particular point about numbers, or Parfit is, it seems that, for many, the most plausible version of maximin will be essentially comparative.

[7] This section's argument is *not* intended to establish that an Internal Aspects View won't *ever* express or capture our views regarding maximin. As indicated in the text, in cases where two outcomes involve completely *different* people, we might think that there is some reason to prefer the outcome in which the worst-off group is better off as would be determined by the Internal Aspects View. Similarly, for at least some cases involving the same *number* of people, we might rank outcomes regarding maximin as they would be ranked on an Internal Aspects View. My discussion here is not only compatible with such claims; I accept them. But my point is to show that there are at least *some* cases where what we care about regarding maximin can only be captured on an Essentially Comparative View. As we have seen, this will be so if two outcomes involve different numbers of people, and all of the people in the smaller outcome exist and are better off in the larger outcome, and the remaining people in the larger outcome have lives that are well worth living. It may be so in other cases as well, but this is sufficient to establish my claim that if one wants to fully capture what people care about insofar as they care about maximin, an Internal Aspects View will not suffice.

It is, perhaps, worth adding here that as pluralists we need not think that only one conception of maximin can be plausible for any given comparison. It may be that for certain comparisons, and perhaps all, we should give weight to *both* an internal aspect conception of maximin *and* an essentially comparative conception of maximin. The important point for my purposes is that there are at least *some* cases where we need to invoke an essentially comparative approach to fully capture our concerns about maximin. Thus, the arguments in the text might be revised to accommodate the view that in *some* (internal aspects) respects we would judge *I* as better than *II* in diagram 12.1.A regarding maximin, but that in *other* (essentially comparative) respects we would judge *I* as worse than *II*.

Having said that, as I have characterized the different outlooks, there is an important asymmetry between the Internal Aspects View and the Essentially Comparative View, namely, that an ideal which is sometimes best captured by an Internal Aspects View but sometimes best captured by an Essentially Comparative View, or an ideal which pluralistically requires us to give weight to *both* Views for certain comparisons, *counts* as an essentially comparative ideal rather than as an internal aspects ideal. This is because on any "hybrid" ideal, the factors that are relevant and significant for assessing any outcome with respect to that ideal won't always depend solely on the internal features of that outcome, and this is the essence of an essentially comparative ideal. This is why, in the text, I have claimed that my arguments show that the version of maximin that most people accept will be essentially comparative. This is compatible with its sometimes, or even always, being the case that in comparing two particular outcomes regarding maximin we should give some weight to an Internal Aspects View of maximin.

I am grateful to Jake Ross, who produced a nice example where maximin seems best captured by an Internal Aspects View, for thus prompting me to clarify the nature and scope of my claims.

[8] I am aware, of course, that not everyone values maximin. Some believe that what is most plausible about maximin can be captured by a view like prioritarianism, or a weighted principle of beneficence that would be compatible with an Internal Aspects View. On such a view, there would be no nonegalitarian basis to prefer case *I* to case *IV* in diagram 12.1.A, for example. Both Shelly Kagan and Derek Parfit hold such a view.

Consider next:

> *The Strong Pareto Principle (SPP)*: One outcome is better than another, *all things considered*, if it is *pareto superior*, where for any two outcomes, A and B, A is *pareto superior* to B if A and B involve the very same people and if A is at least as good as B for everyone, and there is at least *one* person for whom A is better.

Many people accept the Strong Pareto Principle. Indeed, many economists and others believe that the Strong Pareto Principle reflects a fundamental condition of rationality, according to which it is *irrational* to prefer any (pareto inferior) outcome to a pareto superior one. I believe this is a mistake, for reasons I have argued elsewhere and will not repeat here.[9] On my view, an outcome, A, *could* be better than another outcome, B, *all things considered*, even if B is pareto superior to A, and, a fortiori, it needn't necessarily be *irrational* to prefer A to B, even if B is pareto superior to A. Even if I am right, my view is compatible with:

> *The Weak Pareto Principle (WPP)*: One outcome is better than another, *in one important respect*, if it is *pareto superior*, where for any two outcomes, A and B, A is *pareto superior* to B if A and B involve the very same people and if A is at least as good as B for everyone, and there is at least *one* person for whom A is better.

On the Weak Pareto Principle, pareto superiority is *one* important factor that should be given significant weight in our final all-things-considered judgments about how two outcomes compare, but this leaves open the possibility that there may be other morally relevant factors that are also relevant for assessing outcomes and which might, in principle, outweigh the factor of pareto superiority, so that A *could* be worse than B, all things considered, even if A was at least as good as B for everyone, and there was someone for whom A was better. The Weak Pareto Principle should be even more widely accepted than the Strong Pareto Principle. Its advocates can include all of the advocates of the Strong Pareto Principle, as well as anyone who believes that pareto superiority is *relevant* for assessing outcomes, but not *all* that matters, and hence who agrees with me that the Strong Pareto Principle is *too* strong.

In the following, I shall address the Weak Pareto Principle. Everything I say would apply with equal or greater force regarding the Strong Pareto Principle. Intuitively, the thought underlying the Weak Pareto Principle might be put as follows. When comparing outcomes involving the very same people, we should care greatly about how the *particular people* in those outcomes are *affected* for better or worse. It is good if people are affected for the better, and bad if they are affected for the worse.

---

[9] See "Harmful Goods, Harmless Bads," in *Value, Welfare, and Morality*, ed. R. G. Frey and Christopher Morris (Cambridge: Cambridge University Press, 1993), 290–324, and chapter 9 of *Inequality* (New York: Oxford University Press, 1993); also, "Equality, Priority, and the Levelling Down Objection," in *The Ideal of Equality*, ed. Mathew Clayton and Andrew Williams (London: Macmillan; St. Martin's Press, 2000), 126–61, and "Egalitarianism Defended," *Ethics* 113 (2003): 764–82.

Accordingly, at least for outcomes involving the very same people, if one outcome is better for some, and at least as good for everyone else, then that is a powerful reason to favor it; similarly, if one outcome is worse for some, and only equal or worse for everyone else, then that is powerful reason to disfavor it.

Given this reasoning, consider diagram 12.1.C.

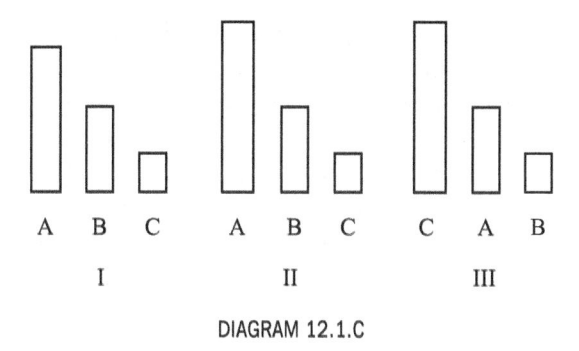

DIAGRAM 12.1.C

I, *II*, and *III* represent three possible outcomes. In each outcome there are three groups consisting of the very same members. So, the same people are in the *A* group in each of *I*, *II*, and *III*, and similarly for the *B* and *C* groups. Thus, outcomes *I*, *II*, and *III* are the kinds of outcomes to which the Weak Pareto Principle is thought to apply. *II* and *III* are exactly alike in terms of their relevant internal features.[10] The only difference between them is that the members of the best-, middle-, and worst-off groups are different. As drawn, the middle- and worst-off groups are equally well off on all three scenarios, but the best-off groups in *II* and *III* are *slightly* better off than the best-off group in *I*. As usual, let us assume that the people in the different outcomes are equally deserving, and that there is no difference between the outcomes in terms of virtue, duty, rights, and so on. In addition, for the purposes of this example, let us assume that there is no difference between the outcomes in terms of perfection,[11] and that everyone in all three outcomes deserves to be at the level of the best-off group in *I*. Moral factors that will be relevant for distinguishing between the alternatives include equality, utility, absolute justice, and maximin.

As drawn, *II* and *III* are slightly better than *I* regarding utility. They will be basically the same regarding maximin, since the worst-off groups fare the same in

---

[10] Of course, there are *some* internal differences between *II* and *III*, namely, the differences in the identities of the members of the different groups in the two outcomes. But, for the reasons given previously, while such differences can be relevant for assessing outcomes on an Essentially Comparative View, they will not be relevant for assessing outcomes on any plausible version of the Internal Aspects View.

[11] Here, I am departing from my usual simplifying assumption that there is a strict correlation between how well off the best-off people are in an outcome, and how good the outcome is regarding perfection. So, for example, the best-off people in *II* and *III* may simply be better off than the best-off people in *I* in virtue of experiencing a greater number of "lower" pleasures that have no bearing on how good their outcomes are regarding perfectionism.

all three outcomes, though *II* and *III* will be ranked slightly better if one accepts a tie-breaking clause which aims to maximize the level of each group, in turn, from the worst-off to the best-off. *II* and *III* will be slightly worse than *I* regarding equality, given the slightly greater inequality that exists in those outcomes between people who are equally deserving. Finally, *II* and *III* will both be slightly worse than *I* in terms of *absolute* justice, since *I*'s, *II*'s, and *III*'s two worse-off groups will all be getting much less than they deserve to the same extent, while *II*'s and *III*'s best-off groups will be objectionably getting *more* than they deserve, though only slightly more, while *I*'s best-off group will be getting exactly what it deserves.

Given these relations, how does *II* compare to *I*? By hypotheses, it is slightly better regarding utility and maximin, slightly worse regarding equality and absolute justice, and equivalent regarding perfection, virtue, duty, rights, and most other ideals relevant to assessing outcomes. So, to this point, it might seem that the ranking of *II* and *I* could go any way, depending on how much we valued the slight differences in utility and maximin versus the slight differences in equality and absolute justice. Given the considerations so far adduced, we might think that *I* is better than *II*, or that *II* is better than *I*, or perhaps that they are roughly comparable or on a par. But, to many, there will be an important *further* factor to consider in comparing *II* and *I*. *II* is *pareto superior* to *I*. Specifically, it is better for *every* member of the *A* group, and at least as good (in fact equally good) for everyone else. Given this, and given the conflicting and only slight differences between *I* and *II* in terms of other morally relevant ideals, many will feel confident that *II* is better than *I*, all things considered. Or, at the very least, given that *II* is pareto superior to *I*, many will feel confident that the Weak Pareto Principle provides a significant reason to favor *II* over *I*, in *addition* to the reasons provided by the fact that *II* would be ranked higher than *I*, regarding utility and regarding a tie-breaking clause of maximin.

Next, consider *III* and *I*. *III* is better for some people, but worse for others. Specifically, it is much better for those in the *C* group, but decidedly worse for those in the *A* and *B* groups. So, neither *I* nor *III* is pareto superior to the other. Accordingly, one of the grounds for ranking *II* better than *I*—and, indeed, perhaps the *strongest* reason in the minds of many for making such a ranking—simply doesn't apply for comparing *III* and *I*. It appears, then, that there is a factor—namely, the factor of pareto superiority—that is relevant and significant for comparing *II* to *I* that isn't relevant and significant for comparing *III* and *I*. But, of course, as we've seen, this is characteristic of an Essentially Comparative View of Moral Ideals, and incompatible with the Internal Aspects View.

Given our suppositions, *II* and *III* should be ranked *exactly the same* on the Internal Aspects View. Thus, in accordance with the Principle of Like Comparability for Equivalents, which is supported by the Internal Aspects View, however *II* compares to *I*, *III* must compare to *I*. But there is no reason to think this, if one believes that *II*'s pareto superiority to *I* is, in fact, relevant to how they compare. In that case, *II* could be ranked one way in relation to *I*, because it is pareto superior, and *III* could be ranked another way, because it is not.

Together, these considerations support the following conclusions. On the Internal Aspects View, pareto superiority cannot *itself* be (independently) relevant to assessing outcomes. Pareto superiority may be an accurate test for how two outcomes compare in some important respects, but if it is, it is only in virtue of an invariable correlation that obtains between pareto superiority and other ideals that can be wholly captured by the Internal Aspects View. In other words, there must be other, deeper factors that actually account for why *II* is better than *I*, that don't appeal to pareto superiority, and those factors must be present in *III* as well, since, by hypothesis, *II* and *III* are the same in terms of all of their relevant internal features. Hence, if we fully understood *why II* is better than *I*, we would also fully understand why *III* is better than *I*, and claims about pareto superiority would play no *fundamental* role in our understanding.

On this view, appeals to claims about pareto superiority are like appeals to algorithms or rubrics that we know work for solving certain complex problems, but we may not actually know why they work. Indeed, given this, we can suggest another rubric that would be entailed by the Internal Aspects View: in comparing any two outcomes, *D* and *E*, even if *D* is *not* pareto superior to *E*, we can treat it *as if* it *were* pareto superior in our deliberations, as long as its internal features are the same as some third outcome, *F*, which would, in fact, be pareto superior to *E*.

Many people will find this picture of the relation between pareto superiority and underlying impersonal ideals hard to accept. They believe that in comparing and assessing outcomes, there is a *fundamental* concern with how the *particular* people who are present in each outcome are *affected* for better or worse in those outcomes. They think that the fact that *II* is better for *some*, and at least as good for *everyone* else, provides direct and powerful reason to favor *II* over *I*, given that *II* and *I* involve the very same people. The fact that *III* is much worse than *I* for two-thirds of the population provides powerful reason to worry about its status vis-à-vis *I*, notwithstanding the fact that *III* is also much better than *I* for one-third of the population. The fact that *III* has the same internal features as *II* does not allay the concerns we have about *III*, nor undermine our positive attitude about *II*.

In sum, the Weak Pareto Principle reflects a position that many find deeply plausible, and both relevant and significant for comparing certain outcomes. But, as indicated, even where it is formulated so as to apply only to outcomes involving the same people, the Weak Pareto Principle is essentially comparative and, for the same reasons, so too is the Strong Pareto Principle. Thus, as with maximin, advocates of the special significance of pareto superiority must look beyond the Internal Aspects View to plausibly avoid this book's worries about the nontransitivity of "all-things-considered better than" (in my wide reason-implying sense).

Let us next consider:

> *An Essentially Comparative View of Utility* (*ECU*): Where, roughly, to improve an outcome regarding utility one must (generally) increase the utility of some of those already living in that outcome.

Jan Narveson defends an Essentially Comparative View of Utility, though he does not call it that and does not consider its implications for the transitivity of "all-things-considered better than." According to Narveson, "Morality has to do with how we treat whatever people there are.... [We] do not... think that happiness is impersonally good. We are in favor of making people happy, but neutral about making happy people."[12] Narveson's view maintains an essential connection between the ideal of utility and our deep concern with how *actual people fare*. On his view it isn't important that there merely *be* lots of utility but, rather, that *people have* as much utility as possible. Thus, on his view, one *doesn't* (generally) improve an outcome regarding utility *merely* by adding new people to that outcome,[13] nor can one (generally) make up for losses in utility to those who exist merely by adding new people to an outcome.[14] As indicated, such a view reflects an Essentially Comparative View of Utility.

On a wholly impersonal view of utility, people are regarded merely as the *producers* or *vessels* of that which is genuinely valuable, namely, utility. They are, as it were, merely the *generators* of utility, or the *containers* into which

---

[12] Jan Narveson, "Moral Problems of Population," *The Monist* 57 (1973): 73, 80.

[13] This position assumes that bringing people into existence with lives worth living does not, itself, benefit the people in question. I, myself, believe this is the most plausible position on the question of whether causing someone to exist can benefit that person, though in appendix G of *Reasons and Persons* Parfit argues that the contrary position is also plausible. Regardless, as I have characterized it here, the Essentially Comparative View of Utility, which reflects Narveson's view, involves the position in question, which is what matters for our present discussion.

Some advocates of the Essentially Comparative View of Utility believe that there is an important asymmetry between bringing someone into existence with a life worth living (which they think does *not* itself *benefit* the person and hence does not, itself, make an outcome better) and bringing someone into existence with a life that is worth *not* living, that is, one below the zero level (which they think *does*, itself, *harm* the person and hence does, itself, make the outcome worse). Whether such a constellation of views is coherent and can be plausibly defended is an open question. This issue and other related ones are broached in section 12.3, as well as in John Broome's *Weighing Lives* (Oxford: Oxford University Press, 2004), and in part 4 of Derek Parfit's *Reasons and Persons*. Unfortunately, to adequately deal with the issues in question would require adding several lengthy chapters to this already long book, so I have regretfully left this for another occasion. Perhaps some readers will take up this interesting and important task.

[14] Oscar Horta notes that my presentation of Narveson's position is compatible with two different interpretations of his view. On one, there is something about being a *person* in virtue of which they merit moral concern—perhaps because they are sentient, or rational, or capable of morality, or whatever, and it is only because an entity possesses such characteristics that we should care about their utility. It is, as it were, because utility is good *for* people, and we care, fundamentally, about people (or sentient beings) that we care about utility, rather than that we care, fundamentally, about utility, and since people are capable of producing and possessing utility, we derivatively care about there being people. On Horta's second interpretation of Narveson's view, we care about people *only* because they are utility producers and recipients, but we only care about *presently existing* utility producers and recipients. Horta suspects that Narveson's view is actually the latter of the two positions. My own interpretation of Narveson sees these two positions as linked, which is why I don't distinguish between them in the text. I suspect that it is because actually existing persons (or sentient beings) have certain properties that we should want what is good for them, and one might think that utility *is* what is good for them. Hence, we care about the utility *of existing beings*, who merit our concern; we don't merely care about utility, and so produce as many beings as possible who are capable of producing and receiving utility.

utility can be poured, and their value, insofar as utility is concerned, lies solely in their ability to generate or contain as much utility as possible. On this view, then, if utility could somehow be produced by windmills, or be like free-floating, unattached atoms of goodness, people could be dispensed with entirely from the standpoint of utility. Narveson and others believe that this gets things backward and terribly wrong. We aren't concerned about people because of our more fundamental concern about utility; we are concerned about utility because of our more fundamental concern about people. On this view, utility is valuable because it is good *for people*, not the other way around.[15]

Consider an outcome that is very poor regarding utility, say, one where millions of people are desperately poor, ill, and hungry. Narveson contends that insofar as we are concerned to improve the outcome's utility, our *real* concern is, and should be, to improve the lives of the badly off people in that outcome. That is, we want to improve the utility by making *those people better off*; we don't simply want there to be *more* utility in the outcome. To see this, consider the fact that mice, like people, are generators and containers of utility. To be sure, they are not as *effective* generators and containers of utility as normal people, but if our concern for utility were wholly impersonal, *one* way of increasing the value of the outcome's utility would be to simply add lots and lots of reasonably contented mice to the outcome! But many believe that increasing utility in *that* way wouldn't, in fact, make the outcome *better*. Not even regarding utility. So, on this view the notions of "*more* utility" and "*better* regarding utility" come apart. As noted, to *improve* an outcome regarding utility, it isn't always sufficient to merely add *more* utility to the outcome.

The point here is not one about the insignificance of mice in comparison with humans, nor is it one about the incommensurability of mice utility and human utility, with human utility having lexical priority over mice utility.[16] Advo-

---

[15] Shelly Kagan balks at the way I motivate Narveson's position. He believes that an impersonal view of utility that is compatible with the Internal Aspects View can resist the "container" or "producer" picture of sentient beings suggested here, and insist that utility or well-being is only good because it is good *for* people or other sentient beings, just as Narveson does. Accordingly, Kagan contends that an impersonal view of utility can deny that "free-floating" utility, if such were possible, would have any value. Frankly, I don't see how to reconcile such claims with other central tenets of the impersonal view of utility that Narveson is opposing. On the impersonal view, "more of the good is better than less of the good," and it doesn't matter *whose* good it is. So why should it matter if the good is *anybody*'s at all?

Kagan can *assert* that free-floating utility wouldn't be good unless it came attached to people, or other sentient beings, but why should one believe this on a wholly impersonal view of utility?

In any event, I presume that if we could introduce brain cell DNA into the cells of a tree or a rock, and thereby create sentient beings capable of having utility, that Kagan would grant that in accordance with the impersonal view of utility, we should do this *whenever* doing so maximized utility, even if this meant destroying *all* of humanity and replacing it with a world inhabited by lots of sentient trees and rocks. This would be enough, I think, to motivate the claim that on the impersonal view of utility people are regarded as, in an important sense, mere "containers" or "producers" of value which are completely *replaceable* by any other possible "containers" or "producers" of value. Most important, Narveson's point is that such a picture distorts what it is that many people really care about insofar as they care about utility.

[16] Oscar Horta convinced me that I should spell out a bit more than I originally did that the issue here has nothing to do with the claim that mice utility and human utility are incommensurable.

cates of the view in question would readily grant that one *could* improve the outcome's utility by improving the lives of already existing poorly off mice, and they might even grant that one could improve the utility *more* by improving the utility of "enough" presently existing mice rather than only a few presently existing humans! (Even if they also thought that there was much greater opportunity to significantly improve the outcome's utility by focusing on humans rather than on mice.) But the point is that they want to improve the lives of sentient beings who already exist; they don't want to merely add more utility to an outcome by adding more producers or containers of utility! Accordingly, as Narveson has seen, it isn't just that adding new *mice* to an outcome won't address the fundamental concern of actually improving the lives of those who exist; the same is true about adding new *people* to an outcome, even if those people would be very well off.

On reflection, many are attracted to Narveson's Essentially Comparative View of Utility, according to which "the principle of utility requires that before we have a moral reason for doing something, it must be because of a change in the happiness [or utility] of some of the affected persons."[17] However, ultimately, I believe that Narveson overstates his position. While Narveson is certainly right that "morality has to do with how we treat whatever people there are," it is a mistake to think, as Narveson seemingly implies, that morality is *only* concerned with how we treat whatever people there are. Surely, if we developed a pill enabling each of us to live wonderful lives for 120 years, it would be terrible for us to take the pill if the cost of doing so were the extinction of humanity.[18] Moreover, this is so even *if* taking the pill were better for each individual who took it, and hence, collectively, for everyone who was alive then or later lived. We think the outcome where people lived wonderful lives for 120 years would be much worse than the outcome where people lived lives of 80 years, but human life continued on for countless centuries. Moreover, *part* of the reason we think the latter outcome would be better is that we think it would be vastly better regarding utility. If right, this undermines Narveson's claim that "we are in favor of making people happy, but neutral about making happy people."[19] But this doesn't mean that Narveson is wrong entirely. He is mistaken to contend that we have no interest in "making happy people" in the context where extinction is the alternative. But he is right, surely, in thinking that *often* our concern about utility

---

[17] This quotation is from Narveson's pioneering work "Utilitarianism and New Generations," *Mind* 76 (1967): 67.

[18] Oscar Horta claims that while he tends to agree with me about this point, he thinks my claim here is far from obvious, and that the issues connected with it are very difficult. I'm inclined to agree that the fundamental issues underlying my claim *are* very difficult, but that nevertheless the claim itself *is* obvious or is almost as obvious as any claim can be in the normative domain. This might be akin to noting that it may be difficult to explain exactly *why* torturing an innocent child for fun is wrong, but nonetheless it *is* obviously wrong. Unfortunately, it is not always easy to *prove* what is obviously true, and this is true in nonnormative as well as normative domains.

[19] This point and its wider significance are discussed further in my article "Is Living Longer, Living Better?" *Journal of Applied Philosophy* 25 (2008): 193–210.

is a concern about improving the lives of already existing people, and that this concern is not allayed *at all* merely by adding more containers or producers of utility to the outcome—whether they be people or mice!

I suggest, then, that while Narveson's view may be overstated, and need some revision or supplementation, the Essentially Comparative View of Utility has tremendous power and appeal. I think, in fact, that many will regard it as the most plausible and important version of utility for a wide range of cases. But it is easy to see that an Essentially Comparative View of Utility raises now familiar worries about nontransitivity.

Consider diagram 12.1.D, a version of the Mere Addition Paradox. Suppose that B contained the same people as those in A, at a significantly lower level, together with another group of people, the Y people, at that same lower level. Suppose, also, that $A+$ involved the same people as those in A in its better-off group, and the same Y people as exist in B in its worse-off group, such that the A people were equally well off in A and $A+$, but that the Y people were sufficiently worse off in $A+$ than in B that, though their lives were still well worth living, the total utility in $A+$ was significantly lower than the total utility in B.

On an Essentially Comparative View of Utility, there is one way of thinking about the relation between A and B where B will be worse than A regarding utility.

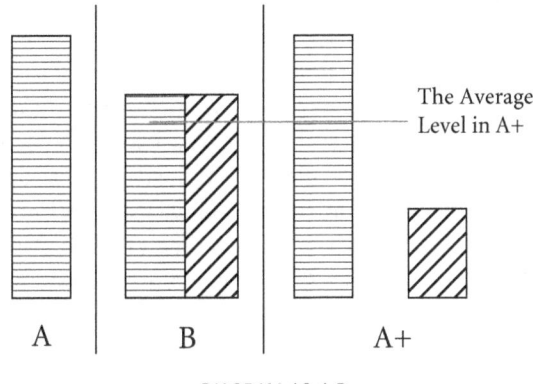

DIAGRAM 12.1.D

In particular, comparing A with that portion of B which just contains the A people at B's lower level, that portion of B would be worse than A regarding utility, since the A people are unequivocally affected for the worse. Then, since the Mere Addition of the Y people to B wouldn't improve the outcome, on an Essentially Comparative View of Utility, thinking about the relation between B and A in this way would lead us to judge B as worse than A regarding utility. In essence, we might say, on an Essentially Comparative View of Utility, loss in people's utility cannot be made up for merely by adding more people.[20] In addition, $A+$ will be worse than B regarding

---

[20] Admittedly, there is another way of thinking about the relationship between A and B where one would think A was worse than B. This is how one would think of it if one thought of B as one's

utility, because loss in some existing people's utility will outweigh the gains of other existing people, when the losses are greater than the gains so that there is a net loss in the outcome's utility. But, on an Essentially Comparative View of Utility, A+ is *not* worse than A regarding utility, as it would have to be if "worse than regarding utility" were a transitive relation. This is because, in the example, the extra people in A+ have lives that are well worth living, and their presence does *not* adversely affect the utility of the people who exist in both A and A+. That is, given that the people who exist in A are *just as well off* in A+, and given that the additional people in A+ have lives that are well worth living, there is no reason, on an Essentially Comparative View of Utility, to regard A+ as *worse* than A *regarding utility*. (For those who might be tempted to regard A+ as worse than A because it has a lower *average* level of utility, see section 10.4.) Indeed, if one imagined diagram 12.1.D slightly redrawn, so that the A people were actually slightly better off in A+ than in A, but the total utility in B were still greater than that in A+, an Essentially Comparative View of Utility would imply that, *regarding utility*, A was better than B, and B was better than A+, but A was *worse* than A+.

So, on an Essentially Comparative View of Utility, a factor that is relevant and significant for comparing B with A+ regarding utility, namely, how the Y people fare in those two outcomes, won't be relevant and significant for comparing B with A, or A+ with A. This is why transitivity either fails, or fails to apply, for the "better than regarding utility" relation, on an Essentially Comparative View of Utility.

It should now be clear why, at the beginning of this section, I claimed that, for many, adopting the Internal Aspects View may not be easy. Doing so would force us to reject what many will regard as the most plausible version of maximin. It will also force us to reject the special significance of the Pareto Principle for assessing outcomes. Moreover, it would undermine the relevance of the kind of view of utility championed by Narveson. Given the strong intuitive plausibility of these positions, and the prominent role they play in many people's assessments of outcomes, it is far from clear that many would regard this as a viable option.

12.2 Narrow Person-Affecting Views

The views I have been discussing—maximin, the Pareto Principle, and the Essentially Comparative View of Utility—all reflect a general conception to which many are attracted. We can call this conception, slightly misleadingly, the *Narrow Person-Affecting View*. In fact, "the" Narrow Person-Affecting View is

---

"default" position, so that A involved a significant loss to B's Y people for far less significant gains to the people who would be in both A and B. The fact that this is so is further evidence that one can't just assign a "score" to an outcome like A or B based solely on their internal features. You have to know the details about how they are supposed to be related. But, this, of course, is just what one should expect on an Essentially Comparative View of Utility, rather than an Internal Aspects View.

not a single view but a *family* of views which assesses outcomes in terms of how a narrow group of *particular* people are *affected* for better or worse, in those outcomes. Different members of the family vary in their characterizations of precisely *which* particular individuals are to count in assessing outcomes, and what counts as *affecting* someone for better or worse. For purposes of discussion, it will be useful to have a particular Narrow Person-Affecting View in mind, and to simply refer to it as "the" Narrow Person-Affecting View. But similar claims and arguments could be made, mutatis mutandis, for any one of the family of views plausibly regarded as a *Narrow* Person-Affecting View.[21]

In order to characterize the Narrow Person-Affecting View I will be discussing, it will be useful to first introduce two terms. In any choice situation between possible outcomes, let us call those people who do exist, or have existed, or will exist in each of the outcomes independently of one's choices *independently existing people*. By contrast, let us call those people whose existence in one or more possible outcomes depends on the choices one makes in bringing about an outcome *dependently existing people*.

We can now state:

> *The Narrow Person-Affecting View*: In assessing possible outcomes, one should (1) focus on the status of independently existing people, with the aim of wanting them to be as well off as possible, and (2) ignore the status of dependently existing people, except that one wants to avoid *harming* them as much as possible. Regarding the second clause, a dependently existing person is harmed *only if* there is at least one available alternative outcome in which that very same person exists and is better off, and the size of the harm will be a function of the extent to which that person would have been better off in the available alternative outcome in which he exists and is best off.

---

[21] In "Does the Moral Significance of Merely Possible People Imply That Early Abortion Is Wrong?" (December 2010, unpublished), Melinda Roberts offers a brilliant analysis of the current state of play regarding population ethics. In doing this, she develops a strikingly original view, which she calls *Variabilism*, arguing that her view is able to solve many of the most intractable problems facing population ethics. Unfortunately, Variabilism has the peculiar feature that even merely possible people who don't exist and never will exist can be harmed or benefited—by not being actualized in a world where their lives would be either worth living, or worth not living, respectively.

I find this feature of Roberts's position deeply counterintuitive (see note 25), but having basically argued throughout this book that every position worth considering in this area has deeply counterintuitive implications, this is hardly sufficient reason, by itself, to reject Roberts's suggestion out of hand. The interesting point about Roberts's view, from my perspective, is that it is clearly an Essentially Comparative one. In particular, the way she is able to "solve" many of the problems of population ethics is to contend that not all benefits and harms *count* in assessing the goodness of outcomes, and, more particularly, that a benefit or harm that *would* count in favor of an outcome given one alternative might *not* count in favor of that very same outcome given another alternative. Suffice it to say, I am very sympathetic with this feature of Roberts's view, for what she has implicitly seen, though she doesn't put it this way, is that *if* we want to capture much of what we actually *believe* in the domain of population ethics, we have to resort to an Essentially Comparative View.

As stated, the Narrow Person-Affecting View is a broader version of Narveson's claim that "we are in favor of making people happy, but neutral about making happy people," namely, that we are in favor of making independently existing people as well off as possible, but neutral about making people exist. But the View spells out a detail that is perhaps only implicit in Narveson's observation that we want to make people happy; to wit: while we are, in general, neutral about making people exist, if we *are* going to make a particular person exist, her interests have to count in the same way as every other existing person's, in that we must seek to make that person, like every other existing person, as well off as possible.

As should be clear, the same kinds of examples that illustrate the plausibility of maximin, the Pareto Principle, and the Essentially Comparative View of Utility can be used to illustrate the more general Narrow Person-Affecting View. Let me briefly offer three such examples.

First, imagine a world with an initial population of 10 billion people, all of whom were at level 1,000, which was contemplating three different population policies. On the first policy, everyone who wanted to have children would have one or two children, and the level of the entire population would remain at 1,000. On the second policy, everyone who wanted to have children would have four children, and the positive effects of the extra children on the parents and first two children would outweigh the negative effects, with the result that everyone would be at level 1,200. On the third policy, everyone who wanted to have children would have eight children, but in this case the negative effects of the extra children on the parents and first four children would outweigh the positive effects, with the result that everyone would be at level 800. Regarding the first policy, I think many, though certainly not all, would agree that the world would be just as good if those people who wanted to have children decided to have just one child instead of two, and this is so even though, by hypothesis, the second children would all have lives that were good *for them*, and so there would be more *total* utility in the latter case. This is because many people believe that, in general, simply adding more or fewer children to a large population does not make the outcome better or worse, *except insofar as their existence would benefit or harm the world's other, independently existing, people*.[22] In addition, many believe that it would be *better* if the second policy were adopted rather than the first, and *worse* if the third policy were adopted rather than the first or second; again, this is so even though each of the children in all of the outcomes would have lives that were good *for them*, and even though the total utility on policy three would be greater than that on policy two, and much greater than that on

---

[22] As we will see shortly, the qualification "in general" is important here. John Broome has called a qualified version of this claim the "neutrality intuition" and observed that it reflects a "person-affecting view." In fact, as it is usually understood, it reflects the kind of *narrow* person-affecting view I have been discussing here. Ultimately, Broome rejects the neutrality intuition for reasons I will discuss later, but he acknowledges that most people, including himself, find it deeply plausible (see chapter 10 of *Weighing Lives*, especially section 10.2).

policy one. To a large extent, I believe that these judgments reflect narrow person-affecting considerations.[23]

My second example concerns the treatment of animals (note that "person-affecting" is a technical term that can include any sentient being within its scope). Many people find the situations obtaining in factory farms morally reprehensible, and believe that such farms should be abolished if their conditions are not significantly improved. In response, factory farmers often claim that while the treatment of their animals may seem harsh, their animals *still* have lives that are worth living. Moreover, they contend that if they were forced to significantly improve the conditions of their farms, it would put them out of business, with the predictable result that *vast* numbers of animals that would otherwise be brought into existence for food production would never be born. Suppose the factory farmers' claims were true. Should that change the demands of their detractors? Some think "yes." But many others think "no," and they think this for narrow person-affecting reasons. They are deeply concerned about the well-being of all those independently existing animals that are adversely affected by the harsh conditions in factory farms; they are not bothered by the prospect of having to miss the "opportunity" of bringing lots of other (dependently existing) animals into similarly squalid conditions![24]

Let us pursue this example further. Suppose that, under good conditions, pigs were *capable* of living lives of value 100, but that factory-farmed pigs had lives of value 10—their lives were worth living, and so of some value *for them*, but not by a lot. Suppose, also, that with a moderate expenditure of funds the factory farmers could improve the conditions in their pens so as to increase the pigs' *quality* of life *five*fold, raising them from level 10 to level 50. But suppose, further, that it were ascertained that for the *same* expenditure, the factory farmers could instead increase the *number* of pigs *ten*fold, but with the predictable result that due to the increased overcrowding *all* of the animals would be even *worse* off than the animals were previously, say, at level 6. Given that a life at level 6 is still minimally worth living, and so is good *for* each new animal, should we accept the conclusion that it would be even *better* for factory farmers to adopt the second plan than the first, on the grounds that there would be even more *total utility* for animals if the second plan were adopted? Again, I think many would reject this contention for narrow-person affecting reasons. For many, if you want to make the outcome *better* with respect to factory farms, you have to *improve* the well-being of those (independently existing) animals living on factory farms, not simply increase the number of animals with positive well-being that live on such farms.

---

[23] I do not deny that our intuitions about this case *could* also be accounted for in other ways. In particular, they could be accounted for by appeal to certain versions of a Wide Person-Affecting View that I will discuss later. But *in fact* I think it is a version of the Narrow Person-Affecting View that best accounts for most people's judgments about such cases.

[24] For the purposes of this example, I am assuming that there would be no positive or negative effects on nonanimals accompanying any changes in factory farming, or that such effects would balance each other out. This, of course, is an implausible assumption, but that does not impact the point of the example.

The third example illustrates the importance of the second part of clause 2 of the Narrow Person-Affecting View, and can be given with the aid of diagram 12.2.A.

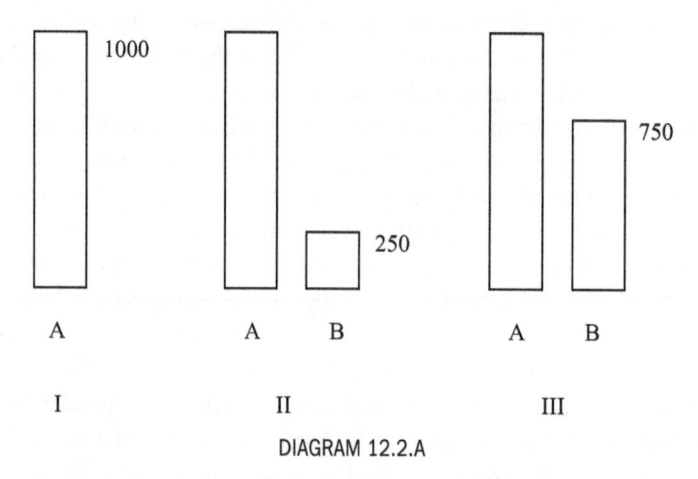

DIAGRAM 12.2.A

In outcome *I*, Group *A* represents a large group of people, say 10 billion, all of whom are very well off at level 1,000. In outcome *II*, the very same people exist in the *A* group, also at level 1,000, and in addition there is another equally large *B* Group whose members all have lives that are well worth living, but only at level 250. outcome *III* is just like outcome *II*, with each group consisting of the very same people in the two outcomes, except that Group *B*'s members are considerably better off, at level 750, though they are still worse off than Group *A*'s members.

Suppose, first, that one could *only* bring about outcome *I* or outcome *II*, or, alternatively, that one could *only* bring about outcome *I* or outcome *III*. Faced with *those* choices, it wouldn't matter *which* outcome one brought about on the Narrow Person-Affecting View. The independently existing people (the members of Group *A*) are equally well off in both outcomes, while the dependently existing people (the members of Group *B*) would not be *harmed* whichever outcome one brought about. If one brings about *I*, one doesn't have to concern oneself with the status of the *B* group, because *they* don't exist in *I* and so they don't *have* a status to be concerned with. This reflects the widely held view that no one is *harmed* by *not* being brought into existence, because *until* someone has been brought into existence there is no one there to *be* harmed.[25] On the

---

[25] To help illustrate this point I once observed, "An average ejaculation contains between 120 and 750 million sperm cells. If one thinks of all of the partners a woman might have sex with during the time each month when she is fertile, and if one thinks that each sperm would combine with her ovum to create a unique individual, the number of possible people she might conceive each month is astronomical. It is surely implausible to think that she acts against each of their interests if she refrains from sex. Moreover, while it might be true that if she had had sex with Tom she might have conceived a particular individual, Tom Jr., it seems implausible to contend that she acted against Tom Jr.'s interest when she had sex with her husband Barry, and conceived Barry Jr. instead." (The quotation is from my "Harmful Goods, Harmless Bads," 319 n. 13.) As noted previously, one person who thinks that a woman *does* act against the interests, and indeed harms, each possible person who she might have conceived, if that person would have had a life worth living, is Melinda Roberts (see note 21).

other hand, one wouldn't harm the members of Group *B* by bringing about *II* or *III*, since, by hypothesis, *I* is the only alternative, and hence there is no available outcome in which the members of the *B* group would be *better* off.

So far, this example is just like many of the others previously discussed, about which many have similar intuitions. As long as Group *A*'s 10 billion members will exist in both outcomes and be well off, many will think that it simply doesn't *matter* if one adds another 10 billion people to the outcome all of whom would have lives worth living, but who would be worse off. Adding the extra 10 billion people won't make the outcome *worse*, they think, since doing so won't *harm anyone*, but, by the same token, *not* adding the extra 10 billion people won't make the outcome worse, either, since that, too, wouldn't *harm anyone*.

Suppose, next, that outcomes *II* and *III* are one's only alternatives. In *this* case, the members of the *A* and *B* groups would *all* be independently existing people, and *III* would clearly be better than *II* in accordance with the first clause of the Narrow Person-Affecting View. Indeed, this is the kind of case where the Narrow Person-Affecting View entails the Pareto Principle, and where most people would accept the judgments of those views in virtue of the reasoning underlying them. That is, focusing on how the particular people who exist in *II* and *III* are *affected* in the different outcomes, they would judge that since the very same people exist in both outcomes, *III* is better than *II*, since it is just as good for some of the people (namely, the *A* group) and better for everyone else (namely, the *B* group).

Finally, consider the important case where *I*, *II*, and *III* are *all* available options. In that case, the Narrow Person-Affecting View would allow the choice of *I* or *III*, but it would rule out the choice of *II*. It would allow the choice of *I* or *III* for now familiar reasons, namely, that no one would be *harmed* by bringing about *I* or *III*. After all, the independently existing people in Group *A* would not be harmed by either alternative, since they are equally well off in each. By the same token, the dependently existing people in Group *B*—and in *this* context they *would* be dependently existing people, since whether or not they exist depends on the choice one makes—would not be harmed by either alternative either, since in *A* they don't exist and never will exist *to be* harmed, while in *B* they are as well off as, and in fact better off than, they would be in any other available alternative in which they exist. On the other hand, *II* is ruled out, precisely because bringing it about *would harm* the dependently existing members of the *B* group, without any compensatory benefits to the independently existing members of the *A* group. The members of the *B* group would be harmed because there *is* another available alternative, *III*, in which they would be better off, while the members of the *A* group are no better off in *II* than in *I* or *III*.

Here, again, I think many people would be attracted to the judgments in question and for narrow person-affecting reasons. Confronted with the alternatives of *I*, *II*, or *III*, many would think that adding the members of the *B* group to the *A* group by bringing about *II* or *III* in the context where *I* was the only alternative wouldn't make the outcome *better*, but it wouldn't make it *worse*, either. On the other hand, while I think many would regard it as optional whether or not to add them at all, they would not think it optional whether or not to add them at level 250 or at level 750. One doesn't *have* to bring extra people into existence, but *if* one is going to bring extra people into existence, then their interests count just as much as anyone else's. In sum, I think many people would agree that given the choice between all three options, *I*, *II*, and *III*, *II* would be the worst option, while *I* and *III* would be better, and equally good, options, and they would think this for narrow person-affecting reasons.

I have suggested that in many cases and contexts people's judgments are influenced by narrow person-affecting considerations. This is important because, as should be evident by now, and as this discussion makes plain, the Narrow Person-Affecting View is an Essentially Comparative View. Focusing as it does on how *particular* people are *affected* for better and worse in different outcomes, the Narrow Person-Affecting View clearly rejects the perspective of the Internal Aspects View. On the Internal Aspects View, the value of *I* in diagram 12.2.A depends *solely* on the internal features of *I*, the value of *II* depends *solely* on the internal features of *II*, and hence how *I* compares to *II* depends *solely* on the internal features of those respective outcomes. But, as we have just seen, on the Narrow Person-Affecting View, the value of *II*'s internal features itself depends on the alternatives with which *II* is compared. In particular, the presence of *II*'s B group at level 250 counts as a *neutral* feature of B if *I* is *II*'s only alternative, but it counts as a *negative* feature of B if *III* is an alternative to *II*. Thus, as we've seen, on the Narrow Person-Affecting View, how *I* and *II* compare depends *not* solely on their internal features, but on the alternatives, if any, to which those alternatives are compared. This, of course, is the characteristic mark of an Essentially Comparative View.

12.3 The Narrow Person-Affecting View: Objections and Responses

So far, my discussion of the Narrow Person-Affecting View has been one-sided. I have been considering examples where the view and its judgments may seem particularly plausible.

But many objections have been raised to the Narrow Person-Affecting View. Let us note some of these objections and then some of the responses that might be given to them.

First, as stated, the Narrow Person-Affecting View says that you only *harm* someone by bringing her into existence, if there was another alternative available which you might have brought about instead, in which that very same person existed and was better off. Many find this to be an unduly restricted and implausible notion of *harm*. In particular, many believe that you can *harm* someone, and thereby make an outcome *worse*, by bringing someone into existence with a life that is so miserable that it is worth *not* living, and that this is so even if there wasn't any available alternative in which that very same person existed with a life worth living. They contend that it would have been *better* for such a person to have never been born, and that this is enough for it to be true that you harmed her, and in so doing made the outcome worse by bringing her into existence.[26]

Second, some believe that there is a *Bad Level*, which is a level of the quality of life at or below which lives are so mean and crimped for a human being that even if they are above the zero level, and so, strictly speaking, not bad *for* the individuals who are living such lives, it would nonetheless be bad, and hence make the outcome worse, to add people to the world who were living such crimped lives.[27] That is, some believe that we should not be neutral about adding crimped human lives to the world; we should oppose such additions on the grounds that it makes the outcomes worse, and even worse regarding well-being, *even if* such lives have minimal value *for* their occupants.

Third, some believe that there is a *Wonderful Level*, which is a level of the quality of a life at or above which lives are so exceptionally good that adding any additional people with such high-quality lives *would* make the outcome better, even if there were already billions of others already existing at or above that level.[28] Many find this view particularly plausible for lives of heavenly quality. So, in particular, they believe that no matter how many angels might already exist, or how many people might already be in heaven, adding more angels to the universe or creating more people in heaven would always make the outcome even better. But many will also be attracted to this kind of position for finite human lives that are far from *heavenly*, but still of exceptionally high quality.

Fourth, some may believe that adding more people with lives worth living will always make the outcome better, if they are better off than everyone else, or if there are only a few others as well off as they are. So, for example, in a world in which the best-off people are at a very low level for humans, say, level 50, adding more people to the world at level 75 would make the outcome better, even if a life of level 75 is not, in fact, of exceptionally high quality.

---

[26] Not necessarily worse all things considered, because there might be indirect good effects on others which outweigh the direct bad effects on the person in question, but worse to the extent that her life is below the zero level.

[27] Derek Parfit discusses this notion of a *Bad Level* in section 147 of *Reasons and Persons*. In doing this, Parfit acknowledges that he is following Gregory Kavka's conception of *Restricted* lives, lives which, though worth living, are sufficiently mean and crimped that, "other things being equal, it is 'intrinsically undesirable from a moral point of view' that such lives be lived. If someone lives a Restricted life, it would have been in itself better if this person had never lived, and no one had existed in his place" (*Reasons and Persons*, 432–33). Kavka's discussion of Restricted lives appears in his pathbreaking article "The Paradox of Future Individuals," *Philosophy and Public Affairs* (1982): 93–112.

[28] I owe the term "Wonderful Level" to early drafts of Derek Parfit's *Reasons and Persons*. For corresponding notions, see Parfit's discussion of the "Valueless Level" and the "Blissful Level" in sections 139, 140, and 145 of *Reasons and Persons*.

Fifth, Derek Parfit famously pointed out that the Narrow Person-Affecting View runs afoul of the *Non-Identity Problem*.[29] For example, Parfit pointed out that given the choice between two policies, Depletion and Conservation, where Depletion would be good for us, but would lower the quality of life for future generations, while Conservation would be slightly worse for us but would improve the quality of life for future generations, the Narrow Person-Affecting View implausibly implies that as long as the actual members of the future generations would be *different* on the two policies, and have lives worth living, the outcome reached by following the policy of Depletion would be *better* than the outcome reached by following Conservation, since there would be some people for whom it was better, namely, us, and no one for whom it was worse.[30]

Sixth, for the same reason that the Narrow Person-Affecting View faces the Non-Identity Problem, it also faces the *Problem of Extinction* that I noted in discussing Narveson's Essentially Comparative View of Utility and the parallel *Problem of Creation*. The Problem of Extinction is that, as stated, the Narrow Person-Affecting View favors slight improvement to presently existing generations at the cost of the future extinction of the human race, over lack of such improvement combined with eons of continued human existence at very high levels. The Problem of Creation is that, as stated, the Narrow Person-Affecting View implies that a deity contemplating an act of creation should be neutral between leaving the universe void and populating it with large numbers of advanced beings all of whom have lives of very high quality.

Seventh, I have offered many further arguments against the Narrow Person-Affecting View, because of its exclusive focus on the *well-being* of particular persons in assessing outcomes. I have argued that such a view fails to give weight to *all impersonal* ideals, and I have pointed out that many people give great weight to ideals like justice, equality, and perfection in their assessment of outcomes—ideals which have a central impersonal component that cannot be adequately captured by any person-*affecting* view that focuses solely on *well-being*. I shall not repeat my arguments here,[31] but I note, for example, that many would agree that

---

[29] See chapter 16 of *Reasons and Persons*.

[30] Parfit offers various arguments in support of the view that adopting the policy of Depletion wouldn't actually be bad *for* anyone, arguments that have been canvassed previously. Thus, Parfit argued that it wouldn't be bad for the future generations who exist under the policy of Depletion, since they have lives worth living, and wouldn't exist if we followed the policy of Conservation; he also argued that it wouldn't be bad for the future generations who *would* have existed had we followed the policy of Conservation, since it isn't bad *for* anyone not to have been born, even if such a *potential* person *would have* had a life worth living *had* she been born. See chapter 16 of *Reasons and Persons*, especially section 123. As noted previously, although many people accept Parfit's view of this matter (including me), Melinda Roberts does not. See note 21.

[31] They are presented in "Harmful Goods, Harmless Bads," chapter 9 of *Inequality*, "Equality, Priority, and the Levelling Down Objection," and "Egalitarianism Defended." For additional considerations relevant to this issue, see also "Personal versus Impersonal Principles: Reconsidering the Slogan," *Theoria* 69 (2003): 20–30.

an outcome in which truly evil people flourish would be *worse* than one in which they fare less well, because it would be more *unjust, even if* the unjust world was better for some, namely, the evil people, and worse for no one. For many, an evil person's getting what he *deserves* is good because it is *just*, not because his getting what he deserves is good *for him*, or anyone else, for that matter.

Individually and collectively, the preceding raise a host of legitimate and compelling points. But what, exactly, do they establish? Some of the objections may succeed in convincing us that we need to modify, supplement, or limit the scope of the Narrow Person-Affecting View to ensure that the judgments it yields are plausible and acceptable. If we do this, we may do so on the basis of reasons that we see as *internal* to the reasoning underlying the Narrow Person-Affecting View; or, alternatively, we may do so on the basis of reasons that we see as *external* to the reasoning underlying the Narrow Person-Affecting View, but reasons which we think powerfully *constrain* the contexts in which the Narrow Person-Affecting View can properly be applied. Still, limiting the scope of a moral principle is a far cry from rejecting it entirely, and I believe that many people will continue to find a suitably modified Narrow Person-Affecting View and its judgments powerfully appealing for a wide range of cases. So, for example, even if one accepts *all* of the first four objections, it remains plausible to believe that there is a large gap, which we can call the *Neutral Range*,[32] between the Bad Level and the Wonderful Level, and that as long as there are already enough people existing who would be as well or better off, it wouldn't matter whether or not one chose to add even *more* people to the world whose lives would fall within the Neutral Range.

On the other hand, even if we ultimately decide that we shouldn't always accept the judgments yielded by the Narrow Person-Affecting View, *even regarding the addition of lives within the Neutral Range*, that does not yet establish that the Narrow Person-Affecting View is *irrelevant* for assessing outcomes and that it should be dismissed entirely. Indeed, this is also the main point to bear in mind in response to the fifth, sixth, and seventh objections.

Like all moral theorists, reasonable advocates of the Narrow Person-Affecting View should be *pluralists*, recognizing that more than one moral factor or ideal is relevant for assessing outcomes. Having done so, they can readily acknowledge that their view cannot capture our considered views about the Non-Identity Problem, Extinction, and Creation. They can also readily acknowledge that in some cases we may judge one outcome as better than another partly on the basis of reasons of justice, equality, or perfection. But they can point out, rightly, that this merely serves to remind us that the Narrow Person-Affecting View is not *all* that matters; it hardly suffices to show that it doesn't matter *at all*.

---

[32] I get the expression the "Neutral Range" from John Broome. See chapters 10 and 14 of Broome's *Weighing Lives* for an important discussion of the Neutral Range.

Consider the analogous claims about equality. Some antiegalitarians have thought that they could refute egalitarianism simply by pointing out that according to the ideal of equality, a perfectly equal world where everyone was miserable would be *just as good* as a perfectly equal world where everyone was flourishing, and even *better* than a world in which just a few of the people were miserable and everyone else was flourishing. But as I have long argued,[33] such claims merely refute the position of radical egalitarianism, which claims that equality is the *only* ideal that matters. But no genuine egalitarian *is* a radical egalitarian; they are all pluralists. Accordingly, reasonable egalitarians can readily acknowledge that a world in which everyone flourishes, or in which most people flourish while just a few people are miserable, would be better than a world in which everyone is miserable, *all things considered*; but still point out that there is *one* important respect, namely, with respect to *equality*, that the latter world is as good as, or better than, the other two. The key for the egalitarian is to defend the claim that there are contexts in which the ideal of equality is relevant and significant for assessing outcomes. He does not have to take on the implausible and impossible task of arguing that equality is *all* that matters, or that egalitarian considerations can never be outweighed by competing considerations of other important ideals.

As indicated, I think any reasonable advocate of the Narrow Person-Affecting View is in the same position as the reasonable egalitarian, or any other reasonable moral theorist for that matter. He does not have to take on the impossible task of arguing that the Narrow Person-Affecting View is *all* that matters, or that narrow person-affecting considerations can never be outweighed by competing considerations representing other important ideals. He merely has to show that in some contexts, at least, narrow person-affecting considerations are relevant and significant for assessing outcomes. And, as we have seen, there are a host of cases for which it does seem both relevant and significant for assessing outcomes, how the *particular* people in those outcomes would be *affected* for better or worse in those outcomes. Specifically, it seems that often in choosing between outcomes there *is* special reason to be concerned about the well-being of any independently existing people, as well as reason to recognize that while it often doesn't matter whether or not we bring others into existence, if we *do* so, we must then treat their interests the same as we would those of any independently existing person. But, of course, as we saw in chapter 7, even if we believe that the Narrow Person-Affecting View is only *one* important factor that is relevant for assessing at least some outcomes, all the worries I have been raising about the implications of Essentially Comparative Views will arise.

---

[33] See my *Inequality*; "Equality, Priority, and the Levelling Down Objection"; "Egalitarianism Defended"; "Egalitarianism: A Complex, Individualistic, and Comparative Notion," in *Philosophical Issues*, vol. 11, ed. Ernie Sosa and Enriquea Villanueva (Boston: Blackwell, 2001), 327–52; and "Equality, Priority, or What?" *Economics and Philosophy* (2003): 61–88.

John Broome and Derek Parfit have both raised another objection to the Narrow Person-Affecting View. They believe that their objection is not merely *damaging* to the Narrow Person-Affecting View, but *fatal*. On the surface, their objection appears to be the same, namely, that the Narrow Person-Affecting View must be rejected because it generates intransitive rankings of alternatives. But Parfit's objection is different than Broome's in an important respect; hence it will be worth considering them each separately.

Broome's objection amounts to recognizing the implications of the Narrow Person-Affecting View for diagram 12.2.A, and then asserting that those implications are sufficient for rejecting the Narrow Person-Affecting View! In making his objection, Broome first suggests that if one accepts that adding someone within the Neutral Zone doesn't make an outcome better or worse, then one should also accept that, regarding diagram 12.2.A, *I* and *II* are equally good, and so are *I* and *III*.[34] But, then, by the transitivity of the "equally as good as" relation, it follows that *II* and *III* must be equally good. However, *II* and *III* are *not* equally good; *II* is *worse* than *III*. Moreover, this argument works even if one is *not* making a claim about how *I*, *II*, and *III* compare *all things considered*, but merely making a claim about how they compare *with respect to the Narrow Person-Affecting View*. The point is that *I* and *II* are equally good in narrow person-affecting terms, and *I* and *III* are equally good in narrow person-affecting terms, but *I* and *III* are not equally good in narrow person-affecting terms. But, Broome contends, this is *impossible*, given the *logic* of goodness and the "equally as good as" relation. Hence, we have grounds of *logic* to reject the Narrow Person-Affecting View, at least insofar as it is supposed to generate rankings reflecting the comparative *goodness* of different outcomes, even if it is just comparative goodness with respect to narrow person-affecting considerations.

Not everyone will be persuaded by Broome's argument that we must, ultimately, regard *I* and *II* as equally good. For example, as we have seen, in discussing his Mere Addition Paradox, Parfit famously claimed that *A+* and *A* were *roughly comparable*, where this explicitly entailed not only that *A+* and *A* were neither better nor worse than each other, but also that *A+* and *A* were *not* equally good. So, regarding diagram 12.2.A, Parfit would contend that *I* and *II* were not worse than each other—meaning roughly comparable—and that *I* and *III* were not worse than each other, but that *II was* worse than *III*. But Parfit isn't worried about this possibility, because he is happy to allow for the possibility that "not worse than" isn't transitive; it is the intransitivity of "equally as good as" or "better than" that he thinks is ruled out by the meanings of those words.

However, for reasons presented in chapter 7, Parfit's view about the intransitivity of "not worse than" is implausibly sanguine, as it fails to appreciate what

---

[34] His arguments for this are interesting and important, but their details need not concern us here. See chapter 10 of Broome's *Weighing Lives*.

428 Rethinking the Good

actually *accounts* for the intransitivity of "not worse than" in his examples. Once one recognizes what actually *generates* the intransitivity in Parfit's Mere Addition Paradox or in diagram 12.2.A, one sees that this also generates intransitivity of the "better than" relation to which Parfit, as well as Broome, objects. Suppose, for example, that in diagram 12.2.A the *A* group were slightly better off in *II* than in *I*, and that the *A* group in *III* were slightly worse off in *III* than in *I*. Then, on the Narrow Person-Affecting View, *II* would be *better* than *I*, when those were the only alternatives, since it would be better for the independently existing *A* group and not worse for the dependently existing *B* group; similarly, *I* would be better than *III*, when those were the only alternatives, since it would be better for the independently existing *A* group and not worse for the dependently existing *B* group, but *II* would *not* be better than *III*, when those were the only alternatives, since in that case the *A* and *B* groups' members are all independently existing people who fare better, *overall*, in *III* than in *II*.

So, considering diagram 12.2.A, Broome would argue that the Narrow Person-Affecting View should be rejected because it is incompatible with the *logic* of goodness and the "equally as good as" relation, while, considering a slight variation of diagram 12.2.A, Parfit would contend that the Narrow Person-Affecting View should be rejected because it is incompatible with the *meanings of the words* "better than."

Before responding to these objections, let me note another example of Parfit's which also appeals to worries about intransitivity, but in an importantly different way. Consider diagram 12.3.A.[35]

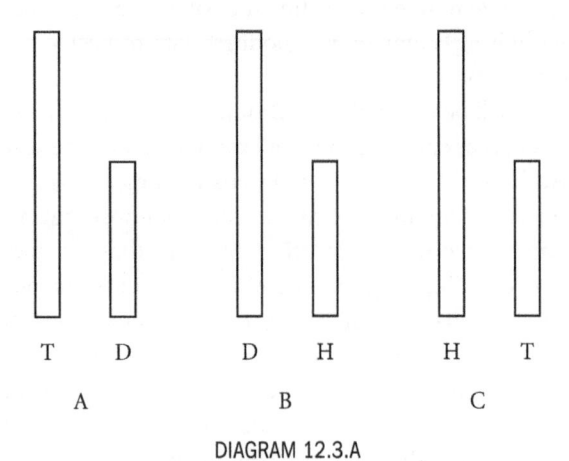

DIAGRAM 12.3.A

A, *B*, and *C* represent three alternative outcomes, each of which contains a healthy person who is very well off to a certain extent, and a handicapped person who is much less well off to a certain extent, but who still has a life well worth living. Three different people are assumed to exist in the three outcomes,

---

[35] Parfit first presented this diagram to me in discussion more than twenty years ago.

Tom, Dick, and Harry. Tom is healthy in *A*, handicapped in *C*, and doesn't exist in *B*; likewise, Dick is healthy in *B*, handicapped in *A*, and doesn't exist in *C*; while Harry is healthy in *C*, handicapped in *B*, and doesn't exist in *A*. As Parfit observes, if *A* and *B* were one's only alternatives, *B* would be better than *A* on the Narrow Person-Affecting View, since it would be better for someone, namely, Dick, and worse for no one. (Recall that Parfit contends that *B* isn't worse than *A* for Harry, because *Harry* doesn't exist in *A*, and though he is handicapped, his life is still well worth living, and *B* isn't bad for Tom, because it isn't bad *for someone* not to have been born.) Analogously, if *B* and *C* were one's only alternatives, *C* would be better than *B* on the Narrow Person-Affecting View, since it would be better for someone, namely, Harry, and worse for no one. But, in an apparent violation of the transitivity of "better than" (about which I'll say more soon), by similar reasoning, *A* would be better than *C*, since it would be better for someone, namely, Tom, and worse for no one.

Suppose, then, that we were confronted with all three alternatives at once. Parfit thought that the Narrow Person-Affecting View would generate the intransitive ranking just noted, that *C* would be better than *B*, *B* better than *A*, and *A* better than *C*, and he thought that this was sufficient reason to reject the Narrow Person-Affecting View. But, here, his appeal isn't solely to a claim about the meanings of the words "better than," or his confidence in the view that "all-things-considered better than" is a transitive relation. Rather, his appeal is partly to our considered judgments about the relative merits of the three alternatives.

Considering diagram 12.3.A, it appears that *A*, *B*, and *C* are *equally good* in terms of any *non*narrow person-affecting considerations that might be thought relevant and significant for comparing outcomes. They are, for example, equally good in terms of any *im*personal conceptions of equality, justice, perfection, or utility, as well as equally good in terms of any *wide* person-affecting conception, which assesses outcomes in terms of the well-being of the people in those outcomes, but pays no heed to how any *particular* people fare within or across outcomes in evaluating the well-being and goodness of those outcomes. Accordingly, since *A*, *B*, and *C* seem to be equally good in all *other* respects, it appears that how they compare *all things considered* will turn on how they compare in terms of any narrow person-affecting considerations that are relevant and significant for comparing outcomes. Thus, since narrow person-affecting considerations support the set of intransitive judgments that *C* is better than *B*, and *B* is better than *A*, but *A* is better than *C*, we *should* accept that ranking as our all things considered judgment about how diagram 12.3.A's three alternatives compare. But, Parfit thinks, considering diagram 12.3.A, that ranking is hard to accept, as intuitively it seems clear that, given the alternatives *A*, *B*, and *C*, each alternative would be *equally* good. Thus, Parfit concludes, we have good reason to think that the Narrow Person-Affecting View is not relevant *at all* for assessing outcomes, and not merely that it is not the *only* position that is relevant for such purposes.

Parfit's argument here implicitly turns on the considerations I presented in section 7.4, when I argued that if an important aspect of a complex notion were nontransitive, the nontransitivity of that aspect is likely to be inherited by the wider notion itself. But he uses that argument as a reductio against the relevance of the Narrow Person-Affecting View for assessing outcomes. As noted, his argument here does not turn on claims about the *logic* of goodness, or the *meaning* of "better than"; it turns on our considered judgment about the relative merits of diagram 12.3.A's *A*, *B*, and *C*. If, on reflection, we deeply believe that *A*, *B*, and *C* really are *equally* good, then, Parfit thinks, we have powerful intuitive reason to reject the relevance of the Narrow Person-Affecting View for assessing outcomes.

Broome's and Parfit's objections are important, but they prompt several possible responses. I'll begin by noting some responses that only apply to Parfit's objection, and then note some responses that apply to both Parfit's and Broome's objections.

First, I have cast Parfit's objection as turning on our intuitions about diagram 12.3.A's *A*, *B*, and *C*. Firm in his intuition about how *A*, *B*, and *C* compare, Parfit believes that we should reject the Narrow Person-Affecting View, since it generates a ranking that is incompatible with that intuition. But, as we have noted previously in this work, one person's modus tollens is another's modus ponens. Advocates of the Narrow Person-Affecting View might use the same kind of argument as Parfit's to argue for a different conclusion. Firm in their intuitions about the importance of the Narrow Person-Affecting View, they could argue that we should reject Parfit's intuition about the rankings of *A*, *B*, and *C*. Indeed, if they are sufficiently caught in the grip of the power and appeal of the Narrow Person-Affecting View, they might not share Parfit's intuitions about *A*, *B*, and *C* in the first place. Instead, echoing Parfit, they might point out that since *A*, *B*, and *C* are equal to each other in every *other* respect, how they compare will turn on how they compare in narrow person-affecting terms, and in those terms *C* is better than *B*, *B* is better than *A*, and *A* is better than *C*; hence we should assess diagram 12.3.A accordingly.

Second, one might accept Parfit's judgment about the alternatives in diagram 12.3.A, but deny that this shows that the Narrow Person-Affecting View should be rejected *entirely*. Appealing to the Principle of Contextual Interaction or the notion of *conditional* factors, values, or ideals, one could argue that the Narrow Person-Affecting View has significance in *some* cases, even if it doesn't have *any* significance in cases like those represented by diagram 12.3.A.[36] In support of this position, one might then present various examples of the sort we have canvassed where the Narrow Person-Affecting View does, indeed, seem powerfully appealing. This response recognizes that the Narrow Person-Affecting View is limited in scope. Perhaps, for example, the view is relevant and significant for comparing any *two* alternatives, but not for comparing three or

---

[36] Frances Kamm's *Principle of Contextual Interaction* and Joseph Raz's notion of *conditional ideals* were introduced previously in note 22 of chapter 2.

more alternatives. Or, alternatively, perhaps the view is relevant and significant for comparing any set of alternatives that involve a large group of independently existing people—particular people who stand to benefit or lose in *each* of the considered alternatives—but not otherwise. This view would account for the Narrow Person-Affecting View's ability to capture many people's judgments about how any *two* of diagram 12.3.A's outcomes would compare all things considered, when those are the *only* available alternatives, but its inability to capture Parfit's intuitive judgment about how all *three* of diagram 12.3.A's outcomes compare all things considered, when all three alternatives are available.

So, there are several moves available to the advocate of the Narrow Person-Affecting View which would grant Parfit the premises of his argument, but deny that they establish that the Narrow Person-Affecting View should be rejected entirely. However, there is another response that is available to Parfit's opponent which is even more central to the issues we have been discussing. That response *agrees* with Parfit regarding the correct all-things-considered judgment about diagram 12.3.A's alternatives, but it denies that the Narrow Person-Affecting View is incompatible with that judgment.

Parfit believes that on the Narrow Person-Affecting View *C* is better than *B*, *B* better than *A*, and *A* better than *C*, and he finds this deeply counterintuitive when assessing diagram 12.3.A. But, on the Narrow Person-Affecting View, the judgments in question only apply when each of those pairs of alternatives is being considered *separately*. And many people *agree* that the judgments in question *are* intuitively plausible, for each pair of alternatives considered alone. However, the Narrow Person-Affecting View does *not* generate the same ranking when all *three* of diagram 12.3.A's alternatives are considered at once. To the contrary, it generates the judgment that in *that* context all three alternatives are *equally good*, exactly as Parfit intuitively believes.[37] The reason for this is that when all three alternatives are considered at once, there are no independently existing people, so comparisons of the different alternatives will turn on the extent to which, if any, the dependently existing people are harmed by the different alternatives. But, as should be plain, from the standpoint of the Narrow Person-Affecting View there will be a single dependently existing person in each outcome who will be harmed, and to the very same extent, no matter *which* outcome is brought about. If *A* is brought about, Dick and only Dick will be harmed, and the extent to which he is harmed

---

[37] In fairness to Parfit, I might observe that he was responding to a different version of the Narrow Person-Affecting View than the one I am discussing here, one according to which one of two outcomes would be worse if it would be worse for some people and better for no one. However, as Parfit puts it in correspondence, I have proposed "a different, improved version." Accordingly, in making the claims I am making here, I am *not* denying that Parfit's version of the Narrow Person-Affecting View had the undesirable and implausible implications that he thought it had; rather, I am contending that the most plausible version of the Narrow Person-Affecting View avoids those implications, and that is the version which I am considering throughout this chapter and which, I contend, needs to be taken seriously.

is a function of how much better off he would be if he were healthy rather than handicapped; if *B* is brought about, Harry and only Harry will be harmed, and the extent to which he is harmed is a function of how much better off he would be if he were healthy rather than handicapped; and if *C* is brought about, Tom and only Tom will be harmed, and the extent to which he is harmed is a function of how much better off he would be if he were healthy rather than handicapped. Since, as drawn, each dependently existing person would be harmed to the same extent whichever alternative was brought about, and since there are no other narrow person-affecting considerations relevant to assessing the outcomes in question, on the Narrow Person-Affecting View we should, in fact, regard *A*, *B*, and *C* as equally good when all three are available alternatives. Hence, Parfit's argument fails. Unfortunately, he has misunderstood the implications of the Narrow Person-Affecting View for diagram 12.3.A.[38]

Parfit has implicitly assumed that if *C* is better than *B* when those are the only alternatives, then *C* must be better than *B* when *A*, *B*, and *C* are all alternatives, and similarly for the other pairwise rankings between *B* and *A*, and *A* and *C*. As we have noted, this assumption is deeply plausible. But it depends on the Internal Aspects View, and while that view is powerfully appealing, it is in competition with another view that is also powerfully appealing, namely, the Essentially Comparative View. And, of course, the Narrow Person-Affecting View is an Essentially Comparative View. It is not compatible with the Internal Aspects View.

So the advocate of the Narrow Person-Affecting View can rightly deny that his view yields an intransitive ranking of diagram 12.3.A's alternatives. In fact, by adopting a fine-grained individuation of outcomes, he can deny that his view ever generates a genuinely *in*transitive ranking of outcomes. For example, he can contend that on his view diagram 12.3.A's *B* corresponds to three *different* outcomes, call them *B'*, *B"*, and *B'''*, depending on whether or not *B* is compared with *A* alone, *C* alone, or both *A* and *C*, respectively. This reflects the fact that on the Narrow Person-Affecting View, the factors that are relevant and significant for assessing *B* vary depending on the alternatives with which it is compared. Similar claims might be made about *A* and *C*. Thus, on the Narrow Person-Affecting View, one might say that *A'* is better than *B'*, *B"* is better than *C'*, and *C'* is better than *A"*. And one might similarly say that *A'''*, *B'''*, and *C'''* are all equally good. Accordingly, on this construal of what is going on, there is, strictly speaking, no *failure* of transitivity for the "better than" relation, and this is so whether or not diagram 12.3.A's alternatives are considered all at once, or in a series of pairwise comparisons.

---

[38] This phrasing is, perhaps, misleading. I am not suggesting that Parfit misunderstood the implications of the version of the Narrow Person-Affecting View that he was considering. Rather, I am suggesting that he misunderstood the position to which an advocate of the Narrow Person-Affecting View should be committed. That is, I think that Parfit's argument against *his* version of the Narrow Person-Affecting View fails against what Parfit himself now regards as my more plausible version of that position. What is philosophically significant is not whether Parfit had good reason to reject a less plausible version of the Narrow Person-Affecting View, but whether there is good reason to reject the most plausible version of the Narrow Person-Affecting View. See note 37.

The preceding remarks also apply, mutatis mutandis, to Broome's example. In diagram 12.2.A, Broome thinks it is clear that we should reject the Narrow Person-Affecting View because it violates the transitivity of the "at least as good as" relation. But this is a mistake. It is *true* that on the Narrow Person-Affecting View *II* is at least as good as *I* if those alternatives are considered alone, that *I* is at least as good as *III* if those alternatives are considered alone, but that *II* is not at least as good as *III* if those alternatives are considered alone. But, on the Narrow Person-Affecting View, the factors that are relevant and significant for assessing *II* are very different depending on whether or not *II* is compared with *I* alone, *III* alone, or both *I* and *II* together. Correspondingly, advocates of the Narrow Person-Affecting View can deny that there is a *failure* of the transitivity of "as good as" in Broome's example, and that this is so whether or not the different alternatives are considered pairwise or all at once.

Arguably, then, advocates of the Narrow Person-Affecting View can resist Broome's and Parfit's objections that their view must be mistaken, on grounds of logic or language, because it implies that "as good as" and "better than" are intransitive relations. Still, in the terminology of chapters 6 and 7, they should grant that on the Narrow Person-Affecting View the "better than" and "equally as good as" relations are *non*transitive because they fail to *apply* across certain sets of alternatives to which we might have thought they *should* apply. That is, looking at diagram 12.2.A, most would have initially thought that if they knew that *II* was as good as *I*, and that *I* was as good as *III*, then they *could* infer, by the transitivity of "as good as," that *II* is as good as *III*. And similarly, looking at diagram 12.3.A, most would have initially thought that if they knew that *C* was better than *B*, and that *B* was better than *A*, then they *could* appeal to the transitivity of "better than" to conclude that *C* was better than *A*. It is only when we understand the nature and structure of Essentially Comparative Views that we understand that such inferences are illegitimate.

The upshot of these remarks is simple. Broome's and Parfit's objections are misleading, insofar as they believe that the real objection to the Narrow Person-Affecting View is that it entails the *in*transitivity of the "better than" or "as good as" relations. But what is certainly the case is that the View *does* entail the *non*transitivity of those notions, in virtue of its being an Essentially Comparative View.[39] Ultimately, then, Broome's and Parfit's objections rest on their conviction that an Internal Aspects View is correct and that an Essentially Comparative View cannot be. Naturally, someone who shares their conviction

---

[39] Recall that here, and elsewhere, I am discussing the notion of an Essentially Comparative View as I was considering it in chapter 11, where the key issue is that the factors that are relevant and significant for assessing the comparative goodness of an outcome may vary depending on the alternatives with which that outcome is compared. I have granted that one may plausibly use the notion of an Essentially Comparative View in other senses which do not open up the possibility that "all-things-considered better than" may be an intransitive relation. See note 24 of chapter 11, and section 13.3.

will have to reject the Narrow Person-Affecting View, while someone who accepts the Narrow Person-Affecting View will have to reject their conviction.

Examining Broome's and Parfit's objections to the Narrow Person-Affecting View, we are once again reminded which positions stand or fall together. But it isn't clear that their objections provide any particularly strong reason to think that we should adopt one constellation of positions rather than the other. The key question remains as to whether or not the factors that are relevant and significant for assessing an outcome can vary depending on the alternatives with which it is compared. Advocates of the Narrow Person-Affecting View think it can. Broome and Parfit think it cannot.

In "Intransitivity and the Person-Affecting Principle,"[40] Alastair Norcross argues that the Narrow Person-Affecting View is implausible for comparing outcomes involving different people. I respond to this argument in appendix E.

12.4 Impersonal Views versus Person-Affecting Views: More Examples Illuminating the Powerful Appeal of Narrow Person-Affecting Considerations

In support of Broome's and Parfit's positions, it is tempting to think that we should reject person-affecting views entirely and only accept views that are not person-affecting (henceforth, *impersonal* views, for short). But while I believe, and have argued, that impersonal views have a crucial role to play in our understanding of the good, I also believe that we cannot dispense with person-affecting views entirely. To illustrate this, consider diagram 12.4.A.

Day 1 P_1 Hell

Day 2 P_1 Heaven; P_2, P_3 Hell

Day 3 P_{1-3} Heaven; P_{4-9} Hell

Day 4 P_{1-9} Heaven; P_{10-27} Hell

⋮

⋮

⋮

W_1

Day 1 P_1 Heaven

Day 2 P_1 Hell; P_2, P_3 Heaven

Day 3 P_{1-3} Hell; P_{4-9} Heaven

Day 4 P_{1-9} Hell; P_{10-27} Heaven

⋮

⋮

⋮

W_2

DIAGRAM 12.4.A

---

[40] *Philosophy and Phenomenological Research* 59 (1999): 769–76.

W_1 represents a world where on day one only one person exists, and he is in Hell; on day two three people exist, with the original person moving to Heaven and two new people existing in Hell; on day three the original three people are in Heaven and six new people are in Hell; on day four the original nine people are in Heaven and eighteen new people are in Hell, and so on. Thus, for each day after day one, everyone who was in Heaven or Hell on the day before is in Heaven—where they will remain henceforth—while for each person in Heaven there are twice as many new people in Hell. W_2 is the "reverse" of W_1. It represents a world where the very same people, P_1, P_2, P_3, and so forth exist, and on day one only person exists, and he is in Heaven; on day two three people exist, with the original person moving to Hell and two new people existing in Heaven; on day three the original three people are in Hell and six new people are in Heaven; on day four the original nine people are in Hell and eighteen new people are in Heaven, and so on. Thus, for each day after day one, everyone who was in Hell or Heaven on the day before is in Hell—where they will remain henceforth—while for each person in Hell there are twice as many new people in Heaven.

The details of this example could be spelled out or changed in many ways. For example, one needn't assume that Hell is infinitely bad and Heaven infinitely good, merely that Hell is bad and Heaven good, and that, considered just by themselves, the goodness of a day in Heaven balances out the badness of a day in Hell, so that, other things equal, a life containing one day of each would be neutral in overall value, and a life containing more days in Heaven than in Hell would be good, and better than a life containing more days in Hell than in Heaven, which would be bad. Moreover, instead of living infinite years, as the example implies, each person might live only a finite number of years. Also, in W_1, instead of there being "only" twice as many people in Hell for each person in Heaven on each day after day one, there could be any finite number times as many people in Hell as in Heaven, for instance, a million times as many; similarly, in W_2, there might be any finite number times as many people in Heaven for each person in Hell. For my present purposes, it is sufficient to consider the example as presented here, bearing in mind the proviso that, considered just by themselves, the goodness of one day in Heaven balances out the badness of one day in Hell, and vice versa.

I think examples like the one depicted in diagram 12.4.A are interesting and illuminating for many reasons. For example, I think it is widely assumed that one can assess the goodness of an outcome regarding utility by simply adding up all of the utility at each moment of *time* in that outcome, or equivalently by adding up all of the utility at each point in *space* in that outcome, or equivalently by adding up all of the utility possessed by each *sentient being* in that outcome. Analogously, I think it is widely assumed that a set of strong Pareto-like dominance principles of the following sort must each be true: for any two outcomes, *A* and *B*, involving the same times, spaces, and people, first, if *A* is better than *B* at *each* moment in *time*, *A* must be better than *B*; second, if *A* is better than *B* at *each* point in *space*, A must be better than B; and third, if A is better than B for *each person*, A must be better than B. But examples like diagram 12.4.A show that these assumptions are dubious and come apart for cases involving infinity.

If one considers W_1 moment by moment, one must grant that, regarding utility, W_1 is a very bad place, since at each moment after day one there is twice as much badness as there is goodness, as there are twice as many people in Hell as there are in Heaven. By the same token, if one considers W_2 moment by moment, one must grant that, regarding utility, W_2 is a very good place, since at each moment after day one there is twice as much goodness as there is badness, as there are twice as many people in Heaven as there are in Hell. Similarly, applying the Pareto-like dominance principle with respect to time, it seems clear that, regarding utility, W_2 should be better than W_1, since at each moment in time W_2 is better. But, however reasonable such thinking may initially appear, it is clearly at odds with the judgments one would arrive at if one assessed each outcome in terms of the way the particular people in those outcomes are affected. In W_1, each person will spend exactly *one* day in Hell, and the *rest of his life*—in this version of the example an infinite amount of time—in Heaven. In contrast, in W_2, each person will spend exactly *one* day in Heaven, and the *rest of his life*—in this version of the example an infinite amount of time—in Hell. So, assessing the value of the outcomes by adding up the utility within each life, W_1 would be an extraordinarily good outcome and W_2 would be an extraordinarily bad outcome, and following the Pareto-like dominance principle with respect to people, W_1 would be better than W_2 since it is better, and indeed vastly so, for each person.

Thinking about diagram 12.4.A, we learn that, at least for cases involving infinity, assessing the value of an outcome's utility moment by moment can generate very different results than assessing the value of the outcome's utility person by person, and that we sometimes have to choose between the judgments yielded by the strong Pareto-like principles with respect to times and people. Moreover, though I shall not present them here, similar considerations could also be presented to show that assessing the value of an outcome's utility point by point (in space) can generate very different results than assessing the value of the outcome's utility moment by moment or person by person, and that we sometimes have to choose between the judgments yielded by the strong Pareto-like principles with respect to space, and the judgments yielded by the strong Pareto-like principles with respect to times and people. But, for my present purposes, the main lesson to be learned from diagram 12.4.A is that we *can't* just dispense with person-affecting considerations in assessing outcomes in favor of impersonal considerations. From a wholly *impersonal* perspective we should either judge W_2 as better than W_1, since for every moment in time there is always twice as much goodness as badness in W_2, while there is always twice as much badness as goodness in W_1, or we should think there is nothing to choose between them, since, over the course of infinity, both outcomes involve an infinite amount of goodness and an infinite amount of badness (of the same order of infinity). But *surely* W_1 is better than W_2, since it is better for each person to spend one day in Hell and an infinite number of days in Heaven, than one day in Heaven and an infinite number of days in Hell. I would choose W_1 for myself, my loved ones, and anyone else (who was not pure evil!). And I am confident that my view of this matter is widely shared. This is because we care about *more* than how *much* utility or goodness obtains in an outcome, we care about how the *people* in an outcome are *affected* by the way in which the outcome's utility or goodness is distributed.

Diagram 12.4.A suggests that in some cases, at least, there is good reason to care about person-affecting considerations and not merely impersonal considerations. But some readers will recognize that, by itself, diagram 12.4.A doesn't give us reason to care about a *Narrow* Person-Affecting View (which focuses on how *particular* people are affected for better or worse) as opposed to a *Wide* Person-Affecting View (which focuses on how *people* are affected for better or worse—understood in terms of the extent to which people have good or bad lives—in different outcomes, whether or not they are the *same* people).[41] After all, while my example assumed that the people in W_1 and W_2 were the same, I think most people would make the same comparative judgments about W_1 and W_2 if different people existed in the two worlds. So, to see whether we need to give weight to a Narrow Person-Affecting View we need to consider a further example.

For this example, we need to note that most people who accept strong Pareto-like dominance principles for assessing outcomes will also accept weaker Pareto-like dominance principles of the following sort: if *A* is better than *B* with respect to at least *one* moment in time, point in space, or person, and at least as good as *B* with respect to every other moment in time, point in space, or person, then *A* must be better than *B*; and also, if everyone who exists in *A* also exists, and is at least as well off, in *B*, with at least one such person being better off in *B* than in *A*, then *B* will be better than *A* as long as any other existing people in *B* have lives that are well worth living. Consider, then, diagram 12.4.B.

---

[41] My characterization of a Wide Person-Affecting View is different from the one Derek Parfit gives in section 136 of *Reasons and Persons* (see, especially, 396–97), where he implies that the difference between the Wide and Narrow Person-Affecting Views is that the former holds, and the latter denies, that causing someone to exist with a life worth living benefits that person, and causing someone to exist with a life that is worth not living (below the zero level at which life ceases to be worth living) harms that person. I have long thought that the question of whether causing someone to exist can benefit or harm that person is extraneous to the notion of a Wide Person-Affecting View. Parfit now agrees. In a recent correspondence he wrote, "On my use, the Wide Person-affecting Principle claims that we ought to do what would benefit people most. I *also* defend the *separate* assumption that, in causing people to exist who would have lives that are worth living, or worth not living, we thereby benefit or harm these people" (emphasis added).

```
-1  -2  -3  -4  -5  -6  -7  -8  -9 -10 -11 -12 -13 -14 -15 -16 -17 -18 -19 -20
T₁  T₂  T₃  T₄  T₅  T₆  T₇  T₈  T₉  T₁₀ T₁₁ T₁₂ T₁₃ T₁₄ T₁₅ T₁₆ T₁₇ T₁₈ T₁₉ T₂₀    ----▶
S₁  S₂  S₃  S₄  S₅  S₆  S₇  S₈  S₉  S₁₀ S₁₁ S₁₂ S₁₃ S₁₄ S₁₅ S₁₆ S₁₇ S₁₈ S₁₉ S₂₀
```

$$W_3$$

```
-11 -12 -13 -14 -15 -16 -17 -18 -19 -20 -21 -22 -23 -24 -25 -26 -27 -28 -29 -30
T₁  T₂  T₃  T₄  T₅  T₆  T₇  T₈  T₉  T₁₀ T₁₁ T₁₂ T₁₃ T₁₄ T₁₅ T₁₆ T₁₇ T₁₈ T₁₉ T₂₀    ----▶
S₁  S₂  S₃  S₄  S₅  S₆  S₇  S₈  S₉  S₁₀ S₁₁ S₁₂ S₁₃ S₁₄ S₁₅ S₁₆ S₁₇ S₁₈ S₁₉ S₂₀
```

DIAGRAM 12.4.B

W_3 and W_4 represent alternative ways an outcome might unfold. Each T_n represents a time period, say 100 years, and each S_n represents a particular area in space. There are no times or areas in space other than those represented in the diagram. In W_3, one person occupies space one, during time period one, and he is suffering severe pains of level –1; a different person occupies space two, during time period two, and is suffering severe pains of level –2; a still different person occupies space three, during time period three, and is suffering severe pains of level –3; and so on. Similarly, in W_4, one person occupies space one, during time period one, and he is suffering severe pains of level –11; a different person occupies space two, during time period two, and is suffering severe pains of level –12; a still different person occupies space three, during time period three, and is suffering severe pains of level –13; and so on. Each higher-level pain is worse than each lower-level pain and, in particular, pain levels –11, –12, –13, and so on are much worse than levels –1, –2, –3, and so on, respectively.

How do the alternative outcomes represented by W_3 and W_4 compare? W_3 is much better than W_4 at *every* moment in time. It is also much better than W_4 at *every* place in space. Correspondingly, I think many people would judge that W_3 was significantly better than W_4, and they might appeal to the strong Pareto-like dominance principles with respect to space and time noted earlier in support of their judgment. Such a judgment has great plausibility *if* one assumes that the people who would exist in W_3 are different from the people who would exist in W_4. On that assumption, one might add the further claim that W_3 is better than W_4 in wide person-affecting terms—that is, that W_3 is better for *people* than W_4 though not better for any *particular* people—though it might also be argued that W_3 is better than W_4 from an *impersonal* perspective as well, given that there is worse suffering at each place and moment of time in W_4 than in W_3.

Suppose, however, that we make a different assumption. In particular, suppose that each person who would exist in W_4 would *also* exist in W_3. More particularly, suppose that the people who would exist at T_1, T_2, T_3, and so on in W_4 would exist at T_{21}, T_{22}, T_{23}, and so on, respectively, in W_3, so that instead of being at pains levels –11, –12, –13, and so on, they would be at pain levels –21, –22, –23, and so on, respectively, and that *in addition* to all the people who would exist in both W_3 and W_4, there would be twenty other people occupying spaces and time periods one through twenty in W_3. On that scenario, I think most people would believe that W_4 was much *better* than W_3, in accordance with a variation of one of the weaker Pareto-like dominance principles for people.[42] Moreover, this judgment seems *correct*. On the assumption in question, I would choose W_4 rather than W_3 for myself, my loved ones, and anyone else who was not thoroughly evil. After all, W_3 is much worse than W_4 for *every* person who would exist in W_4, and *in addition* there are another twenty people who would have to suffer in W_3 but who would not exist, and hence not have to suffer, in W_4.[43]

Importantly, from a purely *impersonal* perspective or a purely *wide* person-affecting perspective, it shouldn't matter whether we assume that the people in W_3 and W_4 are completely different, or whether we assume that the populations of the two worlds overlap in the manner just described. But it seems hard to deny that the latter assumption *does* matter, and is relevant to our judgment about how the worlds compare. I believe that the way in which such an assumption matters is best captured by a *narrow* person-affecting view. In those cases where we want to say that W_3 is worse than W_4, it *isn't* simply because we think it is worse impersonally or worse for *people*; it is because we think it is worse for each *particular* person who exists in the two worlds.[44]

In sum, reflecting on diagram 12.4.A reveals that it would be deeply counterintuitive to forsake person-affecting views entirely in favor of impersonal views. Similarly, reflecting on diagram 12.4.B reveals that it would be deeply counterintuitive to forsake narrow person-affecting views entirely in favor of wide person-affecting views.

Some people worry about examples involving infinity. Although I can appreciate such worries, I don't seriously believe that we might actually be

---

[42] The variation concerns the ranking of outcomes when people's lives are bad rather than good.

[43] Oscar Horta says that he can accept some examples of infinity, but he worries about the one I am discussing here. He writes (in correspondence), "The strength of it relies on a comparison between the suffering of an endless row of individuals versus the suffering of an endless row of individuals *plus* 20 more individuals. This can't be an adequate comparison, I believe, because it relies on the impression that there are 20 *more* individuals suffering in one of the cases, which is not true." However, I don't think the strength of my argument *does* turn on the impression that there are twenty more individuals suffering in the one case than the other. It turns on the fact that everyone who exists in W_4 *also* exists in W_3 where he or she is *clearly worse off*, and that, in addition, anyone who exists in W_3 but not W_4 suffers terribly, and so it would have been much better for them if they'd never existed. The firmness of the intuition that in such a case W_3 would be worse than W_4 does not rest, I believe, on the illegitimate thought that there are *more* people suffering in W_3 than W_4. The point is that we would have rightly judged W_3 as worse than W_4 even if the first twenty people of W_3 didn't exist, and we don't think that the "additional" twenty people who in fact exist in W_3 but not W_4 would in any way make W_3 *better* than it would have been had they not existed. Our firm judgment about the two worlds rests not on our views about whether there are *more* people suffering in the one outcome or the other, or even on whether we think there is *more* total suffering in one outcome or the other, which we may deny, but, rather, on how the particular people are affected, for better or worse, in the two outcomes.

[44] It is certainly worse for each particular person who exists in both worlds, W_3 and W_4. It will also be worse for the twenty people who exist only in W_3, if one assumes that to exist with a life that is worth *not* living is worse for someone than to have never existed at all.

wrong in judging that W_1 would be better than W_2 in diagram 12.4.A, or that W_4 would be better than W_3 in diagram 12.4.B on the assumption that all of W_4's members would also exist in W_3 and be much worse off. Still, it might be worthwhile to consider the following example, which doesn't involve infinity.

> *The Progressive Disease—First Version*: A progressive disease has struck a remote island that is ringed with 100 villages separated by dense jungles and a single outer path between them. Unfortunately, the road is narrow and treacherous, and it is only safe to travel along the road in one direction around the island, clockwise. So, if one starts at village one, one can safely travel to village two, and then, in order, to villages three, four, five, and so on; but if one starts at village two, one can only safely reach village one by traveling clockwise through each of the other villages in turn, three, four, five, and so on. John, who is at an experimental site at the center of the island, learns that two members of the island have been simultaneously struck by the disease, one in village one and the other in village two. John has an antidote for the disease, and a helicopter with just enough gas to enable him to fly to one of the villages. After that, the antidote would have to be delivered via the slow, treacherous, one-way path. Traveling by helicopter to any of the villages takes an hour, as does traveling along the path from any of the villages to the adjacent (clockwise) one. John knows, as does everyone else, that with each passing hour the disease goes untreated the effects of the disease will be worse and longer lasting. Thus, whomever John treats first will have a mild version of the disease, while someone treated an hour later would have a moderately worse version of the disease; someone treated two hours later would have a moderately worse version of the disease than someone treated an hour later, and so on. Unfortunately, the steady progression of the disease is such that someone who is treated 100 hours after the onset of the disease will be in very bad shape for quite a long time, and *vastly* worse than someone who is treated only an hour after the onset of the disease.[45]

In the Progressive Disease—First Version, it seems clear that John should fly his helicopter to the first village and administer his antidote to the infected person there, let's call him *Villager One*, and then travel to the second village, delivering his antidote to the infected person there, who we'll similarly call *Villager Two*. This would produce an outcome where Villager One would suffer a mild version of the disease, and Villager Two would suffer only a moderately worse version of the disease. If, instead, John were to fly to the second village

---

[45] This example was inspired by one that I heard from Gerard Vong, which he attributed to Alex Voorhoeve. The example is similar to a case of "musical chairs" that Derek Parfit and I have been discussing in talks and seminars for many years now, but I think that the version I am now using, which I owe to Voorhoeve via Vong, is more memorable than the ones I previously used to make this point.

first, he could only get the antidote to Villager One via the torturous outer route through *all* of the other villages, and the result would be that while Villager Two would only suffer from a mild version of the disease, Villager One would suffer from a vastly worse version of the disease.

Next, let us consider *Progressive Disease—Second Version*, which is like the First Version except that one villager in *each* of the 100 villages is simultaneously infected by the disease. In the Second Version, it seems clear that it would be equally good for John to fly his helicopter to *any* of the 100 villages first and then travel clockwise around the island, administering his antidote to each of the infected villagers in turn. It wouldn't matter whether John started at village one, village two, village thirty-seven, village eighty-six, or any other village. Wherever he started, he would produce an outcome that was equally as good as any other. In each outcome there would be one person who suffered the mild form of the disease produced when the antidote is delivered after an hour, one person who suffered the moderately worse form of the disease produced when the antidote is delivered after two hours, and so on, up to one person who suffered the really bad form of the disease produced when the antidote is delivered after 100 hours. Notice, in the Second Version our view about whether it would be worse for John to fly to village two first rather than village one is *very* different than in the First Version, even though there is *no* difference between the cases in terms of their effects on Villagers One and Two. What makes the difference in our judgments about the two versions is the way *other* people would or would not be affected by John's actions. In the First Version, *no one* has to suffer from the disease going untreated for more than two hours, while in the Second Version *someone* is going to have to suffer from the disease going untreated for 100 hours, and Villager One has no more claim to its not being him than anyone else.

Finally, let us consider Progressive Disease—Third Version. The Third Version is like the Second Version, in that one villager in *each* of the 100 villages is simultaneously infected by the disease. But in the Third Version, the island's mountains, high winds, and pelting rains make it impossible for John to reach any of the villages by helicopter other than villages one and two. Given this, to which village should John fly?

In one sense, it may seem that this case should be treated like the Second Version. After all, no matter what John does, there will be one villager who suffers the mild form of the disease produced when the antidote is delivered after 1 hour, one villager who suffers the moderately worse form of the disease produced when the antidote is delivered after 2 hours, and so on, up to one person who suffers the really bad form of the disease produced when the antidote is delivered after 100 hours. Moreover, as in the Second Version, it might be claimed that Villager One has no more claim on not having to suffer from the worst form of the disease than anyone else, and in particular that if *he* doesn't suffer from the worst form of the disease, then Villager One Hundred will have to. Accordingly, it might be argued that on the Third Version the outcome in which John flies first to village two would be *just as good* as the outcome where he flies first to village one, and, it should be noted, this would be supported by both an *impersonal* view of the alternatives and a *wide* person-affecting view of the alternatives. After all, in one straightforward sense there would be *just as much* suffering from the disease whichever village John flew to first, and either route would be just as bad for *people*.

So is that the end of the story? *Is* the outcome in which John flies to village one first *just as bad* as the outcome in which he flies to village two first? There is some reason to think the answer to this is "no," when one focuses not merely on how bad the different alternatives are for *people* or from an *impersonal* perspective, but when one also considers how the *particular* people would be affected by the different alternatives. Consider the situation from the perspective of Villager One. Whichever village John flies to first, he will promote the same *overall* amount of good. The only difference will be in *how* that good is distributed. Of the hundred villagers who are infected by the disease, only *one* will be *significantly* affected by John's choice, namely, Villager One. More specifically, whether or not John flies to village one or two first will make only a *moderate* difference in the lives of the other infected villagers, since, for any time, *t*, there is only a moderate difference between getting the antidote at time *t*, and getting it 1 hour later. But which village John flies to first will make a *huge* difference in the first villager's life, since there is a *vast* difference between getting the antidote after an hour and getting it after 100 hours. Thus, it appears that Villager One would have a very *strong* claim on John's flying to village one first, while each of the other villagers would have only a very weak claim on John's flying to village two first. Indeed, the other villagers' claims are *so* much weaker than the first villager's that all of them *together* would just add up, in total, to the size of the first villager's single complaint. Given this, one might reasonably conclude that the outcome in which the first villager had his huge complaint would actually be worse than the outcome in which each of the other villagers had their relatively small complaints; hence the outcome in which John flew first to village one would be better than the outcome in which he flew first to village two (in my wide reason-implying sense).

The preceding reasoning should sound familiar. It reflects the anti-additive-aggregationist reasoning underlying the Disperse Additional Burdens View, discussed at length in chapter 3. I shall not repeat, here, the considerations offered in support of the Disperse Additional Burdens View. Suffice it to say, I think many people do think that, in general, if additional burdens are to be distributed among different people, it is better for a given total burden to be dispersed among a much larger number of people, so the additional burden any single person has to bear is relatively small, than for the entire burden to fall on just a single person, such that the additional burden he would have to bear would be really substantial.

It appears, then, that the reasoning that supports the Disperse Additional Burdens View would be relevant to comparing the alternatives in Progressive Disease—Third Version. But this reasoning only comes into focus, and becomes relevant, if one adopts a *narrow* person-affecting view of the alternatives. That is, it is only when one focuses on the effects of John's choice on the *particular* villagers infected by the disease, which it seems appropriate to do, that it becomes apparent that it would be better for John to fly first to village one.

Before proceeding, let me make several comments about the preceding examples. First, the fact that in Progressive Disease—Second Version we think that the alternative in which John flies first to village two would not be worse than the alternative where he flies first to village one, but that in Progressive Disease—Third Version we think that the alternative in which John flies first to village two would be worse, illustrates that our comparative judgments about those alternatives depends, in part, on what, if any, *other* alternatives are available. This dovetails with the results of section 12.2, illustrating that a Narrow Person-Affecting View entails an Essentially Comparative View of Outcome Goodness.

Second, as should be clear by now, I am *not* arguing that we should accept a Narrow Person-Affecting View *rather* than an impersonal view or a Wide Person-Affecting View. I am a pluralist, and I think that each view may be relevant in different contexts, or even in the same contexts.

Third, for those people who aren't pluralists, Progressive Disease—Third Version would be another example where J. Ross's Principle would be relevant for how we should choose in deciding which outcome to bring about if we wanted to bring about the better outcome. Even if we think it is highly likely that the impersonal view, the Wide Person-Affecting View, or some combinations of those views are the *only* relevant views for assessing outcomes, as long as one grants that there is *some* possibility that the Narrow Person-Affecting View is relevant, that is sufficient reason for one to choose *as if* the Narrow Person-Affecting View is relevant in Progressive Disease—Third Version. In particular, were we in John's situation, we should act *as if* the Narrow Person-Affecting View is true, and hence as if the outcome where we fly to village one first is better than the outcome where we fly to village two first.

By now, the reasoning for this is familiar. If, in fact, the impersonal view and the Wide Person-Affecting View are the only ones relevant for assessing outcomes, then flying to either village first will be *equally good*, and we won't go wrong if we fly to village one first. But if, in fact, the Narrow Person-Affecting View is relevant for assessing outcomes, then flying to village one first will be decidedly better, and we will definitely go wrong if we fly to village two first. Hence, in accordance with the first clause of J. Ross's Principle, even if we think there is only a small chance that the Narrow Person-Affecting View is relevant for assessing outcomes, it would be practically rational in the Progressive Disease—Third Version to act as if it is relevant and to fly to village one first, since doing so will be at least as good as flying to village two first, and may be better.

Fourth, one might wonder whether the Narrow Person-Affecting View might only be relevant as a tiebreaker, so that one should always choose the outcome that would be best according to Impersonal or Wide Person-Affecting Views, but that if two alternatives were equivalent according to such views, then, and only then, would the Narrow Person-Affecting View be relevant for assessing the alternatives. I don't really need to take a stand on this question for my present purposes, but I believe that narrow person-affecting considerations have significant independent weight that give them more than a tie-breaking role in our assessment of outcomes. More particularly, while I'm not prepared to argue *how much* weight narrow person-affecting considerations should have vis-à-vis impersonal or wide person-affecting considerations in contexts where the various considerations point in different directions, I think the considerations presented in chapter 3 in support of the anti-additive-aggregationist Disperse Additional Burdens View support the view that they should be given more than mere tie-breaking weight. Thus, for example, if it would take John half an hour longer to fly to village one than to fly to village two, I think the dire consequences for Villager One if John flies to village two first might still be sufficiently great to offset the increased costs to all of the other infected villagers if John flies to village one first. That is, I think the narrow person-affecting considerations favoring John's flying to village one first might outweigh the impersonal or wide person-affecting considerations that would then clearly favor his flying to village two first.

Finally, I fully recognize that *if* one grants significant independent weight to narrow person-affecting considerations, then one might face problems of iteration; in particular, if one made the same kind of decision each time, one might move through a series of outcomes each of which was better than the one before, but where the last outcome one reached was clearly and unequivocally worse than the very outcome with which one started. This, of course, is exactly what we should expect given the connection between the narrow person-affecting considerations I presented here and the anti-additive-aggregationist reasoning underlying chapter 3's Disperse Additional Burdens View, and my arguments showing that the latter view faces exactly such problems of iteration. Such implications may be practically problematic and theoretically disturbing, but they don't force us to the conclusion that the final (clearly much worse) outcome really is better than the initial (clearly much better) outcome, because, as we have seen, "all-things-considered better than" (in my wide reason-implying sense) is not a transitive relation on Essentially Comparative Views like the Disperse Additional Burdens View or the Narrow Person-Affecting View.

Let me conclude this section by briefly reconsidering the example illustrated by diagram 12.3.A. When Parfit considered alternatives A, B, and C, in diagram 12.3.A, he was convinced that each of the alternatives was *equally good*, and this tempted him to the conclusion that we should simply dispense with the Narrow Person-Affecting View in assessing outcomes (if these aren't outcomes in which all and only the same people exist), since he thought that such a view entailed the intransitive judgments that C was better than B, and B was better than A, but A was better than C. As we saw, Parfit was mistaken about this, for A, B, and C are equally good on the Narrow Person-Affecting View *when all three alternatives are available*. The key question, for my present purposes, is what we should say about A and C when *those* are the only alternatives.

Many believe that in that context *A is* better than *C*, and it is better precisely because it is better in narrow person-affecting terms. Specifically, it is better because *A* and *C* are equal in all *other* respects and, in addition, there is *someone* for whom it is better and *no one* for whom it is worse. If someone brought about *C* when her only alternative was *A*, Tom might legitimately complain that it was bad, or unfair, that he was made worse off when he could have been much better off. But if someone brings about *A* when her only alternative was *C*, there would be no one in a position to lodge a similar complaint. In the context where *A* and *C* are the only alternatives, *C* really *is* bad for Tom, but *A* really *isn't* bad for *anyone*. It obviously isn't bad for Tom, since he is much better off in *A* than in *C*. And, less obviously, it isn't bad for Dick, since, although his life is handicapped, it is well worth living, and *he* wouldn't be alive, with a life worth living, if *C* obtained rather than *A*.

For many, then, narrow person-affecting considerations *are* relevant for comparing different alternatives, and they provide us with a reason for judging *A* as better than *C* when those are the only alternatives, but for judging *A* and *C* as equivalent when *B* is also an alternative.[46] Of course, as we have learned, the fact that our assessment of *A* might vary depending on the alternatives with which it is compared is the distinguishing mark of an Essentially Comparative View. Notice, if we had to choose the better outcome when *A* and *C* were our only alternatives, J. Ross's Principle would once again come into play. Even if we thought it was most likely that only impartial or wide person-affecting considerations were relevant for comparing outcomes, as long as we believed that there was *some* chance that narrow person-affecting considerations were relevant, we should act, in such a case, as if they were relevant. After all, in our example, *A* and *C* are equally good in all other respects, so *if* impartial or wide person-affecting considerations are the only ones relevant for comparing outcomes, we won't go wrong by choosing *A* over *C*. But if, in fact, narrow person-affecting considerations *are* relevant for comparing outcomes, as they *might* be, then *A will* be the better outcome. Hence, were we confronted with such a choice, we should choose as if *A is* the better outcome. By doing so we will be promoting the best or equally best available outcome *whichever* of the different types of considerations (impersonal, wide person-affecting, or narrow person-affecting) are, in fact, relevant.

12.5 Restricting the Scope of Essentially Comparative Ideals

Some people, including Parfit, believe that maximin, the Narrow Person-Affecting View, the Pareto Principle, and the Essentially Comparative View of Utility are all plausible and appropriate for making *some* comparisons, but that they are

---

[46] Jeff McMahan has also argued that narrow person-affecting considerations are relevant for comparing alternatives in his superb book *The Ethics of Killing: Problems at the Margins of Life* (New York: Oxford University Press, 2002).

inappropriate for making *other* comparisons, and that we only face worries about the transitivity of such notions when we allow ourselves to apply such notions to comparisons for which they are ill suited. Specifically, it is claimed that since all of the positions in question focus on how *particular* individuals fare in different outcomes, we must be careful to restrict the scope of such principles to alternatives involving the very same particular individuals, and that if we do this, we won't have to worry about those principles generating nontransitive judgments. A fortiori, we won't have to worry about the nontransitivity of such factors carrying over into our all-things-considered judgments. On this view, we get into trouble in thinking about cases like Parfit's Mere Addition Paradox, precisely because such cases involve different populations in $A+$ and B than in A, and we mistakenly allow ourselves to be influenced by principles that are only relevant for comparing alternatives involving the very same people, like B and $A+$, in forming our judgments about how alternatives involving different people compare, like A and $A+$, or A and B.

Ultimately, I am not sure if such restrictions are plausible. Moreover, as my discussion of the Pareto Principle in section 12.1 illustrates, there is good reason to believe that such restrictions will not always succeed in avoiding the kinds of worries I have raised regarding transitivity with respect to the notions in question. But none of this really matters. The important point is that, although such moves may win a few battles, they are doomed to lose the war. Specifically, even if such moves preserve the transitivity of the particular moral notions in question, they do not preserve—indeed they directly threaten—the transitivity of our all-things-considered judgments (in my wide reason-implying sense). The reason for this should be evident by now. On the view in question, different factors will vary in their relevance and significance for making different comparisons. Specifically, notions like maximin, the Narrow Person-Affecting View, the Pareto Principle, and the Essentially Comparative View of Utility will be relevant and significant for making *certain* comparisons, namely, those involving the very same people, but not relevant and significant for making *other* comparisons, namely, those involving different people. But this is the very recipe for all the doubts that have been raised in this work regarding whether "all-things-considered better than" (in my wide reason-implying sense) is a transitive relation, or applies across different sets of alternatives.

For example, suppose one successfully defends restricting the scope of the Narrow Person-Affecting View, and that A, B, and C are three alternatives such that given its restricted scope the Narrow Person-Affecting View is only relevant for comparing A and C. It could then be the case that all things considered—that is, in terms of the relevance and significance of *all* of the factors for making *each* comparison—A is better than B, and B is better than C, yet C is better than A. After all, even if C is worse than A in terms of the factors relevant for comparing A with B, and B with C, those factors might *not* be relevant or have the same significance for comparing C with A. Moreover, the extent to which C is worse than A in terms of the factors that are relevant for comparing A with B, and B with C

might be *outweighed* by the extent to which C is better than A regarding the Narrow Person-Affecting View, on the assumption that the Narrow Person-Affecting View really is relevant and significant for comparing C with A.

As noted in chapter 7, this point is generalizable and extremely significant. If the scope of a moral factor is restricted, such that it applies when comparing some outcomes but not others, then different factors can be relevant or vary in their significance in comparing alternative outcomes. If this is so, then all of our worries may arise about the transitivity or applicability of our all-things-considered better than judgments even if they don't arise with respect to any of the particular factors underlying such judgments. Thus, restricting the scope of a significant moral ideal opens the possibility that the notion of all-things-considered better than (in my wide reason-implying sense) will either be intransitive, or fail to apply across different sets of alternatives, even if none of its aspects are themselves intransitive.

It is striking that this feature of morality has not been noticed. For example, in *A Theory of Justice* Rawls makes it plain that his two principles of justice are restricted in scope in the sense that "there are surely circumstances in which they fail."[47] More specifically, in his early work Rawls contends that his principles of justice only apply in situations where civilization is "sufficiently" advanced,[48] while in his later work Rawls limits their scope even further, contending that they (may) only apply to situations analogous to modern Western-style democracies. Moreover, Rawls and some of his critics and followers have suggested that maximin may not be applicable to cases involving future generations, particularly where change in population size may be involved. These limitations in the scope of Rawls's principles have been the subject of much discussion and criticism, yet, to my knowledge, no one has noticed their profound implications for transitivity. After all, if maximin really *is* relevant and significant for comparing some outcomes, but not relevant and significant for comparing others, then there is no reason to expect transitivity in our all-things-considered judgments, or to expect the "all-things-considered better than" relation (in my wide reason-implying sense) to apply across all sets of alternatives.

Maximin is hardly the only principle which has been widely regarded as limited in scope. Indeed, a common view is that there are virtually *no* "universal" factors— that is, that virtually *every* moral factor is limited in scope, in the sense that it will be relevant and significant for comparing some, but not all, possible outcomes. Unless one wants to conclude that outcomes are noncomparable *whenever* different factors are relevant to assessing them—a view I find too strong and implausible, as it is likely to result in a *severely* incomplete (partial) ordering of all-things-considered

---

[47] Cambridge, MA: Harvard University Press, 1971, 63.
[48] See, for example, sections 11 and 26 of *A Theory of Justice*.

judgments—one must look elsewhere to avoid the worries about transitivity raised in this book. Restricting the scope of different moral factors is no *solution* to our concerns; it is the very kind of move that *raises* our concerns.

12.6 Another Reason to Accept Essentially Comparative Views: Revisiting "How More Than France Exists"

I have now presented two important reasons for rejecting the Internal Aspects View; namely, that certain moral factors that people find especially powerful and relevant to assessing outcomes seem to be themselves essentially comparative in nature, and that some moral factors may be limited in scope such that they support an Essentially Comparative View of Outcome Goodness. A third important reason lies in certain unpalatable implications of the Internal Aspects View.

In chapter 10, I considered two different models for combining moral ideals. I pointed out that the Standard Model for Utility and the uncapped Standard Model for Combining Ideals seemed plausible for certain comparisons, but that it entailed the Repugnant Conclusion—a deeply implausible position that most people find very difficult to accept. Accordingly, I suggested that if one wanted to avoid the Repugnant Conclusion, as most do, one would have to adopt something like a Capped Model for certain comparisons, where this would involve there being upper (and perhaps lower) limits to how good outcomes were regarding different ideals for at least certain comparisons.

Now, as I tried to make plain, *if* one adopts the Standard Model for Utility and the uncapped Standard Model for Combining Ideals for comparing certain outcomes, and a Capped Model for comparing other outcomes, then one will, in essence, have accepted an Essentially Comparative View. On such a hybrid view, certain factors will be relevant and significant for making certain comparisons, other factors will be relevant or have different significance for making other comparisons, and we will be forced to recognize that "all-things-considered better than" (in my wide reason-implying sense) may not be a transitive relation, or may not apply across the various sets of alternatives that we have been considering in this work.[49]

---

[49] Note, other hybrid views wouldn't be essentially comparative. For example, one might believe that certain ideals have caps, while others do not, and these views might combine with the Standard Model for Combining Ideals in a way that was compatible with the Internal Aspects View. I am grateful to Shelly Kagan for suggesting that I make this clear. (The sense in which a view might be hybrid here is different than the sense in which I suggested that an ideal might be hybrid in note 7. There, an ideal's being hybrid meant that it included an essentially comparative component, and I pointed out that that was enough to ensure that the ideal counted as being essentially comparative. Here, a view's being hybrid means that it might hold that certain ideals are capped, and others are not, and, as noted, this could be true without the view involving an essentially comparative component or entailing the Essentially Comparative View.)

It follows that *if* one wants to avoid the worries about transitivity that I have been raising, *and* one wants to avoid the Repugnant Conclusion, then one will have to combine (something like) the Internal Aspects View with (something like) the Capped Model. Moreover, importantly, one will have to contend that this combination of views is relevant and significant for *all* comparisons between different sets of alternatives.

But this combination of views has deeply implausible implications of its own. To see this, consider diagram 12.6.A, which illustrates the example of "How More Than France Exists" discussed previously in section 12.1.

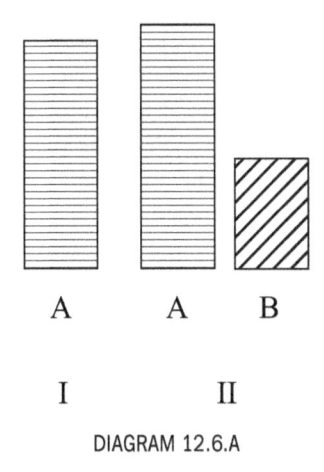

DIAGRAM 12.6.A

Recall that in outcome *I*, there is an *A* group, the French, with lives that are well worth living, but no one else. In outcome *II*, there will be the very *same A* group and, *in addition*, there will be another group, *B, all* of whose members have lives that are *well* worth living. Moreover, unlike Parfit's original example of Mere Addition, it is not the case that the extra group of people in *II* "affect no one else"; to the contrary, their presence makes the *A* people *better off*. As before, perhaps this is because the *B* group produces goods and services that benefit the *A* group. Let us once again assume that the only relevant differences between outcomes *I* and *II* are in terms of equality, maximin, perfection, and utility. In addition, let us once again assume that perfection is correlated with how well off the best-off are. Finally, for simplicity, let's assume that on the Capped Model, the top "score" an outcome could receive regarding each ideal is 100.

In discussing a similar example, Parfit once contended that it would be *absurd* to rank *I* as better than *II* all things considered, *if I* resulted from *II* via group *B* dying off with the *A* group being adversely affected.[50] Parfit is surely right about this, but his introduction of the notion that *I* might *result* from *II* via the *B* group *dying off* is a very misleading feature of his example, if we want

---

[50] See Parfit's discussion of *How Only France Survives* in sections 143 and 144 of *Reasons and Persons* (Oxford: Oxford University Press, 1984), especially 424.

to know how outcomes like *I* and *II* compare. It suggests that we are really comparing a *II/I* outcome with a *II/II* outcome (that is, an outcome that *starts out* like *II* and then is *transformed* into one like *I* via the *B* group *dying off*, with an outcome that *starts out* like *II* and then *remains* like *II* via the *A* and *B* groups *continuing to exist over time*) rather than a *II* outcome with a *I* outcome (that is, an outcome that *starts out* like *II* and then *remains* like *II* with an outcome that *starts out* like *I* and then *remains* like *I*).

But the key point to note, for our purposes, is that even if we just focus on *I* and *II* as possible alternative outcomes that might exist, without thinking that one might be *transformed* into, or from, the other, it *still* seems that, as characterized earlier, outcome *I* would *not* be better than oucome *II*. More specifically, although it may not be *absurd*, it seems *very* hard to believe that if one were going to instantiate one of two outcomes, *I* or *II*, that *I* would be a *better* outcome than *II*, given that *all* of the members of the *B* group have lives that are *well* worth living, and that their existence would actually be *better* for the members of the *A* group.

But notice, if the *A* group is *very* large, and very well off, in some cases *I would* be better than *II* on a combination of the Internal Aspects View and a Capped Model. For example, arbitrarily assigning numbers for the sake of illustration, on the combination of views in question, outcome *I*'s scores might be $U = 90$, $P = 90$, $E = 100$, and $M = 90$ for an all-things-considered score of 370. These scores, which would be based *solely* on *I*'s *internal* features, would reflect the view that if outcome *I* involved a very large population all of whose members were equally and *very* well off, then it would receive scores at or near the top of the scale for each ideal on the Capped Model. On the other hand, outcome *II*'s scores might be $U = 98$, $P = 98$, $E = 40$, and $M = 40$ for an all-things-considered score of 276, 94 points *lower* on a scale of 400. The problem, of course, is that on a Capped Model, *II* may be only slightly better than *I* regarding utility and perfectionism, since *I* will be near the upper limits for how good an outcome can be with respect to those ideals, while on the Internal Aspects View, *II* is almost certain to be *much* worse regarding equality and maximin. This is because if one focuses solely on the internal features of the two outcomes, there is much greater inequality, and the worst-off group is much worse off, in *II* than in *I*.

One might try to avoid this problem by insisting that one attach much greater weight to the ideals of utility and perfection, than to other ideals. That would change the numbers of our example, but not its point. One can always imagine a population like *A* where there are *so* many people in *A* and they are *so* well off that on a Capped Model they would receive an almost perfect score regarding utility and perfection. In that case, an outcome like *II* would almost certainly have to be ranked as worse than outcome *I* on the Internal Aspects View, unless one decided either to abandon the values of equality and maximin entirely, or to effectively give them no weight in the moral assessment of outcomes except, perhaps, in tie-breaking cases. This would be the effect, for example, of preserving the view that *II* is better than *I* by giving *lexical priority* to utility or perfection over equality and maximin.

Reflecting on diagram 12.6.A, one is reminded of the plausibility of an Essentially Comparative View. After all, there is nothing implausible about the idea that an outcome like *I* might be better than an outcome like *II* in *some* cases—for example, if they represented two possible futures with entirely distinct populations. What seems deeply implausible is thinking that *I* would be better than *II* *if they were related in the manner described*. If everyone in *II* has lives that are *well* worth living, it is hard to believe that the outcome would have actually been *better* had half of the population never existed with the result that the remaining half were worse off. In other words, our assessment of outcomes like *I* and *II* seems to depend crucially on the alternatives with which they are compared, and *not* solely on their internal features, exactly as an Essentially Comparative View permits and the Internal Aspects View forbids.

In sum, we see further some of the costs of the Internal Aspects View, and some of the implications of different combinations of views. If we accept the Internal Aspects View and combine it with the Standard Model for Utility and the Standard Model for Combining Ideals, we are committed to the Repugnant Conclusion. On the other hand, if we accept the Internal Aspects View and combine it with the Capped Model so as to avoid the Repugnant Conclusion, then we must either deny significant weight to the values of equality and maximin or accept the implausible ranking of outcomes *I* and *II* in How More Than France Exists. For many, any of these implications will be deeply implausible. Hence there is further reason to accept an Essentially Comparative View.

Combined with the Capped Model, an Essentially Comparative View would enable us to avoid both the Repugnant Conclusion and the implausible ranking of *I* and *II* in How More Than France Exists, while at the same time attaching significant weight to such values as equality and maximin.[51] These constitute powerful reasons to accept such a combination of views. But, of

---

[51] In addition to being able to hold that, in diagram 12.6.A, outcome *I* wouldn't receive a low score for maximin in comparison with outcome *II*, but would receive a low score for maximin in comparison with an outcome where everyone in *I* existed at the level of *I*'s B group, an Essentially Comparative View would enable one to hold that the value of the extra perfection in *I* or the extra utility for *I*'s A group could outweigh the disvalue of *I*'s inequality in the context where *II* was an alternative, but that the extra perfection or extra utility for *I*'s A group would not have been sufficient to outweigh *I*'s inequality, had the alternative been one in which all of *I*'s members existed and were equally well off, but the total utility was less than *I*'s total utility by the amount to which *A*'s total utility is greater in *I* than in *II*. In essence, this view would amount to having an impact on the relative values of the caps for different ideals, depending on the alternatives being compared, in a way that is incompatible with the Internal Aspects View. This is how an Essentially Comparative View could combine with a (changing) Capped Model to resist How More Than France Exists, even if one believes, as I do, that the inequality in *I* of diagram 12.6.A is bad. Though bad, *in the context where the alternative is II*, the badness of *II*'s inequality is outweighed by the positive effects which such inequality makes possible. I am grateful to Jake Ross for suggesting that I say a bit more about this.

course, this is not to deny that such gains come at considerable cost. Whether or not the gains are ultimately worth the costs is by no means clear.

12.7 Two Further Reasons to Accept an Essentially Comparative View

A further reason for rejecting the Internal Aspects View in favor of an Essentially Comparative View is that it may help illuminate, explain, and, in a sense, justify many common cases of apparently inconsistent judgments or behavior.

Here is a real example from my life. Many years ago, I was building an addition to my home in Houston, Texas. Having been raised in the cold climate of Wisconsin, I really wanted to include a wood-burning fireplace in my den. Despite my ecological misgivings about burning wood, there is something about the sight, sound, and smell of burning wood on a cold, crisp day that brings me great pleasure. To add a normal fireplace to the den would have cost around $800. My budget was fairly tight, and it doesn't get very cold in Houston all that often, but even so, all things considered, I thought it would be worth spending $800 to install a fireplace. As it happened, however, my study was on the other side of the den, and for only $300 more, I could add a double-sided fireplace instead of a single-sided one. This would enable me to enjoy a fire while working in my study, and since I typically work in my study many hours each day, it seemed to me clearly worth the extra $300 to install a double-sided fireplace rather than a single-sided one, all things considered. However, every time I thought about spending $1,100 to have a fireplace in Houston, where it is rarely ever cold enough to really warrant a fire, it just didn't seem worth it, all things considered, especially given my fairly tight budget.

In this case, it wasn't that I thought that each of the three alternatives was equally good, or that they were all on a par, or that I may as well just flip a coin to choose between them. When I thought hard about my choices, and what I really wanted, I had the *firm* conviction that having a single-sided fireplace for $800 was a *better* option than having no fireplace and spending the money elsewhere, that having a double-sided fireplace for $1,100 was a *better* option than having a single-sided fireplace for $800 and spending the extra $300 elsewhere, and yet that having no fireplace and $1,100 to spend elsewhere was a *better* option than having a double-sided fireplace for $1,100. I went around and around in my thinking about this issue, unable to rationally resolve it.

Ultimately, my practical dilemma was "resolved" only when my mother, like a deus ex machina, intervened to transform the situation, by offering to pay for the difference between a single-sided fireplace and a double-sided fireplace as a (literal!) housewarming gift.

Here is a common variation. When looking to buy a new car, many believe that, all things considered, it is clearly worth just a few thousand dollars more to buy the car with certain options, $C + O$, than to buy the car without those options,

C. They also believe that, all things considered, it is clearly worth just another few thousand dollars to buy the car "fully loaded" with even further options, $C + O + O$, than to just buy the car with the first set of options, $C + O$. But, on reflection, all things considered, they *don't* believe it is worth all the extra money to buy the car "fully loaded" than to just buy the car without options.

Here is another example from real life.[52] Philosopher S had a really good job at a very prestigious public university, A. He was offered another job that was better in some respects, but worse in others. The new job was at a private university, B, that was less prestigious than his current university, but still quite prestigious. The new job had no graduate students, but really excellent undergraduates. And though his colleagues, on the whole, might not be quite as good, he would teach smaller classes, be in a better city, live closer to his family, and so on. Ultimately, S decided that, all things considered, having a job at B would be better for him than having a job at A, and he accepted the job in question. Sometime later, S was offered a job at another institution, C. C was also a private institution, though not quite as prestigious as B. Its faculty and undergraduates were less good than B's, but it had a graduate program, a lighter teaching load, more research money, a prettier campus, and a nicer office. Ultimately, S decided that, all things considered, having a job at C would be better for him than having a job at B, and he accepted that job as well. Unfortunately, however, when S considered the job at C in comparison with his original job at A, he felt the C job was worse. Although C had several advantages over A, A's advantages over C—including its significantly better faculty and graduate students and significantly greater prestige—were such that S was convinced that, all things considered, having a job at A would be better than having a job at C.

Importantly, S had not changed his attitudes or preferences over the years. Nor did he regret his previous decisions. He remained convinced that, all things considered, B *was* a better job for him than A, and C *was* a better job for him than B. But he *didn't* believe that C was a better job for him than A. To the contrary, he thought that it was worse, and he was acutely aware that had he been without any job, and been offered all three jobs at once, he would be in a deep practical quandary regarding which option to choose. The problem, of course, is that he didn't believe the alternatives were equally good or on a par, and hence wasn't indifferent between the three options. Rather, he felt with great conviction that *any* choice he made in such circumstances would be choosing an option that was *clearly worse* than another available option.

Here is one last example. Some people are convinced that when given the choice between a small, expensive house in the city and a larger, cheaper house in the outskirts, the latter would be the better alternative for them and their family. They are also convinced that when given the choice between a

---

[52] This example was given to me by Alan Hájek regarding a friend of his. I suspect variations of this example apply to many people and their career paths.

larger, cheaper house in the outskirts and an even larger, more expensive house farther out, the latter would be the better alternative. But, when considering the choice between the small, expensive house in the city and the largest, most expensive house farthest out, they are convinced that the former alternative would be better. Accordingly, they find themselves facing a serious practical dilemma, where for each option, another seems better.

In lecturing about these topics over the years, I have had numerous people relate similar examples from their own lives. The phenomenon in question is quite pervasive. Many people have felt, often quite strongly, that they have been caught in a practical dilemma where, *even after full and careful reflection*, each of several choices was clearly better than another, such that there was an intransitive ranking of alternatives.

In the past, many philosophers and others have felt compelled to contend that such preferences were necessarily misinformed, muddleheaded, inconsistent, and/or irrational. As noted previously, the reaction of many economists to such intransitive preferences was to scornfully insist that people must "get their preferences in order"! Moreover, there is no shortage of psychological explanations as to why people might be led astray in certain choice situations. For example, it is arguable that for certain choices certain characteristics are particularly salient, for other choices other characteristics are particularly salient, and that we naturally attend to the more salient features in each choice situation, giving them more weight than they deserve relative to other less salient, but still relevant and significant, features which we undervalue or ignore entirely. Naturally, this can result in inconsistent and mistaken intransitive judgments. An alternative psychological explanation suggests that given the actual conditions of choice under uncertainty, it might be useful, and therefore rational, to adopt "simplification procedures...which approximate one's 'true preference' very well," and hence which *usually* serve one in good stead, but occasionally lead to intransitivities.[53] The heuristics discussed in chapter 9, of similarity-based decision procedures and majority-rule reasoning applied to different factors, are explanations of this ilk.

I believe the reactions just noted to intransitive judgments are often wholly appropriate. No doubt some intransitive judgments *are* muddleheaded, the result of misinformation, or simply irrational. No doubt in some cases people *should* get their preferences in order. And no doubt some intransitive judgments *do* result from heuristics that may serve us in good stead in many cases, but lead us astray in others. Accordingly, I wouldn't be surprised if someone could offer deflationary analyses of each of the particular cases noted earlier, casting doubt on the plausibility of the judgments in question. But, as we have

---

[53] This view was originally expressed by, and the quoted phrase comes from, Amos Tversky's classic article, "Intransitivity of Preferences," *Psychological Review* 76 (1969): 31–48.

seen throughout this work, it is far from obvious that *all* of our intransitive judgments can be plausibly dismissed or "explained away" in this way.

If the relevance or significance of the factors for comparing different outcomes really *can* vary depending on the alternatives being compared, then it will be perfectly rational for people to have intransitive preferences across those sets of alternatives. Indeed, such preferences may be rationally required. Thus, one advantage to rejecting the Internal Aspects View is that doing so may enable us to *make sense* of the apparently inconsistent attitudes and judgments of a lot of (seemingly) sensible, well-informed, clear-thinking, and rational people. Moreover, importantly, it does so in a plausible straightforward way that neither deflates nor explains away the attitudes or judgments in question. Indeed, if an Essentially Comparative View is correct, people sometimes have intransitive judgments because there is, in fact, *good reason* for them both to make and to keep such judgments.[54]

There is another advantage to rejecting the Internal Aspects View that I'll mention but not pursue. Many economists, philosophers, and others have been deeply troubled by Arrow's Impossibility Theorem, according to which, roughly, there can be no decision procedure for arriving at a social ordering among alternatives which simultaneously satisfies certain very plausible assumptions. But Arrow's Theorem and many of its offshoots invoke an Independence of Irrelevant Alternatives Principle, and while Arrow's version of such a principle differs from the one I have presented in this work, there is good reason to believe that such a principle should be rejected, or in any event cannot play the role that Arrow assigns it, if one rejects the Internal Aspects View in favor of something like an Essentially Comparative View. Hence, by rejecting the Internal Aspects View in favor of an Essentially Comparative View, one is in a position to reject Arrow's Theorem and its corollaries.

To be sure, rejecting the Internal Aspects View and the Independence of Irrelevant Alternatives Principle raises new and significant problems regarding decision procedures for both individual and social orderings and, correspondingly, for both individual and collective rationality. Indeed, far from minimizing this fact, part of this book's point is to illustrate the full extent to which this is so. Still, at least the issues, insights, and methods applicable to the individual realm need no longer seem so distinct, much less necessarily irrelevant, to those of the social, or collective, realm. Taking seriously the idea that one should reject the Internal Aspects View may open whole new avenues to explore regarding the rationality of both individual and collective orderings and choices. With luck, some of these avenues will prove to be profoundly rewarding.

---

[54] Of course, this is not the same as saying that there is always good reason to *act* on such judgments, for the reasons given elsewhere in this book.

In sum, in addition to the direct reasons for believing that some important ideals may be essentially comparative, and that some factors may be limited in scope, there may be certain advantages to rejecting the Internal Aspects View. Doing so may enable us to explain what otherwise looks to be nonsensical or inconsistent preferences or behaviors of seemingly rational individuals, and it may open up new ways of thinking about individual and collective orderings.

*****

In this chapter, we have seen that certain ideals that people attach great value to are essentially comparative. This includes the most plausible version of maximin, the Pareto Principle, and a plausible version of utility. More generally, we saw that in many contexts, even if not all, there is great plausibility to a Narrow Person-Affecting View. We also saw that it is plausible to believe that some moral ideals are limited in scope, such that they are relevant and significant for comparing certain alternatives but not others; as we saw, this was Rawls's own view about maximin and his two principles of justice. Each of these positions raises the specter that "all-things-considered better than" (in my wide reason-implying sense) may be a nontransitive relation. Thus, it appears that we can preserve the transitivity of "all-things-considered better than" only by sacrificing our allegiance to these positions. This is a serious cost.

Together, this chapter and the preceding one addressed a central question for practical reasoning. That question concerns the nature of moral ideals, specifically, whether all moral ideals must be understood in accordance with the Internal Aspects View, or whether at least some moral ideals should be understood in accordance with the Essentially Comparative View. I argued that both positions have great intuitive plausibility, but that both also have deeply implausible implications. The main aim of these chapters was to articulate the positions in question, to explore how they might be combined with different combinations of views, some of which may stand or fall together, and to illuminate some of the implications, including both benefits and costs, of the different combinations of views. As with much of the rest of this book, perhaps the main lesson of these chapters is that some of our deepest and most plausible beliefs regarding the nature of the good, moral ideals, and practical reasoning are fundamentally incompatible.

13

Juggling to Preserve Transitivity

I have presented numerous arguments illustrating that a number of beliefs that people hold about ideals and the nature of the good are incompatible. Among these beliefs are various Axioms of Transitivity, which hold that "equally as good as," "at least as good as," and "all-things-considered better than" are transitive relations. Given the central role that the Axioms of Transitivity play in practical reasoning, including the role that they play in Expected Value Theory, and that their analogues play in Expected Utility Theory, many suggestions have been made as to how we might preserve the Axioms of Transitivity even in the face of my various arguments. In this chapter, I shall consider the plausibility and implications of these suggestions. In doing this, I will focus on the view that "all-things-considered better than" is a transitive relation and, for simplicity, refer to that view as the *Axiom of Transitivity* (here, as throughout, I am interpreting this view as involving my wide reason-implying sense of "all-things-considered better than").

13.1 Fine-Grained Solutions

In section 7.5, I presented a response to apparent instances of intransitivity which has, I think, great plausibility. This response is to look for finer-grained individuations of alternatives in the face of apparent counterexamples to the Axiom of Transitivity. In particular, whenever one confronts a case where it appears that there are *three* alternatives, A, B, and C, such that, all things considered, A is better than B, and B is better than C, but A is not better than C, then, if each of the judgments is defensible, there are really always at least *four* alternatives in play, for example, A, B, C, and A', such that the relations that *really* obtain are that, all things considered, A is better than B, and B is better than C, but A' is not better than C. But, of course, as long as A and A' are *different* alternatives, the three "defensible" relations are perfectly compatible with the Axiom of Transitivity; hence, determining that such relations obtain provides one with no reason for even doubting, much less rejecting, the Axiom of Transitivity.

I believe that there are certain cases where an appeal to a fine-grained individuation of alternatives to avoid an apparent counterexample to the Axiom of Transitivity is not only plausible, but is surely *correct*. That is, there are some apparent counterexamples to the Axiom of Transitivity which are, indeed, *only* "apparent," and which are properly understood and resolved by recognizing that they mistakenly treat at least two *distinct* alternatives as if they were a *single* alternative.[1] However, while looking for finer-grained individuations of alternatives can be a powerful and effective weapon in the arsenal of those seeking to defend the Axiom of Transitivity against *some* apparent counterexamples, as a *general* strategy for dealing with *all* of the cases that put pressure on the Axiom of Transitivity, I think the fine-grained approach is problematic.

Consider, for example, the apparent counterexample to transitivity offered by Derek Parfit's Mere Addition Paradox, represented in diagram 13.1.A.[2]

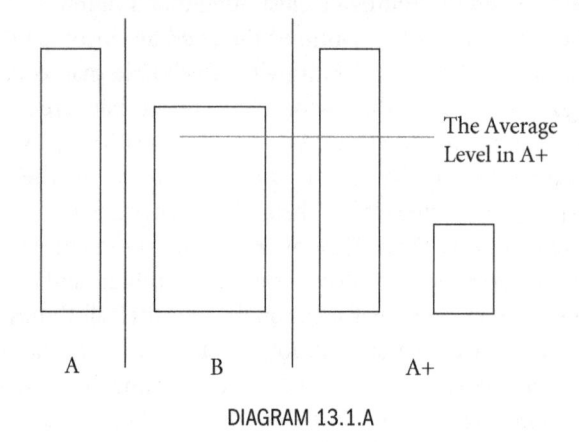

DIAGRAM 13.1.A

According to Parfit, most believe that, all things considered, A is better than B, and B is better than $A+$, but A is not better than $A+$. Assuming that they agree about the plausibility of the judgments in question, advocates of the fine-grained solution to apparent counterexamples to the Axiom of Transitivity will respond by insisting that then there really must be *different* alternatives involved in Parfit's Mere Addition Paradox, corresponding to the judgments in question. For example, they might suggest that in diagram 13.1.A, $A+$ actually represents two *distinct* alternatives, $A+'$ and $A+''$; where, say, $A+'$ is the alternative we have when $A+$ is compared with B, while $A+''$ is the alternative we have when $A+$ is compared with A. In that case, there would be nothing particularly puzzling about the fact that A seems better than B, and B seems better

---

[1] For an appreciation of the power and appeal of such a strategy, and some examples where it is appropriately applied, see John Broome's *Weighing Goods* (Oxford: Basil Blackwell, 1991), especially sections 5.3 and 5.4.

[2] I discuss the Mere Addition Paradox in chapter 11; it is presented by Derek Parfit in chapter 19 of *Reasons and Persons* (Oxford: Oxford University Press, 1984).

than $A+$, but A does not seem better than $A+$, because what we *really* have is simply that A is better than B, and B better than $A+'$, but A is not better than $A+''$, and there is *no* incompatibility between *those* three claims and the Axiom of Transitivity, *on the assumption* that $A+'$ and $A+''$ are actually *different* alternatives.[3]

It is clear how the fine-grained solution would preserve transitivity in the face of Parfit's Mere Addition Paradox. But the question arises as to why we should *believe* the advocate of the fine-grained solution, when she insists that there really *must* be distinct alternatives underlying our judgments about the Mere Addition Paradox.

Recall section 11.4's point that there could be contexts in which it might make perfect sense to say, "I'll have strawberry ice cream, unless you have vanilla, in which case I'll have chocolate." This would make sense, I noted, in the context where the strawberry ice cream would have been made by *one* company if the vanilla were available, and a *different* company if the vanilla were not available, with my example's implicit assumption that the strawberry was of "high" quality if made by the one company, but of "low" quality if made by the other. In that case, the strawberry "alternative" would *in fact* clearly be a *different* alternative depending on whether or not vanilla ice cream was available.

But nothing like this appears to be the case in Parfit's example. $A+$ is composed of the *very same people* at the *very same levels* with, we presume, the *very same underlying properties and relations within A+*. In that context, there seems to be no plausible basis for the claim that *in fact A+* is *one* alternative, $A+'$, in comparison with B, but another, *different*, alternative, $A+''$, in comparison with A.[4] Similar remarks would apply if, instead, the advocate of the fine-grained approach tried to argue that it was really A that

---

[3] Some of Alastair Norcross's arguments that I discuss in appendix E can be interpreted in this way.

[4] Jake Ross agrees that it may be implausible to think that what alternative $A+$ is depends on to which alternative it is compared. But he suggests that there may be a more intelligible fine-grained view in the neighborhood. He writes: "Maybe $A+$ *resulting from a choice between A+ and A* is a different alternative from $A+$ *resulting from a choice between A+ and B*. Thus, while it doesn't seem that the identity of an alternative could depend on what we compare it to, it isn't altogether implausible that the identity of an alternative could depend on how it arose (in the sense that if, in one possible world, outcome X resulted from a choice between a certain set of options, and in another possible world outcome Y resulted from a choice between a different set of options, then X and Y cannot be the same outcome). After all, many people believe that origins are identity-defining for persons (there is no possible world in which I arose from a different sperm and egg), so why couldn't origins, and in particular the choice-situation of origin, be identifying for outcomes?" This is an interesting suggestion. Let me make three quick responses to it.

First, it isn't clear to me that the *way* in which origins make a difference for the identities of people is at all analogous to the way in which choice-situations determine which outcomes obtain. For example, if parents choose to produce a child from a particular sperm and ovum, S_1 and O_1, rather than a different sperm and ovum, S_2 and O_2, there would be *no* temptation to think that the identity of their future child would be *different* than it would have been had they instead chosen to produce a child from the particular sperm and ovum, S_1 and O_1, when given the *different* alternative of producing a child from the sperm and ovum S_3 and O_3. The *same* child would have been produced from the sperm and ovum S_1 and O_1, whether it was chosen in the face of *one* alternative child (the one that would have resulted from S_2 and O_2) or in the face of a different alternative child (the one that would have resulted from S_3 and O_3). So, origins are relevant to the identities of people *in a particular way*, due to the

corresponded to two distinct alternatives, A' and A'', or that it was really B that corresponded to two distinct alternatives, B' and B''.

To be sure, I argued previously that we can imagine alternatives whose abstract features *look* just like $A+$'s, where, despite their similar appearances, they really *do* represent significantly different alternatives. For example, we might regard an $A+$-like outcome as *one* alternative, say $A+'$, if, in comparison with Parfit's original A world, it involved *Mere Addition*, so that, in addition to the A group there was an extra group of people all of whom had lives worth living and who affected no one else, but as a significantly *different* alternative, $A+''$, if it involved the people in Parfit's original A world being at a much *lower* level, with an entirely different group being at the level of the people in Parfit's original A world. In that case, we might plausibly believe that the first $A+$-like alternative was *not* worse than A, but that the second $A+$-like alternative *was* worse than A.

But there are two points to note about this. First, this is *not* how Parfit describes his case. That is, in the Mere Addition Paradox, there is no basis for the claim that $A+$ is a different alternative in the way just described depending on whether we compare it with A or B. Second, and more important, to recognize that an $A+$-like world would be worse than A if its worse-off group included the same people as would be in A, but would not be worse than A if its better-off group included the same people as would be in A is to recognize that we need to abandon the Internal Aspects View.

---

metaphysics of people; there is no reason to believe that there is an analogous metaphysics of outcomes that would make choice-situations relevant to the identities of outcomes in the way that sperm and ovum are relevant to the identities of people. There *might* be, but in the absence of a story that Ross has not given us, I see no reason to think that this is so.

Second, even if the *identities* of outcomes are fixed by the choice-situations which give rise to them, that would not be enough, by itself, to help with the problem that the move to a fine-grained individuation of alternatives is supposed to help us with. Because, for the argument to work, there has to be a *morally relevant difference* between the alternative $A+$ that results from a choice between $A+$ and A, and the alternative $A+$ that results from a choice between $A+$ and B. On an Internal Aspects View, mere difference in the *identities* of two outcomes will be *irrelevant* to an assessment of how good those outcomes are. How good they are will depend solely on the internal features of those outcomes. So, as long as two outcomes have the same internal features, it doesn't matter whether or not one of them results from a choice involving A and the other results from a choice involving B—and hence it doesn't matter whether or not they are the same or different outcomes on the origin/choice account of the identity of outcomes—there will be no basis for assigning one outcome a given value in comparison with A, and the other outcome a different value in comparison with B; nor, for that matter, would there be any basis for assigning one outcome a given value in comparison with A, and the same outcome a different value in comparison with B, but that is what we need to make sense of our various judgments about how A, $A+$, and B compare. To get the morally relevant difference that we think obtains in comparing $A+$ with A, and $A+$ with B, we need to appeal to an Essentially Comparative View; mere difference in *identities* between an $A+$-like alternative that arose from a choice with A, and between an $A+$-like alternative that arose from a choice with B won't help on the Internal Aspects View.

Finally, I'll just note that even if one could defend a fine-grained individuation of outcomes in the way Ross proposes, it will face the problems I discuss later. Specifically, as we'll see, it may provide a way of preserving the transitivity of the "all-things-considered better than" relation, but at the cost of largely undermining its importance and helpfulness for the purposes of practical reasoning.

After all, as I have already argued, any plausible version of the Internal Aspects View will be combined with a view about impartiality that will require us to be neutral between any two outcomes which are exactly the same in all respects except for the actual identities of the different members of their better- and worse-off groups. But, of course, to abandon the Internal Aspects View is a move that raises most of the deep concerns that I have been addressing in this work. Thus, even if one could somehow successfully make out the claim that in Parfit's Mere Addition Paradox we should regard A+ as a *different* outcome depending on whether we compare it with A or B, which I doubt, this will ultimately prove to be a pyrrhic victory.

There is another worry about the resort to the fine-grained solution in the face of apparent counterexamples to the Axiom of Transitivity. However successful such a defense may be of transitivity as a *technical* feature of certain relations, it comes at a high cost. In particular, on such a view the *practical significance* of transitivity will be largely, if not wholly, lost. Let me note two reasons for saying this.

First, as noted previously, transitivity has been regarded as a practically desirable feature of individual preferences over competing alternatives, *in part* because intransitive preferences allow people to be money pumped. However, on the view in question, individuals could be still money pumped *even if they have perfectly transitive preferences*. With *intransitive* preferences, the money pump arises because one might pay to go from A to B, and B to C, only to pay again to return to A from C. On the fine-grained approach, one's *perfectly transitive* judgments might lead one to pay to go from A_1 to B, and B to C, and also from C to A_2. But, on the fine-grained approach, the position that is A_2 *when the alternative* is C in essence reverts to A_1 *when the alternative* is B. That is, A_2 becomes A_1 when one's alternative shifts from C to B. Hence, having paid to return to what is *technically* A_2, and *not* A_1, one will nevertheless *find oneself* in A_1 when reconsidering B. At that point, of course, one might again have reason to pay to go from A_1 to B, and B to C, and yet again from C to A_2. And so on. Thus, adopting a sufficiently fined-grained individuation of alternatives may, indeed, preserve the transitivity of our comparative judgments, but it will not protect us from one of the main reasons people have been worried about having intransitive comparative judgments.

Practically, we need to reject one of our comparative judgments, or refuse to act in accordance with one, whenever we face a money pump situation. But the move to a fine-grained individuation of alternatives is of *no help* guiding us in that decision. To the contrary, such a move *licenses* the theoretical conclusion that *each* of our comparative judgments might, in fact, be coherent and defensible, both individually and in conjunction with the others. Fortified with this theoretical result, our practical dilemma will be to try to make ourselves believe what we take to be false, or, if we are faced with a series of pairwise alternatives, to commit ourselves on at least some occasions to acting contrary to a belief that is normatively justifiable. As strategic and global reasoners, I think we are capable of acting in such ways.[5] Still, it is arguable that from a *practical* standpoint, someone with perfectly transitive comparative judgments over a set of fine-grained alternatives may be no better off than he would have been had his judgments been intransitive.

Second, and even more important, the fine-grained solution preserves transitivity in a way that eviscerates what is perhaps the central role that transitivity plays in everyday decision making. Transitivity isn't supposed to be just a *technically* nice, *logical* feature of certain relations; it is supposed to play a fundamental normative role in guiding practical decisions. In particular, transitivity is supposed to help us to choose when we are faced with an array of competing alternatives, by providing us with a straightforward and manageable way of winnowing down our alternatives.

Thus, faced with a complex decision ranging over an array of competing alternatives, transitivity is supposed to enable us to focus on just two options at a time, and proceed directly to the best option via a series of pairwise comparisons. Specifically, in choosing between any set of options—whether they involve products, careers, job candidates, or whatever—we can begin by focusing on just the first two options, and if the first option is worse than the second, the first is then removed from further consideration, while the second is then compared with the third. Similarly, the better of those options is then compared with the fourth, and so on. If one is lucky, and each pairwise comparison is clear, one can choose the best of n options with only $n-1$ comparisons. But note, this procedure—which is clear, systematic, and implicitly relied on throughout everyday decision making—*presupposes* transitivity, as there is no compelling reason to remove the first option from further consideration *if* it might be better than a later option that itself is better than the second. It is the assumption that "all-things-considered better than" is a transitive relation that rules out such a possibility, and that justifies such reasoning.

But this virtue of transitivity—which makes it such an effective and central tool of practical reasoning and which is, I suspect, the main reason we *care* so much about the Axiom of Transitivity—is basically lost if one adopts the fine-grained solution to the threat of intransitivity.[6] Let me explain.

Consider, for example, the set of options discussed in sections 7.2 and 7.3 between hiring White, Mexican American, and African American. On the fine-

---

[5] See section 6.6.

[6] Mikhail Valdman suggests a more cautious formulation of my present point. Instead of claiming that the virtue of transitivity in question is "basically lost" if one adopts the fine-grained solution, I should merely note that adopting the fine-grained solution leaves one in no better shape with respect to being able to confidently winnow down one's choices on the basis of pairwise comparisons than if one had simply abandoned transitivity. Valdman wants to leave open the possibility that in some contexts, at least, it might be "reasonable" to winnow down one's choices on the basis of pairwise comparisons even if one wasn't *logically entitled* to do so given the failure of the transitivity of "better than" or the adoption of the fine-grained solution given the threat of such failure.

grained approach, we would no longer be able to choose between such options by considering them two at a time. In particular, we could not, for example, compare White with Mexican American, correctly decide that it would be better to hire White given those options, and thus remove the hiring of Mexican American from further consideration, enabling us to focus our attention on the narrower choice of hiring either White or African American. This is because, on a fine-grained approach, we have to recognize that the hiring of White *when the alternative is Mexican American*, is a *different alternative* than the hiring of White *when the alternative is African American*; the hiring of Mexican American *when the alternative is White* is a *different alternative* than the hiring of Mexican American *when the alternative is African American*; and similarly, the hiring of African American *when the alternative is White* is a *different alternative* than the hiring of African American *when the alternative is Mexican American*.

Correspondingly, all the pairwise comparison of White and Mexican American would enable us to do is to remove the hiring of Mexican American *when the alternative is White* from consideration, but it would decidedly *not* settle the issue of whether we should still, perhaps, hire Mexican American! After all, as we've seen, on the fine-grained approach, it might remain true that we should hire Mexican American rather than African American, and African American rather than White. Hence, our pairwise comparison of the different alternatives would, by itself, have brought us no closer to knowing what to do if we faced the different options. Thus, for all we know, we should *still* end up hiring Mexican American, even if we have *rightly* judged that given the choice between White and Mexican American, it would be better to hire White.

This points to the deepest problem about the fine-grained "solution" to the threat of intransitivity. As noted, transitivity is a practically useful feature of the "all-things-considered better than" relation precisely because it offers us, or so we thought, a straightforward decision procedure for narrowing our options and ultimately deciding among a multitude of alternatives via a series of focused pairwise comparisons. But, on the fine-grained approach, it is not clear what role, if any, pairwise comparisons would even be able to play in guiding our decisions. After all, by the *logic* of the fine-grained approach, we couldn't yet rule out the hiring of White as the best alternative *even if we knew* that hiring White would be worse than hiring African American, if those were the only alternatives *and* that hiring White would be worse than hiring Mexican American, if those were the only alternatives. This is because, on the fine-grained approach, the alternative of hiring White when one has *two* other options—namely, to hire either African American *or* Mexican American—is a *different* alternative than hiring White when one has only one other option. That is, the alternative of hiring White rather than either African American *or* Mexican American is a *different* alternative than *both* the alternative of hiring White when the alternative is hiring African American *and* the alternative of hiring White when the alternative is hiring Mexican American. Moreover, importantly, the view recognizes that *different* factors may be relevant for assessing different alternatives. Thus, a factor that might be relevant and significant and tell us to hire White when faced with *both* other options might not be relevant and significant, and so give us no reason to hire White, when faced with either option alone.

The depth of this problem may not be apparent when one compares a simple three-option case—where it might seem that one could reasonably keep all of the options in mind, simultaneously, and perhaps accurately recognize what factors are relevant when all three options are present. But how are we to decide in more complicated situations—where, for example, we must choose between 10 options, or perhaps the 200 options that we typically face when reading dossiers for a philosophy job? On the "old" model, we had a systematic way of wading through 200 dossiers via a series of 199 pairwise comparisons. But this model assumed both the transitivity of the "all-things-considered better than" relation and a courser delineation of alternatives, according to which the nature and value of each alternative remained the same regardless of the other alternatives with which it was compared.[7] But on the fine-grained approach, it is not clear how we should proceed.

Must we have *each* alternative clearly in mind at once? This would surely be practically impossible. Must we compare each alternative with every other, and see who "wins" the most against each of the other alternatives? This, too, would be practically impossible, requiring 19,900 separate pairwise comparisons![8] Moreover, for the reasons just indicated, it isn't even clear that the resulting information would be *relevant* to the decision we actually face. Indeed, on the fine-grained approach there is a serious question as to what criteria *will* be relevant when all the alternatives are considered at once. Will it be the *union* of all the factors that would be relevant if each alternative was compared separately with all the others? Will it be the *intersection* of those factors? Might there be *entirely new* factors that are relevant when a multitude of options are

---

[7] Roger Crisp has claimed, in correspondence, that in fact we wouldn't wade through a list of 200 dossiers via a series of 199 pairwise comparisons. We would simply look at each candidate, one at a time, and arrive at a judgment as to how good of a candidate he or she was, taking account of his or her ethnicity if that was appropriate. But this view assumes that we can give at least a rough score representing how good each candidate is based solely on that candidate's qualifications in a way that is independent of how he or she compares to any other candidates; hence this view is analogous to the one I discuss in presuming that the nature and value of each alternative remains the same whether or not it is compared with any other alternatives.

On Crisp's view, instead of making 199 separate *pairwise* comparisons, we would make 200 separate *individual* evaluations. But whether or not we consciously compared the top candidate with each subsequent candidate after each separate individual evaluation, Crisp's view will be analogous to the one I discuss in that after each evaluation of each new candidate, there will be one or more candidates with the top ranking, and any other candidates will be out of the running. However, as should be clear by now, if "all-things-considered better than" *weren't* a transitive relation, there would be no reason to believe that a stable and reliable ordering of alternatives could be reached in the manner Crisp envisages. Ultimately, both Crisp's view and the one suggested in the text implicitly rely on the same conception of moral ideals for their plausibility, namely, the Internal Aspects View that I discussed in chapter 11.

[8] The formula for determining the number of distinct pairwise comparisons in a group of n alternatives is $(n/2) \times (n - 1)$; so for a group of 200 applicants, there would be $(200/2) \times (200 - 1) = (100) \times (199) = 19,900$ pairwise comparisons.

available that are irrelevant when pairwise comparisons are made? And, if so, how are we to recognize these, and assess their legitimacy and strength?

Perhaps reasonable answers to these questions will be forthcoming. I can't rule out that possibility. But what seems clear is that perhaps the key feature that makes the transitivity of "better than" so fundamentally important for practical reasoning—namely, that it provides a straightforward, systematic method of narrowing our choices and deciding on the best of our options on the basis of a series of pairwise comparisons, where each alternative is fixed independently of the other alternatives with which it is compared, and hence can be assessed, and rejected, on the basis of a single pairwise comparison—is lost once one adopts the fine-grained solution to the threat of intransitivity. Thus, the fine-grained solution is a way of preserving and defending transitivity, but at the cost of the *reason* transitivity is so hugely important for practical reasoning. It is a high cost, indeed.

Let me be clear. The advocate of the fine-grained solution is *no worse off* than someone who rejects the transitivity of the "all-things-considered better than" relation (in my wide reason-implying sense) altogether. Indeed, the objections I have been noting are the very objections that should be raised to those who advocate the latter position. And, as should be clear, they are very serious objections, and give one powerful practical reason to try to defend transitivity against the various threats that might be raised against it. But one shouldn't lose sight of the *reason* it is so important to defend the transitivity of "better than" for the sake of practical reasoning.[9]

Some "cures" leave a patient no better off than she would have been had she not been cured of her disease. I have suggested that this is basically true of the fine-grained alternatives "solution" to the threat of intransitivity. One must seek another solution to that threat, if one wants to both defend the transitivity of "all-things-considered better than" (in my wide reason-implying sense) and to preserve its significance for practical reasoning.

13.2 The Time Trade-off Method

In "Heuristics and Biases in a Purported Counterexample to the Acyclicity of 'Better Than,'"[10] Alex Voorhoeve suggests that we can preserve the Axiom of

---

[9] Oscar Horta suggests that my discussion here is perhaps misleading. The reason we care about the Axiom of Transitivity so much *isn't* just because it is so useful, practically, in winnowing down our options, but because an entire conception of the good hangs in the balance depending on whether or not transitivity obtains, and with it, perhaps, the entire consequentialist approach to thinking about practical reasoning. This comment is fair and important, and I couldn't agree more (see chapter 14). But my point is that some ways of preserving the Internal Aspects View and the possibility of ranking outcomes will prove to be pyrrhic victories, if they do not help us to eliminate or decide between different alternatives that we face. It is dubious what we gain by preserving the possibility of ranking outcomes, if the many rankings we arrive at can't effectively guide our practical deliberations. I have been suggesting that this is the state we may find ourselves in if we adopt the fine-grained solution for preserving the Axiom of Transitivity.

[10] *Politics, Philosophy, and Economics* 7 (2008): 285–99.

Transitivity in the face of my Spectrum Arguments, if we evaluate the different alternatives of my spectrums by employing a version of the *Time Trade-off Method* that is frequently used in the health care literature to evaluate the value of health states. Voorhoeve explicates the Time Trade-off Method and shows how he would appeal to it in order to arrive at a transitive ranking of the various alternatives in my pain spectrum, by suggesting that we evaluate each painful episode, E_i, of my pain spectrum as follows:

> Imagine that you have two possible futures. The first is to live for precisely another T years in good health and without experiencing any significant episode of pain except for the fact that, starting tomorrow, you will have to experience episode E_i.[11] The second is to live for time T_i^* in good health and without having to experience E_i or any other significant episode of pain. How long would T_i^* have to be to render you indifferent between these two futures?[12] You may refuse to answer if you feel unable to come up with an answer you regard as even somewhat reliable.[13]

Voorhoeve rightly observes, and regards it as a positive feature of this approach, that "it requires us to engage in a global evaluation of the badness of each episode separately."[14]

I readily agree that we could adopt such an approach, and that if we did it would generate consistent, transitive rankings of my various spectrum alternatives. The rankings might be severely incomplete—in virtue of the last clause that allows one to make no judgments in cases where one is not confident of the reliability of one's judgment—but any rankings that emerged from such a process *would* be transitive. However, the *important* question is whether we think that the transitive rankings that would emerge from such a process would accurately reflect the *all-things-considered* judgments that *should* be made regarding how all the different alternatives *compare* with each other.

At the end of chapter 7, and again in chapters 11 and 12, I noted that, ultimately, the key question in this area concerns the nature of ideals. As we have seen, on an *Internal Aspects View*, how good an outcome is will depend *solely* on the outcome's internal features. However, on an *Essentially Comparative View*, how good an outcome is may depend on the alternative with which it is compared; so, while there may, in a sense, be a fact of the matter

---

[11] Voorhoeve includes a note here, his note 23, stating, "Period T must be at least as long as the duration of the pain in E_{MILD}." ("Heuristics and Biases," 21).

[12] Voorhoeve includes another note here, his note 24, which reads, "As we assumed at the outset, though enduring episode E_i is bad, living for period T and having to endure episode E_i during some part of that period T is better than dying immediately, so that T_i^* will be larger than 0" ("Heuristics and Biases," 21).

[13] "Heuristics and Biases," 14–15.

[14] "Heuristics and Biases," 15.

about how good an outcome is considered just by itself, and this may be based solely on the outcome's internal features, that fact may have no special privileged status. Thus, as we have seen, on an Essentially Comparative View, an outcome may have one value when considered by itself, another value when compared with another outcome, yet another value when compared with several other outcomes, and so on.

Accordingly, while the Time Trade-off Method *will* give us a transitive ranking of outcomes based on a "global evaluation of the badness of each episode [considered] separately," that ranking won't *settle* the issue of how the different pain episodes compare all things considered, *if* the Essentially Comparative View is correct.

Following the Time Trade-off Method, I might arrive at a reliable "score" for how bad I thought each member of my pain spectrum was considered *just by itself*. Perhaps I would implicitly invoke an additive-aggregationist approach for each member, or an anti-additive-aggregationist approach for each member. Or perhaps I would invoke one approach for some members, the other for other members, and still more complicated approaches for the other members. It doesn't matter. As long as each member gets a *single* score, *however* I arrive at it, I could construct a transitive ranking of the spectrum using those scores. But, *unless an Internal Aspects View is correct*, this won't give me an all-things-considered ranking (in my wide reason-implying sense) of the different alternatives *in comparison with each other*.

In this book, I have argued that an additive-aggregationist approach seems relevant when comparing two years of intense torture with four years of slightly less intense torture, but that an anti-additive-aggregationist approach seems relevant when comparing two years of torture with countless years of one extra mosquito bite per month. The Time Trade-off Method simply ignores the possibility that this may be right. *If* an Essentially Comparative View is correct—if the messy truth about our complex notion of morality is that the relevance or significance of the factors for assessing an alternative can vary depending on the alternatives with which it is compared—then the Time Trade-off Method has no hope of capturing the truth about morality, and Voorhoeve's suggestion that we can arrive at transitive rankings of my spectrums' alternatives by following such a method, though correct, should be ignored. We want to "preserve" the Axiom of Transitivity if and only if it is actually a feature of the normative domain; we don't want to *impose* the Axiom of Transitivity *on* the normative domain, if it is not actually a feature *of* that domain.

I submit, then, that while we may legitimately appeal to a Time Trade-off Method once we've established that an Internal Aspects View is correct, we cannot appeal to such a view to establish that such a view *is* correct. For in the absence of an independent argument that the Internal Aspects View is correct, appealing to the Time Trade-off Method simply begs the question against the Essentially Comparative View and the many considerations supporting it.

13.3 A Sports Analogy

There is another approach one might adopt in response to our challenges to the Axiom of Transitivity. Moreover, this approach may seem especially promising, as it proposes a model for assessing outcomes that is compatible with an Essentially Comparative View while at the same time preserving the Axiom of Transitivity. Let me present this approach with an analogy from sports.

In baseball, it is perfectly possible that the first-place team consistently beats the second-place team, which consistently beats the third-place team, which consistently beats the first-place team. Still, most do not think that "better than" is intransitive regarding baseball teams. Instead, there is general agreement that the better of two teams is the one that wins the most games against *all* of the other teams during the season.[15] Thus, for baseball teams, "all-things-considered better than" remains transitive, notwithstanding the intransitivity of "consistently beats," for if A has more total wins than B, and B more than C, A will have more than C, regardless of their team records against each other.

One might apply a similar model to the judgments we've been discussing. On such a model, which I'll call the *Sports Analogy*, how two outcomes compare *all things considered* will be a function both of how they compare to each other *and* how they compare to other outcomes.

On the Sports Analogy, then, one can accept the Essentially Comparative View, and hence grant that in terms of the relevance and significance of the factors for making each *particular* pairwise comparison, it could be the case that A is better than B, and B is better than C, yet C is better than A. Still, one could deny that these particular pairwise judgments are "all things considered," and hence deny that the "all-things-considered better than" relation (in my wide reason-implying sense) is nontransitive. Specifically, on this view, how A and B each compare to C will, in fact, be relevant to how A and B *themselves* compare, all things considered.

The position sketched has obvious attractions. But is the Sports Analogy ultimately plausible and helpful? In baseball, there is a small, fixed, conventionally agreed upon set of alternatives with which each team is to be compared, namely, the other teams currently in the league. The situation is otherwise regarding most questions of all-things-considered better than, and this raises both practical and theoretical problems.

Consider, again, the simple case of job applications, introduced in section 13.1. As we saw in section 13.1, on the old, standard way of judging candidates, if the first candidate was better than the second considering each of the factors

---

[15] Of course, this is not to deny that a die-hard fan will often insist that his is *really* the best team, even if it didn't win the most games! Nor is it to deny that in *some* cases there might even be general agreement that the best team wasn't the one that won the most games; perhaps it was the victim of terribly bad luck, egregiously poor umpiring, or crippling injuries. For our purposes, we can ignore such complications.

relevant to comparing them directly, the first would be regarded as better all things considered, and the second could be removed from further consideration. Proceeding in this way, if there were *n* applicants for the job, one would theoretically only need to make *n* − 1 judgments to determine the best candidate.

On the Sports Analogy, to know how two candidates compare *all things considered* it is not sufficient to know how they compare directly; one must *also* know how they compare to *each* of the other candidates. So, to determine the best candidate among *n* applicants, each applicant must be compared to every other. As noted in section 13.1, this would require (*n*/2) × (*n* − 1) separate comparisons. Thus, as we saw in section 13.1, while on the old way a search committee that is swamped with 200 applications for a single job "only" has to make a "mere" 199 separate comparisons, on the Sports Analogy, 19,900 separate comparisons would be required to determine the best candidate! The practical impossibility of this will be evident to everyone who has ever served on a search committee.

Recall our earlier claims about the *significance* of the Axiom of Transitivity for practical reasoning. One reason we *care* so much about the transitivity of better than is because of the crucially important role that it plays in *simplifying* our decision procedure. Instead of having to compare each alternative with every other, or somehow keep and assess all of a large number of alternatives in our heads all at once, we can clearly focus on just *two* alternatives at a time, carefully determine which is better, and then remove the worse one from further consideration. Moreover, often we can do this without having to determine, in advance, exactly how much each of the various morally relevant factors matters relative to each other. So, I might be able to determine that *A* is determinately better than *B*, without actually having determined, or even being able to determine, exactly how good *A* and *B* are. In this way, we can, in principle, arrive at a final all-things-considered judgment in a clear, straightforward manner involving the minimal task of making sure that we compare each alternative with but *one* other alternative *once*. This makes the transitivity of better than an enormously powerful and efficient tool for the purposes of practical reasoning. But, on the Sports Analogy, all of the power and efficiency of that tool is lost. Like the fine-grained approach, the Sports Analogy preserves the Axiom of Transitivity, but at the cost of undermining its usefulness for practical reasoning.

There is a further problem exacerbating the one just noted. It may be illustrated as follows. Suppose three baseball teams were up for sale. In assessing which team to buy, one would definitely *not* restrict one's attention to how the available teams fared against each other in direct competition. For example, it *might* be that while *A* consistently lost to *B* and *C*, *A* was the very best team in the league, while *B* and *C* were the two worst.[16] Instead, one would take into

---

[16] Most sports fans are aware of the common phenomenon of a last-place team beating a first-place team more often than their records would lead one to expect. Often, this is because the last-place team really "gets up" for playing the first-place team, while the first-place team is too complacent when

consideration how each team fared against *all* of the other teams, *including all of the teams that were not on the market*. The point has obvious and important implications for applying the Sports Analogy to the normative domain.

Consider again the apparently simple case of selecting the best job candidate, say, for a position in teaching. On the standard way of thinking, it is sufficient to compare the credentials of the applicants *themselves* to determine the best applicant. On the Sports Analogy, this is no longer plausible. To the contrary, one would need to compare each applicant not only with the other actual applicants, but also with the countless other teachers or people who would be qualified to teach who have not applied! But, of course, in the real world we could never do this.

Indeed, the problem may be even worse in the moral realm. In baseball, it makes perfect sense to try to buy the best of all the *actual* teams, since your aim, presumably, is to win a championship, and that will be determined by which team, in fact, wins the most games against the other actual teams in the league. But in the moral realm, if I am really interested in bringing about the *best* outcome all things considered, why should I restrict my comparisons to other *actual* alternatives? Wouldn't the *best* alternative be the one that was best in comparison with *all* other *possible* alternatives, whether or not we might ever actually face them? But, of course, if the Sports Analogy required us to compare each alternative with every other possible alternative, it would be practically impossible to follow, and at that point the notion of "all-things-considered better than" would have completely lost its relevance to practical reasoning.

There is another problem with the Sports Analogy. In baseball, there is basically one criterion employed in comparing teams with other teams, the criterion of wins and losses. Whether we are comparing A with B, B with C, A with C, or A with B and C, our criterion remains the same, namely, who won the most games, overall. But what drives us to consider the Sports Analogy in the first place, in thinking about the notion of "all-things-considered better than," are the problems that arise on an Essentially Comparative View. But, surely, on such a view, even if we *could* successfully compare each alternative with every other actual or possible alternative, there is no particular reason to believe that whichever alternative had the most "wins" in terms of all the pairwise comparisons was necessarily the *best* alternative all things considered.

One reason for this was given in chapter 9's discussion of the shortcomings of majority-rule reasoning. If A just *barely* "won" 1,000 pairwise comparisons, while B "won" 950 pairwise comparisons by a *considerable* margin in each case, then surely it is possible that B would actually be *better* than A, all things considered, and we should reject the ranking generated by the Sports Analogy.

A second deeper, and much more problematic, reason is this. On an Essentially Comparative View, we believe that different factors may be relevant or have

---

playing the last-place team; but sometimes it is due, in part, to the particular "matchups" between the two teams, so that even when the first-place team isn't complacent, it still loses to that particular last-place team.

different significance for assessing an alternative, depending on with which alternatives it is compared. But, as noted in section 13.1, this opens the possibility that the relevance and significance of the factors for comparing three alternatives *together* might *differ* from the relevance and significance of the factors for comparing any two alternatives. So, even if we *knew* how each *pair* of alternatives was ranked according to all of the factors that were relevant and significant for making pairwise comparisons, there is no reason to believe that we could derive the correct ranking of all three alternatives, considered together, from such information alone. The point, of course, is that the relevant factors for making *pairwise* comparisons might not even be relevant for making three-way comparisons, and even if they were relevant they might not have the same significance, given that *other* factors might be relevant and significant for making three-way comparisons that were not relevant or significant for making pairwise comparisons. And, of course, the same might be true, mutatis mutandis, of four-way comparisons, five-way comparisons, and so on. Hence, once we accept an Essentially Comparative View, it is an open question what different factors might come into play in ranking different sets of alternatives, and there is certainly no reason, in advance, to suppose that only those factors that come into play in making pairwise comparisons will be relevant.

This, of course, raises worries about the Sports Analogy. But it also raises much deeper worries about how we determine the correct set of morally relevant factors and their significance for assessing different sets of alternatives, once we abandon the Internal Aspects View.

One might alter the Sports Analogy to try to address some of the problems it faces. Perhaps, for example, one might divide alternatives into different classes, and one might try to develop an argument showing that instead of comparing each alternative with every other, it is sufficient to compare a "representative" alternative from each class with a "representative" alternative from every other class, and then pick the best alternative from the class with the "winning" representative alternative. If one could do this, that would help address some of the foregoing concerns, though not others. Alternatively, one might simply abandon the Sports Analogy and pursue some other way of reconciling the Essentially Comparative View with the Axiom of Transitivity. However, either way, I think one faces an unavoidable problem of which the shortcomings of the Sports Analogy are symptomatic. I shall specify this problem in section 13.5.

13.4 Reflective Equilibrium

John Rawls describes a process whereby moral theorists might try to achieve a state of *reflective equilibrium*, by moving back and forth between different kinds and levels of pre- and posttheoretical intuitions, judgments, arguments, and theories, in order to arrive at a set of firm considered judgments that does the best job, overall, of capturing and illuminating what we ultimately take to be the truth about the moral domain.[17] In seeking a state of reflective equilibrium, there is a constant, ongoing process of revision, pruning, adjustment, reevaluation, and even, if necessary, reconceptualization, taking place at all levels of our thinking, in order to arrive at a stable view that does the best overall job of organizing, accommodating, illuminating, and, if possible, justifying our moral beliefs.

So, to take a well-known example, one might have pretheoretical intuitions, or judgments, at the level of particular cases, including, say, the judgment that it would be wrong to tell the Nazis where your best friend is hiding if you knew that the Nazis would kill her; one might also have pretheoretical intuitions, or judgments, at the level of general moral rules, including, say, the judgment that it is always wrong to tell a lie. In order to arrive at a state of reflective equilibrium with respect to one's overall moral judgments and beliefs, one has to find a way to resolve the tension or inconsistency between one's pretheoretical intuitions or judgments at the different levels. In this case, one presumably has to revise the particular judgment that one should lie to the Nazis, or one has to modify the general moral rule that it is always wrong to tell a lie, or both. Similarly, one might have various pretheoretical intuitions or judgments about the desiderata or criteria that the correct moral theory should meet, and one may determine that Theory X does the best overall job of meeting those criteria. But, if some of Theory X's posttheoretical implications are wildly at odds with some of our considered moral judgments, then, in order to arrive at a state of reflective equilibrium, one has to either abandon or revise the considered moral judgments that conflict with Theory X, or one must abandon or revise Theory X, so that one can retain the considered judgments in question. Naturally, if one chooses the latter option, this may push or require one to abandon or revise some of one's pretheoretical intuitions or judgments concerning the desiderata or criteria that the correct moral theory should meet.

All this is commonplace, and will be familiar to most readers of this book. But notice, if one sticks with such a process long enough, constantly checking and rechecking the various intuitions, judgments, levels, theories, and implications of one's views, and making whatever revisions are necessary at each stage to achieve consistency among all the different levels and elements that are relevant to the moral domain, then one can be confident that the final moral view that one will end up with when one reaches the state of reflective equilibrium will accord with the Axiom of Transitivity. More specifically, and more carefully, *assuming* that the Axiom of Transitivity is *itself* a basic principle of consistency, then one can be confident that our final moral view will embody the Axiom of Transitivity, *if* we are guided by the constraint of consistency throughout the long process of jockeying back and forth between the

---

[17] See Rawls's *A Theory of Justice* (Cambridge, MA: Harvard University Press, 1971), 20–21, 48–51, 120, 432, 434, 579. Rawls presents his notion of reflective equilibrium in the context of his theory of justice, but one can extend the notion to theories of morality or practical reasoning more generally, as I do here.

various elements of our thinking in formulating and shaping our final view. Thus, if one assumes that the moral view one will arrive at when one finally reaches a state of reflective equilibrium is the correct moral view, or at least the best moral view that we can come up with, then one can be confident that the correct or best moral view will, indeed, respect the Axiom of Transitivity.[18]

The preceding reasoning sounds plausible and is fairly seductive, but it begs the question against many of this book's arguments and results.[19] I readily grant, of course, that if, in order to arrive at a state of reflective equilibrium, we engage in a process of jockeying back and forth between the various elements of our thinking long enough, and diligently enough, constantly revising and reformulating our various views in light of a consistency constraint that *includes* the Axiom of Transitivity, then we *will* eventually arrive at a final view that accords with that axiom. That is a logical truth. But, unfortunately, *unless* an Internal Aspects View is correct, such a process will *not* capture the messy truths with which our complex notions of morality and practical reasoning present us. Because if, as seems possible, an Essentially Comparative View is correct, then the Axiom of Transitivity *should* fail, or it should fail to apply across different alternatives to which we might have thought it should apply. In the latter case, as we have seen, we might preserve transitivity even on an Essentially Comparative View, by appealing to a fine-grained approach to individuating outcomes, or by appealing to something like the Sports Analogy for assessing outcomes, but doing so will effectively rob the Axiom of Transitivity of much of its practical relevance and significance.

In this book, I have argued that most people firmly believe that there can be various spectrums of alternatives 1, 2, 3,... $n - 1$, n, such that an additive-aggregationist approach seems relevant for comparing each pair of adjacent alternatives along the spectrums yielding the judgments that the first alternative is better than the second, the second is better than the third, the third is better than the fourth, and so on. I have also argued that most people firmly believe that for

---

[18] Ken Binmore and Alex Voorhoeve rely on a view of this kind in their article "Transitivity, the Sorites Paradox, and Similarity-Based Decision-Making," *Erkenntnis* 64 (2006): 101–14. In their article, Binmore and Voorhoeve propose a complicated method of making lots of different comparisons, and systematically revisiting and revising the various judgments we might come up with until we arrive at a consistent ordering, where, for Binmore and Voorhoeve, the consistency requirement guiding our decision procedure *requires* the Axiom of Transitivity. Having done so, they conclude "Transitivity" with the following remark:

> By a process of jockeying-making judgments under different presentations, checking their consistency, questioning inconsistent judgments and their grounds, discarding orderings resulting from undependable presentations and methods of evaluation in some cases, revising her judgments in others, again checking their consistency, etc.—she should ultimately arrive at an ordering that is consistent across different (non-misleading) presentations and that respects transitivity. (112)

[19] Derek Parfit has suggested, in correspondence, that "on your view, whichever view we take about the problems you discuss, there is some other better view." I'm not sure that my view *entails* this position, however, I confess that, given my arguments, it is hard to see how this bleak possibility can be ruled out.

some such spectrums 1 is not better than *n*, because for making *that* comparison an anti-additive-aggregationist approach seems appropriate. Thus, we know the following: any consistent transitive ranking of such spectrums' alternatives *requires* giving up at least one of the judgments that most people firmly believe. This will require showing that we ought *not* to use an additive-aggregationist approach for comparing some of the adjacent alternatives along the spectrum, or that we ought *not* to use an anti-additive-aggregationist approach for comparing alternatives at the opposite ends of the spectrum. To establish such claims, it is not enough to *insist* that we *force* ourselves to arrive at a transitive ranking of the alternatives by continually reexamining and revising our comparative judgments until they accord with the Axiom of Transitivity.

Similarly, I have argued that many people are strongly attracted to the Essentially Comparative View insofar as they care about maximin, the Pareto Principle, utility, and the Narrow Person-Affecting View, and also insofar as they recognize that many principles or ideals may be limited in scope, such that they may be relevant or significant for assessing certain alternatives in comparison with some alternatives but not others. But such views, which have great plausibility, imply that "all-things-considered better than" (in my wide reason-implying sense) is a nontransitive relation. Thus, one can't simply *insist* that all such views must be rejected because they are incompatible with the Axiom of Transitivity, without simply begging the question against such views.

The Axiom of Transitivity has great plausibility. And it is arguable that it is an important desideratum that we would like our final view of morality to meet, along with other desiderata, such as that morality should be universal, neutral with respect to people, places, and times, concerned with the amelioration of the condition of sentient beings, and so on. However, as we noted earlier, even the desiderata we would *like* our moral theory to meet are ultimately subject to revision, rejection, reevaluation, or reconceptualization as we engage in the difficult and sustained back-and-forth process of trying to arrive at a state of reflective equilibrium with respect to all of the various elements that are relevant to our moral beliefs.

In the quest for reflective equilibrium, some initial positions may be firmer, and hence more secure, than others. And the Axiom of Transitivity may be among these. But so may be our additive-aggregationist views, like chapter 2's First Standard View, chapter 4's Third Standard View, and chapter 5's View One; our anti-additive-aggregationist views, like chapter 2's Second Standard View, chapter 3's Disperse Additional Burdens View, chapter 4's Fourth Standard View, and chapter 5's View Three; as well as the various positions noted earlier in this chapter, and discussed in detail in chapter 12, that entail the Essentially Comparative View.

There are few, if any, sacred or fixed points around which the rest of the moral universe must be made to revolve. But even if there are some, I think this book has done enough to establish that, for all its power and appeal, the Axiom of Transitivity (understood as involving the wide reason-implying sense of "all-things-considered better than") is not among them.

I conclude that if the Axiom of Transitivity is to end up in our final, best picture of the moral and practical realms, as it might, it must *earn* its place in that picture, in full and fair competition with all of the other views with which it conflicts. The Axiom of Transitivity is neither self-evident nor self-validating, nor is it unassailable. Thus, it cannot be used to rule out, in advance, even the *possibility* that our final picture of the moral and practical domains might not include the Axiom of Transitivity within it. Like it or not, as we seek a state of reflective equilibrium, even the Axiom of Transitivity is in play.

13.5 Another Impossibility Result

As indicated in chapter 11, I believe that the Internal Aspects View can accommodate and account for both the Axiom of Transitivity and an especially plausible version of the Independence of Irrelevant Alternatives Principle. I also believe that both positions have enormous appeal, and that most people will continue to find them appealing, even if they reject the Internal Aspects View. Still, *if* one accepts an Essentially Comparative View (in the way that I mainly employ that view in chapter 11, according to which the factors that are relevant and significant for comparing an outcome's goodness relative to other outcomes can vary depending on the alternatives with which that outcome is compared), as we may, on reflection, decide we should, then there is good reason to believe that at least one of the two positions should be rejected.

This is because, on the Essentially Comparative View, A can be better than B, B better than C, and C better than A, in terms of the relevance and significance of the factors for making each pairwise comparison, considered separately. It follows that if, in accordance with the Independence of Irrelevant Alternatives Principle, how two outcomes compare *all things considered* depends solely on how *they* compare in terms of the relevance and significance of the factors for making *that* comparison, considered separately, then the judgments in question *will be* all things considered, and "all-things-considered better than" will not be a transitive relation. On the other hand, if "all-things-considered better than" *is* a transitive relation, then the judgments in question are not all things considered, contrary to what is implied by the Independence of Irrelevant Alternatives Principle.

Thus, once one rejects the Internal Aspects View, if one does, while both the Axiom of Transitivity and the Independence of Irrelevant Alternatives Principle may be false, they cannot both be true. Put differently, we have yet another impossibility result. We must choose between three incompatible positions: the Essentially Comparative View, the Axiom of Transitivity, and the Independence of Irrelevant Alternatives Principle. But, as should be clear by now, to abandon any of these positions would have grave implications for practical reasoning as we currently understand and engage in it.

*****

In this chapter, I have considered four attempts to preserve the Axiom of Transitivity in the face of this book's considerations. I consider a fifth attempt, which appeals to the notion of lexical priority, in appendix F.

Like the rest of this book, this chapter is not intended to show that we must *reject* the Axiom of Transitivity. However, it is intended to show that two ways of trying to defend the Axiom of Transitivity against this book's worries fail to allay those worries; they simply beg the question against them. This is true, I have argued, of the appeals to the Time Trade-off Method and reflective equilibrium. It is also intended to show that two ways that might *successfully* preserve the Axiom of Transitivity in a way that is compatible with the Essentially Comparative View have significant costs of their own. They may leave one open to the possibility of being money pumped, undermine the reason we *care* so much about the Axiom of Transitivity for the purposes of practical reasoning, and effectively invalidate or subvert the practical significance of the Independence of Irrelevant Alternatives Principle. This is true, I have argued, of the fine-grained solution and the Sports Analogy.[20] Finally, I have presented an impossibility result involving the Essentially Comparative View, the Axiom of Transitivity, and the Independence of Irrelevant Alternatives Principle.

Ultimately, then, we may consider or juggle a number of different positions in a valiant attempt to preserve the Axiom of Transitivity, but the aim of trying to reconcile the Axiom of Transitivity with each of the other views that we care deeply about, or retaining it at little or no practical or theoretical cost, is, I think, a fool's quest. Having reached the end of this book's penultimate chapter, the various "impossibility" arguments and worries that I have raised remain unsettled.

---

[20] I only spelled out the point about the Independence of Irrelevant Alternatives Principle in discussing the Sports Analogy. But as should be clear, it also applies to the fine-grained approach.

14

Conclusion

This is a long book, which some readers will have skipped parts of, and which other readers will have read over a long period of time. Accordingly, I shall begin this conclusion, in sections 14.1 through 14.3, by taking stock of the main topics I have canvassed, of some of the lessons learned, and of what remains to be done. I hope that some readers will find this review helpful, but others may want to only skim these sections, or skip straight to section 14.4, depending on how firmly they already have in mind the preceding material. I'll then revisit the question of whether the meaning or logic of "all-things-considered better than" determines that it is a transitive relation, consider some responses to my views, and address the appropriateness of sometimes accepting views that seem incredible or even inconsistent. I shall then discuss the relation between some of my claims and the topic of moral dilemmas or moral dead ends, followed by some thoughts on the relation between my views and skepticism. I end with a final comment on the position I find myself in regarding my results.

For the interested reader, appendix G provides a detailed summary of each chapter.

14.1 Topics Canvassed

This book canvasses many issues related to our understanding of the good, and to comparative evaluations of different outcomes. Sometimes the different outcomes involve different individuals, and sometimes they involve different ways a single life might go. General topics, addressed at length, included aggregation, transitivity, moral ideals, and the nature of practical reasoning.

Regarding aggregation, I presented and assessed various different principles regarding trade-offs between quality and number, or quality and duration, both between lives and within lives.[1] These principles address such questions as when, if at all, it would be better for fewer people to benefit (or suffer) to a greater extent, than for more people to benefit (or suffer) to a lesser extent, and when, if at all, it would be better for one person to have fewer greater-benefits (or greater-harms), or for that person to have more lesser-benefits (or lesser-harms). I discussed, at length, both additive-aggregationist principles and anti-additive-aggregationist principles.

Regarding transitivity, I explored the nature of transitivity and, by examining various examples of both normative and nonnormative notions, identified the underlying conditions that would lead us to judge a notion as referring to a relation that was transitive or nontransitive. I defined "nontransitivity" in such a way as to be neutral between cases where we might say of a notion that it corresponded to a single relation, R, for which transitivity *failed*, and cases where we would say that the notion of transitivity *failed to apply* across the different sets of alternatives for which the notion generated rankings, because, for instance, the notion ranked certain alternatives according to one set of criteria, corresponding, perhaps, to a given relation, R', but other alternatives according to a different set of criteria, corresponding, perhaps, to a different relation, R''.

Regarding moral ideals, I explored the nature, plausibility, and implications of different models for understanding the value of utility, and different models for understanding how ideals combine to generate all-things-considered judgments, a Standard Model and a Capped Model. I also explored the nature, plausibility, and implications of two different ways of understanding the nature of ideals: the Internal Aspects View and the Essentially Comparative View. On the former view, how good an alternative is with respect to any ideal must depend solely on the internal features of that alternative in a manner consistent with impartiality. On the latter view, there are at least some ideals such that how good a given alternative is with respect to that ideal will depend, at least in some cases, on the other alternatives with which that alternative is compared.

Regarding practical reasoning, my discussion of the previous topics illustrated that many assumptions that we routinely employ in practical deliberations are inconsistent. I shall detail this more in the following section, but assumptions "in play" included various Axioms of Transitivity, including the transitivity of "all-things-considered better than" (in my wide reason-implying sense); the Principle of Substitution of Equivalents; a particularly plausible version of an Independence of Irrelevant Alternatives Principle; a Reflection Principle; especially plausible versions of certain moral ideals, like maximin and utility; the Pareto Principle; a Narrow Person-Affecting View; the ideal of equality; and the general view that many moral ideals are limited in scope, such that they are relevant for making certain comparisons but not others, as,

---

[1] In appendix A, I discuss similar principles regarding trade-offs between duration and number, and in appendix B, I discuss the relations between quantity, quality, duration, and number.

for example, appears to be the case with both additive-aggregationist and anti-additive-aggregationist principles.

In addressing the major general topics, a host of other topics were also broached. These included: a series of Spectrum Arguments; the intuitive underpinnings of certain attitudes toward charitable giving; the intuitive plausibility of the Levelling Down Objection; the Repugnant Conclusion and Lollipops for Life case; the Disperse Additional Burdens View; problems of iteration, and how these might confront national and international agencies; Prisoner's Dilemmas, and Each-We Dilemmas more generally; Rawls's and Nozick's views about the separateness of individuals; the distinction between compensation and moral balancing; the goodness of an individual life and Sidgwick's conception of self-interest; McTaggart's Single Life Repugnant Conclusion; principles of decomposition and recombination; proportionality arguments; incommensurability; rough comparability; the money pump; global and strategic reasoning; the nontransitivity of "not worse than," "permissibility," and "moral obligatoriness"; the relation between the right and the good; the inheritability of nontransitivity; the cost of fine-grained solutions for preserving the Axiom of Transitivity; the Principle of Continuity; objections to my Spectrum Arguments spanning such issues as different kinds, Sorites Paradoxes, heuristics, and similarity-based arguments; whether all utility is intrinsically valuable; total versus average utility, and worries about average views generally; neutrality regarding persons, places, and times; whether certain moral ideals may have to share certain formal or structural features and, in particular, whether if numbers count for utility they may also have to count for equality; the Mere Addition Paradox; the impersonal value of equality; How More than France Exists; the plausibility of essentially comparative versions of maximin and utility; the Pareto Principle; a Narrow Person-Affecting View; and various advantages to accepting the Essentially Comparative View, including making sense of normal human preferences and behavior that would otherwise be irrational.

Of course, broaching a topic is easy; doing so in a way that is valuable is another matter. Naturally, I hope that I have often approached, if not fully succeeded, in accomplishing the latter. But the reader must be the judge of this.

14.2 Lessons Learned

One of the principal lessons learned is how difficult it may be to reconcile some of our deepest beliefs about the nature of the good, moral ideals, and practical reasoning. We saw that in many contexts we employ intuitively powerful additive-aggregationist principles in judging how two outcomes compare all things considered. We also saw that in many other contexts we employ intuitively powerful anti-additive-aggregationist principles in judging how two outcomes compare all things considered. This was so, I argued, both within and between lives, that is, for comparisons involving alternative ways a single life might go, and for comparisons involving alternative ways different lives might go. But, we saw that given certain empirical assumptions it would be extremely difficult to deny—namely, that there could be certain spectrums of cases such that the additive-aggregationist principles seemed relevant for comparing alternatives that were "near" each other on the spectrums, while the anti-additive-aggregationist principles seemed relevant for comparing alternatives that were "far apart" from each other on the spectrums—the principles in question were incompatible with the transitivity of the "all-things-considered better than" relation (in my wide reason-implying sense). I claimed that, for many, giving up any of the incompatible positions would be extremely difficult, and would have significant practical and theoretical implications.

A similar problem concerns some widely held beliefs regarding the axioms of Expected Utility Theory. I noted that many people agree that the Completeness Axiom of Expected Utility Theory is implausibly strong, and then argued that it would be hard to reconcile Incompleteness with a number of other very important assumptions of Expected Utility Theory and practical reasoning, including various Principles of Equivalence, a State-by-State Comparison Principle, a Reflection Principle, a Pareto Principle, and the Sure-Thing Principle. I also raised questions about Expected Utility Theory's Principle of Continuity. I noted that many people find the Principle of Continuity extremely plausible for a wide range of cases, including a set of cases that I called "easy" cases. But I also noted that many find the Principle of Continuity extremely *im*plausible for certain other cases, that I called "extreme" cases. Rather than accept a simple, "pure" view, which would insist that continuity be either accepted for *all* cases or rejected for *all* cases, I suggested that here, as elsewhere, many would find a more moderate, intermediate view most plausible, namely, that the Principle of Continuity is plausible for many, but not all, cases. But I pointed out that this seemingly reasonable "compromise" position is incompatible with the Principle of Substitution of Equivalence and the Axioms of Transitivity. Thus, once again, many will be forced to give up a view that they find deeply plausible.

We saw that there is good reason to believe that at least three significant normative relations may be nontransitive: the "permissibility" relation, the "obligatoriness" relation, and the "not worse than" relation. I noted that while most would accept that *such* normative relations could be nontransitive, some continue to insist that "all-things-considered better than" *must* be a transitive relation. Regarding this view I made several points.

First, I observed that if we are already open to the possibility that three significant normative relations are nontransitive, perhaps we should at least be *open* to the possibility that *other* normative relations might *also* be nontransitive, including the "all-things-considered better than" relation (in my wide reason-implying sense).

Second, I pointed out that one reason that *some* people have worried about "all-things-considered better than" not being a transitive relation is that they have worried about the possibility of our being money pumped, at least theoretically, if that were so, and this theoretical possibility has seemed to some to be a mark of irrationality, even if there are strategic *practical* steps people could employ to avoid *actually* being money pumped in the real world. But I pointed out that the possibility of being money pumped, at least theoretically, already arises, both individually and collectively, once one recognizes the nontransitivity of the "obligatoriness" and "not worse than" relations. Accordingly, the money-pump consideration with its attendant worries about irrationality no longer seems to militate against accepting the possibility that "all-things-considered better than" (in my wide reason-implying sense) might be a nontransitive relation, once one has accepted the possibility that "obligatoriness" and "not worse than" might be nontransitive relations.

Finally, and most important, I suggested that the relation between the right and the good is such that there is good reason to believe that the nontransitivity of the "obligatoriness" relation might be carried over into, or "inherited" by, the "all-things-considered better than" relation. So, once one is prepared to accept that the "obligatoriness" relation is nontransitive, as many are, there is good reasons to doubt that "all-things-considered better than" (in my wide reason-implying sense) *must* be a transitive relation.

The last point is an instance of a general truth of great significance. If a complex notion corresponds to a relation, and if an important aspect of that complex notion itself corresponds to a relation, then if the latter relation is nontransitive, the former relation is highly likely to also be nontransitive, as the nontransitivity of the aspect is likely to be inherited by the wider notion of which it is an important element. Thus, in particular, if there is any important aspect of the notion of "all-things-considered better than" which corresponds to a nontransitive relation, the "all-things-considered better than" relation is itself likely to be nontransitive.

Another general truth of great significance concerns the scope of moral ideals. Many people believe that certain ideals are limited in scope, in the sense of applying to, and giving us a basis for comparing, certain alternatives but not others. John Rawls thought this was so of his two principles of justice, and it is arguably true of the Pareto Principle and many other principles.[2] But this, too, raises the possibility that "all-things-considered better than" (in my wide reason-implying sense) will be a nontransitive relation, depending on the manner in which the principle is limited in scope.

Suppose some principle, P, is limited in scope, so that it is relevant for comparing certain alternatives but not others. Suppose, further, that the way in which this is so is such that P is relevant and significant for determining how A and C compare, but not relevant for comparing how A and B compare, or how B and C compare. Then it might well be that A is better than B all things considered—which is to

---

[2] Derek Parfit has told me, in discussion, that he believes it is also true of prioritarianism. According to Parfit, prioritarianism should only be used when comparing outcomes involving the very same people.

say, taking *full* account of *all* of the factors that are relevant and significant for comparing those alternatives—and *B* is better than *C* all things considered, yet *A* is *not* better than *C*, all things considered. This might be so because, by hypothesis, given the limited scope of *P*, there is a factor that is relevant and significant for comparing *A* and *C*, namely, *P*, which might help make it the case that *A* is not better than *C*, that is not relevant for comparing *A* with *B*, or *B* with *C*, and so has no bearing on how *those* alternatives compare, all things considered.

Importantly, the issue here is not simply whether different ideals might be relevant for assessing different outcomes, or whether, in accordance with the Principle of Contextual Interaction, a given ideal might have different significance in different contexts. By themselves, such views are perfectly compatible with "all-things-considered better than" being a transitive relation. The question, rather, is whether the relevance and significance of certain ideals for assessing any given outcome can depend on the other outcomes, if any, with which it might be compared. If so, then the value of *A*, considered by itself, may be different than the value of *A* when it is compared with *B*, which in turn may be different than the value of *A* when it is compared with other alternatives, such as *C*, or *B* and *C*, and so on. In this case, *A* might be better than *B*, and *B* better than *C*, but *A* not better than *C*. Perhaps *A* receives a high value in comparison with *B*, and *B* a high value in comparison with *C*, but *A* receives a low value in comparison with *C*, where, in each case, the value of *A* is determined by *all* of the factors that are relevant and significant for making each comparison.

Some people have thought that worries about transitivity arise when one eschews a simple monistic approach to practical reasoning—according to which outcomes should be assessed in terms of a single factor, ideal, or consideration—in favor of a more complex pluralistic view that gives weight to many different factors, ideals, or considerations in assessing outcomes. Although there is a kernel of truth to this position, it is deeply misleading. One can have an extremely complex, pluralistic view of practical reasoning that gives weight to many different ideals and, as implied earlier, one can even grant that in different contexts one's different ideals would have greatly different weights; but no matter *how* complex one's function might be that assigns values to outcomes, as long as each outcome receives a single value or range of values representing how good it is, all things considered, independently of which alternatives, if any, it is compared with, then the "all-things-considered better than" relation will be transitive.[3] On the other hand, one might adopt a simple "monistic" view that ranks outcomes solely in terms of a single factor, ideal, or consideration, but if the view assigns values to outcomes in part depending on the alternatives with which it is com-

---

[3] This wording is not meant to preclude the possibility that the single value or range of values assigned to an outcome might be imprecise. Whether an outcome's value is precise or imprecise is orthogonal to the question of whether its value is sometimes affected by the alternatives, if any, with which it is compared.

pared, then the possibility arises that "all-things-considered better than" will be a nontransitive relation. So, for example, as we saw in chapter 12, even if all we cared about in comparing outcomes was the single value maximin, or the single value utility, our "all-things-considered better than" judgments might be nontransitive, depending on the versions of those principles that we employ.

To be sure, any view that generates a nontransitive "all-things-considered better than" relation will be pluralistic in *one* sense, namely, it will have more than one way of valuing an outcome depending on the alternatives with which it is compared, and in doing this it will be attending to more than one element that the view deems relevant in assessing outcomes. This is the kernel of truth to the claim that pluralism is relevant to whether the "all-things-considered better than" relation is nontransitive. But the crucial point isn't whether we are monists or pluralists, in the sense of fundamentally valuing one ideal or more than one ideal, but the *nature* of the good and practical ideals that we value.

We have learned that there are two fundamentally different conceptions of practical ideals, an Internal Aspects View and an Essentially Comparative View. If the former view is correct, then how good an outcome is regarding any particular ideal, or all things considered, will depend solely on the internal features of that outcome. If, however, an Essentially Comparative View is correct, then how good any outcome is with respect to any particular ideal, or all things considered, may depend on the alternatives, if any, with which that outcome is compared. In the former case, "all-things-considered better than" will be a transitive relation, but in the latter case, the possibility arises that "all-things-considered better than" (in my wide reason-implying sense) will be nontransitive.

It may be that an Internal Aspects View adequately captures many of our practical ideals. One ideal that I suggested is best captured by such a view is the ideal of equality, but there may be many others as well. On the other hand, I argued that some principles that people find powerfully relevant for assessing outcomes reflect an Essentially Comparative View, for example, the most plausible version of maximin, a version of utility to which many are attracted, the Pareto Principle, and a Narrow Person-Affecting View. Moreover, importantly, given the point about inheritability noted earlier, if there is even *one* important ideal that is relevant to our all-things-considered judgments that is best captured by an Essentially Comparative View, the possibility will arise that the "all-things-considered better than" relation will be nontransitive.

In addition to there being two different conceptions of practical ideals, we considered two different approaches to understanding the value of utility and its relation to other ideals in generating all-things-considered judgments. We considered a Standard Model for Utility and a Standard (uncapped) Model for Combining Ideals that could suitably capture our additive-aggregationist views. We also considered a Capped Model for Ideals that could suitably capture our anti-additive-aggregationist views. Predictably, both models were intuitively plausible for some cases, but intuitively implausible for others.

Another lesson we learned was that there could be serious problems of iteration for anti-additive-aggregationist principles, particularly for national or international organizations. Specifically, we saw that if one repeatedly followed such principles, one could, in certain circumstances, be led to make a series of choices, each of which, *individually*, produced the *best* possible available outcome, but which *collectively* would bring about an outcome that was undeniably *worse* than the outcome that one *would* have been led to had one instead ignored anti-additive-aggregationist reasoning when making one's individual choices, thereby bringing about the *worse* available outcome with respect to each *individual* choice.

Much of this book has tried to illuminate certain views that stand or fall together, as well as the implications of different combinations of views. Although our results in this area are too numerous and complicated to fully detail here, some of them might be summed up as follows.

1. One might adopt the Internal Aspects View and combine it with a version of the Standard Model for Utility and a Standard Model for Combining Ideals, while rejecting the Essentially Comparative View and any version of a Capped Model for Ideals.

Key advantages of this view: It would naturally support our many additive-aggregationist intuitions and the additive-aggregationist principles presented in this work. It would support the view that "all-things-considered better than" is a transitive relation, the Independence of Irrelevant Alternatives Principle, and the Principle of Substitution for Equivalence. It would avoid the problems of iteration to which anti-additive-aggregationist principles can sometimes lead. It is also fully compatible with the Principle of Continuity and Expected Utility Theory.

Key disadvantages of this view: It is at odds with the many anti-additive-aggregationist intuitions and principles presented in this work. So, for example, it entails the Repugnant Conclusion, the desirability of trading off between lollipops and lives, the Single Life Repugnant Conclusion, and the view that if only one lived long enough, it would be better to have two consecutive years of excruciating torture at some point in one's life than one extra mosquito bite per month. As discussed, these are views that the vast majority of people would find very difficult to believe. This view also denies that our assessment of alternatives could ever depend on the kind of factors that Parfit appealed to in presenting his Mere Addition Paradox, for example, whether the fact that an outcome involved Mere Addition could be relevant to how good or bad it was in comparison with another outcome. Accordingly, it entails the rejection of the most plausible version of maximin for comparing outcomes, the version of utility that many people are most attracted to for many cases, the Pareto Principle, and the Narrow Person-Affecting View. More generally, it denies that any principle can be limited in scope, in a way that would be relevant for some comparisons involving an outcome, but not others. Finally, if the view is construed so as to be fully compatible with Expected Utility Theory, it has to accept the Principle of Continuity even in so-called extreme cases, which many find hard to believe.

2. One might adopt the Internal Aspects View, and a version of a Capped Model for Ideals, while rejecting the Essentially Comparative View and any version of the Standard Model for Utility and the Standard (uncapped) Model for Combining Ideals.

Key advantages of this view: It can capture many of the anti-additive-aggregationist intuitions and principles presented in this work, and so enable us to reject the Repugnant Conclusion, the desirability of trading off between lollipops and lives, the Single Life Repugnant Conclusion, and the view that if only one lived long enough, it would be better to have two consecutive years of excruciating torture at some point in one's life, than one extra mosquito bite per month. This view could also capture many, though not all, of our additive-aggregationist intuitions, in particular, in those cases where the values of our ideals have not yet reached or come very near to the upper limits on those ideals of the relevant Capped Model. This view would also support the view that "all-things-considered better than" is a transitive relation, the Independence of Irrelevant Alternatives Principle, and the Principle of Substitution for Equivalence.

Key disadvantages of this view: As with the previous view, this view denies that our assessment of alternatives could ever depend on the kind of factors that Parfit appealed to in presenting his Mere Addition Paradox, for example, whether the fact that an outcome involved Mere Addition could be relevant to how good or bad it was in comparison with another outcome; it entails the rejection of the most plausible version of maximin for comparing outcomes, the version of utility that many people are most attracted to for many cases, the Pareto Principle, and the Narrow Person-Affecting View; and it denies that any principle can be limited in scope, in a way that would be relevant for some comparisons involving an outcome, but not others. In addition, there will be some cases where most people have strong additive-aggregationist intuitions that this view will be unable to capture; these will be cases where an outcome has approached or reached a relevant "cap" regarding one or more ideals. Furthermore, this view requires that either we accept a version of How More Than France Exists—according to which an outcome would have actually been better if some of its members with lives that were well worth living had never existed, and the rest of its members had actually been worse off as a result—or we deny that the ideals of equality and maximin have any significant value. Although this view can capture some of our anti-additive-aggregationist intuitions and principles, it will also have to reject some of them, such as the Disperse Additional Burdens View; otherwise, it will face problems of iteration with implications that are not only deeply implausible, but clearly false. Additionally, this view must cap how bad an outcome can be with respect to different ideals, face deeply implausible implications to the effect that adding new worlds with billions of well-off people could make an outcome worse if those worlds had even one badly off person within them, or reject standard views about neutrality with respect to people, places, and times. Finally, the view may be at odds with the Principle of Continuity and Expected Utility Theory, as its ability to capture our anti-additive-aggregationist intuitions may enable it to capture the view that the Principle of Continuity should be rejected for so-called extreme cases, but, as we saw, the cost of doing so will be that the Principle of Continuity also has to be rejected for at least some so-called easy cases, if the view is to continue to capture the Principle of Substitution for Equivalence and the Axioms of Transitivity.

3. One might adopt an Essentially Comparative View and a version of a Capped Model for Ideals for certain ideals or comparisons, and perhaps an Internal Aspects View and a version of the Standard Model for Utility and the Standard Model for Combining Ideals for other ideals or comparisons.

Key advantages of this view: It can capture the many anti-additive-aggregationist intuitions and principles presented in this work, and so enable us to reject the Repugnant Conclusion, the desirability of trading off between lollipops and lives, the Single Life Repugnant Conclusion, and the view that if only one lived long enough, it would be better to have two consecutive years of excruciating torture at some point in one's life, than one extra mosquito bite per month. It can also capture the many additive-aggregationist intuitions and principles presented in this work, such as the view that among two illnesses, one of which was *slightly* less bad than another, it would be better to eradicate the *less* bad illness if it affected *far* more people, or the view that it would be better to experience a certain intensity of pain for a given duration of time, than a pain that was only *slightly* less intense, but that lasted *much* longer. This view can capture the kind of reasoning Parfit appealed to in presenting his Mere Addition Paradox, as well as the most plausible version of maximin for comparing outcomes, the version of utility that many people are most attracted to for many cases, the Pareto Principle, and the Narrow Person-Affecting View. It can also capture the view that some principles may be limited in scope, in the sense that they may be relevant for some comparisons involving an outcome, but not others. At the same time, this view can avoid How More Than France Exists, while recognizing that both equality and maximin have significant value. It can also capture the view that for some ideals, such as equality, an outcome's value does not depend on the alternatives with which it is compared. Finally, it can capture the widely held intuitive judgments that the Principle of Continuity is plausible for so-called easy cases, but implausible for so-called extreme cases.

Key disadvantages of this view: On this view, "all-things-considered better than" (in my wide reason-implying sense) is nontransitive: either transitivity *fails* or it *fails to apply* across sets of alternatives to which we might previously have thought it did, and should, apply. Strictly speaking, one might preserve the view that the "all-things-considered better than" relation is transitive in one of several ways, for example, by appealing to a sufficiently fine-grained individuation of outcomes or by invoking something like a Sports Analogy for assessing outcomes, according to which the best outcome is the one that is best in the greatest number of pairwise comparisons. But it is intuitively dubious whether such moves are ultimately defensible in all cases for which they would be required, and even if they are, they undermine a particularly intuitive and powerful version of the Independence of Irrelevant Alternatives Principle. Correspondingly, and most important, such moves substantially eviscerate the importance and role that the transitivity of "all-things-considered better than" plays in practical reasoning. Accordingly, such moves deliver a pyrrhic victory at best, one whose practical implications are strikingly similar to those that would obtain if, in fact, "all-things-considered better than" were *not* a transitive relation. This view can capture anti-additive-aggregationist principles like the Disperse Additional Burdens View, but insofar as it does so it will face the problems of iteration generated by such views. Moreover, like the preceding view, this view must cap how bad an outcome can be with respect to different ideals, face deeply implausible implications to the effect that adding new worlds with billions of well-off people could make an outcome worse if those worlds had even one badly off person within them, or reject standard views about neutrality with respect to people, places, and times. Finally, insofar as such a view is developed to capture the position that the Principle of Continuity should be rejected in so-called extreme cases, this view would entail the rejection of the Principle of Continuity in its entirety—even in so-called easy cases—or the Principle of Substitution for Equivalence, or the Axioms of Transitivity. Each of these is centrally important for Expected Utility Theory, the rejection of which would require a significant reconceptualization of the theory itself, those disciplines that depend on it (like game theory, decision theory, and some parts of economics), and practical reasoning more generally.

Other views and combinations of views are also possible. As indicated earlier, I can't detail them all here. But I think it is safe to assume that no matter how many advantages another view may have, it, too, will face serious disadvantages. As we have seen, many people are deeply wedded to a wide range of disparate beliefs about the good, moral ideals, and the nature of practical reasoning, many of which are in tension, and some of which are incompatible. This virtually guarantees that any view that hopes to adequately respond to such beliefs will be very complex and deeply counterintuitive in some respects.

14.3 Work Remaining

There are many questions that this book raises that have not yet been answered, and numerous topics that have been broached but not sufficiently explored. I am acutely aware that the path yet to be traversed is far longer than the path already taken. Without aiming for completeness, let me mention, in no particular order, just some of the many directions that future research might pursue.

I presented two different models for thinking about how different ideals might combine to generate rankings of different alternatives, the Standard Model and the Capped Model. As presented, the Standard Model was fairly developed, but I noted some ways in which one might want to revise some of its elements to avoid certain objections. Other revisions might also be considered. Or an entirely new model might be developed to capture those elements of the Standard Model worth preserving, while attempting to avoid its biggest shortcomings.

The topic of holism was mentioned in this work, but did not receive a lot of attention, as it is largely orthogonal to the main lines I wanted to pursue. However, the issue of holism—which subsumes the importance of interaction effects and the Principle of Contextual Interaction—is central to an adequate understanding of the good, moral ideals, and the nature of practical reasoning. Ultimately, we need a much better understanding of the nature and significance of holism for assessing outcomes, and any models that we develop for assessing outcomes will have to adequately reflect that understanding. It is possible that the revisions necessary for the Standard Model to adequately capture the truth about holism would be so great as to be tantamount to rejecting the Standard Model in favor of a different one.

As presented, the Capped Model was little more than a sketch for how best to capture the value of different ideals alone, and in relation to each other. A host of different questions arose as to how to fill in the details of that sketch. Such questions included whether there might be caps on how good an outcome might be with respect to any given ideal, but no caps on how bad an outcome might be with respect to any given ideal; whether there might be different caps for different ways in which an ideal might be realized—for example, whether the cap for any amount of utility of a "low" quality might be different than the cap for any amount of utility of a "high" quality; whether for certain ideals there might be thresholds such that there would be no caps for instantiations of the ideal above the threshold, but there would be caps for instantiations of the ideal below the threshold in question, and/or vice versa; whether the upper limit in a value for any given ideal could actually be attained, or only approached; and whether the rate at which an upper limit was approached would be increasing, decreasing, constant, or varying with each extra "unit" of the ideal in question. Much work needs to be done in addressing such questions. Also, much work needs to be done to determine how to set the correct caps for different ideals, so that they receive their "due" weight in relation to each other, and this work will be complicated by the necessity of determining the manner and extent to which holistic considerations come into play regarding different outcomes and different comparisons.

As with the Standard Model, one would like to develop the Capped Model so as to maximize the advantages of the model while minimizing its disadvantages. But it is entirely possible that some different model might do a better job of capturing what the Capped Model is intended to capture, and that we should simply reject the Capped Model and replace it with another model instead. This is certainly worth considering.

In this work I made numerous simplifying assumptions, including assumptions about which ideals are relevant for comparing outcomes, and how best to understand those ideals for the cases under consideration. The simplifying assumptions were suitable for my purposes, but ultimately they need to be dropped. If we are really to accurately compare outcomes, at some point we will need to identify and clarify the nature of *all* of the factors relevant for making such comparisons. We will also need to be able to determine how much each of the various factors matter in relation to each other in the context of comparison, taking account of any relevant holistic considerations. Doing this will be no easy task; almost certainly, the best answers available to us in this area will be severely incomplete, and where they are not incomplete, they will generally be imprecise.[4]

I raised numerous worries about appealing to something like the Sports Analogy as a way of preserving the transitivity of the "all-things-considered better than" relation (in my wide reason-implying sense). On the Sports Analogy, the best alternative would be the one that was ranked higher the most number of times in pairwise comparisons against all of the relevant alternatives. If two or more alternatives were tied, they would be equally best. But I suggested that in the moral domain, it would be a mistake to only compare each alternative with

---

[4] These points have been repeatedly and rightly emphasized by Amartya Sen for many years now. See, for example, Sen's "Well-being, Agency, and Freedom: The Dewey Lectures," *Journal of Philosophy* 82 (1985): 169–221, especially the first lecture. Another response to the kinds of worries raised here is to entirely abandon the search for general principles in ethics, in favor of the kind of holistic contextualist approach that Jonathan Dancy calls *particularism* (see, for example, Dancy's *Ethics without Principles* [Oxford: Clarendon Press, 2004]).

every other alternative that one happened, in fact, to be facing, that if one truly wanted to bring about the best alternative, *all things considered*, one should compare each alternative with every other possible alternative one might have faced. This raised a host of practical and theoretical problems, especially if, as seems plausible, for any two alternatives, *A* and *B*, there are an *infinite* number of possible alternatives, such that however *A* compared to *B* in a pairwise comparison, that is how *A* would compare to those infinite alternatives in an infinite number of pairwise comparisons. One might explore various ways of responding to such worries. Perhaps one could defend the claim that if one's concern is to bring about the best available outcome, all things considered, it *is* legitimate to only consider the alternatives one is presently facing. Or perhaps one could defend the claim that for any indefinitely large (or even infinite?) number of alternatives one might face, there is an algorithm that would enable one to select a "manageable representative" subset of those alternatives, such that one could reasonably compare each member of the subset with every other, and whichever alternative(s) was (were) the winner among that set would, in fact, be the winner among the larger set, so would, in fact, be the best alternative all things considered. I am not sanguine about the prospect that such a move is plausible, or that any other adequate answer to the worries I raised is in the offing, but the stakes in this area are sufficiently high that such avenues are worth exploring.

I suggested that equality was best understood in the way suggested by an Internal Aspects View rather than an Essentially Comparative View. An obvious issue to be explored is whether there are any other ideals that are also best captured by such a view, and if so, which ones.

Also, I noted that some ideals may have to share certain formal or structural features, suggesting, for example, that just as there may be a cap on how good an outcome can be with respect to equality, there may have to be a cap on how good an outcome can be with respect to utility, and similarly, if numbers count for utility, they may also have to count for equality. But I also noted that while equality may be best understood with an Internal Aspects View, a large part of what we care about regarding utility is best captured by an Essentially Comparative View. One might wonder if there is a tension between these sets of views, and if so, how, if at all, it should be resolved. My discussion of utility implied that not all of what we care about regarding utility can be captured by the Essentially Comparative View of it that I discussed. Perhaps this means that some of our concerns regarding utility are best captured by an Internal Aspects View. In that case, our concern for equality and *some* of our concerns about utility would share the formal or structural feature of reflecting an Internal Aspects View. Still, one might wonder whether different ideals, or different concerns regarding a single ideal, may have to share certain formal or structural features, but not others, and if so, which ones, and why.

This work broached the possibility that we may have to abandon standard views about the importance of being neutral with respect to sentient beings, space, and time. One question worth pursuing is whether the different possible "locations" in which goodness might obtain—sentient beings, space, and time—should be treated the same or differently regarding neutrality. Another question worth pursuing is whether neutrality is an all-or-nothing requirement, or whether there should be varying degrees of neutrality. Perhaps all "local" sentient beings, places, or times must be treated neutrally, but there is no requirement of neutrality at all regarding "nonlocal" sentient beings, places, or times. Or perhaps the requirement of neutrality lessens as a function of how "far away" sentient beings, locations, or times are from the "local" ones. Such a function might be direct, or, like gravity, reflect an inverse square law, or, like radioactive decay, be exponential; in the first case the "force" of the requirement of neutrality would drop at a constant rate, in the second case at an increasing rate, and in the third case at a decreasing rate, in proportion to how "far away" sentient beings, places, or times were from the "local" ones.

Here, too, questions arise regarding whether different ideals may need to have the same formal or structural requirements of neutrality. For example, in keeping with the kinds of arguments presented throughout this book, it is easy to show that if we think the force of the requirement of neutrality weakens over time for some ideals, but not others, then "all-things-considered better than" (in my wide reason-implying sense) is likely to be a nontransitive relation.[5] More generally, those who continue to be wedded to the notion that "all-things-considered better than" is a transitive relation will have to treat all ideals similarly regarding neutrality. On reflection, then, I suspect that much work needs to be done to even fully identify, much less resolve, the many important questions that arise regarding neutrality.

Most moral theorists ignore questions of infinity. In many ways this is prudent, as there may be no actual choices people face where considerations of infinity would come into play, and perhaps, as importantly, because there are well-known problems and puzzles of infinity that are notoriously difficult to solve. Still, ideally, one would like a theory of practical rationality that would adequately cover all possible cases, and I believe that thinking carefully about examples involving infinity may reveal important shortcomings in certain views.

For example, perhaps we should think it a serious shortcoming of any theory of practical rationality if—as some believe is the case with Expected Utility Theory—it is unable to recommend that we choose an alternative where people would spend all of eternity repeatedly cycling through 1 million days in Heaven followed by one day in Hell, rather than one where people repeatedly cycled through 1 million days in Hell followed by one day in Heaven.[6] Similarly, thinking

---

[5] I present an argument of this kind in "Justice and Equality: Some Questions about Scope," in *The Just Society*, ed. Ellen F. Paul, Fred D. Miller, and Jeffrey Paul (Cambridge: Cambridge University Press, 1995), 72–104.

[6] Arguably, the expected value of an infinite number of periods of 1 million days in Heaven is $+\infty$, which is also the expected value of an infinite number of periods of 1 day in Heaven. Likewise, the expected value of an infinite number of periods of 1 million days in Hell is $-\infty$, which is also the

about cases involving infinity can teach us that we care about *more* than simply maximizing utility, or, alternatively, that we believe that "maximizing" utility involves *more* than merely achieving infinite positive utility. (Of course, most of us already knew this! My point here is merely to help illustrate how thinking about cases involving infinity can shed light on normative positions.) After all, if we somehow learned that the universe had existed infinitely in the past, and that there had always been a positive net utility during each of its moments, I don't believe that would lead many of us to think that it *no longer mattered at all* whether or not all sentient life ended today, whether it continued for many centuries yet to come at a very high level of existence (which most would think highly desirable) or whether it continued for many centuries with everyone suffering intensely (which most would think highly *un*desirable). But, of course, given that for all finite p, $(+\infty + p) = +\infty$, if maximizing utility simply meant achieving infinite utility, there would be nothing to choose between the three alternative ways in which the universe might unfold regarding utility maximization.

I suggest, then, that thinking about cases involving infinity may illuminate certain desiderata for theories of practical rationality, and possible ways in which we need to understand the good, moral ideals, and practical reasoning to meet those desiderata.

On the Essentially Comparative View, the factors that are relevant and significant for assessing an alternative can vary depending on the other alternatives with which that alternative is compared. Correspondingly, I noted that it is unclear what relevance, if any, pairwise comparisons between various alternatives might be, when more than two alternatives are considered together. More generally, in principle, knowing how A compares with any fixed set of alternatives won't tell us how A compares to the members of that set in the context where additional (or fewer) alternatives are also considered along with the initial set. Accordingly, an important line to pursue is whether one can determine under what conditions new factors will, in fact, come into play in assessing a set of alternatives with the addition (or contraction) of alternatives and, more particularly, if one can say in advance what those factors will be and their relative significance in assessing the expanded (or contracted) set of alternatives. At the

---

expected value of an infinite number of periods of 1 day in Hell. Seemingly, then, the expected value of an eternal cycle of 1 million days in Heaven followed by 1 day in Hell, and the expected value of an eternal cycle of 1 million days in Hell followed by 1 day in Heaven would both be the same, namely $+\infty + -\infty$. Mind you, we may decide that where cases involving infinities are involved, we can't make the usual arithmetical assumptions that work perfectly well in finite cases and that would license calculating the expected values of the two alternatives in the preceding manner. But if this is so, it would be an example of the kind of important lesson we need to learn in developing a full theory of practical rationality that we might only recognize by considering alternatives involving infinity. I am grateful to Derek Parfit, who first brought this particular example of a worry about infinity to my attention, many years ago. (Ironically, Parfit, himself, is dubious about how much of genuine significance we can learn about normative theory by reflecting on cases involving infinity.)

same time, one would like to be able to say under what conditions the addition (or contraction) of alternatives would alter the relevance and significance of previously relevant and significant factors and how, exactly, this would go. Perhaps there are a relatively limited number of ways and cases in which variations in the alternatives with which a given alternative are compared can alter the factors that are relevant and significant for assessing an alternative, and perhaps we can discover a few simple rules that govern this matter. But perhaps not. This is a topic that will bear careful consideration if we decide that an Essentially Comparative View is correct for at least some ideals and contexts.

A related topic that bears careful scrutiny is whether one can circumscribe this work's more worrying results. For example, even if one is persuaded that there are *some* cases where the "all-things-considered better than" relation is nontransitive, one might try to show that these are rare, and very special, cases, so that for the most part we don't have to worry about this work's worries in our daily practical reasoning. Perhaps one could show that in most real-world cases the factors that give rise to the nontransitivity of "all-things-considered better than" are not present. Alternatively, one might try to argue that while *strictly speaking* the "all-things-considered better than" relation is nontransitive, for most real-world cases we can safely and rationally proceed *as if* it is transitive, just as one might contend that while *strictly speaking* Newtonian physics needs to be replaced by relativity theory and quantum mechanics, for most real-world cases we can safely and rationally proceed *as if* Newtonian physics were true.

As with some of the other lines suggested in this section, I am not, myself, particularly optimistic that one will achieve great success pursuing this line.[7] But it is certainly worth pursuing. In the face of a view with seemingly far-reaching and devastating implications, one's first choice is always to *refute* the view, but if that proves unfeasible, one's next choice is always to try to limit the damage as much as possible.

Finally, having shown that some of our beliefs are inconsistent, much more work needs to be done to determine which of them, if any, should be given up. This will involve further exploration of the practical and theoretical consequences of giving up any of the beliefs in question. For example, I have observed that the Axioms of Transitivity and the Principle of Continuity underlie Expected Utility Theory, which in turn underlies game theory, decision theory, and some parts of economics. This naturally raises the questions of how Expected Utility Theory might be revised, or what it might be replaced with, if we ultimately decided that the Axioms of Transitivity or the Principle of Continuity must be rejected, and of what the implications of this would be for our understanding of game theory, decision theory, and economics. Similarly, much more thought needs to be given regarding the full impact of such moves as abandoning addi-

---

[7] One reason for pessimism about this line will be presented in section 14.8.

tive-aggregationist principles, or anti-additive-aggregationist principles, or the view that at least some ideals either are limited in scope or have a nature that is best captured by an Essentially Comparative View.

In sum, in my judgment this book opens up a large number of avenues that need exploring. It raises a host of difficult questions but settles few, if any, of them. However, not everyone shares this view. Some believe that the book effectively closes off the avenues that I think need exploring, by showing that pursuing such avenues would be fruitless. I'll briefly touch on this position, among others, in the following sections.

14.4 On the (Ir)Relevance of Meaning or Logic to Whether "All-Things-Considered Better Than" Is a Transitive Relation

In this section, I want to follow up on a point broached in my introduction. When I first began thinking about the issues raised in this book, I knew of no one who questioned the view that "all-things-considered better than" was a transitive relation. Indeed, as noted in my preface, when I first broached the idea that perhaps "all-things-considered better than" wasn't transitive, Tom Nagel told me that he wouldn't understand what someone *meant* who claimed that *all things considered A* is better than *B*, and *all things considered B* is better than *C*, but *all things considered A* is not better than *C*. So, at the time, Nagel thought that it was an *analytic* truth that "all-things-considered better than" was a transitive relation, and this view was held by many, including Tim Scanlon and Derek Parfit. Others, like John Broome, held that it was a *logical*, rather than analytic, truth that "all-things-considered better than" was a transitive relation.

I believe that these positions had the unchallenged dominance that they did, in part, because people were *assuming* that some version of the Internal Aspects View was correct, and on such a view it is, indeed, true that "all-things-considered better than" *must* be a transitive relation. At this point, people hadn't recognized that some of our deepest normative views reflect an alternative conception of ideals, which I have called the Essentially Comparative View. Indeed, in my own case, at least, and I suspect for some others as well, it wasn't until Parfit gave us his ingenious Mere Addition Paradox, and I explored the underlying foundations of that Paradox, that it became apparent that an Essentially Comparative View plays a significant role in our normative reasoning.[8]

Prior to understanding the possibility that some ideals could be essentially comparative, and the full nature of such ideals, it made perfect sense for someone to fail to understand how it could possibly be that "all-things-considered better than" might not be a transitive relation. But, once one understands the *possibility*

---

[8] My original exploration of these issues appeared in my "Intransitivity and the Mere Addition Paradox," *Philosophy and Public Affairs* 16 (1987): 138–87.

that some of our ideals might be essentially comparative, it no longer seems either analytically or logically impossible that "all-things-considered better than" might not be a transitive relation. To the contrary, for those who, on reflection, are prepared to accept that at least *some* of our ideals *are* essentially comparative, it can seem perfectly straightforward how it could be that "all-things-considered better than" (in my wide reason-implying sense) might not be a transitive relation. Accordingly, I suggest that the possibility of coming to calmly accept what seemed previously impossible quite naturally accompanies a (paradigm?) shift in our conception of ideals, from one that is exclusively an Internal Aspects View, to one that is at least in part an Essentially Comparative View.

I have claimed that whether or not "all-things-considered better than" (in my wide reason-implying sense) is a transitive relation depends on the nature of moral ideals. *If* an Internal Aspects View is correct, then "all-things-considered better than" must be a transitive relation, but *if* an Essentially Comparative View is even partly correct, then "all-things-considered better than" may be nontransitive. However, whether or not an Essentially Comparative View is partly correct is *not* determined by the *meanings of the words* "all-things-considered better than." Likewise, it doesn't seem that the logic of "better than" guarantees that an Essentially Comparative View of Ideals *must* be false. It is a central, and important, *substantive* question for normative theory what view of ideals is correct. This is not a question that *could* be settled by terminological analysis, nor does it seem to be the kind of question that *is* settled by the logic of "better than."

This point is worth emphasizing. Consider those who contend that an Essentially Comparative View is relevant when making at least *some* moral comparisons. They might claim that maximin is relevant for comparing certain outcomes, but that the only plausible version of maximin is an essentially comparative one. Or they might claim that an essentially comparative version of utility is relevant for comparing certain outcomes, that the Pareto Principle provides an independent consideration that is both powerful and relevant for comparing certain same-people cases, or that for *certain* comparisons a Narrow Person-Affecting View is relevant. Such claims represent *substantive* normative positions. Such positions may be *wrong*, but surely someone who wants to argue against such claims has to do more than just insist that such positions *have* to be wrong, because such positions open the possibility that "all-things-considered better than" is a nontransitive relation, and it is analytically or logically true that "all-things-considered better than" is a transitive relation. So, to focus on one particular claim, if the Pareto Principle lacks the independent weight some people think it has, this *won't* be true because of the meanings of the words "all-things-considered better than." Nor will it be true, I believe, because of the logic of "better than."

In sum, I remain open to the possibility that we must ultimately reject the Essentially Comparative View. Perhaps people *are* mistaken when they implicitly appeal to such a view. But if they are, they are making a *substantive* mistake about the nature of the good, moral ideals, and normative reasoning. They are not making a terminological mistake involving a failure to understand the words "all-things-considered better than," nor is their mistake a failure to understand the logic of "better than."

Some people believe that one of this work's main lessons is that the notion of "all-things-considered better than" is *incoherent*.[9] Their thought can be expressed as follows. We *do* use the words "all-things-considered better than" to mean that if, all things considered, A is better than B, and B is better than C, then, all things considered, A is better than C. But we *also* use the words "all-things-considered better than" to mean that if A is better than B taking proper account of *all* of the factors that are relevant and significant for making *that* comparison, then A is better than B all things considered. Moreover, importantly, in and of itself, the latter meaning does not rule out the possibility that *some* ideals might be essentially comparative, and so it opens up the possibility that, for the reasons I have shown, "all-things-considered better than" is *not* a transitive relation. Thus, the notion of "all-things-considered better than" is *incoherent*, because its meaning entails both that "all-things-considered better than" must, and yet may not be, a transitive relation.

Others continue to believe that the notion of "all-things-considered better than" is *coherent* and that it is either analytically or logically true that the "all-things-considered better than" relation is transitive. But they grant that this cannot settle the substantive normative question of whether certain ideals are essentially comparative. More specifically, they admit that it is at least *possible* that in certain contexts the factors that are relevant and significant for assessing an outcome will depend on the alternative(s), if any, with which that outcome is compared. On this view, the comparisons that would be made in such cases might be of great normative significance, but they would not be "all-things-considered better than" comparisons. They couldn't be. Perhaps, in such cases, we might say that one outcome was "preferable" to another, or "more choiceworthy," but we couldn't say that it was "all-things-considered better than." The latter notion would be restricted in scope so as to only apply across alternatives for which the resulting rankings were transitive. Unfortunately, on this view it is unclear to how many alternatives the notion of "all-things-considered better than" could usefully be applied. In addition, it is unclear what the significance of the notion of "all-things-considered better than" would still be for practical reasoning. If, for example, it were possible for A to be better than B "all things considered," yet for B to be more "choiceworthy" than A, it isn't clear how much weight, if any, the former ranking should have in our normative deliberations.

In my introduction, I acknowledged that some people may use the words "all-things-considered better than" in such a way as to make it analytically or logically true that "all-things-considered better than" is a transitive relation. And since people can use words however they see fit, they may continue with

---

[9] This has been suggested to me by many people over the years, though as I recall the first person to suggest it to me, many years ago now, was my former colleague Baruch Brody.

such usage in the face of this book's considerations. For such people, I suggest that one of the two preceding views is in order.

On the other hand, I believe that some people already use the notion of "all-things-considered better than" in the wide reason-implying sense of the sort assumed throughout this work, and that others will come to accept such usage as reflecting the best way of understanding the notion for the purposes of practical reasoning. Understood in the wide reason-implying sense, the notion of "all-things-considered better than" leaves open both the possibility that an Internal Aspects View captures the full truth about the good and normative ideals, and the possibility that an Essentially Comparative View captures at least *part* of the truth about the good and normative ideals. If the former turns out to be correct, then it will turn out that the "all-things-considered better than" relation is, in fact, transitive, as most have thought all along, but this will *not* simply be because of the meanings of the words "all-things-considered better than," nor will it simply be because of the logic of "better than." If, on the other hand, the latter turns out to be correct, then the possibility arises that "all-things-considered better than" (in my wide reason-implying sense) will be a nontransitive relation, for the reasons given in this work.

14.5 Some Responses to My Views

I have contended that despite the advantages of the Internal Aspects View, it is extremely difficult to reject the view that at least *some* principles are essentially comparative, and I have suggested a fundamental incompatibility between the Essentially Comparative View, the view that "all-things-considered better than" *must* be transitive (the Axiom of Transitivity), and the view that how two alternatives compare all things considered depends solely on how *they* compare in terms of the relevant and significant factors for making *that* comparison, and not on how one or both compare to some other independent alternative(s) (the Independence of Irrelevant Alternatives Principle).

Not everyone will be troubled by my results. To the contrary, some virtue theorists and deontologists might relish insuperable difficulties with ranking outcomes. Already convinced that the question "Which outcome would be best?" receives too much attention, they might welcome its relegation to the scrap heap of the unanswerable, enabling the "genuinely" important questions—such as "How ought one *to be*?" or "What ought one *to do*?"—to receive more consideration in the domain of practical reasoning. And, of course, people like Nozick and Foot might welcome my results as further vindication of their view that claims about one outcome being better than another are ultimately unintelligible. (I've heard Foot say, in discussion, that she simply doesn't understand what someone *means* in claiming that one outcome is better than another.)

These positions cannot be taken lightly. Perhaps my arguments are best interpreted as a frontal assault on the very intelligibility of consequentialist reasoning about morality and rationality. Perhaps, at the end of the day, we should restrict our attention in the normative realm to such notions as virtue, duty, care, rights, and so on, abandoning our concerns about the good or bringing about the best available outcome. But this is not a position I readily endorse.

As I noted at the very beginning of this book, I concur with Rawls that any "ethical doctrines worth our attention [must] take consequences into account.... One which did not would be simply irrational, crazy."[10] I continue to believe that it is both intelligible, and normatively significant, that an outcome where millions of people flourish but one person suffers a scratched finger would be a better outcome than one where the millions of people suffered greatly but the one person was spared his scratch. However we come to terms with this book's arguments, it must leave room for the intelligibility and significance of such claims.

Others who will not be troubled by my results will include certain consequentialists, like total utilitarians, or average utilitarians, or certain perfectionists. Such theorists will simply reject Essentially Comparative Views and "bite the bullet" when it comes to accepting the unintuitive consequences of doing so. I have never been attracted to such theories, but I confess that I now appreciate their simplicity and elegance as I never did before. Still, I continue to believe, with Nagel, that "simplicity and elegance are never reasons to think that a philosophical theory is true: on the contrary, they are usually grounds for thinking it false."[11] Such views are perfectly consistent, and they avoid the morass of problems raised in this book. These virtues are not to be sniffed at. Still, such views are far too simpleminded, and I believe one should seek other "messier" and more complex solutions to the problems we confront.

Some people are troubled by my book's arguments, but not sufficiently so as to shake their confidence in certain fundamental assumptions, including the axioms of Expected Utility Theory. Thus, they hold fixed their conviction that "all-things-considered better than" is a transitive relation, the Principle of Substitution for Equivalence, the Principle of Continuity, and so on. Impressed by the scope and explanatory power of Expected Utility Theory, such people use that theory, and its underlying axioms, as a modern-day Ockham's razor, to shave off any principles or intuitions incompatible with the theory, thereby guaranteeing a resulting view that is coherent. If the result of doing this is to accept certain deeply unintuitive consequences, such as the Repugnant Conclusion, they are prepared to do this as the price of consistency. This is the kind of view espoused by John Broome.[12]

---

[10] John Rawls, *A Theory of Justice* (Cambridge, MA: Harvard University Press, 1971), 30. As the reader may recall, Rawls's full claim is slightly more detailed, but the point I attribute to him here is both compatible with, and implied by, his more detailed claim, which is that "all ethical doctrines worth our attention must take consequences into account in judging rightness. One which did not would simply be irrational, crazy."

[11] Thomas Nagel, *Mortal Questions* (Cambridge: Cambridge University Press, 1979), x.

[12] In *Weighing Goods* (Oxford: Basil Blackwell, 1991), and in *Weighing Lives* (Oxford: Oxford University Press, 2004).

There is much to be admired about this view. And perhaps, at the end of the day, it, or something like it, will be the best that we can do in the face of the problems I have raised. But, for the reasons that I have conveyed previously, I am leery about jumping into the comforting arms such an approach seems to offer. For all its power and accomplishments, I fear that Expected Utility Theory is, in its own way, too rigid, simplistic, and monolithic to do justice to the full complexity and even morass of normative thinking. Like cost-benefit analysis, Expected Utility Theory is a powerful and effective tool for certain restricted domains, but it may obscure or run roughshod over important insights and truths if it is employed beyond those domains.

Long ago, Aristotle offered the sage warning "that in every subject... [one must look] for only so much precision as its subject matter permits."[13] My worry about Expected Utility Theory echoes Aristotle's concerns. I believe that the normative realm is messy and incredibly complex. Accordingly, any theory that hopes to accurately reflect the normative realm must reflect such features. I fear that Expected Utility Theory fails to adequately do that.

As noted in chapter 1, following Nagel, "I believe one should trust problems over solutions, intuition over arguments, and pluralistic discord over systematic harmony."[14] This makes me wary of too readily wielding the powerful tool of Expected Utility Theory, as a way of "resolving" the problems and discord that seemingly engulf much of the normative realm.

14.6 On the Appropriateness of (Sometimes) Embracing Incredible or Inconsistent Views

Suppose we accept an Essentially Comparative View, and as a result come to believe that "all-things-considered better than" (in my wide reason-implying sense) is not a transitive relation. More particularly, suppose that there are three alternatives A, B, and C, such that we come to believe that it really *is* the

---

[13] *Nicomachean Ethics*, book 1, chapter 3, trans. J. A. K. Thompson. (London: George Allen and Unwin, 1953). Aristotle's warning has been ably amplified and defended by people like David Lewis and Amartya Sen. Lewis notes that it is a strength of his account of causation that it does not identify the cause of an event in those cases where it is indeterminate what the cause of the event really is, while it is a shortcoming of some rival accounts that for every event they always identify its cause even in those cases where it is, in fact, indeterminate what the cause of the event is! (see Lewis's *Counterfactuals* [Oxford: Basil Blackwell; Cambridge, MA: Harvard University Press, 1973]). Similarly, Sen believes that the normative realm is vague and incomplete, and hence that our normative theory must accurately reflect that vagueness and incompleteness in its pronouncements and implications. Accordingly, he believes that it is a shortcoming of certain normative theories, such as certain versions of total utilitarianism, that they offer precise and complete answers to every possible question about what we ought to do (see Sen's "Well-being, Agency, and Freedom: The Dewey Lectures," *Journal of Philosophy* 82 [1985]: 169–221, especially the first lecture).

[14] Nagel, *Mortal Questions*, x.

case that, all things considered, *A* is better than *B*, and *B* is better than *C*, but, all things considered, *A* is *not* better than *C*. Would this mean that we have inconsistent beliefs or that we thought the world was inconsistent?

No! It *would* mean this if we *also* thought that "all-things-considered better than" was a transitive relation. But if we accept an Essentially Comparative View, and hence *reject* the view that "all-things-considered better than" (in my wide reason-implying sense) is a transitive relation, then where is the inconsistency in our beliefs, or the world, if it turns out that there *are* three alternatives *A*, *B*, or *C* that are actually related to each other in the manner our beliefs suggest?

Consider any other relation that is not transitive, for example, the "being the father of" relation. Clearly there is nothing inconsistent about us, or the world, if we rightly believe that John is the father of Henry, and Henry is the father of Elliot, but John is not the father of Elliot. There would only be something inconsistent about those three beliefs and the propositions corresponding to them if, in fact, "being the father of" were a transitive relation. But it is not! Why isn't the same thing true of beliefs or propositions about how different alternatives compare with each other all things considered, if, in fact, "all-things-considered better than" isn't a transitive relation?

But some people may balk at such reasoning. They may insist that there is a *conceptual* connection between the notions of consistency and the transitivity of the "all-things-considered better than" relation such that any set of all-things-considered rankings that is transitive is consistent, and any set of all-things-considered rankings that is intransitive is inconsistent. On this view, if an Essentially Comparative View were correct, we might come to believe that, all things considered, *A* is better than *B*, and *B* is better than *C*, but, all things considered, *A* is *not* better than *C*; but, if we did, our beliefs *would* be inconsistent. And if, caught in the grip of this book's arguments, we came to believe that such a triad of beliefs were actually *true*, that would involve our believing that the world, *itself*, was inconsistent. Suppose one thought this way, as some do. What, if anything, would that show about the reasonableness of our ever accepting an intransitive and (thus) inconsistent all-things-considered ranking of different alternatives?

I don't want to take a stand on whether there can be genuine metaphysical inconsistencies, but I'm willing to accept that in some cases there can be good reason to *accept* inconsistency as part of our best current understanding of the world, while we continue to seek an even better understanding which would be devoid of inconsistencies. Moreover, I'd like to remind the reader that this is, in fact, a familiar, and rather modest, proposal.

W. V. O. Quine famously argued that we could, conceivably, revise *any* of our beliefs in the face of new evidence about the world, *including* our beliefs in the most fundamental laws of logic.[15] Of course, Quine believed that our pic-

---

[15] See, for example, *From a Logical Point of View* (Cambridge: Cambridge University Press, 1953).

ture of the world would have to change *radically* before we would ever give up a fundamental law of logic, but the point is that he believed that we couldn't rule out *in advance* that one day our picture of the world might so change. I think Quine is right. Right now it seems *impossible* to believe that A and not A could ever both be true at the same time, but humans have shown an amazing capacity not only to believe the impossible, but to substantially revise their conceptions of the world, so as to come to believe what previously seemed impossible.

Let me set aside people's incredible capacity to believe the impossible in the religious realm—that a single being could be both mortal man and immortal God, that a single being might at one and the same time be three beings—God the Father, God the Son, and the Holy Spirit—and so on. The "miracles" of religion are generally accepted as articles of faith, rather than on the basis of reason. Instead, let me focus on radical transformations that have occurred in our understanding of science, or mathematics, or perhaps language itself.

For much of human history, it seemed impossible for an event occurring on the other side of the solar system, galaxy, or even universe to have any impact on events on Earth. People greeted such a possibility with derision, violating the seemingly a priori truth that there can be "no action at a distance." However, with advances in physics, and the paradigm shifts accompanying them, we learn that such interactions are possible because of the presence of gravitational and electromagnetic fields. Note, in this case we were able to retain the "a priori" view that there is no "true" action at a distance, but only via radical reconceptualization of how objects are connected in space and time.

On the other hand, on quantum mechanics, a new challenge to the a priori principle of no action at a distance arises, with the famous Einstein-Podolsky-Rosen Paradox.[16] Here, too, we might ultimately be able to preserve the claim

---

[16] A *rough* characterization of the EPR Paradox might be put as follows. Two subatomic particles, a positron and an electron, might be emitted from a single source, a pion decay. The positron may travel down a tube to the right, say, and the electron may travel down a tube to the left, say. The positron and electron are related in such a way that one particle's spin about any axis will be the opposite of the other particle's spin about that axis. So if, say, we characterize the positron's spin as "up" along the x-axis, then the electron's spin will be "down" along the x-axis. But, according to quantum mechanics, no particle's spin will be "fixed" along any axis prior to our measurement of it. That is, if we measure the positron's spin, we might find it to be "up," but we also might find it to be "down." Both are genuine possibilities prior to our measurement of the particle. So, if we measure the positron's spin in the tube to the right along the x-axis at a particular time t, we could, according to quantum mechanics, find out that it is "up," but we could *also* find out that it is "down." But, importantly, the same is true if we measure the electron's spin in the tube to the left along the x-axis at a particular time t, we could, according to quantum mechanics, find out that it is "up," but we could also find out that it is "down." But, Einstein, Podolsky, and Rosen predicted that if one measured the positron in the right tube and thereby "fixed" its spin along the x-axis as "up," this would guarantee that the spin of the electron along the x-axis in the left tube would be simultaneously "fixed" as "down," prior to any measurement of it. This seems to imply that quantum mechanics is mistaken or incomplete, in contending that the direction of spin of any particle is genuinely indeterminate prior to the measurement of that spin, or that there is "action at a distance" in the sense that the measurement of the positron in the right tube instantly fixed the direction of the spin of the electron in the left tube before any information could have arrived from our

that there is no "true" action at a distance, but this requires further radical revision in our understanding of the nature of reality, including, perhaps, our understanding of causality and how information can be conveyed across the space/time continuum. Perhaps this should not be surprising, given that the move to quantum mechanics already represents a radical departure from previous understandings of causality and the nature of reality.

For example, for most of human history it was considered to be an a priori truth that every event had a cause, and this was interpreted to imply that if two sets of causal conditions were identical, the resulting effects would be identical. But, on quantum mechanics, the a priori truth that every event has a cause can be preserved only by radically reconceptualizing what that involves. After all, quantum mechanics teaches us that from any given causal conditions a multitude of effects might ensue. Thus, on one occasion an apple might fall when it is detached from its branch, on another it might remain suspended in the air, and on a third it might disappear entirely, with *no variation at all* in the antecedent conditions producing these events. Of course, quantum mechanics will predict that the former effect is *vastly* more probable than either of the latter two, but it allows for the possibility that *any* of the three effects, as well as an indefinite number of other ones, *could* ensue from the *very same* antecedent conditions.

Similarly, for much of history people would have thought that waves and particles had distinctive natures and properties, indeed, that the *definitions* of "wave" and "particle" were such that an entity could be a wave *or* a particle, but *not* both. However, according to modern physics, *all* matter and energy possess the nature and properties of *both* waves and particles, though to varying degrees. Here, a radical reconceptualization of our understanding of the world makes possible a reconciliation between seemingly inconsistent and even contradictory views, such as the view that electrons are waves with wavelike natures and properties, and the view that electrons are particles with particle-like natures and properties. Prior to advances in our understanding of physics, a wave-particle conception of electrons might have seemed as unintelligible as a round-square.

Next, consider "nihil ex nihilo fit"—the view that "nothing comes from nothing"—which was long regarded as yet another a priori, and perhaps even logical, truth. It appears the Big Bang Theory presents a counterexample to that claim, at least as the claim would have been understood by most of its advocates. Yet many scientists and others believe that something like the Big Bang Theory is, or at least might be, true. Hence they are either rejecting what

---

measurement in the one locale to the other locale. Put differently, it appears that quantum mechanics is incomplete, committed to the possibility of action at a distance, or committed to rejecting the fundamental principle that no information can travel faster than the speed of light. Einstein, Podolsky, and Rosen's original predictions have since been confirmed by experimental data, and their article and the results confirming it have been widely discussed. Their original article, "Can Quantum-Mechanical Description of Physical Reality Be Considered Complete?" appeared in *Physics Review* 47 (1935): 777–80.

previously seemed to many to be an a priori, possibly logical, truth, or reconceptualizing what such a truth commits one to.

Or consider the view that for any two events, A and B, there must be a single fact of the matter as to whether A preceded B, B preceded A, or they were simultaneous. For most of history, this view would have been regarded as a logical or conceptual truth. But, on special relativity, we learn that for spacelike separated events—that is, events outside of each other's light cones—different reference frames will disagree about which of two events came first, so that for two events, A and B, outside of each other's light cones, A and B will be simultaneous in one inertial frame, A will precede B in another inertial frame, and B will precede A in yet another inertial frame, and the right way to view all this is that there is no fact at all about which of A and B came first![17]

Similarly, for most of human history it would have been thought intuitively obvious that it was a necessary metaphysical truth that if two people were born at the exact same moment they would always be the exact same age until one of them died (and so stopped aging). But on special relativity, we learn that two people born at the exact same moment could meet late in life having aged different amounts, depending on their trajectories through space-time.[18]

Next consider the concept of infinity. For much of history, people thought that it was a conceptual truth that the infinite was without end, that nothing could be bigger than the infinite, and that there couldn't be different sizes of infinity. But our understanding of mathematics has progressed, and with it our understanding of the concept of infinity has evolved. It is now widely accepted that there can be different sizes or orders of infinity, for example, that the order or size of the real numbers is different from that of the natural numbers, so that there are *more* real numbers than natural numbers, indeed, infinitely more. In fact, it is now widely accepted that there are an infinite number of different orders of magnitude of infinity.[19]

Or consider the connection between the notion of a property and the notion of a set. Some people thought it was conceptually true that for every property, there had to be a set of all objects which had that property. But Russell's Paradox forced us to revise our understanding of the relation between properties and sets, since "being a set" is itself a property, yet there is no set of all objects which has the property of being a set, as the "set of all sets" is logically impossible.[20]

---

[17] I am grateful to Tim Maudlin and Stuart Kurtz for correcting my original formulation of this example.

[18] Again, I am grateful to Tim Maudlin and Stuart Kurtz for their input regarding this example. Indeed, the last half of the noted sentence is taken, word for word, from Maudlin's correspondence on this point.

[19] I am grateful to Shelly Kagan for suggesting this example, as well as the following one.

[20] Russell's first published formulation of his paradox, and his initial attempt to respond to it, appears in "Appendix B: The Doctrine of Types," in his *Principles of Mathematics* (Cambridge: Cambridge University Press, 1903), 523–28. His most developed response to the paradox appears in his monumental masterpiece, coauthored with Alfred North Whitehead, *Principia Mathematica*, 3 vols. (Cambridge: Cambridge University Press, 1910).

The upshot of these remarks is simple. Many propositions which once seemed to be a priori necessary truths, including some which may have at one time seemed to be logical or conceptual truths, are no longer even accepted as true, let alone necessarily true. Our modern worldview is teeming with claims that seemed impossible, *until* we made certain (paradigm?) shifts in our understanding of the world. Once one makes such a shift, if one is able to, the impossible may no longer seem so. Moreover, and importantly, the claims I have been discussing may yet be true (or not!) even if we are not able to make the conceptual and intuitive shifts necessary to truly get our heads around them.

My point here is simply to offer a modest reminder that the mere fact that a current set of views strikes us as impossible or inconsistent doesn't necessarily mean that it is. Perhaps with a sufficient advance in our understanding of the world, we'll come to see how our views can be reconciled. Of course, the more radical Quinian possibility remains: perhaps with a sufficient advance in our understanding of the world, we'll come to see that we should accept our views even though they *are* inconsistent and cannot be "reconciled."

Let me next say a bit more about inconsistency itself. I believe there are contexts in both the normative and nonnormative realms where there is more reason to maintain an inconsistent view or set of views than to revise one's view or views merely to avoid the inconsistency. Of course, this is compatible with hoping, or even expecting, that eventually knowledge will progress, enabling us to revise, resolve, or surpass our inconsistent views. But until we actually reach that stage, we should maintain those views that there are "sufficiently" powerful reasons to accept, even when doing so involves inconsistency.

Consider, for example, Niels Bohr's model of the atom at the beginning of the twentieth century. Scientists were well aware that Bohr's model was internally inconsistent. Despite this, his model was the reigning model of the atom for more than a decade because it was better than any other available model in making successful predictions and explaining certain observed phenomena.[21] Eventually, the quantum mechanical model of the atom replaced Bohr's, but I suggest that this is mainly because of its greater predictive and explanatory success, not because it was seen to be consistent and Bohr's inconsistent. After all, presumably, there were lots of models of the atom that were *consistent* but not preferred to Bohr's, because they were less able than Bohr's to account for the relevant data.[22]

Next, consider the conflict between general relativity and quantum mechanics. My understanding is that so far as scientists can currently tell, there is no consistent way of combining them both, as the two theories are fundamentally incompatible. But there are powerful reasons to accept both general relativity and quantum

---

[21] I am grateful to my former colleague Richard Grandy for this example.

[22] My presentation and discussion of this example, as well as the following one about the conflict between consequentialist and deontological approaches, is taken from chapter 10 of *Inequality* (New York: Oxford University Press, 1993), 295–96.

mechanics, as both theories have enormous predictive and explanatory power. Accordingly, it is reasonable to continue to employ both theories in doing science, even *if* one accepts that at the most fundamental level they are incompatible. Of course, in doing this one may be assuming that *eventually* the apparent incompatibility will be resolved, or the two theories superseded by another equally or more powerful consistent theory. But one can't assume that that day will necessarily arrive, and unless or until it does, scientists are better served giving weight to both of the theories than they would be if they abandoned one, or both, in the name of consistency.

As is well known, Einstein spent much of the latter portion of his life seeking a unified field theory. The aim of such a theory is to give a unified coherent account of four fundamental forces in nature, strong nuclear interaction, electromagnetic interaction, weak nuclear interaction, and gravitational interaction.[23] Some people regard the unified field theory as the Holy Grail of science, and like the Holy Grail, it has so far eluded everyone who has sought it. It may continue to do so. It may be that there simply *isn't* a theory that can provide a coherent unified account of all of the fundamental forces of nature. But if this is so, it raises the following possibility. Perhaps the *very best* account that we can come up with for explaining gravitational interaction—which is to say the one there is *most* reason to accept based on its predictive and explanatory success—will be fundamentally incompatible with the very best account that we can come up with for explaining one or more of the other fundamental forces. In that case, I submit that it would be rational to maintain the inconsistent set of views—hoping something better might come along, but recognizing that it might not—rather than to reject one or more of the views solely on the grounds of inconsistency.

Lastly, a point about singularities. There are at least two kinds of singularity that mathematicians and physicists describe. There is the kind of singularity that is presumed to have obtained at the very beginning of the Big Bang, and there is the kind of singularity that is presumed to obtain at the center of a black hole. As I understand it, the laws of physics go entirely out the window at the "points" of singularity, and at moments and spaces *extremely* close to those points. I don't pretend to understand such claims, but I think they imply that the mathematical and physical descriptions that we employ to describe most of the known or postulated universe are inconsistent with the mathematical and physical descriptions that we employ to describe the very beginning, and possibly the very end, of the universe. This may not be right. But suppose it is. Suppose there is no consistent account we can yet give that adequately explains *everything* we want to explain about the beginning and end of the universe and everything in between. That

---

[23] Einstein, himself, was focused on unifying electromagnetism and gravitational fields, and he had a number of partial successes, but also some important failures. The current effort is to unite gravitational fields with the three other forces noted in the text. I am grateful to Stuart Kurtz for this clarification.

would not be enough, I believe, to abandon our current models of the universe. We should continue to accept and develop the *best* models we have for the phenomena we are studying until better models of those phenomena arise, and this is so even if the models we have most reason to accept are inconsistent.

Suffice it to say, I believe similar considerations apply in the normative realm. Here, I'll note just one example. Consider the conflict between consequentialist and deontological approaches. Most pluralists blithely assume that while such approaches conflict, they are not incompatible. But suppose this were not true. Suppose that when one carefully explored the *foundations* of the two theories they were, in fact, inconsistent. Perhaps they rest on competing and conflicting conceptions of the nature of duties, or autonomy, or moral agency. Would this be sufficient reason to abandon either or both approaches in normative reasoning? I think not. I believe that consequentialism has a powerful and important role to play in normative reasoning. It captures a great deal of what needs to be captured in such reasoning. But the same is true of deontology. At least until a fuller, richer theory is available that does as good or better job of capturing the crucially important tenets of morality that these theories capture, it would be a mistake to forsake either of them in the name of consistency.

Finally, consider the *Preface Paradox*.[24] An author writes a book that he has carefully researched. The book includes countless claims, each of which he has good evidence for, and each of which he strongly believes is true. Nevertheless, the author knows that he is fallible, and he has read countless other books with errors by authors who were at least as expert in their fields as he is in his. Hence, in his preface, he includes a disclaimer, apologizing, in advance, for his book's mistakes. Here we have a logical inconsistency between his perfectly rational belief that at least one of his book's claims is false, and his perfectly rational belief in the truth of each of his book's individual claims for which, by hypothesis, he has good evidence. If we refer to the author's set of beliefs as his overall worldview, or theory, we can then say the following. The author can *know* that his beliefs are inconsistent, and hence know that his overall theory is *false*, without having a clue as to where the falsity in his theory lies. Accordingly, it is perfectly rational for the author to continue to use each of the various bits of his theory in the contexts where they work well, all the while hoping that he might eventually identify and rectify the false bits later, but recognizing that despite his very best efforts, and those of others, he may, in fact, never be in a position to completely do so.

Ralph Waldo Emerson once wrote that "a foolish consistency is the hobgoblin of little minds, adored by little statesmen and philosophers and divines."[25] Emer-

---

[24] The Preface Paradox was introduced by D. C. Makinson, in "The Paradox of the Preface," *Analysis* 25 (1965): 205–7. I am grateful to Tim Maudlin for suggesting that I include this paradox in my discussion, as especially relevant to this section's point, and have basically incorporated his suggestions, wholesale, as to how I might do that.

[25] Ralph Waldo Emerson, from his *Essays, New England Reformer*, Ib. ii. *Self-Reliance*, in *Essays and Lectures*, ed. Joel Porte (New York: Library of America, 1983), 259–82.

son's contention seems unduly harsh, but the key word here is "foolish." Consistency is a laudable desideratum to seek in one's views and theories. Assuming alternative theories do roughly as well in other respects, it would be crazy to be neutral between consistent and inconsistent theories. But it is foolish to abandon a view that there is powerful reason to accept merely because it is inconsistent with some other view that there is *also* powerful reason to accept. In many cases, accepting an inconsistent view or theory may be the best we can do in the short run. And, unless the world cooperates, it may be the best we can do in the long run as well.

We may vehemently assume, fervently expect, or desperately hope that at the end of the day the world is, and must be, consistent, and thus that the ideal theory will also be consistent. But our assumptions, expectations, and hopes won't make it so, in either the normative or nonnormative realms. Depending on the nature of reality, the ideal theory may not be consistent. But even if the *ideal* theory is, *that* theory may be unavailable to us, now or ever.

I conclude that there are many contexts in which it would be perfectly reasonable and appropriate to accept (apparently?) inconsistent beliefs, at least until further advances in our understanding enable us resolve or abandon such beliefs. So, *even if we accept* the view that it would be inconsistent to accept an intransitive all-things-considered ranking of alternatives, that is not yet enough to establish that we should abandon such rankings. Given our current understanding of the normative realm, an intransitive and inconsistent ranking of alternatives may be more reasonable than any other ranking that currently suggests itself.

But having said all that, I want to reiterate a point I made at the beginning of this section. I think we should *not* accept that any intransitive all-things-considered ranking is inconsistent. Such a ranking will only be inconsistent if we *also* accept the Axiom of Transitivity. But if we accept an Essentially Comparative View, we may reject the Axiom of Transitivity—which means that we can accept any intransitive all-things-considered ranking without being inconsistent.[26]

Let me conclude this section with a slightly different, but related, point. Economists, psychologists, and philosophers have long held that it is a paradigmatic mark of irrationality to believe that, all things considered, *A* is better than *B*, and *B* better than *C*, but not to believe that, all things considered, *A* is better than *C*, and, similarly, to prefer *A* to *B*, and *B* to *C*, but not to prefer *A* to *C*. This long-standing view has assumed that the world is such that the correct ranking of all alternative outcomes would correspond to a transitive ordering. However, if one construes the "world" to include both the normative and nonnormative realms, as I do, then this book raises the serious possibility that it need not be irrational to have such beliefs or preferences. To the contrary, if an Essentially

---

[26] I am grateful to Shelly Kagan for urging that I reemphasize this point, lest the preceding discussion obscure the fact that this is my considered view of this matter. To explore how one could respond to someone who *insisted* that intransitive all-things-considered rankings must be inconsistent is not to suggest that one thinks that such a person is right. He is not.

Comparative View is correct, then it might be the case that, all things considered, *A* is better than *B*, and *B* is better than *C*, but, all things considered, *A* is not better than *C* (in my wide reason-implying sense). In that case, someone who is fully rational—in the sense of being fully responsive to all the reasons that there are—should accurately reflect that ordering in her beliefs and preferences. This is so even if the necessity of avoiding money pumps, personal ruin, and social disaster may dictate that we adopt effective practical strategies for actually dealing with such intransitive beliefs and preferences.[27]

14.7 Moral and Practical Dilemmas

Tom Nagel once wrote, "We have always known that the world is a bad place. It appears that it may be an evil place as well."[28] Nagel makes this remark in the context of having argued for the possibility of moral dilemmas, or what are sometimes referred to as moral blind alleys or moral dead ends, understood as circumstances in which people might find themselves, through no fault of their own, such that no matter *what* they do they will be acting *wrongly*. As Bernard Williams makes clear, this kind of view involves a particularly egregious form of moral luck, striking deeply at the Kantian conception that each person is always ultimately in control of, and hence responsible for, whether he acts rightly or wrongly, a conception which, as Williams puts it, has "an ultimate form of justice at its heart."[29] Of course, many would argue that only rational *agents* can be evil, or unjust, so that talk of the *world's* being "evil" or "unjust" is at best metaphorical and misleading and more likely mistaken or nonsensical. But without getting bogged down in terminological wrangling, the *point* of Nagel's and Williams's views seems plain enough. There seems to be something especially objectionable about the possibility that we might find ourselves in a predicament, not of our making, such that no matter *what* we did we would be acting wrongly.

To illuminate how a moral dilemma might be possible, we might distinguish between *prima facie* duties and *genuine* duties. Roughly, a *prima facie duty* to do a given action *X* provides one with *some* reason to do *X*, but this reason might be outweighed or canceled by other, countervailing reasons, in

---

[27] Of course one practical strategy that naturally suggests itself and that we might deem appropriate to adopt in many, if not all, cases, would be to impose a *transitivity* constraint on our preferences and actions! But we must not forget that the *usefulness* of a strategy or convention does not make it *right*, and entails nothing about what it is regarding reality that *makes* it useful. We should also remember that in imposing a transitivity constraint on one's preferences and actions, one may, for good rational reasons, be effectively rendering oneself less than fully rational. See part 1 of Derek Parfit's *Reasons and Persons* (Oxford: Oxford University Press, 1984) for an excellent discussion of the kinds of issues associated with such a position.
[28] "War and Massacre," chapter 5 in Nagel, *Mortal Questions*, 74.
[29] See "Moral Luck," chapter 2 in William's *Moral Luck*. The quoted phrase appears on page 21.

which case it would not be wrong to fail to do *X*; while a *genuine duty* to do *X* provides one with a *compelling* reason to do *X* which cannot be outweighed, canceled, or rendered moot by any other competing reasons, no matter how powerful, so that failure to do *X* is *wrong*. Clearly, moral dilemmas will be possible *if* there can be two conflicting genuine duties, that is, two genuine duties which prescribe different actions that cannot both be done, and hence which cannot both be satisfied. In that case, one would be at a moral dead end, as there would be *nothing* one could do to avoid acting *wrongly*.

Here is the kind of example which Nagel thought might be a moral dilemma: we find ourselves confronted with the possibility of mercilessly torturing an innocent child as our sole means of preventing a terrorist from blowing up a city. Here, one might think that there are overwhelmingly powerful consequentialist reasons to torture the child, which ground a genuine duty to torture the child; on the other hand, one might also think that there are overwhelmingly powerful deontological restrictions against torturing an innocent child "come what may," which ground a genuine duty not to torture the child. Thus, it may seem that no matter *what* one does, one will be acting wrongly.[30]

---

[30] On Nagel's account of the nature and source of normative reasons, the fact that we can confront such conflicts reflects a deep truth about *us*; specifically, it reflects the fact that humans can take both objective and subjective perspectives on the world, such that from a certain (relatively) "objective" perspective there will be reason to act as consequentialism dictates, but from a different (relatively) "subjective" perspective there will be reason to act as deontology dictates. Crucially, for Nagel, each perspective is equally *our* perspective, and a perspective that we can only forsake at the cost of an etiolation or radical disassociation of ourselves. In those cases where consequentialism delivers an especially powerful and unequivocal verdict, and (hence?) where it may be particularly appropriate or compelling to take up or "occupy" the objective perspective, the reasons provided by that perspective may assert "primacy" or "dominance" over all other reasons provided by any other perspective, and thus it may be that we genuinely act *wrongly* if we fail to abide by that verdict; but, likewise, in those cases where deontology delivers an especially powerful and unequivocal verdict, and (hence?) where it may be particularly appropriate or compelling to take up or "occupy" the subjective perspective, the reasons provided by that perspective may *also* assert "primacy" or "dominance" over all other reasons provided by any other perspective, and thus it may also be that we genuinely act wrongly if we fail to abide by *that* verdict. We see, then, that for Nagel the possibility of facing moral dilemmas arises from our capacity to (more or less simultaneously) take different perspectives on the world and be motivated by the reasons that hold for us from each of those perspectives, together with the fact that in some cases the rival perspectives can generate conflicting reasons each of which is compelling. My interpretation of Nagel is gleaned from a number of his works. In addition to "War and Massacre," see Nagel's "Subjective and Objective" (in Nagel, *Mortal Questions*, 196–213), and *The View from Nowhere* (New York: Oxford University Press, 1986). On the point about etiolation or disassociation of the self, see "The Absurd" (in Nagel, *Mortal Questions*, 11–23), and *The Possibility of Altruism* (Princeton, NJ: Princeton University Press, 1970).

Though interesting and suggestive, the ensuing discussion suggests that Nagel's account at best captures the source of *some* moral dilemmas. In the classic Sophie's Choice case, discussed next, a moral dilemma appears to arise solely within the deontological realm; hence it cannot be attributed to a conflict arising from our taking two different perspectives on the world, one of which (the more objective) gives rise to compelling consequentialist considerations, and one of which (the more subjective) gives rise to compelling deontological considerations. As important, we will later see that some moral dilemmas may arise because of how alternatives in the world are related in terms of what matters in ways that have nothing to do with facts about *us* and the different possible perspectives with which we may view the world.

Here is one other example which many regard as a paradigmatic example of a moral dilemma or moral dead end. In *Sophie's Choice*, Sophie faced a dilemma in which she had to choose which of her two children would live, or let both be killed by the Nazis.[31] Here, Sophie's dilemma does not involve a conflict between her deontological duties toward her children and her consequentialist duty to bring about the best outcome. Her dilemma arises solely within the deontological realm. Sophie seemingly has a genuine duty to save her son if she can, which she can, and does. But Sophie *also* seemingly has a genuine duty to save her daughter if she can, which she can, but doesn't. Accordingly, some believe that Sophie acts wrongly in failing to save her daughter when she could have done so. But, of course, on this thinking, had she saved her daughter, she would have acted wrongly in failing to save her son, when she could have done so. Hence, the sense, for some, that Sophie was facing a moral dead end.

The basic thought here is that while Sophie couldn't have a duty to save *both* of her children—since ought implies can, and it isn't possible for her to save *both*—for *each* of her children she has an equally strong duty to save that child *if* it possible for her to do so, and *it is*. Moreover, some think, the duty to save one's child, if one can, is not merely a *prima facie* duty; it is a *genuine* duty, that is, one that is not outweighed, canceled, or rendered moot even by the presence of an equally strong conflicting duty to save another of one's children. On such thinking, Sophie found herself in a situation, not of her making, where *whatever* she chose, she would be acting wrongly.

My point in commenting on *Sophie's Choice* is not to endorse the view that Sophie was facing a genuine moral dilemma. Nor am I wedded to the preceding analysis as the best interpretation of what is going on if we think Sophie was facing a moral dilemma. My point is merely to illustrate how moral dilemmas would arise for any view that allows for the possibility of two conflicting genuine duties.

Consequentialists have long thought it a virtue of their theory that it avoids the problem of moral dead ends, with its attendant problem of moral luck that many find deeply problematic.[32] On their view, there is only one genuine duty—in each circumstance, to promote the best outcome among all of one's available options, or (to handle cases of ties or imprecise equality) if there is no uniquely best outcome, produce any one of the available outcomes such that there is no other available outcome that would be better than it. Accordingly, consequentialists have long assumed that it is *always* possible for individuals to avoid acting wrongly, and hence that there are no genuine moral dilemmas. So, for example, if torturing an innocent child would promote the best consequences, then doing so would be *tragic* but not *wrong*. Similarly, if Sophie's saving her son produced consequences that were no worse than those

---

[31] William Styron, *Sophie's Choice* (New York: Random House, 1979).
[32] In addition to Williams's *Moral Luck* (Cambridge: Cambridge University Press, 1981), see Tom Nagel's "Moral Luck" for a seminal discussion of the topic (see note 29).

that would have been produced had she saved her daughter, then however tragic and heartrending her choice undoubtedly was, it was not *wrong*.

I'm not sure what to say about the deeply problematic possibility of moral dilemmas and its profound implications for moral luck and our understanding of morality. But I think this book's considerations raise serious doubts about the consequentialists' blithe assumption that their view avoids moral dilemmas, and in this respect is clearly superior to any deontological or other view that allows for the possibility of moral dilemmas.

My point here is not the familiar one, levied by some advocates of moral dilemmas, that since, on reflection, it appears that there really are *some* moral dilemmas, it is a *weakness* and not a *strength* of consequentialism that it cannot accommodate and account for such situations. My point here is the altogether different one that consequentialism may, in fact, face moral dilemmas.

Suppose, at the end of the day, that this book's considerations lead us to accept that there are sets of cases for which "all-things-considered better than" (in my wide reason-implying sense) is an intransitive relation. More specifically, suppose that we decide that there are cases where, all things considered, A is better than B, and B is better than C, but, all things considered, C is better than A; or that there are spectrums of outcomes such that the spectrum's first outcome is better than the second, the second is better than the third, the third is better than the fourth, and so on, but that the last outcome is better than the first.

In such cases, it appears that there will be no *best* outcome that consequentialism could direct us to select, and *not* because the outcomes are equally good, roughly comparable, or utterly incomparable. The outcomes *are* comparable, but they don't admit of a transitive ordering.[33] Accordingly, consequentialism will be impotent to guide us in contexts where we face such choices. Worse, it appears that consequentialists facing such choices would be facing a moral dilemma. For the problem isn't "merely" that there is no single best, or equally best, or imprecisely equally best choice. The problem is much deeper, in that *whatever* choice the consequentialist might make would, by hypothesis, be *worse* than an available alternative that he *might* have made. Hence, by standard consequentialist lights, in such circumstances the consequentialist is doomed to act wrongly *whatever* he chooses.[34] But this, of course, is the mark of a moral dilemma.

---

[33] Technically, this is redundant, since it is a defining feature of orderings that they are transitive, but for some readers it may be a helpful redundancy. I employ such redundancy often in this work; hopefully, the degree to which it is helpful for the non-technically minded outweighs the degree to which it may be annoying to the technically minded.

[34] For some time now, it has been recognized that maximizing doctrines can face moral or rational dilemmas in cases involving an *infinite* number of alternatives. But our discussion entails that if the Essentially Comparative View is correct, maximizing doctrines could face such dilemmas even in cases involving a *finite* number of alternatives. Moreover, the standard cases involving infinite alternatives allow one to confidently throw out certain options, whereas throwing out any option is much more problematic among intransitive alternatives. (cont.)

Although the point here should be clear, let me illustrate it by way of the kind of pain spectrum discussed in chapter 2. If it really would be *worse* to bring about an outcome where many people suffered to some extent, than to bring about an outcome where only *half* as many people suffered to a *slightly* greater extent, then there will be spectrums of cases where, according to consequentialism, it would be *wrong* to bring about the second outcome rather than the first, the third rather than the second, the fourth rather than the third, and so on. But, by the same token, if it really would be *worse* to bring about an outcome where some people suffered *immensely* for many years, than an outcome where innumerable people suffered *one* extra mosquito bite per month for the course of their lives, then, according to consequentialism, it would be wrong to bring about the former outcome rather than the latter one. If the Essentially Comparative View is correct, all of these judgments might be true. But, of course, together these judgments imply that consequentialists could face a spectrum of cases such that no matter *what* outcome they chose, they would be acting wrongly.

Here is an amusing case facing anyone who subscribes to a maximizing theory of individual rationality, according to which the rational action is the one that maximizes one's overall welfare or utility, or a maximizing theory of morality, according to which the right action is the one that maximizes overall well-being or utility. John is standing at the gates of Heaven. Saint Peter informs him that he may enter Heaven immediately, in which case he will live in Heaven for one day, followed by annihilation; or he may wait outside of Heaven, in a state of limbo for one day, in which case he will then enter and live in Heaven for two days, followed by annihilation; or he may wait outside of Heaven, in a state of limbo for two days, in which case he will then enter and live in Heaven for four days, followed by annihilation; or he may wait outside of Heaven, in a state of limbo for three days, in which case he will then enter and live in Heaven for six days, followed by annihilation; and so on. If John waits outside the gates of Heaven, in a state of limbo, forever, he will act irrationally and wrongly by the lights of the two maximizing theories, since he will be worse off and have promoted less utility on that option than if he had chosen *any* other available option. But for *any* day that John chooses to enter Heaven, he will act irrationally and wrongly by the lights of the two maximizing theories, since he will be worse off and have promoted less utility on that option than if he had chosen to enter Heaven the following day. Hence, faced with an infinite sequence of alternatives of the sort in question, it appears that John faces a rational and moral dilemma, since *any* action that John performs will be irrational and wrong given that there will be another *available* option that he *might* have chosen instead that would be *better* according to the two maximizing theories.

Notice, however, that in this example there is a clear ordering of the infinite alternatives that lets one confidently say of each alternative that it is worse than *all* subsequent alternatives and better than each alternative, if any, which precedes it. This desirable, well-ordered feature of the cases involving infinite alternatives, which provides John with a definitive reason to prefer some alternatives to others, is not a feature of cases involving intransitive rankings.

Since there are many deep and difficult problems of infinity, some people are not especially bothered if their favorite maximizing theory faces moral dilemmas in cases involving infinity, including cases where there are an infinite number of alternatives. I think this complacent response is dubious, but in any event it is not available to the worries I have raised, since I have shown that if the Essentially Comparative View is correct, moral dilemmas can arise for consequentialist theories even in cases where there are only a finite number of alternatives.

I grateful to Alan Hájek, who first brought an example of the preceding sort to my attention, but I'm afraid I don't know who deserves credit for first coming up with such an example. I suspect it is some mathematician whose name has long since been lost to us. A devilish (!) variation of the example, where the protagonist remains in Hell for all of eternity as a result of what seems to be his own rational (at least by the lights of Expected Utility Theory!) free will can be found in Frank Arntzenius, Adam Elga, and John Hawthorne's "Bayesianism, Infinite Decisions, and Binding," *Mind* 113 (2004): 251–83.

It appears, then, that the problem of moral dilemmas is not only a possible problem for deontologists and their ilk. *If* "all-things-considered better than" (in my wide reason-implying sense) is not a transitive relation—and this remains a big "if," but one that we may eventually come to accept—then it may also be a problem for consequentialists.

Many people have rejected the notion of moral dilemmas, including many deontologists as well as many consequentialists. But if the preceding considerations are correct, and *if* "all-things-considered better than" is not a transitive relation, then there is good reason to believe that virtually every plausible moral and practical theory will face dead ends of the sort we have been discussing.

It is arguable, for example, that any plausible theory of *individual* rationality will contend that there are at least *some* cases where, if one wants to act *rationally*, one ought to bring about the outcome that would be best for oneself or one's loved ones, so that in such cases, at least, one would be acting *irrationally* if one knowingly chose to bring about an inferior outcome when a superior one was available. However, such theories have always presupposed that there will be a transitive ranking of the alternatives one faces. If "all-things-considered better than" (in my wide reason-implying sense) is not a transitive relation, then one may face three alternatives, *A*, *B*, and *C*, such that, in terms of what would, in fact, be better for oneself or one's loved ones, all things considered, *A* is better than *B*, and *B* is better than *C*, but, all things considered, *C* is better than *A*. In that case, we would face a practical dilemma or dead end of the sort I have been discussing on *all* such theories, as no matter which alternative one chose, one would be acting irrationally, as there would be another available alternative that one might have chosen instead which was superior to the alternative that one in fact chose.

Similar claims might be made, mutatis mutandis, about any plausible theory of *collective* rationality.

By the same token, it is arguable that any plausible moral theory will contend that there are at least *some* cases where, if one wants to act *morally*, one ought to bring about the best available (relevant) outcome, so that in such cases, at least, one would be acting *wrongly* if one knowingly chose to bring about an inferior (relevant) outcome when a superior (relevant) one was available. For example, a deontologist who believes that parents have special obligations toward their children might hold that as long as parents were not violating any other deontological duties or constraints, there would be some cases where what they *ought* to do is bring about the best available outcome for their children. Similarly, deontologists and virtue theorist would agree that there would be some cases where as long as one was not violating any deontological constraints, and it would not require too much effort or sacrifice on one's part, and as long as one would not be acting viciously in doing so, there would be some cases where one *ought* to bring about the best available outcome. But, again, such theories have always presupposed that there will be a transitive ranking of the alternatives one faces. *If* "all-things-considered better than" is not a transitive relation, then one may face three alternatives, A, B, and C, such that, in terms of what would, in fact, be better for one's children, or better for the sentient beings whose interests were at stake, all things considered, A is better than B, and B is better than C, but, all things considered, C is better than A. In that case, as before, we would face a moral dilemma or dead end of the sort I have been discussing on *all* such theories, as no matter which alternative one chose, one would be acting wrongly, as there would be another available alternative that one might have chosen instead which was superior to the alternative that one in fact chose.

In sum, if "all-things-considered better than" (in my wide reason-implying sense) is not a transitive relation, then any moral or practical theory which prohibits us, on at least some occasions, from acting in some way, when this act would be worse than one of the other possible acts (and this might be true in the reason-implying sense if, whichever way we act, we had more reason to act in some other way) will face the possibility of moral or practical dead ends, where anything we choose would be wrong or irrational. But it is reasonable to assume—or at least has been up to now!—that *all* plausible moral or practical theories would include some such prohibitions. Hence, unless or until we radically revise our understanding of what we should expect from our moral and practical theories, we should expect such theories to face dead ends if, in fact, "all-things-considered better than" (in my wide reason-implying sense) is *not* a transitive relation.

14.8 Skepticism

Are the arguments of this book an argument for skepticism? Do they have deeply skeptical implications? To some extent, any genuinely intriguing impossibility argument raises skeptical doubts about how much we can trust even those judgments that we feel most confident about. I think my arguments do raise skeptical doubts of this kind, but in that respect they are like numerous other arguments that are already prevalent in contemporary thought. Where my arguments raise new, and possibly deep, skeptical worries is where they suggest that we may need to reject the Internal Aspects View, and as a result, may come to recognize that "all-things-considered better than" (in my wide reason-implying sense) is not a transitive relation.

Of course, as recognized previously, no argument can force us, by logic alone, to forsake the transitivity of the "betterness" relation. Accordingly, as I have stressed throughout this work, there are various options available that would enable us to hang on to the view that "all-things-considered better than" is a transitive relation. Still, I think it is not too bold to claim that this work at least raises doubts as to whether we can be quite so confident that "all-things-considered better than" (in my wide reason-implying sense) *is* a transitive relation. Given that, let me say a bit about the nature and scope of the skeptical worries that would arise *if*, in the end, we reject the transitivity of "all-things-considered better than" (in my wide reason-implying sense). In doing this, it may help to contrast the skeptical worries such a view engenders with the nature and source of a few other major skeptical positions. So let me begin with a brief presentation of the latter.

For many, skepticism is associated with a lack of faith in God. Nietzsche famously claimed that God is dead, implying, among other things, that there is no God, and Dostoevsky famously contended that if there is no God, everything is permitted.[35] Many believe that Dostoevsky was right—that morality, and values more generally, ultimately depend on the existence of God as their Creator and/or Foundation. For such people, coming to believe that Nietzsche was also right propels them into the abyss of skepticism, a skepticism that the universe lacks Value, and that life is meaningless and absurd.

For others, skepticism reflects a lack or loss of faith in the fundamental aims and presuppositions of the Enlightenment Project. Believing in the importance and attainability of human progress, Enlightenment thinkers sought the amelioration of the human condition with great confidence in the power of human Reason to recognize the Good; in the nature of man as basically good, ensuring that the "better angels of our nature"[36] would seek the Good that our Reason recognized; and in the power of science and education to transform and ultimately perfect both man and society. For many, twentieth-century events—including, but by no means limited to, World War I, the Holocaust, the firebombing of Dresden, the atomic bombings of Hiroshima and Nagasaki, the deportations and mass starvations of Stalinist Russia, and the development and use of chemical and biological weapons—sounded the death knell of the Enlightenment Project and gave rise to the conviction that the universe lacks Value and that life is meaningless and absurd.

Finally, for many, skepticism arises from a kind of Humean, empiricist, or scientific worldview that emphasizes the ontological primacy of the natural world. Believing that the world consists of primary material objects—atoms and subatomic particles—and the natural forces and laws that govern their behavior, some people believe that we are "mere atoms in a void" and that there is no place for ontologically significant nonnatural facts or values.[37] On this view, "values are not objective, are not part of the fabric of the world"; they are manmade inventions, to be rejected, manipulated, or changed as it suits our desires and purposes.[38] Some people who hold such a view will deny that they

---

[35] Nietzsche expresses his view in section 108 of *The Gay Science*, trans. Walter Kaufmann (New York: Vintage Books, 1974). Dostoevsky expresses his view via his character Ivan Karamozov, in *The Brothers Karamozov*, trans. Andrew MacAndrew (New York: Bantam Classics, 1984).

[36] This quoted phrase is from the end of Abraham Lincoln's *First Inaugural* (Presidential) *Address*, delivered on March 4, 1861. It is an eloquent expression of the Enlightenment thought that there is a "higher" nature that is in each of us which is basically good, and which can be appealed to and direct our actions.

[37] The view that there are only atoms in a void is not a new one. It is commonly attributed to the ancient Greek philosopher Democritus, who lived from 460 to 370 B.C.

[38] The cited phrase is from John Mackie's *Ethics: Inventing Right and Wrong* (New York: Penguin Books, 1977), 15. The expressed view is shared by Mackie, Gilbert Harman, and many others (see Harman's *The Nature of Morality* [New York: Oxford University Press, 1977]).

are moral skeptics, pointing out that on their view it is perfectly appropriate to make such claims as "I ought not to eat meat," or "Henry ought not to lie to his mom," and that such claims can even have truth value. But despite such protestations, on their view they can change their desires and intentions at any point and for any reason so as to change the truth value of the statements in question. Anyone who believes that moral values and truths are so malleable and wholly dependent on us in such a way is a moral skeptic as I use that notion.

As should be clear, if the results of this work are skeptical, they rest on entirely different foundations than these other familiar brands of skepticism. Nothing in this work presupposes that a Supreme Being must serve as the creator and/or foundation of values. Nothing in this work presupposes that man is essentially good or that man and society are perfectible. And nothing in this work presupposes a narrow naturalistic conception of the world that precludes the possibility of significant normative facts that we may recognize. To be sure, like many, in reflecting on the countless twentieth-century examples of "man's inhumanity to man," I feel a sense of despair about where we are as a species and our prospects for human progress. But even more so, I feel an acute sense of outrage, shame, and resentment that so many evil and unjust actions were perpetrated, and this reinforces, rather than undermines, my belief that there are important values that we are *capable* of recognizing and abiding by, even if all too often we fail to do so for an assortment of selfish, chauvinistic, lamentable, and wicked reasons.

Nothing in this book supports the view that life is meaningless and absurd, that there are no values, or that if there are values, we are incapable of recognizing or being moved by them. Indeed, I completely reject (though don't *argue* for the rejection of) all forms of nihilism. Insofar as this book leads to a form of skepticism, it does so on the basis of the view that there are, as it were, too *many* values, rather than *none*. More specifically, the results of this work are skeptical precisely insofar as they suggest that there *are* normative facts and values that we recognize and which provide us with significant reasons for acting, but that the values and reasons that there are *conflict* in such a way as to preclude there being a coherent, transitive ordering of certain sets of alternative outcomes.

The scope of such skepticism then depends on just how far such worries extend. If it can be successfully argued that there is a fairly limited, and perhaps peculiar, set of outcomes, such that no transitive ordering obtains of *those* outcomes, but that for the vast majority of sets of outcomes there *is* a transitive ordering, then this work's implications will not be too ominous or skeptical. But I suspect it will be difficult to develop a successful argument for the view in question. Let me briefly indicate one reason why.

Suppose one contends, as some do, that while there is intransitivity across some "special" sets of cases—like a spectrum of cases from *very long* lives that include two years of torture to *very long* lives that include one extra mosquito bite a month for the duration of the life—such cases are radically different from the kinds of alternatives that we normally confront in our lives. For most *regular* alternatives, these people are confident, if A is better than B, and B better than C, then A will, indeed, be better than C, and, moreover, this is because the factors that make it the case that A is better than B, and B better than C, will also ensure that A is better than C. Here is a worry about this widely accepted article of faith.

Take any three outcomes, J, K, and L, such that in terms of each of the factors that seem relevant and significant for each comparison, we might judge J better than K, K better than L, and J better than L. On the preceding reasoning, we can then be confident that we should choose J rather than K or L, and K rather than L. But can we be confident of this?

Suppose that J, K, and L are all negative experiences. We might then be able to embed the three outcomes, J, K, and L, in a larger spectrum of cases, say, from A to Z, where the negative experience of A is equivalent in its degree of badness to the negative experience of two years of excruciating torture, and the negative experience Z is equivalent in its degree of badness to the negative experience of one extra mosquito bite per month for countless years and where, in accordance with the Essentially Comparative View, we would judge that, all things considered, A is better than B, B is better than C,..., J is better than K, K is better than L,..., X is better than Y, Y is better than Z, and Z better than A. The possibility of our doing so may be enough to undermine our confidence in the view there is a coherent ranking of outcomes that supports the definitive judgment that J is, in fact, better than L, *all things considered*. After all, by hypothesis, we know that L is *better* than some other alternatives, which are in turn *better* than some other alternatives, which are in turn *better* than some other alternatives, and so on, which are in turn *better* than J!

If we know that J, K, and L actually stand in the way described to the other alternatives in the spectrum from A to Z, how can we simply ignore this fact in our evaluation of how J, K, and L compare? To borrow from our discussion of the Sports Analogy in chapter 13, that would seem to be akin to deciding which of three baseball teams to buy by considering only how they fared in competition with each other, and ignoring how they fared against all of the other teams in the league. But we know that doing this might be a recipe for disaster, as it could lead us to buy the very *worst* team in the league when the very best one was available!

If one actually *knows* that one team that is up for sale actually loses to every other team that is not up for sale, how can one rationally ignore that in deciding which of the teams that is up for sale is actually best? Likewise, if one actually *knows* that J is worse than some other alternatives that in turn are worse than some other alternatives, and so on, and that some of the alternatives in this progression are actually worse than K, how can one simply ignore *that* in deciding which, if any, of J, K, and L is actually best?

Similar considerations might apply, mutatis mutandis, if J, K, and L were all positive experiences, if we thought that they could be embedded in a sequence of positive experiences ranging from A to Z, where the positive experience of A is equivalent in its degree of goodness to the positive experience of two years of extraordinarily high-quality pleasure and the positive experience Z is equivalent in its degree of goodness to the positive experience of one tiny bit of low-quality pleasure per month for countless years and where, in accordance with the Essentially Comparative View, we would judge that, all things considered, A is worse than B, B is worse than C,..., J is worse than K, K is worse than L,..., X is worse than Y, Y is worse than Z, and Z is worse than A.

Such considerations are by no means conclusive, but they give some indication of why it may not be easy to circumscribe my results. Once it is accepted that "all-things-considered better than" (in my wide reason-implying sense) is not a transitive relation for *some* sets of cases, if it ever is, I suspect that the considerations supporting such a conclusion will also support the much broader conclusion that "all-things-considered better than" is not a transitive relation for *many* sets of cases, and perhaps even *most* sets of cases. Indeed, ultimately, there may prove to be no defensible "middle-ground" position that is relatively unthreatening. It may well be that in *all* cases "all-things-considered better than" is a transitive relation, or, alternatively, that in *all* cases it is not.

The preceding remarks are speculative, but they suggest that in the worst-case scenario, there may be no coherent ranking of alternatives with respect to goodness. This would obviously have profound implications for consequentialism, which understands the right as that which is conducive to the good. Whether one adopts a maximizing conception of consequentialism (according to which one only acts rightly if one brings about the best [or equally best, or imprecisely equally best] outcome) or a satisficing conception of consequentialism (according to which one only acts rightly if one brings about an outcome that is "sufficiently" good), it appears that there would be no basis to choose, or rule out, one alternative rather than any other if there is no coherent ranking of alternatives with respect to goodness. It appears, then, that on the worst-case scenario, either "everything would be permitted" or "nothing would be permitted" according to consequentialism, if "all-things-considered better than" isn't a transitive relation. Put differently, there would be no basis for seeing some actions as right and others as wrong relative to any other actions.

Similar remarks apply to Expected Utility Theory, which tells us that one acts rationally only insofar as one maximizes the expected value of one's actions. Such a view presupposes that there is a coherent transitive ranking of alternatives. Without such a ranking, it is hard to see how Expected Utility Theory could either approve, or disapprove, of one action over any other. Likewise, similar remarks apply to both maximizing and satisficing conceptions of prudential action, which see people as acting prudently only insofar as they bring about either the best (or equally best or imprecisely equally best), or a "sufficiently" good, available outcome in self-interested terms. Such views embody a consequentialist perspective, and like other versions of consequentialism, they depend on there being a coherent ranking of alternative outcomes on the basis of which people are supposed to make their choices. In the absence of such coherent rankings, such views can provide no guidance for rationally choosing one alternative over any other.

It appears, then, that rejecting the transitivity of "all-things-considered better than" may have devastating implications for both moral and prudential consequentialist theories. But, then, as I tried to make plain in the previous section, it is hardly only consequentialist theories for which such a result would have devastating implications. *All* plausible moral theories would face devastating implications in the absence of a transitive ordering of outcomes.

Recall, once more, Rawls's words cited at the very beginning of chapter 1, and again in section 14.5: "All ethical doctrines worth our attention take consequences into account in judging rightness. One which did not would be simply irrational, crazy."[39] The same might be said for all *prudential* doctrines worth our attention. Yet, plainly, such theories won't be able to take consequences into account in the way Rawls and most people would have wanted and expected them to, if there is no coherent ranking of outcomes with respect to goodness.

One can see, then, why Parfit, who is to a large extent a consequentialist, once suggested that my arguments present the most serious case for skepticism about practical reasoning since Hume.[40] He thought this because, although he ultimately rejected them, he thought that my arguments lent considerable plausibility to the view that "all-things-considered better than" (in my wide reason-implying sense) isn't a transitive relation, and hence that there is no coherent ranking of outcomes. Having said this, however, it is worth emphasizing, again, that my arguments do not support skepticism about the *reality* of the normative domain. Rather, they may, on the worst-case scenario, present us with a skeptical *crisis* about how to decide what to *do* in the moral and prudential domains.

I have been discussing the outer boundaries of what may be at stake if "all-things-considered better than" (in my wide reason-implying sense) is not a transitive relation. But I continue to reject extreme skepticism in all its forms. Accordingly, if necessary, I would reject the importance of consequentialist reasoning for normative theory, before concluding that "everything is permitted" in the moral or prudential domains. In section 14.5, I mentioned the view that "perhaps, at the end of the day, we should restrict our attention in the normative realm to such notions as virtue, duty, care, rights, and so on, abandoning our concerns about the good or bringing about the best available outcome." As I noted then, this is not a position I readily endorse, but I certainly would endorse it if the alternative was extreme skepticism about practical reasoning.

I believe there are many sources of reasons that can guide our behavior besides the category of the good. At present, I continue to regard the good as a fundamental category for normative theory. So if, in the end, we determine that there is no

---

[39] Rawls, *A Theory of Justice*, 30.
[40] Parfit has suggested this to me in conversation on several occasions.

coherent ranking of alternatives with respect to goodness, I would seek, and expect to find, another role for the good to play in normative theory than the one that we have customarily assigned to it. But if that proved futile, then I think we would have to revise our theories of practical reasoning accordingly. We have learned to develop "Godless" theories of practical reasoning. Though I am not yet persuaded that we will need to, I am confident that we could, and should, develop "Goodless" theories of practical reasoning, if that proves necessary.

14.9 Final Remarks

Some readers will no doubt be surprised, perplexed, or dismayed that in a book as long as this one, I haven't taken a stand on which combination of views I think is the *right* one. No doubt, many readers will think it is absolutely clear which views should be accepted or rejected, and they will assume that I am being dense in not also seeing this, or perhaps simply being coy or disingenuous in not admitting to it. While density on my part is certainly a possibility here, I assure the reader that I am being neither coy nor disingenuous in this matter. I find the issues raised in this book incredibly complex and difficult, and despite having thought about them for many years now, I remain at a loss as to what I should ultimately believe. As Nagel put it so succinctly and I noted in my introduction, "I do not feel equal to the problems treated in this book."[41]

So, as I described in my introduction, I feel in a position a bit like that of a juggler who is trying to juggle too many balls at once, and who knows he will eventually have to let some of them drop, but who, regarding each ball as incredibly precious, cannot see how he could possibly let *any* of them drop. Thus, the juggler frantically continues his juggling in a desperate attempt—which he knows must ultimately prove futile—to keep all of them in the air, forever. Having said that, however, let me note three important respects in which the juggler analogy is misleading.

First, as I described his situation, the juggler has only two options with respect to each ball: he can keep it in the air, or let it drop. With respect to the important positions discussed in this work, however, we actually have *three* options: we can retain them as is, we can reject them entirely, or we can revise them. Perhaps, with sufficient development of our thought, we will be able to revise our views so as to render them compatible, while at the same time preserving most, if not all, of what is important about them.

Second, as I described his situation, the juggler's predicament really is futile. He will eventually tire and let something drop. But the position with respect to inconsistent ideas is different. Nothing can *force* someone to give up a set of inconsistent views. Moreover, as I noted in section 14.6, although there

---

[41] Nagel, *The View from Nowhere*, 12.

is always reason to seek a richer conceptual and theoretical understanding of the world that is consistent, until we have actually arrived at such an understanding we may be better served by hanging on to our present, inconsistent views, than by moving to any consistent set of views currently available.

Third, in the end, it is solely up to the juggler to decide which balls are most important to him, and which ones he will let drop. On my realistic conception of the normative realm, it is not similarly up to *us* to simply *decide* which positions should be accepted and which revised or rejected. This is important. I know of some people who are so attached to certain views that they find plausible and useful, that they are prepared to reject *any* views that are inconsistent with them, "no matter what." Some have this attitude toward Expected Utility Theory, because it has proved to be *such* a powerful and helpful tool in so many domains of practical reasoning. But no matter how useful a view or theory may be, it may be incompatible with another view whose truth does not depend *on us*. Our theories should reflect the world as it actually is, and on my view, whether or not the normative realm is vague, incomplete, or even inconsistent depends on facts about the normative realm, not on what is useful for us, or on how we use certain words, or on how we think the normative realm "should" be.[42]

There is an old joke about the prevailing attitudes in England in the first part of the twentieth century.[43] The pessimists at the time looked around them and thought that the world was in such a mess that civilization as they knew it would soon come to an end. The optimists looked at the very same set of events and thought they were right! I am reminded of this joke, because pessimists reading this work may conclude that, if my arguments are sound, we must reject or drastically revise our current understandings of the good, moral ideals, and the nature of practical reasoning. Optimists, in turn, may think they are right.

---

[42] This is not to deny, of course, as Shelly Kagan notes in correspondence, that "we might think that various options in response to your arguments would be *much* easier to accept if we abandon realism in ethics (or never had it). After all, if morality, etc., is just a tool that we use to serve various purposes, it might be that the best such tool is an inconsistent model! (If we aren't describing an independent realm, why think that the best tools are consistent?) Or, we might think that since it is *just* a tool, we might keep transitivity, knowing that in some cases it will misfire, but so what, what tool is perfect?" Kagan is certainly right about this. But for all that, I can't, myself, reject realism about the normative domain, and neither does Kagan.

[43] Conveyed to me by Derek Parfit many years ago.

Appendix A

Worries about Duration and Number

In chapter 2, I presented worries about the consistency of certain standard views about trade-offs between quality and number and the transitivity of the "all-things-considered better than" relation (in my wide reason-implying sense). Let me next note that analogous worries can be raised concerning certain standard views about trade-offs between duration and number. Having considered the positions regarding quality versus number at length, I can be briefer here.

Analogous to chapter 2's First Standard View, I believe that most would accept the following view:

The Fifth Standard View (FiSV)—Trade-offs between Duration and Number Are Sometimes Desirable: In general, an outcome where a larger number of people receive a benefit for a shorter duration is better than an outcome where a smaller number of similarly situated people receive the same or a similar benefit for a longer duration, *if* the number of people benefited in the former outcome is "sufficiently" greater than the number benefited in the latter outcome, and *if* the differences in the durations of the benefits received in the two outcomes are not "too" great.

In holding such a position, one rejects:

The Second No Trade-offs View (SNTOV)—No Trade-offs between Duration and Number Are Desirable: An outcome where a larger number of people have benefits for a shorter duration is not better than an outcome where a smaller number of similarly situated people have the same or similar benefits for a longer duration, *even if* the number of people benefited in the former outcome is "much" greater, and *even if* the differences in the durations of the benefits in the two outcomes are "very" small.

Consider the following. Other things equal, it would be better if 5,000 people suffered from manic depression for ten years, than if 15,000 people suffered from manic depression for eight years; if 100 people suffered from broken arms for six months, than if 200 people suffered from broken arms for five months; and if 7,000 people suffered from acne for two years, than if 20,000 people suffered from acne for twenty months. As in chapter 2, the particular illnesses I've chosen, along with the numbers of people and lengths of duration, are not significant, and not everyone will necessarily make the same judgments about these particular alternatives. But I think these examples are sufficient to illustrate the appeal of the Fifth Standard View that Trade-offs Between Duration and Number are Sometimes Desirable across the *full range* of medical conditions.

Just as most people would accept a view about duration and number analogous to chapter 2's First Standard View, I think most people would accept a view about duration and number analogous to chapter 2's Second Standard View. Specifically, I think most would accept:

> *The Sixth Standard View (SiSV)—Trade-offs between Duration and Number Are Sometimes Undesirable Even When Vast Numbers Are at Stake*: In general, an outcome where a smaller number of people had a certain type of benefit for a longer duration would be better than an outcome where virtually any number of people had that type of benefit for a "short" duration, *if* the duration in the latter outcome is short "enough" and *if* the duration in the former outcome is "sufficiently" longer.

Opposing such a position is:

> *The Second Unlimited Trade-offs View (SUTOV)—Trade-offs of Number for Duration Are Always in Principle Desirable*: An outcome where a "sufficiently" large number of people have benefits of short duration will be better than an outcome where a smaller number of people receive the same or similar benefits of longer duration, *even if* the duration of benefits in the former outcome is "very" short, and no matter *how much* longer the duration of benefits in the latter outcome might be.

On the Sixth Standard View, it might be worse if 10 people suffered from intense pain, depression, paralysis, blindness, arthritis, headaches, limping, or acne for *fifty years* than if 10 million or even 100 million people suffered from such illnesses for a day. This view is, perhaps, more controversial than the other "Standard" Views I've described. Nevertheless, I believe that, on reflection, many people will find it compelling. Here, as before, the view seems plausible across a wide range of medical conditions.[1]

---

[1] But let me grant that there may be some "illnesses" or medical conditions that are so trivial that the Sixth Standard View would lose its force. This acknowledges that the Sixth Standard View may be

As should be apparent, together the Fifth and Sixth Standard Views are inconsistent with the transitivity of the "all-things-considered better than" relation (in my wide reason-implying sense). At least, this will be so given the plausible assumption that there is, or at least could be, a spectrum of durations, ranging from the very long to the very short, such that one could make a series of pairwise comparisons of benefits across the spectrum, where the Fifth Standard View would apply to all pairwise comparisons involving benefits that were "near" each other on the spectrum, while the Sixth Standard View would apply to all pairwise comparisons of benefits at opposite ends of the spectrum.

Consider the following spectrum of cases.

A 10 people suffer from a given illness or disability for 50 years
B 40 people suffer from a given illness or disability for 40 years
C 120 people suffer from a given illness or disability for 30 years
D 300 people suffer from a given illness or disability for 20 years
E 900 people suffer from a given illness or disability for 10 years
F 2,700 people suffer from a given illness or disability for 5 years
G 8,000 people suffer from a given illness or disability for 2.5 years
H 20,000 people suffer from a given illness or disability for 1.25 years
I 60,000 people suffer from a given illness or disability for 8 months
J 150,000 suffer from a given illness or disability for 4 months
K 450,000 suffer from a given illness or disability for 2 months
L 1.35 million suffer from a given illness or disability for 1 months
M 4 million suffer from a given illness or disability for 2 weeks
N 12 million suffer from a given illness or disability for 1 week
O 50 million suffer from a given illness or disability for 3 days
P 200 million suffer from a given illness or disability for 1 day

As described, I think many would agree that for "near" members of the preceding spectrum (*A* and *B*, *B* and *C*, *C* and *D*, etc.) the Fifth Standard View would apply, so that trade-offs between number and duration would be appropriate. In particular, other things equal, I think many might agree that, all things considered, *A* would be better than *B* and, similarly, that, all things considered, *B* would be better than *C*, *C* better than *D*, and so on, with *O* being better than *P*. It follows that if "all-things-considered better than" were a transitive relation, *A* must be better than *P*. But I believe many would deny this. The difference in duration of the illness or disability between *A* and *P* is *so* great that many would think that the Sixth Standard View applies, and that trade-offs between number and duration are undesirable. In particular, for many illnesses and disabilities at least, many would contend that *P* is better than *A*.

---

limited in scope. But all I need for my argument is that there are some illnesses or medical conditions for which the Sixth Standard View is plausible, as is the case with serious illnesses and conditions.

Now, as earlier, people may well differ about exactly how many more people would have to suffer a certain illness or disability for a shorter duration of time, for the outcome to be worse than one in which fewer people suffered that illness or disability for a longer duration of time. And their judgments about this may vary depending on the exact nature of the illness or disability in question. So, some might want to change the durations, numbers of people, or total number of outcomes involved in the spectrum before they would accede to the judgments I've suggested. Nevertheless, the foregoing is sufficient to illustrate the fundamental inconsistency between the Fifth Standard View, the Sixth Standard View, and the transitivity of "all-things-considered better than" (in my wide reason-implying sense). As long as there is, or could be, a spectrum of cases, ranging from cases involving very long durations to cases involving very short durations, such that the Fifth Standard View would apply to all cases "near" each other on the spectrum, and the Sixth Standard View would apply to cases at opposite ends of the spectrum, one must choose between the Fifth Standard View, the Sixth Standard View, or the transitivity of the "all-things-considered better than" relation.

Appendix B

On the Relations between Quantity, Quality, Duration, and Number

In chapter 2, and appendix A, I treated quality and duration separately, and suggested that each may be distinguished from, and traded off against, number. In fact, the boundaries between quality, duration, and number are easily blurred, as are their relations to quantity. In this appendix, I note some of the complexities in the relations between quantity, quality, duration, and number.

One way of thinking about an outcome's *quantity* of benefits or burdens is as a function of the *number* of instances of benefits or burdens of given *qualities* and *durations*. For example, suppose 10 people each experienced a value of great benefit for 3 years each. We might select a number to represent the quality of that benefit, relative to other benefits and burdens, and then calculate the total quantity (QN) of that benefit in that outcome, as a function of the quality (QL), times the duration (D), times the number of people (N) having that benefit. So, in this simple case, our formula for calculating the total quantity of the great benefit in the outcome would be $QN = (QL \times D) \times N$. If we decided the benefit had a value of 100 units of quality, we would determine that the quantity of benefit in the outcome was (100×3) × 10 or 3,000 units of benefit. Notice, calculated this way, the same *quantity* of benefit would be in an outcome where one person had a benefit of quality 100 for 30 years, or 10 people had a benefit of quality 300 for 1 year, or 1,000 people had a benefit of quality 1 for 3 years.

Also, while in this example N represents the number of people that have the benefit for a certain duration, in general, N might just represent the number of distinct instances that the benefit occurs for a certain duration. So, for example, if one person had a benefit of quality 100 for 1 year early in her life, and another benefit of quality 100 for 1 year later in her life, the total quantity of that benefit in the person's life might be measured as (100×1) × 2 = 200, reflecting the quality of each benefit and its duration times the number of instances of that benefit that occurred for that duration.

Suppose, next, that there were 10 people in an outcome receiving benefits of different quality during different periods of their lives. Specifically, suppose that 8 of them had a benefit of quality 100 for 2 years, 5 had a benefit of quality 50 for 6 years, and 4 had a benefit of quality 25 for 10 years. Then, on the approach being considered, the total quantity of benefits in that outcome might be calculated as $((100(QL) \times 2(D)) \times 8(N)) + ((50 \times 6) \times 5) + ((25 \times 10) \times 4) = 4{,}100$. Moreover, on this way of measuring *quantity* it doesn't matter how the different instances of benefits are distributed among the different people. They might be relatively equally distributed, or some people might have each of the different kinds of benefits within their lives, while others might have none.

There are other conceptions of quantity people might have, including conceptions that drive a firm wedge between quantity and quality. But I think the conception suggested here is a natural and plausible one, and one that frequently underlies people's claims about the quantity of benefits or burdens that obtain in outcomes. So, for example, if in one outcome 10 people have high-quality benefits of level 100 for 2 years each, and in another outcome 10 people have medium-quality benefits of level 75 for 2 years each, it is natural to claim that there are *fewer* benefits in the latter outcome than in the former one. Similarly, it would be natural to say that there is *less* pain in an outcome where someone experiences mild pain for 1 hour than where someone experiences intense pain for 1 hour. Here, one might say that while the *number* of instances and *duration* of the pains experienced by someone would be the same in the two cases, the *total quantity* of pain is greater in the outcome where the *quality* of the pain is worse.

Analogous points might be made regarding duration and number. It is natural to say that there is a greater quantity of pain in an outcome where 10 people have a mild pain for 2 years each, than in an outcome where 10 people have a mild pain of the same quality for 1 year each. Likewise, it is natural to say that there is a greater quantity of pain in an outcome where 10 people have a mild pain for 2 years each, than in an outcome where 5 people have a mild pain of the same quality for 2 years each.

It appears, then, that on one natural conception of *quantity*, the quantity of benefits or burdens in an outcome will be a function of the quality, duration, and number of instances of benefits and burdens in that outcome, and that variations in the latter properties can produce variation in the former property. Correspondingly, one can see how one might easily blur, or confuse, the distinction between the quantity of benefits or burdens in an outcome and the quality, duration, or number of instances of those benefits or burdens.

I have tried to give examples where it seems relatively easy to keep the notions of quality, duration, and number distinct. But, importantly, this isn't always the case. Consider the case of someone who experiences a mild pain for 3 years running. As I described it previously, there would be 1 instance of mild pain, lasting for a duration of 3 years. But the outcome might be equally well described as one involving 3 consecutive instances of mild pain, each lasting 1 year, or 36 consecutive instances of mild pain, each lasting 1 month, or....

Or consider the case of someone who experiences a mild pain over the course of 2 hours, but who receives relief from that pain for 10 minutes in the middle. Should we say that that person has experienced 1 instance of interrupted pain lasting 110 minutes, or that the person has experienced 2 instances of uninterrupted pain each lasting 55 minutes? In such cases, it seems largely arbitrary how we carve up the distinction between the number of instances of pain and the duration of those instances. Fortunately, nothing much hinges on how we choose to do so. On the approach to measuring quantity of benefits or burdens suggested earlier, there will be the same quantity of benefit or burdens in the different cases however we carve them up in terms of numbers of instances versus duration.

Does this mean that duration and number are interchangeable, and that we could dispense with one category or the other? No. Duration and number are complementary notions. Although one can sometimes count fewer instances of longer duration, or more instances of shorter duration, one needs both notions to capture the "places"—whether understood as space-time coordinates or as sentient beings who travel through space and time—where benefits and burdens of different quality "occur."[1] Moreover, as long as we continue to think of benefits and burdens as coming to individuals and enduring through time, there will be a lower limit on the number of instances of benefits and burdens that we might count as obtaining in any given outcome, equal to the number of people who receive benefits or burdens in that outcome. So while there may be some degree of arbitrariness as to how we decide between the numbers of benefits or burdens versus the duration of those benefits or burdens *within* lives, such issues seem much less arbitrary when we're tallying benefits and burdens occurring in *different* lives.

Put crudely, my pain now may or may not be counted as an instance of the "same" pain, extended through time, later, but it will never be plausibly counted as an instance of the same pain, extended through space or persons, that *you* are experiencing now or later. Your pain and mine will always be counted as two instances of pain, of similar or different quality, and of similar or different duration.

---

[1] For the best discussion of the different "locations" at which the good may appear, and the implications of taking a stand on this matter, see John Broome's *Weighing Goods* (Oxford: Basil Blackwell, 1991). I might add that I am not, myself, committed to the view that all goods occur in space and time, though if they do not, that may complicate the rubric we need to accurately measure an outcome's overall goodness. Suppose, for example, as some people believe, that satisfying someone's deepest other-regarding preferences can benefit that person, or be a good thing, even after the person is dead. It is an interesting issue to try to determine *where* such a benefit or good is "located" or what its "duration," if any, might be.

Just as there may be some blurring of lines between duration and number, there may be some blurring of lines between duration and quality. In particular, it might be thought that large differences in the duration of a benefit or burden may amount to a difference in the quality of the benefit or burden. So, for example, it might be argued that the difference between walking with a painful limp for a day and walking with a painful limp over the course of one's life *isn't* merely a difference in the duration of the painful limp; it is the difference between having a sore foot and being *crippled*. Moreover, importantly, it might be argued that being crippled is *qualitatively* distinct from having a sore foot. Likewise, it might be argued, there is a large qualitative difference between being clinically depressed for twenty years and being down in the dumps for a day, even though there is a sense in which someone who is "down in the dumps" every day for twenty years just is someone who is clinically depressed.

Of course, someone who is crippled, or clinically depressed, will have had their life radically altered in ways that someone who merely has a sore foot or is down in the dumps for a day will not have, and one can plausibly argue that the qualitative differences alluded to previously lie in these *effects* of having the conditions in question for different durations, rather than in the *conditions* themselves. Still, it isn't clear that the conditions are appropriately separable from their effects, and even if they are, it seems clear that it is both the conditions and their effects that underlie our judgments about the relative desirability of different trade-offs between quality and number, or duration and number. Thus, it is arguable that appendix A's Sixth Standard View, that Trade-offs between Duration and Number Are Sometimes Undesirable Even When Vast Numbers Are at Stake, isn't really distinct from chapter 2's Second Standard View, that Trade-offs between Quality and Number Are Sometimes Undesirable Even When Vast Numbers Are at Stake, because differences in duration of sufficient size, together with the effects attendant on such differences, sometimes amount to differences in quality. Similarly, it is arguable that even small differences in the duration of a benefit or burden, together with the effects of those differences, may amount to a small difference in the quality of those benefits or burdens, together with their effects. Correspondingly, it is arguable that appendix A's Fifth Standard View, that Trade-offs between Duration and Number Are Sometimes Desirable, may just be a variation of chapter 2's First Standard View, that Trade-offs between Quality and Number Are Sometimes Desirable.

In sum, there is a natural way of measuring quantity as a function of quality, duration, and number. Moreover, while quantity, quality, duration, and number are distinct notions, they are related in ways that make it easy to blur the lines between them. For one, variations in quality, duration, and number may be correlated with variations in quantity, making it easy to conflate any of the former notions with the latter notion. For another, in different cases, duration, or duration together with its effects, may seem interchangeable with either number or quality. Finally, given the suggested relation between quality and duration, it shouldn't be surprising if most who find chapter 2's First and Second Standard Views plausible also find appendix A's Fifth and Sixth Standard Views plausible. Nor should it be surprising that, together, appendix A's Fifth and Sixth Standard Views have similar implications and raise similar problems as chapter 2's First and Second Standard Views.

Appendix C

A New Version of the Paradox of the Heap

In chapter 9, I presented the standard Hairiness/Baldness Sorites Paradox and showed, following a suggestion of Ryan Wasserman's, how it might be revised or reinterpreted so that it paralleled my Spectrum Arguments. In this appendix, I note how Wasserman's considerations might also apply to another well-known Sorites Paradox, the Paradox of the Heap.

The standard version of the Paradox of the Heap runs roughly as follows. Start with a large heap of sand. Surely, it is thought, one grain of sand will not be enough, by itself, to make a difference to whether or not there is a heap of sand. Call this the *Crucial Premise for the Standard Sorites Paradox of the Heap*, or *CPH*, for short. So, start with a pile of sand that is clearly a heap. Remove one grain. In accordance with *CPH*, it will still be a heap. Iterate. After each iteration, it will still be a heap, according to *CPH*. After enough iterations one will be left with a single grain of sand. This argument supposedly shows that a single grain of sand is a heap of sand. But that is obviously false. Hence the argument has clearly gone wrong, and the question is where.

Wasserman's revised version of the Paradox of the Heap proceeds differently. Wasserman contends that our criteria for determining whether or not a pile of sand is a heap are complex, and they vary depending on the alternatives being compared. Roughly, we think that two criteria must be met for a pile of sand to count as a heap. First, it must have a large number of grains of sand. Second, it must have a roughly mound-like shape. So, for example, a flat beach would not count as a heap of sand, no matter how many grains of sand it might contain. Neither would a large pile of sand roughly one inch deep, even if it had a few uneven undulations across its surface.

But then Wasserman suggests the following. Start with a relatively large pile of sand that is sufficiently mound-like in appearance as to clearly count as a heap. Suppose, for the sake of argument, that the sand heap is some twenty feet high. Wasserman suggests that given the fact that we have *two* criteria for assigning "heapness" to a sand pile—roughly the *number* of sand grains and the *shape* of the grains—we might all rightly agree that a *slight* worsening of a pile in terms of one criterion, say shape, could be more than made up for by a "sufficient" gain in the second criterion, say number.

So, Wasserman suggests, if we pushed down the top of a sand pile, lowering it by a few inches, but *doubled* the total number of grains in the pile, we might rightly agree that the second pile was even more of a heap than the first. The thought, of course, is that the second pile would be less like the first in terms of being a heap regarding its shape, but even more of a heap in terms of its number of grains of sand, and that in *this* case, since the change in shape was slight and the gain in numbers great, *all things considered*, the second would be even more of a heap than the first. Let us say that if one sand pile is even more of a heap than another, then it is "heapier." So, in the example, the second pile is "heapier than" the first.

Wasserman then repeats the kind of transformation in question many times. Each time, he makes a *slight* alteration in the pile's heap-like *shape*, but he adds *many* times more grains of sand, so that everyone might agree that whether or not either of the piles was, in fact, a heap, the second would be heapier than the first. Of course, after many such iterations, one would be left with a flat beach-like surface, perhaps with some undulations, but less than one inch deep. As noted earlier, although everyone could agree that there were now *far* more grains of sand than one originally began with, the sand would *not* be a heap, and it would not be heapier than the original mound, which *was*, clearly, a heap.

One can see how this version of the Paradox of the Heap runs. There is a spectrum of piles of sand, ranging from the first to the last, such that the second is heapier than the first, the third is heapier than the second, and so on. If "heapier than" is a transitive relation, as one might have thought it *must* be, then the last pile must also be heapier than the first. But the last pile is like a beach. Correspondingly, we must either give up the view that the last pile is not a heap, and is not heapier than the first pile, which clearly *is* a heap; we must reject the view that "heapier than" is a transitive relation; or we must find at least one spot along the spectrum of alternatives where the spectrum's $(n + 1)$th member was not heapier than the nth.

The key to this argument, of course, is that we seem to apply *different* criteria in making different comparisons of sand piles. When we compare piles whose shapes are "sufficiently" similar, we give significant weight to the *number* of sand grains in determining which of two piles is heapier. But when the difference in shapes is large enough—and, more specifically, if one is clearly mounded, while the other is basically flat—then as long as there are *enough* grains of sand in the mounded pile, we will count that as a heap, and heapier than the flat-shaped pile, no matter *how* many more grains of sand there may be in the flat pile than in the mounded one.

As should be clear, analogues of this argument could be presented for any Standard Sorites Paradox, as long as there were at least two dimensions underlying the Paradox's central notion, and we thought that they were related along the lines in question: specifically, if "sufficiently" small losses along one dimension could be made up for by "sufficiently" large gains along other dimensions, but "sufficiently" large losses along the first dimension could not be made up for by gains along the other dimensions, no matter how large those gains might be. As noted in chapter 9, such Revised Sorites Paradoxes will raise all the difficulties of my Spectrum Arguments and not be amenable to the same kind of solutions as Standard Sorites Paradoxes.

Appendix D

Three Further Objections to Spectrum Arguments

In this appendix, I want to comment on three further arguments that have been raised against my Spectrum Arguments. The first was presented by Christopher Knapp, who argued that my Spectrum Arguments could be resolved via a proper understanding of vagueness and indeterminacy. The second was presented by Ken Binmore and Alex Voorhoeve, who once argued that my Spectrum Arguments were a version of one of Zeno's Paradoxes. The third was presented by Erik Carlson, who argued that we can find a uniquely best alternative along my spectrums.

D.1 Vagueness and Indeterminacy

Many believe that the root of most paradoxes involving spectrums, including Sorites Paradoxes, lies in a failure to properly understand vagueness and indeterminacy. Specifically, they believe that it is because we misunderstand and misapply vague and indeterminate notions that we get into trouble when considering spectrums of alternatives involving such notions. A fortiori, many suspect that a careful understanding of vagueness and indeterminacy will enable us to reject my Spectrum Arguments.

One person who has argued for such a position is Christopher Knapp, in his article "Trading Quality for Quantity."[1] Ultimately, as Knapp himself recognizes,[2] his objection reduces to a version of the "different kinds, different criteria" objection that I have already discussed, and rejected, in section 9.1. However, since Knapp's argument is couched in terms of vagueness and indeterminacy, I believe

---

[1] *Journal of Philosophical Research* 32 (2007): 211–33.
[2] "Trading Quality for Quantity," 225.

that some may initially find it attractive, or at least assume that his objection is on the right track. Accordingly, it is perhaps worth a direct response.

Consider chapter 9's pain spectrum, ranging from the mildest possible pain, which gets a score of 1, to the most intense possible pain, which gets a score of 600.

Knapp started out by distinguishing between pains of the *same* or *different* kinds, and his corresponding notions of mere *quantitative* versus *qualitative* differences in pain. Roughly, for Knapp, any two pains at the *same* end of the pain spectrum will be pains of the *same* kind, and there will be mere *quantitative* differences between them, while any two pains at *opposite* ends of the pain spectrum will be pains of *different* kinds, and there will be a *qualitative* difference between them. Knapp then contended that chapter 5's View One—for any unpleasant or "negative" experience, no matter what the intensity and duration of that experience, it would be better to have that experience than one that was only a "little" less intense but twice (or three or five times) as long—was appropriate for comparing two pains of the *same* kind, such as two very intense pains or two very mild pains; while chapter 5's View Three—the mild discomfort of a mosquito bite would be better than two years of excruciating torture, no matter how long one lived and no matter how long the discomfort of a mosquito bite persisted—was appropriate for comparing two pains that were *different* in kind, such as a very intense pain and a very mild pain. So, Knapp begins his argument by granting that trade-offs between intensity and duration are desirable for alternatives involving mere quantitative differences, but not for alternatives involving qualitative differences.

Knapp then claimed that for *middle* members of the pain spectrum, such as pains 300 or 301, it was *indeterminate* whether they were very intense or very mild. He then argued, and this is the *key* step in his argument, that since pain levels of 300 and 301 are *borderline* cases of being "very intense" and *also borderline* cases of being "very mild," then the choice between a life containing pain 300 for a certain duration or pain 301 for a much longer duration is *itself* "a borderline case of a choice in which the relevant qualitative difference is at stake. This is because ... *one* of our option's being a borderline case of a qualitative distinction is *enough* to *guarantee* that *any* tradeoff involving that option will be a borderline case of a tradeoff in which that difference is at stake."[3]

Intuitively, Knapp's thought seems to be that if there is no fact of the matter whether pains 300 and 301 are or are not "very intense" or "very mild," then there *can't* be a fact of the matter as to whether or not View One or View Three applies to them. So, for example, since it isn't *false* that pain 301 is very intense, and since it also isn't *false* that pain 300 is very mild, then it isn't *false* that View

---

[3] "Trading Quality for Quantity," 220–21, emphases added. Knapp puts this claim in terms of borderline cases of happiness along the contentment spectrum, but he clearly intends to apply it, as I have, mutatis mutandis, to borderline cases of very intense or very mild pains along the pain spectrum.

Three is applicable for comparing them and, likewise, it isn't *true* that View One is applicable for comparing them. Of course, Knapp readily admits that on his view it *also* isn't *true* that View Three is applicable for comparing them, and isn't *false* that View One is applicable for comparing them, but that is okay with him. For *my* argument to succeed, Knapp argues, I need it to be *true* that View One applies to all "nearby" pains along the pain spectrum, including 300 and 301. Thus, Knapp thinks he has shown that View One should be rejected.

So, according to Knapp, the vagueness of our notions about pain explains why even though View One applies when comparing pains that are on the same ends of the pain spectrum, it is neither true nor false that it applies for comparing certain pains in the middle of the spectrum. Hence, there will be at least some alternatives for which it is *indeterminate* whether a pain of greater intensity for a shorter period of time is better or worse than a pain of *slightly* less intensity for a much longer period. This is enough to break the "chain" of pairwise comparisons that would imply, if the transitivity of "all-things-considered better than" were true, that a life involving two years of excruciating torture would actually be *better* than a life containing *one* extra mosquito bite per month for *many* months. Thus, Knapp concluded that once we really understand the nature of vagueness, we can see how it provides a way of responding to my Spectrum Arguments and preserving the transitivity of the "all-things-considered better than" relation.

Knapp's argument fails. We must clearly reject its key premise that a pain's being a borderline case of a qualitative distinction guarantees that it would be indeterminate whether or not View One or View Three applied for *any* comparisons involving that pain. This is simply not so. After all, even if one grants that pain 301 is both indeterminately very intense and indeterminately very mild, and so a borderline case of a qualitative distinction, it *doesn't* follow that a trade-off between *one* year of pain 301 and *five* years of pain 301 would involve a borderline case *where a qualitative difference* was at stake! Since there is *no* difference between the intensity of pain in the two cases, only a difference in duration, it cannot be indeterminate whether a qualitative difference is at stake.

For Knapp, a qualitative difference is at stake when comparing a very intense pain, like torture, with a very mild pain, like that of a mosquito bite. This is a *big* difference in intensity. It is *not* indeterminate whether a big difference in intensity is at stake between a pain of intensity 301 lasting one year and a pain of intensity 301 lasting five years. Likewise, crucially, even if it *is* indeterminate whether pains 300 and 301 are very intense or very mild, it is *not* indeterminate whether there is a small or big *difference* in intensity between such pains. There is, in fact, only a *small* difference.

View Three is appropriate for comparing pains between which there is a *big* difference in intensity. View One is appropriate for comparing pains between which there is a *small* difference in intensity. Although it may be indeterminate whether View One is appropriate for comparing pain 301 with pains 597 or 3—because it may be indeterminate whether the difference between *those* pains is big or small—it is *not* indeterminate whether View One is appropriate for comparing pains 300 and 301. Thus, as indicated, the key premise of Knapp's argument is false, and hence his argument against me is fallacious.

As suggested earlier, Knapp himself recognized that although his argument is couched in terms of vagueness and indeterminacy, it is, in fact, a version of the different kinds argument rejected in section 9.1. Accordingly, it should be rejected for the same reasons. Basically, to review the relevant arguments from chapter 9, it is a mistake to contend, as Knapp essentially does, that the *reason* View One applies for comparing some alternatives is that they are the *same* kind; that the *reason* View Three applies to other alternatives is that they are *different* kinds; and that it is *indeterminate* whether View One or View Three applies to alternatives when it is indeterminate what *kinds* of pain they are. After all, whether two pains count as the same, different, or indeterminately the same or different *kind* of pain depends on the *kind* in question. Pains 551 and 597 may be the *same* for the kind "very intense" pain, but *indeterminately the same* for the kind "super very intense" pain. Likewise, pains 597 and 3 may be the *same* for the kind "experience there is some reason to avoid," but *different* for the kinds "very intense" pain and "very mild" pain. Similarly, pains 300 and 301 may be *indeterminately the same* for the kinds "very intense" pain and "very mild" pain, but the *same* for the kind "moderate" pain.

Thus, to determine what principle is relevant for comparing two pains, we can't simply ask ourselves whether the pains are the same, different, or indeterminately the same kind of pain. Rather, we have to determine what *makes it the case* that a principle applies, doesn't apply, or indeterminately applies. On reflection, it seems clear that View One applies for comparing pains that are "sufficiently" similar in intensity; this, ultimately, explains *why* it is plausible for comparing two pains both of which are very intense, or both of which are very mild. But then View One is also plausible for comparing pains 300 and 301, and *n* and *n* + 1 more generally, since such pains will *also* be "sufficiently" similar in intensity for View One to apply. Thus, I conclude that Knapp's claims about vagueness and indeterminacy fail to provide any reason for rejecting the plausibility of View One and its role in my argument.

One final remark. There is a different argument Knapp hints at in his paper, having nothing to do with vagueness or indeterminacy.[4] Instead of trying to show that View One is mistaken or implausible, or that we have powerful independent reason to reject it, one might claim that View One is *less* plausible than the *other* premises of my impossibility argument. That is, one might recognize that *something* has to go, but contend that it is too difficult to reject the empirical premise, View Three, or the transitivity of the "all-things-considered better than" relation (in my wide reason-implying sense).

---

[4] "Trading Quality for Quantity," 225–26.

I doubt that View One *is* the least plausible of the premises of my impossibility argument. But I accept that this is the kind of argument that we may ultimately be forced to appeal to in the face of my arguments. Perhaps, one day, we will conclude that View One *has* to go, not because we have shown where it goes wrong, but because we are unable to accept its implications *given the other views to which we are committed*. I am not ready to make that move yet. But if we do, ultimately, make such a move, we need to recognize that the "lesser evil" argument is a completely different argument than the kinds of arguments that most people have offered against View One, and that I have considered, and rejected, in this book. And while the "lesser evil" argument may ultimately be the strongest argument we can muster in this area, it is a rather unsatisfying argument, not least because different people have very different views about what the lesser evil actually is.

D.2 Zeno's Paradox

In "Defending Transitivity against Zeno's Paradox," Ken Binmore and Alex Voorhoeve argued that the kinds of arguments that Stuart Rachels and I have offered challenging the Axiom of Transitivity fail, and claimed to make "clear where the argument goes wrong, by showing that it is a version of Zeno's Paradox of Achilles and the tortoise."[5] Binmore and Voorhoeve contended that our arguments *depended* on making the same kind of mistake that Zeno made in his famous paradox.

I mention Binmore and Voorhoeve's article here mainly because some readers may be acquainted with it, and may wonder why, in a book as long as this one, I haven't bothered to respond to it. The answer is simple. Because Erik Carlson has already shown that Binmore and Voorhoeve were mistaken in claiming that our arguments depended on a mistake akin to Zeno's,[6] and Binmore and Voorhoeve already recognize and accept this.[7]

In my article "A Continuum Argument for Intransitivity,"[8] I presented three claims that I contended were jointly incompatible with each other and the Axiom of Transitivity. Binmore and Voorhoeve correctly saw that *if* one considered a convergent series, of the sort which enables one to avoid Zeno's Paradox of Achilles and the tortoise, then each of my three claims could be true without entailing a violation of the Axiom of Transitivity.

---

[5] *Philosophy and Public Affairs* 31 (2003): 272–79; the quoted remark is from page 272.

[6] See Carlson's "Intransitivity without Zeno's Paradox," in *Recent Work in Intrinsic Value*, ed. T. Rønnow-Rasmussen and Michael Zimmerman (Dordrecht: Springer, 2005), 273–77.

[7] Voohoeve acknowledged this to me in personal conversation following a lecture I gave at the University of London in the spring of 2006. He has also acknowledged this in print, in note 4 of his "Heuristics and Biases in a Purported Counterexample to the Acyclicity of 'Better Than,'" *Politics, Philosophy, and Economics* 7 (2008): 285–99.

[8] *Philosophy and Public Affairs* 25 (1996): 175–210.

They were right. But as Carlson correctly pointed out, this does *not* show that Rachels's and my Spectrum Arguments *depended* on a mistake akin to Zeno's. All it showed is that I was being slightly sloppy in my initial formulation of some of my claims. Indeed, if one looks at the various examples that I presented in my paper, it is fairly clear how I intended my claims to be interpreted, and how they would need to be revised to reflect the way that I was actually understanding and employing them.

Instead of my original:

Claim 1: For any unpleasant or "negative" experience, no matter what the intensity and duration of that experience, it would be better to have that experience than one that was only a little less intense but that lasted much longer.[9]

I should instead have written some variation of the following:

Claim 1: There exists some fixed and finite degree of intensity of pain, k, which is sufficiently small, that for any unpleasant or "negative" experience, no matter what the intensity and duration of that experience, it would be better to have that experience than one that was only less intense by degree k, but that lasted much longer.

Likewise, instead of my original:

Claim 2: There is a finely distinguishable range of unpleasant or "negative" experiences ranging in intensity from mild discomfort to extreme agony.

I should instead have written something like the following:

Claim 2: There is, or at least could be, a finely distinguishable range of unpleasant or "negative" experiences ranging in intensity from mild discomfort to extreme agony, such that one could make a series of pairwise comparisons of benefits across the spectrum, where claim *1* would apply to all pairwise comparisons involving benefits that were "near" each other on the spectrum, while claim *3* would apply to all pairwise comparisons of benefits at opposite ends of the spectrum.[10]

In fact, the revised version of claim *2* is all I really need for my argument; but though not necessary, the revised version of claim *1* is also a view I accept, and it,

---

[9] Claim *1* and the first claim *2* I am about to present are from page 273 of Binmore and Voorhoeve's "Defending Transitivity against Zeno's Paradox." These claims appear in their reconstruction of the Rachels/Temkin argument challenging the Axiom of Transitivity. They cite pages 72–75 and 78–79 of Stuart Rachels's "Counterexamples to the Transitivity of Better Than," *Australasian Journal of Philosophy* 76 (1998): 71–83; and page 179 of my "A Continuum Argument for Intransitivity," *Philosophy and Public Affairs* 25 (1996): 175–210, as the original sources of their reconstructed argument.

[10] In Binmore and Voorhoeve's reconstruction of the Rachels/Temkin argument, *Claim 3* is: No matter how long it must be endured, mild discomfort is preferable to extreme agony for a significant amount of time. See the previous note, 9.

too, would directly address Binmore and Voorhoeve's worry about Zeno's Paradox. Although I already had versions of the "revised" claims *1* and *2* in mind in my earlier papers and examples, in this book I have tried to be more careful in my presentation of such claims, to avoid prompting Binmore and Voorhoeve's worry.

In sum, while I am grateful to Binmore and Voorhoeve for pointing out one way in which I needed to tighten up the presentation of my arguments,[11] their objection about Zeno's Paradox was not, in fact, relevant to the actual examples that Rachels and I offered, nor did it have any bearing on the *substance* of the challenges for the Axiom of Transitivity that Rachels and I were raising.

D.3 Finding a Uniquely Best Alternative along a Spectrum

In his article "On Some Recent Examples of Intransitive Betterness,"[12] Erik Carlson argued that there was, in fact, a solution to my Spectrum Arguments, and those offered by Stuart Rachels.[13] Carlson addresses his solution to those Spectrum Arguments, like Rachels's and mine, that have the following structure: there is a spectrum of alternatives, say, from x_1 to x_n, whose members vary along two dimensions, say, *intensity* of pain and *duration* of pain, such that (1) the alternatives go from best to worst along the first dimension, and (2) the alternatives go from worst to best along the second dimension; and we think the trade-offs between the different dimensions are such that (3) for each *pairwise* judgment of any two adjacent alternatives, x_j and x_k, where $k > j$, we would judge x_k as *worse* than x_j, and yet (4) we would make the *pairwise* judgment that x_n is *better* than x_1.

Carlson suggests that the *appearance* that "all-things-considered better than" is an intransitive relation along such a spectrum is misleading, because in fact we can locate a best alternative along the spectrum. Roughly, according to Carlson, the best, or most "choiceworthy," alternative along the spectrum will be the first alternative as one moves along the spectrum from x_1 toward x_n, which is *pairwise* better than *each* alternative that comes after it along the spectrum, that is, it must be the first alternative, x_i, which is pairwise better than each alternative x_j through x_n. Carlson claims that the alternative which

---

[11] I should mention that soon after my "A Continuum Argument for Intransitivity" was published, John Broome sent me a note pointing out the flaw in my argument's original presentation, and how I should recast it so as to accurately reflect my views and avoid the sort of worries that Binmore and Voorhoeve later raised. Broome's suggestion was essentially the same as the response that Carlson later published in my defense. So, while I am grateful to Binmore, Voorhoeve, and Carlson for their responses to my work, thanks to Broome, I was already aware of the flaw in my presentation and was reformulating my arguments accordingly.

[12] In *Logic, Law, Morality*, ed. K. Segerberg and R. Sliwinski (Uppsala: Department of Philosophy, Uppsala University, 2003), 181–95.

[13] I am grateful to Tim Campbell for urging that I address Carlson's article directly.

meets his suggested criterion is the spectrum's "uniquely most choiceworthy alternative," and he claims that it is "maximally better-than-x_n."[14]

Carlson's solution is similar to others that have been offered, and in the face of the skeptical concerns that this book raises it is certainly worth pursuing.[15] However, it prompts a number of responses, many of which have already been given in the book, and so which I'll only mention here.

First, as Carlson himself recognizes in his article, it is unclear whether his "solution" is really a solution to the theoretical challenges this book raises for the transitivity of the "all-things-considered better than" relation, or whether it is best understood as providing a *practical* suggestion for how best to proceed in the face of those challenges.[16] This is not to deny the significance of the latter, if we think it succeeds, but as I noted at the end of chapter 6, it is important not to conflate a practical response to a theoretical problem with a theoretically satisfactory solution to that problem.

Second, although it may seem somewhat "natural" to list the alternatives of the spectrum in the way that Rachels, I, and Carlson have, so that the "first" member of the spectrum is best along the first dimension and worst along the second dimension, and the "last" member of spectrum is best along the second dimension and worst along the first dimension, for the purposes of *ranking* the various alternatives of the spectrum it may seem *arbitrary* to give the "last" member of the spectrum, so conceived, *privileged status* for the purposes of ranking each of the alternatives vis-à-vis each other.

Suppose, for example, that one "rearranged" the alternatives of the spectrum, so that the first member of the spectrum, x_1, was the alternative with a "medium" intensity of pain lasting a "medium" duration; the second member of the spectrum, x_2, involved a pain of slightly less intensity, but one that lasted twice as long; one of the "middle" members of the spectrum, x_g, had a pain the intensity of a mosquito bite with a duration of a few days, every month, for *many* years; the next member of the spectrum, $x_{(g+1)}$, had a pain the intensity of horrible torture with a duration of two years; the next member of the spectrum, $x_{(g+2)}$, had a pain which was slightly less intense than that of horrible torture, but which lasted twice as long; and so on, with the last member of the spectrum, x_n, having a pain that was a little more intense than the "medium" intensity of pain in x_1, but whose duration was only half as long as the duration of the pain in x_1.

Here, as before, we might agree that for each *pairwise* judgment of any two adjacent alternatives, x_j and x_k, where $k > j$, along the spectrum of alternatives from x_1 through x_n, we would judge x_k as *worse* than x_j, and yet we would also

---

[14] "On Some Recent Examples of Intransitive Betterness," 111.

[15] I have heard similar suggestions from a number of people over the years, including both Stuart Rachels and Frances Kamm.

[16] "On Some Recent Examples of Intransitive Betterness," 111–12.

make the *pairwise* judgment that x_n is *better* than x_1. But notice, if we applied Carlson's approach for determining the best alternative along *this* spectrum, starting with x_n, we would, according to Carlson, arrive at the "uniquely most choiceworthy alternative" of the spectrum, namely, the one that was "maximally better-than-x_n." Clearly, however, the alternative we would arrive at in this case would be *different* than the alternative we would have arrived at in the other case, given that x_n is different in the two cases. That is, the alternative that is maximally better than the alternative which involves the pain of a mosquito bite which lasts for *many* years will be different than the alternative that is maximally better than the alternative which involves a pain of slightly more than "medium" intensity whose duration is only half that of a "medium" duration of time.

The problem, of course, is that the set of alternatives is *exactly the same* in the two cases; they have just been arranged in a different order! More generally, Carlson's approach will yield a *different* answer to the question of which alternative in the spectrum is best, for each possible ordering of the spectrum's alternatives that would respect the pairwise comparisons represented by clauses 3 and 4 presented earlier. And, in fact, if there are n members of the spectrum there will be n such orderings! Thus, I suggest that in the absence of an independent justification for *privileging* the particular ordering that he has focused on, in trying to determine which of the various alternatives of the spectrum is best, Carlson's approach will be of no help either theoretically *or* practically.

The worry I am raising here is similar to familiar worries that are raised about the importance of *order of presentation* in majority-rule pairwise decision procedures. As is well known, if one-third of a population prefers option *A* to option *B* and option *B* to option *C*, a second third of the population prefers option *B* to option *C* and option *C* to option *A*, and the remaining third of the population prefers option *C* to option *A* and option *A* to option *B*, then, collectively, the population will have intransitive preferences following the principle of majority rule, with two-thirds of the population preferring *A* to *B*, two-thirds preferring *B* to *C*, and yet two-thirds preferring *C* to *A*.

This means that if the population's final choice is determined by a sequence of two pairwise votes—where the population is asked to first consider their top choice between two of the options, and then to choose between that option and the third remaining option—the eventual winner will depend on the order in which the options are presented. If the population is first presented with the choice between *A* and *B*, *C* will be the eventual winner; if the population is first presented with the choice between *B* and *C*, *A* will be the eventual winner; and if the population is first presented with the choice between *A* and *C*, *B* will be the eventual winner.

But no one believes that which option is actually *best* between *A*, *B*, and *C*, if there is one, depends in this way on the particular order in which the various options happen to be considered and voted upon. Similarly, in the absence of a story that Carlson has not yet given us, it seems implausible to think that the question of which alternative among a spectrum of alternatives is actually *best* should depend on the particular order in which the various options are placed or considered. But, as we have seen, it is *crucial* for Carlson's approach that there be a single, privileged order in which we consider the spectrum's alternatives, so that starting with the favored candidate, x_n, there is a "uniquely most choiceworthy alternative" along the spectrum which is the one that is "maximally better-than-x_n."

Suppose that Carlson could provide us with a plausible justification for ordering any given spectrum of alternatives one way rather than another, for the purposes of applying his "solution" to my Spectrum Arguments. There are still various worries to be noted about his solution.

First, as Carlson himself recognizes,[17] his solution is only helpful, if at all, against the various challenges to the Axiom of Transitivity raised by Spectrum Arguments. All of the worries about the Axiom of Transitivity raised by the Essentially Comparative View are *untouched* by Carlson's solution, including those raised in chapter 12 by plausible versions of maximin, utility, the Pareto Principle, and the Narrow Person-Affecting View, as well as by those raised by the possibility that different principles might be limited in scope such that a given principle might be relevant and significant for comparing *A* with *B* (say, when *A* and *B* have the same people or the same number of people), but not for comparing *A* with *C* (say, when *A* and *C* have different people or a different number of people).

Second, Carlson's solution will face many of the same worries as those I raised against the Sports Analogy in chapter 13. For example, as Carlson himself clearly recognizes, his solution will violate the plausible version of the Independence of Irrelevant Alternatives Principle that I discussed in chapters 11 and 13. Relatedly, Carlson's solution raises the worry that even if I know that option *A* would be the best of a number of options that I currently face, I might want or have to consider other options that I don't currently face, including, perhaps, all other *possible* options, to determine which of my available options is actually the best *all things considered*. In addition, this kind of solution eviscerates much of the power, appeal, and importance of the Axiom of Transitivity for the purposes of practical reasoning. In particular, if we accept Carlson's solution, then we cannot appeal to the Axiom of Transitivity to help us winnow down a large complex set of alternatives on the basis of a relatively manageable set of pairwise comparisons. For Carlson, I may know that option *J* is pairwise better than option *K*, but I still can't rule option *K* out, since it might yet be the case that option *K* is better than all subsequent alternatives but option *J* is not, in which case option *K* would be best all things considered. So, for Carlson, I not only have to compare options *J* and *K* directly, I also have to compare them with every other alternative to be sure where they fit in along

---

[17] "On Some Recent Examples of Intransitive Betterness," 100.

the spectrum so that I can then determine how they compare, pairwise, with each "subsequent" member of the spectrum.

I think, then, that it is unclear whether Carlson's approach is ultimately defensible, but even if it is, for reasons presented in chapter 13, it faces a wide array of serious difficulties that have significant implications for practical reasoning.

*****

Between this appendix and chapter 9, I have now considered each of the main objections that have been raised to my Spectrum Arguments. I have argued that none of them is compelling. I conclude that the Spectrum Arguments raise deep problems that are not easily evaded.

Appendix E

Norcross's Argument for Restricting the Scope of the Narrow Person-Affecting View

In "Intransitivity and the Person-Affecting Principle,"[1] Alastair Norcross offers several objections to my "Intransitivity and the Mere Addition Paradox."[2] For the most part, I am not giving Norcross's objections separate treatment in this book, since I have already responded to them—and shown that they were either question-begging or compatible with my views—in my article "Intransitivity and the Person-Affecting Principle: A Response,"[3] and, more important, since I think they no longer apply to, or are already adequately dealt with by this book's arguments, especially those presented in sections 12.1 through 12.5. However, in this appendix, I think it may be worth directly addressing Norcross's argument that the Narrow Person-Affecting View is only plausible when comparing outcomes involving the very same people.[4]

First, I agree, and have myself argued, that the Narrow Person-Affecting View is implausible, at least as an "all-things-considered" principle, for comparing outcomes involving completely different people.[5] I also think that Norcross has given us powerful reason to believe that the Narrow Person-Affecting

---

[1] *Philosophy and Phenomenological Research* 59 (1999): 769–76.
[2] *Philosophy and Public Affairs* 16 (1987): 138–87.
[3] *Philosophy and Phenomenological Research* 59 (1999): 777–84.
[4] This response is a revised version of the one I originally gave in my "Intransitivity and the Person-Affecting Principle: A Response." Also, in the following discussion, I have slightly recast Norcross's claims to bring them in line with my current terminology. In particular, the position that I now call the "Narrow Person-Affecting View" I originally just called the "person-affecting view." I have revised Norcross's claims accordingly, but obviously this change in terminology does not affect either of our substantive positions.
[5] See my "Intransitivity and the Mere Addition Paradox," *Philosophy and Public Affairs* 16 (1987): 138–87, and also section 12.3. This was one of the main lessons to be learned from Derek Parfit's Non-Identity Problem; see part 4 of *Reasons and Persons* (Oxford: Oxford University Press, 1984).

View is not plausible, at least as an "all-things-considered" principle, for comparing *all* situations where some people are the same, but some people are different. Norcross's argument is simple. Consider diagram E.1.

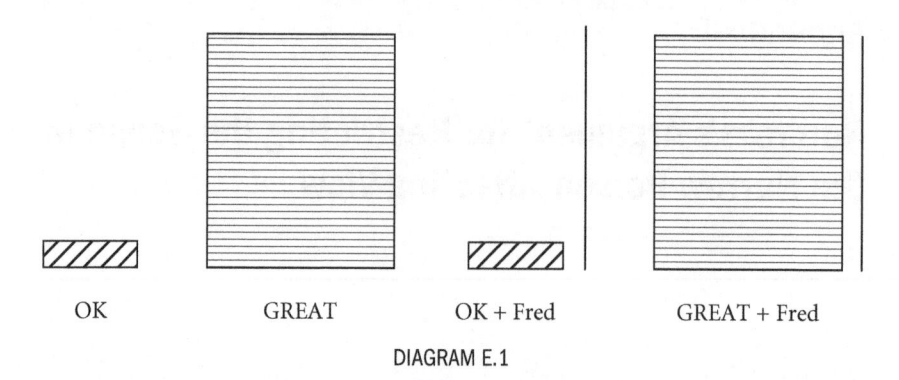

OK   GREAT   OK + Fred   GREAT + Fred

DIAGRAM E.1

Norcross starts by asking us to consider two of the four possible outcomes represented in diagram E.1: *OK*, in which there are a large number of people with lives worth living, and *GREAT*, in which there are *twice* as many *completely different* people *all* of whom are *much* better off. Norcross asserts, and I agree, that we should all agree that *GREAT* is a *much* better outcome than *OK*. So far, of course, this is just the kind of case, involving completely different people, where there is general agreement that the Narrow Person-Affecting View is implausible, at least as an "all-things-considered" principle. After all, if we brought about *OK* rather than *GREAT*, there would be *no one* (no particular people) *affected* for the worse, since the *OK* people would then be alive, with lives worth living, while the *GREAT* people would simply not exist, and, as I noted in chapter 12, most of us don't think that merely failing to bring people into existence *affects* them for the worse.

Norcross then asks us to consider a slight variation of his case, where there is *one* additional person, Fred, who would exist in both possible outcomes. In the *GREAT + Fred* outcome, Fred would be as well off as everyone else. In the *OK + Fred* outcome, Fred would be slightly better off than he would be in the *GREAT + Fred* outcome. In this case, if we brought about the *OK + Fred* outcome, there would be someone we would be affecting for the better, namely, Fred, while if we brought about the *GREAT + Fred* outcome, there would be someone we would be affecting for the worse, again, Fred.[6] But, Norcross contends, nobody believes that the difference in the existence and very slight

---

[6] As per our discussion of the Narrow Person-Affecting View in chapter 12, the claim that we would be affecting Fred "for the worse" in bringing about *GREAT + Fred* is not a claim about how well off he is in absolute terms, since, by hypothesis, Fred would be highly well off in *GREAT + Fred*. Rather, we would be affecting him "for the worse" in comparison with how well off he would have been in *OK + Fred*, which, by hypothesis, we could have brought about instead and where he would have been slightly better off. Similarly, if I could do *X*, which would save your life but at the cost of your legs, or do *Y*, which would save your life with no cost to you, then even though doing either action would benefit you in absolute terms, since it would save your life, doing *X* would affect you for the worse relative to doing *Y*.

quality of a *single* person's life should alter our judgments about which outcome would be better. Surely, the presence of *one additional* highly well-off person among *billions* of people wouldn't be enough to transform a *vastly* worse outcome into a better one, merely because, in the otherwise *vastly* inferior outcome, that *one* person would be *slightly* better off! Hence, Norcross concludes, we must admit that the Narrow Person-Affecting View is not only implausible as an "all-things-considered" principle for comparing outcomes involving *completely* different people, as in the cases of *OK* and *GREAT*, it is *also* implausible as an "all-things-considered" principle for comparing outcomes where *some* people are the same but other people are different, as in the cases of *OK + Fred* and *GREAT + Fred*.

I completely agree with Norcross's view about the relative all-things-considered merits of *OK* and *GREAT* with or without the presence of Fred. But, for the reasons given in section 12.3, all this kind of argument *establishes* is that the Narrow Person-Affecting View is not *all* that matters for comparing outcomes that involve some people who are the same and some people who are different. It certainly isn't enough to show that the Narrow Person-Affecting View isn't relevant *at all* for such comparisons. Moreover, even if we *agreed*, which I doubt we should, that the Narrow Person-Affecting View isn't relevant or plausible *at all* for comparisons between outcomes like *OK + Fred* and *GREAT + Fred*, it is dubious whether one should conclude from that that the Narrow Person-Affecting View is *never* relevant or plausible for comparing *any* outcomes where some people are different, and that much stronger conclusion is what Norcross is contending (and what he actually needs for his argument against me that the Narrow Person-Affecting View doesn't pose a threat to Axioms of Transitivity).

Perhaps the lesson of Norcross's argument regarding Fred's significance, or lack thereof, is simply that we shouldn't let our judgments about outcomes *involving many people* be *radically* influenced by the mere presence or absence of *one* individual or small group. Ironically, I illustrated this same lesson via an analogous argument in my book *Inequality*.[7]

Arguably, then, the upshot of Norcross's argument is that the Narrow Person-Affecting View is problematic for cases where only one person, or small group, is the focus of the Narrow Person-Affecting View's assessment, in contexts where many other people are also involved. This conclusion is important, but not surprising. After all, for reasons both Parfit and I have noted, the Narrow Person-Affecting View is *not* plausible, at least not as an "all-things-considered" principle, for some cases where just a *few* people are involved. Norcross's argument *extends* this point to cases where *many* are involved, but only a *few* would be the *focus* of the Narrow Person-Affecting View.

So, acknowledging that the Narrow Person-Affecting View's judgments are problematic when only a few are the focus of the Narrow Person-Affecting View's assessments, let us consider a variation of Norcross's example, where we

---

[7] New York: Oxford University Press, 1993, see pp. 103–11.

OK	GREATER		GREAT	ALSO GREAT
A		B

DIAGRAM E.2

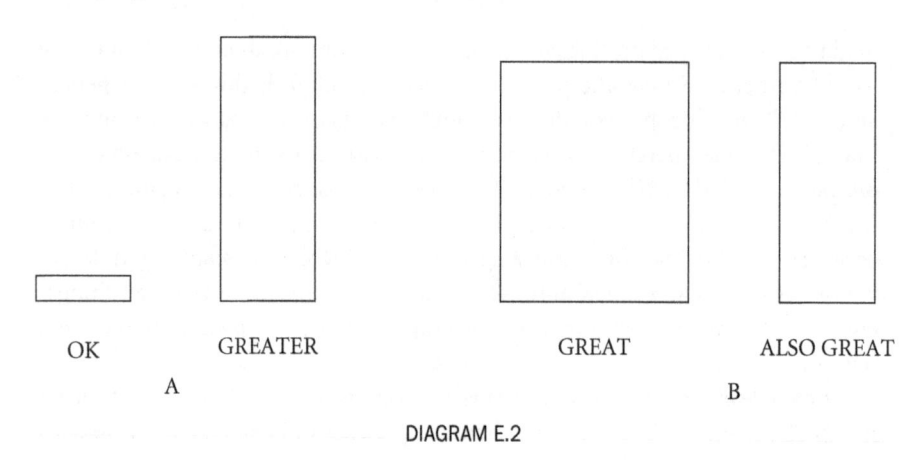

needn't worry about one person, or just a few people, distorting our overall judgments. Consider diagram E.2.

A and *B* are similar to Norcross's *OK + Fred* and *GREAT + Fred*, except that in *A*, instead of there being a single person, Fred, who is really well off, there is a large group, *GREATER*, which is the same size as *A*'s *OK* group and which is at the same level as Fred is in *OK + Fred*; and in *B*, instead of there being a single person, Fred, as well off as *B*'s *GREAT* group, there is a large group, *ALSO GREAT*, which is the same size as *A*'s *OK* and *GREATER* groups, and which is at the same level as Fred and the *GREAT* group are in *GREAT + Fred*. Assume that the *OK*, *GREATER*, and *ALSO GREAT* groups number 10 billion each, and that the *GREAT* group numbers 20 billion. How do *A* and *B* compare?

At first, it may seem clear that *B* is better than *A*, all things considered, since *B* appears to only be a little worse than *A*, regarding perfection, but has more total utility, is much more equal, and its worst-off group fares so much better. But is this judgment stable, and independent of how we think the particular members of the various groups fare in the different alternatives? In particular, is it certain that the Narrow Person-Affecting View is not plausible or relevant for comparing *A* and *B*, just because we know that some people will be different in the two alternatives?

On an Internal Aspects View, which Norcross undoubtedly accepts, the answer to this question *is* clear. But at issue here is precisely whether we should accept an Internal Aspects View; hence, we must be careful not to beg the question against proponents of the Essentially Comparative View who accept the Narrow Person-Affecting View. And I suggest that, for many, whether *B* is better than *A* will, in fact, depend on the precise relation between them; in particular, it will depend on how the particular members of *A* and *B* are affected, for better or worse, in the different alternatives. To see this, we shall consider two different ways in which the members of *A* and *B* might be related.

| | OK | GREATER | GREAT | ALSO GREAT |
| | | A | | B |

DIAGRAM E.3

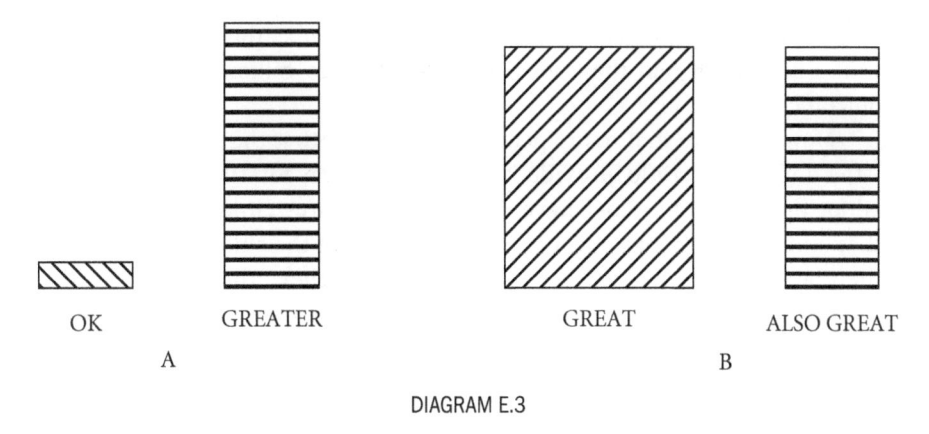

One way in which the members of A and B might be related is depicted in diagram E.3.

In diagram E.3, the very same people would exist in both A's *GREATER* group and B's *ALSO GREAT* group, while different people would exist in A's *OK* group and B's *GREAT* group. In this case, if we brought about A, there would be 10 *billion* people for whom that would be *better*, and *no one* for whom it was worse. (Here, as discussed in chapter 12, we are assuming that bringing about A rather than B is not *bad for* the members of A's *OK* group, if their lives are well worth living, nor is it *bad for* the members of B's *GREAT* group, since it is not bad for people never to have been born, and the members of B's *GREAT* group don't exist, and never will exist, if A is brought about.) On the other hand, if one brings about B, rather than A, there will be 10 *billion* people for whom that will be worse, namely, all of the members who exist in B's *ALSO GREAT* group, but who would also have existed, and been better off, in A, where they would have been the members of A's *GREATER* group. If A and B were related in *this* way, then, I think many people might think that there was a powerful reason to judge A as better than B, in accordance with the Narrow Person-Affecting View. That is, I think many people would agree that the Narrow Person-Affecting View would be plausible and relevant for comparing A and B *if* they were related in the manner in question, even though *some* members of A and B are different.

Let me add a few details to the preceding example. Suppose a population were considering two reproduction policies. On one, they would produce an outcome like *GREATER*, each couple who wanted to have children would have 3 children, there would be 10 *billion* such children total, and *all* of the children would be exceptionally well off. On a second policy, they would produce B. Each couple who wanted to have children would have 9 children, where, let us assume, the first 3 would be the very same children who would have been born had they stopped at 3, and produced *GREATER*, but rather than stopping at 3, each couple decides to bring an additional 6 children into the world, knowing that this will produce an outcome where there are a total of 30 billion children all of whom are very well off, though not as well off as their first 3 children would have been had they not added the extra 20 billion children to the outcome.

Now I believe that many people would agree that the Narrow Person-Affecting View would provide *a* powerful reason for the population to adopt the first policy, and have people stop at three children each rather than nine, since doing so would be better *for all* of the children who would then be alive, and worse for *no one*. Indeed, I believe that, for many, the Narrow Person-Affecting View would not only be relevant and plausible, for such a comparison, but dominant in their thinking, supporting the judgment that, all things considered, GREATER would be a *better* outcome than *B*.

But now, suppose that having chosen to bring about GREATER rather than *B*, the parents discover a way to bring extra children into the world without in *any* way harming their first three children. Or, alternatively, suppose that having brought about GREATER, the parents all accidentally have three more children, all of whom have lives that are worth living, and which do not in *any* way negatively impact the lives of the first three children. The result might be the outcome depicted by *A* in diagram E.3.

As we saw in chapter 12, many people believe that adding more people to an already large population won't necessarily make an outcome *better*, but they *also* believe that *if their lives are worth living and they don't adversely affect the quality of lives of anyone else*, it won't make the outcome *worse*, either. That is, many people would be tempted to agree that in *this* case, *A* would be no worse than GREATER. But, of course, this suggests that many people would agree that *if A* and *B* were related in the way described, then *A* would be *better* than *B*, since GREATER would be better than *B*, and *A* is no *worse* than GREATER.

Note, this argument makes an appeal to a principle of transitivity that we may ultimately reject if the argument succeeds! But while rejecting the relevant principle of transitivity is an option for those who accept an Essentially Comparative View like the Narrow Person-Affecting View, it is not an option for Norcross, so he can hardly avail himself of this response against my argument. Note, also, that I am not committed to the view that the preceding considerations entail the view that if *A* and *B* were related in the way in question, *A* would be better than *B*, all things considered. Perhaps, for example, some would appeal to *A*'s inequality, in support of the view that *A* was worse than *B*, all things considered. My point is simply to emphasize that, Norcross's claims to the contrary, the Narrow Person-Affecting View might indeed be plausible and relevant for comparing alternatives where some people exist in both alternatives, but others do not. To underscore this point, further, consider next diagram E.4.

OK	GREATER	GREAT	ALSO GREAT
A		B

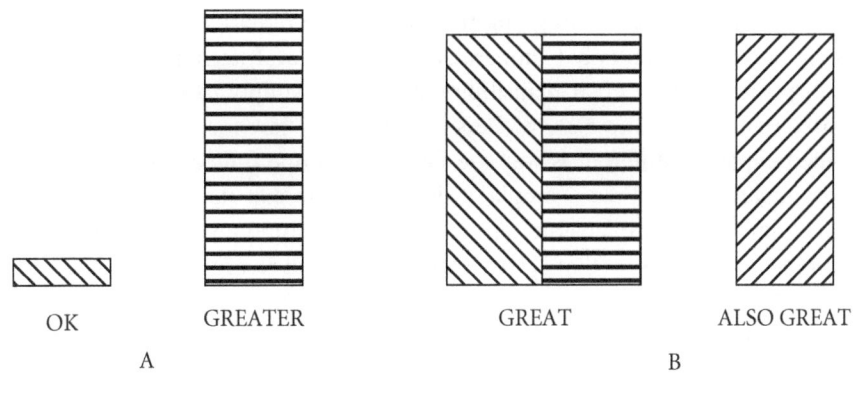

DIAGRAM E.4

Suppose that one could bring about an outcome like B's *GREAT*, or an outcome like A, where the very same people would exist in the two outcomes, with half of the people being *much* worse off in A than in *GREAT* (the members of A's *OK* group) and half of the people being slightly better off in A than in *GREAT* (the members of A's *GREATER* group). In this case, I think many would agree that *GREAT* was much better than A, and in holding this they might be paying attention, among other things, to how the particular people who exist in both outcomes fare in each outcome. If they then considered adding 10 billion new people to *GREAT*, and, more specifically, if they then considered bringing about B rather than *GREAT*, by adding the members of B's *ALSO GREAT* group, they might be confident that B would be no worse than *GREAT*, since B is just as good as *GREAT* regarding equality and maximin, since all of the members of *ALSO GREAT* have lives that are well worth living, and since adding the members of *ALSO GREAT* in *no way* adversely affects the members of *GREAT*, or anyone else for that matter. So, if one thinks of the members of A and B as related in the way depicted in diagram E.4, I think there would be strong reason, including reasons provided by narrow person-affecting considerations, to regard B as much better than A, all things considered.

I suggest, then, that if the members of A and B were related in the way depicted by diagram E.4, many people would clearly regard B as better than A, while if the members of A and B were related in the way depicted by diagram E.3, many people would at least be tempted to the view that A was better than B, and one reason for their difference in attitude to the two scenarios would be the plausibility and relevance of the Narrow Person-Affecting View for making such comparisons. But, as should be apparent, on the Internal Aspects View, we should think A and B compare the same way, whether their members are related in the way depicted in diagram E.3 or in the way depicted in diagram E.4. This is because on any plausible doctrine of impartiality, there is no relevant difference in the internal features of A and B in the two diagrams.

As I have stressed throughout this book, these remarks are not intended to vindicate an Essentially Comparative View over an Internal Aspects View. Both positions have great plausibility. My aim is simply to show that Norcross's rejection of the Narrow Person-Affecting View for outcomes where some people are different is way too fast. Even if one fully agrees with Norcross regarding his Fred example, it doesn't follow that the Narrow Person-Affecting View is implausible for *all* cases where some people are different. On reflection, I suggest that Norcross has not offered an argument that would shake the confidence of the Narrow Person-Affecting View's proponents for at least some cases like A and B. But if the Narrow Person-Affecting View is plausible for *any* such cases, then the worries I have raised in this book remain, concerning the transitivity of the judgments generated by the Narrow Person-Affecting View, and hence the transitivity of our "all-things-considered better than" judgments (in my wide reason-implying sense).[8]

I have been arguing that the Narrow Person-Affecting View is sometimes plausible for comparing outcomes where some people are the same and some people are different. But, as we saw in section 12.5, there will be worries about the Axioms of Transitivity even if one thinks that the Narrow Person-Affecting View only applies to cases where the very same people are involved, *as long as* one believes that the Narrow Person-Affecting View has *independent* weight in such cases, and is not simply a lemma of a more general view, like total utilitarianism, that applies equally in all cases.

---

[8] In keeping with the spirit of pluralism prevalent throughout this book, Jake Ross has suggested (in correspondence) that we might want to always attach some weight to both total utility, which is best captured by an Internal Aspects View, and what we might call differential utility, which is best captured by an Essentially Comparative View. Differential utility reflects how any outcomes being compared differentially affect the welfare levels of those who exist in each outcome. On this view, differential utility matters even in cases where there is only a small overlapping group—as in Norcross's case where there is only a single overlapping person, Fred. But how much it matters is proportional to the size of the overlapping group, so that where the group is very small relative to the total size of the groups in the different outcomes, as in Norcross's case, the significance of differential utility will be swamped by the significance of total utility.

As Ross recognizes, as long as we grant independent weight to the value of differential utility, our overall view of utility will be essentially comparative, and the worries that I have raised about the Axiom of Transitivity will arise.

Also, as Ross notes, if one believes, as many do and as I have argued for many years, that one should care about both absolute and comparative fairness, then why not allow that one should also care about both absolute and comparative (differential) utility? Indeed, this would not be a surprising result, given the argument of section 10.10, that certain ideals may share certain formal or structural features. (On the view that one should care about both absolute and comparative fairness, see my "Equality, Priority, and the Levelling Down Objection," in *The Ideal of Equality*, ed. Matthew Clayton and Andrew Williams [London: Macmillan; St. Martin's Press, 2000], 126–61; "Weighing Goods: Some Questions and Comments," *Philosophy and Public Affairs* 23 [1994]: 350–80; "Egalitarianism Defended," *Ethics* 113 (2003): 764–82; and "Justice, Equality, Fairness, Desert, Rights, Free Will, Responsibility, and Luck," in *Distributive Justice and Responsibility*, ed. Carl Knight and Zofia Stemplowska [Oxford: Oxford University Press, 2011], 51–76.)

At the end of the day, Norcross's arguments are plausible, but not conclusive. More important, they do not adequately recognize the *costs* of preserving the Axioms of Transitivity. In this book, I have argued that those costs are high, much more so than most people have realized. So, while we may ultimately decide to preserve the Axioms of Transitivity, and to reject the Essentially Comparative View and positions like the Narrow Person-Affecting View, for many this will require some major shifts in their thinking. That is one of this book's central lessons, and that lesson is untouched by Norcross's arguments.

Appendix F

Lexical Priority in Defense of the Axiom of Transitivity

In this book, I have argued that on an Essentially Comparative View, where the relevance and significance of the factors for assessing an outcome can vary depending on the alternatives with which that outcome is compared, "all-things-considered better than" (in my wide reason-implying sense) may be a nontransitive relation. David Bourget has challenged my claim, claiming that the Axiom of Transitivity is compatible with an Essentially Comparative View.[1]

Here is the kind of example that Bourget had in mind.

Zeke's Preferences among Apples and Oranges: Zeke prefers every apple to every orange. Among apples, he prefers those which are crispest, caring about nothing else. Among oranges, he prefers those which are juiciest, again, caring about nothing else.

In the preceding case, it *appears* that different factors are relevant and significant for making different comparisons, and yet, as should be evident, Zeke could still have a perfectly transitive ranking of all apples and oranges. Given this, is it possible that an analysis of Bourget's example might reveal a general solution to my worries about nontransitive rankings?

Here is a thought one might initially entertain. The fact that Zeke gives *lexical priority* to apples over oranges seems to play an important role in the transitivity of his preferences over all apples and oranges. Perhaps, if one gave lexical priority to certain factors, at least in some contexts, one could similarly preserve the transitivity of our all-things-considered judgments.

Here is one way this might be true, on analogy with Bourget's example. Suppose one thought that a certain moral ideal was restricted in scope, such

---

[1] David made this point during discussion in the spring of 2008, when I was a visiting scholar at the Australian National University.

that it only applied for comparing certain alternatives, *S*, but not others, *T*. But suppose, as it happened, one also had reason to believe that all of the alternatives to which it applied were better than all of the alternatives to which it didn't apply. Then, depending on the nature of all of the other ideals that were relevant and significant for comparing the different kinds of alternatives, it could well be the case that the rankings of *S* were transitive, and similarly that the rankings of *T* were transitive. In that case, the rankings of all alternatives *S* and *T* would be transitive, despite the fact that different factors seem relevant or vary in their significance for assessing different alternatives.

I don't want to rule out this possibility, but I don't find it promising. Let me mention several sources of concern.

First, I am not convinced that Bourget's example even illustrates a genuine case where the factors that are relevant and significant for assessing an outcome vary depending on the alternatives with which it is compared. That is, I'm not convinced that an Essentially Comparative View even applies to Bourget's example, rather than an Internal Aspects View. If I am right about this, it won't be surprising that Zeke would have a transitive ranking of apples and oranges, and Bourget's example won't have a bearing on how we should respond to worries about transitivity if we *do* adopt a genuinely Essentially Comparative View for assessing outcomes.

Arguably, it isn't *crispness* and *juiciness* that Zeke values, but *apple crispness* and *orange juiciness*. This explains why Zeke would give no preference to a crispier orange over a less crisp orange (if that were possible), or to a juicier apple over a less juicy apple. Accordingly, Zeke might simply have three criteria that he applies to each alternative apple or orange, where the three criteria are, roughly, apples over oranges, degree of apple crispness, and degree of orange juiciness. Appealing to those criteria, Zeke might assign a score to each apple or orange based solely on that piece of fruit's "internal" features.[2] For example, in accordance with his first criterion, he might assign a score of 100 to any piece of fruit that is an apple, and a score of 0 to any piece of fruit that is an orange; and in accordance with his second and third criteria, he might assign scores from 0 to 50 reflecting the degree to which a piece of fruit is "apple crispy" or "orange juicy." In this way, every apple will get a score ranging from 100 to 150, reflecting the three relevant criteria for assessing apples and oranges: it will get a 100 on the first criterion of apples over oranges, a score from 0 to 50 on the second criterion of apple crispness, and a zero on the third criterion of orange juiciness. Similarly, every orange will get a score ranging from 0 to 50, again reflecting the three relevant criteria for assessing apples and oranges: it will get a 0 on the first and second criteria, and a score from 0 to 50 on the third criterion.

---

[2] This discussion would need to be slightly revised if one understood "apple crispness" and "orange juiciness" as relations obtaining between apples or oranges and people's sensibilities. But this would not affect the substance of my claims.

The point, of course, is that such a model could completely accommodate Bourget's example in terms of an Internal Aspects View. Each apple or orange would receive an "all-things-considered" score based solely on its internal features; a fortiori, there would be a transitive ranking of all apples and oranges. Correspondingly, on such a model it would not be the case that an apple or orange might receive a different score representing how good it was, depending on with what alternative piece of fruit it was compared. I suggest, then, that initial appearances to the contrary, Bourget's example does not really involve a genuine case where an Essentially Comparative View is involved. Likewise, I suggest that a similar analysis could be given for the case where one ideal applied only to certain outcomes, but all outcomes to which it applied had lexical priority over all outcomes to which it didn't apply.

Given the problems raised by Essentially Comparative Views, one might try to urge that all apparent examples of essentially comparative reasoning should ultimately be explained away along the lines that I have just followed with Bourget's example. But for those who find essentially comparative reasoning compelling for at least certain comparisons, there is no particular reason to believe that his example will shed light on how to respond to the questions about transitivity raised by such reasoning.

As for giving lexical priority to some alternatives or principles over others, it isn't clear how this would help, unless it were combined with the kind of restriction in scope noted previously. But giving lexical priority to one set of alternatives over another, based solely on whether a particular factor is or is not relevant and significant for comparing such alternatives, seems deeply implausible, at least for the kinds of essentially comparative factors we have been discussing.

Consider, for example, the Pareto Principle. As I noted in chapter 12, many believe that the Pareto Principle is deeply plausible, and of these, many might also believe that it is restricted in scope, such that it is only relevant and significant for comparing alternatives involving exactly the same people. On this view, if A and B have the same people, but C and D do not, the Pareto Principle would apply for comparing A and B, but not for comparing A or B with C or D. This restriction of the Pareto Principle's scope seems plausible. But what does *not* seem plausible is the further claim that we should give lexical priority to all alternatives involving the same people over all alternatives involving different people, or vice versa. That is, there is absolutely no reason to believe, and every reason to deny, that no matter what else is true of the different alternatives in terms of ideals like justice, equality, utility, perfection, and so on, we can know that A, B, and every other alternative involving the same people would be better (or worse), than C, D, and every other alternative involving different people from those in A and B.

Furthermore, suppose C and D involved the same people, who were different from those in A and B. How could it be the case that A and B had lexical priority over C and D, or vice versa, *in virtue of the fact* that A and B contained the same people, and C and D contained people who were different from them?

After all, *C* and *D also* contain the same people, while *A* and *B* contain people who are different from them. Not even *I*, who am open to all sorts of *crazy* views, can make sense of this position!

Finally, there are many well-known difficulties with lexical orderings, and I do not see how a set of second-order dominance principles can be arrived at which (1) will not be ad hoc, (2) will plausibly respond to the theoretical difficulties raised by the Essentially Comparative View, and (3) will not themselves be subject to non-transitive rankings (thus requiring a set of third-order dominance principles, which in turn may be nontransitive, etc.). That is, I just don't see how to plausibly motivate, develop, and defend an appeal to giving lexical priority to some moral factors in a way that would actually *help* with the problems posed by the Essentially Comparative View. Thus, I'll leave this avenue for others to explore. Perhaps those who are more sympathetic to lexical orderings than I am will find a way to put them to good use in addressing our concerns. But I seriously doubt it.

Appendix G

Book Summary

This appendix contains summaries of each chapter and appendix.

G.1 Chapter 1

In chapter 1, I presented an overview of the book and a guide to the material. I discussed the role that intuitions play in my book, and noted that I will be presenting a number of impossibility arguments throughout the book, some of which span several pages, and some of which span many chapters. I observed that I find myself in the position of someone who is juggling a number of very important or valuable items, and who realizes that he cannot hang on to them all, but is loath to let any of them drop. I suggested that others may also find themselves in my position, in reading this book.

I introduced some important terminology, including the distinction between a relation's being transitive, intransitive, and nontransitive, where saying that a relation R is *nontransitive* is neutral between the case where R is *in*transitive, and so we might say that transitivity *fails* for R, and the case where instead we would merely want to say that transitivity *fails to apply* across different sets of alternatives to which R applies, and to which we might think transitivity should apply.

I pointed out that many of this book's arguments are relevant both to judgments about the goodness of outcomes and to judgments about the goodness of individual lives. Thus, since virtually everyone accepts the intelligibility of the latter sort of judgments, I claimed that even those who are suspicious about the intelligibility of the former sort of judgments—a view that I barely understand and have little sympathy with—need to take account of this book's arguments.

I expressed my conviction that in the normative domain, as elsewhere, one should be careful not to apply tools that are useful and powerful for certain questions and domains to other questions and domains for which they are ill suited.

Likewise, I warned against being content with simple, clean, clear answers in contexts where complex, messy, and murky answers are, unfortunately, required.

I acknowledged that I am not, myself, up to solving the various problems that this book raises. But I expressed the hope that perhaps others will find my problems interesting and important, and have better success than I in addressing them. Regardless, I suggested that coming to terms with this book's arguments may require us to substantially rethink and revise our understanding of the good, moral ideals, and the nature of practical reasoning.

G.2 Chapter 2

In chapter 2, I introduced and discussed two Standard Views about aggregation that focus on how we should make trade-offs involving benefits or burdens between quality and number in assessing outcomes involving different individuals. These views offer answers to such questions as whether it would improve or worsen an outcome more if a large number of people were benefited or harmed a little, or if a small number of people were benefited or harmed a lot.

The First Standard View—Trade-offs between Quality and Number Are Sometimes Desirable involves an *additive-aggregationist* approach to assessing outcomes that allows trade-offs between quality and number, while the *Second Standard View—Trade-offs between Quality and Number Are Sometimes Undesirable Even When Vast Numbers Are at Stake* involves an *anti-additive-aggregationist* approach to assessing outcomes that prohibits trade-offs between quality and number. I claimed that each of the Standard Views is extremely plausible in different contexts, and that many people are firmly committed to them for making certain comparisons.

I noted that most people firmly believe that "all-things-considered better than" is a transitive relation, which means that for any three alternatives *A*, *B*, and *C*, if all things considered *A* is better than *B*, and all things considered *B* is better than *C*, then all things considered *A* is better than *C*. I then presented several *Spectrum Arguments*, each of which involves a spectrum of outcomes, such that the First Standard View applies for comparing certain, nearby outcomes along the spectrum, while the Second Standard View applies for comparing certain other, far apart outcomes along the spectrum. I then showed that, together, the rankings of outcomes generated by the Standard Views are incompatible with the view that "all-things-considered better than" (in my wide reason-implying sense) is a transitive relation. It follows that unless one can show that there *couldn't* be a spectrum of cases of the sort I presented—a claim that will be very hard to defend—one will have to give up at least one of the Standard Views about aggregation or the view that "all-things-considered better than" (in my wide reason-implying sense) is a transitive relation. I noted that, for many, it will be extremely difficult to give up *any* of the views in question, and that giving up any of them would have serious practical and theoretical implications.

In addressing these issues, I discussed a number of anti-additive-aggregationist examples, including, among others, Derek Parfit's Repugnant Conclusion, Thomas Scanlon's case of Jones receiving electrical shocks from a television transmitter, and my own Lollipops for Life case. I also introduced J. Ross's Principle, which I returned to throughout the book. According to J. Ross's Principle, there are cases where it would be most rational to act *as if* the Second Standard View was true, even if we have most reason to believe that the First Standard View is true, and vice versa. Roughly, this would be the case if there was little or no difference between two alternatives according to one of the Standard Views, but there was a big difference between two alternatives according to the other Standard View. I also noted that we should distinguish between two notions that are often conflated, the notions of incommensurability and incomparability. Finally, I discussed the view that there can be discontinuities in value, suggesting that the view is both deeply plausible and coherent, but that in some cases for which we might invoke it, it is inconsistent with other deeply held views.

G.3 Chapter 3

In chapter 3, I presented and assessed a "new" principle of aggregation, an anti-additive-aggregationist view which I called the *Disperse Additional Burdens View*. I noted that, like many principles, the Disperse Additional Burdens View is incomplete, applying to some alternatives but not others. I also noted that the view is a natural extension of chapter 2's Second Standard View, and that, like the Second Standard View, it has great plausibility.

Unfortunately, the Disperse Additional Burdens View faces a serious problem of iteration. Specifically, I argued that, in principle, if one repeatedly follows the Disperse Additional Burdens View in those cases where it seems both relevant and plausible, one might end up making a series of choices *each* of which, individually, produces the best possible available outcome, but which *together* produce an outcome that is clearly inferior to the outcome that one would have produced had one consistently refused to allow oneself to be guided by the Disperse Additional Burdens View in the individual cases to which it applies. I suggested that the problem of iteration facing the Disperse Additional Burdens View resists a stable solution and challenges the transitivity of the "all-things-considered better than" relation (in my wide reason-implying sense).

In discussing the Disperse Additional Burdens View, I noted that the View may help account for some of the intuitive attractiveness of the antiegalitarian's Levelling Down Objection, as well as certain prevalent attitudes toward charitable giving. I also claimed that the View may give rise to practical problems for national or international organizations in such areas as health care and famine relief. In addition, I suggested that my analysis of the Disperse Additional Burdens View and its implications challenges Derek Parfit's claim that agent-neutral theories can't face moral analogues of Prisoner's Dilemmas, and requires us to reevaluate Parfit's claims about, and our understanding of, the nature and scope of Each-We Dilemmas.

G.4 Chapter 4

In chapter 4, I argued that anti-additive-aggregationist reasoning applies *within* lives as well as *between* lives, and that, accordingly, most people accept a view analogous to chapter 2's Second Standard View and chapter 3's Disperse Additional Burdens View for assessing individual lives. Specifically, I argued that most people accept the *Fourth Standard View—Even within Lives, Trade-offs between Quality and Duration Are Sometimes Undesirable Even When Vast Differences in Duration Are at Stake*, a view that prohibits trade-offs, in certain contexts, between benefits and duration within a life.

I suggested that the source and scope of anti-additive-aggregationist views may have been obscured by two important factors: one, compensation's being possible within lives but not between lives; and two, the substantial influence on contemporary thought of John Rawls's and Robert Nozick's claims about the separateness of individuals. Although the facts in question provide some important reasons to treat certain cases involving multiple lives differently than analogous cases involving a single life, I argued that they do not ultimately support the common assumption that trade-offs are always permissible within lives, even though they are not always permissible between lives.

In addition to presenting a number of examples involving a single life which were analogues of examples from chapters 2 and 3 involving multiple lives, I also presented a number of examples showing that, in assessing lives, many people care about such factors as the shape, pattern, and direction of lives, as well as the sum total of individual units of good possessed at each moment of the lives.

I discussed an analogue of Derek Parfit's Repugnant Conclusion, which I called the *Single Life Repugnant Conclusion*. I noted that a variation of my Single Life case was first discussed by J. M. E. McTaggart, and considered and rejected his various arguments for the view that we should judge an extraordinarily flourishing human life lasting a million years as worse than a barely contented oyster-like life if the latter life persists long enough.

Together, chapter 4's considerations suggested that we should reject Henry Sidgwick's conception of individual self-interest, which measures the goodness of an individual life as a simple additive function of how much utility it has at each moment, treating each moment equally. Arguably, versions of Sidgwick's conception have dominated Western thought from Plato through the present.

G.5 Chapter 5

In chapter 5, I claimed that, in certain contexts, most people accept an additive-aggregationist approach for assessing trade-offs within lives. Specifically, I claimed that for certain kinds of comparisons, most people accept the *Third Standard View—Trade-offs between Quality and Duration Are Sometimes Desirable*, a view that allows trade-offs within lives between benefits and duration. I then showed that analogous to the inconsistency highlighted in chapter 2, there is an inconsistency between the Third Standard View's additive-aggregationist approach within lives, the Fourth Standard View's anti-additive-aggregationist approach within lives, and the transitivity of the "all-things-considered better than" relation (in my wide reason-implying sense). At least, there is an inconsistency between those views and the plausible assumption that there could be a spectrum of cases such that the Third Standard View was plausible and appropriate for comparing nearby members of the spectrum, but the Fourth Standard View was plausible for comparing other, far apart members of the spectrum. Thus, I showed that problems of consistency arise with respect to trade-offs between quality and duration *within* a life, for the same reasons that problems of consistency arise with respect to trade-offs between quality and number *across* lives, namely, that for some such comparisons additive-aggregationist reasoning seems plausible, but for others anti-additive-aggregationist reasoning seems plausible.

I then considered a particularly forceful example, owing to Stuart Rachels,[1] illuminating the power, appeal, and inconsistency of the views that most people have regarding trade-offs between quality and duration within a life. Following that, I discussed numerous objections that might be raised to my example. This discussion canvassed a host of issues, including whether there might be sharp boundaries between lives worth living and lives not worth living; whether there might be unpleasant experiences so slight that it wouldn't matter *at all* how long they lasted; whether some of our firm intuitions about when trade-offs are permissible have to be limited in scope; whether we must distrust our intuitions about cases involving countless years of life; whether there may be interaction effects between certain unpleasant experiences within a life that are relevant to our judgments; whether principles of decomposition, additive aggregation, and recombination apply to the normative realm; and whether the badness of an unpleasant experience of any given duration is proportional to the length of the life in which that experience obtains. Ultimately, I argued that none of the objections discussed is telling against the worries raised by my example or the general problem of inconsistency presented in chapter 5.

I concluded that as with the case of trade-offs between lives, the issue of trade-offs within lives is deeply problematic. I noted that, almost certainly, most people will have to give up a view that they find deeply plausible to avoid inconsistency in their thinking. I also noted that doing this would not be easy, and that it is far from clear what view should be given up.

---

[1] Rachels's original example appeared in his unpublished Philosophy, Politics, and Economics thesis, "A Theory of Beneficence" (Oxford University, 1993). Rachels later modified his example, as well as offered other arguments for intransitivity in "Counterexamples to the Transitivity of *Better Than*," *Australian Journal of Philosophy* 76 (1998): 71–83.

G.6 Chapter 6

In chapter 6, I began a careful exploration of the notion of transitivity. I looked at a number of different notions that are, or are not, transitive, in order to illuminate the nature and foundation of transitive relations. This clarified the conditions that would have to obtain for the "all-things-considered better than" relation to be either transitive or nontransitive, where the notion "nontransitive" is a technical one, defined in section 1.5.

My discussion canvassed a number of topics, including whether all "...er than" relations are transitive; the connection between a property's being *gradable* in the linguists' sense, the possibility of ranking objects on a single linear scale in terms of the degree to which they possess a gradable property, and transitivity; the fact that incommensurable or incomparable objects cannot be placed on a common scale; and that transitivity fails to apply in cases where different alternatives are compared in terms of different relations, and hence by appeal to different scales.

In discussing these issues, I argued that a relation, R, would be intransitive for the very same reason that transitivity fails to apply across different relations. I first noted that if aR_1b, and bR_2c, *nothing* follows about how a and c compare with respect to R_1, R_2, or in any other respect. This is because transitivity simply *fails to apply* to comparisons involving *different* relations. I then pointed out that *if* there were a relation, R, such that the comparison of certain alternatives with respect to R depended on how those alternatives ranked on one scale, while the comparison of other alternatives with respect to R depended on how those alternatives ranked on a different, independent scale, then R might be *intransitive*, and would certainly be *nontransitive*, for the *very same reason* that transitivity *fails to apply* to comparisons involving *different* relations. That is, I claimed that R could be nontransitive whenever the factors that were relevant and significant for comparing a given outcome with respect to R varied depending on the alternatives with which that outcome was compared. So, for example, if the relevance and significance of the factors for determining whether a stands in relation R to b differed from the relevance and significance of the factors for determining whether a stands in relation R to c, then R might be a nontransitive relation.

Chapter 6 included an extended discussion of the notion of "not worse than" understood as the category of "rough comparability," "imprecise equality," or "being on a par with." I noted that many people accept the category of rough comparability, and that those who do, accept that "not worse than" is an intransitive relation. I then argued that once one has fully understood the conditions that would account for the possibility that some alternatives stand in the "not worse than" relation, and for the subsequent possibility that the "not worse than" relation is intransitive, one would see that those same conditions would open up the possibility that "all-things-considered better than" (in my wide reason-implying sense) might be an intransitive relation. Thus, I suggested that *if* one is willing to accept that there is a "not worse than" relation which is intransitive, as many are, one should also be willing to accept that the "all-things-considered better than" relation (in my wide reason-implying sense) is intransitive.

I also pointed out that one reason that many people have resisted the notion that "all-things-considered better than" could be intransitive is because they have recognized and worried about the possibility that if that were the case, then perfectly rational people could, at least theoretically, be *money pumped*. That is, if "all-things-considered better than" were an intransitive relation, it could be rational, at least in theory, to pay to go around in a circle—constantly paying to move from one alternative to another available better alternative, only to end up where one started. However, I suggested that some who reject the view that "all-things-considered better than" could be intransitive for this reason nevertheless *accept* that "not worse than" is an intransitive relation, and I argued that the theoretical possibility of being money pumped arises in the latter situation as well as the former. So, if the theoretical possibility of being money pumped is not enough to rule out the possibility that "not worse than" is an intransitive relation, it can't be enough to rule out the possibility that "all-things-considered better than" is an intransitive relation.

I concluded chapter 6 by granting that global and strategic reasoning may offer a *practical* solution to the possibility of being money pumped in either case, but I suggested that one should not conflate a practical solution with a theoretical one, in situations where a theoretical problem is posed and for which a theoretical solution is, ideally, desired.

G.7 Chapter 7

In chapter 7, I continued my exploration of transitivity. I began by considering an argument of Frances Kamm's purporting to show that the "permissible to do rather than" relation is intransitive.[2] I noted that Kamm's argument may not be as worrisome as some of my other purported counterexamples to transitivity, and actually shows that the "permissible to do rather than" relation is *non*transitive rather than *in*transitive, but that Kamm's analysis of *why* the "permissible to do rather than" relation seems not to be transitive is important and instructive. Kamm rightly saw that different factors are relevant to the permissibility of an action depending on what alternatives are available to that action, and that it is this feature that ultimately accounts for the fact that it can be permissible to do A rather than B, and permissible to do B rather than C, and yet it might not be permissible to do A rather than C.

I next discussed the "moral obligatoriness" relation, "ought to be done rather than," suggesting that it, too, may be nontransitive for the same reason

---

[2] Kamm's example appeared in "Supererogation and Obligation," *Journal of Philosophy* 82 (1985): 118–38.

that the "not worse than" and "permissible to do rather than" relations are nontransitive. Specifically, I contended that it could be the case that A ought to be done rather than B, and B ought to be done rather than C, and yet it might not be the case that A ought to be done rather than C, and that this is because the relevance and significance of the factors for determining whether I ought to do an action can vary depending on the alternatives with which it is compared.

This naturally raised the following thought. If, indeed, as I argued and many accept, there are already *three* significant normative relations that are nontransitive—namely, the "not worse than," the "permissible to do rather than," and the "ought to be done rather than" relations—on reflection, is it not plausible to believe that the fourth normative relation, "all-things-considered better than" (in my wide reason-implying sense), might *also* be nontransitive, despite many people's *initial* conviction that this *couldn't* be so?

I then argued that if, as many believe, the right is at least *relevant* to the good—in the sense that acting rightly is itself a good-making feature of outcomes—there is good reason to suspect that the nontransitivity of the "ought to be done rather than relation" will be *inherited* by the "all-things-considered better than" relation. Indeed, I observed that this would be a particular instance of a significant general truth: that if an important aspect of a practical notion is nontransitive, the notion itself is likely to be nontransitive.

Chapter 7 is where I first introduced the terminology of the *Internal Aspects View* and the *Essentially Comparative View*, corresponding to two different views we might have about how to assess and compare different outcomes. Ultimately, I claimed that whether the "all-things-considered better than relation" is transitive or not is correlated with which, if either, of these two views is correct. On the Internal Aspects View, every outcome can be assessed by reference to a common scale reflecting how desirable that outcome is, and the value of an outcome is unchanging, and entirely dependent on its internal features. On this view, "all-things-considered better than" will, indeed, be a transitive relation. On the Essentially Comparative View, there is no single fact of the matter as to how valuable an outcome is; rather, there are a plurality of such facts, as different factors can be relevant and significant for assessing an outcome's value depending on the alternatives with which it is compared. On this view, "all-things-considered better than" may not be a transitive relation.

Together, the considerations of chapters 6 and 7 illuminated the nature of the conflicts presented in chapters 2 through 5, showing, among other things, that the Essentially Comparative View is implicit in our maintaining both of the differing views about additive-aggregation discussed in chapters 2 through 5. Thus, chapters 6 and 7 clarified why, ultimately, we must either reject the view that in assessing the value of a given outcome an additive-aggregationist approach can be appropriate for some comparisons, but an anti-additive-aggregationist approach can be appropriate for others, or abandon the view that the "all-things-considered better than" relation is transitive.

G.8 Chapter 8

In chapter 8, I offered a brief characterization of Expected Utility Theory, and an analogous theory which I called *Expected Value Theory*. I then noted that many people reject the Completeness assumption which underlies these theories, accepting the category of rough comparability, or "not worse than," discussed in chapter 6. I suggested that most people probably assume that it should be easy enough to modify Expected Utility Theory and Expected Value Theory to accommodate Incompleteness, but I argued that this assumption is dubious. In particular, I argued that it would be difficult or impossible to reconcile Incompleteness with all of a number of other very important assumptions of Expected Utility Theory and practical reasoning, including various Principles of Equivalence, a State-by-State Comparison Principle, a Reflection Principle, a Pareto Principle, and the Sure-Thing Principle.

I also raised questions about another assumption underlying Expected Utility Theory and Expected Value Theory, the Principle of Continuity. I noted that many people find the Principle of Continuity extremely plausible for a wide range of cases, including a set of cases that I called "easy" cases. But I also noted that many find the Principle of Continuity extremely *im*plausible for certain other cases, that I called "extreme" cases. I suggested that rather than accept a simple "pure" view, which would insist that continuity be either accepted for *all* cases or rejected for *all* cases, many would believe that the Principle of Continuity is plausible for many, but not all, cases. But I pointed out that this seemingly reasonable "compromise" position is incompatible with the Principle of Substitution of Equivalence and the Axioms of Transitivity.

Together, my arguments in this chapter suggested that one will not be able to easily modify Expected Utility Theory and Expected Value Theory in order to capture the widely held views that the Completeness Axiom is implausible and that the Principle of Continuity is implausible for "extreme" cases. Once one makes such concessions, other important positions will also have to be given up that are central to our understanding of the theories in question and practical reasoning. Given this, I suggested, that one should be dubious of any claims to the effect that we can be confident that "all-things-considered better than" (in my wide reason-implying sense) must be a transitive relation, because it is one of various Axioms of Transitivity that underlie Expected Utility Theory, and because of the role and success that Expected Utility Theory plays in other important areas, such as game theory, decision theory, and large parts of economics.

G.9 Chapter 9

Some of the most natural and important worries that people have about my Spectrum Arguments are anticipated, and responded to, when I first develop them. However, in chapter 9, I dealt with the most serious remaining objections.

The first objection responds to my arguments by appealing to the significance of there being different *kinds* of alternatives along my spectrums. According to this objection, cases at one end of one of my spectrums are different in kind from cases at the other end, so there must be some point along the spectrum where there is a break, or discontinuity, from one kind to another. It is claimed that this fact undermines one of the key premises underlying my Spectrum Arguments.

The second objection claims that my arguments are versions of the Standard Sorites Paradox, familiar examples of which purport to "prove" that hairiness is the same as baldness and that a heap of sand is the same as a grain of sand. Although there is much dispute about exactly *where* Sorites Paradoxes go wrong, there is *no* dispute that they *do* go wrong, and must be rejected. Hence, it is claimed that my Spectrum Arguments should also be rejected, along with the other obviously fallacious Standard Sorites Paradoxes.

The third objection suggests that my arguments rest on certain heuristics and similarity-based reasoning schemes well known to produce intransitive judgments. But psychologists have amply demonstrated that the heuristics and reasoning schemes in question can lead our intuitions astray, and, in particular, that they do so precisely in those cases where they generate intransitive judgments. Hence, it is concluded, there is good reason to reject my arguments.

Convinced that there *must* be something wrong with my Spectrum Arguments, many people are attracted to some version or other of these different objections. I argued that none of them succeeds. If we ultimately decide to reject my arguments, we will have to do so on grounds other than those considered in chapter 9.

G.10 Chapter 10

In chapter 10, I presented a *Standard Model for Utility*, which expresses one natural way of understanding and valuing utility. On this model, utility is noninstrumentally and intrinsically valuable; neutral with respect to sentient beings, places, and times; and impartial. In addition, how good an outcome is regarding utility is a function of how much total utility the outcome has. I also presented a *Standard Model for Combining Ideals*, which holds that there is no limit on how good an outcome can be regarding various ideals, like utility, and that how good an outcome is all things considered is a simple additive function of how good it is with respect to each ideal relevant to assessing outcomes. I suggested that the two Standard Models are intuitively plausible and implicitly accepted by many. I also noted that, together, the Standard Models capture and express our additive-aggregationist views.

I next showed that, together, the Standard Models entail Parfit's Repugnant Conclusion and, more generally, that we need another model for capturing our anti-additive-aggregationist views. I presented and explored one schema for doing this, which I called the *Capped Model for Ideals*. The Capped Model can share the element of the Standard Model for Combining Ideals which holds that how good an outcome is all things considered is a simple additive function of how good it is with respect to each ideal relevant to assessing outcomes. However, on the Capped Model, there will be some cases where in comparing one outcome with another we must impose an upper limit on how good an outcome can be regarding any particular ideal, and so an upper limit on how good the alternatives can be all things considered. Thus, for example, I noted that on the Capped Model, after a point, mere increases in the *amount* of utility will not substantially increase the outcome's *value*, even regarding utility. Accordingly, such increases, however great, will not be sufficient to outweigh significant losses in other morally important respects. I showed how this kind of model would enable us to capture our intuitions about the Repugnant Conclusion, as well as our anti-additive-aggregationist views more generally.

I explored the points of agreement and disagreement between the two Standard Models and the Capped Model. I also noted a number of ways in which one might try to flesh out the details of a Capped Model. I acknowledged that the Capped Model faced numerous serious problems, and that ultimately we may need to pursue another model entirely, including one more sensitive to holistic considerations, to adequately capture our anti-additive-aggregationist views.

Among other things, my discussion raised important questions about the sense in which we should be neutral with respect to sentient beings, places, and times, casting doubt on the plausibility of standard assumptions about such issues. In addition, I argued that moral ideals cannot be fully and adequately characterized in isolation from each other, that, for certain comparisons, at least, some ideals must share certain formal or structural features. In particular, in addition to those considerations already presented—which showed that, for certain comparisons, at least, just as there may be an upper limit on how good an outcome can be regarding equality, there may also have to be an upper limit on how good an outcome can be regarding other ideals, like utility—I presented further considerations which suggested that if numbers count for utility, as most believe, they may also have to count for equality, contrary to what many have assumed.

G.11 Chapter 11

In chapters 11 and 12, I explored the key question raised by my Spectrum Arguments: whether different factors may be relevant and significant for assessing and comparing outcomes, depending on the alternatives with which those outcomes are compared. According to the *Essentially Comparative View*, the answer to that question is "yes"; according to the *Internal Aspects View* the answer to that question is "no," as the assessment of an outcome will depend solely on the internal features of that outcome, and hence be independent of any other alternatives to which that outcome is compared.

Chapter 11 began with an extended discussion of Derek Parfit's Mere Addition Paradox. I showed that, in presenting his paradox, Parfit implicitly relied on an *Essentially Comparative View*. I noted that if one accepts an Essentially Comparative View the three judgments constituting Parfit's Mere Addition Paradox will no longer be incompatible, since, on such a view, "all-things-considered better than" (in my wide reason-implying sense) will not be a transitive relation.

I then explored the Internal Aspects View, which Parfit has since come to accept. I claimed that the Internal Aspects View has great intuitive appeal and showed that it has many advantages. It entails the view that "all-things-considered better than" is a transitive relation; it licenses the Principle of Like Comparability for Equivalents and it captures a particularly plausible version of an Independence of Irrelevant Alternatives Principle, according to which for any two alternatives A and B, neither adding to, nor subtracting from, a set of alternatives whose members include A and B should affect how A and B compare with each other. I also showed how the Internal Aspects View would enable us to plausibly respond to the Mere Addition Paradox, by rejecting one or more of the three judgments constituting the paradox.

I claimed that the real paradox illuminated by the Mere Addition Paradox lies not in the inconsistency between the three particular judgments that technically produce the paradox, but in the inconsistency between the two conflicting ways of understanding ideals. The role that "Mere Addition" plays in our judgment about how $A+$ compares to A in Parfit's Paradox speaks to the tremendous power and appeal of the Essentially Comparative View. But the firm conviction, that many hold, that "all-things-considered better than" must be a transitive relation, speaks to the tremendous power and appeal of the Internal Aspects View. It is, I claimed, really these two conflicting views that underlie the Mere Addition Paradox, and that ultimately make it so significant and deeply problematic.

G.12 Chapter 12

In chapter 12, I explored the Essentially Comparative View. I argued that the Essentially Comparative View has great plausibility, and that, for many, it would be extremely difficult to abandon. I noted that, for many, the most plausible versions of maximin and utility are essentially comparative. I also argued that if one wants to give independent weight to the Pareto Principle, as many do, one has to accept an Essentially Comparative View. In addition, I presented an extended discussion of a *Narrow Person-Affecting View*, showing that such a principle is also essentially comparative. I considered numerous objections and worries that could be raised to the Narrow Person-Affecting View, but showed that, ultimately, it is extremely plausible to think that the Narrow Person-Affecting View is both relevant and significant for making certain comparisons, even if it is not the only ideal that is relevant and significant for making such comparisons.

I noted that many people have thought that certain principles are restricted in scope, such that they are relevant and significant for comparing certain outcomes but not others. I then showed that such a view typically involves a commitment to the Essentially Comparative View. I further showed that one needed to appeal to an Essentially Comparative View to capture our judgments about certain kinds of cases, including one which I called *How More Than France Exists*. I also noted that appealing to an Essentially Comparative View could help us make sense out of the many instances of intransitive judgments that are made on a regular basis by people who are seemingly clear-thinking, well-informed, and perfectly rational.

Together, the considerations presented in chapters 11 and 12 support this book's main lesson. Many of us have beliefs that are deeply plausible but incompatible with each other. Moreover, the beliefs are such that giving up any of them would have grave implications for practical reasoning as we currently understand and engage in it.

G.13 Chapter 13

In chapter 13, I considered four different approaches to trying to preserve the transitivity of the "all-things-considered better than" relation in the face of this book's arguments. The first approach adopts a fine-grained individuation of the different alternatives in my examples. This approach enables one to claim that transitivity doesn't *fail* in my examples, but merely *fails to apply*. I argued that such a move might enable one to defend transitivity as a *technical* feature of certain outcomes, but would leave one open to being rationally money pumped. More important, I argued that such a move would basically undermine the fundamental role that transitivity plays in practical reasoning.

The second approach adopts something akin to the "time trade-off method" often employed in the health literature in order to evaluate the different outcomes presented in my Spectrum Arguments. I readily granted that this approach would result in a transitive ranking of alternatives, but argued that this approach simply begs the question against the many arguments and considerations offered in support of the Essentially Comparative View. More important, I pointed out that the costs of such a move would, inevitably, be great, as they would involve all of the costs involved in giving up the Essentially Comparative View.

The third approach is to adopt a Sports Analogy, whereby one would accept an Essentially Comparative View for assessing outcomes, but contend that in order to rank any two outcomes one would need to compare them not only with each other, but with *all* of the other outcomes. I observed that this view committed one to rejecting one of the most plausible versions of the Independence of Irrelevant Alternatives Principle. More important, I argued that this approach raised a host of difficulties, especially in the moral domain, some of which were theoretical and some of which were practical. I suggested that the practical difficulties might be insuperable, but that even if they were not, such an approach would be similar to the fine-grained approach, in that it would effectively eviscerate the role and importance of transitivity for the purposes of practical reasoning.

The fourth approach is to argue that one can preserve the transitivity of the "better than" relation if one engages in a back-and-forth process of re-evaluating and revising one's views, as necessary, so as to arrive at a state of reflective equilibrium with respect to one's overall set of beliefs. I argued that such a process will only guarantee the result in question if, from the outset, one builds into the process a "consistency" requirement that the Axiom of Transitivity be met. I argued that building such a requirement into the process from the outset would beg the question against any arguments challenging the Axiom of Transitivity, and would be contrary to the spirit with which one should seek to arrive at a state of reflective equilibrium with respect to one's beliefs. I also noted that no process can avoid the costs that such a result would ensure, which is partly what this book is intended to highlight.

G.14 Chapter 14

In my conclusion, chapter 14, I began by taking stock of the main topics presented. I then listed some of the key lessons learned and in doing this indicated a number of the different combinations of views that stand or fall together. I then noted some of the work that remains to be done if one hopes to arrive at a full understanding of how to assess outcomes, suggesting, among other things, that more attention would need to be paid to the issues of holism and infinity.

I returned to a topic first broached in chapter 1 and argued that we were now in a better position to understand why, even if the "all-things-considered better than" relation *is* transitive, it is not so merely in virtue of the meanings of the words or the logic of "goodness," at least, not given my wide reason-implying sense of "all-things-considered better than."

I considered a number of possible responses to this book, including whether we should abandon considerations of goodness entirely in the practical domain, or abandon the view that one can intelligibly compare outcomes in terms of goodness, or instead opt for a monistic approach to assessing goodness like that offered by total utilitarianism. I expressed my antipathy to each of these approaches, but acknowledged that they may seem more attractive in light of my results than they did previously.

I broached the question of whether it might be appropriate to embrace incredible or even inconsistent views. Considering a host of examples drawn from science, math, and philosophy, I suggested that it might well be more rational to embrace a set of inconsistent views, at least temporarily, than to forsake any of the views merely on the basis of the inconsistency that obtains between them. My remarks implied that at this stage of our understanding, it might be more rational to accept both the Internal Aspects View and the Essentially Comparative View in thinking about the normative realm, than to abandon either; and that similarly, for now, at least, it might be more rational to continue to appeal to additive-aggregationist reasoning, anti-additive-aggregationist reasoning, *and* various Axioms of Transitivity, in our practical deliberations, rather than to choose between them simply because we recognize that they are inconsistent.

I discussed the topic of moral and practical dilemmas. I argued that contrary to what has long been assumed, if this book's arguments are correct, then even consequentialist theories might face moral and practical dilemmas. Specifically, I noted that any consequentialist might face a series of finite alternatives, such that no matter what alternative he chose he would have acted wrongly according to consequentialism, as there would have been another available alternative that he might have chosen instead which would have been better than the alternative he chose. I also suggested that the kinds of moral and practical dilemmas which might arise for consequentialist theories would also arise for *any* moral theory which granted that in some contexts, at least, one would be acting wrongly if one chose a worse outcome over another available outcome that was better than it. I further suggested that, at least prior to this book's results, we would have thought that *all plausible* moral theories would have made such a claim, and hence would face moral and practical dilemmas.

I next raised the question of whether this book supports a form of skepticism. I acknowledged that it might, insofar as it seems to call into question the possibility of plausibly ranking outcomes in terms of goodness. But I noted that this form of skepticism is very different from other familiar forms of skepticism. My view doesn't challenge the reality of moral facts; it questions whether the moral facts that exist permit a very important kind of judgment that we previously thought we could make. This raises a serious crisis regarding how we ought to make choices in the normative domain, but it isn't a version of nihilism.

I ended my conclusion with some final remarks, regarding the position I find myself in with respect to this book's claims. I noted that I remain very perplexed, recognizing that many of the views I care most deeply about are inconsistent, but not seeing how to give any of them up. I also noted that, on my view of the normative realm, it isn't up to *me* to just *choose* which views to keep and which to give up. I suggested that pessimists may claim that this book forces us to seriously rethink and revise our understanding of the good, moral ideals, and the nature of practical reasoning. And that optimists, like me, may agree.

G.16 Appendices

In appendix A, I showed that the same sort of considerations that apply to trade-offs between *quality* and *number* in cases involving different people also apply to trade-offs between *duration* and *number* in cases involving different people.

In appendix B, I explored the relations between quantity, quality, duration, and number. I noted that there is a sense of quantity, which I employ, according to which the *quantity* of pleasure or pain in an outcome *includes* considerations of the *quality*, *duration*, and *number* of pains in that outcome. So, at least as I understand the notion, quantity is not in fact distinct from quality, as is often supposed. I also showed that the lines between the notions of quality, duration, and number are blurred, though one can't simply dispense with one or two of the notions in favor of the other two or one.

In appendix C, I noted how, given certain assumptions, one could revise the standard Sorites Paradox of the Heap along the same lines that I revised the standard Hairiness/Baldness Sorites Paradox in chapter 9, so as to convert it into the sort of Spectrum Argument that I presented in chapters 1 through 5.

In appendix D, I considered and rejected three further objections to my Spectrum Arguments. The first objection appeals to claims about vagueness and indeterminacy, but I show that it amounts to a version of chapter 9's "different kinds" objection, and should be rejected for the same reason already given against that objection in chapter 9. The second objection claims that my Spectrum Arguments are a version of Zeno's Paradox, and fail for the same reason that Zeno's Paradox fails. I argued that this is not the case, and is based on a misinterpretation of my argument. I pointed out that this objection, which was originally lodged against an early formulation of my argument, doesn't apply to this book's arguments, and that if I had spelled out my original premises more carefully, as I now do, this misinterpretation would not have arisen. The third objection claims that we are, in fact, able to find a uniquely best alternative along my spectrums. I pointed out that this solution dubiously favors one particular ordering of the spectrum over alternative orderings that might be equally legitimate. I further argued that the position in question faces many of the same problems facing the Sports Analogy, discussed in chapter 13, and that as such it faces a wide array of serious difficulties that have significant implications for practical reasoning. Finally, I pointed out that the proposed solution to my Spectrum Arguments has no traction against my other worries, raised in chapters 11 and 12, regarding the transitivity of the "all-things-considered better than" relation (in my wide reason-implying sense).

In appendix E, I considered an argument for the claim that the Narrow Person-Affecting View should be restricted in scope so as to apply only to alternatives involving the very same people. I pointed out that this argument is based on a misleading example that cannot support the conclusion in question. It is true, I admitted, that the Narrow Person-Affecting View can render deeply implausible judgments in alternatives involving large populations where there is only a single person in common in the two populations. But this hardly shows, nor, I argued, is it plausible to believe, that the Narrow Person-Affecting View should be abandoned entirely in comparing *any* two populations where some people are the same and some people are not.

In appendix F, I considered whether one might appeal to lexical priority to preserve the Axiom of Transitivity in the face of this book's arguments. I showed that the initial reason for thinking that this might be possible is mistaken and unhelpful. I further expressed my doubts that appealing to lexical priority would, in fact, be of any relevance to the arguments I have presented, or would help to avoid the worries I have raised.

Appendix G summarizes the book, but of course, if you are reading this line you already know that! Finally, I am pleased to add that I have nothing more to add.

BIBLIOGRAPHY

Adams, Robert. "Motive Utilitarianism." *Journal of Philosophy* 73 (1976): 467–81.
Aldred, Jonathan. "Intransitivity and Vague Preferences." *Journal of Ethics* 11 (2007): 377–403.
Anand, Paul. "Are the Preference Axioms Really Rational?" *Theory and Decision* 23 (1987): 189–214.
———. *Foundations of Rational Choice under Risk*. Oxford: Oxford University Press, 1993.
———. "The Philosophy of Intransitive Preference." *Economic Journal* 103 (1993): 337–46.
———. "Rational and Intransitive Preference, Money Pumps and Counterexamples: Two Recent Arguments." Unpublished, 1997.
———. "The Rationality of Intransitive Preferences: Foundations for the Modern View." In *Handbook of Rational and Social Choice*, edited by P. Pattanaik and C. Puppe, 156–73. Oxford: Oxford University Press, 2009.
Anscombe, Elizabeth. "Modern Moral Philosophy." *Philosophy* 33 (1958): 1–19.
Aristotle. *Nicomachean Ethics*. Translated by J. A. K. Thompson. London: George Allen and Unwin, 1953.
———. *Metaphysics*. Translated by Hippocrates G. Apostle. Bloomington: Indiana University Press, 1966.
———. *Poetics*. Abridged and translated by N. G. L. Hammond. Copenhagen: Museum Tusculanum, 2001.
Arntzenius, Frank, Adam Elga, and John Hawthorne. "Bayesianism, Infinite Decisions, and Binding." *Mind* 113 (2004): 251–83.
Arrow, Kenneth. *Social Choice and Individual Values*. New York: Wiley, 1951.
Axelrod, Robert. "The Emergence of Cooperation among Egoists." *American Political Science Review* 75 (1981): 306–18.
———. *The Evolution of Cooperation*. New York: Basic Books, 1984.
Bar-Hillel, Maya, and Avishai Margalit. "How Vicious Are Cycles of Intransitive Choice?" *Theory and Decision* 24 (1988): 199–145.
Beckstead, Nick. "Problems for Capped Models of Moral Ideals." Unpublished, December 2009.
Benbaji, Yitzhak. "Parity, Intransitivity and a Context-Sensitive Degree Analysis of Gradability." *Australasian Journal of Philosophy* 87 (2009): 313–35.
Bendor, Jonathan. "In Good Times and Bad: Reciprocity in an Uncertain World." *American Journal of Political Science* 31 (1987): 531–58.
Binmore, Kenneth. *Playing Fair: Game Theory and the Social Contract 1*. Cambridge, MA: MIT Press, 1994.
Binmore, Kenneth, and Alex Voorhoeve. "Defending Transitivity against Zeno's Paradox." *Philosophy and Public Affairs* 31 (2003): 272–79.

Brandt, Richard. "Toward a Credible Form of Utilitarianism." In *Morality and the Language of Conduct*, edited by Hector-Neri Castañeda and George Nakhnikian, 107–43. Detroit, MI: Wayne State University Press, 1963.

Brentano, Franz. *The Origin of Our Knowledge of Right and Wrong*. Translated by Roderick M. Chisholm and Elizabeth Schneewind. London: Routledge and Kegan Paul, 1969.

Broome, John. *Weighing Goods*. Oxford: Basil Blackwell, 1991.

———. "Are Intentions Reasons? And How Should We Cope with Incommensurable Values?" In *Practical Rationality and Preference: Essays for David Gauthier*, edited by Christopher Morris, and Arthur Ripstein, 98–120. Cambridge: Cambridge University Press, 2001.

———. "Measuring the Burden of Disease by Aggregating Well-being." In *Summary Measures of Population Health: Concepts, Ethics, Measurement and Applications*, edited by Christopher J. L. Murray, Joshua A. Salomon, Colin D. Mathers, and Alan D. Lopez, 91–114. Geneva: World Health Organization, 2002.

———. *Weighing Lives*. Oxford: Oxford University Press, 2004.

Carlson, Erik. "Cyclical Preferences and Rational Choice." *Theoria* 62 (1996): 144–60.

———. "On Some Recent Examples of Intransitive Betterness." In *Logic, Law, Morality*, edited by K. Segerberg, and R. Sliwinski, 181–95. Uppsala: Department of Philosophy, Uppsala University, 2003.

———. "Intransitivity without Zeno's Paradox." In *Recent Work on Intrinsic Value*, edited by T. Rønnow-Rasmussen and M. Zimmerman, 273–77. Dordrecht: Springer, 2005.

Carter, Alan. "A Solution to the Purported Non-transitivity of Normative Evaluation." Unpublished, 2009.

Chang, Ruth. "Introduction." In *Incommensurability, Incomparability and Practical Reason*, edited by Ruth Chang, 1–34. Cambridge, MA: Harvard University Press, 1997.

———. "The Possibility of Parity." *Ethics* 112 (2002): 659–88.

———. "All Things Considered." *Philosophical Perspectives* 18 (2004): 1–22.

———. "Parity, Interval Value and Choice." *Ethics* 114 (2005): 331–50.

Chisholm, Roderick. *Brentano and Intrinsic Value*. Cambridge: Cambridge University Press, 1986.

Dancy, Jonathan. *Ethics without Principles*. Oxford: Clarendon Press, 2004.

———. "Essentially Comparative Concepts." *Journal of Ethics and Social Philosophy* 1 (2005): 1–15.

De Grey, Aubrey. "We Will Be Able to Live to 1,000." *BBC News*, December 3, 2004.

Dostoevsky, Fyodor. *The Brothers Karamazov*. Translated by Andrew MacAndrew. New York: Bantam Classics, 1984.

Dreifus, Claudia. "A Conversation with Michael R. Rose: Live Longer with Evolution? Evidence May Lie in Fruit Flies." *New York Times*, science section, December 6, 2005.

Einstein, A., N. Podolsky, and N. Rosen. "Can Quantum-Mechanical Description of Physical Reality Be Considered Complete?" *Physics Review* 47 (1935): 777–80.

Elster, Jon. *Ulysses and the Sirens: Studies in Rationality and Irrationality*. Cambridge: Cambridge University Press, 1979.

Emerson, Ralph Waldo. "Self-Reliance." In *Essays and Lectures*, edited by Joel Porte, 259–82. New York: Library of America, 1983.
Foot, Philippa. "Utilitarianism and the Virtues." In *Moral Dilemmas: And Other Topics in Moral Philosophy*, 59–77. Oxford: Clarendon Press, 2002.
Frankena, William. *Ethics*. 2nd ed. Englewood Cliffs, NJ: Prentice-Hall, 1973.
Gauthier, David. *Morals by Agreement*. Oxford: Oxford University Press, 1986.
Glover, Jonathan. "It Makes No Difference Whether or Not I Do It." *Proceedings of the Aristotelian Society, Supplementary Volumes* 49 (1975): 171–209.
Griffin, Jim. *Well-being: Its Meaning, Measurement, and Moral Importance*. Oxford: Clarendon Press, 1986.
Hardin, Garrett. "The Tragedy of the Commons." *Science* 162 (1968): 1243–48.
Hare, Caspar. "Rationality and the Distant Needy." *Philosophy and Public Affairs* 35 (2007): 161–78.
———. "Take the Sugar." *Analysis* 70 (2010): 237–47.
Hare, R. M. "Ethical Theory and Utilitarianism." In *Contemporary British Philosophy IV*, edited by H. D. Lewis, 113–31. London: Allen and Unwin, 1976.
Harman, Gilbert. *The Nature of Morality*. New York: Oxford University Press, 1977.
Hooker, Brad. *Ideal Code, Real World: A Rule-Consequentialist Theory of Morality*. Oxford: Oxford University Press, 2000.
Howard, J. V. "Cooperation in the Prisoner's Dilemma." *Theory and Decision* 24 (1988): 203–13.
Howard, Nigel. *Paradoxes of Rationality*. Cambridge, MA: MIT Press, 1971.
Huemer, Michael. "In Defense of Repugnance." *Mind* 117 (2008): 899–933.
Hurka, Thomas. "Value and Population Size." *Ethics* 93 (1983): 496–507.
———. "Two Kinds of Organic Unity." *Journal of Ethics* 2 (1998): 299–320.
Hurley, Susan. "Newcomb's Problem, Prisoners' Dilemma, and Collective Action." *Synthese* 86 (1991): 173–96.
Jensen, Karsten K. "Discontinuity in Value and the Repugnant Conclusion." Unpublished, June 1998.
Kagan, Shelly. "The Additive Fallacy." *Ethics* 99 (1988): 5–31.
———. *The Limits of Morality*. Oxford: Oxford University Press, 1989.
———. "Rethinking Intrinsic Value." *Journal of Ethics* 2 (1998): 277–97.
Kahneman, Daniel. "Maps of Bounded Rationality: A Perspective on Intuitive Judgment and Choice." *Nobel Prize Lecture* 8 (2002): 449–89.
Kahneman, Daniel, Paul Slovic, and Amos Tversky, editors. *Judgment under Uncertainty: Heuristics and Biases*. Cambridge: Cambridge University Press, 1982.
Kahneman, Daniel, and Amos Tversky. "The Framing of Decisions and the Psychology of Choice." *Science* 211 (1981): 453–58.
———. "The Psychology of Preferences." *Scientific American* 246 (1982): 160–73.
Kahneman, Daniel, Peter Wakker, and Rakesh Sarin. "Back to Bentham? Explorations of Experienced Utility." *Quarterly Journal of Economics* 112 (1997): 375–405.
Kamm, Frances. "Supererogation and Obligation." *Journal of Philosophy* 82 (1985): 118–38.
———. *Morality, Mortality, Volume I: Death and Whom to Save From It*. New York: Oxford University Press, 1993.

———. "Does Distance Matter Morally to the Duty to Rescue?" *Law and Philosophy* 19 (1999): 655–81.
———. "Health and Equity." In *Summary Measures of Population Health*, edited by C. J. L. Murray et al., 685–706. Geneva: WHO, 2002.
———. *Intricate Ethics: Rights, Responsibilities, and Permissible Harm*. New York: Oxford University Press, 2007.
———. "Aggregation, Allocating Scarce Resources, and the Disabled." *Social Philosophy and Policy* 26 (2009): 148–97.
Kant, Immanuel. *Groundwork for the Metaphysics of Morals*. Translated by James W. Ellington. Indianapolis, IN: Hackett, 1981.
Kavka, Gregory. "The Paradox of Future Individuals." *Philosophy and Public Affairs* 11 (1982): 93–112.
———. *Hobbesian Moral and Political Theory*. Princeton, NJ: Princeton University Press, 1986.
Knapp, Christopher. "Trading Quality for Quantity." *Journal of Philosophical Research* 32 (2007): 211–33.
Korsgaard, Christine. "Two Distinctions in Goodness." *Philosophical Review* 92 (1983): 169–95.
Kramer, Peter. *Against Depression*. New York: Viking, 2005.
Lemos, Noah M. *Intrinsic Value: Concept and Warrant*. Cambridge: Cambridge University Press, 1994.
Lewis, David. *Counterfactuals*. Cambridge, MA: Harvard University Press, 1973.
———. "Prisoner's Dilemma Is a Newcomb Problem." *Philosophy and Public Affairs* 8 (1979): 235–40.
Lyons, David. *Forms and Limits of Utilitarianism*. Oxford: Clarendon Press, 1965.
Mackie, John. *Ethics: Inventing Right and Wrong*. New York: Penguin Books, 1977.
———. "Parfit's Population Paradox." In *Persons and Values*, edited by Joan Mackie and Penelope Mackie. Oxford: Oxford University Press, 1985.
Makison, D. C. "The Paradox of the Preface." *Analysis* 25 (1965): 205–7.
McCarthy, David. "On Interpersonal Aggregation." Unpublished, 2003.
———. "Saving One vs. Saving Many." Unpublished, 2003.
McLennen, Edward. *Rationality and Dynamic Choice: Foundational Explorations*. New York: Cambridge University Press, 1990.
McMahan, Jeff. *The Ethics of Killing: Problems at the Margins of Life*. New York: Oxford University Press, 2002.
McTaggart, J. M. E. *The Nature of Existence*. 2 vols. Cambridge: Cambridge University Press, 1921.
Moore, G. E. *Principia Ethica*. Cambridge: Cambridge University Press, 1903.
Naeh, Shlomo, and Uzi Segal. "The Talmud on Transitivity." *Boston College Working Papers in Economics* 687 (2009): 1–23.
Nagel, Thomas. *The Possibility of Altruism*. Oxford: Oxford University Press, 1970.
———. "The Fragmentation of Value." In *Mortal Questions*, 128–41. Cambridge: Cambridge University Press, 1979.
———. *The View from Nowhere*. New York: Oxford University Press, 1986.
Narveson, Jan. "Utilitarianism and New Generations." *Mind* 76 (1967): 62–72.
———. "Moral Problems of Population." *The Monist* 57 (1973): 63–86.

Nietzsche, Friedrich. *The Gay Science*. Translated by Walter Kaufmann. New York: Vintage Books, 1974.
Norcross, Alastair. "Comparing Harms: Headaches and Human Lives." *Philosophy and Public Affairs* 26 (1997): 135–67.
———. "Great Harms from Small Benefits Grow: How Death Can Be Outweighed by Headaches." *Analysis* 58 (1998): 152–58.
———. "Speed Limits, Human Lives, and Convenience: A Reply to Ridge." *Philosophy and Public Affairs* 27 (1998): 59–64.
———. "Intransitivity and the Person-Affecting Principle." *Philosophy and Phenomenological Research* 59 (1999): 769–76.
Nozick, Robert. *Anarchy, State, and Utopia*. New York: Basic Books, 1974.
———. *Philosophical Explanations*. Cambridge, MA: Harvard University Press, 1981.
Otsuka, Michael. "Scanlon and the Claims of the Many versus the One." *Analysis* 60 (2000): 288–93.
Parfit, Derek. "Innumerate Ethics." *Philosophy and Public Affairs* 7 (1978): 285–301.
———. "Future Generations: Further Problems." *Philosophy and Public Affairs* 11 (1982): 113–72.
———. *Reasons and Persons*. Oxford: Oxford University Press, 1984.
———. "Equality or Priority?" The Lindley Lecture, University of Kansas, 1991. Reprinted in *The Ideal of Equality*, edited by Matthew Clayton and Andrew Williams, 81–125. London: Macmillan; New York: St. Martin's Press, 2000.
———. *On What Matters*. Oxford: Oxford University Press, 2011.
Persson, Ingmar. "Why There Cannot Be Transitivity with Respect to Supervenient Properties." In *Kvantifikator för en Dag*, Philosophical Communications Web Series, no. 35, Department of Philosophy, Gothenburg University (2006): 231–49.
Plato. *Phaedrus*. Translated R. Hackforth. Cambridge: Cambridge University Press, 1952.
———. "Protagorus." In *Protagorus and Meno*, translated by William Keith Chambers Guthrie, 27–100. London: Penguin Books, 1956.
———. *Gorgias*. Translated with commentary by Eric Robertson Dodds. Oxford: Clarendon Press, 1959.
———. *The Republic*. Translated with commentary by Allan Bloom. New York: Basic Books, 1968.
Poddiakov, Alexander. "Intransitivity of Superiority Relations and Decision Making." *Psychology: The Journal of the Higher School of Economics* 3 (2006): 88–111.
Qizilbash, Mozaffar. "Transitivity and Vagueness." *Economics and Philosophy* 21 (2005): 109–31.
Quine, W. V. O. *From a Logical Point of View*. Cambridge: Cambridge University Press, 1953.
Quinn, Warren. "The Puzzle of the Self-Torturer." *Philosophical Studies* 59 (1990): 79–90.
Rabinowicz, Wlodek. "The Size of Inequality and Its Badness: Some Reflections around Temkin's *Inequality*." *Theoria* 69 (2003): 60–84.
Rabinowicz, Wlodek, and Gustaf Arrhenius. "Value and Unacceptable Risk: Temkin's Worries about Continuity Reconsidered." *Economics and Philosophy* 21 (2005): 177–98.

Rachels, Stuart. "Counterexamples to the Transitivity of Better Than." *Australasian Journal of Philosophy* 76 (1998): 71–83.

———. "A Set of Solutions to Parfit's Problems." *Noûs* 35 (2001): 214–38.

———. "Repugnance or Intransitivity." In *The Repugnant Conclusion: Essays on Population Ethics*, edited by Jesper Ryberg and Torbjorn Tannsjo, 163–86. Dordrecht: Kluwer Academic Publishers, 2004.

Rawls, John. *A Theory of Justice*. Cambridge, MA: Harvard University Press, 1971.

Raz, Joseph. *The Morality of Freedom*. Oxford: Oxford University Press, 1986.

Redelmeier, Daniel, and Daniel Kahneman. "Patients' Memories of Painful Medical Treatments: Real-Time and Retrospective Evaluations of Two Minimally Invasive Procedures." *Pain* 66 (1996): 3–8.

Roberts, Melinda. "Does the Moral Significance of Merely Possible People Imply That Early Abortion Is Wrong?" Unpublished, December 2010.

Ross, Jacob. "Rejecting Ethical Deflationism." *Ethics* 116 (2006): 742–68.

Ross, W. D. *The Right and the Good*. Oxford: Clarendon Press, 2002.

Rubinstein, Ariel. "Similarity and Decision-making under Risk (Is There a Utility Theory Resolution of the Allais Paradox?)." *Journal of Economic Theory* 46 (1988): 145–53.

———. "Economics and Psychology? The Case of Hyperbolic Discounting." *International Economic Review* 44 (2003): 1207–16.

Russell, Bertrand. *Principles of Mathematics*. Cambridge: Cambridge University Press, 1903.

Samuelson, Paul. "Probability, Utility, and the Independence Axiom." *Econometrica* 20 (1952): 670–78.

Scanlon, Thomas. *What We Owe to Each Other*. Cambridge, MA: Harvard University Press, 1998.

Schelling, Thomas. *The Strategy of Conflict*. Cambridge, MA: Harvard University Press, 1960.

Schreiber, Charles, and Daniel Kahneman. "Determinants of the Remembered Utility of Aversive Sounds." *Journal of Experimental Psychology: General* 129 (2000): 27–42.

Schumm, George. "Transitivity, Preference and Indifference." *Philosophical Studies* 52 (1987): 435–37.

Sen, Amartya. *On Economic Inequality*. Oxford: Clarendon Press, 1973.

———. "Rational Fools: A Critique of the Behavioral Foundations of Economic Theory." *Philosophy and Public Affairs* 6 (1977): 317–44.

———. "Well-being, Agency, and Freedom: The Dewey Lectures." *Journal of Philosophy* 82 (1985): 169–221.

———. "Internal Consistency of Choice." *Econometrica* 61 (1993): 495–521.

Sidgwick, Henry. *The Methods of Ethics*. 7th ed. London: Macmillan, 1907.

Silver, Lee M. "Remaking Human Nature: The Ethics of Genetic Enhancement." Hinna Stahl Memorial Lecture in Bioethics. Presented at Robert Wood Johnson Medical School, New Brunswick, New Jersey, March 28, 2007.

Skyrms, Brian. *The Dynamics of Rational Deliberation*. Cambridge, MA: Harvard University Press, 1990.

Slote, Michael. *Beyond Optimizing: A Study of Rational Choice*. Cambridge, MA: Harvard University Press, 1989.

Stratton-Lake, Phillip. "Introduction." In *The Right and the Good*, by W. D. Ross, x-l. Oxford: Clarendon Press, 2002.
Styron, William. *Sophie's Choice*. New York: Random House, 1979.
Taurek, John. "Should the Numbers Count?" *Philosophy and Public Affairs* 6 (1977): 293-316.
Temkin, Larry. "Intransitivity and the Mere Addition Paradox." *Philosophy and Public Affairs* 16 (1987): 138-87.
———. "Additivity Problems." In *Encyclopedia of Ethics*, edited by Lawrence C. Becker and Charlotte B. Becker, 15-18. New York: Garland Press, 1992.
———. "Intergenerational Inequality." In *Philosophy, Politics, and Society*, 6th series, edited by Peter Laslett and James Fishkin, 169-205. New Haven, CT: Yale University Press, 1992.
———. "Harmful Goods, Harmless Bads." In *Value, Welfare, and Morality*, edited by R. G. Frey and Christopher Morris, 290-324. Cambridge: Cambridge University Press, 1993.
———. *Inequality*. New York: Oxford University Press, 1993.
———. "Weighing Goods: Some Questions and Comments." *Philosophy and Public Affairs* 23 (1994): 350-80.
———. "Justice and Equality: Some Questions about Scope." In *Social Philosophy and Policy*, edited by Ellen F. Paul, Fred D. Miller, and Jeffrey Paul, 72-104. Cambridge: Cambridge University Press, 1995.
———. "A Continuum Argument for Intransitivity." *Philosophy and Public Affairs* 25 (1996): 175-210.
———. "Rethinking the Good, Moral Ideals and the Nature of Practical Reasoning." In *Reading Parfit*, edited by Jonathan Dancy, 290-344. Oxford: Basil Blackwell, 1997.
———. "Intransitivity and the Person-Affecting Principle: A Response." *Philosophy and Phenomenological Research* 59 (1999): 777-84.
———. "An Abortion Argument and the Threat of Intransitivity." In *Well-being and Morality: Essays in Honour of James Griffin*, edited by Roger Crisp and Brad Hooker, 336-56. Oxford: Oxford University Press, 2000.
———. "Equality, Priority, and the Levelling Down Objection." In *The Ideal of Equality*, edited by Matthew Clayton and Andrew Williams, 126-61. London: Macmillan; New York: St. Martin's Press, 2000.
———. "Egalitarianism: A Complex, Individualistic, and Comparative Notion." In *Philosophical Issues*, vol. 11, edited by Ernie Sosa and Enrique Villanueva, 327-52. Boston: Blackwell, 2001.
———. "Worries about Continuity, Transitivity, Expected Utility Theory, and Practical Reasoning." In *Exploring Practical Philosophy*, edited by Dan Egonsson et al., 95-108. Burlington: Ashgate, 2001.
———. "Determining the Scope of Egalitarian Concerns: A Partial Defense of Complete Lives Egalitarianism." *Theoria* 69 (2003): 45-58.
———. "Egalitarianism Defended." *Ethics* 113 (2003): 764-82.
———. "Equality, Priority, or What?" *Economics and Philosophy* 19 (2003): 61-88.
———. "Exploring the Roots of Egalitarian Concerns." *Theoria* 69 (2003): 124-50.
———. "Measuring Inequality's Badness: Does Size Matter? If So, How, If Not, What Does?" *Theoria* 69 (2003): 85-107.

———. "Personal versus Impersonal Principles: Reconsidering the Slogan." *Theoria* 69 (2003): 20–30.

———. "A 'New' Principle of Aggregation." *Philosophical Issues* 15 (2005): 218–34.

———. "Is Living Longer, Living Better?" *Journal of Applied Philosophy* 25 (2008): 193–210.

———. "Aggregation within Lives." In *Utilitarianism: The Aggregation Question*, edited by Ellen F. Paul, Fred D. Miller, and Jeffrey Paul, 1–29. Cambridge: Cambridge University Press, 2009.

———. "Justice, Equality, Fairness, Desert, Rights, Free Will, Responsibility, and Luck." In *Distributive Justice and Responsibility*, edited by Carl Knight and Zofia Stemplowska, 51–76. Oxford: Oxford University Press, 2011.

Thomson, Judith Jarvis. "A Defense of Abortion." *Philosophy and Public Affairs* 1 (1971): 47–66.

Trivers, Robert. "The Evolution of Reciprocal Altruism." *Quarterly Review of Biology* 46 (1971): 35–57.

Tversky, Amos. "Intransitivity of Preferences." *Psychological Review* 84 (1967): 31–48.

———. "Features of Similarity." *Psychological Review* 84 (1977): 327–52.

Tversky, Amos, and Daniel Kahneman. "Rational Choice and the Framing of Decisions." *Journal of Business* 59 (1986): 251–78.

Tversky, Amos, Shmuel Sattath, and Paul Slovic. "Contingent Weighting in Judgment and Choice." *Psychological Review* 95 (1988): 371.

Tversky, Amos, and Eldar Shafir. "Decision under Conflict: An Analysis of Choice Aversion." *Psychological Science* 6 (1992): 358–61.

Unger, Peter. *Living High and Letting Die: Our Illusion of Innocence*. New York: Oxford University Press, 1996.

Vallentyne, Peter. "The Connection between Prudential and Moral Goodness." *Journal of Social Philosophy* 24 (1993): 105–28.

Varey, Carol, and Daniel Kahneman. "Experiences Extended across Time: Evaluation of Moments and Episodes." *Journal of Behavioral Decision Making* 5 (1992): 169–85.

Velleman, David. "Well-being and Time." *Pacific Philosophical Quarterly* 71 (1991): 48–77.

Vonnegut, Kurt. *Welcome to the Monkey House*. New York: Dell, 1970.

von Neumann, John, and Oskar Morgenstern. *The Theory of Games and Economic Behavior*. 2nd ed. Princeton, NJ: Princeton University Press, 1944.

Voorhoeve, Alex, and Ken Binmore. "Heuristics and Biases in a Purported Counterexample to the Acyclicity of 'Better Than.'" *Politics, Philosophy, and Economics* 7 (2008): 285–99.

———. "Transitivity, the Sorites Paradox, and Similarity-Based Decision Making." *Erkenntnis* 64 (2006): 101–14.

Wasserman, Ryan. "Paradoxes of Transitivity." Unpublished, December 2004.

Williams, Andrew D. "The Revisionist Difference Principle." *Canadian Journal of Philosophy* 25 (1995): 257–82.

Williams, Bernard. "A Critique of Utilitarianism." In *Utilitarianism For and Against*, by J. J. C. Smart and Bernard Williams, 77–150. Cambridge: Cambridge University Press, 1973.

———. *Moral Luck*. Cambridge: Cambridge University Press, 1981.

Williamson, Timothy. *Vagueness*. New York: Routledge, 1994.

Wittgenstein, Ludwig. *Philosophical Investigations*. 2nd ed. Edited and translated by G. E. M. Anscombe. Oxford: Blackwell, 1958.

INDEX

affirmative action
  and the transitivity of the moral obligatoriness relation, 197–202, 212–16
  and justice, 199, 215–16
agent-neutral duties: characterized, 391 n. 36
  and Each-We Dilemmas, 88–92, 92–94 n. 19
  and the relation between the right and the good, 206–7
  and moral dilemmas, 513–14
agent-relative duties: characterized, 391 n. 36; referenced, 10, 52, 78, 81, 89–92, 105 n. 21, 332 n. 18
  and Each-We Dilemmas, 88–92, 92–94 n. 19
  and the moral "obligatoriness" relation, and rightness as a good-making feature of outcomes, 204–7
  and moral dilemmas, 508–11
aggregation: characterized, 24
  See aggregation, additive; aggregation, anti-additive; aggregation within lives; and anti-additive aggregationist position
aggregation, additive: characterized, 25, 37–38; referenced, 4, 99–101, 108–27, 129, 146–47, 161, 385, 467, 473–74, 478–80, 483–87, 494
  and total utilitarianism, 25, 34–35, 38
  and the Unlimited Trade-offs View, 38
  and the First Standard View, 38, 61–66, 64 n. 38, 130–32, 162, 222–23, 474
  and Parfit, 80–85
  and Sidgwick, 96–98
  and principles of decomposition/recombination, 145–52
  and the Sure-Thing Principle, 239–40
  and the Principle of Continuity, 257–60
  and Sorites Paradox, 277–283, 307–9, 312
  and the Standard Model for Utility, 316
  and second additive aggregationist's position, 523
  See also Standard Model for Combining Ideals; Standard Model for Utility; Standard View, Fifth; Standard View, First; Standard View, Third; View One
aggregation, anti-additive: characterized, 34, 37–38; referenced, 124, 129, 161, 222–23, 313, 316, 319, 324–28, 473–74, 477–80, 484–88, 493–94
  and the Repugnant Conclusion, 34–35, 37, 41, 42 n. 26, 324–28
  and Lollipops for Life, 34–35, 42
  and the Second Standard View, 34–38, 61–66, 73 n. 8
  and discontinuities of value, 35–36, 282–83
  and Headaches versus Lives, Kamm, 36
  and Jones and the TV transmitter, and Scanlon, 36–37
  See also anti-additive aggregationist position
aggregation within lives: 20–22, 129–30, 155–56, 292, 312
  and impartiality, 96–98
  and Sidgwick, 96–98
  and anti-additive aggregation, 100, 109, 114–15, 124–28
  and the Disperse Additional Burdens View, 100–1, 113–18, 115–16 n. 29, 125–28
    and the status quo, 115–18
  and the shape of a life, 111–13, 113–14 n. 26, 125–26
    and Kamm, and Velleman, 111 n. 24

583

aggregation within lives (*continued*)
   and holism/organic unity, 112
   and hedonism, 113–14 n. 26
   and the Single Life Repugnant Conclusion, 118–23, 127
      and McTaggart's error theory of, 119–22
   and the Capped Model for Ideals, 333–34
   See also Standard View, Fourth; Standard View, Third; View One; View Three
Aman, David, and the significance of numbers for the value of equality: 356–60, 356 n. 31
Anscombe, Elizabeth, and the moral significance of numbers: 27 n. 4, 354 n. 28
anti-additive-aggregationist position: 38–39, 41–44, 44–45 n. 27
   and limited scope of, 38, 65–66, 140–45
   and freedom, 61–62
   and equality, and the Repellant Conclusion, 62–64, 64 n. 38
   and the Disperse Additional Burdens View, 68, 70, 75, 82–83, 92–94 n. 19, 95, 442
   and Each-We Dilemmas, 88–95
   and aggregation within lives, 100, 109, 114–115, 124–128
   and the Fourth Standard View, 124
   and the Principle of Continuity, 259, 263–64
   and the Capped Model for Ideals, 333–43, 350–51, 361–62
   See also aggregation, anti-additive; Disperse Additional Burdens View; Standard View, Fourth; Standard View, Second; Standard View, Sixth; View Three
Aristotle: 111 n. 24, 268 n. 6, 499, 499 n. 13
   and the unity of the virtues, 334–35
Arntzenius, Frank: 511–12 n. 34
Arrow, Kenneth, and the Independence of Irrelevant Alternatives Principle: 387–88, 387 n. 33, 388 n. 84, 455

Beckstead, Nick
   and the regress objection to the claim that rightness is a good-making feature of outcomes, 207 n. 9
   and rough comparability and Expected Value Theory, 244 n. 16
   and utilitarianism and impossibility results, 264 n. 34
   and the Capped Model for Ideals, 361–62 n. 33
Bentham, Jeremy: 328 n. 13
"better than" relation
   and impartiality of, 10–11, 10 n. 8, 228–30
   and meaning of, 10–18, 494–97
      reason-implying sense of, 12–16
   See also transitivity of the "all-things-considered better than" relation
bias toward the near, and the Single Life Repugnant Conclusion: 122
Binmore, Ken: 296–310, 297 n. 20, 473 n. 18, 538–40, 538 n. 5, 539 nn. 9–10, 540 n. 11
Bourget, David; and lexical orderings and the Essentially Comparative View of Ideals: 554–57
Brentano, Franz, and holism: 148 n. 6
Brody, Baruch: 496 n. 9
Broome, John: 233 n. 1, 351 n. 24, 412 n. 13, 528 n. 1
   and the transitivity of the "all-things-considered better than" relation, 11 n. 9, 12–13, 16 n. 14, 494
   and the Pareto Principle/principle of personal good, 122
   and Career Choices: Lawyer versus Academic, 178–79
   and rough comparability of alternatives, 178–83, 178 n. 10, 178–79 n. 11, 181 n. 12, 182–83 n. 13, 238 n. 10
   and the transitivity of the "not worse than" relation, 178–88, 182–83 n. 13, 222–27
   and A "Not Worse Than" Money Pump, 183–86
   and the fine-grained individuation of alternatives, 215 n. 11, 458, 458 n. 1
   and the transitivity of the "all-things-considered better than" relation, 232–33, 233–35 nn. 1–7
   and Expected Utility Theory/Expected Value Theory, 233–34, 233 nn. 2–3, 238 n. 10, 239–40, 254, 498
   and the Sure-Thing Principle, 239–40
   and the significance of numbers for the value of equality, 351–60
   and the Mere Addition Paradox, 384 n. 30

and the Narrow Person-Affecting View and the neutral range, 418 n. 22, 425 n. 32, 427–34, 427 n. 34
and objections to Spectrum Arguments based on Zeno's Paradox, 540 n. 11

Campbell, Tim: 540 n. 13
    and rough comparability and Expected Value Theory, 244 n. 16
    and Internal Aspects View and the Essentially Comparative View, 375 n. 19
    and How Only France Survives, 404 n. 4
Capped Model for Ideals: characterized, 328–29; referenced, 5, 366–67 n. 10, 449–52, 451 n. 51, 478, 484–89
    and gymnastics analogy, Olga and Nadia, 328–29
    and equality, 328–29, 332–35
    and as applied to different kinds of utility
        with the Repugnant Conclusion, 328–31
        with the Single Life Repugnant Conclusion, 336–37
        with the pain spectrum, 337
        with Headaches versus Lives, 337
        with lollipop licks versus watching the birth of one's child, 339–40
    and the Repugnant Conclusion, 328–31, 336–37, 351–52, 360–62
    and infinite utility, 330
    and the diminishing marginal value of utility, 331
    and *Harrison Bergeron*, 331–32
    and the Single Life Repugnant Conclusion, 333–34, 337
    and anti-additive aggregation, 333–43, 350–51, 361–62
    and virtue, and Attila the Hun, 334–35
    and the transitivity of the "all-things-considered better than" relation, 337–38, 361–62, 448–52
    and difficulties with, and Parfit, 339–42
    and contrasted with the Standard Model for Utility
        with respect to the marginal value of utility, 343
        with respect to the non-instrumental value of utility, 343
        with respect to impartiality over people, places, and times, 343–44
        with respect to the value of total utility, 349
        with respect to additive aggregation, 349–51
    and the Internal Aspects View of Moral Ideals, 351, 448–52, 485–86
    and the Essentially Comparative View of Moral Ideals, 351, 448–52, 451 n. 51, 486–88
Carlson, Erik: 538, 538 n. 6, 540–44, 540 nn. 11–12, 541 n. 14, 543 n. 17
Chang, Ruth: 176 n. 7, 178–79 n. 11, 182–83 n. 13
charitable giving
    and the Disperse Additional Burdens View, 78–79
    and Unger, 137–38 n. 5
choiceworthiness: 11–12, 11 n. 10
Code, Alan: 268 n. 6, 335 n. 19
Cohen, G.A.: 8 n. 6
Compensation: *See* separateness of individuals; compensation
consequentialism: 11–12, 328, 497–98, 506–20, 511–12 n. 34
    and the Principle of Irrelevant Utilities, 36 n. 18, 44 n. 27
    and Each-We Dilemmas, 88–95, 92–94 n. 19
    and the relation between the right and the good, 204
    and conflict with deontology, 504 n. 22
    and moral dilemmas, 510–14
Consolidate Additional Benefits View: characterized, 68; referenced, 68, 69 n. 4, 75
    and equivalence with the Disperse Additional Burdens View, and Shelly Kagan, 68–70, 69 n. 4
Contextual Interaction, Principle of: 116 n. 29
    and Kamm, 38 n. 22, 323, 430 n. 36
    and utilitarianism, 323–24
    and the Narrow Person-Affecting View, 430–31
    and the transitivity of the "all-things-considered better than relation," 482

Continuity, Principle of: characterized, 236; referenced, 245–64, 479, 480, 484–88, 493, 498
  and easy cases, 245–46
  and extreme cases, 247–48, 253–59
    everyday risk, 253–56
    the importance of certainty, 255–56
    global versus local optimization, 255–56
    unimaginably small probabilities, 256–57
    rational regret, 257–58
    iteration and anti-additive aggregation, 258–59
    Super Extreme Case and J. Ross's Principle, 261–62
  and satisficing, 248
  and Vallentyne's counterexample to, 248–49
  and Spectrum Argument connecting easy cases and extreme cases, 249–51
  and the Essentially Comparative View of Moral Ideals, 252
  and the Internal Aspects View of Moral ideals, 252
  and Parfit, 256–57
  and additive aggregation, 257–60
  and the Second Standard View, 259, 262–63
  and anti-additive aggregation, 259–60, 263–64
Crisp, Roger: 205 n. 7
  and adaptive preference formation, 51 n. 32
  and the transitivity of permissibility, 195 n. 2
  and total utilitarianism and additive aggregation, 328 n. 13
  and the usefulness of the fine-grained solution to preserving transitivity, 464 n. 7

Dancy, Jonathan: 489 n. 4
decision theory: *See* Expected Utility Theory
Democritus: 515 n. 37
deontology: 332 n. 18, 506, 509 n. 30
  and the Principle of Irrelevant Utilities, 44 n. 27
  and Each-We Dilemmas, 88–95
  and the relation between the right and the good, 105–106 n. 21, 204
  and skepticism about impersonal value, 497–98, 513–14, 519
  and conflict with consequentialism, 504 n. 22
  and moral dilemmas, 510–14
discontinuities of value: 336–38
  and anti-additive aggregation, 34–37, 247 n. 19, 283
  and Griffin, 35–37, 52–57, 123, 336–38
  and the First and Second Standard Views, 52–58
  and kinds of value, 53–55, 265–74
  and the Single Life Repugnant Conclusion, 122–24
  and Spectrum Arguments
    objections to From Torture to Mosquito Bites, 140–42
    comparison with discontinuities in Sorites Paradoxes, 280–84
    Knapp's objections to Spectrum Arguments based on vagueness, 534–38
Disperse Additional Burdens View: characterized and illustrated, 67–68, 70–76; referenced, 67–95, 100, 113–18, 115–16 n. 29, 125–27, 129, 324, 474
  and the Second Standard View, 67–69, 73 n. 8, 82, 95
  and anti-additive aggregation, 68, 70, 75, 82–83, 92–94 n. 19, 95, 442
  and contrast with other anti-additive-aggregationist moral ideals
    equality, 70–78, 73 n. 8, 89
    maximin, 70–79, 73 n. 8
    perfectionism, 71–78
    prioritarianism, 71 n. 5
  and additive aggregation, 71, 113–14
  and Jones and the TV Transmitter, variant of, 71–73

    and the Levelling Down Objection, 75–79
    and charitable giving, 78–79
    and the status quo bias, 78 n. 12, 116–18
    and the transitivity of the "all-things-considered better than" relation, and iteration, 79–85
    and Prisoner's Dilemma, 85–89
    and Each-We Dilemmas, 85–95
        for consequentialists, 88–95, 92–94 n. 19
        Distinct Aims versus Distinct Factors Each-We Dilemmas, 90–95
    and the separateness of individuals, 100–1, 113–14
    and aggregation within lives, 100–1, 113–18, 115–16 n. 29, 125–28, 292
    and the Principle of Continuity, 259, 263–64
Doris, John: 225 n. 15
Dostoevsky, Fyodor: 515
Dworkin, Ronald: 198 n. 4

Each-We Dilemmas
    and Parfit, 85–88, 92–94 n. 19
    and the Disperse Additional Burdens View, 85–95
    and Kant, 86
    and Agent-Neutrality/Agent-Relativity, 88–94, 92–94 n. 19
    and anti-additive aggregation, 88–95
    and Consequentialism/Deontology, 88–95, 92–94 n. 19
    and Distinct Aims versus Distinct Factors Each-We Dilemmas, 91–95
Einstein, A.: 501–2, 501–2 n. 16, 505 n. 23
Elga, Adam: 511–12 n. 34
Elster, Jon, and global versus local optimization: 84 n. 15, 188–93, 188 n. 16, 191 n. 20
Emerson, Ralph Waldo, and inconsistency: 506–7, 506 n. 25
EPR Paradox: 501–2, 501–2 n. 16
equality: characterized, 314; referenced, 404 n. 5, 410, 424–26, 429, 547, 550–51, 451 n. 51
    and the Levelling Down Objection, 25 n. 1, 75–79
    and contrast with prioritarianism, 25 n. 1, 331–32 n. 16
    and tension between First and Second Standard Views, 62–64
    and First Standard View, and additive aggregation, 62–64, 64 n. 38
    and Second Standard View, 63
    and simplicity in normative theory, 63 n. 37
    and anti-additive aggregation, 64–65, 64 n. 38
    and the Repellant Conclusion, 64 n. 38
    and the Disperse Additional Burdens View, 70–77, 89
    and the separateness of individuals, 103–9
    and the Standard Model for Combining Ideals, 324–28, 448–51
    and the Repugnant Conclusion, 324–28, 449–51
    and the Capped Model for Ideals, 328–29, 332–33, 448–51
    and *Harrison Bergeron*, 332
    and the relevance of numbers of people, 350–60, 356 n. 32
        and Broome, and Aman, 356
    and Sen, 352–53 n. 25
    and the Mere Addition Paradox/Mere Addition, 365–69, 366–67 n. 10, 372–84, 391–92, 395–98, 401, 404
    and the Essentially Comparative View of Moral Ideals, 380–81
Essentially Comparative View of Moral Ideals: characterized, 229–31, 369, 371–74; referenced, 5, 13, 116 n. 30, 252, 478–80, 483–85, 490–94, 497–501, 507–8, 517
    illustrated and contrasted with the Internal Aspects View of Moral Ideals
    The Mere Addition Paradox, 364–66
    Saints, Sinners, and the Inadequacy of Purely Abstract Diagrams, 374–75
    How Variations in Group Membership Matter, (Or Not): Internal Aspects versus Essentially Comparative Views, 377–78

Essentially Comparative View of Moral Ideals (*continued*)
  How an Essentially Comparative View of Equality Challenges Transitivity, 380–81
  Vanilla, Chocolate, or Strawberry: On the Independence of Irrelevant Alternatives Principle, 389
  Mere Addition Paradox Variations, 397
  How More Than France Exists, 402–4, 448–52
  Another Variation of the Mere Addition Paradox: On the Plausibility of an Essentially Comparative View of Utility, 411–16
  The Wood-Burning Fireplace, 452
  intransitive rankings of cars, jobs, and homes, 452–54
Essentially Comparative View of Outcome Goodness: characterized, 371; referenced, 371, 385, 399–400, 443, 446–48
  and the transitivity of the "all-things-considered-better-than" relation and other axioms of transitivity, 13, 221 n. 13, 230–31, 364–65, 369, 379–85, 399–400, 406 n. 6, 407, 411, 416, 432–34, 444–56, 459–60 n. 4, 466–76, 494–97, 542–43, 548–52, 552 n. 8
  and contrast with Internal Aspects View of Moral Ideals, 229–31, 369–74
  and the Capped Model for Ideals, 350–51, 448–52, 448 n. 49, 451 n. 51, 486–88
  and the Mere Addition Paradox, 363–85, 394–96, 399–400, 401–4, 415–16, 446, 459–60 n. 4
  and the Independence of Irrelevant Alternatives Principle, 364, 455, 475–76, 486–88
  and maximin, 365–67, 402–7, 416, 447–52, 451 n. 51, 456, 473–74, 483, 486, 495
  and equality, 365–69, 395–96, 401–5, 404 n. 5, 450–51, 451 n. 51
  and the Repugnant Conclusion, 366–67 n. 10, 448–52
  and utility, 402–3 n. 2, 410–16, 417 n. 21, 446, 448–52, 456, 473–74, 554–57
    and an Essentially Comparative View of Utility, 411–16, 412 n. 13, 417 n. 21, 424, 446
  and the Narrow Person-Affecting View, 416–47, 418 n. 22, 431 n. 37, 432 n. 38, 437 n. 41, 456, 473–74
    and Norcross's objections, 548–52, 552 n. 8
  and the Standard Model for Combining Ideals, 448–52, 448 n. 49, 486–88
  and the Standard Model for Utility, 448–52, 486–88
  and the Sports Analogy, 468–71
  and moral dilemmas, 512
Expected Utility Theory: characterized, 233–34; referenced, 5, 18, 478–80, 484–88, 491–93, 498–99, 518, 521
  and simplicity in normative theory, 18–19
  and the Essentially Comparative View of Moral Ideals, 230–31
  and transitivity, 230–33, 457
  and Expected Value Theory, 231, 233–34, 457
  and Valdman, 264 n. 34
  See also Expected Value Theory
Expected Value Theory: characterized, 233–37; referenced, 5–6
  and the transitivity of the "all-things considered better than" relation, 232–33, 235, 235–36 n. 8, 243–46, 253, 262–63, 363, 457
  and John Broome, 232–33, 238 n. 10, 239–40, 254, 498
  and Expected Utility Theory, 233–34, 457
  and Axioms of Transitivity, 235, 457
  and Principle of Continuity, 236
  and Completeness, 236–37
  and Principle of Like Comparability for Equivalents, 237
    and rough comparability, 237–45
  and Principle of Substitution of Equivalents, 237
  and First Principle of Equivalence, 238
  and Second Principle of Equivalence, 238
  and the State-by-State Comparison Principle, 239
    and incompleteness, 239
    and a Reflection Principle, 240
  and the Sure-Thing Principle, 239
  and holism, 245

Feldman, Fred: 154 n. 10
Ferrari, Geoffrey: 182–83 n. 13
Fifth Standard View: *See* Standard View, Fifth
fine-grained individuation of alternatives: characterized, 214–18
    and a defense of the transitivity of the moral "obligatoriness" and "all-things-considered better than" relations, 214–18, 215 n. 11, 230, 432–33, 457–65, 459–60 n. 4, 469, 472–73, 475
    and objections to, 217–18, 230–31, 459–60 n. 4, 460–65, 462 n. 6, 472–73, 475–76, 487
First Standard View: *See* Standard View, First
Foot, Philippa: 8 n. 6
    and skepticism about impersonal value, 21 n. 21, 74 n. 9, 497
    and the moral significance of numbers, 27 n. 4
Fourth Standard View: *See* Standard View, Fourth
freedom: 74, 103–5, 108, 180
    and First and Second Standard View, 61–62
    and tension between First and Second Standard Views, 61–62
    and anti-additive aggregation, 62
From Torture to Mosquito Bites: characterized, 134–39
    objections and responses
        based on the claim that life containing extreme torture is not worth living, 140–41
        based on the disintegration of the self, 140–41
        based on the distinction between differences in degrees of pain and differences in kinds of pains, 141–42, 265–77
        based on the temporal order of pains, 142–43
        based on the claim that additive aggregationist views do not apply to very mild harms, or to harms of very short duration, 143–45
        argument against View Three based on principles of decomposition and recombination, 145–52
        proportionality argument against View Three, 152–54
        based on skepticism of intuitions about large numbers, 155–61

Gauthier, David: 84 n. 15, 191 n. 20
global versus local optimization: 479
    and the Disperse Additional Burdens View, 79–80, 82–85
    and practical reasoning, 80
    and McClennen, and Gauthier, and Parfit, and Nagel, 84 n. 15
    and Elster, 84 n. 15, 188–93, 191 n. 20
    and the money pump, 188–93, 461–62
    and the Principle of Continuity, 255–56
Glover, Jonathan: 81 n. 3
Grandy, Richard: 504 n. 21
Green, Preston: 236 n. 9
Griffin, James: 26 n. 2
    and discontinuities of value, 35–37, 52–57, 123, 336–38
    and anti-additive aggregation, 35–37, 247 n. 19
    and the First and Second Standard Views, 52–57

Hájek, Alan: 453 n. 52, 511–12 n. 34
Hanser, Matthew: 21 n. 21
Hare, Caspar, and rough comparability and Expected Value Theory: 244 n. 16
Harman, Gilbert: 515 n. 38
Hausman, Dan: 274 n. 9
Hawthorne, John: 511–12 n. 34
Hedonism, and aggregation within lives: 114 n. 26
holism/organic unity: illustrated, 148–49; referenced, 147, 148 n. 6, 210 n. 10, 489, 489 n. 4
    and aggregation within lives, 112
    and examples of

holism/organic unity (*continued*)
    Wine and Food Complementarity, 148
    The Beauty of a Face, 149
    and Expected Value Theory, 245
    and the Capped Model for Ideals, 350, 355–56
Horta, Oscar
    and the Repellant Conclusion and additive aggregation, 64 n. 38
    and anti-additive aggregation, 115 n. 27, 115–16 n. 29, 124 n. 38
    and the appropriateness of meat-eating examples, 148 n. 7
    and How Only France Survives, 404 n. 4
    and the maximin principle of equality, 404 n. 5
    and Jan Narveson's view of utility, 412 n. 14, 414 nn. 16 and 18
    and intuitions about infinite utility cases, 439 n. 43
    and the importance of the Axioms of Transitivity, 465 n. 9
How More Than France Exists: 485, 486–87
    and the Essentially Comparative View of Moral Ideals, and maximin, 402–7, 448–52, 451 n. 51
    and How Only France Survives, 404 n. 4, 449 n. 50
Hume, David: 391
    and skepticism about impersonal value, 21–22
    and moral skepticism, 515, 519
Hurka, Thomas: 8 n. 6
    and McTaggart, 120 n. 33
    and holism/organic unity, 148 n. 6

ideals: *See* Capped Model for Ideals; Essentially Comparative View of Moral Ideals; Internal Aspects View of Moral Ideals; moral ideals; prudential ideals; Standard Model for Combining Ideals
impartiality
    and the "better than" relation, 10–11, 10 n. 8, 228–30
    and the Principle of Irrelevant Utilities, 44 n. 27
    and aggregation within lives, 96–8
    and Sidgwick, 98
    and the Internal Aspects View of Moral Ideals, 230, 377–78, 460–61, 551–52
    and the Standard Model for Utility, 315, 318
    and people, places, and times, 343–49, 479, 486, 487, 490–91
        and the Capped Model for Ideals, 343–49
incommensurability: characterized and illustrated, 35–36, 171–73; referenced, 35–36, 52–53, 55–56
    and contrast with incomparability, 53 n. 34, 54, 171
    and the drab life, and wildly fluctuating life, 109–11
    and transitivity, and conditions where it fails/fails to apply, 171–76, 182–83 n. 13
    See also discontinuities of value; rough comparability
inconsistency
    and the juggling analogy, 10, 520–21
    and the meaning of "better than," 10–18, 494–97
    and discontinuities of value, 56
    and whether morality could be inconsistent, 499–508
    and whether it can be reasonable to accept inconsistent views, 504–8
        and physics, 502–7
        and the Preface Paradox, 506
    and Ralph Waldo Emerson, 506–7, 506 n. 25
Independence of Irrelevant Alternatives Principle: characterized and illustrated, 201 n. 5, 389–90
    and practical reasoning, 201 n. 5
    and the Essentially Comparative View of Moral Ideals, 364–65, 455, 475–76, 486–88
        Vanilla, Chocolate, or Strawberry: On the Independence of Irrelevant Alternatives Principle, 389–91
    and Internal Aspects View of Moral Ideals, 388–91, 475
        and Arrow's Impossibility Theorem, 387–88, 455
    and transitivity of the "all-things-considered better than" relation, 475–76

infinity and value: 491–92, 491 n. 6
　and the Capped Model for Combining Ideals, 330
　and pareto-like principles, 434–40, 439 n. 43
Internal Aspects View of Moral Ideals: characterized, 228–30, 369–74; referenced, 5, 478–80, 490–95, 497, 514, 556–57
　and contrast with Essentially Comparative View of Moral Ideals, 229–30, 369–74
　See also Essentially Comparative View of Moral Ideals, illustrated and contrasted with the Internal Aspects View of Moral Ideals
Internal Aspects View of Outcome Goodness: characterized, 370, 378, 385–91
　and transitivity of the "all-things-considered better than" relation, 13, 229 n. 18, 230–31, 383–88, 395–400, 401–16, 406 n. 6, 432–34, 445–56, 464 n. 7, 466–67, 472–73, 475–76
　and the Principle of Continuity, 251–52
　and the Standard Model for Combining Ideals, 350–51, 448–52, 448 n. 49, 484–88
　and the Capped Model for Ideals, 350–51, 448–52, 485–56
　and the Mere Addition Paradox, 364–88, 391–416, 459–61
　and Independence of Irrelevant Alternatives Principle, 388–91, 475
　　and Arrow's Impossibility Theorem, 387–88, 455–56
　and the Standard Model for Utility, 448–52, 484–88
　and maximin, 401–416, 402–3 n. 2, 404 n. 5, 406 n. 6, 406–7 n. 7, 448–52, 451 n. 51, 456, 484, 485, 495–97
Intransitivity: *See* nontransitivity; transitivity
Intuitions: 8 n. 6, 19
　and rational intuitionism, 6–8
　and Sidgwick, 6–8, 7 n. 3, 8 n. 5, 154–55
　and reflective equilibrium, 6–8, 471–75, 473 n. 18
　and Rawls, 7, 7 n. 4, 471–72, 472 n. 17
　and Nagel, 18–19, 18 nn. 16–17, 19 n. 18, 499
　and explaining them away
　　and big numbers, 35, 120–23
　　and shape of a life, 113
　　McTaggart and the Single Life Repugnant Conclusion, 118–22
　　and inordinate lengths of time 154–61
　and framing effects, and the Disperse Additional Burdens View, 68
　and Unger, 138 n. 5
　and inordinate lengths of time, 154–61
　and Feldman, 154 n. 10
　and similarity-based decision-making, and Voorhoeve and Binmore, 296–310
　Anchoring and Adjustment Heuristic, and Voorhoeve, 309–12
　and neutrality intuition, and Broome, 418 n. 22
Irrelevant Utilities, Principle of
　and Kamm, 36 n. 18, 44 n. 27
　and impartiality, and consequentialism/deontology, and J. Ross's Principle, 44 n. 27
iteration, problems of: 479, 484, 487
　and the Disperse Additional Burdens View, 79–83, 444–45
　and the infinite regress objection to the claim that rightness contributes to the value of an outcome, 209–10
　and the Standard Sorites Paradox, 277–78
　and the revised Sorites Paradox, 291–92
　and the Mere Addition Paradox, and the Repugnant Conclusion, 366–67 n. 10
　and the Narrow Person-Affecting View, 444–45

J. Ross's Principle: characterized and illustrated, 35–36, 40–41, 171–73
　and anti-additive aggregation, 39–44, 41 n. 25, 42 n. 26, 125–27, 126 n. 40, 261–62
　and practical reasoning, 40
　and the Sure-Thing Principle, 40 n. 24
　and the Repugnant Conclusion, 41, 42 n. 26

J. Ross's Principle (*continued*)
   and Pascal's Wager, 41–42 n. 25
   and Lollipops for Life, 42
   and the Principle of Irrelevant Utilities, 44–45 n. 27
   and the Principle of Continuity, 261–62, 261 n. 31, 262 n. 33
   and the Narrow Person-Affecting View, 443, 445
Jones and the TV transmitter, and anti-additive aggregation/the Second Standard View, 36–37
   and the Disperse Additional Burdens View, 71–74
justice: 424–25, 429
   and Rawls, 30–31, 31 n. 10, 98–101, 108–9, 447, 456
   and maximin/No Trade-offs View, 30–32
   and Nozick, 98–108
   and the number two, on incommensurability, 172, 177
   and affirmative action, 199, 215–16
   and the Mere Addition Paradox, 364–65
   and the Weak Pareto Principle, 409–10

Kagan, Shelly: 8 n. 6, 38 n. 21, 73 n. 8, 86 n. 17, 116 n. 30, 117 n. 31, 134 n. 2, 228 n. 17, 246 n. 17, 253 n. 26, 283–84, 283 n. 13, 284 n. 14, 308 n. 25, 317–18 n. 2, 326 n. 10, 337 n. 20, 448 n. 49, 503 n. 19, 507 n. 26, 521 n. 42
   and the moral significance of numbers, 27 n. 4, 354 n. 28
   and maximin, 32 n. 11
      and the Repugnant Conclusion, 326–27 n. 11
      and the Internal Aspects View of Moral Ideals, 402–3 n. 2, 407 n. 8
   and the equivalence of the Disperse Additional Burdens View and the Consolidate Additional Benefits View, 69 n. 4
   and the Second Standard View, 78 n. 8
   and the separateness of individuals and compensation, 107 n. 22
   and rough comparability, 176 n. 7
   and money pumps, 186 n. 15
   and mathematical representation of ethical claims, 253 n. 26
   and the Internal Aspects and Essentially Comparative Views of Moral Ideals, 375 n. 19, 378–79 n. 23, 386–87 n. 32
   and How Only France Survives, 404 n. 4
   and Narveson's view of utility, 413 n. 15
Kahneman, Daniel: 302, 302 n. 23
Kamm, Frances: 8 n. 6, 541 n. 15
   and the Principle of Irrelevant Utilities, 36 n. 18, 44–45 n. 27
      and utilitarianism, and J. Ross's Principle, 44–45 n. 27
   and anti-additive aggregation, and Headaches versus Lives, 36–37, 36 n. 18
   and the Principle of Contextual Interaction, 38 n. 22, 323, 323 n. 8, 430 n. 36
   and aggregation within lives, 111 n. 24
   and the transitivity of the "permissibility" relation, 195–97, 195 nn. 1–2, 198 n. 4, 200, 222
Kant, Immanuel
   and the moral significance of numbers, 27 n. 4
   and Each-We Dilemmas, 86
   and the separateness of individuals, 100, 105
   and the instrumental/non-instrumental value of utility, 316, 317 n. 1
   and moral luck, 508
Kavka, Gregory: 423 n. 27
Knapp, Christopher, and an objection to Spectrum Arguments appealing to vagueness and indeterminacy: 534–38, 534 nn. 1–2, 535 n. 3, 537 n. 4
Kramer, Peter, on depression: 49 n. 31
Kurtz, Stuart: 503 nn. 17–18, 505 n. 23

Levelling Down Objection: characterized and illustrated, 75–76
   and prioritarianism, 25 n. 1

and equality, 25 n. 1, 75–78
and the Disperse Additional Burdens View, 75–78
Lewis, David: 499 n. 13
lexical orderings
   and maximin, 30–31, 31 n. 10, 32 n. 11, 71 n. 5, 76
   and the separateness of individuals, 107
   and the Essentially Comparative View of Ideals, 554–57
Lincoln, Abraham: 515 n. 36
Lollipops for Life: characterized, 34; referenced, 484–88
   and anti-additive aggregation, 35, 42
   and J. Ross's Principle, 42
   and the Principle of Continuity, 259–61, 263–64
   and the Capped Model for Ideals, 339

Mackie, John: 515 n. 38
Macpherson, Fiona, and rough comparability and Expected Value Theory: 244 n. 16
Makinson, D.C.: 506 n. 24
Maudlin, Tim: 503 nn. 17–18, 506 n. 24
maximin: characterized, 30–31, 314, 402–6; referenced, 25, 31 n. 10, 326 n. 10, 332 n. 18, 478, 479, 483
   and Rawls, 30–31, 31 n. 10, 261, 402 n. 1, 447, 456
   and justice/the No Trade-offs View, 30–32
   and the lexical version, 30–32, 31 n. 10, 32 n. 11, 71 n. 5, 76
   and the First Standard View, 30–32, 32 n. 12
   and Kagan, 32 n. 11
      and the Internal Aspects View of Moral Ideals, 402–3 n. 2, 407 n. 8
   and the Disperse Additional Burdens View, 70–78, 73 n. 8
   and the separateness of individuals, 103–5, 108–9
   and average utilitarianism versus total utilitarianism, 325
   and the Repugnant Conclusion, 325–30, 326 n. 10, 366–67 n. 10, 402–3 n. 2, 448–52
   and the Essentially Comparative View of Moral Ideals, 365–67, 402–7, 416–17, 445–52, 451 n. 51, 456, 473–74, 483, 486–87, 495
   and the Internal Aspects View of Moral Ideals, 395–97, 401–16, 404 n. 5, 448–52, 451 n. 51, 456, 484, 485
   and Parfit, and How Only France Exists, 402–6
   and prioritarianism, 407 n. 8
McLenden, Edward: 84 n. 15, 191 n. 20
McMahan, Jeff: 8 n. 6
   and the Narrow Person-Affecting View, 445 n. 46
McTaggart, J.M.E., and the Single-life Repugnant Conclusion: 119–24, 333
Meacham, Chris, and the Principle of Continuity and unimaginably small numbers: 256 n. 28
Mere Addition Paradox: characterized, 364–66; referenced, 484–86, 494
   and the transitivity of the "all-things-considered better than" relation, 34 n. 15, 364–84, 394–416, 427–29, 446, 457–61
   and Parfit, 363–84, 391–403, 427–29, 457–61
   and the Essentially Comparative View of Moral Ideals, 364–85, 394–96, 399–404, 415–16, 446, 459–60 n. 4
   and the Internal Aspects View of Moral Ideals, 364–88, 391–416, 459–61
   and justice, 365, 374–75
   and equality, 365–69, 372–84, 391–92, 395–404
   and the Repugnant Conclusion, 366–67 n. 10, 395 n. 40, 402–3 n. 2
   and perfectionism/perfection, 367 n. 11, 394–96
Mill, John Stuart: 328 n. 13
money pump: 163, 183–88, 244 n. 16, 480–81, 508
   and the nontransitivity of the "not worse than" relation, 183–85
      and a "Not Worse Than" Money Pump, 178–80, 183–86
   and global versus local optimization, 188–93

money pump (*continued*)
    and the nontransitivity of the moral "obligatoriness" relation
        and an "Obligatoriness" Money Pump, 201–3
    and fine-grained individuation of alternatives, 461–62, 475
Moore, G.E., and organic unity: 148 n. 6
moral dilemmas
    and Nagel, 508–9
    and Sophie's Choice, 509 n. 30, 510, 510 n. 31
    and agent-relativity, 510–14
    and consequentialism/deontology, 510–14
    and the transitivity of the "all-things-considered better than" relation, 511–14
    and maximizing doctrines, 511–12 n. 34
moral ideals: 3–5, 20, 38, 60, 65, 264 n. 34, 477–79, 488, 495–96, 521
    and the separateness of individuals, 103–8
    and trade-offs between utility and other moral ideals, 313–62
    and illustrative lists of moral ideals
        for impersonal value, 314
        for well-being, 333–34
        for virtue, 334
    and the inheritability of nontransitivity, 481–83
    See also Capped Model for Ideals; Essentially Comparative View of Moral Ideals; Impartial Internal Aspect View of Moral Ideals; Standard Model for Combining Ideals
moral "obligatoriness" relation, transitivity of: 5, 163, 194–203, 480
    and an "obligatoriness" money pump, 201–3
    and the inheritability of nontransitivity, 203–24
    and fine-grained individuation of alternatives, 215–18, 215 n. 11, 230
Morgenbesser, Sidney: 388 n. 35
Morgenstern, Oskar: 239 n. 13

Nagel, Thomas: 22, 22 n. 22, 498, 499, 520
    and intuitions, and pluralism, and simplicity in normative theory, 8 n. 6, 18–19, 18 nn. 16–17, 19 n. 18, 498–499
    and global versus local optimization, 84 n. 15, 191 n. 20
    and the transitivity of the "all-things-considered better than" relation, 494
    and moral dilemmas, 508–9, 509 n. 30, 510 n. 32
Narrow Person-Affecting View: characterized, 416–18; referenced, 416–45, 418 n. 22, 431 n. 37, 432 n. 38, 437 n. 41, 456, 473–74
    examples of
        Three Population Policies, 418–19
        Factory Farms and the Narrow Person-Affecting View, 419
        Three Cases Illustrating the Intuitive Plausibility of the Narrow Person-Affecting View, 420–22
        Hell-to-Heaven versus Heaven-to-Hell: Infinite Utility Cases *1* and *2*, 434–35
        The Wide Person-Affecting View is Not Enough: Infinite Utility Cases *3* and *4*, 437–39
        Progressive Disease—First, Second, and Third Versions, 440–42
    and Narveson, 411–47
    and Roberts, 417 n. 21, 420 n. 25
    and objections and responses, 422–34
        Conservation and Depletion, 424
        Problem of Creation, 424
        Good, Evil, and Desert, 424–25
        The Neutrality Intuition: Broome's Counterexample to the Narrow Person-Affecting View, 427–28
        Tom, Dick, and Harry: Parfit's Counterexample to the Narrow Person-Affecting View, 428–29
    and Wide Person-Affecting View, 419 n. 23, 434–45
    and Norcross's Argument for Restricting the Scope of, Does One Person's Existence Undermine the Narrow Person-Affecting View?: 545–47, 546 n. 6
        Why One Person's Existence Does Not Undermine the Narrow Person-Affecting View, 547–51

Narveson, Jan
    and an Essentially Comparative View of Utility, 411–16, 412–13
        nn. 13–15, 424
    and the Narrow Person-Affecting View, 416–47
Nietzsche, Friedrich: 394–95 n. 39, 515, 515 n. 35
nontransitivity: characterized, 17; referenced, 5, 17–18, 178–82
    examples of
        Novelist versus Two Poets, 177–78, 223–25
        Career Choices: Lawyer versus Academic, 178–79
        Affirmative Action Case, 197
        Hiring Conflicts involving Parents and Strangers, 198
    and nontransitivity versus intransitivity, 16–17, 59–60, 66
    and transitive versus nontransitive relations, 163–71
    and the underlying conditions that make a relation nontransitive, 171–77
    and the inheritability of nontransitivity, 203–14
        and affirmative action and the inheritability of nontransitivity, 212–14
    See also transitivity, and the moral "obligatoriness" relation, and the "permissibility" relation, and the "not worse than" relation,
No Trade-offs View: characterized, 30
    and maximin, 30–32
    and Second No Trade-off View, 522
    and contrasts with the Second Standard View, 523
Norcross, Alastair, and an argument for restricting the scope of the Narrow Person-Affecting View: 459 n. 3, 545–52, 545 nn. 1, 3, 4, 546 n. 6
"not worse than" relation: *See* Broome, John; money pump; nontransitivity; rough comparability; transitivity
Nozick, Robert: 8 n. 6
    and skepticism about impersonal value, 20–21, 74 n. 9, 99, 497
    and the moral significance of numbers, 27 n. 4
    and the separateness of individuals/justice, 99–109, 99 n. 9, 100 n. 12
    and side-constraints, 100
    and conception of rational self-interest, 100 n. 13
    and the right and the good, 105–6 n. 21
    and holism/organic unity, 148 n. 6, 210 n. 10
        and the value of fitting attitudes, 210 n. 10
numbers, the moral significance of: 26–32
    and Foot, Kagan, Kant, Nozick, Thomson, 27 n. 4
    and Anscombe, Taurek, Williams, 27 n. 4, 354 n. 8
    and Parfit, 28 n. 5
    and for equality, 350–60

objective perspective: 509 n. 30
Ord, Toby: 170 n. 5
    and the "larger than" relation, 164 n. 1
organic unity: *See* holism/organic unity

Pareto Principle
    and Broome's Principle of Personal Good, 102–3
    and compensation, 102–3
    and the inheritability of nontransitivity, 211–15
    and prospects, 242–43
    and Strong and Weak versions of, 408–11
    and Person-Affecting Views, 416–21, 436–39, 456
    and lexical orderings, 556–57
Pareto-Like Principles: 478–81, 483–86, 495–96
    and infinite value, 436–39

Parfit, Derek: 8 n. 6, 11 n. 10, 25 n. 1, 87–94, 100 n. 13, 118, 123, 198 n. 4, 203 n. 6, 205 n. 7, 330 n. 15, 331–32 n. 16, 370 n. 15, 412 n. 13, 423 nn. 27–28, 424 n. 30, 440 n. 45, 473 n. 19, 481 n. 2, 484–86, 491–2 n. 6, 494, 508 n. 27, 519, 519 n. 40, 521 n. 43
   and moral skepticism, 3 n. 2, 8 n. 5, 519 n. 40
   and Sidgwick, 8 n. 5
   and the transitivity of the "all-things-considered better than" relation, 11 n. 9, 16 nn. 13–14, 182–83 n. 13, 186–87, 203–4, 224–25, 394–400, 427–34
   and the moral significance of numbers, 28 n. 5
   and the Repugnant Conclusion, 34–35, 34 n. 15, 37, 41, 42 n. 26, 64 n. 38, 327–28, 366–67 n. 10
   and his notion of pain intensity, 36 n. 4
   and additive aggregation, 80–85
   and global versus local optimization, 84 n. 15, 191 n. 20
   and Each-We Dilemmas, 85–88, 92–94 n. 19
   and the conception of rational self-interest, 100 n. 13
   and the separateness of individuals, 101–3
   and rough comparability, 176 n. 7, 177–83, 178–79 n. 11, 181 n. 12, 182–83 n. 13, 223 n. 14
   and nontransitivity of the "not worse than" relation, 177–83, 223–28, 223 n. 14
   and the Principle of Continuity, 256–57
   and average versus total utility, and Hells One, Two, and Three, 319–20, 321–22 n. 6
   and perfectionism, 325
   and asymmetries between pleasure and pain, 338–41
   and the Capped Model for Ideals, 338–41, 338, n. 22
   and the Mere Addition Paradox, 363–84, 365 n. 3, 367 n. 11, 391–400, 392 n. 37, 401–3, 403 n. 3, 427–29, 457–61
   and his brilliant mistake, 383 nn. 26–27
   and maximin, and How Only France Exists, 402–6, 404 n. 4, 406–7 n. 6, 407 n. 8
   and the Narrow Person-Affecting View, 428–33, 428 n. 35, 431 n. 37, 432 n. 38, 545 n. 4, 547–48 vesus Wide Person-Affecting View, 437 n. 41
parity: *See* rough comparability
particularism: 489 n. 4
perfectionism/perfection: characterized, 314; referenced, 24–25, 27, 27 n. 3, 326–27 n. 11, 498
   and contrast with the Disperse Additional Burdens View, 72–8
   and the separateness of individuals, 103–8
   and average and total perfection, and Michelangelo, Rembrandt, and Da Vinci, and Parfit, 320–21, 321 n. 6
   and the Repugnant Conclusion, 327–30
   and Evan Williams, 394 n. 39
   and the Mere Addition Paradox, 394–97
permissibility relation: characterized, 195
   and nontransitivity of, 195 n. 2, 195–97
   and transitivity of the "all-things-considered better than" relation, 194–95, 222–23, 230–31
   and transitivity of the moral "obligatoriness" relation, 194–8, 201–2, 222, 230
   and Kamm, 194–7, 200, 222
Personal Good, Principle of: *See* Pareto-like Principles
Plato: 8 n. 5, 100 n. 13
   and holism, 148 n. 6, 149 n. 8
   and rationality, 190 n. 19
pluralism, ethical: 482–83, 506
   and Nagel, 18–19, 18 nn. 16–17, 19 n. 18, 499
   and simplicity in normative theory, 322–23
   and relevance to moral ideals
     of average and total utility, 324
     of maximin, 406–7 n. 7
     of the Narrow Person-Affecting View, 425, 443–44
     of equality, 426
   and the transitivity of the "all-things-considered better than" relation, 482–83

Podolsky, N.: 501-2, 501-2 n. 16
practical reasoning: *See* Expected Utility Theory; Expected Value Theory; global versus local optimization; Independence of Irrelevant Alternatives Principle; J. Ross's Principle; transitivity of the "all-things-considered better than" relation
Preface Paradox: 506, 506 n. 24
preferability: 11-12, 11 n. 10
Principle of Contextual Interaction: *See* Contextual Interaction, Principle of
Principle of Continuity: *See* Continuity, Principle of
Principle of Irrelevant Utilities: *See* Irrelevant Utilities, Principle of
Principle of Like Comparability for Equivalents: characterized, 237, 378
  and rough comparability, 243-44
  and the Essentially Comparative and Internal Aspects Views of Moral Ideals, 378-88, 401, 406-11
Principle of Substitution of Equivalents: characterized, 237
  and the Principle of Continuity, 246, 250-53, 260-63
  and the Principle of Like Comparability of Equivalents, 378 n. 22
Prioritarianism
  and contrast with Egalitarianism, and the Levelling Down Objection, 25 n. 1
  and the Disperse Additional Burdens View, 70-6
  and the diminishing marginal value of utility, 331-32 n. 16
  and equality, 331-32 n. 16
  and Parfit, 331-32 n. 16, 407 n. 8, 481 n. 2
  and maximin, 407 n. 8
Prisoner's Dilemma: 85-90, 85 n. 16
  and rational decision-making, 193
  See also Each-We Dilemmas
prudential ideals
  and contrast with moral ideals, 8 n. 5, 19-20
  and the Essentially Comparative and Internal Aspects Views of Moral Ideals, 369 n. 13
  See also aggregation within lives

quantity of benefits or burdens as a function of quality, duration, and number: 526-28
  and blurriness of the relationships between duration and number, and duration and quality, 527-30
  and the potential equivalence of the Second and Fourth Standard Views, and the First and Third Standard Views, 529-30
Quine, W.V.O.: 500-1, 504
Quinn, Warren, and The Puzzle of the Self-Torturer: 296

Rabinowicz, Wlodek: 376 n. 21
Rachels, Stuart, and Spectrum Arguments: 135, 279 n. 11, 296-97, 302, 538-40, 539 nn. 9-10, 541 n. 15
rationality/rational decision-making: *See* aggregation within lives; Each-We Dilemmas; Expected Value Theory; global versus local optimization; money pump; Prisoner's Dilemma
Rawls, John: 8 n. 6, 98-99 nn. 6-9, 481, 498, 498 n. 10, 519
  and skepticism about impersonal value, 3, 21, 519
  and intuitions/reflective equilibrium, 7, 471-72, 472 n. 17
  and justice, 30-31, 31 n. 10, 98-101, 108-9, 447, 456
  and maximin, 30-31, 31 n. 10, 261, 402 n. 1, 447, 456
  and utilitarianism, 98, 109
  and the separateness of individuals, 98-101, 100 n. 12, 108-9
  and conception of rational self-interest, 100 n. 13
Raz, Joseph, and conditional ideals: 8 n. 6, 38 n. 22, 430 n. 36
Reflection, Principle of, and the State-by-State Comparison Principle: 240-41
reflective equilibrium, and Rawls: 7, 471-72, 472 n. 17
Repugnant Conclusion: characterized, 34; referenced, 118-19, 124
  and the Second Standard View, 34-35
  and Parfit, 34-35, 37, 41, 42 n. 26, 64 n. 38, 327-28

Repugnant Conclusion (*continued*)
  and anti-additive aggregation, 34–35, 37, 41–42, 42 n. 26, 324–28
  and the transitivity of the "all-things-considered better than" relation, 34 n. 15
  and total utilitarianism, 34–35, 260, 328–29
  and J. Ross's Principle, 41–42, 42 n. 25
  and the Repellant Conclusion, 64 n. 38
  and the Principle of Continuity, 260, 262–63
  and the Standard Model for Utility, 324–28, 327 n. 12, 330 n. 15, 448–52
  and utility, 324–28, 337
  and the Standard Model for Combining Ideals, 324–28, 361–62 n. 33, 448–52
  and maximin, 325–30, 448–52, 401–2 n. 2
  and the Capped Model for Ideals, 328–31, 336–37, 351–52, 360–62, 448–52
  and the Mere Addition Paradox, 366–67, 395 n. 40, 402–3 n. 2
  See also Single Life Repugnant Conclusion
Roberts, Melinda, and the Narrow Person-Affecting View: 417 n. 21, 420 n. 25
Rosen, N.: 501–2, 501–2 n. 16
Ross, Jacob: 39 n. 23, 111 n. 25, 404 n. 4, 407 n. 7, 552 n. 8
  and moral uncertainty, 39–44, 44–45 n. 27, 125–27, 126 n. 40, 261–62
  and rough comparability and Expected Value Theory, 244 n. 16
  and the Essentially Comparative and Internal Aspects Views of Moral Ideals, 371 n. 16, 375 n. 19, 451 n. 51
  and the fine-grained solution for preserving transitivity in the Mere Addition Paradox, 459–60 n. 4
  See also J. Ross's Principle
Ross, W.D.: 374
rough comparability of alternatives: characterized and illustrated, 176–81; referenced, 480
  and the drab life and the wildly fluctuating life, 110–11
  and nontransitivity of the "not worse than" relation, 177–88, 183–84 n. 13, 223–27
  and Expected Utility Theory/Expected Value Theory, 237–45, 244 n. 16
  and the Principle of Like Comparability of Equivalents, 243–44
Rubenstein, Ariel: 296–97
Russell, Bertrand, and Russell's Paradox: 503, 503 n. 20

Samuelson, Paul: 239, 239 n. 13
satisficing: 518
  and Slote, 101 n. 14, 190 n. 18, 248 n. 22
  and global versus local optimization, 190–91
  and the Principle of Continuity, 248
Scanlon, Thomas: 8 n. 6, 28 n. 6
  and the scope of morality, 19 n. 19
  and anti-additive aggregation
    and Jones and the TV Transmitter, 36–37, 37 n. 20
    and the Disperse Additional Burdens View, 71–74
  and the Buck-Passing Account of Goodness, 205 n. 7
  and the transitivity of the "all-things-considered better than" relation, 494
Second Standard View: *See* Standard View, Second
self-interest: *See* aggregation within lives
Sen, Amartya: 8 n. 6, 489 n. 4, 499 n. 13
  and Sidgwick's theory of rationality, 190 n. 19
  and equality, 352–53 n. 25
separateness of individuals
  and utilitarianism, 96–108
  and justice, 98–107
  and Nozick, 99–109
  and Kantian roots of, 100, 105
  and anti-additive aggregation, 100–1
  and the Second Standard View, 100–1

and Parfit, 100–1, 103
and the Disperse Additional Burdens View, 100–1, 113–14
and compensation, 101–7
   and the Principle of Personal Good/Pareto Principle, 102–3
and other moral ideals, maximin, equality, and perfectionism, 103–9
and Kagan, 107 n. 22
Sidgwick, Henry: 96–101, 108–9, 328 n. 13
   and intuitions, 7–8, 154–55
   and the dualism of practical reason, 8 n. 5
   and aggregation within lives, 96–98, 129, 155–56
   and impartiality, 98
   and rationality, 190 n. 19
simplicity in normative theory
   and Expected Utility Theory, 18–19
   and utilitarianism, 18–19
   and Nagel, 18–19, 18 nn. 16–17, 19 n. 18, 498–99
   and equality, 63 n. 37
   and pluralism, 322–24
Single Life Repugnant Conclusion: 127, 479, 484–88
   and utilitarianism, 111 n. 25, 125
   and anti-additive aggregation, 118, 121
   and McTaggart, 119–22, 333–34
   and additive aggregation, 120–22
   and discontinuities of value, 121–23
   and the bias toward the near, 122
   and the Fourth Standard View, 123
   and the Capped Model for Ideals, 333–34, 337
skepticism: 3–4, 8 n. 5, 21–22, 284–85, 295
   and about impersonal value
      and Rawls, 3, 3 n. 1, 21, 498
      and Nozick, 20–22, 74 n. 9, 99, 497
      and Foot, 21 n. 21, 74, 497
      and Hume, 21–22
      and Thomson, 74
      and deontology/virtue ethics, 497–98, 513–14, 519
   and Parfit, 3 n. 2, 519
   and atheism, 515
   and Hume, 515, 519
   and naturalism, 515–16
   and the nontransitivity of the "all-things-considered better than" relation, 516–20
Slote, Michael, and satisficing: 101 n. 14, 190 n. 18, 248 n. 22
Sophie's Choice
   and anti-additive aggregation, 311–12
   and moral dilemmas, 509 n. 30, 510, 510 n. 31
Sorites Paradox, revised version, and Wasserman: 284–96, 531–33
   See also Spectrum Arguments, objections and replies
Sorites Paradox, standard version: 265, 277–85, 295–96, 534
   and vagueness, 266 n. 2, 268 n. 5, 278–83, 534
   and Crucial Premise of the Standard Hairiness/Baldness Sorites Paradox, 277–84, 295, 531–33
   See also Spectrum Arguments, objections and replies
Spectrum Arguments: illustrated, 45–52; referenced, 4–5, 66, 135–38, 479–80, 512–13
   and transitivity of the "all things considered better than" relation, 4–5, 45–52, 59–66, 129, 132–143, 158, 161, 221–25, 226 n. 16, 265–67, 272–309, 363–64, 383–84, 465–67, 472–74, 534–44
   examples of
      Depression Spectrum, 47–50
      Missing Limbs Spectrum, 50–51

Spectrum Arguments (*continued*)
    Torture to Limp Spectrum, 157–58
    Electrical Service Disruption Spectrum, 159
    Traffic Jam Spectrum, 159
    Missed Garbage Pick-ups Spectrum, 159–60
    illnesses, 524
  and discontinuities of value, 52–8
    and vagueness, 534–38
  and objections and replies
    based on the distinction between differences of degree and differences of kind, 266–77
    based on an analogy with the Sorites Paradox, 277–84
    and Sorites Paradox, revised version, 284–96, 531–33
    based on heuristics and similarity-based reasoning, 296–310
    based on anchoring bias and duration neglect, 309–401
    Knapp's claims about pain and vagueness, 534–38
    based on Zeno's Paradox, 538–40, 540 n. 11
  See also From Torture to Mosquito Bites, objections and responses
Sports Analogy: 487, 489–90, 517, 543–44
  and the Essentially Comparative View of Moral Ideals, 468–71
Standard Model for Combining Ideals: characterized, 315; referenced, 5, 448–49, 448 n. 49, 451, 478, 485–86, 488–89
  and additive aggregationist nature of, 316
  and scope of, 316, 361–62
  and equality, 324–28
  and the Repugnant Conclusion, 324–28, 327 n. 12
  and infinity and value, 330, 448–52
  and the Single Life Repugnant Conclusion, 333–34
  and the transitivity of the "all-things-considered better than" relation, 337–38, 361–62
  and the Internal Aspects View of Moral Ideals, 350–51, 448–52, 484–85
  and the relevance of numbers to the value of equality, 352–56, 354 n. 28
  and the Standard Model for Utility, 484–85
  and the Essentially Comparative View of Moral ideals, 486–88
  and contrasted with the Capped Model for Ideals: *See* Capped Model for Ideals, contrasted with Standard Model for Combining Deals
  See also aggregation, additive; aggregation, anti-additive; utilitarianism; utility
Standard Model for Utility: characterized, 315; referenced, 448, 451
  and additive aggregation, 316
  and the scope of, 316–17, 338–39
  and the instrumental/non-instrumental value of utility, 317–19
  and total versus average utility, 319–35
  and the Repugnant Conclusion, 324–28, 327 n. 12
  and the Single Life Repugnant Conclusion, 333–34
  and contrasted with the Capped Model for Ideals
    with respect to the non-instrumental value of utility, 343
    with respect to the marginal value of utility, 343–44
    with respect to impartiality over people, places, and times, 343–49
    with respect to the value of total utility, 349–50
    with respect to additive aggregation, 349–51
  and the relevance of numbers to equality, 356–57 n. 32
  and the Internal Aspects View of Moral Ideals, 448–52, 483–88
  and the Standard Model for Combining Ideals, 483–88
Standard View, Fifth: characterized and illustrated, 522–23; referenced, 522–25
  and contrasts with the Second No Trade-offs View, 522
Standard View, First: characterized and illustrated, 30–31; referenced, 129–30
  and maximin, 30–32, 32 n. 12
    and the Second Standard View, and tension between, 38, 45–52, 58–60, 64–66
  and additive aggregation, 38, 66, 130–31, 221–22, 474

    and discontinuities of value, 52–58
    and freedom, 61
        tension with other widely held views, 62
    and equality, 62
        tension with other widely held views, 63–64
        and the Repellent Conclusion, 64 n. 38
    and the Third Standard View, 123
    and tensions with other widely held views, 130–32, 221–22, 474
    and intuitions, 310
    and the Fifth Standard View, 522
Standard View, Fourth: characterized and illustrated, 118–19, 123–27
    and the Second Standard View, 123–24, 127
    and anti-additive aggregation, 124
    and the Single Life Repugnant Conclusion, 124
    and tension with other widely held views, 133–37, 221–22, 474
    and discontinuities of value, 144–45
    and the Principle of Continuity, 259, 263
Standard View, Second: characterized and illustrated, 32–33
    and the Unlimited Trade-offs View, 33–34, 33–34 n. 14, 37–38
    and Lollipops for Life, 34–35
    and the Repugnant Conclusion, 34–35
    and total utilitarianism, 34–35
    and anti-additive aggregation, 34–38, 62–65, 73 n. 8
    and Jones and the TV Transmitter, 36–37
    and the First Standard View, and tension with other widely held views, 38, 45–52, 58–60, 64–66
    and discontinuities of value, 52–58
    and freedom, 61–62
        tension with the First Standard View for Freedom, 62
    and equality, 63
        tension with the First Standard View for Equality, 63–64
    and the Repellent Conclusion, 64 n. 38
    and the Disperse Additional Burdens View, 67–69, 69 n. 8, 73, 95, 442–44
    and the separateness of individuals, 100–1
    and the status quo, 116–18
    and the Fourth Standard View, 123, 128
    and tension with other widely held views, 129–32, 221–22, 474
    and the Principle of Continuity, 259, 263
    and the Sixth Standard View, 522–23
    and contrasts with the Unlimited Trade-offs View, 523
    See also Standard View, First Standard View, Sixth: characterized and illustrated, 523–24; referenced, 523–25, 523–24 n. 1
    and contrasts with the Second Unlimited Trade-offs View, 523
Standard View, Third: characterized and illustrated, 123, 129–32
    and the First Standard View, 123
    and discontinuities of value, 123–24, 144–45
    and tension with other widely accepted views, 132–37, 221–22, 474
Stanley, Jason: 166 n. 2
Stratton-Lake, Philip: 205 n. 7
Styron, William: 311–12 n. 30, 510
subjective perspective: 509 n. 30
Sure-Thing Principle
    and J. Ross's Principle, 40 n. 24
    and Broome, 239
    and Expected Value Theory, 239
    and additive aggregation, 239–40
    See also Expected Value Theory; rough comparability

Taurek, John, and the moral significance of numbers: 27 n. 4, 354 n. 28
Third Standard View: *See* Standard View, Third
Thomson, Judith Jarvis: 8 n. 6
    and the moral significance of numbers, 27 n. 4
    and skepticism about impersonal goodness, 74 n. 9
transitivity: characterized, 9
    and the moral "obligatoriness" relation, 5, 17, 194–95, 197–201, 222
    and the "permissibility" relation, 5, 17, 194–95, 222
    and relations in general
        fails versus fails to apply, 16–17, 59–60, 66
        transitive and nontransitive relations, 163–71
        conditions where it applies or fails to apply, 171–77
    and the "not worse than" relation
        and Novelist versus Two Poets, 177, 223–25
        and rough comparability of alternatives, 177–88, 182–83 n. 13, 223, 227
        and Career Choices: Lawyer versus Academic, 178–79
        and A "Not Worse Than" Money Pump, 183–86
        and rational decision-making, 183–93
    and as a practical constraint, 508, 508 n. 27
    See also transitivity of the "all-things-considered better than" relation
transitivity of the "all-things-considered better than" relation: characterized, 9; referenced, 3–4, 9–18
    and Spectrum Arguments, 4–5, 45–52, 59–60, 129, 132–44, 158, 161, 221–25, 226 n. 16, 265–67,
        272–310, 363–64, 383–84, 465–67, 472–75, 534–44
    and "better than" relation, meaning of, 10–18, 494–97
    and Parfit, 11 n. 9, 16 nn. 13–14, 182–83 n. 13, 186–87, 203, 223–24, 394–96, 399–400, 427–34
    and Broome, 11 n. 9, 16 n. 14, 232–34, 233–35 nn. 1–7, 494
    and the Essentially Comparative View of Moral Ideals, 13, 228–31, 364–65, 369, 379–85, 399–400,
        405–6, 406 n. 6, 411, 415–16, 428–29, 432–34, 433 n. 39, 445–56, 451 n. 51, 459–60 n. 4, 465–76,
        494–97, 542–43, 548–56, 552 n. 8
    and the Internal Aspects View of Moral Ideals, 13, 228–31, 383–88, 395–416, 406 n. 6, 432–34, 446–56,
        465 n. 9, 466–67, 472–73, 475–76, 548–52, 552 n. 8, 555–56
    and the Repugnant Conclusion, 34 n. 15
    and the Mere Addition Paradox, 34 n. 15, 364–84, 394–416, 427–28,
        445–46, 457–61
    and tension with the First and Second Standard Views, 45–52, 58–66
    and the Disperse Additional Burdens View, 79–85
    the inheritability of nontransitivity, 203–23, 479, 481–83
    and the fine-grained individuation of alternatives, 214–17, 230, 432, 457–65, 459–60 n. 4, 462 n. 6,
        464 n. 7, 469, 472–73, 475–76, 479, 487
    and Expected Utility Theory, 231–33, 457
    and Expected Value Theory, 232–33, 235, 235–36 n. 8, 243–46, 253, 262–63, 363, 457
    and the Capped Model for Ideals, 337–39, 361–62, 448–52
    and Independence of Irrelevant Alternatives Principle, 475–76
    and moral dilemmas, 512–14
    and moral skepticism, 516–20
Tversky, Amos: 296–97, 297 nn. 20 and 22, 454, 454 n. 53

Unger, Peter: 155 n. 12
    and charitable giving, and intuitions, 137–38 n. 5
Unlimited Trade-offs View: characterized, 33
    and the Second Standard View, 33–34, 33 n. 14, 37–38
    and additive aggregation, 38
    and the Second Unlimited Trade-offs View, 523
utilitarianism: 491–92 n. 6, 498
    and total utilitarianism, 18, 324–25, 328–29, 498, 499 n. 13
        and simplicity in normative theory, 18–19

and additive aggregation, 25, 34–35, 37–38, 70
and the Repugnant Conclusion, 34–35, 259–60, 328–29
and the separateness of individuals, 96–98
and the Single Life Repugnant Conclusion, 111 n. 25, 124
and the shape of a life, 125–26
and average utilitarianism, 316, 324–25
and aggregation, 25
and Hells One, Two, and Three, 319–20
and average versus total utilitarianism, 319–25
and Hells One, Two, and Three, 319–20
and maximin, 324–25
and the Principle of Contextual Interaction, 324–25
and multi-level utilitarianism, and global versus local optimization, 193
utility: 313–17, 361–62, 365–66, 374, 388–89, 392, 396–98, 409–10, 429, 435–37, 446, 478–79, 482–94, 511–12 n. 34
and objective versus subjective value of, 317–19
and non-instrumental value of, 317–19, 342–43
and Kant, 316, 317 n. 1
and desert, 318–19
and the Repugnant Conclusion, 324–28, 337
and the Single Life Repugnant Conclusion, 333–34, 337
and the Essentially Comparative View of Moral Ideals, 402–3 n. 2, 411–19, 415–16 n. 20, 446, 448–52, 456, 473–74, 554–57
and an Essentially Comparative View of Utility, 411–16, 413 n. 15, 424, 446
See also aggregation within lives; Capped Model for Ideals; Standard Model for Utility

Vagueness, and the Standard Sorites Paradox: 279–83
See also Spectrum Arguments, objections and replies, and Knapp
Valdman, Mikhail: 67 n. 1, 72 n. 7, 122 n. 34
and the Levelling Down Objection, 78 n. 12
and the shape of a life, 113–14 n. 26
and the regress objection to the claim that rightness can be a good-making feature of outcomes, 206–7, 207 n. 9
and Expected Utility Theory, 264 n. 34
and How Only France Survives, 404 n. 4
and preserving the practical significance of the fine-grained solution to preserving transitivity, 462 n. 6
Vallentyne, Peter, and counterexample to the Principle of Continuit: 248–49, 248 n. 23
van Neumann, John: 239 n. 13
Velleman, David, and aggregation within lives: 111 n. 24
View One: characterized, 135
and the Third Standard View, and tension with other widely-held views, 136–37, 221–22, 474
and Spectrum Arguments, 266–67, 271–77, 273 n. 8, 286
and Wasserman's Premise One, 286
and Knapp's claims about pain and vagueness, 535–38
View Three: characterized, 135; referenced, 535–37
and Spectrum Arguments, 135–55, 161, 271–77, 286
and the Fourth Standard View, 136–37, 144–45
and tension with other widely held views, 136–39, 221–22, 474
and the Principle of Continuity, 259–63
and Knapp's claims about pain and vagueness, 535–37
See also From Torture to Mosquito Bites, objections and replies, View Three
View Two: characterized, 135
and inconsistency with other widely held views, 135–38
and the Fourth Standard View, 136–37
and Wasserman's Premise Three, 287

virtue/virtue ethics
    and the Capped Model for Ideals, 334–35
    and the unity of virtues, 334–39
    and skepticism about impersonal value, 497–98, 513–14, 519
Vong, Gerard: 440 n. 45
Vonnegut, Kurt, and *Harrison Bergeron* and equality: 331–32, 332 nn. 17–18
Voorhoeve, Alex: 296–312, 297 n. 20, 440 n. 45, 466 nn. 11–12, 473 n. 18, 538–40, 538 nn. 5 and 7, 539 nn. 9–10, 540 n. 11

Wasserman, Ryan, and the Revised Sorites Paradox: 284–96, 531–33
    See also Sorites Paradox; Spectrum Arguments, objections based on an analogy with the Sorites Paradox
Wide Person-Affecting View: characterized and illustrated, 434–37, 437 n. 41; referenced, 419 n. 23, 437–45, 437 n. 41
    and the Narrow Person-Affecting View, 419 n. 23, 434–35
Williams, Bernard: 8 n. 6, 508, 510 n. 32
    and the moral significance of numbers, 27 n. 4, 354 n. 28
Williams, Evan
    and rough comparability and Expected Value Theory, 244 n. 16
    and the Essentially Comparative View of Moral Ideals, 373 n. 17, 382 n. 25
    and perfectionism/perfection, 394–95 n. 39
Williamson, Timothy: 268 n. 5
Wittgenstein, Ludwig, and "meaning is use": 12

Zeno's Paradox: *See* Spectrum Arguments, objections and replies, based on Zeno's Paradox

LIST OF DIAGRAMS

3.2.A	75
3.2.B	77
4.2.A	101
4.3.A	124
6.3.A	178
9.2.2.A	279
10.4.A	319
10.5.A	325
10.10.A	352
10.10.B	352
11.1.A	365
11.2.A	374
11.2.B	379
11.5.A	390
11.6.A	396
12.1.A	403
12.1.B	406
12.1.C	409
12.1.D	415
12.2.A	420
12.3.A	428
12.4.A	434
12.4.B	438
12.6.A	449
13.1.A	458
E.1	546
E.2	548
E.3	549
E.4	551

LIST OF CASES AND EXAMPLES

The Juggler, 10
Lollipops for Life, 34
Repugnant Conclusion, 34
Fine Art versus Kitsch, 36
Jones and the TV Transmitter, 36–37
Jones and the TV Transmitter Variation, 71–72
Headaches versus Lives, 36
Gnats versus Cannibals, *Case I*, 39
Gnats versus Cannibals, *Case II*, 39
Depression Spectrum, 47
Missing Limbs Spectrum, 50–51
Grading Example: Few *A*'s versus Many *C*'s, 56
Pain Trade-offs between the Many and the Few, 70
Levelling Down, 75
Longevity Trade-offs between the Many and the Few, 79–80
Bad Old Days, 80–81
Harmless Torturers, 81
Quality versus Duration Trade-offs within a Life, 109
Drab Life, 109–10
Wildly Fluctuating Life, 110
Ascending Quality of Life, 125–26
Descending Quality of Life, 125–26
Single Life Repugnant Conclusion, 119
Massage Choices, 130–31
Salary Choices, 131
Life Quality versus Longevity, 131
Warts or Acne for Longer?, 131–32
A Broken Arm or a Broken Leg for Longer?, 132
Psychosis or Depression for Longer?, 132
From Torture to Mosquito Bites, 135–39
Wine and Food Complementarity, 148
The Beauty of a Face, 149
Harmful Goods, Harmless Bads, 150
The Straw that Broke the Camel's Back, 150
Snow Dustings versus Blizzards, 150–51
Hell and Earth Case Against a Proportionality Argument, 153–54
Height Spectrum, Tall to Short in Relatively Few Steps, 155
Shortened Pain Spectrum, 155–56
Color Spectrum, End to End in Relatively Few Steps, 156
Torture to Limp Spectrum (*Case I*), 157–58
Electrical Service Disruption Spectrum (*Case II*), 159
Traffic Jam Spectrum (*Case III*), 159
Missed Garbage Pick-ups Spectrum (*Case IV*), 159–60
Larger Than: Heavier Than or Taller Than, 164
Justice and the Number Two: On Incommensurability, 172
Tennis Players and Husbands, 173–74

Novelist versus Two Poets, 177
Career Choices: Lawyer versus Academic, 178–79
A "Not Worse Than" Money Pump, 183–86
A Standard Money Pump, 185–86
Jon Elster's "Two Hills" Case, 189
Ulysses and the Sirens, 189
The Smoker, 190
How Larry Watches His Weight, 190
Intransitivity of Permissibility, 195
Affirmative Action Case, 197
Hiring Conflicts involving Parents and Strangers, 198
An "Obligatoriness" Money Pump, 201–3
My Drowning Mother *I*, 205
My Drowning Mother *II*, 207
Boxes and Bows, 208–9
Affirmative Action and the Inheritability of Nontransitivity, 212–14
Risking Everything for a Dollar, 248–49
Small Risks to Big Risks: Objection to the Principle of Continuity, 250–52
Slightly Risky Life Choices, 254
Super Extreme Case, 261–62
Kinds of Hairiness, 268–69
Intransitivity of "Neighborhood," 276
Hairiness/Baldness Sorites Paradox, Standard Version, 277–78
Spectrum Arguments versus Standard Sorites Paradoxes, 279–83
Hairiness/Baldness Sorites Paradox, Revised Version, 285–89
Choosing Between Hairy Heads, 289–90
Baldness Spectrum, 291–92
Miracle Hair Growth Salesman, 293
Job Candidates *I*: Similarity-based Reasoning and Intransitivity, 298–99
Job Candidates *II*: Similarity-based Reasoning, Majority-rule Reasoning, and Intransitivity, 300–1
Pleasure versus Evil-Doing: Similarity-based Reasoning and Transitivity, 304–5
Trade-Offs Between Quality and Duration *I*: Similarity-based Reasoning and Transitivity, 304–5
Torture versus Mosquito Bites: Similarity-based Reasoning and Transitivity, 305–6
Pain Trade-offs: Similarity-based Reasoning and Transitivity, 306–7
Disease Trade-offs: Similarity-based Reasoning and Transitivity, 307–8
Evil Space Invader Forces a Sophie's Choice Scenario, 311
Hells One, Two, and Three, 319–20
Michelangelo, Rembrandt, and Da Vinci, 320–21
Olga, Nadia, and the Capped Model for Ideals, 329
Harrison Bergeron, 332
Attila the Hun, 334–35
Lollipop Licks versus Watching Your Child's Birth, 339–40
The Mere Addition Paradox, 364–66
Saints, Sinners, and the Inadequacy of Purely Abstract Diagrams, 374–75
How Variations in Group Membership Matter, (Or Not): Internal Aspects versus Essentially Comparative Views, 377–78
How an Essentially Comparative View of Equality Challenges Transitivity, 380–81
Vanilla, Chocolate, or Strawberry: On the Independence of Irrelevant Alternatives Principle, 389
Mere Addition Paradox Variations, 397
How More Than France Exists, 404–5
Why the Weak Pareto Principle is Plausible, 408–11
Hungry People or Happy Mice?, 413–14
Life-Extending Pill or Human Extinction?, 414
Variation of the Mere Addition Paradox: On Plausibility of an Essentially Comparative View of Utility, 415–16

Three Population Policies, 418
Factory Farms and the Narrow Person-Affecting View, 419
Three Cases Illustrating the Intuitive Plausibility of the Narrow Person-Affecting View, 420–22
Conservation and Depletion, 424
Problem of Creation, 424
Good, Evil, and Desert, 424–25
The Neutrality Intuition: Broome's Counterexample to the Narrow Person-Affecting View, 427
Tom, Dick, and Harry: Parfit's Counterexample to the Narrow Person-Affecting View, 428–29
Hell-to-Heaven versus Heaven-to-Hell: Infinite Utility Cases *1* and *2*, 434–37
The Wide Person-Affecting View is Not Enough: Infinite Utility Cases *3* and *4*, 438–39
Progressive Disease—First Version, 440–41
Progressive Disease—Second Version, 441
Progressive Disease—Third Version, 441–42
How More Than France Exists and the Capped Model, 449–51
The Wood-Burning Fireplace, 452
Intransitive Ranking of Cars, 452–53
Intransitive Ranking of Jobs, 453
Intransitive Ranking of Homes, 453–54
The Mere Addition Paradox and the Fine-Grained Individuation of Alternatives, 458–59
Affirmative Action and the Fine-Grained Individuation of Alternatives, 462–63
The Swamped Philosophy Search Committee, 464, 468–69
Ranking Alternative Lives: The Time Trade-off Method, 466
Ranking Baseball Teams: The Sports Analogy, 468
Different Cycles between Heaven and Hell, 491
Sophie's Choice, 510
Spectrum of Illnesses: On the Appeal of the Fifth and Sixth Standard Views, 524
Does One Person's Existence Undermine the Narrow Person-Affecting View?: Norcross's Objection, 546–47
Why One Person's Existence Does Not Undermine the Narrow Person-Affecting View: Response to Norcross, 547–51
Zeke's Preferences among Apples and Oranges, 554

LIST OF PRINCIPLES AND VIEWS

For further references for the following principles and views, see the index.

Additive-Aggregationist Position, 37–38

1. Benefits and burdens, or well-being, or what has traditionally been called *utility* is morally significant and relevant for comparing outcomes.
2. In comparing outcomes, *more* utility is *better* than *less* utility.
3. How *much* utility an outcome contains, as a whole, is a simple *additive* function of the utilities of *each* sentient individual in that outcome.
4. The total utility of each sentient being is determined by a simple *additive* function of the "local" utilities possessed by that individual over the course of her life, day by day, or perhaps moment by moment.
5. The relation between how good an outcome is regarding utility and how good it is regarding other ideals is thought to be such that as long as one outcome is better than another regarding utility by *enough*, then the one outcome will also be better all things considered.
6. Perhaps, how good an outcome is, all things considered, is an additive function of how good it is with respect to each individual ideal that is relevant to assessing the goodness of outcomes.

Anti-additive Aggregationist Position, 38
    The contrary of the Additive-Aggregationist Position
Capped Model for Ideals, 328–30

1. For each ideal relevant to assessing outcomes, each outcome merits a rough numerical "score" representing how good that outcome is with respect to that ideal.
2. How good the outcome is all things considered is represented by the numerical score arrived at by summing the individual scores of each relevant ideal.
3. There is an upper limit on how much better any individual ideal can make an outcome, all things considered, and hence an upper limit on the maximum score that can be given for any ideal, representing how good an outcome is regarding that ideal.
4. Therefore, there is an upper limit on how good an outcome can be all things considered, and hence an upper limit on the maximum score representing how good an outcome can be all things considered.

Consolidate Additional Benefits View, 68
    In general, if additional benefits are dispersed among different people, it is better for a given total benefit to be consolidated among a few people, such that each person's additional benefit is substantial, than for a larger total benefit to be dispersed among a vastly larger number of people, so that the additional benefit any single person receives within her life is "relatively small."

Continuity, Principle of, 236
    For any three outcomes A, B, and C, such that A is better than B and B is better than C, there must be some probability, p, between 0 and 1, such that one should be rationally indifferent between having B occur for sure and having A occur with probability p or C occur with probability $(1 - p)$.

Crucial Premise of the Standard Hairiness/Baldness Sorites Paradox, 277
    One hair, more or less, will not make a difference to whether or not one is hairy or bald.

Disperse Additional Burdens View, 67–68
    In general, if additional burdens are dispersed among different people, it is better for a given total burden to be dispersed among a vastly larger number of people, so that the additional burden any

single person has to bear within her life is "relatively small," than for a smaller total burden to fall on just a few, such that their additional burden is substantial.

Essentially Comparative View of Moral Ideals, 371
Roughly, there is at least one moral ideal, F, and at least one outcome, O, such that there is no answer to the question of how good O is regarding F, based solely on F's internal features; or, even if, for each moral ideal, F, and each outcome, O, there is an answer to the question of how good O is regarding F based solely on O's internal features, there is at least one ideal, F, and two outcomes O_1 and O_2, such that how O_1 compares with O_2 regarding F is not simply a function of the extent to which O_1 is good with respect to F based solely on O_1's internal features and the extent to which O_2 is good with respect to F based solely on O_2's internal features.

Essentially Comparative View of Outcome Goodness, 371
Roughly, there is at least one outcome, O, such that there is no answer to the question of how good O is all things considered based solely on O's internal features; or, even if, for each outcome, O, there is an answer to the question of how good O is all things considered based solely on O's internal features, there are at least two outcomes, O_1 and O_2, such that how O_1's goodness compares with O_2 all things considered is not simply a function of the extent to which O_1 is good, all things considered, based solely on O_1's internal features and the extent to which O_2 is good, all things considered, based solely on O_2's internal features.

Essentially Comparative View of Utility, 411
To improve an outcome regarding utility one must (generally) increase the utility of some of those already living in that outcome.

First Principle of Equivalence, 238
For any two prospects, A and B, if for every possible outcome, w_i, that might arise with a given probability, p_i, if A is chosen, the same outcome, w_i, might arise with the same probability, p_i, if B is chosen, and vice versa, then prospects A and B are equally good (that is, $V(A) = V(B)$).

Independence of Irrelevant Alternatives Principle, (Version 1), 201 n. 5
Roughly, this principle holds that the relative goodness of two outcomes, A and B, is determined solely on the basis of how they compare with each other, and cannot depend on how either or both of those outcomes compare with respect to some other outcome or set of outcomes.

Independence of Irrelevant Alternatives Principle, (Version 2), 387–88
For any two outcomes, A and B, to know how A compares to B all things considered it is, at least in principle, sufficient to compare them directly in terms of each of the ideals about which we care. More particularly, if one accurately knew how A compared to B in terms of each ideal relevant to our all-things-considered judgments, and if one granted each ideal its due weight, then one would be in a position to know how A compared to B all things considered.

Internal Aspects View of Moral Ideals, 369–70
Roughly, for each outcome, O, and each moral ideal, F, there is an extent to which outcome O is good with respect to F which depends solely on O's internal features. Moreover, for any two outcomes, O_1 and O_2, and any moral ideal F_1, O_1 will be better than O_2 regarding F_1, if and only if the extent to which O_1 is good regarding F_1, as determined solely on the basis of O_1's internal features, is greater than the extent to which O_2 is good regarding F_1, as determined solely on the basis of O_2's internal features. In addition, if O_1 is better than O_2 regarding any moral ideal F_1, the extent to which this is so will depend solely on the extent to which O_1 is good regarding F_1 is greater than the extent to which O_2 is good regarding F_1.

Internal Aspects View of Outcome Goodness, 370
Roughly, for each outcome, O, how good that outcome is *all things considered* depends solely on how good it is with respect to each moral ideal that is relevant for assessing the goodness of outcomes, and on how much all of the relevant ideals matter vis-à-vis each other, where these depend solely on O's internal features. Moreover, for any two outcomes, O_1 and O_2, O_1 will be better than O_2 *all things considered* if and only if the extent to which O_1 is good all things considered, as determined solely on the basis of O_1's internal features, is greater than the extent to which O_2 is good all things considered, as determined solely on the basis of O_2's internal features. In addition, if O_1 is better than O_2 all things considered, the extent to which this is so will depend solely on the extent to which O_1 is good, all things considered, is greater than the extent to which O_2 is good, all things considered.

J. Ross's Principle, 40–41
    Clause *1*: Given any two theories, T_1 and T_2, it is rational to *follow* T_2 in one's practical deliberations, even if one believes that T_1 is more likely to be true than T_2, as long as one gives *some* credence to the possibility of T_2's being true, and T_1 evaluates all of one's options as equally desirable. So, given options O_1, O_2, O_3, ..., O_n, if T_1 judges all the options as equivalent, while T_2 judges one of the options, say O_p, as superior to the others, as long as one has some credence in T_2 it is rational to *follow* T_2 and choose O_p, *even if* one has most reason to *believe* that T_1 is the correct theory. In such a case, one has everything to gain and nothing to lose by acting *as if* T_2 were the correct theory and following its dictates. Clause ²: similarly, if T_1 judges that there is little to choose between one's options, while T_2 judges that it makes a great difference which of one's options one chooses, then as long as one believes there is a "decent" chance that T_2 might be true, it will often be rational to follow the dictates of T_2, even if in fact one has more credence in T_1 than in T_2.

Like Comparability for Equivalents, Principle of, 237
    According to this principle, if two outcomes or prospects are equivalent (meaning equally good) in some respect, then however the first of those outcomes or prospects compares to a third outcome or prospect in that respect, that is how the second of those outcomes or prospects compares to the third outcome or prospect in that respect.

maximin, 402
    The best outcome is the one in which the worst-off people are best off.

Narrow Person-Affecting View, 417
    In assessing possible outcomes, one should, (1) focus on the status of independently existing people, with the aim of wanting them to be as well off as possible, and, (2) ignore the status of dependently existing people, except that one wants to avoid *harming* them as much as possible. Regarding the second clause, a dependently existing person is harmed *only if* there is at least one available alternative outcome in which that very same person exists and is better off, and the size of the harm will be a function of the extent to which that person would have been better off in the available alternative outcome in which he exists and is best off.

No Trade-offs View, 30
    An outcome where a larger number of people have a lower quality benefit is not better than an outcome where a smaller number of similarly situated people have a higher quality benefit, *even if* the number of people receiving benefits in the former outcome is "much" greater than the number of people receiving benefits in the latter outcome, and *even if* the differences in the degrees to which the similarly situated people in the different outcomes are benefited are "very" small.

Pain Argument's Important Additive-Aggregationist Premise, 278
    For each pair of adjacent members of the pain spectrum, the slightly less intense pain is worse than the slightly more intense one, if it lasts two, or three, or five times as long.

Pareto Principle, 211
    If how two outcomes, X and Y, compare with respect to a given notion, N, depends on how they compare with respect to three factors, A, B, and C, often, there will be a positive correlation between the factors A, B, C, and N, such that if X is better than Y in one important respect, say A, and at least as good as Y in the other respects, then all things considered X is better than Y with respect to N.

Pareto Principle (Standard Version), 242
    For any two prospects A and B, if the value of A's outcome is at least as good as the value of B's outcome for *each* possible state of nature, and, in addition, there is at least one state of nature where the value of A's outcome is greater than the value of B's outcome, then prospect A is better than prospect B.

Pareto Principle (Strong Version), 408
    One outcome is better than another, *all things considered*, if it is *pareto superior*, where for any two outcomes, A and B, A is *pareto superior* to B if A and B involve the very same people and if A is at least as good as B for everyone, and there is at least *one* person for whom A is better.

Pareto Principle (Weak Version), 408
    One outcome is better than another, *in one important respect*, if it is *pareto superior*, where for any two outcomes, A and B, A is *pareto superior* to B if A and B involve the very same people and if A is at least as good as B for everyone, and there is at least *one* person for whom A is better.

Reflection Principle, 240
> If, on reflection, I know that at some point in the future I'll have more knowledge than I currently have, and I now know that given that future knowledge it will be reasonable to assess two prospects in a certain way, then it is *now* reasonable for me to assess the two prospects in that way.

Second No Trade-offs View, 522
> An outcome where a larger number of people have benefits for a shorter duration is not better than an outcome where a smaller number of similarly situated people have the same or similar benefits for a longer duration, *even if* the number of people benefited in the former outcome is "much" greater, and *even if* the differences in the durations of the benefits in the two outcomes are "very" small.

Second Principle of Equivalence, 238
> For any two prospects A and B, if for every possible state of nature, s_i, the very same outcome, w_i, will occur if A is chosen or if B is chosen, then prospects A and B are equally good, ($V(A) = V(B)$).

Second Unlimited Trade-offs View, 523
> *Trade-offs of Number for Duration Are Always in Principle Desirable*: An outcome where a "sufficiently" large number of people have benefits of short duration will be better than an outcome where a smaller number of people receive the same or similar benefits of longer duration, *even if* the duration of benefits in the former outcome is "very" short, and no matter *how much* longer the duration of benefits in the latter outcome might be.

Standard Model for Combining Ideals, 235
> How good an outcome is all things considered is an additive function of how good it is regarding each ideal, so that insofar as an outcome gets better regarding any particular ideal it will, to that extent, be getting better all things considered.

Standard Model for Utility, 315
> 1. Utility is noninstrumentally valuable—meaning that there is some value to utility over and above the extent to which it promotes other valuable ideals.
> 2. Utility is intrinsically valuable—meaning that each unit of utility contributes to the value of an outcome, and each unit contributes the same amount of value as every other, so that two units of utility add twice as much value to the goodness of an outcome as one, three units of utility add three times as much value to the goodness of an outcome as one unit and 50 percent more value to the goodness of an outcome as two units, and so on.
> 3. The ideal of utility is strictly neutral with respect to sentient beings, places, and times—meaning that a given amount of utility will count just as much no matter who experiences it, where it is experienced, or when it is experienced.
> 4. The ideal of utility is strictly impartial—meaning that each sentient being's utility counts as much as any other's.
> 5. Insofar as one cares about utility, one should care about total utility.
> 6. How good an outcome is regarding utility is a simple additive function of how much utility sentient beings have in that outcome.

Standard View, First, 30
> *Trade-offs between Quality and Number Are Sometimes Desirable*: In general, an outcome where a larger number of people have a lower quality benefit is better than an outcome where a smaller number of people have a higher quality benefit, *if* the number receiving the lower quality benefit is "sufficiently" greater than the number receiving the higher quality benefit, and *if* the differences in the initial situations of the people benefited and the degrees to which they are benefited are not "too" great.

Standard View, Second, 32
> *Trade-offs between Quality and Number Are Sometimes Undesirable Even When Vast Numbers Are at Stake*: If the quality of one kind of benefit is "sufficiently" low, and the quality of another kind of benefit is "sufficiently" high, then an outcome in which a relatively small number of people received the higher quality benefit would be better than one in which virtually any number of (otherwise) similarly situated people received the lower quality benefit.

Standard View, Third, 123
> *Trade-offs between Quality and Duration Are Sometimes Desirable*: In general, it is better for an individual to receive a lower-quality benefit for a longer period of time than a higher-quality benefit for a shorter period of time, *if* the difference in the quality of the benefits and its impact on the person's life are not "too" great, and *if* the duration of the lower-quality benefit would be "sufficiently" longer than the duration of higher-quality benefit.

Standard View, Fourth, 123-4
> *Even within Lives, Trade-offs between Quality and Duration Are Sometimes Undesirable Even When Vast Differences in Duration Are at Stake*: If the difference in the quality of benefits is "sufficiently" large, it would be preferable for someone to receive a larger, (higher quality) benefit, as long as it persisted for a "sufficiently" long duration, than for that person to receive a smaller, (lower quality) benefit for any period of finite duration.

Standard View, Fifth, 522
> *Trade-offs between Duration and Number Are Sometimes Desirable*: In general, an outcome where a larger number of people receive a benefit for a shorter duration is better than an outcome where a smaller number of similarly situated people receive the same or a similar benefit for a longer duration, *if* the number of people benefited in the former outcome is "sufficiently" greater than the number benefited in the latter outcome, and *if* the differences in the durations of the benefits received in the two outcomes are not "too" great.

Standard View, Sixth, 523
> *Trade-offs between Duration and Number Are Sometimes Undesirable Even When Vast Numbers Are at Stake*: In general, an outcome where a smaller number of people had a certain type of benefit for a longer duration would be better than an outcome where virtually any number of people had that type of benefit for a "short" duration, *if* the duration in the latter outcome is short "enough" and *if* the duration in the former outcome is "sufficiently" longer.

State-by-State Comparison Principle, 239
> For any two prospects A and B, if the value of A's outcome stands in a particular comparative relation, R, to the value of B's outcome for *each* possible state of nature, then prospect A stands in relation R to B. More specifically, for any two prospects A and B, if the value of A's outcome is, respectively, greater than, (>), equal to, (=), at least as good as, (≥), or roughly comparable to, (~), the value of B's outcome for *each* possible state of nature, then prospect A will be, respectively, better than, as good as, at least as good as, or roughly comparable to prospect B.

Substitution of Equivalents, Principle of, 237
> For any x and y, where x and y are numbers or mathematical formulas, if $x = y$, then x and y are interchangeable in any formulas where they occur.

Unlimited Trade-offs View, 33
> *Trade-offs of Number for Quality Are Always, in Principle, Desirable*: No matter *how* low the quality of one kind benefit (as long as it is positive), and no matter *how* high the quality of another kind of benefit (as long as it is finite), an outcome with a "sufficiently" large number of people receiving the low-quality benefits will be better than an outcome with a smaller number of (otherwise) similarly situated people receiving the high-quality benefits.

View One, 135
> For any unpleasant or "negative" experience, no matter what the intensity and duration of that experience, it would be better to have that experience than one that was only a "little" less intense but twice (or three or five times) as long.

View Two, 135
> There is, or could be, a spectrum of unpleasant or "negative" experiences ranging in intensity, for example, from extreme forms of torture to the mild discomfort of a mosquito bite, such that one could move from the harsh end of the spectrum to the mild end in a finite series of steps, where each step would involve the transformation from one negative experience to another that was only a "little" less intense than the previous one.

View Three, 135
> The mild discomfort of a mosquito bite would be better than two years of excruciating torture, no matter how long one lived and no matter how long the discomfort of a mosquito bite persisted.

View Four, 135
> "All-things-considered better than" is a transitive relation. So, for any three outcomes, A, B, and C, which involve unpleasant experiences of varying intensities and durations, if, all things considered, A is better than B, and B is better than C, then A is better than C.

Wide Person-Affecting View, 437
> In assessing possible outcomes, one should focus on how *people* are affected for better or worse—understood in terms of the extent to which people have good or bad lives—in different outcomes, whether or not they are the *same* people, with the aim of wanting whichever people will exist to be as well off as possible.